Microsoft Power BI Complete Reference

D1546607

Bring your data to life with the powerful features of
Microsoft Power BI

Devin Knight
Brian Knight
Mitchell Pearson
Manuel Quintana
Brett Powell

BIRMINGHAM - MUMBAI

Microsoft Power BI Complete Reference

Copyright © 2018 Packt Publishing

All rights reserved. No part of this book may be reproduced, stored in a retrieval system, or transmitted in any form or by any means, without the prior written permission of the publisher, except in the case of brief quotations embedded in critical articles or reviews.

Every effort has been made in the preparation of this book to ensure the accuracy of the information presented. However, the information contained in this book is sold without warranty, either express or implied. Neither the authors, nor Packt Publishing or its dealers and distributors, will be held liable for any damages caused or alleged to have been caused directly or indirectly by this book.

Packt Publishing has endeavored to provide trademark information about all of the companies and products mentioned in this book by the appropriate use of capitals. However, Packt Publishing cannot guarantee the accuracy of this information.

First published: December 2018

Production reference:1171218

Published by Packt Publishing Ltd.
Livery Place
35 Livery Street
Birmingham
B3 2PB, UK.

ISBN 978-1-78995-004-5

www.packtpub.com

About Packt

mapt.io

Mapt is an online digital library that gives you full access to over 5,000 books and videos, as well as industry leading tools to help you plan your personal development and advance your career. For more information, please visit our website.

Why subscribe?

- Spend less time learning and more time coding with practical eBooks and Videos from over 4,000 industry professionals

- Improve your learning with Skill Plans built especially for you

- Get a free eBook or video every month

- Mapt is fully searchable

- Copy and paste, print, and bookmark content

PacktPub.com

Did you know that Packt offers eBook versions of every book published, with PDF and ePub files available? You can upgrade to the eBook version at www.PacktPub.com and as a print book customer, you are entitled to a discount on the eBook copy. Get in touch with us at service@packtpub.com for more details.

At www.PacktPub.com, you can also read a collection of free technical articles, sign up for a range of free newsletters, and receive exclusive discounts and offers on Packt books and eBooks.

Contributors

About the authors

Devin Knight a Microsoft Data Platform MVP and the Training Director at Pragmatic Works. At Pragmatic Works, Devin determines which courses are created, delivered, and updated for customers, including 10+ Power BI courses. This is the seventh SQL Server and Business Intelligence book that he has authored. Devin often speaks at conferences such as PASS Summit, PASS Business Analytics Conference, SQL Saturdays, and Code Camps. He is also a contributing member to several PASS Virtual Chapters. Making his home in Jacksonville, FL, Devin is the Vice President of the local Power BI User Group and SQL Server User Group (JSSUG). His personal blog can be found at Devin Knight's website.

Brian Knight is the owner and founder of Pragmatic Works, and is a serial entrepreneur, having also started up other companies. Brian is a contributing columnist at several technical magazines. He is the author of 16 technical books. Brian has spoken at conferences such as PASS Summit, SQL Connections, TechEd, SQLSaturdays, and Code Camps. He has received a number of awards from the State of Florida, from both the governor and press, including the Business Ambassador Award (governor) and Top CEO (Jacksonville Magazine). His blog can be found at Pragmatic Works website.

Thanks to everyone who made this book possible. As always, I owe a huge debt to my wife, Jenn, for putting up with my late nights, and to my children, Colton, Liam, Camille, and John, for being so patient with their tired dad who has always overextended himself. Finally, I would like to thank Shawn Trautman, my line dancing instructor. This will be the year that we complete the United Country Western Dance Council's goal of making line dancing a competitive sport worldwide.

Mitchell Pearson has worked for Pragmatic Works for six years as a Business Intelligence Consultant and Training Content manager. Mitchell has experience developing enterprise level BI Solutions using the full suite of products offered by Microsoft (SSRS, SSIS, SSAS, and Power BI). Mitchell is very active in the community presenting at local user groups, SQL Saturday events, PASS virtual chapters and giving free webinars for Pragmatic Works. He can also be found blogging at Mitchellsql website. Mitchell is also the president of the local Power BI User Group in Jacksonville, Florida. In his spare time, Mitchell spends his time with his wife and three kids. For fun, Mitchell enjoys playing tabletop games with friends.

I would like to thank God for the gifts and opportunities afforded me and most of all for sending his son Jesus Christ. I would like to thank my wife and children for their patience and support as I worked on this book. I would also like to thank Brian Knight for the opportunity to learn and grow in the field of Business Intelligence. Finally, I would like to thank Anthony Martin, Dustin Ryan, Bradley Schacht, Devin Knight, Jorge Segarra, and Bradley Ball, each one of these individuals have provided guidance and mentoring through the years and have had a profound impact on my career.

Manuel Quintana is a Training Content Manager at Pragmatic Works. Previously, he was a senior manager working in the hotel industry. He joined the Pragmatic Works team in 2014 with no knowledge in the Business Intelligence space, but now speaks at SQL Saturdays and SQL Server User Groups locally and virtually. He also teaches various BI technologies to many different Fortune 500 companies on behalf of Pragmatic Works. Since 2014, he has called Jacksonville home and before that Orlando, but he was born on the island of Puerto Rico and loves to go back and visit his family. When he isn't working on creating new content for Pragmatic Works, you can probably find him playing board games or watching competitive soccer matches.

Thank you to all my family and friends who support me in all of my endeavors. Special praise must be given to my wife for supporting me during late hours working and some weekends being dedicated to writing this book, without her I wouldn't be the person I am proud of being today. Also, I must say thank you to all my coworkers at Pragmatic Works; each one of them has mentored me in one way or another, and all my success can be traced back to them. I hope to make everyone mentioned here proud of what I have done and what I will achieve.

Brett Powell is the owner of Frontline Analytics, a data and analytics consulting firm and Microsoft Power BI partner. He has worked with Power BI technologies since they were first introduced with the Power Pivot add-in for Excel 2010 and has contributed to the design and delivery of Microsoft BI solutions across retail, manufacturing, finance, and professional services. He is also the author of *Microsoft Power BI Cookbook* and a regular speaker at Microsoft technology events such as the Power BI World Tour and the Data & BI Summit. He regularly shares technical tips and examples on his blog, Insight Quest, and is a co-organizer of the Boston BI User Group.

I'd like to thank Packt for giving me this opportunity, the content and technical editing teams, and particularly Divya Poojari, acquisition editor, and Amrita Noronha, senior content development editor. As Power BI continues to evolve, it is necessary to be flexible with the outline and page counts, and I greatly appreciated this autonomy.

About the reviewers

Nick Lee is a Business Intelligence Consultant and trainer for Pragmatic Works' training team. He comes from a customer service background and has an ample amount of experience in presenting and interacting with large Organizations. His focus at Pragmatic Works is creating Power BI content and delivering Power BI classes to our customers.

Ruben Oliva Ramos is a computer engineer from Tecnologico of León Institute, with a master's degree in computer and electronics systems engineering and networking specialization from the University of Salle Bajio. He has more than 5 years' experience of developing web apps to control and monitor devices connected to Arduino and Raspberry Pi, using web frameworks and cloud services to build IoT applications. He has authored *Raspberry Pi 3 Home Automation Projects*, *Internet of Things Programming with JavaScript*, *Advanced Analytics with R and Tableau*, and *SciPy Recipes* for Packt.

Packt is searching for authors like you

If you're interested in becoming an author for Packt, please visit `authors.packtpub.com` and apply today. We have worked with thousands of developers and tech professionals, just like you, to help them share their insight with the global tech community. You can make a general application, apply for a specific hot topic that we are recruiting an author for, or submit your own idea.

Table of Contents

Preface

Microsoft Power BI Complete Reference gets you started with business intelligence by showing you how to install the Power BI toolset, design effective data models, and build basic dashboards and visualizations that make your data come to life.

In this Learning Path, you will learn to create powerful interactive reports by visualizing your data and learn visualization styles, tips and tricks to bring your data to life. You will be able to administer your organization's Power BI environment to create and share dashboards. You will also be able to streamline deployment by implementing security and regular data refreshes.

Next, you will delve deeper into the nuances of Power BI and handling projects. You will get you acquainted with planning a Power BI project, development, and distribution of content, and deployment. You will learn to connect and extract data from various sources to create robust datasets, reports, and dashboards. Additionally, you will learn how to format reports and apply custom visuals, animation and analytics to further refine your data.

By the end of this Learning Path, you will learn to implement the various Power BI tools such as on-premises gateway together along with staging and securely distributing content via apps.

This Learning Path is packaged up keeping your journey in mind. The curator of this Learning Path has combined some of the best that Packt has to offer in one complete package. It includes content from the following Packt products:

- Microsoft Power BI Quick Start Guide by Devin Knight et al.
- Mastering Microsoft Power BI by Brett Powell

Who this book is for

This Learning Path is for those who want to learn and use the Power BI features to extract maximum information and make intelligent decisions that boost their business. If you have a basic understanding of BI concepts and want to learn how to apply them using Microsoft Power BI, this Learning Path is for you. It consists of real-world examples on Power BI and goes deep into the technical issues, covers additional protocols, and much more.

What this book covers

Chapter 1, *Getting Started with Importing Data Options*, begins by getting the audience oriented with the Power BI Desktop. Next, they will learn how to connect to various common data sources in Power BI. Once a data source is chosen, the options within will be explored, including the choice between data import, direct query, and live connection.

Chapter 2, *Data Transformation Strategies*, explores the capabilities of the Power Query Editor inside the Power BI Desktop. Using this Power BI Query Editor, the reader will first learn how to do basic transformations, and they will quickly learn more advanced data-cleansing practices. By the end of this chapter, the audience will know how to combine queries, use parameters, and read and write basic M queries.

Chapter 3, *Building the Data Model*, discusses one of the most critical parts of building a successful Power BI solution—designing an effective data model. In this chapter, readers will learn that while designing a data model, they are really setting themselves up for success when it comes to building reports. Specifically, this chapter will teach the audience how to establish relationships between tables, how to deal with complex relationship designs, and how to implement usability enhancements for the report consumers.

Chapter 4, *Leveraging DAX*, teaches that the Data Analysis Expression (DAX) language within Power BI is critical to building data models that are valuable to data consumers. While DAX may be intimidating at first, readers will quickly learn that its roots come from the Excel formula engine. This can be helpful at first, but as you find the need to develop more and more complex calculations, readers will learn that having a background in Excel formulas will only take them so far. This chapter will start with an understanding of basic DAX concepts but quickly accelerate into more complex ideas, such as Time Intelligence and Filter Context.

Chapter 5, *Visualizing Data*, describes how to take a finely tuned data model and build reports that properly deliver a message that clearly and concisely tells a story about the data.

Chapter 6, *Using a Cloud Deployment with the Power BI Service*, examines deploying your solution to the Power BI Service to share what you've developed with your organization. Once deployed, you can build dashboards, share them with others, and schedule data refreshes. This chapter will cover the essential skills a BI professional would need to know to top off a Power BI solution they have developed.

Chapter 7, *Planning Power BI Projects*, discusses alternative deployment modes for Power BI, team and project roles, and licensing. Additionally, an example project template and its corresponding planning and dataset design processes are described.

Chapter 8, *Connecting to Sources and Transforming Data with M*, depicts the data access layer supporting a Power BI dataset, including data sources and fact and dimension table queries. Concepts of the Power Query M language, such as query folding and parameters, are explained and examples of custom M queries involving conditional and dynamic logic are given.

Chapter 9, *Designing Import and DirectQuery Data Models*, reviews the components of the data model layer and design techniques in support of usability, performance, and other objectives.

Chapter 10, *Developing DAX Measures and Security Roles*, covers the implementation of analysis expressions reflecting business definitions and common analysis requirements. Primary DAX functions, concepts, and use cases such as date intelligence, row-level security roles, and performance testing are examined.

Chapter 11, *Creating and Formatting Power BI Reports*, describes a report planning process, data visualization practices, and report design fundamentals, including visual selection and filter scopes. Top report development features, such as slicer visuals, tooltips, and conditional formatting are also reviewed.

Chapter 12, *Applying Custom Visuals, Animation, and Analytics*, examines powerful interactive and analytical features, including drillthrough report pages, bookmarks, the Analytics pane, ArcGIS Maps, and the waterfall charts. Additionally, examples of custom visuals, such as the Power KPI, and the capabilities of animation to support data storytelling are provided.

Chapter 13, *Designing Power BI Dashboards and Architectures*, provides guidance on visual selection, layout, and supporting tiles to drive effective dashboards. Alternative multi-dashboard architectures, such as an organizational dashboard architecture, are reviewed, is the configuration of dashboard tiles and mobile-optimized dashboards.

Chapter 14, *Managing Application Workspaces and Content*, features the role and administration of app workspaces in the context of Power BI solutions and staged deployments. Additionally, the Power BI REST API, content management features, and practices are reviewed, including field descriptions and version history.

Chapter 15, *Managing the On-Premises Data Gateway*, covers top gateway planning considerations, including alternative gateway architectures, workloads, and hardware requirements. Gateway administration processes and tools are described, such as the manage gateways portal, gateway log files, and PowerShell Gateway commands.

Chapter 16, *Deploying the Power BI Report Server*, contrasts the Power BI Report Server with the Power BI cloud service and provides guidance on deployment topics such as licensing, reference topology, configuration, administration, and upgrade cycles.

Chapter 17, *Creating Power BI Apps and Content Distribution*, walks through the process of publishing and updating apps for groups of users. Additionally, other common distribution methods are covered, such as the sharing of reports and dashboards, email subscriptions, data-alert-driven emails, and embedding Power BI content in SharePoint Online.

Chapter 18, *Administering Power BI for an Organization*, highlights data governance for self-service and corporate BI, Azure Active Directory features such as Conditional Access Policies, and the Power BI admin portal. Details are provided about configuring Power BI service tenant settings, managing Power BI Premium capacities, and the tools available to monitor Power BI activities.

Chapter 19, *Scaling with Premium and Analysis Services*, reviews the capabilities of Power BI Premium and alternative methods for allocating premium capacity. Additionally, Power BI datasets are contrasted with Analysis Services models, Azure Analysis Services is contrasted with SQL Server Analysis Services, and the migration of a Power BI dataset to an Analysis Services model is described.

To get the most out of this book

A Power BI Pro license and access to the Power BI service is necessary to follow many of the topics and examples in this book. The assignment of the Power BI Service Administrator role within the Office 365 admin center, as well as administrative access to an On-premises data gateway, would also be helpful for the second half of this book. It's assumed that readers are familiar with the main user interfaces of Power BI Desktop and have some background in business intelligence or information technology.

The primary data source for the examples in this book was the AdventureWorks data warehouse sample database for SQL Server 2016 CTP3. A SQL Server 2017 Developer Edition database engine instance was used to host the sample database. For the import mode dataset, an Excel workbook stored the sales plan data. For the DirectQuery dataset, the sales plan data was stored in the sample SQL Server database.

The AdventureWorksDW2016CTP3 sample database can be downloaded from the following URL:
https://www.microsoft.com/en-us/download/details.aspx?id=49502.

Editions of SQL Server 2017 are available for download from the following URL:
https://www.microsoft.com/en-us/sql-server/sql-server-downloads.

The Power BI Desktop files and specific queries and scripts utilized in the book are included in the code bundle. However, the source data and database are not included in the code bundle. Additionally, the database used by the book contains objects not included in the downloadable sample database, such as SQL views for each fact and dimension table. Therefore, even with access to a SQL Server 2017 database engine instance and the sample AdventureWorks data warehouse database, the examples in the book cannot be completely reproduced.

Download the example code files

You can download the example code files for this book from your account at www.packtpub.com. If you purchased this book elsewhere, you can visit www.packtpub.com/support and register to have the files emailed directly to you.

You can download the code files by following these steps:

1. Log in or register at www.packtpub.com.
2. Select the **SUPPORT** tab.
3. Click on **Code Downloads & Errata**.
4. Enter the name of the book in the **Search** box and follow the onscreen instructions.

Once the file is downloaded, please make sure that you unzip or extract the folder using the latest version of:

- WinRAR/7-Zip for Windows
- Zipeg/iZip/UnRarX for Mac
- 7-Zip/PeaZip for Linux

The code bundle for the book is also hosted on GitHub at `https://github.com/PacktPublishing/Learning-Path-Microsoft-Power-BI-Complete-Reference`. In case there's an update to the code, it will be updated on the existing GitHub repository.

We also have other code bundles from our rich catalog of books and videos available at `https://github.com/PacktPublishing/`. Check them out!

Conventions used

There are a number of text conventions used throughout this book.

`CodeInText`: Indicates code words in text, database table names, folder names, filenames, file extensions, pathnames, dummy URLs, user input, and Twitter handles. Here is an example: "This function is used by the **Web Data Connector** (**WDC**) (**Get Data | Web**) to return the contents of an HTML web page as a table, as shown in the following M Query:"

A block of code is set as follows:

```
// Retrieve table of data access M functions and their descriptions
let
  Source =
Web.Page(Web.Contents("https://msdn.microsoft.com/en-US/library/mt2966
15.aspx")),
  PageToTable = Source{0}[Data],
  ChangedType = Table.TransformColumnTypes(PageToTable,
 {{"Function", type text}, {"Description", type text}})
in
    ChangedType
```

Bold: Indicates a new term, an important word, or words that you see onscreen. For example, words in menus or dialog boxes appear in the text like this. Here is an example: "The **Data Gateway** item from the download menu in the preceding image currently links to a **Power BI Gateway** page with a large **Download Gateway** button at the top."

Warnings or important notes appear like this.

 Tips and tricks appear like this.

Get in touch

Feedback from our readers is always welcome.

General feedback: Email feedback@packtpub.com and mention the book title in the subject of your message. If you have questions about any aspect of this book, please email us at questions@packtpub.com.

Errata: Although we have taken every care to ensure the accuracy of our content, mistakes do happen. If you have found a mistake in this book, we would be grateful if you would report this to us. Please visit www.packtpub.com/submit-errata, selecting your book, clicking on the Errata Submission Form link, and entering the details.

Piracy: If you come across any illegal copies of our works in any form on the Internet, we would be grateful if you would provide us with the location address or website name. Please contact us at copyright@packtpub.com with a link to the material.

If you are interested in becoming an author: If there is a topic that you have expertise in and you are interested in either writing or contributing to a book, please visit authors.packtpub.com.

Reviews

Please leave a review. Once you have read and used this book, why not leave a review on the site that you purchased it from? Potential readers can then see and use your unbiased opinion to make purchase decisions, we at Packt can understand what you think about our products, and our authors can see your feedback on their book. Thank you!

For more information about Packt, please visit packtpub.com.

Getting Started with Importing Data Options

1

Power BI may very well be one of the most aptly named tools ever developed by Microsoft, giving analysts and developers a powerful business intelligence and analytics playground while still packaging it in a surprisingly lightweight application. Using Microsoft Power BI, the processes of data discovery, data modeling, data visualization, and sharing are made elegantly simple using a single product. These processes are so commonplace when developing Power BI solutions that this book has adopted sections that follow this pattern. However, from your perspective, the really exciting thing may be that development problems that would previously take you weeks to solve in a corporate BI solution can now be accomplished in only hours.

Power BI is a **Software as a Service (SaaS)** offering in the Azure cloud, and, as such, the Microsoft product team follows a strategy of *cloud first* as they develop and add new features to the product. However, this does not mean that Power BI is only available in the cloud. Microsoft presents two options for sharing your results with others. The first, most often-utilized method is the cloud-hosted Power BI Service, which is available to users for a low monthly subscription fee. The second option is the on-premises Power BI Report Server, which can be obtained through either your SQL Server licensing with Software Assurance or a subscription level known as Power BI Premium. Both solutions require a development tool called Power BI Desktop, which is available for free, and is where you must start to design your solutions.

Using the **Power BI Desktop** application enables you to define your data discovery and data preparation steps, organize your data model, and design engaging data visualizations on your reports. In this first chapter, the development environment will be introduced, and the data discovery process will be explored in depth. The topics detailed in this chapter include the following:

- Getting started
- Importing data
- Direct query
- Live Connection

Getting started

The Power BI Desktop is available free and can be found via a direct download link at Power BI(https://powerbi.microsoft.com/), or by installing it as an app from Windows Store. There are several benefits in using the Windows Store Power BI app, including automatic updates, no requirement for admin privileges, and making it easier for planned IT roll-out of Power BI.

If you are using the on-premises Power BI Report Server for your deployment strategy, then you must download a different **Power BI Desktop**, which is available by clicking the advanced download options at https://powerbi.microsoft.com/en-us/report-server/ . A separate install is required because updates are released more often to Power BI in the cloud. This book will be written primarily under the assumption that the reader is using the cloud-hosted Power BI Service as their deployment strategy.

Once you download, install, and launch the Power BI Desktop, you will likely be welcomed by the Start screen, which is designed to help new users find their way. Close this start screen so we can review some of the most commonly used features of the application:

Power BI Desktop

Following the numbered figures, let's learn the names and purposes of some of the most important features in the Power BI Desktop:

- **Get Data**: Used for selecting and configuring data sources.
- **Edit Queries**: Launches the **Power Query Editor**, which is used for applying data transformations to incoming data.
- **Report View**: The report canvas used for designing data visualizations. This is the default view open when the Power BI Desktop is launched.
- **Data View**: Provides a view of the data in your model. This looks similar to a typical Excel spreadsheet, but it is read-only.
- **Relationship View**: Primarily used when your data model has multiple tables and relationships need to be defined between them.

Importing data

Power BI is best known for the impressive data visualizations and dashboard capabilities it has. However, before you can begin building reports, you first need to connect to the necessary data sources. Within the Power BI Desktop, a developer has more than 80 unique data connectors to choose from, ranging from traditional file types, database engines, big data solutions, cloud sources, data stored on a web page, and other SaaS providers. This book will not cover all 80 connectors that are available, but it will highlight some of the most popular.

When establishing a connection to a data source, you may be presented with one of three different options on how your data should be treated: Import, DirectQuery, or Live Connection. This section will focus specifically on the Import option.

Choosing to import data, which is the most common option, and default behavior, means that Power BI will physically extract rows of data from the selected source and store it in an in-memory storage engine within Power BI. The Power BI Desktop uses a special method for storing data, known as xVelocity, which is an in-memory technology that not only increases the performance of your query results but can also highly compress the amount of space taken up by your Power BI solution. In *some* cases, the compression that takes place can even lower the disk space required up to one-tenth of the original data source size. The xVelocity engine uses a local unseen instance of **SQL Server Analysis Services** (**SSAS**) to provide these in-memory capabilities.

There are consequences to using the import option within Power BI that you should also consider. These consequences will be discussed later in this chapter, but as you read on, consider the following:

- How does data that has been imported into Power BI get updated?
- What if I need a dashboard to show near real-time analytics?
- How much data can really be imported into an in-memory storage system?

Excel as a source

Believe it or not, Excel continues to be the most popular application in the world and as such, you should expect that at some point you will be using it as a data source:

1. To get started, open the Power BI Desktop and close the start-up screen if it automatically appears.

2. Under the **Home** ribbon, you will find that **Get Data** button, which you already learned is used for selecting and configuring data sources. Selecting the down arrow next to the button will show you the most common connectors, but selecting the center of the button will launch the full list of all available connectors. Regardless of which way you select the button, you will find Excel at the top of both lists.

3. Navigate to and open the file called `AdventureWorksDW.xlsx` from the book resources. This will launch the **Navigator** dialog, which is used for selecting the objects in the Excel workbook you desire to take data from:

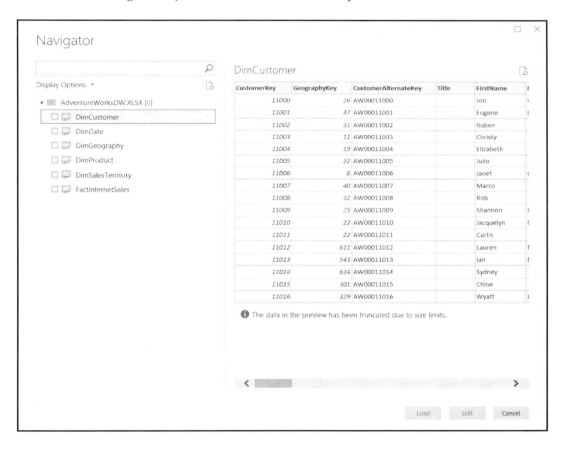

4. In this example, you see six separate spreadsheets you can choose from. Clicking once on the spreadsheet name will give you a preview of the data it stores, while clicking the checkbox next to the name will include it as part of the data import. For this example, select the checkboxes next to all of the available objects, then notice the options available in the bottom right.

5. Selecting **Load** will immediately take the data from the selected spreadsheets and import them as separate tables in your Power BI data model. Choosing **Edit** will launch an entirely new window called the **Power Query Editor** that allows you to apply business rules or transforms to your prior to importing it. You will learn much more about the **Power Query Editor** in Chapter 2, *Data Transformation Strategies*. Since you will learn more about this later, simply select **Load** to end this example.

Another topic you will learn more about in Chapter 6, *Using a Cloud Deployment with the Power BI Service*, is the concept of data refreshes. This is important because, when you import data into Power BI, that data remains static until another refresh is initiated. This refresh can either be initiated manually or set on a schedule. This also requires the installation of a Data Gateway, the application in charge of securely pushing data into the Power BI Service. Feel free to skip to Chapter 6, *Using a Cloud Deployment with the Power BI Service*, if configuring a data refresh is a subject you need to know now.

SQL Server as a source

Another common source designed for relational databases is Microsoft SQL Server:

1. To connect to SQL Server, select the **Get Data** button again, but this time choose **SQL Server**. Here, you must provide the server, but the database is optional and can be selected later:

2. For the first time, you are asked to choose the type of **Data Connectivity mode** you would like. As mentioned previously, **Import** is the default mode, but you can optionally select **DirectQuery**. DirectQuery will be discussed in greater detail later in this chapter. Expanding the **Advanced** options provides a way to insert a SQL statement that may be used as your source. For the following example, in the server is the only one property populated before clicking **OK**:

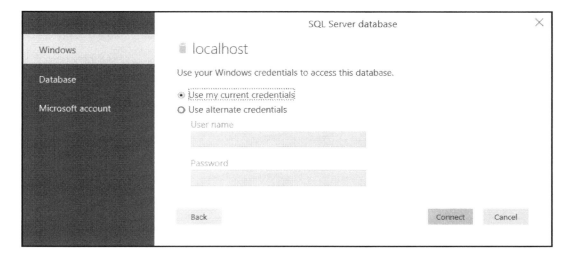

3. Next, you will be prompted to provide the credentials you are using to connect to the database server you provided on the previous screen.

4. Click **Connect** after providing the proper credentials to launch the same **Navigator** dialog that you may remember from when you connected to Excel. Here, you will select the tables, views, or functions within your SQL Server database that you desire to import into your Power BI solution. Once again, the final step in this dialog allows you to choose to either **Load** or **Edit** the results.

Web as a source

One pleasant surprise to many Power BI Developers is the availability of a web connector. Using this connection type allows you to source data from files that are stored on a website or even data that has been embedded into an HTML table on the web page. Using this type of connector can often be helpful when you would like to supplement your internal corporate data sources with information that can be publicly found on the internet.

For this example, imagine you are working for a major automobile manufacturer in the United States. You have already designed a Power BI solution using data internally available within your organization that shows historical patterns in sales trends. However, you would like to determine whether there are any correlations in periods of historically higher fuel prices and lower automobile sales. Fortunately, you found that the United States Department of Labor publicly posts historical average consumer prices of many commonly purchased items, including fuel prices.

1. Now that you understand the scenario within the Power BI Desktop, select the **Get Data** button and choose **Web** as your source. You will then be prompted to provide the URL where the data can be found. In this example, the data can be found by searching on the website Data.Gov (`https://www.data.gov/`) or, to save you some time, use the direct link: `https://download.bls.gov/pub/time.series/ap/ap.data.2.Gasoline`. Once you provide the URL, click **OK**:

2. Next, you will likely be prompted with an **Access Web Content** dialog box. This is important when you are using a data source that requires a login to access. Since this data source does not require a login to find the data, you can simply select anonymous access, which is the default, and then click **Connect**:

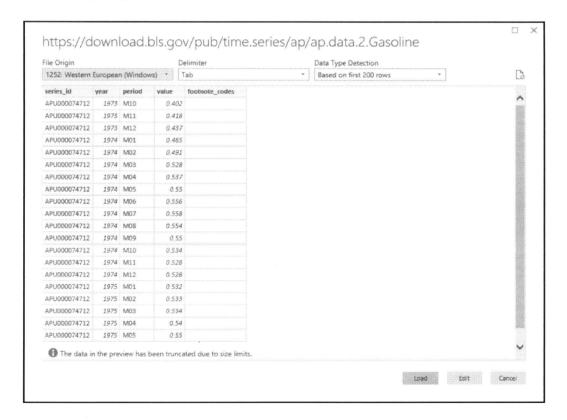

Notice on the next screen that the Power BI Desktop recognizes the URL provided as a tab-delimited file that can now easily be added to any existing data model you have designed.

DirectQuery

Many of you have likely been trying to envision how you may implement these data imports in your environment. You may ask yourself questions such as the following:

- If data imported into Power BI uses an in-memory technology, did my company provide me a machine that has enough memory to handle this?
- Am I really going to import my source table with tens of billions of rows into memory?
- How do I handle a requirement of displaying results in real time from the source?

These are all excellent questions that would have many negative answers if the only way to connect to your data was by importing your source into Power BI. Fortunately, there is another way. Using **DirectQuery**, Power BI allows you to connect directly to a data source so that no data is imported or copied into the Power BI Desktop.

Why is this a good thing? Consider the questions that were asked at the beginning of this section. Since no data is imported to the Power BI Desktop, that means it is less important how powerful your personal laptop is because all query results are now processed on the source server instead of your laptop. It also means that there is no need to refresh the results in Power BI because any reports you design are always pointing to a live version of the data source. That's a huge benefit!

Enabling this feature can be done by simply selecting **DirectQuery** during the configuration of a data source. The following screenshot shows a connection to an SQL Server database with the **DirectQuery** option selected:

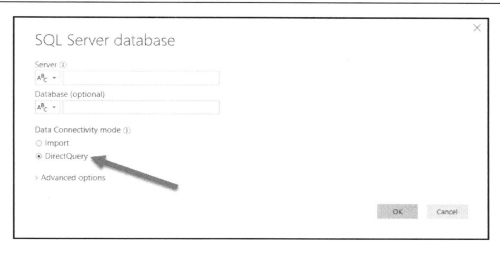

Earlier in this chapter, the Data Gateway application was mentioned as a requirement to schedule data refreshes for sources that used the import option. This same application is also needed with DirectQuery if your data is an on-premises source. Even though there is no scheduled data refresh, the Data Gateway is still required to push on-premises data into the cloud. Again, this will be discussed in more depth in Chapter 6, *Using a Cloud Deployment with the Power BI Service*.

Limitations

So, if DirectQuery is so great, why not choose it every time? Well, with every great feature you will also find limitations. The first glaring limitation is that not all data sources support DirectQuery. As of the time this book was written, the following data sources support DirectQuery in Power BI:

- Amazon Redshift
- Azure HDInsight Spark
- Azure SQL Database
- Azure SQL Data Warehouse
- Google BigQuery
- IBM Netezza
- Impala (Version 2.x)
- Oracle Database (Version 12 and above)
- SAP Business Warehouse Application Server

- SAP Business Warehouse Message Server
- SAP HANA
- Snowflake
- Spark (Version 0.9 and above)
- SQL Server
- Teradata Database
- Vertica

Depending on the data source you choose, there is a chance of slower query performance when using DirectQuery compared to the default data import option. Keep in mind that when the import option is selected it leverages a highly sophisticated in-memory storage engine. When selecting **DirectQuery**, performance will depend on the source type you have chosen from the list above.

Another limitation worth noting is that not all Power BI features are supported when you choose **DirectQuery**. For example, depending on the selected source, *some* the **Power Query Editor** features are disabled and could result in the following message: **This step results in a query that is not supported in DirectQuery mode**. Another example is that some DAX functions are unavailable when using DirectQuery. For instance, several Time Intelligence functions such as TotalYTD would generate the following type error when using DirectQuery:

```
YTD = TotalYTD(SUM('FactInternetSales'[SalesAmount]),'DimDate'[FullDateAlternateKey])
```
Function 'DATESYTD' is not supported in DirectQuery mode.

The reason for this limitation is because DirectQuery automatically attempts to convert DAX functions such as this one to a query in the data source's native language. So, if the source of this solution was SQL Server, then Power BI would attempt to convert this DAX function into a comparable T-SQL script. Once Power BI realizes the DAX function used is not compatible with the source, the error is generated.

You can turn on functions that DirectQuery blocks by going to **File | Options and settings | Options | DirectQuery | Allow restricted measures in DirectQuery Mode**. When this option is selected, any DAX expressions that are valid for a measure can be used. However, you should know that selecting this can result in very slow query performance when these blocked functions are used.

Live Connection

The basic concept of Live Connection is very similar to that of DirectQuery. Just like DirectQuery, when you use a Live Connection no data is actually imported into Power BI. Instead, your solution points directly to the underlying data source and leverages Power BI Desktop simply as a data visualization tool. So, if these two things are so similar, then why give them different names? The answer is because even though the basic concept is the same, DirectQuery and Live Connection vary greatly.

One difference that should quickly be noticeable is the query performance experience. It was mentioned in the last section that DirectQuery can often have poor performance depending on the data source type. With Live Connection, you generally will not have any performance problem because it is only supported by the following types of data sources:

- SQL Server Analysis Services Tabular
- SQL Server Analysis Services Multidimensional
- Power BI Service

The reason performance does not suffer from these data sources is because they either use the same xVelocity engine that Power BI does, or another high-performance storage engine. To set up your own Live Connection to one of these sources, you can choose the **SQL Server Analysis Services** database from the list of sources after selecting **Get Data**. Here, you can specify that the connection should be live:

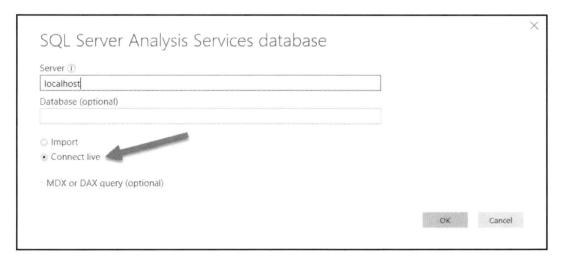

If a dataset is configured for a Live Connection or DirectQuery, then you can expect automatic refreshes to occur approximately every hour or when interaction with the data occurs. You can manually adjust the refresh frequency in the Scheduled cache refresh option in the Power BI service.

Limitations

So far, this sounds great! You have now learned that you can connect directly to your data sources, without importing data into your model, and you won't have significant performance consequences. Of course, these benefits don't come without giving something up, so what are the limitations of a Live Connection?

What you will encounter with Live Connections are limitations that are generally a result of the fact that Analysis Services is an Enterprise BI tool. Thus, if you are going to connect to it, then it has probably already gone through significant data cleansing and modeling by your IT team.

Modeling capabilities such as defining relationships are not available because these would be designed in an Analysis Services Model. Also, the Power Query Editor is not available at all against a Live Connection source. While at times this may be frustrating, it does make sense that it works this way because any of the changes you may desire to make with relationships or in the query editor should be done in Analysis Services, not Power BI.

Which should I choose?

Now that you have learned about the three different ways to connect to your data, you're left to wonder which option is best for you. It's fair to say that the choice you make will really depend on the requirements of each individual project you have. To summarize, some of the considerations that were mentioned in this chapter are listed in the following table:

Consideration	Import Data	DirectQuery	Live Connection
Best performance	X		X
Best design experience	X		
Best for keeping data up-to-date		X	X
Data sources availability	X		
Most scalable		X	X

Some of these items to consider may be more important than others to you. So, to make this more personal, try using the Decision Matrix file that is included with this book. In this file, you can rank (from 1 to 10) the importance of each of these considerations to help give you some guidance on which option is best for you.

Since the Data Import option presents the most available features, going forward, this book primarily uses this option. In `Chapter 2`, *Data Transformation Strategies*, you will learn how to implement data transformation strategies to ensure all the necessary business rules are applied to your data.

Summary

Power BI provides users a variety of methods for connecting to data sources with natively built-in data connectors. The connector you choose for your solution will depend on where your data is located. Once you connect to a data source, you can decide on the type of query mode that best suits your needs. Some connectors allow for zero latency in your results with the options of Direct Query or Live Connection. In this chapter, you learned about the benefits and disadvantages of each query mode, and you were given a method for weighting these options using a decision matrix. In the next chapter, you will learn more about how data transformations may be applied to your data import process so that incoming data will be properly cleansed.

2
Data Transformation Strategies

Within any BI project, it is essential that the data you are working with has been properly scrubbed to make for accurate results on your reports and dashboards. Applying data cleansing business rules, also known as transforms, is the method for correcting inaccurate or malformed data, but the process can often be the most time-consuming part of any corporate BI solution. However, the data transformation capabilities built into Power BI are both very powerful and user-friendly. Using the Power Query Editor, tasks that would typically be difficult or time-consuming in an enterprise BI tool are as simple as right-clicking on a column and selecting the appropriate transform for the field. While interacting with the user interface in this editor, a language called M is being written automatically for you behind the scenes.

Through the course of this chapter, you will explore some of the most common features of the Power Query Editor that make it so highly regarded by its users. Since one sample dataset cannot provide all the problems you will run into, you will be provided several small disparate examples to show you what is possible. This chapter will detail the following topics:

- The Power Query Editor
- Transform basics
- Advanced data transformation options
- Leveraging R
- M formula language

The Power Query Editor

The **Power Query Editor** is the primary tool that you will utilize for applying data transformations and cleansing processes to your solution. This editor can be launched as part of establishing a connection to your data, or by simply clicking **Edit Queries** on the **Home** ribbon of the Power BI Desktop. When the Power Query editor is opened, you will notice that it has its own separate environment for you to work in. The environment encapsulates a user-friendly method for working with all of the queries that you will define. Before you dive deep into the capabilities of the Power Query Editor, let's first start by doing an overview of the key areas that are most important:

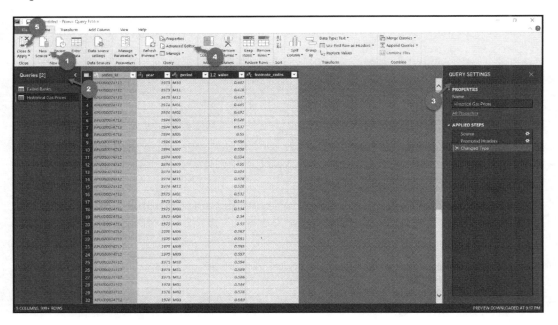

Power BI Desktop

Following the numbered figures, let's review some of the most important features of the Power Query Editor:

- **New Source**: This launches the same interface as the **Get Data** button that you learned about in `Chapter 1`, *Getting Started with Importing Data Options*.

- **Queries Pane**: A list of all the queries that you have connected to. From here, you can rename a query, disable the load and refresh capabilities, and organize your queries into groups.
- **Query Settings**: Within this pane, you can rename the query, but more importantly you can see and change the list of steps, or transforms, that have been applied to your query.
- **Advanced Editor**: By launching the **Advanced Editor**, you can see the M query that is automatically written for you by the Power Query Editor.
- **Close & Apply**: Choosing this option will close the **Power Query Editor** and load the results into the data model.

Transform basics

Applying data transformations within the **Power Query Editor** can be a surprisingly simple thing to do. However, there are few things to consider as we begin this process. The first is that there are multiple ways to solve a problem. As you work your way through this book, the authors have tried to show you the fastest and easiest methods of solving the problems that are presented, but these solutions certainly will not be the only ways to reach your goals.

The next thing you should understand is that every click you do inside the **Power Query Editor** is automatically converted into a formula language called M. Virtually all the basic transforms you will ever need can be accomplished by simply interacting with the **Power Query Editor** user interface, but for more complex business problems there is a good chance you may have to at least modify the M queries that are written for you by the editor. You will learn more about M later in this chapter.

Finally, the last important consideration to understand is that all transforms that are created within the editor are stored in the **Query Settings** pane under a section called **Applied Steps**. Why is this important to know? The **Applied Steps** section has many features, but here are some of the most critical to know for now:

- **Deleting transforms**: If you make a mistake and need to undo a step, you can click the **Delete** button next to a step.
- **Modifying transforms**: This can be done with any step that has a gear icon next to it.
- **Changing the order of transforms**: If you realize that it is better for one step to execute before another one, you can change the order of how the steps are executed.

- Clicking on any step prior to the current one will allow you to see how your query results would earlier in the process.

With this understanding, you will now get hands-on with applying several basic transforms inside the Power Query Editor. The goal of these first sets of example is to get you comfortable with the Power Query user interface before the more complex use cases are covered.

Use First Row as Headers

Organizing column names or headers is often an important first task when organizing your dataset. Providing relevant column names makes many of the downstream processes, such as building reports, much easier. Often, column headers are automatically imported from your data source, but sometimes you may be working with a more unique data source that makes it difficult for Power BI to capture the column header information. This walkthrough will show how to deal with such a scenario:

1. Launch the Power BI Desktop, and click **Get Data** under the **Home** ribbon.
2. Choose **Excel**, then navigate and select Open on the Failed Bank List.xlsx file that is available in the book source files.
3. In the **Navigator** window, select the table called Data, then choose **Edit**. When the **Power Query Editor** launches, you should notice that the column headers are not automatically imported. In fact, the column headers are in the first row of the data.
4. To push the column names that are in the first row of data to the header section, select the transform called **Use First Row as Headers** from the **Home** ribbon:

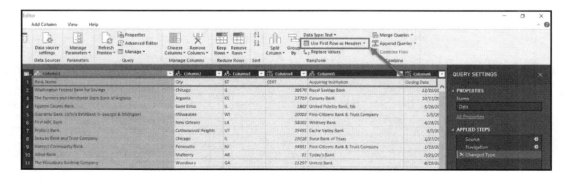

Remove Columns

Often, the data sources you will connect to will include many columns that are not necessary for the solution you are designing. It is important to remove these unnecessary columns from your dataset because these unused columns needlessly take up space inside your data model. There are several different methods for removing columns in the Power Query Editor. This example will show one of these methods using the same dataset from the prior demonstration:

1. Multi-select (*Ctrl* + click) the column headers of the columns you wish to keep as part of your solution. In this scenario, select the columns **Bank Name**, **City**, **ST**, and **Closing Date**.
2. With these four columns selected, right-click on any of the selected columns and choose **Remove Other Columns**. Once this transform is completed, you should be left with only the columns you need:

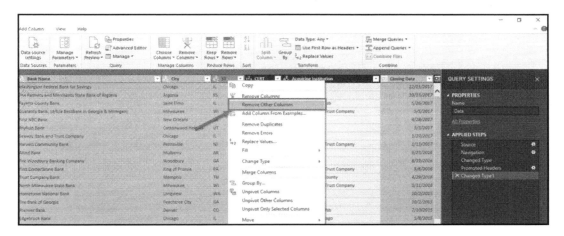

Option to Remove Other Columns

Another popular method for removing columns is clicking the **Choose Columns** button on the **Home** ribbon of the **Power Query Editor**. This option provides a list of all the columns, and you can choose the columns you wish to keep or exclude.

You can also select the columns you wish to remove; right-click on one of the selected columns and click Remove. This seems like the more obvious method. However, this option is not as user-friendly in the long run because it does not provide an option to edit the transform in the **Applied Steps** section like the first two methods allow.

Change type

Defining column data types properly early on in your data scrubbing process can help to determine the type of values you are working with. The **Power Query Editor** has various numeric, text, and date-time data types for you to choose from. In our current example, all of the data types were automatically interpreted correctly by the **Power Query Editor**, but let's look at where you could change this if necessary:

1. Locate the data type indicator on the column header to the right of the column name
2. Click the data type icon, and a menu will open that allows you to choose the new data type you desire:

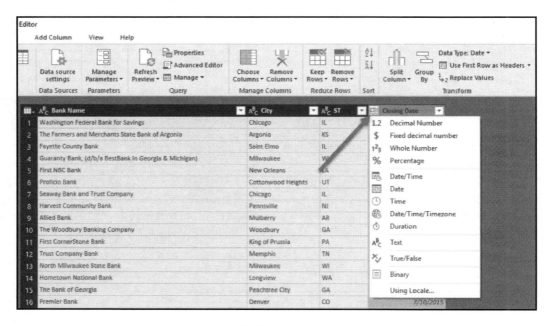

Choosing the Datatype

Another method you can use for changing column data types is to right-click on the column you wish to change, then select Change Type and choose the new data type you desire.

 If you want to change multiple column data types at once, you can multi-select the necessary columns, then select the new data type from the Data Type property under the **Home** ribbon.

Many of the transforms you will encounter in the future are contextually based on the column data types you are working with. For example, if you have a column that is a date then you will be provided special transforms that can only be executed against a date data type, such as extracting the month name from a date column.

Add Column From Examples

One option that can make complex data transformations seem simple is the feature called Add Column From Examples. Using Add Column From Examples, you can provide the Power Query Editor a sample of what you would like your data to look like, and it can then automatically determine which transforms are required to accomplish your goal. Continuing with the same failed banks example, let's walk through a simple example of how to use this feature:

1. Find and select the **Add Column** tab in the Power Query Editor ribbon.
2. Select the **Column From Example** button and, if prompted, choose **From All Columns**. This will launch a new **Add Column From Examples** interface.
3. Our goal is to leverage this feature to combine the City and ST columns together. In the first empty cell, type Chicago, IL and then hit Enter. You should notice that below the text you typed Power BI has automatically translated what you typed into a transform that can be applied for every row in the dataset.

4. Once you click **OK**, the transform is finalized and automatically added to the overall M query that has been built through the user interface:

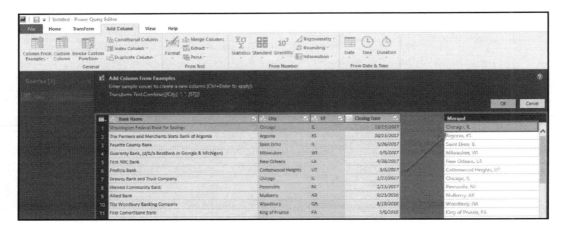

Adding Columns from Examples

Sometimes, you may encounter scenarios where the **Add Column From Examples** feature needs more than one example to properly translate your example into an M query function that accomplishes your goal. If this happens, simply provide additional examples of how you would like the data to appear, and the **Power Query Editor** should adjust to account for outliers.

Advanced data transformation options

Now that you should be more comfortable working within the Power Query Editor, let's take the next step in working with it. Often, you will find the need to go beyond these basic transforms when dealing with data that requires more care. In this section, you will learn about some of the more common advanced transforms that you may have a need for, which include Conditional Columns, Fill down, Unpivot, Merge Queries, and Append Queries.

Conditional Columns

Using the **Power Query Conditional Columns** functionality is a great way to add new columns to your query that follow logical if/then/else statements. This concept of if/then/else is common across many programming languages, including Excel formulas. Let's review a real-world scenario where you would be required to do some data cleansing on a file before it can be used. In this example, you will be provided a file of all the counties in the United States, and you must create a new column that extracts the state name from the county column and places it in its own column:

1. Start by connecting to the FIPS_CountyName.txt file that is found in the book files using the Text/CSV connector.
2. Launch the **Power Query Editor**, and start by changing the data type of Column1 to Text. When you do this, you will be prompted to replace an existing type conversion. You can accept this by clicking **Replace current**.
3. Click the arrow next to the column header for Column2 and uncheck **United States** from the list, then click **OK**.
4. Now, on Column2, filter out **United States** from the field to remove this value from the column.
5. Remove the **state abbreviation** from Column2 by right-clicking on the column header and selecting **Split Column | By Delimiter**. Choose **-- Custom --** for the delimiter type, and type **,** , then click **OK**:

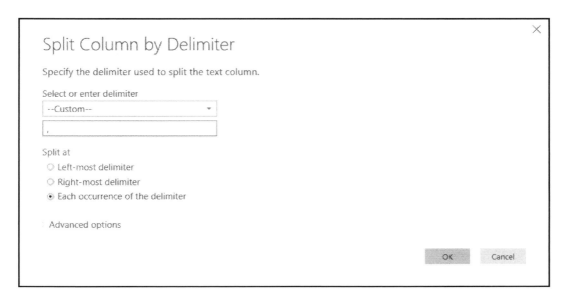

6. Next, rename the column names `Column1`, `Column2.1`, and `Column 2.2`, to `County Code`, `County Name`, and `State Abbreviation`, respectively.

7. To isolate the full state name into its own column, you will need to implement a **Conditional Column**. Go to the **Add Column** button in the ribbon and select **Conditional Column**.

8. Change the New column name property to `State Name` and implement the logic *If State Abbreviation equals null Then return County Name Else return null* as shown in the following screenshot. To return the value from another column, you must select the icon below the text **Output**, then choose **Select a column**. Once this is complete, click **OK**:

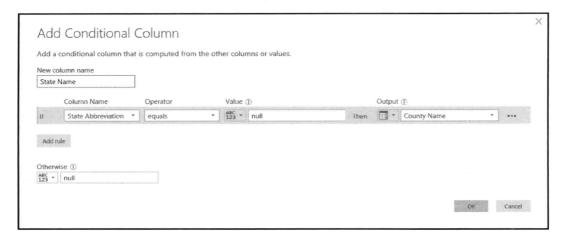

This results in a new column called `State Name`, which has the fully spelled-out state name only appearing on rows where the `State Abbreviation` is `null`.

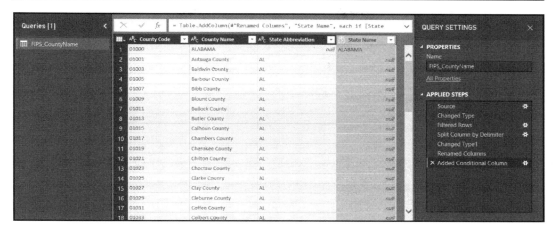

This is only setting the stage to fully scrub this dataset. To complete the data cleansing process for this file, read on to the next section. However, for the purposes of this example, you have now learned how to leverage the capabilities of the Conditional Column transform in the **Power Query Editor**.

Fill Down

Fill Down is a rather unique transform in how it operates. By selecting **Fill Down** on a particular column, a value will replace all Null values below it until another non-null appears. When another non-null value is present, that value will then fill down to all Null values. To examine this transform, you will pick up from where you left off with the Conditional Column example in the previous section.

1. Right-click on the **State Name** column header and select **Transform ||
   Capitalize Each Word**. This transform should be self-explanatory.
2. Next, select the State Name column and, in the Transform ribbon, select **Fill
   || Down**. This will take the value in the **State Name** column and replace all
   non-null values until there is another State Name value that it can switch
   to. After performing this transform, scroll through the results to ensure that
   the value of Alabama switches to Alaska when appropriate.

3. To finish this example, filter out any Null values that appear in the State Abbreviation column. The final result should look like this:

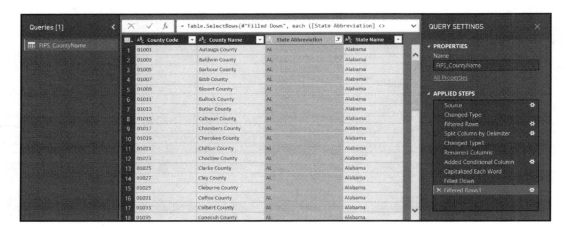

In this example, you learned how you can use **Fill Down** to replace all of the `null` values below a `non-null` value. You can also use **Fill Up** to do the opposite, which would replace all the `null` values above a `non-null` value.

Unpivot

The Unpivot transform is an incredibly powerful transform that allows you to reorganize your dataset into a more structured format for Business Intelligence. Let's discuss this by visualizing a practical example to help understand the purpose of Unpivot. Imagine you are provided a file that has the last three years of population by US States, and looks like this:

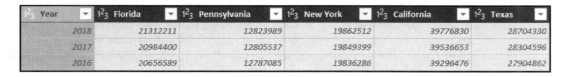

Year	Florida	Pennsylvania	New York	California	Texas
2018	21312211	12823989	19862512	39776830	28704330
2017	20984400	12805537	19849399	39536653	28304596
2016	20656589	12787085	19836286	39296476	27904862

The problem with data stored like this is you cannot very easily answer simple questions. For example, how would you answer questions like, *What was the total population for all states in the US in 2018* or *What was the average state population in 2016?* With the data stored in this format, simple reports are made rather difficult to design. This is where the Unpivot transform can be a lifesaver. Using Unpivot, you can change this dataset into something more acceptable for a BI project, like this:

Data stored in this format can now easily answer the questions posed earlier. To accomplish this in other programming languages can often require fairly complex logic, while the **Power Query Editor** does it in just a few clicks.

There are three different methods for selecting the Unpivot transform that you should be aware of, and include the following options:

- **Unpivot Columns**: Turns any selected columns headers into row values and the data in those columns into a corresponding row. With this selection, any new columns that may get added to the data source *will* automatically be included in the Unpivot transform.

- **Unpivot Other Columns**: Turns all column headers that *are not* selected into row values and the data in those columns into a corresponding row. With this selection, any new columns that may get added to the data source will automatically be included in the Unpivot transform.
- **Unpivot Only Selected Columns**: Turns any selected columns headers into row values and the data in those columns into a corresponding row. With this selection, any new columns that may get added to the data source *will not* be included in the Unpivot transform.

Let's walk through two examples of using the Unpivot transform to show you a few of these methods, and provide an understanding of how this complex problem can be solved with little effort in Power BI.

1. Launch a new instance of the Power BI Desktop, and use the Excel connector to import the workbook called `Income Per Person.xlsx` found in the book source files. Once you select this workbook, choose the spreadsheet called `Data` in the **Navigator** window, and then select **Edit** to launch the **Power Query Editor**.

2. Now, make the first row of data column headers by selecting the transform called **Use First Row as Headers** under the **Home** Ribbon.

3. Rename the column `GDP per capita PPP, with projections` column to `Country`.

4. If you look closely at the column headers, you can tell that most of the column names are actually years and the values inside those columns are the income for those years. This is not the ideal way to store this data because it would be incredibly difficult to answer the question, *What is the average income per person for Belgium?* To make it easier to answer this type of question, right-click on the Country column and select **Unpivot Other Columns**.

5. Rename the `columns` **Attribute** and `Value to Year and Income`, respectively.

6. To finish this first example, you should also rename this query Income.

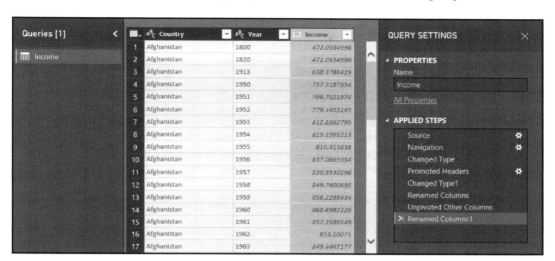

This first method walked you through what can often be the fastest method for performing an Unpivot transform, which is by using the Unpivot Other Columns option. In this next example, you will learn how to use the Unpivot Columns method.

1. Remain in the Power Query Editor, and select New Source from the Home Ribbon to use the Excel connector to import the workbook called Total `Population.xlsx` found in the book source files. Once you select this workbook, choose the spreadsheet called Data in the Navigator window, and then select OK.

2. Like the last example, you will again need to make the first row of data column headers by selecting the transform called Use First Row as Headers under the Home Ribbon.

3. Then, rename the column Total population to Country.

4. This time, multi-select all the columns except Country, then right-click on one of the selected columns and choose Unpivot Columns. The easiest way to multi-select these columns is to select the first column then hold *Shift* before clicking the last column.

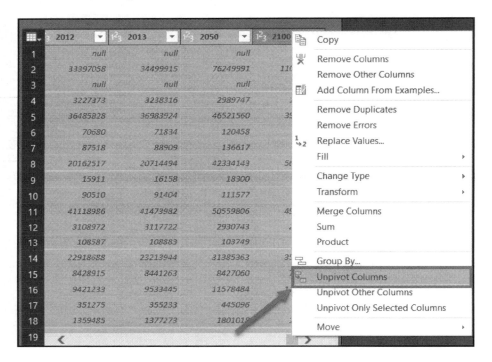

5. Rename the columns Attribute and Value to Year and Population, respectively.
6. To finish this first example, you should also rename this query Population.

In this section, you learned about two different methods for performing an Unpivot. To complete the data cleansing process on these two datasets, it's recommended that you continue through the next section on Merging Queries.

Merging Queries

A common requirement when building BI solutions is the need to join two tables together to form a new result that includes some columns from both tables in a single query. Fortunately, Power BI makes this task very simple with the **Merge Queries** feature. Using this feature requires that you select two tables and then determine which column or columns will be the basis of how the two queries are merged. After determining the appropriate columns for your join, you will select a join type. The join types are listed here with the description that is provided within the product.

- Left Outer (all from first, matching from second)
- Right Outer (all from second, matching from first)
- Full Outer (all rows from both)
- Inner (only matching rows)
- Left Anti (rows only in first)
- Right Anti (rows only in second)

Many of you may already be very familiar with these different join terms from SQL programming you have learned in the past. However, if these terms are all new to you I recommend reviewing Visualizing Merge Join Types in Power BI, courtesy of Jason Thomas in the Power BI Data Story Gallery: `https://community.powerbi.com/t5/Data-Stories-Gallery/Visualizing-Merge-Join-Types-in-Power-BI/m-p/219906`. This visual aid is a favorite of many users that are new to these concepts.

To examine the **Merge Queries** option, you will pick up from where you left off with the Unpivot examples in the previous section.

1. With the **Population query** selected, find and select **Merge Queries | Merge Queries as New** under the **Home** Ribbon.
2. In the **Merge dialog box**, select the **Income query** from the dropdown selection in the middle of the screen.
3. Then, multi-select the **Country** and **Year** columns under the **Population query**, and do the same under the **Income query**. This defines which columns will be used to join the two queries together. Ensure that the number indicators next to the column headers match. If they don't, you could accidentally attempt to join on the incorrect columns.

4. Next, select **Inner (only matching rows)** for the Join Kind. This join type will return rows only when the columns you chose to join on exist in both queries. Before you click **OK**, confirm that your screen looks like this:

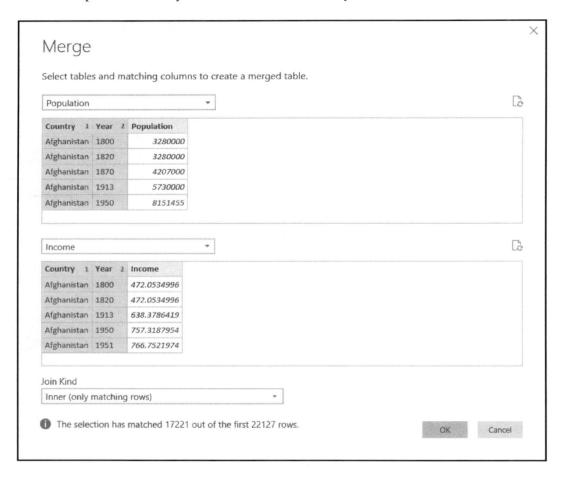

5. Once you select **OK**, this will create a new query called `Merge1` that combines the results of the two queries. Go ahead and rename this query **Country Stats**.

6. You will also notice that there is a column called `Income` that has a value of Table for each row. This column is actually representative for the entire `Income` query that you joined to. To choose which columns you want from this query, click the **Expand** button on the column header. After clicking the **Expand** button, uncheck `Country`, `Year`, and Use original column name as the prefix then click **OK**.

7. Rename the column called `Income.1` to `Income`.

8. Finally, since you chose the option `Merge Queries` as New in Step 1, you can disable the load option for the original queries that you started with. To do this, right-click on the `Income` query in the **Queries** pane and click **Enable Load** to disable it. Do the same thing for the **Population** query. Disabling these queries means that the only query that will be loaded into your Power BI data model is the new one, called **Country Stats**:

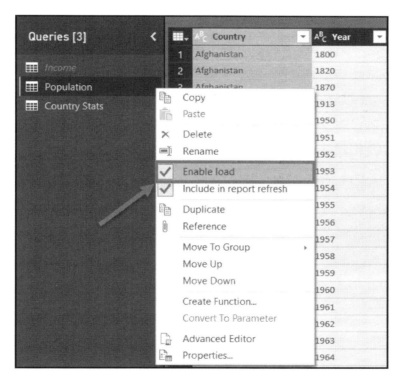

To begin using this dataset in a report, you would click Close & Apply. You will learn more about building reports in `Chapter 5`, *Visualizing Data*.

In this section, you learned how the **Merge Queries** option is ideal for joining two queries together. In the next section, you will learn how you could solve the problem of performing a union of two or more queries.

Appending Queries

Occasionally, you will work with multiple datasets that need to be appended to each other. Here's a scenario: you work for a customer service department for a company that provides credit to customers. You are regularly provided .csv and .xlsx files that give summaries of customer complaints regarding credit cards and student loans. You would like to be able to analyze both of these data extracts at the same time but, unfortunately, the credit card and student loan complaints are provided in two separate files. In this example, you will learn how to solve this problem by performing an append operation on these two different files.

1. Launch a new instance of the Power BI Desktop, and use the **Excel** connector to import the workbook called **Student Loan Complaints.xlsx** found in the book source files. Once you select this workbook, choose the spreadsheet called **Student Loan Complaints** in the Navigator window, and then select **Edit** to launch the Power Query Editor.

2. Next, import the credit card data by selecting **New Source | Text/CSV**, then choose the file called Credit Card Complaints.csv found in the book source files. Click **OK** to bring this data into the **Power Query Editor**.

3. With the **Credit Card Complaints** query selected, find and select **Append Queries | Append Queries as New** under the **Home** Ribbon.

4. Select **Student Loan Complaints** as the table to append to, then select **OK**.

5. Rename the newly created query **All Complaints**.

6. Similar to the previous example, you would likely want to disable the load option for the original queries that you started with. To do this, right-click on the Student **Load Complaints query** in the **Queries** pane, and click **Enable Load** to disable it.

7. Do the same to the **Credit Card Complaints** query, and then select **Close & Apply**.

Leveraging R

R is a very powerful scripting language that is primarily used for advanced analytics tools, but also has several integration points within Power BI. One such integration is the ability to apply business rules to your data with the R language. Why is that important? Well, with this capability you can extend beyond the limits of the Power Query Editor and call functions and libraries from R to do things that would not regularly be possible. In the next two sections, you will explore how to set up your machine to leverage R within Power BI and then walk through an example of using an R Script transform.

 There are many additional books and references you can read to learn more about the R scripting language, but for the purposes of this book, our goal is to inform you on what is possible when R and Power BI are combined.

Installation and configuration

To use R within Power BI, you must first install an R distribution for you to run and execute scripts against. In this book, we will leverage Microsoft's distribution, Microsoft R Open. It is an open source project and free for anyone to use. Once Microsoft R Open has been installed, you can then configure Power BI to recognize the home directory where R libraries may be installed. Let's walk through these setup steps together:

1. Navigate to the website `https://mran.microsoft.com/download/` to download and install Microsoft R Open.
2. For the purposes of our example, you will select **Download next to Microsoft R Open for Windows**.
3. Once the download has completed, run the installation and accept all default settings and user agreements.
4. Next, launch a new instance of the Power BI Desktop to set up the R integration with Power BI. Click the menu options **File | Options and settings | Options**.

5. Choose the R scripting section and ensure that the Detected R home directories property is filled with the R instance you just installed:

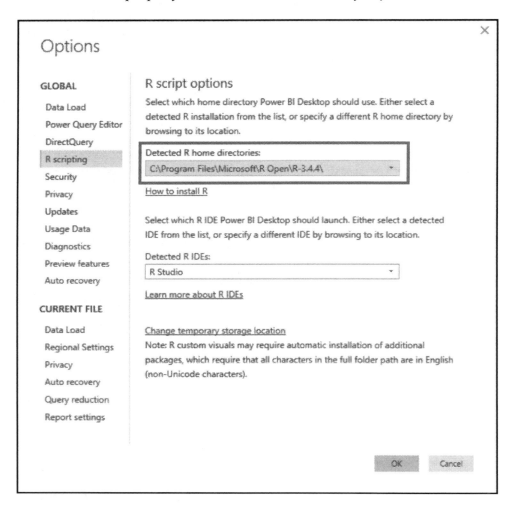

6. Once this is completed, click OK to begin using the capabilities of R within Power BI.

The R Script transform

With the R distribution now installed and configured to integrate with Power BI, you are now ready to see what's possible with these new capabilities. In this example, you will be looking at data from the European Stock Market. The problem with this dataset, that must be corrected with R, is that the file provided to you is missing values for certain days. So, to get a more accurate reading of the stock market, you will use an R package called MICE to impute the missing values:

1. Before beginning in Power BI you should ensure that the MICE library is installed and available in the R Distribute you installed in the last section. To do this, launch Microsoft R Open from your device. This is the basic RGui that was installed for you to run R scripts with. Microsoft R Open may need to be run as administrator. To do this right-click on the application and select Run as administrator.

 For many developers, the preferred method for writing R scripts is a free open source tool called RStudio. RStudio includes a code editor, debugging, and visualization tools that many find easier to work with. You can download RStudio from `https://www.rstudio.com/`.

2. Type the following script in the **R Console** window, and then hit *Enter*:

   ```
   install.packages("mice")
   ```

3. You can close the **R Console** and return to the Power BI Desktop after it returns back `package 'mice' successfully unpacked and MD5 sums checked`.

4. In the Power BI Desktop, start by connecting to the required csv data source called `EuStockMarkets_NA.csv` from the book source files. Once you connect to the file, click **Edit** to launch the **Power Query Editor**.

5. You will notice that there are a few days that are missing a **SMI (Stock Market Index)** value. The values that show NA we would like to replace using an R script. Go under the **Transform** ribbon, and select the **Run R Script** button on the far right.

6. Use the following R script to call the MICE library that you recently installed to detect what the missing values in this dataset should be:

   ```
   # 'dataset' holds the input data for this script
   library(mice)
   tempData <- mice(dataset,m=1,maxit=50,meth='pmm',seed=100)
   ```

```
completedData <- complete(tempData,1)
output <- dataset
output$completedValues <- completedData$"SMI missing values"
```

7. Click **OK**, and then click on the hyperlink for the table next to the **completedData** row to see the result of the newly implemented transform for detecting missing values.

This new output has replaced the missing values with new values that were detected based on the algorithm used within the R script. To now build a set of report visuals on this example, you can click **Close & Apply** under the **Home** ribbon.

This is just one simple way that R can be used with Power BI. You should note that in addition to using R as a transform, it can also be used as a data source and as a visual within Power BI.

M formula language

The **Power Query Editor** is the user interface that you have now learned is used to design and build data imports. However, you should also know that every transform you apply within this editor is actually, quietly and behind the scenes, writing an M query for you. The letter M here is a reference to the languages data mashup capabilities.

For simple solutions, it is unlikely that you will ever need to even look at the M query that is being written, but there are some more complex cases where it's helpful to understand how to read and write your own M. For the purposes of this book, covering just the Power BI essentials, you will learn how to find the M query editor within your solution and then understand how to read what it is doing for you. For the purposes of this example, you can open up any previously built example, however, the screenshot used here is coming from the very first example in this chapter on basic transforms.

1. Using any Power BI solution you have designed, launch the **Power Query Editor**.
2. Under the **Home** Ribbon, select **Advanced Editor** to see the M query that has been written by the user interface:

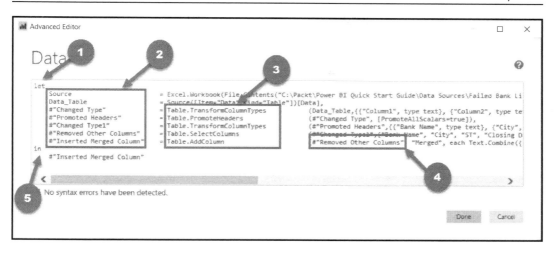

This query has been formatted to make it easier to read. Let's review the key elements that are present here:

1. **Let Expression**: Encapsulates a set of values or named expressions to be computed.

2. **Named Expressions or Variables**: The name given to a set of operations in a step. These names can be anything, but you should note that if you wish to have a space in the name of a step then it must be surrounded by #"". For example, If I wanted something to be called Step 1, then I would have to name an expression #"Step 1".

3. **M Functions**: The operations that are used to manipulate the data source.

4. **Prior Step Reference**: The M Query language generally executes its functions as serial operations, meaning each operation is executed one after the other sequentially. You can see this when you look at a query because each call to an M function always references the prior-named expression, to pick up where it left off.

5. **In Expression**: Oddly, the In expression is actually a reference to what the query will output. Whichever name expression is referenced in the In expression will be what is returned back in the Power Query Editor preview.

 It is important to realize that M is case-sensitive. That means if you ever make a change to a query or write one from scratch, you should be careful because there is a difference between "a" and "A".

#shared

As mentioned previously, this book will not dive deep into writing your own M queries since that would be far beyond the essentials of Power BI. However, there is a great method for exploring the M functions that are available, and how to use them. Within the **Power Query editor**, you can use the #shared function to return back documentation on every available function in the M library. Let's walk through how you can leverage this tool:

1. In a new instance of the Power BI Desktop, select **Get Data** and then choose **Blank Query**. This will launch the **Power Query Editor** with an empty formula bar waiting for you to provide your own M.

2. In this formula bar, type = #shared, then hit *Enter*. Remember that M is case-sensitive so you must use a lower case "s" when typing shared.

3. This will return a list of all the available M functions. By selecting the cell that has the hyperlink text of function, you can see documentation on how to use each function:

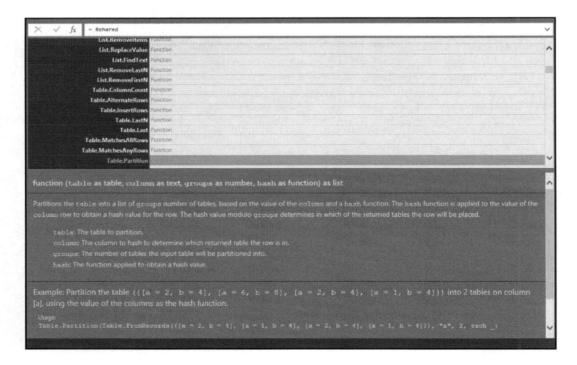

This is a great method for learning what M functions are available, and how each may be used.

Summary

In this chapter, you learned that the Power Query Editor is an extremely powerful tool for applying business rules to incoming data. Implementing data cleansing techniques can be as simple as right-clicking on a column, or more complex such as when building a Conditional Column. While the Power Query Editor does have a vast library of transforms available, you also learned that you can tap into the capabilities of R to extend what's possible when designing queries. Finally, this chapter also helped you learn that the decisions you make while building your queries can impact Query Folding, which can be incredibly important for the performance of your queries.

Building the Data Model 3

In this chapter, you are now going to create a coherent and intelligent data model by creating the necessary relationships to bring those data sources together. The topics detailed in this chapter are as follows:

- Building relationships
- Working with complex relationships
- Usability enhancements

Self Service BI would not be possible without a functional data model. Historically, BI projects focused on building data models could take months and even years to develop when working within the rigid structure and constraints of a corporate business intelligence environment. Unfortunately, studies show that about fifty percent of all BI projects fail, and that these projects either do not complete or don't deliver on promised deliverables at the completion of the project.

Fortunately, Power BI Desktop provides you with a much more agile approach to building your data model, and instead of months or years, you can now build your data model in hours or days.

Building relationships

One could argue that the building of relationships is the most important piece of Power BI Desktop. It is this process, the building of relationships, that makes everything else work like magic in Power BI. The automatic filtering of visuals and reports, the ease in which you can author DAX measures, and the ability to quickly connect disparate data sources are all made possible through properly built relationships in the data model.

Sometimes, Power BI Desktop will create the relationships for you automatically. It is important to verify these *auto-detected relationships* to ensure accuracy.

There are a few characteristics of relationships that you should be aware of, and that will be discussed in this section:

- Auto-detected relationships
- There may be only one active relationship between two tables
- There may be an unlimited number of in-active relationships between two tables
- Relationships may only be built on a single column, not multiple columns
- Relationships automatically filter from the one side of the relationship to the many side
- Relationships cannot be built directly between tables that have a many-to-many relationship

Open up the .pbix file Chapter 3 - Building the Data Model.pbix found in your class files.

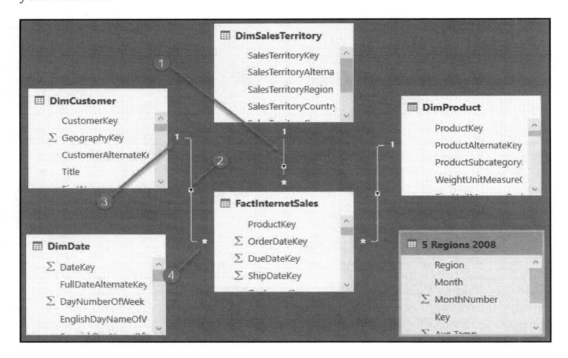

Figure 1-pbix file___

Let's take a closer look at each of the four items highlighted in the preceding screenshot:

1. **Relationship**: The line between two tables represents that a relationship exists
2. **Direction**: The arrow indicates which direction that filtering will occur
3. **One side**: The 1 indicates the `Customer table` as the one side of the relationship
4. **Many side**: The * indicates that the `FactInternetSales` table is the many side of the relationship

The first thing you should do after importing data is to verify that all auto-detected relationships have been created correctly. From the modeling ribbon, select **Manage Relationships**:

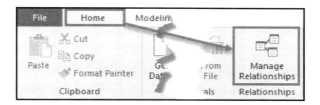

Figure 2-Manage Relationships

This will open up the **Manage Relationships** editor. The relationship editor is where you will go to create new relationships and edit or delete existing relationships. In this demo, the relationship editor will be used to verify the relationships that were automatically created by Power BI Desktop.

Let's take a look at the **Manage Relationships** editor, in which you can manage or perform the following:

- Current relationships in the data model
- Create a new relationship
- Edit existing relationships

- Delete a relationship

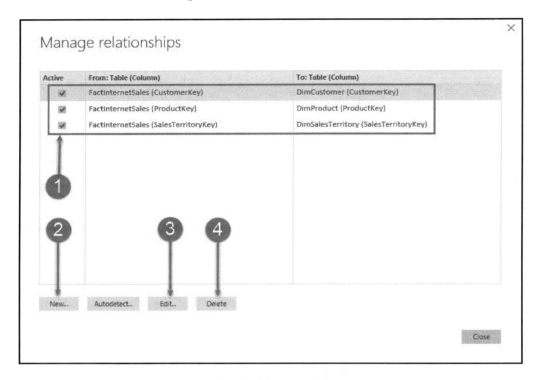

Figure 3- Deleting a Relationship

First, you need to verify auto-detected relationships. The top half of the relationship editor gives you a quick and easy way to see what tables have relationships between them, what columns the relationships have been created on, and if the relationship is an active relationship. We will discuss active and inactive relationships later in this chapter:

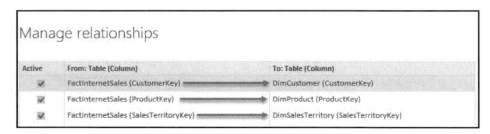

Figure 4-Active Relationshops

Take a look at *Figure 4*, You will see that there are currently three relationships, and all three relationships are currently active. The first relationship is the relationship between the CustomerKey column in the FactInternetSales table and the CustomerKey column in the DimCustomer table. This relationship was created automatically by Power BI Desktop when the tables were imported into the data model, and this is a valid relationship. In fact, all three relationships are valid.

Editing relationships

Now, let's take a look at how to edit an existing relationship. In this example, you will edit the relationship between **FactInternetSales** and **DimCustomer**. To edit an existing relationship, select that relationship and then click on **Edit...**. See *Figure 5*, here:

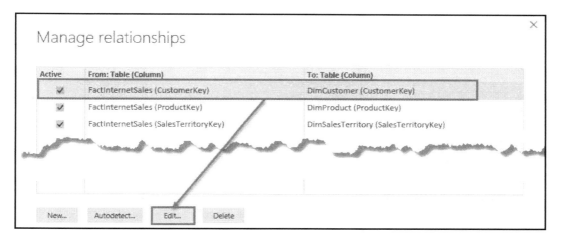

Figure 5-Editing a relationship

Once you select **Edit...** you will receive a new dialog box; this is the **Edit Relationship** editor. In this view, you will see how to change an existing relationship, how to change a relationship to active or inactive, and the cardinality of the current relationship; this is also where you can change the cross filter direction:

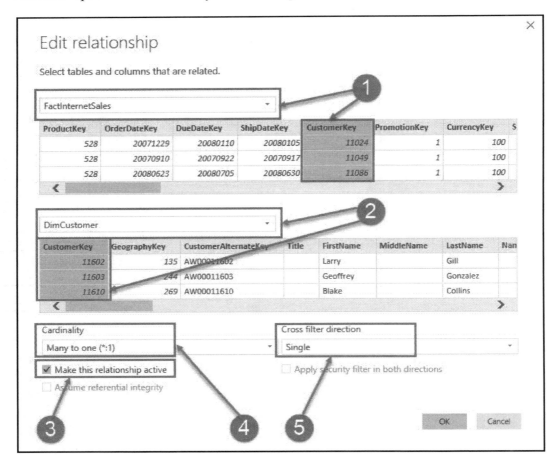

Figure 6-Editing a relationship

There are five things we want to look at in the edit relationship window:

1. This identifies the **FactInternetSales** table and the column that the relationship was built on.
2. This identifies the DimCustomer table and the column that the relationship was built on.

3. This checkbox identifies whether the relationship is active or inactive.

4. This is the current cardinality between the two tables. Here we see that there is a many-to-one relationship between FactInternetSales and DimCustomer. Power BI does an excellent job of identifying the correct cardinality, but it is important to always verify that the cardinality is correct.

5. The cross filter direction can be single or both. The one side of a relationship always filters the many side of the relationship, and this is the default behavior in Power BI. The cross filter option allows you to change this behavior. Cross filtering will be discussed later in this chapter.

If you need to change the relationship of an existing relationship, then you would do that in the edit relationship editor seen in *Figure 6*. To change the column that a relationship has been created on, simply select a different column. It is important to point out that a relationship between two tables may only be created on a single column. Therefore, if you have a multiple column key, also known as a composite key, then you would need to first combine those keys into a single column before creating your relationship. You saw how to combine columns in the previous chapter.

Creating a new relationship

In the previous section, you saw how to verify existing relationships, and even how to edit them. In this section, you are going to learn how to create a new relationship. There are six tables in the data model so far, and Power BI created a relationship for all the tables, except for two. Let's start by creating a relationship to the DimDate table.

The FactInternetSales table stores three different dates: OrderDate, ShipDate, and DueDate. There can be only one active relationship between two tables in Power BI, and all filtering occurs through the active relationship. In other words, which date do you want to see your total sales, profit, and profit margin calculations on? If it's OrderDate, then your relationship will be on the OrderDate column from the FactInternetSales table to the FullDateAlternateKey column in the DimDate table. To create a new relationship, open "manage relationships" from the home ribbon.

Now, let's create a relationship from the `OrderDate` column in `FactInternetSales` to the `FullDateAlternateKey` column in `DimDate`. With the manage relationship editor open, click on **New...** to create a new relationship:

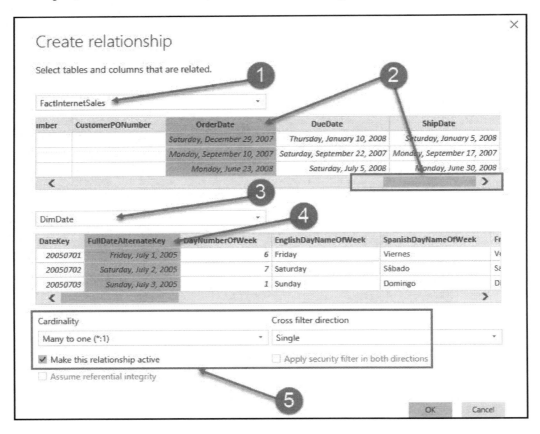

Figure 7- Creating a new relationship

Complete the following steps to create a new relationship:

1. Select `FactInternetSales` from the list of tables in the dropdown
2. Select `OrderDate` from the list of columns, and use the scroll bar to scroll all the way to the right
3. Select `DimDate` from the next in the drop-down list
4. Select `FullDateAlternateKey` from the list of columns

5. The cardinality, cross filter direction, and whether the relationship is active or inactive is updated automatically by Power BI; remember to always verify these items.
6. Click **OK** to close the editor

Congratulations, you have created your first relationship with Power BI!

Working with complex relationships

There are many complex scenarios that need to be addressed when building a data model, and Power BI is no different in this regard. In this section, you will learn how to handle many-to-many relationships and role-playing tables in Power BI.

Many-to-many relationships

Once relationships have been defined in your data model, filtering occurs automatically and this adds a tremendous amount of value to Power BI. However, the analytical value achieved through many-to-many relationships does not happen automatically.

Before you can learn how to handle many-to-many relationships in Power BI, you must first understand the basic behavior of filtering. Let's take a minor detour to explain how filtering works. Filtering will be discussed in more detail in the next chapter. In *Figure 8*, the total **SalesAmount** of all transactions is $29,358,677.22. The table visual you see in *Figure 8* is simply the sum of the column **SalesAmount** from the **FactInternetSales** table:

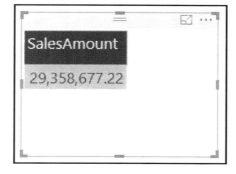

Figure 8- SalesAmount

To view the total **SalesAmount** for all transactions broken down by country, all you would need to do is simply add the **SalesTerritoryCountry** column from the **DimSalesTerritory** table. This behavior in Power BI is awesome, and this is automatic filtering at work. Take a look at *Figure 9*:

Figure 9-Viewing total sales amount

Please note that this only works because a valid relationship exists between the **FactInternetSales** and **DimSalesTerritory** tables. If a relationship had not been created, or if the relationship created was invalid, then you would get entirely different results and they would be confusing. Let's take a look at what would happen if no relationship had previously existed. In *Figure 10*, the country has been removed and replaced with the Temperature Range column from the **5 Regions 2008** table:

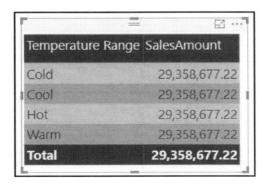

Figure 10-Replacing Country with Temperature range

Notice how the total sales amount is repeated for each temperature range. This behavior indicates that the **5 Regions 2008** table is unable to filter the **FactInternetSales** table. This inability to filter can happen for a number of different reasons, and here are a few:

- Because a relationship does not exist between the tables
- Because an existing relationship is invalid
- Because an existing relationship does not allow the filtering to pass through an intermediate table

If you see the repeated value behavior demonstrated in Figure 10, then go back to the relationship view and verify that all relationships have been created and are valid.

Cross-filtering direction

Now that you understand the basics of automatic filtering in Power BI, let's take a look at an example of a many-to-many relationship. **DimProduct** and **DimCustomer** have a many-to-many relationship. A product can be sold to many customers. For example, bread can be sold to Jessica, Kim, and Tyrone. A customer can purchase many products. Kim could purchase bread, milk, and cheese.

A bridge table can be used to store the relationship between two tables that have a many-to-many relationship, just like tools you have worked with in the past.

The relationship between **DimProduct** and **DimCustomer** is stored in the **FactInternetSales** table. The **FactInternetSales** table is a large many-to-many bridge table:

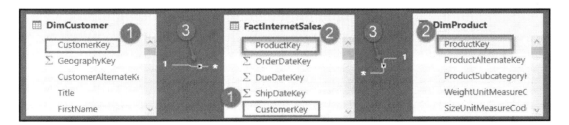

Figure 11-Relationship between DimCustomer and FactInternetSales

Figure 11 shows the relationship between these two tables; see the following explanation for the numbered points:

1. The relationship between **DimCustomer** and **FactInternetSales**
2. The relationship between **DimProduct** and **FactInternetSales**
3. The cross filter direction is set to single

The following report displays the total sales, total transactions, and customer count for each product:

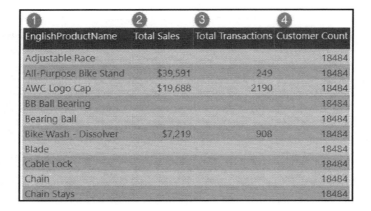

Figure 12- Customer Count for each product

Let's take a closer look at Figure 12, and note the numbered points:

1. **Product Name** from the **DimProduct** table
2. **Total Sales** is the SUM of the **Sales Amount** column from the **FactInternetSales** table
3. **Total Transactions** is the number of corresponding transactions from the **FactInternetSales** table
4. Customer Count is the COUNT of the **CustomerKey** column from the **DimCustomer** table

Total Sales and Total Transactions are returning the correct results for each product. Customer Count is returning the same value for all products (18,484). This is due to the way that filtering works. The calculations for **Total Sales** and **Total Transactions** are derived from columns or rows that come from the **FactInternetSales** table. The Product table has a one-to-many relationship with Internet Sales, and therefore filtering occurs automatically. This explains why those two calculations are being filtered properly, but it does not explain why the count of customers is returning the same repeated value for all products, not entirely anyway.

Let's take another look at the relationship between **DimProduct** and **DimCustomer**. You will notice in the following image that the relationship between these two tables flows through the **FactInternetSales** table. This is because they have a many-to-many relationship. In this scenario, the table **FactInternetSales** is acting as a large many-to-many bridge table. DimProduct filters FactInternet Sales. DimCustomer also filters FactInternetSales, and FactInternetSales is currently unable to filter the customer table:

Figure 13

The repeated value for customer count occurs because **FactInternetSales** is unable to filter the **DimCustomer** table. **DimProduct** filters **FactInternetSales**, and a list of transactions are returned for each product. Unfortunately, the filtering does not pass from **FactInternetSales** to **DimCustomer**. This is because **FactInternetSales** is on the many side of the relationship with **DimCustomer**. Therefore, when our calculation performs a count on the customer key, the table is not filtered and the calculation sees every customer key in the **DimCustomer** table (18,484).

Do you remember the cross-filter direction property that was briefly covered earlier in this chapter? That little property is there to provide many-to-many support. By simply enabling cross-filtering in both directions, the **FactInternetSales** table will be able to filter the customer table and the customer count will work.

Enabling filtering from the many side of a relationship

 To enable cross-filtering, click on Manage Relationships from the home ribbon; this will launch the manage relationship editor. Find the relationship between **FactInternetSales** and **DimCustomer**, and then click **Edit**.

Once the relationship editor has launched, change the cross-filter direction from single to both:

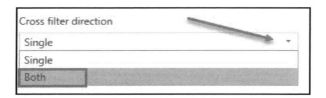

Figure 14- Changing the Cross filter direction

Back in the report view, you will now see the correct customer count for each product:

EnglishProductName	Total Sales	Total Transactions	Customer Count
All-Purpose Bike Stand	$39,591	249	243
AWC Logo Cap	$19,688	2190	2132
Bike Wash - Dissolver	$7,219	908	875
Classic Vest, L	$12,383	195	195
Classic Vest, M	$12,637	199	199
Classic Vest, S	$10,668	168	168
Fender Set - Mountain	$46,620	2121	2110
Half-Finger Gloves, L	$10,849	443	437

Figure 15-Customer Count for each product

Do not enable cross-filtering for your date table. In order for some DAX calculations to work properly, the date table must have a contiguous range of dates.

Role-playing tables

A role-playing table is a table that can play multiple roles, and this helps to reduce data redundancy. Most often, the Date table is a role-playing table. For example, the **FactInternetSales** table has three dates to track the processing of an order. There is the Order Date, Ship Date, and Due Date and, without role-playing tables, you would need to have three separate date tables instead of just one. The additional tables take up valuable resources, such as memory, as well as add an extra layer of administrative upkeep.

Each of these dates is very important to different people and different departments within an organization. For example, the finance department may wish to see total sales and profit by the date that a product was purchased, the order date. However, your shipping department may wish to see product quantity based on the ship date. How do you accommodate requests from different departments in a single data model?

One of the things I loved about working with SQL Server Analysis Services Multidimensional was the ease with which it handled role-playing tables; perhaps you also come from a background where you have worked with tools that had built-in support for Role-Playing tables. Unfortunately, Role-Playing tables are not natively supported in Power BI; this is because all filtering in Power BI occurs through the active relationship and you can only have one active relationship between two tables.

There are generally two ways you can handle role-playing tables in Power BI:

1. Importing the table multiple times and creating individual active relationships.
2. Using DAX and inactive relationships to create calculations that show calculations by different dates.

The first way, and the method we will show here, is importing the table multiple times. Yes, this means that it will take up more resources. The data model will have three date tables, one table to support each date in the FactInternetSales table. Each date table will have a single active relationship to the FactInternetSales table.

Some of the benefits of importing the table multiple times are as follows:

- It is easier to train and acclimate end users with the data model. For example, if you want to see sales and profit by the ship date, then you would simply use the date attributes from the ship date table in your reports.
- Most, if not all, DAX measures will work across all date tables, so no need for creating new measures.
- The analytical value of putting different dates in a matrix. For example, sales ordered and sales shipped by date.

Some of the cons of importing the table multiples times are:

- Resources. Additional memory and space will be used.
- Administrative changes. Any modifications made to one table will need to be repeated for all tables, as these tables are not linked. For example, if you create a hierarchy in one table, then you would need to create a hierarchy in all date tables.

The report in Figure 16 shows total sales and total transactions by year, but which year? Is this the year that a product was purchased or the year a product was shipped? The active relationship is on order date, so the report is displaying the results based on when the product was purchased:

CalendarYear	Total Sales	Total Transactions
2005	$3,266,374	1013
2006	$6,530,344	2677
2007	$9,791,060	24443
2008	$9,770,900	32265
Total	**$29,358,677**	**60398**

Figure 16-Total sales and total transactions by year

Importing the date table

In this section, we are going to import a date table to support analyzing data based on when an order shipped. From the get data option, select excel and open the AdventureWorksDW excel file; the file can be found in the directory location, C:\Packt\Power BI Quick Start\Data\

Next, select **DimDate** from the list of tables, and then click load:

	DateKey	FullDateAlternateKey	DayNumberOfWeek
◢ ▦ AdventureWorksDW.XLSX [6]			
☐ ▦ DimCustomer	20050101	1/1/2005	7
☑ ▦ DimDate	20050102	1/2/2005	1
	20050103	1/3/2005	2
☐ ▦ DimGeography	20050104	1/4/2005	3
☐ ▦ DimProduct	20050105	1/5/2005	4
☐ ▦ DimSalesTerritory	20050106	1/6/2005	5
☐ ▦ FactInternetSales	20050107	1/7/2005	6
	20050108	1/8/2005	7

Load

Figure 17- Select DimDate from the list of tables

Now that the data has been imported, the next step is creating a valid relationship. Select Manage Relationships, found on the home ribbon, to launch the relationship editor. Click new to create a new relationship. Complete the following steps:

1. Select **FactInternetSales** from the drop-down list.
2. Select the **ShipDate** column; use the scroll bar to scroll all the way to right.
3. Select **DimDate** (2) from the drop-down list.
4. Select the **FullDateAlternateKey** column.
5. Click **OK** to close the create relationship window.

I took the liberty of changing the table and column names here, for clarity. You will learn how to rename tables and columns in the following *Usability enhancements* section.

1. **DimDate** has been renamed **Order Date.**
2. **DimDate** (2) has been renamed Ship Date.

The data model now has two date tables, each with an active relationship to the **FactInternetSales** table. If you wish to see sales by order year then you would bring in the year column from the **Order Date** table, and if you wish to see sales by the ship year, then you would bring in the year column from the Ship Date table:

Total Sales and Transactions by Order Year			Total Sales and Transactions by Ship Year		
Year (Order)	Total Sales	Total Transactions	Year (Ship)	Total Sales	Total Transactions
2005	$3,266,374	1013	2005	$3,105,587	962
2006	$6,530,344	2677	2006	$6,576,979	2665
2007	$9,791,060	24443	2007	$9,517,549	23313
2008	$9,770,900	32265	2008	$10,158,562	33458
Total	**$29,358,677**	**60398**	**Total**	**$29,358,677**	**60398**

Figure 18-Displaying ship year column

Importing the same table multiple times is generally the preferred method when two tables have multiple relationships between them. This method is easy to explain to end users and allows you to reuse most, if not all, of your existing DAX calculations.

The alternative method is to create inactive relationships and then create new calculations (measures) using the Data Analysis Expression (DAX) language. This method of leveraging inactive relationships can become overwhelming from an administrative point of view. Imagine having to create copies of the existing measures in the data model for each relationship between two tables. In the current data model, **FactInternetSales** stores three dates, and this would possibly mean having to create and maintain three copies of each measure, one to support each date.

Usability enhancements

Usability enhancements are those enhancements that can significantly improve the overall user experience when interacting with the data model. In order to ensure a successful handoff and adoption of the work you have done, it is important to not overlook these rather basic improvements.

In this section, we are going to cover the following usability enhancements:

1. Hiding tables and columns
2. Renaming tables and columns
3. Changing the default summarization property
4. How to display one column but sort by another
5. Setting the data category of fields
6. How to create hierarchies

Hiding tables and columns

Some tables are available in the data model simply in a support capacity, and would never be used in a report. For example, you may have a table to support many-to-many relationships, weighted allocation, or even dynamic security. Likewise, some columns are necessary for creating relationships in the data model but would not add any value when added to a report. Tables or columns that will not be used for reporting purposes should be hidden from the report view to reduce complexity and improve the user experience.

To hide a column or table, simply right-click on the object you wish to hide, and then select **Hide in report view**. If you are in the report view already, the available option will simply say **Hide**.

Navigate to the relationship view, find the **FactInternetSales** table, and right-click on **ProductKey,** then select **Hide in report view**:

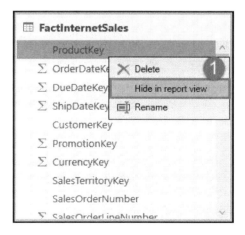

Figure 19-Select Hide in report view

Columns that are hidden are still visible in the data and relationship views, but they have slightly lighter text than columns that are not hidden, as you can see in Figure 20:

Figure 20-Hidden Columns

Next, go to each table and hide all remaining key columns, except for **FullDateAlternateKey**.

Renaming tables and columns

The renaming of tables and columns is an important step in making your data model easy to use. Different departments often have different terms for the same entity, therefore it is important to consider multiple departments when renaming objects. For example, you may have a column with a list of customer names and you decide to name this column Customer. However, the sales team may have named that column Prospect or Client, or any number of other terms. Remember to keep your end users and consumers of your reports in mind when renaming tables and columns.

You may rename tables or columns in the report, data, or relationship view. Navigate to the relationship view and right-click on FactInternetSales, then select Rename:

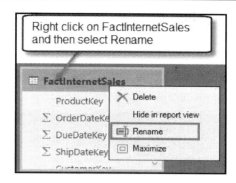

Figure 21-Renaming FactInternetSales

Rename this table to Internet Sales. Now, rename the other tables, removing the Dim prefix and adding spaces where applicable. You can use the table here for reference:

FactInternetSales	Internet Sales
DimDate	Date (Order)
DimDate (2)	Date (Ship
DimProduct	Product
DimCustomer	Customer
DimSalesTerritory	Sales Territory
5 Regions 2008	Temperature

The next step is necessary, but could be a somewhat tedious process. If you come from a programming or development background, then you are used to eliminating spaces in table and column names. End users and consumers of reports will expect to see spaces and, for that reason, it is recommended to add spaces where applicable. Spaces need to be added to any column that is visible, not hidden, in the report view. To rename a column, right-click on it and then select **Rename**. In the following screenshot, spaces have been added to **SalesOrderNumber** and **SalesOrderLineNumber**.

Complete the following steps to rename the rest of your columns:

1. Repeat this process of adding spaces for the remaining columns in each table
2. Rename **FullDateAlternateKey** to simply `Date`:

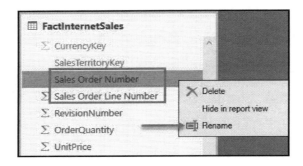

Figure 22-Renaming columns in each table

Default summarization

By default, Power BI assigns a default summarization to numeric columns, and this default summarization is usually a sum operation. Columns that have been assigned a default summarization are denoted by Power BI with a Sigma symbol (Σ). **DateKey, Day Number of Week, Day Number of Month, Day Number of Year**, and **Week Number of Year** have all been assigned a default summarization by Power BI in the following screenshot:

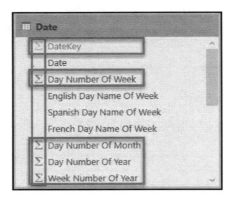

Figure 23-Default assigned columns for summarization

This automatic assignment of default summarizations can cause a lot of confusion to report developers in Power BI. Columns that have a default summarization assigned will be automatically aggregated with their assigned default summarization when added to a report. The columns identified in Figure 23 are generally descriptive attributes that help to explain the data; these columns would rarely be aggregated. Take a look at the following screenshot:

Figure 24-Year column from date table

In *Figure 24*, the **Year** column from the date table has been added into a table visual, and the expected behavior is to see a distinct list of years (2005, 2006, 2007, 2008, 2009, and 2010). Instead, a value of 4,398,433 is returned. Instead of returning a distinct list, the report returns a sum of all records from the year column in the date table. See the screenshot and steps shown next to adjust the default summarization:

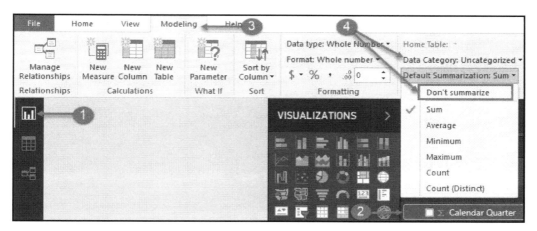

Figure 25-Adjust the default summarization

The preceding screenshot walks through changing the default summarization, with detailed steps listed here:

1. Select the report view from the left navigation bar.
2. Expand the date table and select Calendar Quarter, highlighted by a yellow box.
3. Select the modeling ribbon.
4. Click the dropdown for Default Summarization, and select Don't summarize.

Repeat the above process for each column in the date table that has been assigned a default summarization by Power BI.

How to display one column but sort by another

Oftentimes, you want to display the name of one column but sort by another. For example, the month name is sorted alphabetically when added to a report visual; see the following screenshot as an example:

Figure 26-Month names sorted alphabetically when added to a report visual

The desired behavior is for the month to be sorted chronologically instead. Therefore, the report should display the month name but sort by the month number of year. Let's take a look at how to change the sorting:

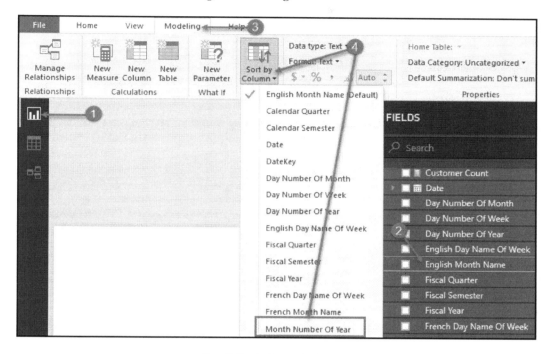

Figure 27-Changing the sort order of a column

In order to change the sort order of a column, complete the following steps:

1. Select the report view from the left navigation bar.
2. Expand the date table and select **English Month Name**, highlighted by a yellow box.
3. Select the modeling ribbon.
4. Click the dropdown for **Sort by Column**, and select **Month Number of Year**.

Data categorization

Power BI makes some assumptions about your columns based on data types, column names, and relationships in the data model. These assumptions are used in the report view when building visualizations to improve your default experience with the tool. Once you start building visualizations, you will notice that Power BI selects different types of visuals for different columns; this is by design. Power BI also decides column placement within the fields section of a visual, and you will learn more about the creation of visuals in Chapter 5, *Visualizing Data*. As you saw previously in this chapter, when Power BI detects a column that has numeric values, a default aggregation is assigned. Power BI assumes you will want to aggregate that data, and will automatically place these numeric columns into the Values area of a report visual.

The classification of data allows you to improve the user experience as well as improve accuracy. There are quite a few different options available for data categorization, thirteen in fact. Take a look at the options available in the following screenshot:

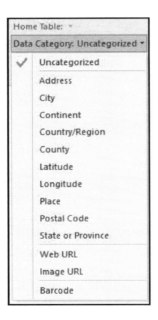

Figure 28-Options for data categorization

The most common use for data categorization is the classification of geographical data. When geographical data is added to a map, Bing maps may have to make some assumptions about how to map that data. This can sometimes cause inaccurate results. However, through data classification, you can reduce and possibly eliminate inaccurate results.

One method I have found extremely useful is combining multiple address columns (City, State) into a single column, and assigning the new column a data categorization of "Place". I have used this method with great success. See the following blog post for more tips on mapping geographical data:
`https://tinyurl.com/pbiqs-categoryplace`.

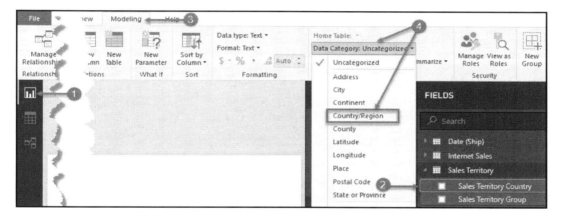

Figure 29-Modifying the date category

Follow the steps here to modify the data category:

1. Select the report view from the left navigation bar.
2. Expand the **Sales Territory** table and select **Sales Territory Country**, highlighted by a yellow box.
3. Select the modeling ribbon.
4. Click the dropdown for **Data Category**, and select **Country/Region**.

Creating hierarchies

Predefining hierarchies can provide several key benefits. Some of those benefits are listed here:

1. Hierarchies organize attributes and show relationships in the data
2. Hierarchies allow for easy drag and drop interactivity
3. Hierarchies add significant analytical value to the visualization layer through drilling down and rolling up data, as necessary

Hierarchies store information about relationships in the data, that users may not have otherwise known. I remember when I was working for a client in the telecommunication industry and they had Base Transceiver Stations (BTS) and Sectors, and without looking at my notes, I could never remember the correct order. Did a BTS contain multiple sectors, or did a sector contain multiple base transceiver stations? Once the hierarchy was added to the data model, I no longer had to worry about remembering the relationship because the relationship was stored in the hierarchy. Here is a list of common hierarchies:

1. **Category | Subcategory | Product**
2. **Country | State | City**
3. **Year | Quarter | Month | Day**

Hierarchies may only be created in either the report or data view. In order to create a new hierarchy, complete the following steps:

1. Expand the **Sales Territory** table.
2. Right-click on the **Sales Territory Country** column.
3. Select **New Hierarchy**:

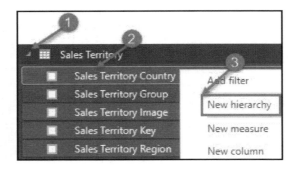

Figure 30-Create a new hierarchy

A new hierarchy has been created with a single column, and given a default name of **Sales Territory Country Hierarchy**:

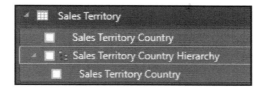

Figure 31-New hierarchy created

First, right-click on the Sales Territory Country Hierarchy and rename it to **Sales Territory Drilldown**. The next step is to add additional columns/attributes to the hierarchy. Complete the following steps:

1. Right click on **Sales Territory Region**.
2. Click on **Add to Hierarchy**.
3. Select **Sales Territory Drilldown.**
4. Repeat steps 1-3 for Sales Territory Group:

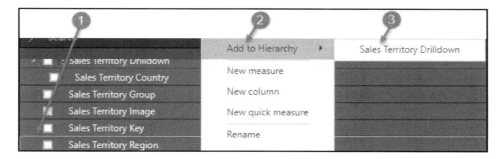

Figure 32-Adding columns/attributes to the hierarchy

The completed hierarchy can be seen in the following screenshot. However, the order of the attributes is incorrect; the order should be **Sales Territory Group** I **Sales Territory Country** I **Sales Territory Region**:

Figure 33-Completed hierarchy

To correct the order of the attributes:

1. Right-click on **Sales Territory Group**.
2. Click **Move Up**.
3. Repeat steps 1 and 2:

Figure 34-Correct the order of attributes

Summary

In this chapter, you learned how to build relationships between the different tables within your data model. These relationships, combined with simple, yet critical, usability enhancements, allow you to build a data model that is both coherent and intelligent. Historically, business intelligence projects cost significant resources in terms of time and money. Through a self-service approach to BI, you now have the tools necessary to build your own BI project within hours or even minutes.

4
Leveraging DAX

Data analysis expressions (DAX) is a formula language that made its debut back in 2010 with the release of Power Pivot within Excel. Much of DAX is similar to Excel's functions, and therefore learning DAX is an easy transition for Excel users and power users. In fact, DAX is so similar to Excel that I have seen new students become comfortable with the language and begin writing DAX within minutes.

The goal of this chapter is to introduce you to DAX and give you the confidence to start exploring this language on your own. Because of the brevity of this chapter, there will not be any discussions on in-depth DAX concepts and theory. There are, of course, many other books that are dedicated to just that.

Now, let's take a look at what is covered in this chapter:

- Building calculated columns
- Calculated measures – the basics
- Calculated measures – filter context
- Calculated measures – time intelligence

Building calculated columns

Open the pbix file Chapter 4 – Leveraging DAX from the book files

Calculated columns are stored in the table in which they are assigned, and the values are static until the data is refreshed. You will learn more about refreshing data in a later chapter.

There are many use cases for calculated columns, but the two most common are as follows:

- Descriptive attributes
- Concatenated key columns

Now you are going to create your first calculated column. Before you get started, though, you need to first know that Power BI Desktop has IntelliSense. IntelliSense will help you out a lot when writing code, as you will discover very soon. This built-in functionality will autocomplete your code as you go, and will also help you explore and discover new functions in the DAX language. In order to take advantage of IntelliSense, you simply need to start typing in the formula bar. Now you are ready to start writing DAX!

Click on the **Data View**—this is located on the left side of the Power BI Desktop screen. Next, click on the customer table from the **Fields** list. Once the customer table has been selected, click **New Column**—this is found under the modeling ribbon, as shown in the following screenshot:

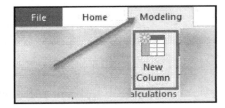

Figure 1- New column

You will now see the text **Column** = in the formula bar. First, name the new column by replacing the default text of **Column** with **Full Name**. Then, move your cursor to after the equals sign and type a single quote character. Immediately after typing the single quote character, a list of autocomplete options will appear preceding the formula bar. This is IntelliSense at work. The first option in this list is the name of the table you currently have selected—**Customer**. Click the *Tab* key and the name of the table will automatically be added to the formula bar, as shown in the following screenshot:

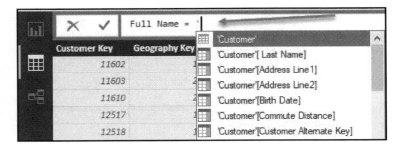

Figure 2-Adding name of the table

At some point, you will inevitably discover that you can reference just the column name. As a best practice, we recommend always referencing both the table and column name anytime you use a column in your DAX code.

Next, type an opening square bracket into the formula bar followed by a capital letter F, making **[F**. Once again, you will immediately be presented with autocomplete options. The list of options has been limited to only columns that contain the letter f, and the first option available from the dropdown is **First Name**. Click *tab* to autocomplete. The formula bar should now contain the following formula:

Full Name = 'Customer'[First Name]

The next step is to add a space, followed by the last name. There are two options in DAX for combining string values. The first option is the concatenate function. Unfortunately, concatenate only accepts two parameters; therefore, if you have more than two parameters, your code will require multiple concatenate function calls. On the other hand, you also have the option of using the ampersand sign (&) to combine strings. The ampersand will first take both input parameters and convert them into strings. After this data conversion step, the two strings are then combined into one. Let's continue with the rest of the expression. Remember to use the built-in autocomplete functionality to help you write code.

Next, add a space and the last name column. To add a space—or any string literal value for that matter—into a DAX formula, you will use quotes on both sides of the string. For example, " " inserts a space between the first and last name columns. The completed DAX formula will look like the following:

```
Full Name = 'Customer'[First Name] & " " & 'Customer'[Last Name]
```

String functions – Month, Year

Now that you have completed your first calculated column, let's build a calculated column that stores the month–year value. The goal is to return a month–year column with the two-digit month and four-digit year separated by a dash, making "MM-YYYY". Let's build this calculation incrementally.

Select the **Date** (order) table and then click **New Column** from the modeling ribbon. Write the following code in the formula bar and then hit *Enter*:

```
Month Year = 'Date (Order)'[Month Number of Year]
```

As you begin validating the code, you will notice that this only returns the single-digit month with no leading zero. Your next attempt may look something like the following:

```
Month Year = "0" & 'Date (Order)'[Month Number of Year]
```

This will work for single-digit months; however, double-digit months will now return three digits. Take a look at the following screenshot:

Figure 3-Displaying Month Year

To improve upon this and only return the two-digit month, you can use the RIGHTfunction. The RIGHT function returns a specified number of characters from the right side of a string. Modify your existing DAX formula to look like the following:

```
Month Year = RIGHT("0" & 'Date (Order)'[Month Number of Year], 2)
```

 For a full list of text functions in DAX, please go to the following link:
https://tinyurl.com/pbiqs-text

The rest of this formula can be completed quite easily. First, to add a dash, the following DAX code can be used:

```
Month Year = RIGHT("0" & 'Date (Order)'[Month Number of Year], 2)
& "-"
```

Complete the Month Year formula by combining the current string with the calendar year column:

```
RIGHT("0" & 'Date (Order)'[Month Number of Year], 2) & "-" & 'Date
(Order)'[Year])
```

You may have noticed that the Year column has a data type of a whole number, and you may have expected that this numeric value would need to be converted to a string prior to the `combine` operation. However, remember that the ampersand operator will automatically convert both inputs into a string before performing the combine operation!

Format function – Month Year

As with any other language, you will find that there are usually multiple ways to do something. Now you are going to learn how to perform the calculation that we saw in the previous section using the FORMAT function. The FORMAT function allows you to take a number or date column and customize it in a number of ways. A side effect of the FORMAT function is that the resulting data type will be text. Let's perform the preceding calculation again, but this time using the FORMAT function.

Make sure you have the **Date** (order) table selected, and then click on **Create a New Calculated Column** by selecting **New Column** from the modeling ribbon. In the formula bar, write the following expression:

```
Month Year Format = FORMAT('Date (Order)'[Date], "MM-YYYY")
```

If you would like to take a full look at all the custom formatting options available using the FORMAT function, please take a look at https://tinyurl.com/pbiqs-format.

Age calculation

Next, you are going to determine the age of each customer. The **Customer** table currently contains a column with the birth date for each customer. This column, along with the TODAY function and some DAX, will allow you to determine each customer's age. Your first attempt at this calculation may be to use the DATEDIFF function in a calculation that looks something like the following:

Customer Age = DATEDIFF('Customer'[Birth Date], TODAY(), YEAR)

The TODAY function returns the current date and time. The DATEDIFF function returns the count of the specified interval between two dates; however, it does not look at the day and month, and therefore does not always return the correct age for each customer.

Let's rewrite the previous DAX formula in a different way. In this example, you are going to learn how to use conditional logic and the FORMAT function to return the proper customer age. Please keep in mind, that there are many ways to perform this calculation.

Select the **Customer Age** column from the previous step and rewrite the formula to look like the following:

```
Customer Age =
IF(
    FORMAT('Customer'[Birth Date], "MMDD") <= FORMAT(TODAY(), "MMDD"), //Logical Test
    DATEDIFF('Customer'[Birth Date], TODAY(), YEAR),               //Result If True
    DATEDIFF('Customer'[Birth Date], TODAY(), YEAR) -1)            //Result If False
```

Figure 4-Select Customer age and rewrite the formula

Formatting code is very important for readability and maintaining code. Power BI Desktop has a built-in functionality to help out with code formatting. When you type *Shift + Enter* to navigate down to the next line in your formula bar, your code will be indented automatically where applicable.

When completed, the preceding code returns the correct age for each customer. The FORMAT function is used to return the two-digit month and two-digit day for each date (the birth date and today's date). Following the logical test portion of the IF statement are two expressions. The first expression is triggered if the logical test evaluates to true, and the second expression is triggered if the result of the test is false. Therefore, if the customer's month and day combo is less than or equal to today's month and day, then their birthday has already occurred this year, and the logical test will evaluate to true, which will trigger the first expression. If the customer's birthday has not yet occurred this year, then the second expression will execute.

In the preceding DAX formula, I added comments by using two forward slashes in the code. Comments are descriptive, and are not executed with the rest of the DAX formula. Commenting code is always encouraged, and will make your code more readable and easier to maintain.

SWITCH() – age breakdown

Now that you have the customer's age, it's time to put each customer into an age bucket. For this example, there will be four separate age buckets:

- 18-34
- 35-44
- 45-54
- 55 +

The SWITCH function is preferable to the IF function when performing multiple logical tests in a single DAX formula. This is because the SWITCH function is easier to read and makes debugging code much easier.

With the **Customer** table selected, click New Column from the modeling ribbon. Type in the completed DAX formula for the following example:

```
Age Breakdown =
SWITCH(TRUE(),
    'Customer'[Customer Age] >= 55,  "55 +", //If 55 or older then 55 +
    'Customer'[Customer Age] >= 45, "45-54", //If 45-54 then 45-54
    'Customer'[Customer Age] >= 35, "35-44", //If 35-44 then 35-44
    "18-34")                                 //ELSE, 18-34
```

Figure 5-Completed DAX formula

The preceding formula is very readable and understandable. There are three logical tests, and if a customer age does not evaluate to true on any of those logical tests, then that customer is automatically put into the 18-34 age bucket.

The astute reader may have noticed that the second and third logical tests do not have an upper range assigned. For example, the second test simply checks whether the customer's age is 45 or greater. Naturally, you may assume that a customer whose age is 75 would be incorrectly assigned to the 45–54 age bucket. However, once a row evaluates to true, it is no longer available for subsequent logical tests. Someone who is 75 would have evaluated to true on the first logical test (55 +) and would no longer be available for any further tests.

If you would like a better understanding of using the SWITCH statement instead of nesting multiple IF statements, then you can check out a blog post by Rob Collie at https://tinyurl.com/pbiqs-switch.

Navigation functions – RELATED

It's finally time to create a relationship between the temperature table and internet sales table. The key on the **Temperature** table is a combination of the region name and the month number of the year. This column combination makes a single row unique in this table, as shown in the following screenshot:

Region	Month	MonthNumber	Key	Avg Temp	Temperature Range
Northeast	Jan	1	Northeast1	26.3	Cold
Northeast	Feb	2	Northeast2	25.4	Cold
Northeast	Mar	3	Northeast3	31.4	Cold
Northeast	Apr	4	Northeast4	48.1	Cool

Figure 6-Column combination that makes a single row unique

Unfortunately, neither of those two columns currently exist in the **Internet Sales** table. However, the **Internet Sales** table has a relationship to the **Sales Territory** table, and the **Sales Territory** table has the region. Therefore, you can determine the region for each sale by doing a simple `lookup` operation. Well, it should be that simple, but it's not quite that easy. Let's take a look at why.

Calculated columns do not automatically use the existing relationships in the data model. This is a unique characteristic of calculated columns; calculated measures automatically see and interact with all relationships in the data model. Now let's take a look at why this is important.

In the following screenshot, I have created a new column on the **Internet Sales** table and I am trying to return the region name from the **Sales Territory** table. Take a look at the following screenshot:

```
Temperature Key =
'Sales T
```

Figure 7-Sales Territory table

Note that there is no IntelliSense, and that the autocomplete functionality is unavailable as I type in "**Sales Territory**". The reason for this is because the calculated column cannot see the existing relationships in the data model, and therefore does not automatically return the column you want from another table. There is a much more complicated explanation behind all this, but for now, suffice to say that navigation functions (`RELATED` and `RELATEDTABLE`) allow calculated columns to interact with and use existing relationships.

If I rewrite the following DAX formula with the RELATED function, then you will notice that IntelliSense has returned, along with the autocomplete functionality that was previously discussed:

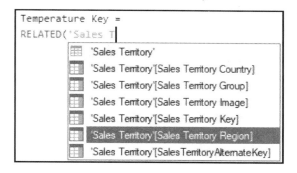

Figure 8-Temperature key column

Now it's time to create a **Temperature Key** column on the **Internet Sales** table. Create a new column on the **Internet Sales** table and then type in the following DAX formula:

```
Temperature Key =
RELATED('Sales Territory'[Sales Territory Region]) & //Return the region from Sales Territory table
RELATED('Date (Order)'[Month Number Of Year])       //Return the Month number of year from the Date table
```

Figure 9-Temperature Key column on the Internet Sales table

Now that the temperature key has been created on the **Internet Sales** table, let's create the relationship. Click **Manage Relationships** from the home ribbon and then click **New...** to open the **Create Relationship** window. Then complete the following steps to create a new relationship. The relevant fields and entries for each step are marked out on the following screenshot:

1. Select **Internet Sales** from the first drop-down selection list
2. Select the **Temperature Key** from the list of columns
3. Select **Temperature** from the second drop-down selection list (scroll right)
4. Select **Key** from the list of columns

5. Click **OK** to save your new relationship:

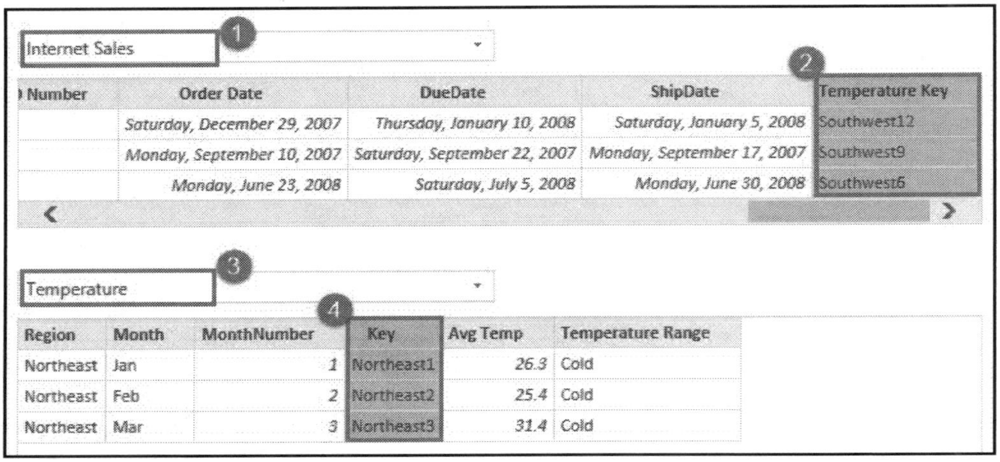

Figure 10-Creating new relationship

Calculated measures – the basics

Calculated measures are very different than calculated columns. Calculated measures are not static, and operate within the current filter context of a report; therefore, calculated measures are dynamic and ever-changing as the filter context changes. You were introduced to filter context in the previous chapter. The concept of the filter context will be slightly expanded on later in this chapter. Calculated measures are powerful analytical tools, and because of the automatic way that measures work with filter contexts they are surprisingly simple to author.

Before you start learning about creating measures, let's first discuss the difference between implicit and explicit measures.

Implicit aggregations occur automatically on columns with numeric data types. You saw this in the previous chapter when the year column was incorrectly aggregated after being added to a report. There are some advantages to this default behavior—for example, if you simply drag the **Sales Amount** column into a report, the value will be automatically aggregated and you won't have to spend time creating a measure. As discussed in the next section, it's generally considered a best practice to create explicit measures in lieu of implicit measures.

An explicit measure allows a user to create a calculated measure, and there are several benefits to using explicit measures:

- Measures can be built on each other
- They encapsulate code, making logic changes less time-consuming
- They centrally define number formatting, creating consistency

Calculated measures can do the following:

- They can be assigned to any table
- They interact with all the relationships in the data model automatically, unlike calculated columns.
- They are not materialized in a column, and therefore cannot be validated in the **Data View**

Calculated measure – basic aggregations

In this section, you are going to create four simple calculated measures:

- Total Sales
- Total Cost
- Profit
- Profit Margin

Total Sales

To create your first measure, select the **Internet Sales** table and then click **New Measure...** from the modeling ribbon. In the formula bar, type the following code and hit *Enter*:

```
Total Sales = SUM('Internet Sales'[Sales Amount])
```

One of the benefits of creating explicit measures is the ability to centralize formatting. Once the measure has been created, navigate to the modeling ribbon and change the formatting to **$ English (United States)**, as shown in the following screenshot:

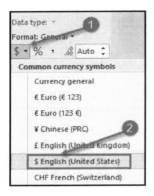

Figure 11-Change formatting to $ English(United States)

Total Cost

Now let's create the Total Cost measure. Once again, this is a simple SUM operation. Click **New Measure...** from the modeling ribbon and type in the following DAX formula:

```
Total Cost = SUM('Internet Sales'[Total Product Cost])
```

Remember to apply formatting to this new measure; it is easy to miss this step when learning to create measures. The formatting should be **$ English (United States)**.

Profit

Profit is the next measure you will create. You may attempt to write something such as the following:

```
Profit = SUM('Internet Sales'[Sales Amount]) - SUM('Internet Sales'[Total Product Cost])
```

This calculation would be technically correct; however, it's not the most efficient way to write code. In fact, another benefit of building explicit measures is that they can be built on top of each other.

Reusing existing calculated measures will make the code more readable, and make code changes easier and less time consuming. Imagine for a moment that you discovered that the Total Sales calculation is not correct. If you encapsulated all this logic in a single measure and reused that measure in your other measures, then you need only change the original measure, and any updates would be pushed to all other measures.

Now it's time to create the Profit measure. select your **Internet Sales** table and then click on **New Measure...** from the modeling ribbon. Type the following into the formula bar—remember to format it:

```
Profit = [Total Sales] - [Total Cost]
```

This calculation returns the same results as the original attempt. The difference is that now you are reusing measures that were already created in the data model. You may have noticed that I referenced the name of the measure without the table name. When referencing explicit measures in your code, it is considered a best practice to exclude the table name.

Profit Margin

Now it's time to create the **Profit Margin** calculation (the profit margin is simply profit divided by sales). For this measure, you are going to use the DIVIDE function. The DIVIDE function is recommended over the divide operator (/) because the DIVIDE function automatically handles divide by zero occurrences. In the case of divide by zero occurrences, the DIVIDE function returns blank.

Create a new measure on the **Internet Sales** table using the following code:

```
Profit Margin = DIVIDE([Profit], [Total Sales])
```

Next, set the formatting as a percentage. From the modeling ribbon, click on the % icon, as shown in the following screenshot:

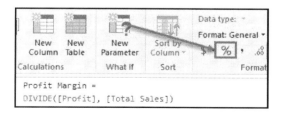

Figure 12-Setting formatting as a percentage

Optional parameters

You may have noticed that the DIVIDE function accepted three parameters and you only provided two. The third parameter allows you to set an alternative result for divide by zero occurrences. This alternate result is optional. Optional parameters are denoted by square brackets on both sides of the parameter. These optional parameters are prevalent in many DAX functions. Take a look at the following screenshot:

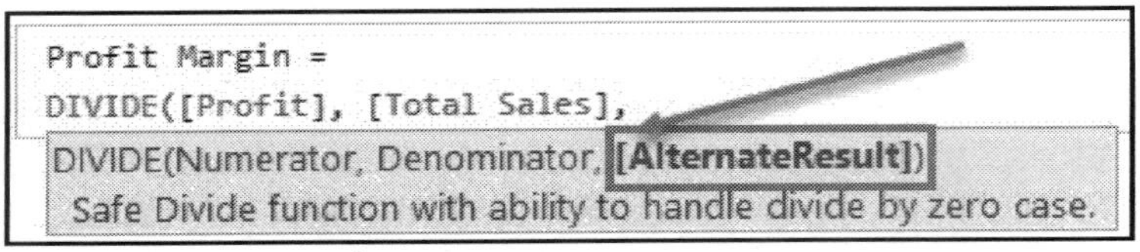

```
Profit Margin =
DIVIDE([Profit], [Total Sales],
DIVIDE(Numerator, Denominator, [AlternateResult])
Safe Divide function with ability to handle divide by zero case.
```

Figure 13-Optional parameters in DAX functions

Filter context

The automatic filtering that occurs in Power BI is a really awesome feature, and is one of the reasons that so many companies are gravitating to this tool. Automatic filtering is directly tied to the concept of the filter context. You were introduced to the filter context in the previous chapter. I want to briefly expand on the previous chapter here before discussing the **CALCULATE** function.

A simple definition of the filter context would be that it is simply anything in your report that is filtering a measure. There are quite a few items that make up the filter context. Let's take a look at a few of them:

- Any attributes in the rows; this includes the different axes in charts
- Any attributes in the columns
- Any filters applied by slicers (visual filters); slicers are discussed in the next chapter
- Any filters applied explicitly through the **Filters** pane
- Any filters explicitly added to the calculated measure

Calculate

The CALCULATE function is an extremely powerful tool in the arsenal of any DAX author. This is because the CALCULATE function can be used to ignore, overwrite, or change the existing filter context. You may be asking yourself why—why would anyone want to ignore the default behavior of Power BI? Let's take a look at an example.

Let's assume you want to return the total sales of each country as a percentage of all countries. This is a very basic percent of total calculation: **Total Sales** per country divided by **Total Sales** for all countries. However, how do you get the total sales of all the countries so that you can perform this calculation? This is where the CALCULATE function comes into the picture. Take a look at the following screenshot:

Sales Territory Country	Total Sales	Total Sales all Countries
Australia	9,061,000.58	29,358,677
Canada	1,977,844.86	29,358,677
France	2,644,017.71	29,358,677
Germany	2,894,312.34	29,358,677
United Kingdom	3,391,712.21	29,358,677
United States	9,389,789.51	29,358,677
Total	**29,358,677.22**	

Figure14-Calculating total sales of all the countries

To do the percent of total calculation, you need to get **Total Sales all Countries** on the same row as Total Sales. This means you need to create a new calculated measure that ignores any filters that come from the country attribute. Create a new calculated measure on your **Internet Sales** table using the following DAX formula:

```
Total Sales all Countries =
CALCULATE(
    [Total Sales],
    ALL(
        'Sales Territory'[Sales Territory Country]))
```

Figure 15-Create a new calculated measure on Internet sales table using DAX formula

The preceding calculation will return all sales for all countries, explicitly ignoring any filters that come from the **Country** column. Let's briefly discuss why this works.

The first parameter of the CALCULATE function is an expression, and you can think of this as an aggregation of some kind. In this example, the aggregation is simply Total Sales. The second parameter is a filter that allows the current filter context to be modified in some way. In the preceding example, the filter context is modified by *ignoring any filters* that come from the country attribute. Let's take a look at the definition for the **ALL** function used in the second parameter of the CALCULATE function:

ALL: Returns all the rows in a table, or all the values in a column, *ignoring any filters* that may have been applied.

Percentage of total calculation

Now, create another calculated measure on the **Internet Sales** table using the following code. Make sure that you format the measure as a percentage:

```
% of All Countries = DIVIDE([Total Sales], [Total Sales all
Countries])
```

In the following screenshot, you can see the completed example with both of the new measures created in this section. Without a basic understanding of the CALCULATE function, this type of percent of total calculation would be nearly impossible:

Sales Territory Country	Total Sales	Total Sales all Countries	% of All Countries
Australia	9,061,000.58	$29,358,677.22	30.86%
Canada	1,977,844.86	$29,358,677.22	6.74%
France	2,644,017.71	$29,358,677.22	9.01%
Germany	2,894,312.34	$29,358,677.22	9.86%
NA		$29,358,677.22	
United Kingdom	3,391,712.21	$29,358,677.22	11.55%
United States	9,389,789.51	$29,358,677.22	31.98%
Total	**29,358,677.22**	**$29,358,677.22**	**100.00%**

Figure 16- Completed example with both of the new measures

Time intelligence

Another advantage of Power BI is how easily time intelligence can be added to your data model. Within **data analysis expressions (DAX)**, you have a comprehensive list of built-in time intelligence functions to make this very easy. In this section, you are going to use these built-in functions to create the following measures:

- Year to Date Sales
- Year to Date Sales (Fiscal Calendar)
- Prior Year Sales

Built-in time intelligence calculations do not work if you are using a direct query connection to your data source rather than importing data. Take a look at the alternative methods for calculating time intelligence in the DAX cheatsheet at `https://tinyurl.com/pbiqs-daxcheatsheet`.

Year to Date Sales

Create a new calculated measure on your **Internet Sales** table using the following DAX formula. Remember to format the measure as **$ English (United States)**:

```
YTD Sales = TOTALYTD([Total Sales], 'Date (Order)'[Date])
```

YTD Sales (Fiscal Calendar)

Maybe your requirement is slightly more complex, and you need to see the year-to-date sales based on your fiscal year end rather than the calendar year end date. The TOTALYTD function has an optional parameter that allows you to change the default year end date from "12/31" to a different date. Create a new calculated measure on your **Internet Sales** table using the following DAX formula:

```
Fiscal YTD Sales = TOTALYTD([Total Sales], 'Date (Order)'[Date], "03/31")
```

Now, let's take a look at both of these new measures in a table in Power BI:

Year	English Month Name	Total Sales	YTD Sales	Fiscal YTD Sales
2005	July	473,388.16	$473,388	$473,388
2005	August	506,191.69	$979,580	$979,580
2005	September	473,943.03	$1,453,523	$1,453,523
2005	October	513,329.47	$1,966,852	$1,966,852
2005	November	543,993.41	$2,510,846	$2,510,846
2005	December	755,527.89	① $3,266,374	$3,266,374
2006	January	596,746.56	② $596,747	$3,863,120
2006	February	550,816.69	$1,147,563	$4,413,937
2006	March	644,135.20	$1,791,698	③ $5,058,072
2006	April	663,692.29	$2,455,391	④ $663,692
2006	May	673,556.20	$3,128,947	$1,337,248
Total		**29,358,677.22**		

Figure 17-Both the new measure in a table

The newly created measures **YTD Sales** and **Fiscal YTD Sales** have both been added to the preceding table. Let's take a closer look at how these two measures are different; the relevant sections in the table are annotated with the numbers one to four, corresponding to the following notes:

1. The amount displayed for December 2005 is $3,266,374. This is the cumulative total of all sales from January 1, 2005 to December, 2005.

2. As expected, the cumulative total starts over as the year switches from 2005 to 2006; therefore, the YTD Sales amount for January 2006 is $596,747.

3. In the **Fiscal YTD Sales** column, the cumulative total works slightly differently. The displayed amount of $5,058,072 is the cumulative total of all sales from April 1st, 2005 to March 31, 2006.

4. Unlike the YTD Sales measure, the Fiscal YTD Sales measure does not start over until April 1. The amount displayed for April 2006 of $663,692 is the cumulative total for April. This number will grow each month until May 31, at which point the number will reset again.

Prior Year Sales

A lot of time series analysis consists of comparing current metrics to the previous month or previous year. There are many functions in DAX that work in conjunction with the CALCULATE function to make these types of calculations easy. You are going to create a new measure to return the total sales for the prior year.

Create a new calculated measure on your **Internet Sales** table using the following DAX formula:

```
Prior Year Sales =
CALCULATE(
    [Total Sales],          // SUM('Internet Sales'[Sales Amount])
    SAMEPERIODLASTYEAR(     // Change the filter context to go back one year
        'Date (Order)'[Date]))
```

Figure 18-Create a new calculated measure on your Internet sales

CALCULATE allows you to ignore or even change the current filter context. In the preceding formula, CALCULATE is used to take the current filter context and change it to one year ago. This calculated measure also works at the day, month, quarter, and year level of the hierarchy. For example, if you are looking at sales for June 15, 2018, then the **Prior Year Sales** measure would return sales for June 15, 2017. However, if you were simply analyzing your sales aggregated at the month level for June 2018, then the measure would return the sales for June 2017.

For a comprehensive list of all the built-in time intelligence functions, please take a look at https://tinyurl.com/pbiqs-timeintelligence.

Summary

In this chapter, you learned that DAX allows you to significantly enhance your data model by improving the analytical capabilities with a relatively small amount of code. You also learned how to create calculated columns and measures and how to use DAX to perform useful time series analysis on your data. This chapter merely scratched the surface of what is possible with DAX. As you further explore the DAX language on your own, you will quickly become a proficient author of DAX formulas. As with everyone who learns DAX, you will inevitably learn that there is a layer of complexity to DAX that will require further education to really master. When you get to this point, it would be advantageous to look for classes or books that will help you to truly master DAX!

5
Visualizing Data

Up to this point, you have spent some time importing data and modeling it to your specifications. In this chapter, we will take that hard work and begin to visualize the data in efficient and effective ways. The most common association with Power BI for consumers is the ability to create very impactful visualizations of data, and there are many options available to do this. In this chapter, we will look at all the various options that are available to you within the Power BI Desktop application. Additionally, we will take a brief glimpse at the additional visualization options that are available through the Custom Visuals Marketplace. The topics detailed in this chapter are as follows:

- Data visualization basics
- Visuals for filtering
- Visualizing tabular data
- Visualizing categorical data
- Visualizing trend data
- Visualizing KPI data
- Visualizing geographical data
- Leveraging Power BI custom visuals
- Data visualization tips and tricks

At the time of this book's publication, there are 30 readily available visuals in the Power BI Desktop application; this includes the Shape map visual that is in the preview options. We will be exploring most of them and how they best work with certain types of data sets to bring the model we have worked on until this point to life!

With Power BI's rapid update cycle, there will be many visuals added to the application over time. If you would like to leverage these as soon as they are available, you can find them in the **Preview** section of the application's options. *Figure 5-1* shows how to access the **Preview Features** area. Once you have enabled something in this area, it usually requires you to restart the Power BI application, so make sure to save your work! The path is `File||Options and Settings||Options||Preview Features`.

How to turn on **Preview Features** can be seen here:

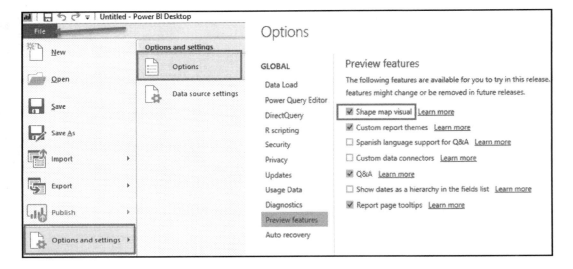

Figure 5-1

Data visualization basics

As soon as you launch the Power BI desktop application and close out of the initial splash screen, you will find yourself in the Report View, which is where we will stay for the duration of this chapter. In the previous chapter, you explored the Relationship view as well as the Data view, but these areas are not necessary for the visualization work we will be doing. There are many items of interest in this initial Report view area that we need to discuss so that we can work efficiently. Let's open the completed Power BI file from `Chapter 4`, *Leveraging DAX*, which includes all of the calculated columns and calculated measures that we will use in the upcoming visuals.

Let's review the key items from *Figure 5-2*:

For this chapter, you can build on top of the completed PBIX file from `Chapter 4`, *Leveraging DAX*. If you would like to keep your work from each chapter separate, please follow the noted steps here. Open the completed PBIX file called `Chapter 5`, *Visualizing Data*. Then, under the File option, choose Save As and give this file a new name for the work we will be doing in `Chapter 5`, *Visualizing Data*.

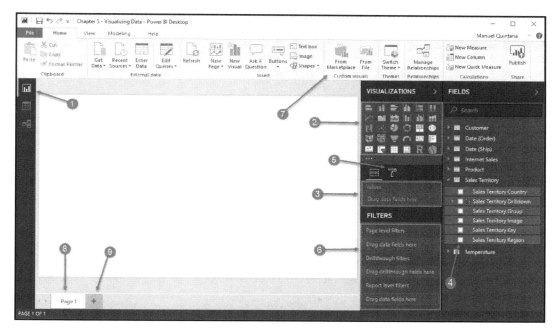

Figure 5-2

1. **Report view**: This is the button that will place us in the Report canvas and allow us to create visuals.
2. **Visuals area**: This is where we can choose which visual, we would like to use. Once custom visuals are added, they will appear here as well.

3. **Field area**: This area will change depending on the visual but it is where we place the fields we will use within the selected visual.

4. **Field pane**: These are all the available fields we have to choose from to add to our visuals.

5. **Format area**: Here is where we can decide on many things specific to either the entire report page or the selected visual, such as text size, font style, titles, and so on.

6. **Filters area**: This is where we can apply filters of various scopes:

   - **Page-level filters**: Any filters applied here will affect every single visual on the selected page.
   - **Drillthrough filters**: This option allows users to pass a filter value from a different report page to this one. This will be discussed in further detail.
   - **Report-level filters**: Filters applied here will affect every single visual for the entire Power BI report.
   - **Visual-level filters**: This category will only appear when you have a visual selected, and the applied filters will only affect the selected visual.

7. **Custom visuals**: By selecting this button, you will have a menu appear that has access to all the custom visuals from the Microsoft store. You can then add whichever visual you would like to the Visuals area.

8. **Report page**: Here is where you can select which report page you would like to work with. Each page has a limited work area where we can use visuals, so it is common to have more than one page in a Power BI report.

9. **Add Report page**: By selecting this symbol, you can add a new report page to add more area in which we can add visuals.

It is important to note that when working with Visual level filters, the Fields area, and the Format area, you must have the specific visual selected. You can verify this when you see the various anchor points around the visual in question. Now that we have familiarized ourselves with the Report page features and layout, its time to start visualizing!

Visuals for filtering

Filtering the data that users will see within a Power BI report is the most effective way to answer very specific questions about that data, and there are many ways to accomplish this. One of Power BI's best features is its default capability to allow users to interact with a visual, which will then apply that as a filter to the rest of the visuals on that page, and this is known as interactive filtering. This behavior really puts the power into the user's hands, and they can decide how they want to filter the visuals. This now makes a report so much more robust because it can answer so many more questions about the data. Along with this functionality, we, report developers, can add more explicit forms of filtering using the Slicer visual that is available to us in the visuals area. This allows us to choose a very specific field from our data, that we know our end users will want to manipulate to see that data in various different states. So now, lets dive in and get a better understanding of these two filtering options, as they will most definitely be elements we will see in our finished reports.

Interactive filtering

Almost every single visual that is readily available to us within Power BI has some sort of element that users can interact with. At the same time, every visual can be impacted by these very same elements. This really gives us a lot of room when it comes to deciding which visuals we would like in a report page. We will cover Interactive filtering again later on in this chapter, but it is important to understand how this feature works so that we can leverage it throughout the following examples. Let's create two very simple visuals based off our current data model so we can see exactly how this interactive filtering works. For right now, let's not worry about the details of these visuals as they will be fully described in later sections of this chapter.

Let's look at, setting up the example:

1. Select the **Stacked Column Chart** visual that will appear in the report canvas. Make sure you can see the anchor points we talked about earlier so that the following steps will work.
2. Now, let's add a couple of fields to the visual. In the Fields pane under the Internet Sales table, choose the **Total Sales** calculated measure by placing a check in the box to the left. You will notice that the field shows up under the **Value** section of the Field area.

3. Do the same thing for the **Sales Territory Country** field located under the **Sales Territory** table. This time, the field shows up under the **Axis** section of the **Field** area. Reference figure 5-3 here to validate that everything is set correctly:

Figure 5-3

 You may notice that some of the visual elements do not meet your standards. For example, the size of the text for various items in this visual are far too small to read. These are the types of changes that we would make in the Format area but will not be doing in this specific example. We will be examining the most common Format changes for each of the visuals within their respective section in this chapter. Right now, we just want to see how interactive filtering works.

4. We can already start to interact with any of the columns we currently have, but since this is the only visual it really isn't that exciting. So, let's add another visual to the report canvas; make sure you left-click somewhere in the empty space so that no visual is currently selected.

5. Now, we can select the Pie Chart visual, which will be added to the report canvas. You may have to move the visual to a location more to your liking.

6. We will now add two fields to this visual, and the first will be the **Age Breakdown** calculated column. We can either place a check in the box next to the field, or we can drag that field on top of the correct visual; both methods will have the same effect and we should see the **Age Breakdown** field located under the **Legend** section.

7. Using either of the two methods just described, let's add the **Profit** calculated measure to this visual as well, which should populate under the **Values** section. See figure 5-4 to verify the setup. Remember, don't worry about formatting right now:

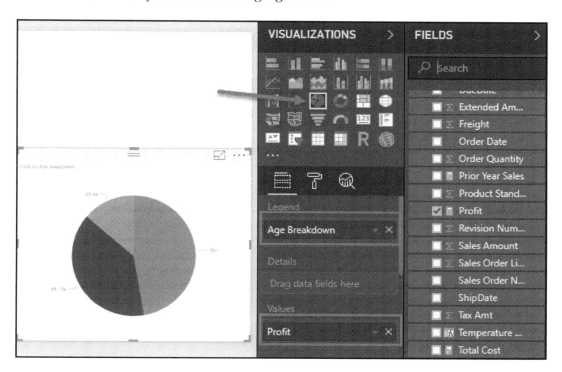

Figure 5-4

Now that the example is all set and there are two visuals in the report canvas, we can really see how interactive filtering works. Go ahead and select (left-mouse-click) the column labeled **United States** in the stacked column chart. You will immediately see that the pie chart changes to having a much smaller highlighted area. By hovering over the *35-44* section of the pie chart, we can now see that the United States makes up $413,617.35 of the $1,661,776.43 total for that category. This same type of filtering can be done by the pie chart, which will then affect the stacked column chart. Just with this simple example, you can see how effective interactive filtering is in answering questions about our data. Keep this in mind as we move forward with our other examples so you can keep seeing the impact this filtering has. We will cover additional option settings around interactive filtering at the end of this chapter.

The Slicer visual

So now that we know that interactive filtering will always be an option for users, what do we do when our end users want to filter by something that isn't used inside our visuals? This is where the **Slicer** visual comes into play. The **Slicer** visual only allows one field to be assigned to it but, depending on what data type that field is, we will have different presentation options. The first option will be if we wanted to use a field of a **String/Text** date type. The second option will appear if we use any of the **Numeric** data types, which include: **Decimal Number**, **Fixed Decimal Number**, **Whole Number** and any of the **Date** data types. This second option is referred to as a **Numeric Range Slicer**. Let's take a look at these two different options with the visuals we already have.

Let's look at, setting up the visual:

1. Select the **Slicer** visual and move it to someplace convenient within the report canvas. You can use the anchor points to resize the visual as you see fit.
2. In our first example, let's add in the **Temperature Range** field from the **Temperature** table to our selected **Slicer** visual.

What we are seeing within our slicer is known as the List view. This allows users to see a distinct list of all the options they can now filter on from that specific field. For us, we can see that we now have four temperature options to choose from, and we can either single-select from our list, or multi-select. By simply left-clicking any of the boxes next to our options, we can see that both of our visuals become filtered based on the selected criteria. So, if we were to select the **Cold** option, the stacked column chart would be showing the Total Sales by Country when the weather was cold; see *Figure 5-5*:

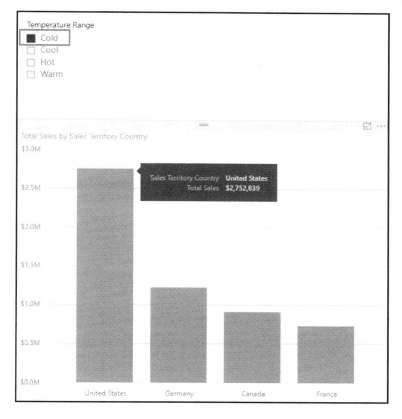

Figure 5-5

 In order to multi-select, you have two options. The first is to hold down the *Ctrl* key on your keyboard while making your selections. The second option lies within the *Format* area under the *Selection Controls* expandable menu. Here, you will find an option called *Single Select*, which is set to *On* by default, and by turning this off you no longer need to hold the *Ctrl* key to multi-select.

Now, let's add another slicer to our current report page, which uses a field of a numeric data type, so we can explore the *Numeric Range Slicer*.

Let's look at, setting up the visual:

1. Ensure that you have no other visual selected, and choose the **Slicer** visual once again. Resize and move the slicer to your liking.
2. For this slicer, let's add the `Year` field from the `Date (Order)` table.

Immediately, you will see a very different presentation for our filter options. We have a sliding bar that can be moved from either side to give us a range of values, which will be used to filter the other visuals on our page. By moving the left slider one value to the right, we can see that the year 2005 has now been removed from our range and the data in our visuals have changed; see *Figure 5-6*. It should be noted that this slicer that we are using to filter by year could also be set to use the **List** format that our temperature slicer is using. Imagine, though, if rather than choosing the **Year** field as we did, we selected the **Date** field. The **Date** field has so many unique choices for filtering that using the **List** format would be impossible. This is really where the range format for the slicer makes the most sense. As well, there are a couple other formats available to us within the slicer. We can find those options in the upper right-hand corner of the slicer visual. Let's take a look at what those formats are and when they are available to us:

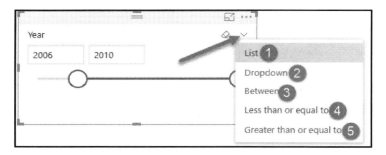

Figure 5-6

Format options from figure 5-6 are as follows:

1. **List**: This option is available no matter what field you select. It is a distinct list of values from the selected field. This is better used when there is a small number of options to choose from.
2. **Dropdown**: This gives the user a drop-down menu that will contain a distinct list of values from the selected field. This is very similar to the List option, but our choices are hidden until we hit the drop-down option. This is still meant for a smaller set of values so that users don't have to scroll through hundreds of choices.
3. **Between**: Here we have the option from our second example using the *Year* field. This choice will only present itself for fields that are of a numeric data type, and this includes dates. It allows users to specify a range of values to leverage as the filter by the use of a sliding bar.

4. **Less than or equal to***: Very similar to the Between option, but the sliding scale can only be adjusted from the left side.

5. **Greater than or equal to**: This is the same as the previous option, except you can only adjust the sliding scale from the right side.

When using the *List* option for a smaller set of filter choices, try changing the orientation from vertical to horizontal. If you add a background color to this setup, it gives the feeling of having buttons to filter with. To set this up, just go to the *Format* area of the slicer. Expand the *General* area and switch the value within the *Orientation* section to Horizontal. Then, expand the *Items* area and select a font color and background color of your choice, and you will see the design feels like a set of buttons.

So, now we know a couple different ways to allow our users to filter the visuals we have created for them. Interactive filtering will always be there for our users, but we can take a more traditional route with the *Slicer* visual and present them specific options they would find meaningful to filter the data. The last thing we will do is rename this report page from *Page 1* to *Slicers.*

Visualizing tabular data

We will see that there are many options within Power BI to visually represent data, but sometimes our users may want to see and compare detailed data and exact values. In these scenarios, using the *Table* or *Matrix* visual ends up being our best choice. When leveraging either of these two visuals, it is important to take advantage of the *Format* area to ensure that users can easily interpret the detailed data that is being presented. One of the best ways to bring attention to values of importance with these visuals is by using *Conditional Formatting.* We will explore this option, as well as take advantage of the hierarchies we created in Chapter 3, *Building the Data Model*, to allow for drill downs within the visuals.

The table visual

The table visual is perfect for looking at many values (measures) for a category. To really make the table shine, we will also want to take advantage of the *Conditional Formatting* option that is available to us. In our example, we will be using the *Sales Territory Region* as our category and looking at four different values for it.

Let's look at, setting up the visual:

1. Rename the blank page we are working on from `Page 1` to `Tabular Data`.
2. Select the Table visual and resize it to take up a little less than half the report canvas. Notice, similar to the slicer, that there is only one area in which to populate fields, called `Values`.
3. The first field we will want to select will be `Sales Territory Region` from the `Sales Territory` table; this will be our category.
4. Next, navigate to the `Internet Sales` table and select the `Total Sales` measure. Also, select the `Profit`, `Total Cost`, and `Total Transactions` measures. See *Figure 5-7* for reference:

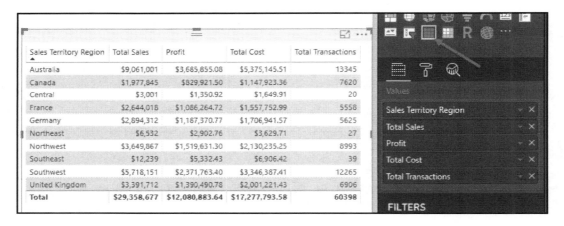

Figure 5-7

Already, we can see how this table provides great insights into our selected category, `Sales Territory Region`. By default, though, there are many formatting options that we will want to adjust. One of the first items will want to change is the size of the text for the data, as well as the headers. With the Table visual selected, go into the **Format** area (roller-brush icon) and expand the **Column Headers** section. We will see there are many options here for us, but for now let's simply adjust the *Text Size* option to something larger, making it easier to read the headers. Next, let's expand the *Values* area and make the same change here for the *Text Size* option. Now that our table is easier to read, let's explore the **Conditional Formatting** option, which will let us customize text or background colors based off values. If we return back to the **Fields** area where we can see our five options, you will note a small drop-down arrow next to each of our fields.

Select the arrow next to our `Total Sales` measure, and you will see the option
for **Conditional Formatting,** as shown in *Figure 5-8*. When you place your mouse icon
over the **Conditional Formatting** option, you will see that we are presented with
three choices that are similar in functionality and setup. The one we will focus on is
the **Background color scales** option, so go ahead and select that option. A menu will
appear in which we will simply only change one option; place a check mark in the
box that is in the bottom left that says **Diverging.** After hitting okay, we will now see
that our *Total Sales* column is color-coded so that we can easily identify the regions
that are good (green) and bad (red) performers. This is something that we can choose
to apply to whichever columns we feel would benefit most from **Conditional
Formatting,** but it is not necessarily required. With the use of this table visual, we can
get a very quick and detailed understanding of performance for our `Sales
Territory Region` category.

 It is important to also remember about Interactive Filtering with the
table visual. Any of the rows that are present within the table can be
selected, and will apply a filter to all other visuals on the same page.

Figure 5-8

The Matrix visual

Where a table does a great job of allowing users to consume tons of detailed data about a single category, the *Matrix* visual can accomplish this for more than one category. The *Matrix* visual allows users to not only select a category for the rows, but means we can also select a field to populate the columns, which allows us to see detailed data at a cross section for two categories. *Conditional formatting* is also available for use within the *Matrix* visual, and is incorporated in the same fashion as we accomplished in the previous example. Other than *Conditional Formatting*, the *Matrix* visual can take advantage of established hierarchies to give users that capability of drilling down into more granular data. Many of the other visuals can also take advantage of hierarchies, but for tabular data the *Matrix* visual does a great job with this.

Let's look at, setting up the visual:

1. Ensure that you do not have any other visual selected, and choose the *Matrix* visual from the visual's area.
2. Firstly, we will populate the *Rows* area with our Sales Territory Drilldown, which you will find under the Sales Territory table. You will see that when we place a check mark next to the Sales Territory Drilldown option, it brings in three different fields, starting with Sales Territory Group.
3. Next, we will select what is known as a natural hierarchy which Power BI automatically creates from our Date (Order) table. Place a check mark next to the Date field, which will bring in the Year, Quarter, Month, and Day fields. If these fields do not automatically become populated in the *Columns* area, just drag them to that location. Now, we have our two categories with options to drill down to get more granular data.
4. Lastly, let's add two measures to the *Matrix* under the *Values* area. Select both the *Total Sales* and *Profit* measures. See *Figure 5-9* for reference. Move and resize the *Matrix* as you see fit:

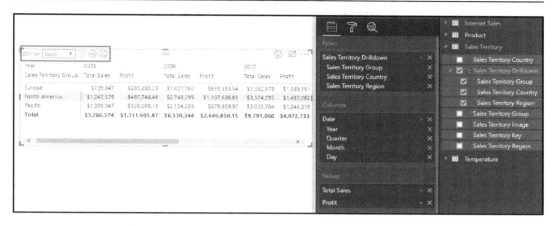

Figure 5-9

Now, we can see that the amount of data available to us is even greater than that of the *Table* visual. We should apply the same format changes to the *Text Size* as we did for the table at this point. The *Matrix* allows us to see fantastically detailed information about the different geographic regions, as well as a breakdown per year. Also, you will see that there are some new icons in the upper left of the visual which relate to the drilldown feature we spoke of earlier. Because we have hierarchies on both the rows and columns, we must decide which we would like to expand for further details. We will focus solely on the rows option and expand upon the geographical category. The first upward pointing arrow, which should be currently grayed out, allows users to move up a level in the hierarchy, but we are currently at the highest level. The option just to the right of this, which is depicted by two disconnected downward arrows, will change the category to the next level of the hierarchy, which is the *Sales Territory Country* in our example. Let's go ahead and select this option two times so that we are displaying the *Sales Territory Region*. The third option, which is depicted by two connected downward arrows will also go down one level at a time through the hierarchy, but it will also retain the previous (higher) category. By having the *Matrix* and *Table* next to each other, you can see the difference in detail that can be achieved by each of them. Both, though, can benefit greatly from *Conditional Formatting*.

Visualizing categorical data

Where the *Table* and *Matrix* visuals allow for a detailed look at multiple measures across a category, the following visuals are best for displaying data values across categories. In the upcoming visuals, we will be displaying Bars, Columns, and other visual elements, which will be proportional to the data value. These visuals have a far less detailed few of the data, but it is very easy to distinguish the differences of the values within the chosen category. All of the visuals allow for interactive filtering and the use of drilldowns, which we will not focus on since it was covered in the previous examples. We will focus on how to understand and configure the following visuals:

- Bar and Column Charts
- Pie and Donut Charts
- The Treemap Visual
- Scatter Charts

We will continue using the same Power BI report from the previous examples, but we will want to create a new report page and call it *Categorical Data*.

Bar and Column charts

Both the *Bar* and *Column* charts are very similar in setup and how they visual data. The only difference here will be the orientation: the *Bar* chart uses rectangular bars horizontally where the length of the bar is proportional to the data, while the *Column* chart displays the bars vertically, but both are used to compare two or more values. Both of these visualizations have three different formats; *Stacked*, *Clustered*, and *100% Stacked*. For our example, we will focus on the *Bar* chart, but users can easily switch over to the *Column* just with the click of a button.

There are some situations where the *Bar* chart will better display data, and the same thing can be said of the *Column* chart. The biggest limitation for the *Column* chart would be the limited space on the *x*-axis where the category would go. So, if you have a lot of data labels or if they are very long, you may find that the *Bar* chart is the better option. An example where you might choose the *Column* chart over the *Bar* chart is if your dataset contains negative values. In a *Bar* chart, the negative values will show on the left side while in a *Column* chart they will display on the bottom. Users generally associate negative values with a downward direction.

Let's look at, setting up the visual:

1. Select the *Stacked Bar Chart* option and move and resize the visual to take up a quarter of the report canvas.
2. The first field we will want to select is `Sales Territory Country`; this should populate in the *Axis* area.
3. Next, let's add our `Profit` measure, which should populate in the `Value` section.

Just with these two fields, we can very easily comprehend which countries make the most profit and which makes the least. As you can see though, there are more sections of the *Fields Area* that we can supply values for, namely the *Legend* section. By adding a category to this area, we can add sections to our original category, which shows the countries. Let's go ahead and add the *Age Breakdown* column to the legend for this visual (see *Figure 5-10*). Just like that, we have a very exciting display of our company's profit broken down by country and age group. Users can now hover over any section of the bar chart and the tooltip will display the values for that specific section. There is, though, another great format option that we can enable to make it even easier to understand the data, and it is called *Data Labels*. To enable this, simply select the *Format Area* and you will see an option called *Data Labels* that can be toggled on and off. By turning this option to *On*, we now can see the profit breakdown for each country by age category, as seen in *Figure 5-10*:

Figure 5-10

In regards to the other two options, *Clustered* and *100% Stacked*, you can simply select those visuals to experience the different presentations. You will notice the *Data Labels* remain and add great value regardless of the visual selection. As well with the addition of the *Legend*, we have another way to do interactive filtering.

Pie and Donut charts

Both the *Pie* chart and *Donut* chart are meant to visualize a particular section to the whole, rather than comparing individual values to each other. The only difference between the two is that the *Donut* chart has a hole in the middle, which could allow for some sort of label. Both of these visuals can be very effective in allowing interactive filtering, but if there are too many categories it can become difficult to read and interpret.

Let's look at, setting up the visual:

1. Ensure that no other visual is currently highlighted, and select the *Donut* chart visual. Move and resize the visual so as to take up a quarter of the report canvas, preferably above or below the *Bar* chart.
2. We will be populating two fields for this visual; the first will be *Temperature Range*, which should populate under the *Legend* section. The second field, which we want to show up in the *Values* section, is the *Total Sales* measure.

Because there are only four values within the *Temperature Range* category, this chart looks very clean and easy to understand. There is something, though, that we can add that will make it even easier to read: *Detail Labels*. This option is very similar to *Category Labels* in that we can display the data of each of the quadrants without having to use the tooltips. One thing that is different though is that it is already on, and all we need to do is decide how much detail we would like to have displayed. The more values that are present this can cause even more clutter though. To access these options go to the *Format Area* and expand the *Detail Labels* category, and manipulate the *Label Style* dropdown. For our example, let's choose the *All Detail Labels* option. As you can see in figure 5-11, we have a very nice and easy way to understand the presented data, as well as use it for interactive filtering:

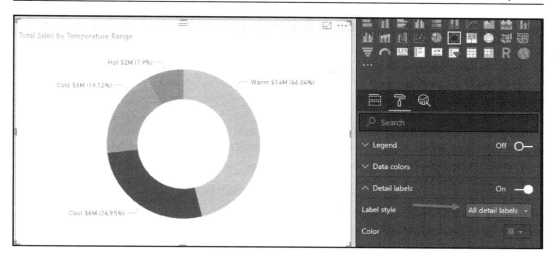

Figure 5-11

The Treemap visual

A fantastic visual for displaying hierarchies is definitely the *Treemap* visual. It accomplishes this by nesting the data in rectangles, which are represented by color, and this is commonly known as a "branch". If you add a category into the *Details* section of the visual you will note smaller rectangles within the "branches" and these are known as "leaves", hence the name *Treemap*. In order to really maximize this visual, we will need to do a little extra setup and bring in a new table, and create a new hierarchy. Let's go through this process now:

Let's look at, setting up the example:

1. We need to bring in the `DimGeography` table from the `AdventureWorksDW` excel workbook. Since we accomplished this during `Chapter 3`, *Building the Data Model*, you should be able to see this source under the *Recent Sources* option. If not, you can connect to this source by pointing to this location: `C:\Packt\Data Sources\AdventureWorksDW.xlsx`.

2. Once the *Navigator* appears, we will want to place a check mark next to the `DimGeography` table and hit **Load**.

3. We need to do a couple quick fixes to this new table before we can leverage it. Navigate to the Relationship View and delete the inactive relationship between `Sales Territory` and `DimGeography`.

4. Also let's rename this new table to `Geography` and hide the following fields: `FrenchCountryRegionName` and `SpanishCountryRegionName`.

5. Lastly, let's create a new hierarchy that we will use inside of this *Treemap* visual, as well as the Map visuals later on. Right-click on the `EnglishCountryRegionName` column and select New Hierarchy from the dropdown. Rename the new hierarchy `Region Drilldown`.

6. Add StateProvinceName to the hierarchy by right-clicking on it and selecting Add to Hierarchy from the dropdown. Repeat this step for the `City` field. See *Figure 5-12* for reference:

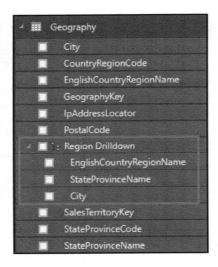

Figure 5-12

Now that we have a new geographical hierarchy that goes all the way down to a city level, we can see how this will display with our *Treemap* visual.

Let's look at, setting up the visual:

1. Click on any of the white space on the report canvas to ensure no visual is selected, and bring in the *Treemap* visual.

2. Move and resize this visual so that it takes up a quarter of the remaining report canvas.

3. First. we must decide on what we will be grouping on, and in our situation. that will be the newly defined `Region Drilldown`.

4. Next. we will add the `Total Sales` measure to the *Values* area and we start to see the beauty of this visual.

5. The last thing we will add is to the *Details* area so that we can see some "leaves". Bring in the `Year` field from the `Date (Order)` table.

The size of each of the rectangles is determined by the value being measured, which in our case is `Total Sales`. The "leaves" in this visual are portrayed by the `Year` category while our `Region Drilldown` creates the "branches". Because we are using a hierarchy, we have full access to the Drilldown capabilities shown earlier. You should also now be able to tell that the *Treemap* visual arranges the rectangles by size from top left (largest) to bottom right (smallest).

The Scatter chart

The last visual we will look at the is used for categorical data is the *Scatter* chart, sometimes referred to as the *Bubble* chart. This visual allows us to show the relationships between two or three numerical values. We are given the opportunity to place values for the x and y axis, but what is different about this visual is that we can add a third value for the size, and this is where the name *Bubble* chart comes from. There is also a very unique option available to us within the *Format Area* to really bring this data to life, and it is called the *Play Axis*. Let's go ahead and create our *Scatter* chart first, and then we will talk about the *Play Axis*.

Let's look at, setting up the visual:

1. Make sure no other visual is currently selected and choose the *Scatter* chart. Move and resize the visual to take up the remainder of the report canvas.

2. The first field we will select is the `Total Sales` measure, and this will serve as the value for our *X* axis.

3. For the *Y* axis, let us select the `Profit` measure.

4. The third value that we will use for the size of the bubbles will be the `Order Quantity` field.

5. Finally, we must choose the category that we would like to see all these measure for, and we will use the `EnglishCountryRegionName` field from the `Geography` table. Make sure that this field is displayed under the *Legend* section, which should give you a visual like in *Figure 5-13*:

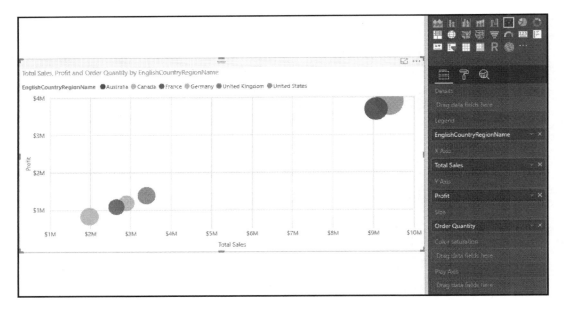

Figure 5-13

Now, the last part that we will add to this visual will be the *Play Axis*, which is unique to the *Scatter* chart. By adding some category of time, we can bring a little animation to this visual. For our example, let's add the *English Month Name* field to the *Play Axis* section, and you will see a *Play* button appear along with our 12 months. By hitting the button, you will now be able to watch the bubbles move to display their values at the specific moments in time.

Visualizing trend data

When we use the term *Trend Data*, we are talking about displaying and comparing values over time. Power BI gives us many options in this category, each with their own focus. The idea for each of the visuals, though, is to draw attention to the total value across a length of time. Let's create a new report page and call it *Trend Data*, and dive right in to see what the differences are between the following options:

- Line and Area Charts
- Combo Charts
- Ribbon Charts
- Waterfall and Funnel Charts

Line and Area charts

The *Line* chart is the most basic of our options when it comes to looking at data over time. The *Area* chart and *Stacked Area* chart are based on the line chart; the difference is that the area between the axis and the line is filled in with colors to show volume. Because of this, we will focus on the *Line* chart for our example. Since we have a very nice *Date* hierarchy, we will use this alongside a couple of measures to see trending.

Let's look at, setting up the visual:

1. Select the *Line* chart visual and move it to take up a quarter of the report canvas.
2. The axis is where we dictate our time category and, for this example, we will use the built-in *Date* hierarchy by selecting the `Date` field from the `Date(Order)` table.
3. We will be using this chart to compare two different measures over time; they will be the `Total Sales` and `Prior Year Sales` measures. Select both of these, and they should populate under the `Values` section.

4. To make it a bit more of an exciting visual, let's take advantage of the hierarchy and it expand it down two levels to include the quarter and month, as seen in *Figure 5-14*:

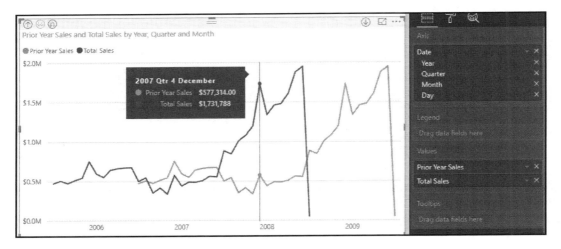

Figure 5-14

With this *Line* chart, we can clearly see there was a large growth in sales between 2007 and 2008. Visuals that focus on *Trend Data* can very easily illustrate any outliers, which can allow users to further investigate the cause of the seen trend. This visual can also benefit from some of the formatting options we have talked about previously, such as *Data Labels*.

Combo charts

As the name states, *Combo* charts combine the *Line* chart and *Column* chart together in one visual. Users can choose to have either the *Stack Column* format or the *Clustered Column* format. By combining these two visuals together, we can make a very quick comparison of the data. The main benefit of this type of chart is that we can have one or two *Y axes*. What this means is that we can either display two measures that would have the same Y-axis, something like *Total Sales and Profit.* Or, we could show two measures that are based on completely different values such as *Order Quantity and Profit;* let's use the two for our example.

Let's look at, setting up the visual:

1. For this example, we will be using the *Line and Stacked Column Chart* visual. Select and resize it to take up a quarter of the report canvas.
2. For the *Shared Axis* area, let's select the `Date` field from the Date (Order) table.
3. We will then select the Order Quantity field to populate the *Column Values* section.
4. The last field we will select is the `Profit` measure, but when we check mark this item you will see that it is placed under the *Column Values* section, which is incorrect. Simply drag the *Profit* measure to the *Line Values* section.

In this example, you can see that we have two Y axes; the left one relates to the *Order Quantity* while the right one corresponds with our *Profit* measure. Go ahead and expand the hierarchy one level; this will give us more data points to see the trending between the two measures, as seen in *Figure 5-15*. From this visual, it's fairly easy to validate that when we sell more items we make more profit. This, like many other visuals, can also benefit from *Data Labels*:

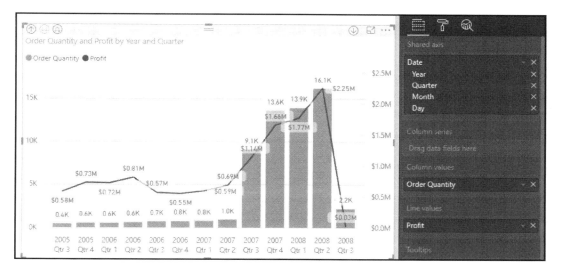

Figure 5-15

The Ribbon Chart

The *Ribbon Chart* is no different than the other visuals we just worked with; it is good at viewing data over time. What makes *Ribbon Charts* effective though is their ability at showing rank change; the highest range or value is always displayed on the top for each of the time periods. The chart also does have a unique visual flowing appeal to it that is different than the other visuals. Let's take a look that the *Ribbon Chart*.

Let's look at, setting up the visual:

1. Select the **Ribbon Chart** to add as a new visual, and resize it to take up a quarter of the report canvas.
2. For the *Axis* area, let's choose the *Date* field from the `Date (Order)` table so that we have a hierarchy available for drilldown.
3. The next field we will add to the visual is the *Total Sales* measure, which should populate under the *Value* section. At this point, you will see that it pretty much looks like a **Column Chart**.
4. Once we add a category to the *Legend* area, we will get that flowing ribbon presentation. For our example, let's add the `EnglishCountryRegionName` to the *Legend* area.

The first thing you may notice is the lighter areas between time periods; this is really one of the best parts of the **Ribbon Chart**. This area shows the value for the category for the previous period and the upcoming one. Also, the tooltip does give each value a rank and shows any increases as well as decreases. This, like many other visuals, also gets a nice visibility bump by adding *Data Labels*, as seen in *Figure 5-16*:

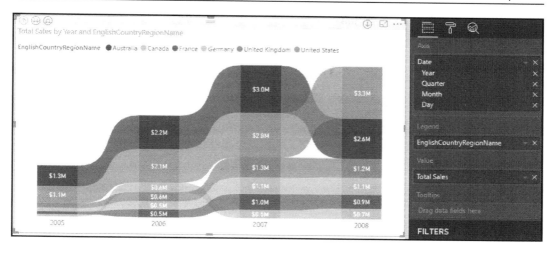

Figure 5-16

The Waterfall Chart

This next visual, the *Waterfall Chart,* is very helpful in understanding the changes that occur from an initial value. It displays a running total in relation to values being added or subtracted. By populating a field in the *Breakdown* option of the visual, we can see if it has had a positive or negative impact from value to value. Let's set up an example of the *Waterfall Chart.*

Let's look at, setting up the visual:

1. In our current report page, we should have a quarter of the area still available. We will use half of this for the *Waterfall Chart.* Let's go ahead and now add this visual to the report page.
2. The first area we want to populate is Category, and for this, we will select the Date field from the Date (Order) table. As before, this will bring in a hierarchy.
3. Next, select the Profit measure to represent the *Y-axis.* With this, we can see how much each year has contributed to the total profit.
4. The last field we will select is Age Breakdown. Upon selecting this field, you will need to move it to populate the *Breakdown* section.

Now, we can see the strength of the *Waterfall Chart*, and we can see how much contribution each age group provided between years. By default, the visual uses the green color to indicate positive changes and red to illustrate negative ones, but this can be changed from the *Format Area* if you are so inclined. Depending on how many values are within your breakdown category, enabling *Data Labels* can be useful in this visual, as seen in *Figure 5-17*:

Figure 5-17

The Funnel Chart

The *Funnel Chart* allows users to see the percentage difference between values. Normally, the highest value is at the top and the lowest is at the bottom, which gives the look of a funnel. Each stage of the funnel with tell the percentage difference between itself and the previous stage, as well as compared to the highest stage. With this type of design, it makes sense that the *Funnel Chart* is very effective when visualizing a linear process with at least three or four stages. Our data set does not have a process with multiple stages, but we can still create something that gives us value.

Let's look at, setting up the visual:

1. With the remaining space we have on this report page, go ahead and add in the last visual for this section, the Funnel Chart.
2. For this visual, we will only be adding two fields. The first will be the `CountryRegionCode`, which will be what we use for the *Group* section.
3. The second item that we will add to the `Values` section will be the **Profit** measure.

The way we have set up this visual allows us to very easily identify which countries make the most profit and which make the least, but this is something we can achieve with many other visuals. What gives the *Funnel Chart* an edge is when we hover over one of the sections within the funnel and note the items that appear within the tooltip. You will see, when we hover over the section for France, that the tooltip lets us know how it compares to the section directly above it, as well as how it compares to the highest section, which is represented by the United States.

Visualizing KPI data

Key Performance Indicator is what KPI stands for. It is a measurable value that demonstrates how well a company is achieving a certain objective. With Power BI, we have a couple of options to measure the progress being made towards a goal for operational processes. The strength of a KPI visual lies in its simplicity. It displays a single value and its progress toward a specific goal. Let's create a new *Report Page* called *KPI Data*, and take a closer look at the *Gauge and KPI* visuals.

The Gauge visual

The *Gauge* visual displays a single value within a circular arc and its progress towards a goal or target value that we specify. The *Target Value* is represented by a line within the arc. With our current data set, we do not have a measure that we can use to illustrate an accurate business goal, so we will have to create it. Before we set up this visual, we will need to create a new calculated measure.

Let's look at, setting up the example:

1. We will be using the `Total Sales` measure as our value in the *Gauge* visual. Our target will be 10% more than the previous year's total sales, so we need to use DAX to create this measure.
2. Right-click the `Internet Sales` table and select the *New Measure* option, which would bring us to the formula bar.
3. Name the measure `Sales Target`, and use the following DAX formula to get our target:

```
Sales Target = [Prior Year Sales] * 0.1
```

Now that we have all the measures we need, lets set up the gauge visual and create our first KPI.

Let's look at, setting up the visual:

1. Select the *Gauge* visual and move/resize it as you see fit.
2. For the **Value** section, select the `Total Sales` measure.
3. Select our newly created `Sales Target` measure for the `Target Value` area. Upon selecting this measure, it will not automatically be populated for the *Target Value,* so you will need to move it.

Using a *Slicer* visual alongside this KPI will be really helpful with our data set. Go ahead and add the *Slicer* visual using the *Year* field for the value. If you choose the year 2008, you will see that the value changes along with the target, as seen in *Figure 5-18*. With our dataset, the year 2008 is where we have our most recent transactions, and because of this visual, we can see that we have still not met our goal. If you look at any of the other previous years, we can validate that we were able to surpass our target every time:

Figure 5-18

The KPI visual

Where the *Gauge* visual uses the circular arc to show the current progress,
the *KPI* visual takes a more explicit approach and just shows the value in plain text,
along with the goal. The only real visual elements that are in play with this visual
occur when the indicator value is lower than the goal and the text is shown in red,
and when it has surpassed the goal and the text is in green. This is definitely one of
the more direct visuals and perfectly exemplifies what we want for a KPI.

Let's look at, setting up the visual:

1. Ensure that no other visual is selected, and bring in the *KPI* visual, and
   move it as you see fit.
2. For the *Indicator* section, go ahead and select the Total Sales measure.
3. Next, choose the Prior Year Sales measure to represent the *Target Goals*
   section.
4. The last piece that we need to add is for the *Trend Axis,for* which we will be
   using the Year option from the Date (Order) table.

If, after following the preceding steps, the visual displays a value of *Blank* for the indicator, do not worry. This is because it is trying to show the total sales for the year 2010, the most recent value in our dataset. Unfortunately, we do not have any sales for 2009 or 2010, so to have this visual display correctly simply choose any other year from the slicer that we added in the previous section. Once you have accomplished this, you will now be able to view the *KPI* visual, and it should look like *Figure 5-19*:

Figure 5-19

Visualizing geographical data

One of the most exciting ways to visualize data in Power BI is through the various map options that we have. All the maps serve the same purpose to illustrate data in relation to locations around the world, but there are some small differences between each of them. All of the maps, except the *Shape Map*, have the option to provide the latitude and longitude coordinates, which will be the best way to ensure the appropriate location is being displayed. The reason for this is because the information that we provide the visual will be sent to *Bing Maps* to verify the positioning on the map. If we do not provide enough detail, then *Bing* may not return the desired results. For example, if we were to provide the map visual with a field that contains only the city name, that could result in some confusion because there may be multiple cities in the US with that name. In these scenarios, we will either want to supply some sort of geo-hierarchy to give better definition, or we can create new columns with more detailed information. Power BI also has a built-in feature when dealing with geographic data that allows users to help identify the type of data that is being provided: this is called *Data Category*. Let's go ahead and take advantage of this for our data set to make the map visuals more accurate.

Let's look at, setting up the example:

1. Within the **Fields** Pane, expand the `Geography` table.

2. The first field that we will categorize will be the `City` field. Highlight this field and then navigate to the **Modeling** ribbon. Once here, you will see the **Data Category** option.

3. Inside the drop-down menu, we will select the `City` option. Upon accomplishing this, you will see that there is now a globe icon next to the `City` field.

4. Repeat the steps above for the `StateProvinceName` field, but choose the `State` or `Province` option for the data category dropdown.

5. The final field that we need to perform these steps for is `EnglishCountryRegionName`; select the `Country/Region` option from the dropdown.

Now that we have given a better description of our geographical data, we can proceed with using the various map visuals. One thing of note is that using any of these visuals does require internet access because we are going to be sending data to *Bing Maps*. Before we begin, create a new *Report Page* called `Geographical Data`.

The Map visual

The first visual we will use to illustrate geographical data is simply called the *Map* visual. This visual is also referred to as the *Bubble Map* because it plots the points of data with circles that can be set to change in size based off a supplied measure. With this visual, if you have the latitude and longitude coordinates in your data set, then nothing needs to be sent to *Bing Maps*. We do not have such detailed data, so we will need to supply the necessary information through the *Location* section, which will be sent to *Bing Maps*.

Let's look at, setting up the visual:

1. For this new report page, let's select the *Map* visual to get things started, and move it to take up a quarter of the report canvas.

2. To ensure there is no confusion about the locations we want to map, we will provide the geo-hierarchy, which we have created within the `Geography` table. Go to this table and select the `Region Drilldown` option, which will populate the **Location** section. Just with this, we can see the six countries represented by a bubble.

3. Next, we will add a measure that will dictate the size of the bubbles we are currently seeing. Let's use the `Total Sales` measure for the *Size* section, so that larger bubbles will show countries with higher sales amounts.

4. The last thing we will add to this visual is the Age Breakdown to the *Legend* section. With this, the bubbles start to look like little pie charts, as seen in *Figure 5-20*:

Figure 5-20

 When using a geo-hierarchy with a map, enabling the Drill Mode, which is signified by the down arrow in the upper right, can make this visual even more enjoyable. Remember this for any visual where we have a hierarchy selected; you should explore the different views it gives you.

The Filled Map visual

Unlike the traditional *Map* visual, which uses a bubble to indicate locations, the *Filled Map* visual uses shading to display the geographic data. So, the lighter an area looks, the lower the representative value. For this visual, it is recommended to visit the *Format Area* and dictate the range of colors for the shading so it will appear more apparent.

Let's look at, setting up the visual:

1. Select the *Filled Map* visual and move it to take up a quarter of the report page.
2. Just like the previous example, we will use the `Region Drilldown` from the `Geography` table to populate the *Location* section.
3. The only other field we will add to this visual is the *Profit* measure, which will control the *Color Saturation* option.

With just these setting, we can see the effect of this map, but because of the color selection it is very difficult to see the lighter shades; let's fix this. By going into the *Format Area* and expanding the *Data Colors* section, we will be presented with a couple of options. The first one we should turn on is the option labeled *Diverging*. Next, we should change the colors so that they are more distinguishable. For this example, let's use a more traditional option for our colors; red for M*inimum*, yellow for *Center*, and green for M*aximum*.

The Shape Map visual

Similar to the *Filled Map*, the *Shape Map* visual uses shading/saturation to show the geographic data. One thing that does make the *Shape Map* unique is that it allows users to upload their own maps to be illustrated. In order to accomplish this, you must have a JSON file which contains all the necessary information required by Power BI. By default, the visual does offer some standard maps but currently does not have an option to show the entire world. Let's take a look at the *Shape Map* visual.

Let's look at setting up the visual:

1. Select the *Shape Map* visual and move it to take up a quarter of the report page.
2. This map does not allow for multiple fields to be placed in the *Location* section, so we cannot use the *Region Drilldown* as before. For this example, we will use the *StateProvinceName*. Do not be alarmed if nothing appears initially, as we still have to tell Power BI which map we want to use.
3. Before we go into the *Format Area* to choose a map, let's add the *Profit* measure, which will control the shading/saturation.
4. Now, we can look at the *Format Area* and expand the *Shape* option, where there will be a dropdown selection for the *Map* category. For our example, we will want to choose *USA: states*.

5. This is another example where taking control of what colors will be used for the shading can be helpful, so let's apply the same changes that we did for the *Filled Map* under the *Data Colors* section.

The ArcGIS Map visual

The final map we will talk about is the *ArcGIS Map* visual; this one is very different in that there is an option to pay for additional features. Also, the location where you can make visual changes to the map is different as well. Normally, we would access the *Format Area* but for this map, you must hit the ellipsis in the upper-right corner of the visual and choose the *Edit* option. We will be focusing on a couple of areas here, but there are lots of options that are worth exploring. Let's take a look on how to configure the *ArcGIS Map* visual.

Let's look at, setting up the visual:

1. We should have one more section available within the report canvas to place this last visual, so let's select the *ArcGIS Map* visual.
2. Just like the *Shape Map*, we are unable to select multiple fields to populate the *Location* section; we will use *StateProvinceNanme* for our example. You will notice that after loading the information there will be a small yellow ribbon at the bottom saying that it failed to load some of the information. This is fine because this field contains provinces that are outside the United States.
3. The only other field that we will map for this visual will be the *Total Sales* measure, and we will use this for the *Color* section.

This visual is ready to go with the configuration that we have set, but if we want to change how things look we must go a new route. In the upper right-hand corner you will see an ellipsis; left-click this and choose the *Edit* option. This brings us to a display that looks very similar to *Focus Mode,* but you will notice there are quite a few options at the top of the map. The first area we will visit to make a slight change will be the *Symbol Style* option. Here, we can control the level of transparency as well as the color palette being used. Select the dropdown menu for the *Color Ramp* option, and choose whatever selection you find enjoyable. This is the only change we will be making for our example, but you should take the time and examine all the other options available to you. Remember, there are even more options to choose from if you decided to subscribe and pay for this visual. All of these maps are very similar but each has a specific functionality that does not exist in the others. The traditional *Map* and *Filled Map* visuals are the most common ones used, but you will need to decide when one might illustrate your data set better than the other.

Leveraging Power BI custom visuals

Throughout this chapter, we have seen many different visuals and how they work with specific types of data. Although we already have many options readily available with Power BI, we have access to 100+ more visuals from the Microsoft store right at our fingertips. Users can either navigate to the Microsoft app store via any web browser or while inside of the Power BI desktop application they can select the *From Marketplace* option in the home ribbon. Once you select this option, a menu will appear where you can simply search the entire collection of custom visuals available. Once you have found a visual that you would like to use, just hit the *Add* button shown in yellow. Users can also download the physical file as well, which can be uploaded into Power BI by using the *From File* option, which is also in the home ribbon. It is important to understand that when you select a custom visual, it saves as part of the Power BI report file and doesn't remain inside of the application. So, if you just downloaded a custom visual and then closed down Power BI, when you restart the application you will not see that custom visual unless you open the report you saved the custom visual to. This is a fantastic feature, and it only continues to grow so it is definitely worthwhile to check out the marketplace.

Data visualization tips and tricks

We have created six different report pages filled with different visuals and looked into different configuration options for each of them. That being said, we have barely scratched the surface of all the features that are available to us, and with the very quick update cycle Power BI has, that list of features will keep growing. In this final section, we will look at a couple of features that are not exclusive to just one visual, but can really help out when designing a report. It is highly recommended to watch the monthly videos that the Power BI team produces alongside the actual product update. This way, you can know exactly what is new and how to use it.

Edit interactions

Throughout all of our examples, we have had the capability of using interactive filtering. We know that almost everything we see inside a visual can be selected, and it will affect all the other visuals within that same report page. This behavior can be altered though, and there will be situations where you do not want a specific visual to be filtered by any others. The way we can control this is through an option called *Edit Interactions*, which can be found under the *Format* ribbon when a visual is selected. When you select the *Edit Interactions* button, you will see new icons for all of the other visuals that are currently not selected, as seen in figure 5-21. In this example, I have the *Pie Chart* selected and I can now decide if any of the other visuals will be affected by interactive filtering from the *Pie Chart*. The two primary icons are a funnel which lets us know that the visual will be filtered, and then a circle with a line through it designates that it will not be filtered. Occasionally, there will be an icon that looks like a pie chart, which we can see for the *Stacked Column Chart*. This means that the visual will be filtered by highlighting the filtered portion, as shown in *Figure 5-21*. This option is something that you will have to do for each individual visual:

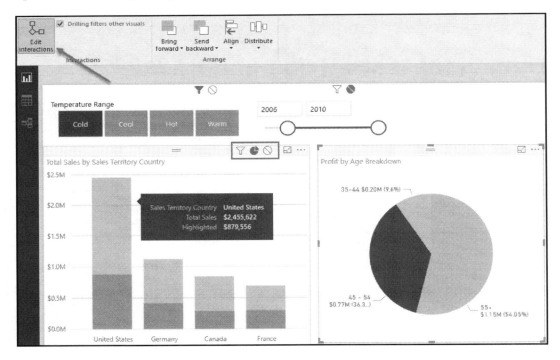

Figure 5-21

The Analytics pane

For every visual, we worked with the *Field Area* and the *Format Area* but there is an option you may have noticed that is called the *Analytics Pane*. This option is available for most visuals, but some of the options will not appear; for our example, we will look at the *Line Chart* example we created. Once we have that visual selected, we can choose the *Analytics Pane* and see that we are presented with seven different lines that can be added to the visual. All we have to do is decide which one we would like to be displayed and turn it on. For our visual, let's add an *Average Line* by expanding that section and selecting the *Add* option. Once the line has been added, we can change the color, name, transparency, style, and position from this same area, as seen in *Figure 5-22*. Users can add as many of these lines as they so choose, but remember, more is not necessarily better:

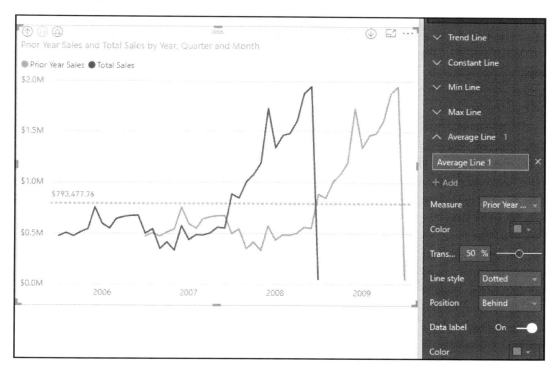

Figure 5-22

The Top N filter

At the very beginning of this chapter, we briefly talked about the *Filter Area* and how we can apply filters to different scopes. There are a couple of choices available to users for the filter fields, but we are going to look at the *Top N* option. Even though it is called the *Top N* filter, this option allows us to create a filter that will show either the top or bottom number of values. For example, if we look at the *Ribbon Chart* we created, we can see that there are six countries that appear in the visual. With this filter, we can set it so that it only displays the top four countries based off a measure that we choose. So, in this situation, we could have that measure be `Total Sales`, which is what the visual is showing, or really anything we want. Let's go ahead and hit the dropdown next to the `EnglishCountryRegion` field in *Visual Level Filters*. If *Top N* isn't showing by default in the *Filter Type* section, go ahead and select it from the dropdown. For the *Show Items* section, we will leave the value of *Top* and manually input the number 4, as shown in *Figure 5-23*. The last thing that needs to be done is to decide what measure will be used to determine the top four countries; we will keep things simple and drag in the `Total Sales` measure, and hit **Apply Filter**. The most important thing to remember is that you can use any measure you want for this filter:

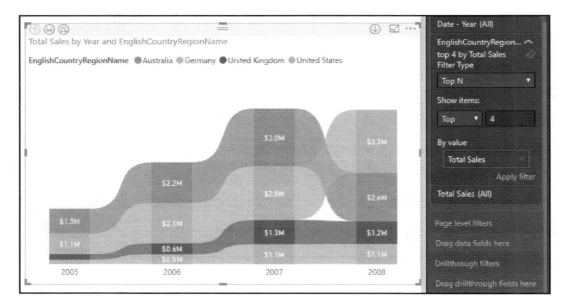

Figure 5-23

Show value as

Earlier in this chapter, we went through an example to take advantage of *Conditional Formatting*. This option can be found by hitting the downward arrow next to a field that is being used in a visual. Within this area is where we will find another option that is labeled *Show Value As*. This option will only be available for numeric data types and allows us to show the values as a percentage of the grand total. The best way to take advantage of this is to place an identical column side by side and then use this option to display one of them as a percentage. For our example, let's revisit the *Matrix* visual we created for the *Tabular Data* section. Locate the `Profit` measure in the `Fields` Pane and drag it into the `Values` section for the visual, and place it directly after the `Profit` measure that we already had in place, referencing *Figure 5-24*. The visual looks a little odd since there is a duplicated column, but let's change it to show a percentage. Within the dropdown for the second representation of `Profit`, choose the **Show Value** As option and select **Percent of Grand Total**. The *Matrix* was already a great visual to quickly see a lot of metric information about the `Sales Territory Regions`, but now we have a firm understanding of what percentage each country is contributing to the grand total:

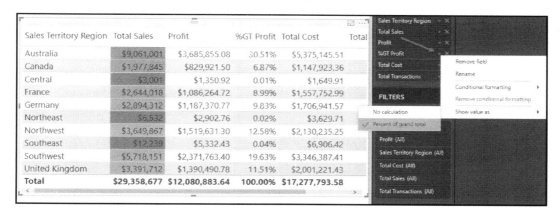

Figure 5-24

Summary

In this chapter, we focused on how to configure visuals and what data they best illustrate. We also saw a couple of the most common formatting options that are used with these visuals. In the next chapter, we will look into the concept of digital storytelling. Power BI has a strong set of options that we can leverage to allow users to experience and navigate through the data in an adventurous and exploratory manner.

6
Using a Cloud Deployment with the Power BI Service

You've spent the course of this book creating amazing reports using the Power BI Desktop client. Now, it's time to share those reports with your team, company, or customers. In this chapter, you're going to learn about the Power BI service and how to use it to do the following:

- Deploy reports to the Power BI service
- Create and interact with dashboards
- Share dashboards
- Secure your reports with row-level security
- Schedule refreshes of your data

The Power BI service operates a freemium model. You can get most of the features in the free model, but when you want to share data with others and use team development, it will need to be upgraded to the pro edition. Other features requiring the pro edition are the ability to store larger datasets and more frequently refresh, to name a few.

 Before you begin this chapter, make sure you sign up for a free account at Power BI (https://powerbi.microsoft.com/). Some sections of this book will require a pro license, such as the section dealing with workspaces.

Deploying to the Power BI service

There are numerous ways to publish a report to the `PowerBI.com` service, but the easiest way is by using the Power BI desktop. To do this, you'll need to simply click the **Publish** button in the desktop application, as shown in the following screenshot. If you have not previously signed in with your free `PowerBI.com` account, you will be prompted to create one or sign in with an existing account:

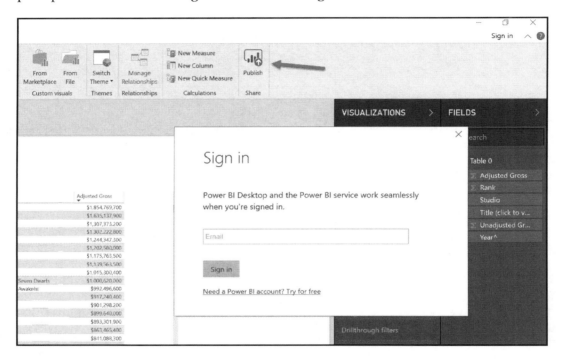

You'll then be asked which workspace you want to deploy to. A *workspace* is an area in the Power BI service that is much like a folder, where you can bundle your reports, datasets, and dashboards. You can also assign security to the workspace and not have to worry about securing each item. Most importantly, it allows for team development of a Power BI solution, where you can have multiple authors on a solution. We'll cover much more about workspaces in the *Sharing Your Dashboards* section of this chapter.

At this point, select the **My Workspace** item, which will send the report and its data to your personal workspace. The report will then deploy to the Power BI service. The amount of time this takes will depend on how large your dataset is. You'll then be presented with two options: **Open the Report** or **Get Quick Insights**.

Quick Insights is an amazing feature in Power BI that will try to find additional interesting insights about your data that you may not have known you had. For example, in the following screenshot of the sample report, it found that Disney dominated all other film studios in 2016. You'll notice that it not only provides a graphic of the anomaly in your data, but also a narrative to the right of the graphic. If you find any of the insights especially interesting, you can click the push pin on the top right of the graphic to save it into a dashboard. We'll cover dashboards in the next section of this chapter:

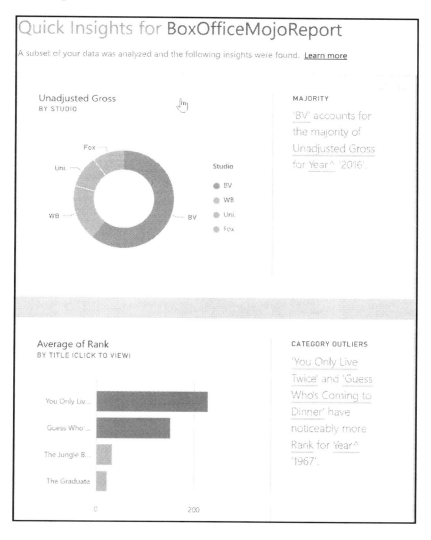

If you open the report, `PowerBI.com` will launch and show you the same report that you were viewing in the desktop in a web browser. You'll also be able to immediately see the report in the Power BI mobile app from your Android or iPhone. `PowerBI.com` has four key areas that you can interact with:

- **DATASETS**: This is the raw data that you have built in the Power BI desktop. You can also build a new dataset by clicking **Get Data** in the bottom-left corner of your browser. When you click the datasets, you can also build new reports from that dataset.
- **WORKBOOKS**: You can upload Excel workbooks into this area. These Excel workbooks can be used as a dataset or can form pieces of the workbook that can be pinned to a dashboard.
- **REPORTS**: This refers to what you have built in the Power BI desktop. These reports can be explored, modified, or downloaded in this section.
- **DASHBOARDS**: You can pin the best elements from multiple reports into a unified set of dashboards. These dashboards are the first thing most of your casual users will interact with:

DATASETS

The **DATASETS** area of Power BI holds the raw data that makes up your reports. When you left-click on one of your datasets, the designer opens to build reports from the dataset. The designer can be used to do the following things:

- Create more Quick Insights
- Create new reports
- Refresh or schedule refreshes
- Manage permissions
- Download the Power BI Desktop file (.pbix)

When you start with a dataset, users can create new reports from your data, even when accessing it through the web. The entire user interface will feel nearly identical to Power BI Desktop, but you will be lacking the ability to modify the model, query, and relationships. The best part of building reports here is that you have a central dataset that IT can own, modify, and make human-readable so that the entire organization can build reports off of it.

WORKBOOKS

The **WORKBOOKS** section gives you the ability to upload Excel workbooks, which can be used as datasets for a report or to pin selected parts of that workbook to a dashboard. Workbooks can be updated by either reuploading the workbook, using the database management gateway or using OneDrive. OneDrive is Microsoft's cloud-hosted hard drive system. With OneDrive, you can simply share or save your Excel workbooks, and if you're using the workbook in a Power BI report, it can also refresh.

Creating and interacting with dashboards

Once you have deployed your datasets and are using them in reports, you're ready to bring together the many report elements into a single dashboard. Often, your management team is going to want to have a unified executive dashboard that combines elements such as your sales numbers, bank balances, customer satisfaction scores, and more into a single dashboard. The amazing thing about dashboards in Power BI is that data can be actionable and reacted to quickly. You can click on any dashboard element and be immediately taken to the report that makes up that number. You can also subscribe to the dashboard and create mobile alerts when certain numbers on the dashboard reach a milestone.

Creating your first dashboard

To create your first dashboard, start by opening a report that has some interesting data. On each of the charts, tiles, and other elements, you'll see a pin icon in the top right of that object. After you click on the pin, it will ask you what dashboard you wish to pin that report element to. You can, at that point, select a new dashboard to create or choose an existing dashboard to add the element to, as shown in the following screenshot. This is what makes Power BI so magical—you're able to append data from your accounting department next to data from your sales and customer service teams, giving your executives one place to look:

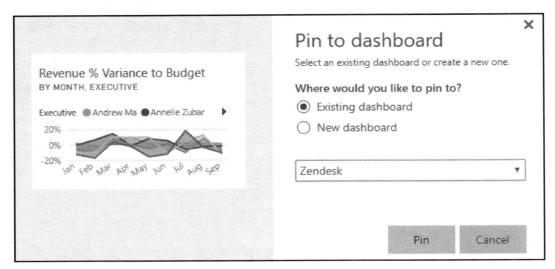

Once you pin the first item to the dashboard, you'll be prompted with a link to the dashboard. The newly created dashboard will allow you to resize elements and add additional tiles of information. You can click **Add Tile** in the upper-right corner to add additional interesting data, such as web content, images—such as logos—text data, and videos to the dashboard. Most people use this in the line-manager dashboard to insert a company logo and a small video talking about the initiative of the quarter that relates to the dashboard from the executive team.

You can also pin real-time data as a tile, as well as use custom streaming data. Once you click **Custom Streaming Dataset**, you have the option to add a new dataset from Azure Stream Analytics or PubNub, or a developer can use the API to push data directly in via the API. Azure Stream Analytics is the most common of these live data streams. In this mechanism, devices could stream data through Azure Event Hub, for example, and then get aggregated with Azure Stream Analytics. Imagine a smart power grid sending thousands of records a second to the cloud, and then Azure Stream Analytics aggregating this to a single record every five seconds, the status shown by a moving needle in a gauge or line graph in Power BI.

One of the key ways to view Power BI is from a phone either in web view or in the native Power BI client, which is downloadable from the App Store for Android or iPhone. There are going to be some dashboard elements that you'll want to exclude from a phone device because the surface area is too small. By the very nature of the device, most people sign into Power BI on their phone to get a quick look at the numbers. For those consumers, you can create a specialized phone view of the dashboard.

Simply click on the **Web View** drop-down box in the top right and select **Phone View**. The default phone view will contain every element from the web view. To remove items, hover over each report element and click the push pin to move it to the **Unpinned Tiles** section, as shown in the following screenshot. Once you're done, you can click the phone icon (or **Phone View** name, based on your resolution) and flip it back to the **Web View** again:

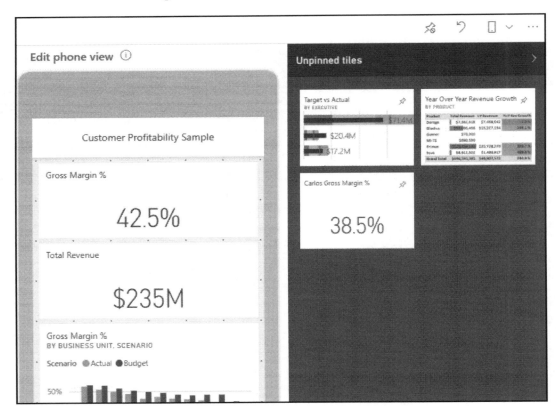

Asking your dashboard a question

Once the dashboard is complete, you're able to ask questions of your data. Right above the dashboards' data, you'll see the area where you can **Ask a question about your data**. For example, you can ask the question "Show me the total stores by state", and Power BI will typically produce a geography answer from that question. If you'd prefer to see your answer as a bar chart instead of a map, you can explicitly ask for it as a graph element—for example, "Show me the total stores by the state in a bar chart".

If you like the answer that comes back, you can click **Pin Visual** in the top-right corner to pin the report item to a dashboard. You can also expand the **Filters** and **Visualizations** on the right to be very precise with your report item. For example, you may only want to see stores with sales above a certain level. While Power BI is great at answering questions with filters, it sometimes needs fine tuning. If you're curious as to where Power BI pulled this data from, below your newly created report, you'll see the source of the data from which the report was derived.

A great way to encourage your users to utilize this feature is to seed Power BI with some sample questions. To do this, select the settings gear box on the upper-right corner of your screen. Once there, click the dataset that you wish to create sample questions for in the **Datasets** tab, as shown in the following screenshot. Expand the **Featured Q&A Questions** section, click **Add a Question,** and add several questions that might interest your user:

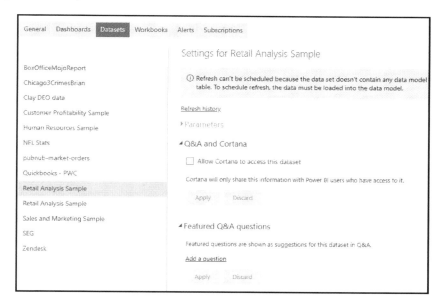

Creating featured questions will help your users to start to use the vocabulary of the report. For example, your sales team may be used to calling someone a "client", but your marketing team uses the term "customer". Featured questions will encourage all users to refer to customers as clients. If you want to have your cake and eat it too, you can create synonyms inside the Power BI desktop. You can do this in the modeling tab when looking at your relationships. You can also create more advanced linguistic models in the Power BI desktop by importing linguistic models. This can help with questions that you think users might ask, such as "Who is my best customer in New York?" or "Show me the worst employees by office." The linguistic model would translate what "best" and "worst" means to the company.

One of the amazing features you can do inside of Power BI is to ask questions through Cortana, Windows's voice-operated assistant. With Cortana integration enabled in the **Settings** tab, your users will be able to ask questions in Windows without logging into Power BI, and can get quick answers right from the **Start** menu. To do this, the user must have their company account (typically Office 365) associated with Windows by going to **Settings** | **Account** in Windows. You must also connect Office 365 to Cortana as a connected service.

Subscribing to reports and dashboards

To discourage users from printing reports and dashboards, you can have them subscribe to the reports and dashboards instead. This will email the report or dashboard when the data changes on the report, typically daily or weekly. Select **Subscribe** in the upper-right corner of the browser. Power BI will read the account you're signed in with and subscribe you using that email address. When subscribing to reports, you must select the report page that you wish to be emailed to you. With dashboards, the entire dashboard will be emailed.

You can also set up alerts from your mobile device to alert you when a critical number changes on a report. While looking at a dashboard, you can click the alert icon (it looks like a bell) to create an alert. This will monitor the data on the report, and upon that number hitting a certain threshold, it will send you a phone alert and, optionally, an additional email. Alerts are great mechanisms to let you know if a given critical number, such as a profit margin, has fallen.

Subscriptions and alerts can be managed in the Power BI settings area under the **Alerts** and **Subscriptions** tabs. You can turn off alerts and subscriptions here, as well as edit the subscriptions. By default, the frequency of subscriptions will be whenever the data is updated, but this happens typically no more than once per day (although this can be altered).

Sharing your dashboards

Sharing in Power BI is quite simple, but you'll want to consider what your goal is first. If your goal is simply to share a view-only version of a report or dashboard that users could engage with, the basic sharing mechanism can do that. If your goal is instead to allow users to also edit the report, you will want to use workspaces. Lastly, if you want to logically package reports and dashboards together, and have the ability to have fine-control over which reports can be seen by default, consider using Power BI apps.

The easiest way to share a dashboard or report is to simply click **Share** in the upper-right corner of any report or dashboard. Simply type the email address of the user that you want to share with and what type of access you want to give them. While you can't allow them to edit the report or dashboard, they will be able to view and reshare the report themselves. At any time, you can also see what assets are shared with you by clicking **Shared with Me** from the left menu. Then, you will see a list of users that have shared items with you. You can click on this list to filter the report lists that are shared with you.

Workspaces

Workspaces are areas where groups of users can collaborate with datasets, reports, and dashboards. You can create a workspace if you have a pro license of the Power BI service. This is the main way that your BI developers will be able to co-develop the same sets of data and reports. Typically, you'll create a workspace for each department in your company for the teams to store their items and data.

To create one, simply expand the **Workspaces** section in the left navigation menu and click **Create App Workspace**. Name the workspace that you wish to create and define whether members can edit the content or just view the content, as shown in the following screenshot. You can also define whether users will be able to see the content of what's inside the workspace without being a member. This doesn't mean they'll be able to see the reports, but they will be able to see the metadata. If you're running the Power BI premium edition, you can also assign the dedicated capacity to a given workspace.

This is handy for those executive reports that must always return their visuals in a few seconds:

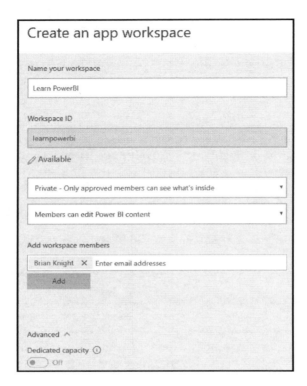

 At any time, you can change the permissions or add users by editing the workspace if you have permission to do so. To do this, select the ellipsis button next to the workspace name and click **Edit Workspace**.

Setting up row-level security

In most organizations, security is not just a report-level decision. Organizations want more granular decisions, such as whether a sales executive can only see his or her own data. Another example is the ability for a teacher to see his or her own students, but the school's principal can see all the teachers at their school and the school board members can see all of the data. This level of granularity is quite possible in Power BI, but will require some thought ahead of time on how to lay the data out.

To show an example of this, we'll need to go back to the Power BI Desktop and open `Chapter 5 - Visualizing Data Completed.pbix` from a previous chapter's example; this file can be downloaded from this book's web page at `http://packtpub.com`. The goal of this example is to ensure that United States sales managers can only see US sales, and likewise for Australian sales managers. We'll only use two countries in our example, but the same example can apply to the entire world, and can be expanded to be made more dynamic.

To create this type of automated filter based on your user's credentials, you'll need to use DAX language snippets. Open the Power BI Desktop and click **Manage Roles** from the **Modeling** ribbon in the report. Then, click **Create** to make a new role called **US**. Then, select **Sales Territory** as your table to filter on and click **Add Filter | [Sales Territory Country]**, as shown in the following screenshot. This will create a stub of code in the **Table Filter DAX Expression** box that shows **[Sales Territory Country] = Value**. Simply replace **Value** with **United States**, and your first role is created. Do the same for Australia to complete the example:

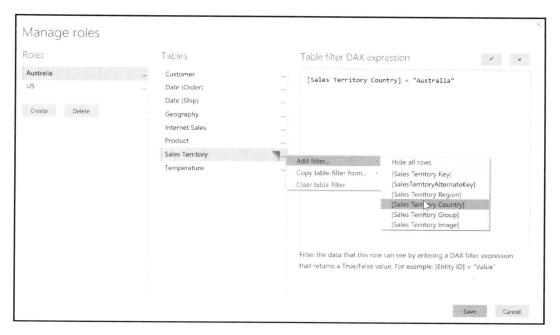

Now that we've created the two rules, let's test them out. The Power BI desktop will not automatically filter the data for you, since you have access to the underlying data anyway, but it can be used to test it. Click **View as Role** from the **Modeling** tab and select the role you wish to test. You'll notice after you click on Australia, for example, that every report element on each report page filters at that point to only show Australian data. Power BI Desktop also warns you that you're filtering the data and that you can click **Stop Viewing** to stop viewing as the role. Once you're ready to see what you've done on the Power BI service, publish to your Power BI account and open the report there.

Navigate to the dataset matching your report and select **Security**. You can then select each role and type the email address of each member of that role. Click **Add** and then **Save** to start using the role, as shown in the following screenshot. You can also add groups (such as your Australian Employee group) to this role if you have one created already in Office 365's directory. After clicking **Save**, members of that role will only see their own data in dashboards, reports, and any new reports that they build from the dataset:

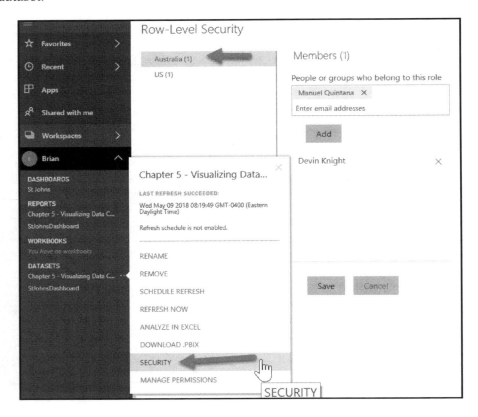

If your user has edit rights to the workspace or dataset, then these roles will not work since they already have the ability to see the underlying data. However, roles do work if the user is connecting to Power BI Desktop to see the data through Excel. Make sure the members of the workspace only have **View** rights selected if this feature is important to you. Additionally, when row-level security is turned on, Q&A will no longer work as of the publication of this book.

Scheduling data refreshes

Once you have a report that everyone depends on, you're not going to want to refresh it manually each day. The Power BI service has the ability to refresh your datasets up to every half an hour for the Power BI pro edition when you're not doing real-time analysis. If all of your data lives in the cloud, refreshing is very simple. However, if you have some data or files on premise, you must install the on-premises gateway.

Don't forget that if you want to see data in real time, you have the option to perform a direct query, where clicks run queries against your source system. Doing this will slow your reports down by large factors. You can also do real-time analysis of your data by using Azure services, such as Stream Analytics, where elements in your dashboards refresh every second.

The on-premises gateways can be used across multiple cloud services, such as Power BI, PowerApps, Logic Apps, and Microsoft Flow. You can download the free gateway from the top-right download icon on PowerBI.com once you're signed in. The first question that will be asked during the installation is whether you want to install the data gateway in personal mode or on-premises gateway mode.

The largest difference between the on-premises data gateway and the on-premises data gateway in personal mode is that personal mode runs as an application versus a Windows service. By installing in personal mode, you risk your data becoming stale if the application is not open when your PC starts. It is handy for those users who may not have admin access to their machine, or users who want easier data refreshes. It is recommended for ease of management and reliability that most users install the on-premises data gateway.

After installation, you'll need to provide your Power BI login credentials. Next, you'll need to name your gateway and provide a recovery key, as shown in the following screenshot. The recovery key is used to encrypt your connection strings and your configuration. Make sure that this key is kept in a safe place and is backed up. If you wish to make this gateway highly available, you can add the gateway into a cluster, allowing multiple machines to act as a single gateway to Power BI:

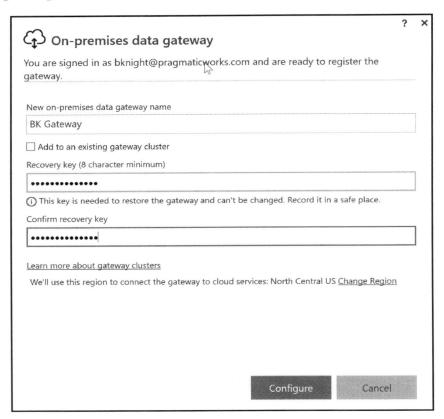

With the on-premises work now complete, you will need to complete the configuration on PowerBI.com. Click the settings gear box from the top-right corner and select **Manage Gateways**. At that point, you should see the gateways on the left. You can add more administrators (who have permission to configure data sources that can use this connection) in the **Administrators** tab.

Most importantly, you will want to test the gateway before proceeding.

Now, we need to create a connection with each of your files or databases that are used in your report that are on-premises. Click the **Add Data Source** button from the top-left corner. Give the data source a name that can enable you to easily identify it later. Typically, that name should match the filename or database name to help with debugging later. For Excel files or any other type of files used in your report, select **File** from the **Data Source Type** drop-down box. Then, type the full path for the filename or a network path (UNC path). Lastly, give the Windows credentials that are needed to access the file on the share or folder. Once you're finalized, click **Test all Connections** again to ensure you have a proper connection, as shown in the following screenshot:

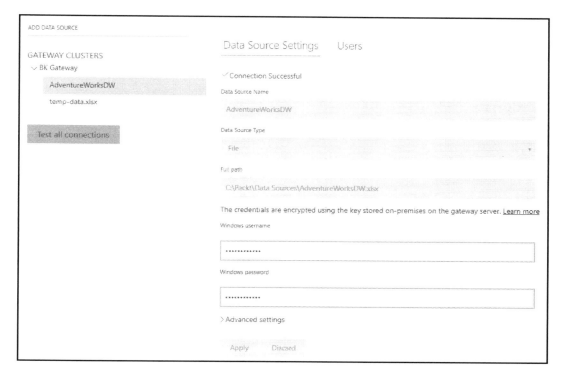

The **Users** tab also allows you to have a more refined control of who can access this data source. Once you've saved those settings, you're ready to schedule the refresh. If you wish to just refresh the data immediately, select the ellipsis button next to the dataset and select **Refresh Now**. To schedule a refresh, click **Schedule Refresh**. This will take you to the dataset configuration screen. Expand the **Gateway Connection** section, select **Use an On-Prem Data Gateway**, and click **Apply**. You should see your gateway name in this section, with a status reading **Online**. If you don't see **Online**, check whether there are any proxy settings or firewall issues preventing Power BI from seeing your machine.

Next, expand the **Scheduled Refresh** section in this **Datasets** tab and switch the setting **Keep Your Data Up to Date** to **On**. You can then schedule the refresh to occur as often as every half an hour. Once you test the refresh, you can see the **Refresh History** in this same tab to see whether the data was successfully refreshed. You can also get email notifications of when refreshing fails.

 If your data is already in Azure or OneDrive, then the on-premises gateway is not required. You just need to make sure the firewall will allow you to communicate with the Power BI service.

Summary

The Power BI service allows your users to see the same reports on a web or mobile platform with the same type of interactivity as they experience in Power BI Desktop. It also allows users to build reports quickly, straight from a web platform. Once your reports are deployed to the service, you can use row-level security to see data at a granular level, allowing a sales manager to only see their own territory. The data can also be refreshed every 30 minutes. If you're using on-premises data sources, then you can use the on-premises gateway to bring data from on-premise to the cloud.

Planning Power BI Projects 7

In this chapter, we will walk through a Power BI project planning process from the perspective of an organization with an on-premises data warehouse and a supporting nightly **extract-transform-load** (**ETL**) process but no existing SSAS servers or IT-approved Power BI datasets. The business intelligence team will be responsible for the development of a Power BI dataset, including source queries, relationships, and metrics, in addition to a set of Power BI reports and dashboards.

Almost all business users will consume the reports and dashboards in the Power BI online service and via the Power BI mobile apps, but a few business analysts will also require the ability to author Power BI and Excel reports for their teams based on the new dataset. Power BI Pro licenses and Power BI Premium capacity will be used to support the development, scalability, and distribution requirements of the project.

In this chapter, we will review the following topics:

- Power BI deployment modes
- Project discovery and ingestion
- Power BI project roles
- Power BI licenses
- Dataset design process
- Dataset planning
- Import and DirectQuery datasets

Power BI deployment modes

Organizations can choose to deliver and manage their Power BI deployment through IT and standard project workflows or to empower certain business users to take advantage of Self-Service BI capabilities with tools such as Power BI Desktop and Excel. In many scenarios, a combination of IT resources, such as the On-premises data gateway and Power BI Premium capacity, can be combined with the business users' knowledge of requirements and familiarity with data analysis and visualization.

Organizations may also utilize alternative deployment modes per project or with different business teams based on available resources and the needs of the project. The greatest value from Power BI deployments can be obtained when the technical expertise and governance of Corporate BI solutions are combined with the data exploration and analysis features, which can be made available to all users. The scalability and accessibility of Power BI solutions to support thousands of users, including read-only users who have not been assigned Power BI Pro licenses, is made possible by provisioning Power BI Premium capacity, as described in the final three chapters of this book.

Corporate BI

The Corporate BI delivery approach in which the BI team develops and maintains both the Power BI dataset (data model) and the required report visualizations is a common deployment option, particularly for large-scale projects and projects with executive-level sponsors or stakeholders. This is the approach followed in this chapter and throughout this book, as it offers maximum control over top BI objectives, such as version control, scalability, usability, and performance.

However, as per the following Power BI deployment modes diagram, there are other approaches in which business teams own or contribute to the solution:

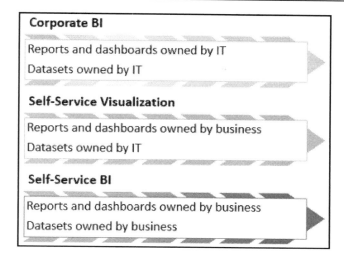

Power BI deployment modes

A Power BI dataset is a semantic data model composed of data source queries, relationships between dimensions and fact tables, and measurement calculations. The Power BI Desktop application can be used to create datasets as well as merely connect to existing datasets to author Power BI reports. The Power BI Desktop shares the same data retrieval and modeling engines as the latest version of **SQL Server Analysis Services (SSAS)** in tabular mode and Azure Analysis Services, Microsoft's enterprise BI modeling solution. Many BI/IT organizations utilize Analysis Services models as the primary data source for Power BI projects and it's possible to migrate Power BI Desktop files (.pbix) to Analysis Services models, as described in Chapter 19, *Scaling with Premium and Analysis Services*.

Self-service approaches can benefit both IT and business teams, as they can reduce IT resources, project timelines, and provide the business with a greater level of flexibility as their analytical needs change. Additionally, Power BI projects can be migrated across deployment modes over time as required skills and resources change. However, greater levels of self-service and shared ownership structures can also increase the risk of miscommunication and introduce issues of version control, quality, and consistency.

Self-Service Visualization

In the Self-Service Visualization approach, the dataset is created and maintained by the IT organization's BI team, but certain business users with Power BI Pro licenses create reports and dashboards for consumption by other users. In many scenarios, business analysts are already comfortable with authoring reports in Power BI Desktop (or, optionally, Excel) and can leverage their business knowledge to rapidly develop useful visualizations and insights. Given ownership of the dataset, the BI team can be confident that only curated data sources and standard metric definitions are used in reports and can ensure that the dataset remains available, performant, and updated, or refreshed as per business requirements.

Self-Service BI

In the Self-Service BI approach, the BI organization only contributes essential infrastructure and monitoring, such as the use of an On-premises data gateway and possibly Power Premium capacity to support the solution. Since the business team maintains control of both the dataset and the visualization layer, the business team has maximum flexibility to tailor its own solutions including data source retrieval, transformation, and modeling. This flexibility, however, can be negated by a lack of technical skills (for example, DAX measures) and a lack of technical knowledge such as the relationships between tables in a database. Additionally, business-controlled datasets can introduce version conflicts with corporate semantic models and generally lack the resilience, performance, and scalability of IT-owned datasets.

 It's usually necessary or at least beneficial for BI organizations to own the Power BI datasets or at least the datasets which support important, widely distributed reports and dashboards. This is primarily due to the required knowledge of dimensional modeling best practices and the necessary technical skills in the M and DAX functional languages to develop sustainable datasets. Additionally, BI organizations require control of datasets to implement **row-level security (RLS)** and to maintain version control. Therefore, small datasets initially created by business teams are often migrated to the BI team and either integrated into larger models or rationalized given the equivalent functionality from an existing dataset.

Choosing a deployment mode

Larger organizations with experience of deploying and managing Power BI often utilize a mix of deployment modes depending on the needs of the project and available resources. For example, a Corporate BI solution with a set of standard IT developed reports and dashboards distributed via a Power BI app may be extended by assigning Power BI Pro licenses to certain business users who have experience or training in Power BI report design. These users could then leverage the existing data model and business definitions maintained by IT to create new reports and dashboards and distribute this content in a separate Power BI app to distinguish ownership.

An app workspace is simply a container of datasets, reports, and dashboards in the Power BI cloud service that can be distributed to large groups of users. A Power BI app represents the published version of an app workspace in the Power BI service and workspace. Members can choose which items in the workspace are included in the published Power BI app. See Chapter 14, *Managing Application Workspaces and Content,* and Chapter 17, *Creating Power BI Apps and Content Distribution,* for greater detail on app workspaces and apps, respectively.

Another common scenario is a **proof-of-concept (POC)** or small-scale self-service solution developed by a business user or a team to be transitioned to a formal, IT-owned, and managed solution. Power BI Desktop's rich graphical interfaces at each layer of the application (query editor, data model, and report canvas) make it possible and often easy for users to create useful models and reports with minimal experience and little to no code. It's much more difficult, of course, to deliver consistent insights across business functions (that is, finance, sales, and marketing) and at scale in a secure, governed environment. The IT organization can enhance the quality and analytical value of these assets as well as provide robust governance and administrative controls to ensure that the right data is being accessed by the right people.

The following list of fundamental questions will help guide a deployment mode decision:

1. Who will own the data model?
    - Experienced dataset designers and other IT professionals are usually required to support complex data transformations, analytical data modeling, large data sizes, and security rules, such as RLS roles, as described in `Chapter 10`, *Developing DAX Measures and Security Roles*
    - If the required data model is relatively small and simple, or if the requirements are unclear, the business team may be best positioned to create at least the initial iterations of the model
    - The data model could be created with Analysis Services or Power BI Desktop

2. Who will own the reports and dashboards?
    - Experienced Power BI report developers with an understanding of corporate standards and data visualization best practices can deliver a consistent user experience
    - Business users can be trained in report design and development practices and are well-positioned to manage the visualization layer, given their knowledge of business needs and questions

3. How will the Power BI content be managed and distributed?
    - A staged deployment across development, test, and production environments, as described in `Chapter 14`, *Managing Application Workspaces and Content*, helps to ensure that quality, validated content is published. This approach is generally exclusive to Corporate BI projects.
    - Sufficient Power BI Premium capacity is required to support distribution to Power BI Free users and either large datasets or demanding query workloads.
    - Self-Service BI content can be assigned to Premium Capacity, but organizations may wish to limit the scale or scope of these projects to ensure that provisioned capacity is being used efficiently.

Project discovery and ingestion

A set of standard questions within a project template form can be used to initiate Power BI projects. Business guidance on these questions informs the BI team of the high-level technical needs of the project and helps to promote a productive project kickoff.

By reviewing the project template, the BI team can ask the project sponsor or relevant **subject matter experts (SMEs)** targeted questions to better understand the current state and the goals of the project.

Sample Power BI project template

The primary focus of the project-planning template and the overall project planning stage is on the data sources and the scale and structure of the Power BI dataset required. The project sponsor or business users may only have an idea of several reports, dashboards, or metrics needed but, as a Corporate BI project, it's essential to focus on where the project fits within an overall BI architecture and the long-term **return on investment (ROI)** of the solution. For example, BI teams would look to leverage any existing Power BI datasets or SSAS tabular models applicable to the project and would be sensitive to version-control issues.

Sample template – Adventure Works BI

The template is comprised of two tables. The first table answers the essential *who* and *when* questions so that the project can be added to the BI team's backlog. The BI team can use this information to plan their engagements across multiple ongoing and requested Power BI projects and to respond to project stakeholders, such as Vickie Jacobs, VP of Group Sales, in this example:

Date of Submission	10/15/2017
Project Sponsor	Vickie Jacobs, VP of Group Sales
Primary Stakeholders	Adventure Works Sales Adventure Works Corp
Power BI Author(s)	Mark Langford, Sales Analytics Manager

The following table is a list of questions that describe the project's requirements and scope. For example, the number of users that will be read-only consumers of Power BI reports and dashboards, and the number of self-service users that will need Power BI Pro licenses to create Power BI content will largely impact the total cost of the project.

Likewise, the amount of historical data to include in the dataset (2 years, 5 years?) can significantly impact performance scalability:

Topic	#	Question	Business Input
Data sources	1	Can you describe the required data? (For example, sales, inventory, shipping).	`Internet Sales`, `Reseller Sales`, and the `Sales and Margin Plan`. We need to analyze total corporate sales, online, and reseller sales, and compare these results to our plan.
Data sources	2	Is all of the data required for your project available in the data warehouse (SQL Server)?	No
Data Sources	3	What other data sources (if any) contain all or part of the required data (for example, Web, Oracle, Excel)?	The `Sales and Margin Plan` is maintained in Excel.
Security	4	Should certain users be prevented from viewing some or all of the data?	Yes, sales managers and associates should only see data for their sales territory group. VPs of sales, however, should have global access.
Security	5	Does the data contain any PCII or sensitive data?	No, not that I'm aware of
Scale	6	Approximately, how many years of historical data are needed?	3-4
Data refresh	7	How often does the data need to be refreshed?	Daily
Data refresh	8	Is there a need to view data in real time (as it changes)?	No
Distribution	9	Approximately, how many users will need to view reports and dashboards?	200
Distribution	10	Approximately, how many users will need to create reports and dashboards?	3-4

| Version control 11 | Are there existing reports on the same data? If so, please describe. | Yes, there are daily and weekly sales snapshot reports available on the portal. Additionally, our team builds reports in Excel that compare actuals to plan. |
| Version Control 12 | Is the Power BI solution expected to replace these existing reports? | Yes, we would like to exclusively use Power BI going forward. |

A business analyst inside the IT organization can partner with the business on completing the project ingestion template and review the current state to give greater context to the template. Prior to the project kickoff meeting, the business analyst can meet with the BI team members to review the template and any additional findings or considerations.

Many questions with greater levels of detail will be raised as the project moves forward and therefore the template shouldn't attempt to be comprehensive or overwhelm business teams. The specific questions to include should use business-friendly language and serve to call out the top drivers of project resources and Corporate BI priorities, such as security and version control.

Power BI project roles

Following the review of the project template and input from the business analyst, members of the Power BI team can directly engage the project sponsor and other key stakeholders to officially engage in the project. These stakeholders include subject matter experts on the data source systems, business team members knowledgeable of the current state of reporting and analytics, and administrative or governance personnel with knowledge of organizational policies, available licenses, and current usage.

New Power BI projects of any significant scale and long-term adoption of Power BI within organizations require **Dataset Designers**, **Report Authors**, and a **Power BI Admin(s)**, as illustrated in the following diagram:

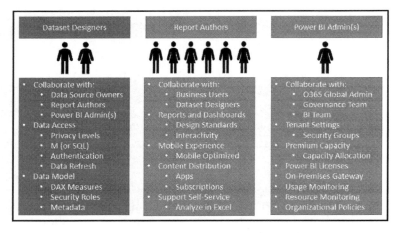

Power BI team roles

Each of the three Power BI project roles and perhaps longer-term roles as part of a business intelligence team entail a distinct set of skills and responsibilities. It can be advantageous in a short-term or POC scenario for a single user to serve as both a dataset designer and a report author. However, the Power BI platform and the multi-faceted nature of Corporate BI deployments is too broad and dynamic for a single BI professional to adequately fulfill both roles. It's therefore recommended that team members either self-select or are assigned distinct roles based on their existing skills and experience and that each member develops advanced and current knowledge relevant to their role. A BI manager and/or a project manager can help facilitate effective communication across roles and between the BI team and other stakeholders, such as project sponsors.

Dataset designer

Power BI report visualizations and dashboard tiles are built on top of datasets, and each Power BI report is associated with a single dataset. Power BI datasets can import data from multiple data sources on a refresh schedule or can be configured to issue queries directly to a single data source to resolve report queries. Datasets are therefore a critical component of Power BI projects and their design has tremendous implications regarding user experience, query performance, source system and Power BI resource utilization, and more.

The dataset designer is responsible for the data access layer of the Power BI dataset, including the authentication to data sources and the M queries used to define the tables of the data model. Additionally, the dataset designer defines the relationships of the model and any required row-level security roles, and develops the DAX measure expressions for use in reports, such as **year-to-date (YTD)** sales. Given these responsibilities, the dataset designer should regularly communicate with data source owners or SMEs, as well as report authors. For example, the dataset designer needs to be aware of changes to data sources so that data access queries can be revised accordingly and report authors can advise of any additional measures or columns necessary to create new reports. Furthermore, the dataset designer should be aware of the performance and resource utilization of deployed datasets and should work with the Power BI admin on issues such as Power BI Premium capacity.

As per the *Power BI team toles* diagram, there are usually very few dataset designers in a team while there may be many report authors. This is largely due to the organizational objectives of version control and reusability, which leads to a small number of large datasets. Additionally, robust dataset development requires knowledge of the M and DAX functional programming languages, dimensional modeling practices, and business intelligence. Database experience is also very helpful. If multiple dataset designers are on a team they should look to standardize their development practices so that they can more easily learn and support each other's solutions.

 A Power BI dataset designer often has experience in developing SSAS models, particularly SSAS tabular models. For organizations utilizing both SSAS and Power BI Desktop, this could be the same individual. Alternatively, users with experience of building models in Power Pivot for Excel may also prove to be capable Power BI dataset designers.

Report authors

Report authors interface directly with the consumers of reports and dashboards or a representative of this group. In a self-service deployment mode or a hybrid project (business and IT), a small number of report authors may themselves work within the business. Above all else, report authors must have a clear understanding of the business questions to be answered and the measures and attributes (columns) needed to visually analyze and answer these questions. The report author should also be knowledgeable of visualization best practices, such as symmetry and minimalism, in addition to any corporate standards for report formatting and layout.

Power BI Desktop provides a rich set of formatting properties and analytical features, giving report authors granular control over the appearance and behavior of visualizations.

Report authors should be very familiar with all standard capabilities, such as conditional formatting, drilldown, drillthrough, and cross-highlighting, as they often lead demonstrations or training sessions. Additionally, report authors should understand the organization's policies on custom visuals available in the MS Office store and the specific use cases for top or popular custom visuals.

Power BI admin

A Power BI admin is focused on the overall deployment of Power BI within an organization in terms of security, governance, and resource utilization. Power BI admins are not involved in the day-to-day activities of specific projects but rather configure and manage settings in Power BI that align with the organization's policies. A Power BI admin, for example, monitors the adoption of Power BI content, identifies any high-risk user activities, and manages any Power BI Premium capacities that have been provisioned. Additionally, Power BI admins use Azure Active Directory security groups within the Power BI admin portal to manage access to various Power BI features, such as sharing Power BI content with external organizations.

Users assigned to the **Power BI service administrator** role obtain access to the Power BI admin portal and the rights to configure Power BI **Tenant settings**. For example, in the following image, **Anna Sanders** is assigned to the Power BI service administrator role within the Office 365 admin center:

Assigning Power BI service admin role

The **Power BI service administrator role** allows Anna to access the Power BI admin portal to enable or disable features, such as exporting data and printing reports and dashboard. BI and IT managers that oversee Power BI deployments are often assigned to this role, as it also provides the ability to manage Power BI Premium capacities and access to standard monitoring and usage reporting. Note that only global administrators of Office 365 can assign users to the Power BI service administrator role.

The Power BI admin should have a clear understanding of the organizational policy on the various tenant settings, such as whether content can be shared with external users. For most tenant settings, the Power BI service administrator can define rules in the Power BI admin portal to include or exclude specific security groups. For example, external sharing can be disabled for the entire organization except for a specific security group of users. Most organizations should assign two or more users to the Power BI service administrator role and ensure these users are trained on the administration features specific to this role. Chapter 18, *Administering Power BI for an Organization*, contains details on the Power BI admin portal and other administrative topics.

Project role collaboration

Communicating and documenting project role assignments during the planning stage promotes the efficient use of time during the development and operations phases. For organizations committed to the Power BI platform as a component of a longer-term data strategy, the project roles may become full-time positions.

For example, BI developers with experience in DAX and/or SSAS tabular databases may be hired as dataset designers while BI developers with experience in data visualization tools and corporate report development may be hired as report authors:

Name	Project role
Brett Powell	Dataset Designer
Jennifer Lawrence	Report Author
Anna Sanders	Power BI Service Admin
Mark Langford	Report Author
Stacy Loeb	QA Tester

Power BI licenses

Users can be assigned either a Power BI Free or a Power BI Pro license. Power BI licenses (Pro and Free) can be purchased individually in the Office 365 admin center, and a Power Pro license is included with an Office 365 Enterprise E5 subscription. A Power BI Pro license is required to publish content to Power BI app workspaces, consume a Power BI app that's not assigned to Power BI Premium capacity, and utilize other advanced features, as shown in the following table:

Feature	Power BI Free	Power BI Pro
Connect to 70+ data sources	Yes	Yes
Publish to web	Yes	Yes
Peer-to-peer sharing	No	Yes
Export to Excel, CSV, PowerPoint	Yes	Yes
Email subscriptions	No	Yes
App workspaces and apps	No	Yes
Analyze in Excel, Analyze in Power BI Desktop	No	Yes

With Power BI Premium, users with Power BI Free licenses are able to access and view Power BI apps of reports and dashboards that have been assigned to premium capacities. This access includes consuming the content via the Power BI mobile application. Additionally, Power BI Pro users can share dashboards with Power BI Free users if the dashboard is contained in a Premium workspace. Power BI Pro licenses are required for users that create or distribute Power BI content, such as connecting to published datasets from Power BI Desktop or Excel.

In this sample project example, only three or four business users may need Power BI Pro licenses to create and share reports and dashboards. Mark Langford, a data analyst for the sales organization, requires a Pro license to analyze published datasets from Microsoft Excel. Jennifer Lawrence, a Corporate BI developer and report author for this project, requires a Pro license to publish Power BI reports to app workspaces and distribute Power BI apps to users.

The following image from the Office 365 admin center identifies the assignment of a Power BI Pro license to a report author:

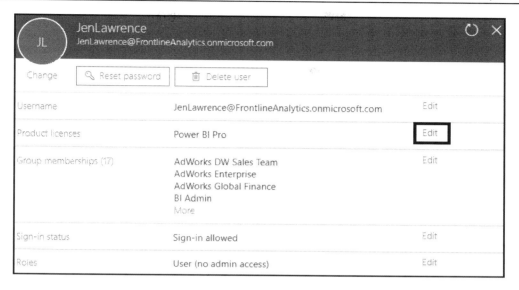

Power BI Pro license assignment

As a report author, Jennifer doesn't require any custom role assignment as per the **Roles** property of the preceding image. If Jennifer becomes responsible for administering Power BI in the future, the `Edit` option for the Roles property can be used to assign her to the Power BI service administrator role, as described in the *Power BI project roles* section earlier.

The approximately 200 Adventure Works sales team users who only need to view the content can be assigned Free licenses and consume the published content via Power BI apps associated with Power BI Premium capacity. Organizations can obtain more Power BI Pro licenses and Power BI Premium capacity (virtual cores, RAM) as usage and workloads increase.

> Typically, a Power BI service administrator is also assigned a Power BI Pro license, but a Power BI Pro license is not required to be assigned to the Power BI service administrator role.

The administration and governance of Power BI deployments at scale involve several topics (such as authentication, activity monitoring, and auditing), and Power BI provides features dedicated to simplifying administration.

These topics and features are reviewed in `Chapter 18`, *Administering Power BI for an Organization.*

Given the broad controls associated with the Power BI service administrator role, such as managing Power BI Premium capacities and setting policies for the sharing of external content, some organizations may choose to limit this access to defined time periods. **Azure Active Directory Privileged Identity Management (PIM)** can be used to provide short-term, audited access to this role. For example, a decision could be made to allow one security group of users to export data from Power BI. A user, such as a BI manager, could be granted Power BI service administrator rights for one day to implement this policy in the Power BI admin portal.

Power BI license scenarios

The optimal mix of Power BI Pro and Power BI Premium licensing in terms of total cost will vary based on the volume of users and the composition of these users between read-only consumers of content versus Self-Service BI users. In relatively small deployments, such as 200 total users, a Power BI Pro license can be assigned to each user regardless of self-service usage and Power BI Premium capacity can be avoided. Be advised, however, that, as per the following *Power BI Premium features* section, there are other benefits to licensing Power BI Premium capacity that may be necessary for certain deployments, such as larger datasets or more frequent data refreshes.

If an organization consists of 700 total users with 600 read-only users and 100 self-service users (content creators), it's more cost effective to assign Power BI Pro licenses to the 100 self-service users and to provision Power BI Premium capacity to support the other 600 users. Likewise, for a larger organization with 5,000 total users and 4,000 self-service users, the most cost-effective licensing option is to assign Power Pro licenses to the 4,000 self-service users and to license Power BI Premium for the remaining 1,000 users.

Several factors drive the amount of Power BI Premium capacity to provision, such as the number of concurrent users, the complexity of the queries generated, and the number of concurrent data refreshes. The Power BI Premium calculator provides an initial estimate of the mix of Power BI Pro and Power BI Premium capacity needed for a given workload and can be found at `https://powerbi.microsoft.com/en-us/calculator/`.

See `Chapter 18`, *Administering Power BI for an Organization,* and `Chapter 19`, *Scaling with Premium and Analysis Services,* for additional details on aligning Power BI licenses and resources with the needs of Power BI deployments.

Power BI Premium features

An organization may choose to license Power BI Premium capacities for additional or separate reasons beyond the ability to distribute Power BI content to read-only users without incurring per-user license costs. Significantly, greater detail on Power BI Premium features and deployment considerations is included in `Chapter 19`, *Scaling with Premium and Analysis Services.*

The following table identifies several of the top additional benefits and capabilities of Power BI Premium:

Feature	Detail
Large Datasets	• Without Power BI Premium, a dataset is limited to 1 GB. • Per the Power BI Premium roadmap, Power BI Premium will support datasets up to the size of the given capacities such as 100 GB (compressed) and beyond.
No User Quotas	• Without Power BI Premium, an individual user is limited to 10 GB of storage. • Power BI Premium provides 100 TB of storage for each capacity.
Frequent Dataset Refreshes	• Without Power BI Premium, an import dataset can only be refreshed 8 times per day. • Power BI Premium supports 48 refreshes per day.
Isolation	• Without Power BI Premium, the activities of another organization could impact performance or responsiveness of the Power BI Service (aka 'Noisy Neighbour'). • With Power BI Premium, dedicated hardware helps to ensure a consistent, stable experience.
Power BI Report Server	• The v-cores licensed via Power BI Premium can also be used to deploy the Power BI Report Server on-premises. • Power BI Premium v-cores do not have to be split between the on-premises deployment and the Power BI Service.
Power BI Embedding	• Power BI Premium capacity can be used to embed Power BI content into corporate applications.

Additional Power BI Premium capabilities

Beyond the six features listed in the preceding table, the roadmap included in the Power BI Premium white paper has advised of future capabilities including read-only replicas, pin to memory, and geographic distribution. See the Power BI Premium white paper (http://bit.ly/2wBGPRJ) and related documentation for the latest updates.

Data warehouse bus matrix

The fundamentals of the dataset should be designed so that it can support future BI and analytics projects and other business teams requiring access to the same data. The dataset will be tasked with delivering both accurate and consistent results across teams and use cases as well as providing a familiar and intuitive interface for analysis.

To promote reusability and project communication, a data warehouse bus matrix of business processes and shared dimensions is recommended:

					SHARED DIMENSIONS					
BUSINESS PROCESSES	Account	Customer	Data	Department	Employee	Organization	Products	Promotion	Reseller	Sales Territory
Customer Service Calls		✓	✓		✓		✓			
Customer Surveys		✓	✓				✓			
General Ledger	✓		✓	✓		✓				
Internet Sales		✓	✓				✓	✓		✓
Intventory			✓				✓			
Reseller Sales			✓		✓		✓	✓	✓	✓
Sales Plan			✓				✓			✓

Data warehouse bus matrix

Each row reflects an important and recurring business process, such as the monthly close of the general ledger, and each column represents a business entity, which may relate to one or several of the business processes. The shaded rows (Internet Sales, Reseller Sales, and Sales Plan) identify the business processes that will be implemented as their own star schemas for this project. The business matrix can be developed in collaboration with business stakeholders, such as the corporate finance manager, as well as source system and business intelligence or data warehouse SMEs.

The data warehouse bus matrix is a staple of the Ralph Kimball data warehouse architecture, which provides an incremental and integrated approach to data warehouse design. This architecture, as per *The Data Warehouse Toolkit (Third Edition)* by Ralph Kimball, allows for scalable data models, as multiple business teams or functions often require access to the same business process data and dimensions.

Additional business processes, such as maintaining product inventory levels, could potentially be added to the same Power BI dataset in a future project. Importantly, these future additions could leverage existing dimension tables, such as a **Product** table, including its source query, column metadata, and any defined hierarchies.

 Each Power BI report is tied to a single dataset. Given this 1:1 relationship and the analytical value of integrated reports across multiple business processes, such as `Inventory` and `Internet Sales`, it's important to design datasets that can scale to support multiple star schemas. Consolidating business processes into one or a few datasets also makes solutions more manageable and a better use of source system resources, as common tables (for example, `Product`, `Customer`) are only refreshed once.

Dataset design process

With the data warehouse bus matrix as a guide, the business intelligence team can work with representatives from the relevant business teams and project sponsors to complete the following four-step dataset design process:

1. Select the business process.
2. Declare the grain.
3. Identify the dimensions.
4. Define the facts.

Selecting the business process

Ultimately each business process will be represented by a fact table with a star schema of many-to-one relationships to dimensions. In a discovery or requirements gathering process it can be difficult to focus on a single business process in isolation as users regularly analyze multiple business processes simultaneously or need to. Nonetheless, it's essential that the dataset being designed reflects low level business activities (for example, receiving an online sales order) rather than a consolidation or integration of distinct business processes such as a table with both online and reseller sales data:

- Confirm that the answer provided to the first question of the project template regarding data sources is accurate:
    - In this project, the required business processes are `Internet Sales`, `Reseller Sales`, `Annual Sales and Margin Plan`
    - Each of the three business processes corresponds to a fact table to be included in the Power BI dataset
- Obtain a high-level understanding of the top business questions each business process will answer:
    - For example, "What are total sales relative to the `Annual Sales Plan` and relative to last year?"
    - In this project, `Internet Sales` and `Reseller Sales` will be combined into overall corporate sales and margin KPIs
- Optionally, reference the data warehouse bus matrix of business processes and their related dimensions:
    - For example, discuss the integration of inventory data and the insights this integration may provide
    - In many projects, a choice or compromise has to be made given the limited availability of certain business processes and the costs or timelines associated with preparing this data for production use:
        - Additionally, business processes (fact tables) are the top drivers of the storage and processing costs of the dataset and thus should only be included if necessary.

A common anti-pattern to avoid in Power BI projects is the development of datasets for specific projects or teams rather than business processes. For example, one dataset would be developed exclusively for the marketing team and another dataset would be created for the sales organization. Assuming both teams require access to the same sales data, this approach naturally leads to a waste of resources, as the same sales data would be queried and refreshed twice and both datasets would consume storage resources in the Power BI service. Additionally, this isolated approach leads to manageability and version control issues, as the datasets may contain variations in transformation or metric logic. Therefore, although the analytical needs of specific business users or teams are indeed the priority of BI projects, it's important to plan for sustainable solutions that can ultimately be shared across teams.

Declaring the grain

All rows of a fact table should represent the individual business process from step *1* at a certain level of detail or grain such as the header level or line level of a purchase order. Therefore, each row should have the same meaning and thus contain values for the same key columns to dimensions and the same numeric columns.

The grain of fact tables ultimately governs the level of detail available for analytical queries as well as the amount of data to be accessed:

- Determine what each row of the different business processes will represent:
    - For example, each row of the `Internet Sales` fact table represents the line of a sales order from a customer
    - The rows of the `Sales and Margin Plan`, however, are aggregated to the level of a `Calendar Month`, `Products Subcategory`, and `Sales Territory Region`

If it's necessary to apply filters or logic to treat certain rows of a fact table differently than others, the fact table likely contains multiple business processes (for example, shipments and orders) that should be split into separate tables. Although it's technically possible to build this logic into DAX measure expressions, well-designed fact tables benefit Power BI and other data projects and tools over the long term. The same metrics and visualizations can be developed via separate fact tables with their own relationships rather than consolidated fact tables.

- Review and discuss the implications of the chosen grain in terms of dimensionality and scale:

    - Higher granularities provide greater levels of dimensionality and thus detail but result in much larger fact tables

    - If a high grain or the maximum grain is chosen, determine the row counts per year and the storage size of this table once loaded into Power BI datasets

    - If a lower grain is chosen, ensure that project stakeholders understand the loss of dimensionalities, such as the inability to filter for specific products or customers

In general, a higher granularity is recommended for analytical power and sustainability. If a less granular design is chosen, such as the header level of a sales order, and this grain later proves to be insufficient to answer new business questions, then either a new fact table would have to be added to the dataset or the existing fact table and all of its measures and dependent reports would have to be replaced.

Identifying the dimensions

The dimensions to be related to the fact table are a natural byproduct of the grain chosen in step 2 and thus largely impact the decision in step 2. A single sample row from the fact table should clearly indicate the business entities (dimensions) associated with the given process such as the customer who purchased an individual product on a certain date and at a certain time via a specific promotion. Fact tables representing a lower grain will have fewer dimensions.

For example, a fact table representing the header level of a purchase order may identify the vendor but not the individual products purchased from the vendor:

- Identify and communicate the dimensions that can be used to filter (aka *slice and dice*) each business process:
    - The foreign key columns based on the grain chosen in the previous step reference dimension tables.
    - Review a sample of all critical dimension tables, such as **Product** or **Customer**, and ensure these tables contain the columns and values necessary or expected.
- Communicate which dimensions can be used to filter multiple business processes simultaneously:
    - In this project, the **Product, Sales Territory**, and **Date** dimensions can be used to filter all three fact tables.
    - The data warehouse bus matrix referenced earlier can be helpful for this step
- Look for any gap between the existing dimension tables and business questions or related reports:
    - For example, existing IT-supported reports may contain embedded logic that creates columns via SQL which are not stored in the data warehouse
- Strive to maintain version control for dimension tables and the columns (attributes) within dimension tables:
    - It may be necessary for project stakeholders to adapt or migrate from legacy reports or an internally maintained source to the Corporate BI source

A significant challenge to the identity of the dimensions step can be a lack of **Master Data Management (MDM)** and alternative versions. For example, the sales organization may maintain their own dimension tables in Excel or Microsoft Access and their naming conventions and hierarchy structures may represent a conflict or gap with the existing data warehouse. Additionally, many corporate applications may store their own versions of common dimensions, such as products and customers. These issues should be understood and, despite pressure to deliver BI value quickly or according to a specific business team's preferred version, the long-term value of a single definition for an entire organization as expressed via the bus matrix should not be sacrificed.

Defining the facts

The facts represent the numeric columns to be included in the fact table. While the dimension columns from step 3 will be used for relationships to dimension tables, the fact columns will be used in measures containing aggregation logic such as the sum of a quantity column and the average of a price column:

- Define the business logic for each fact that will be represented by measures in the dataset:
    - For example, gross sales are equal to the extended amount on a sales order, and net sales are equal to gross sales minus discounts
- Any existing documentation or relevant technical metadata should be reviewed and validated
- Similar to the dimensions, any conflicts between existing definitions should be addressed so that a single definition for a core set of metrics is understood and approved
- Additionally, a baseline or target source should be identified to validate the accuracy of the metrics to be created.
    - For example, several months following the project, it should be possible to compare the results of DAX measures from the Power BI dataset to an SSRS report or a SQL query
    - If no variance exists between the two sources, the DAX measures are valid and thus any doubt or reported discrepancy is due to some other factor

 See Chapter 8, *Connecting to Sources and Transforming Data with M*, Chapter 9, *Designing Import and DirectQuery Data Models*, and Chapter 10, *Developing DAX Measures and Security Roles*, for details on the fact table columns to include in Power BI datasets (for import or DirectQuery) and the development of DAX metric expressions. The fact definitions from this step relate closely to the concept of base measures described in Chapter 10, *Developing DAX Measures and Security Roles*. Ultimately, the DAX measures implemented have to tie to the approved definitions, but there are significant data processing, storage and performance implications based on how this logic is computed. In many cases, the Power BI dataset can provide the same logic as an existing system but via an alternative methodology that better aligns with Power BI or the specific project need.

Data profiling

The four-step dataset design process can be immediately followed by a technical analysis of the source data for the required fact and dimension tables of the dataset. Technical metadata, including database diagrams and data profiling results, such as the existence of null values in source columns, are essential for the project planning stage. This information is used to ensure the Power BI dataset reflects the intended business definitions and is built on a sound and trusted source.

For example, the following SQL Server database diagram describes the schema for the reseller sales business process:

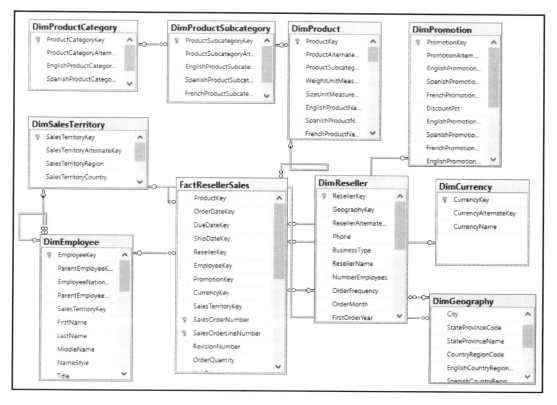

SQL Server Database diagram: reseller sales

The foreign key constraints identify the surrogate key columns to be used in the relationships of the Power BI dataset and the referential integrity of the source database. In this schema, the product dimension is modeled as three separate dimension tables—`DimProduct`, `DimProductSubcategory`, and `DimProductCategory`. Given the priorities of usability, manageability, and query performance, a single denormalized product dimension table that includes essential `Product Subcategory` and `Product Category` columns is generally recommended. This will reduce the volume of source queries, relationships, and tables in the data model and will improve report query performance, as fewer relationships will need to be scanned by the dataset engine.

Clear visibility to the source system, including referential and data integrity constraints, data quality, and any MDM processes, is essential. Unlike other popular BI tools, Power BI is capable of addressing many data integration and quality issues, particularly with relational database sources which Power BI can leverage to execute data transformation operations. However, Power BI's ETL capabilities are not a substitute for data warehouse architecture and enterprise ETL tools, such as **SQL Server Integration Services (SSIS)**. For example, it's the responsibility of the data warehouse to support historical tracking with slowly changing dimension ETL processes that generate new rows and surrogate keys for a dimension when certain columns change. To illustrate a standard implementation of slowly changing dimensions, the following query of the `DimProduct` table in the Adventure Works data warehouse returns three rows for one product (`FR-M94B-38`):

ProductKey	ProductAlternateKey	EnglishProductName	StandardCost	ListPrice	DealerPrice	StartDate	EndDate	Status
304	FR-M94B-38	HL Mountain Frame - Black, 38	617.0281	1191.1739	714.7043	2011-07-01 00:00:00.000	2007-12-28 00:00:00.000	NULL
305	FR-M94B-38	HL Mountain Frame - Black, 38	653.6971	1226.9091	736.1455	2012-07-01 00:00:00.000	2008-12-27 00:00:00.000	NULL
306	FR-M94B-38	HL Mountain Frame - Black, 38	739.041	1349.60	809.76	2013-07-01 00:00:00.000	NULL	Current

Historical tracking of dimensions via slowly changing dimension ETL processes

It's the responsibility of the Power BI team and particularly the dataset designer to accurately reflect this historical tracking via relationships and DAX measures, such as the count of distinct products not sold. Like historical tracking, the data warehouse should also reflect all master data management processes that serve to maintain accurate master data for essential dimensions, such as customers, products, and employees. In other words, despite many lines of business applications and ERP, CRM, HRM, and other large corporate systems which store and process the same master data, the data warehouse should reflect the centrally governed and cleansed standard. Creating a Power BI dataset which only reflects one of these source systems may later introduce version control issues and, similar to choosing an incorrect granularity for a fact table, can ultimately require costly and invasive revisions.

Different tools are available with data profiling capabilities. If the data source is the SQL Server, SSIS can be used to analyze source data to be used in a project.

In the following image, the **Data Profiling Task** is used in an SSIS package to analyze the customer dimension table:

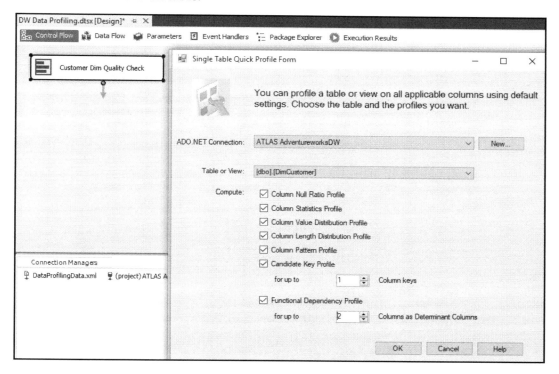

Data Profiling Task in SQL Server integration services

The Data Profiling Task requires an ADO.NET connection to the data source and can write its output to an XML file or an SSIS variable. In this example, the ADO.NET data source is the Adventure Works data warehouse database in SQL Server 2016 and the destination is an XML file (`DataProfilingData.xml`). Once the task is executed, the XML file can be read via the SQL Server Data Profile Viewer as per the following example. Note that this application, Data Profile Viewer, requires an installation of the SQL Server and that the Data Profiling Task only works with SQL Server data sources.

All fact and dimension table sources can be analyzed quickly for the count and distribution of unique values, the existence of null values, and other useful statistics.

Each data profiling task can be configured to write its results to an XML file on a network location for access via tools such as the **Data Profile Viewer**. In this example, the **Data Profile Viewer** is opened from within SSIS to analyze the output of the **Data Profiling Task** for the **Customer** dimension table:

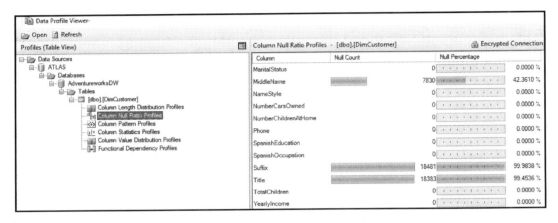

Data Profile Viewer: column null ratio profiles of DimCustomer table

Identifying and documenting issues in the source data via data profiling is a critical step in the planning process. For example, the cardinality or count of unique values largely determines the data size of a column in an import mode dataset. Similarly, the severity of data quality issues identified impacts whether a DirectQuery dataset is a feasible option.

Dataset planning

After the source data has been profiled and evaluated against the requirements identified in the four-step dataset design process, the BI team can further analyze the implementation options for the dataset. In almost all Power BI projects, even with significant investments in enterprise data warehouse architecture and ETL tools and processes, some level of additional logic, integration, or transformation is needed to enhance the quality and value of the source data or to effectively support a business requirement. A priority of the dataset, planning stage is to determine how the identified data transformation issues will be addressed to support the dataset. Additionally, based on all available information and requirements, the project team must determine whether to develop an import mode dataset or a DirectQuery dataset.

Data transformations

To help clarify the dataset planning process, a diagram such as the following can be created that identifies the different layers of the data warehouse and Power BI dataset where transformation and business logic can be implemented:

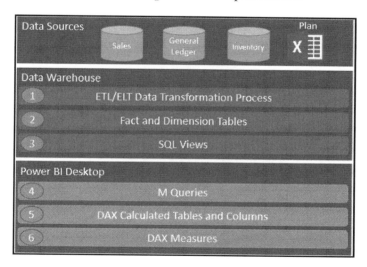

Dataset planning architecture

In some projects, minimal transformation logic is needed and can be easily included in the Power BI dataset or the SQL views accessed by the dataset. For example, if only a few additional columns are needed for a dimension table and there's straightforward guidance on how these columns should be computed, the IT organization may choose to implement these transformations within Power BI's M queries rather than revise the data warehouse, at least in the short term.

 If a substantial gap between BI needs and the corporate data warehouse is allowed to persist and grow due to various factors, such as cost, project expediency, and available data warehouse skills, then Power BI datasets will become more complex to build and maintain. Dataset designers should regularly analyze and communicate the implications of datasets assuming greater levels of complexity.

However, if the required transformation logic is complex or extensive with multiple join operations, row filters, and data type changes, then the IT organization may choose to implement essential changes in the data warehouse to support the new dataset and future BI projects. For example, a staging table and a SQL stored procedure may be needed to support a revised nightly update process or the creation of an index may be needed to deliver improved query performance for a DirectQuery dataset.

Ideally, all required data transformation and shaping logic could be implemented in the source data warehouse and its ETL processes so that Power BI is exclusively used for analytics and visualization. However, in the reality of scarce IT resources and project delivery timelines, typically at least a portion of these issues must be handled through other means, such as SQL view objects or Power BI's M query functions.

 A best practice is to implement data transformation operations within the data warehouse or source system. This minimizes the resources required to process an import mode dataset and, for DirectQuery datasets, can significantly improve query performance, as these operations would otherwise be executed during report queries. For many common data sources, such as Oracle and Teradata, M query expressions are translated into equivalent SQL statements (if possible) and these statements are passed back to the source system via a process called Query Folding. See Chapter 8, *Connecting to Sources and Transforming Data with M*, for more details on query folding.

As per the dataset planning architecture diagram, a layer of SQL views should serve as the source objects to datasets created with Power BI Desktop. By creating a SQL view for each dimension and fact table of the dataset, the data source owner or administrator is able to identify the views as dependencies of the source tables and is, therefore, less likely to implement changes that would impact the dataset without first consulting the BI team. Additionally, the SQL views improve the availability of the dataset, as modifications to the source tables will be much less likely to cause the refresh process to fail.

As a general rule, the BI team and IT organization will want to avoid the use of DAX for data transformation and shaping logic, such as DAX calculated tables and calculated columns. The primary reason for this is that it weakens the link between the dataset and the data source, as these expressions are processed entirely by the Power BI dataset after source queries have been executed. Additionally, the distribution of transformation logic across multiple layers of the solution (SQL, M, DAX) causes datasets to become less flexible and manageable. Moreover, tables and columns created via DAX do not benefit from the same compression algorithms applied to standard tables and columns and thus can represent both a waste of resources as well as a performance penalty for queries accessing these columns.

In the event that required data transformation logic cannot be implemented directly in the data warehouse or its ETL or **extract-load-transform** (**ELT**) process, a second alternative is to build this logic into the layer of SQL views supporting the Power BI dataset. For example, a SQL view for the product dimension could be created that joins the `Product`, `Product Subcategory`, and `Product Category` dimension tables, and this view could be accessed by the Power BI dataset. As a third option, M functions in the Power BI query expressions could be used to enhance or transform the data provided by the SQL views. See `Chapter 8`, *Connecting to Sources and Transforming Data with M,* for details on these functions and the Power BI data access layer generally.

DirectQuery mode

A DirectQuery dataset is limited to a single data source and serves as merely a thin semantic layer or interface to simplify the report development and data exploration experience. DirectQuery datasets translate report queries into compatible queries for the data source and leverage the data source for query processing, thus eliminating the need to store and refresh an additional copy of the source data.

A common use case of Power BI and SSAS Tabular DirectQuery datasets is to provide reporting on top of relatively small databases associated with OLTP applications. For example, if SQL Server 2016 or later is used as the relational database for an OLTP application, nonclustered columnstore indexes can be applied to several tables needed for analytics. Since nonclustered indexes are updateable in SQL Server 2016, the database engine can continue to utilize existing indexes to process OLTP transactions, such as a clustered index on a primary key column while the nonclustered columnstore index will be used to deliver performance for the analytical queries from Power BI. The business value of near real-time access to the application can be further enhanced with Power BI features, such as data-driven alerts and notifications.

Sample project analysis

As per the data refresh questions from the project template (#7-8), the Power BI dataset only needs to be refreshed daily—there's not a need for real-time visibility of the data source. From a dataset design perspective, this means that the default import mode is sufficient for this project in terms of latency or data freshness. The project template also advises that an Excel file containing the Annual Sales Plan must be included in addition to the historical sales data in the SQL Server data warehouse. Therefore, unless the Annual Sales Plan data can be migrated to the same SQL Server database containing the Internet Sales and Reseller Sales data, an import mode dataset is the only option.

The data security requirements from the project template can be implemented via simple security roles and therefore do not materially impact the import or DirectQuery decision. DirectQuery datasets can support dynamic or user-based security models as well but, given restrictions on the DAX functions that can be used in security roles for DirectQuery datasets, import mode datasets can more easily support complex security requirements. However, depending on the data source and the security applied to that source relative to the requirements of the project, organizations may leverage existing data source security through a DirectQuery dataset via a single sign-on with Kerberos delegation.

Finally, the BI team must also consider the scale of the dataset relative to size limitations with import mode datasets. As per the project template (#6), 3–4 years of sales history needs to be included, and thus the dataset designer needs to determine the size of the Power BI dataset that would store that data. For example, if Power BI Premium capacity is not available, the PBIX dataset is limited to a max size of 1 GB. If Power BI Premium capacity is available, large datasets (for example, 10 GB+) potentially containing hundreds of millions of rows can be published to the Power BI service.

The decision for this project is to develop an import mode dataset and to keep the Excel file containing the `Annual Sales Plan` on a secure network location. The BI team will develop a layer of views to retrieve the required dimension and fact tables from the SQL Server database as well as connectivity to the Excel file. The business will be responsible for maintaining the following `Annual Sales Plan` Excel file in its current schema, including any row updates and the insertion of new rows for future plan years:

Calendar Yr-Mo	Year	Sales Territory Region	Product Subcategory	Internet Net Sales	Reseller Net Sales	Internet Net Sales Margin %	Reseller Net Sales Margin %
2018-Apr	2018	Northwest	Mountain Bikes	$54,638.43	$38,979.37	40.79%	8.59%
2018-Apr	2018	Southeast	Mountain Bikes	$0.00	$60,448.09	0.00%	10.77%
2018-Apr	2018	Southwest	Mountain Bikes	$42,515.11	$224,846.25	50.94%	10.72%
2018-Apr	2018	United Kingdom	Mountain Bikes	$30,214.33	$44,984.28	39.40%	8.19%

Annual Sales Plan in Excel data table

By using the existing Excel file for the planned sales and margin data rather than integrating this data into the data warehouse, the project is able to start faster and maintain continuity for the business team responsible for this source. Similar to collaboration with all data source owners, the dataset designer could advise the business user or team responsible for the sales plan on the required structure and the rules for maintaining the data source to allow for integration into Power BI. For example, the name and directory of the file, as well as the column names of the Excel data table, cannot be changed without first communicating these requested revisions.

Additionally, the values of the `Sales Territory Region`, `Product Subcategory`, and `Calendar Yr-Mo` columns must remain aligned with those used in the data warehouse to support the required actual versus plan visualizations.

The sales plan includes multiple years and represents a granularity of the month, sales territory region, and product subcategory. In other words, each row represents a unique combination of values from the `Calendar Yr-Mo`, `Sales Territory Region`, and `Product Subcategory` columns. The *Bridge tables* section in Chapter 9, *Designing Import and DirectQuery Data Models*, describes how these three columns are used in integrating the Sales Plan data into the dataset containing `Internet Sales` and `Reseller Sales` data.

Summary

In this chapter, we've walked through the primary elements and considerations in planning a Power BI project. A standard and detailed planning process inclusive of the self-service capabilities needed or expected, project roles and responsibilities, and the design of the dataset can significantly reduce the time and cost to develop and maintain the solution. With a sound foundation of business requirements and technical analysis, a business intelligence team can confidently move forward into a development stage.

In the next chapter, the two data sources identified in this chapter (SQL Server and Excel) will be accessed to begin development of an import mode dataset. Source data will be retrieved via Power BI's M language queries to retrieve the set of required fact and dimension tables. Additionally, several data transformations and query techniques will be applied to enhance the analytical value of the data and the usability of the dataset.

8
Connecting to Sources and Transforming Data with M

This chapter follows up on the dataset planning process described in the previous chapter by implementing M queries in a new Power BI Desktop file to retrieve the required fact and dimension tables. Parameters and variables are used to access a set of SQL views reflecting the data warehouse tables inside a SQL Server database and the `Annual Sales Plan` data contained in an Excel workbook. Additional M queries are developed to support relationships between the sales plan and dimension tables and to promote greater usability and manageability of the dataset.

Three examples of implementing data transformations and logic within M queries, such as the creation of a dynamic customer history segment column, are included. Finally, tools for editing and managing M queries, such as extensions for Visual Studio and Visual Studio Code, are reviewed.

In this chapter, we will review the following topics:

- Query design per dataset mode
- Data sources
- Power BI Desktop options
- SQL views
- Parameters
- Staging queries
- Data types
- Query folding
- M query examples
- M query editing tools

Query design per dataset mode

Many common M queries can be written for both import and DirectQuery datasets, but with widely different implications for the source system resources utilized and the performance of the analytical queries from Power BI. It's essential that the mode of the dataset (import or DirectQuery) has been determined in advance of the development of the data access queries and that this decision is reflected in the M queries of the dataset.

The M queries supporting a Power BI dataset import mode should exclude, or possibly split, columns with many unique values, such as a `Transaction Number` column, as these columns consume relatively high levels of memory. A standard design technique for import mode models is to exclude derived fact table columns with relatively more unique values when these values can be computed via simple DAX measure expressions based on columns of the same table with fewer unique values.

In the following example, the `SUMX()` DAX function is used to compute the `Sales Amount` measure based on the `Order Quantity` and `Unit Price` columns of the `Internet Sales` fact table, thus avoiding the need to import the `Sales Amount` column:

```
Internet Sales Amount (Import) =
SUMX('Internet Sales','Internet Sales'[Order Quantity]*'Internet
Sales'[Unit Price])

Internet Sales Amount (DirectQuery) =
SUM('Internet Sales'[Sales Amount])
```

As per the second measure, the `Sales Amount` column would be included in a DirectQuery data model and the DAX measure for the sales amount would exclusively utilize this column to generate a more efficient SQL query for the data source.

 The import mode model is able to efficiently compute similar `SUMX()` expressions at scale with basic arithmetic operators (+, −, *, /) as these operations are supported by the multithreaded storage engine of the xVelocity in-memory analytics engine. For greater detail on DAX measures for import and DirectQuery datasets, see `Chapter 10`, *Developing DAX Measures and Security Roles*.

The M queries supporting a DirectQuery dataset should generally contain minimal to no transformation logic as the complexity of the resulting SQL statement may negatively impact the performance of Power BI report queries as well as increase the resource usage of the data source.

This is especially important for the fact tables and any large dimension tables of the DirectQuery dataset. Given the central role of the data source for query performance and scalability of DirectQuery solutions, the Power BI dataset designer should closely collaborate with the data source owner or subject matter expert, such as a database administrator, to make the best use of available source system resources.

As noted in the *To get the most out of this book* section of the Preface, an AdventureWorks data warehouse sample database (AdventureWorksDW2016CTP3) hosted on a local instance of the SQL Server 2017 database engine was the primary data source for the examples in this book. The PBIX files included in the code bundle reference ATLAS as the name of the database server and AdventureWorksDW as the name of the database. Therefore, any attempt to refresh the queries within these PBIX files or create new queries against this data source will return errors as the user doesn't have access to this source.

Additionally, certain objects of the AdventureWorksDW database used in this book such as views are not included in the downloadable sample database. For this reason, the exact results depicted in this book cannot be perfectly reproduced via a SQL Server 2017 (or later) database instance and the sample database alone. Moreover, the code examples in the book are intended to highlight essential concepts and use cases. The corresponding code included in the code bundle may, for example, include additional columns not referenced in the book as these columns weren't essential to the given example.

Import mode dataset queries

All M queries of an import mode dataset are executed only once per scheduled refresh. Therefore, if sufficient resources are available during these scheduled intervals, the M queries can contain more complex and resource-intensive operations without negatively impacting report query performance. In fact, well-designed data retrieval processes can benefit from report query performance as the source data is prepped to take greater advantage of the compression algorithms applied to import mode datasets. The systems impacted by these retrieval operations depend on the data source, whether the data sources is located on-premises or in a public cloud, such as MS Azure, and the operations of the query itself.

In this project example with an on-premises SQL Server database, the M queries can utilize the database server's resources during each refresh via the query folding process described later in this chapter. In the event that certain M expressions cannot be translated into an equivalent SQL statement for the given source, these expressions will be evaluated by the in-memory M engine of the On-premises data gateway, which is installed on-premises. If the source database was in the cloud and not within an **Infrastructure-as-a-Service (IaaS)** virtual machine, a gateway would not be required for the refresh, and resources in Power BI, such as Power BI Premium capacity hardware, would be used to execute any M expressions that can't be folded to a source.

For import mode datasets, M queries can be partially folded such that a source database is used to execute only part of the required logic. For example, an M query may contain both simple transformation steps, such as filtering out rows, as well as more complex logic that references a custom M function. In this scenario, a SQL statement may be generated for the initial steps of the query, and the results of this SQL query could be used by another system's resources, such as the On-premises data gateway to process the remaining logic. All steps (variables) within an M query following a step that cannot be folded are also not folded. Likewise, any M step following a `Value.NativeQuery()` function that passes a SQL statement to a source system will also not be folded. See the *Query folding section* later in this chapter for more details.

DirectQuery dataset queries

For DirectQuery datasets, every M query is folded to exclusively utilize the resources of the single data source. Therefore, certain M functions and query logic that lack an equivalent SQL expression for the given data source, such as Oracle or Teradata, are not supported. In these scenarios, the dataset designer can develop alternative M queries that produce the same target data structure and are supported by the source system or implement the necessary logic within the layer of SQL views supporting the dataset.

An additional and fundamental limitation to the scope of M queries for DirectQuery datasets is the impact on query performance and user experience. Since the SQL statements representing M queries must be executed by the source system during report viewing sessions, common transformations such as converting data types and sorting tables can cause significant performance degradation.

Additionally, a high volume of sub-optimal SQL queries passed from Power BI reports can quickly drive up the resource usage of the source system. Therefore, although it's often technically possible to implement similar data transformation logic in the SQL views and M queries of DirectQuery datasets as with import mode datasets, the performance and resource implications of these transformations frequently prove unacceptable.

Dataset designers of DirectQuery datasets should document the SQL statements generated by their M queries. As shown in the Query folding section later in this chapter, these queries can be accessed from the **View Native Query** command within the **Applied Steps** pane of the Power Query Editor in Power BI Desktop. Sharing and reviewing these queries with the data source owner, or a subject matter expert on the data source can often lead to new ideas to improve performance or data quality. For example, the data source owner can analyze the indexes of the source fact table and determine whether the WHERE clause of the query can take advantage of existing indexes.

Data sources

Data source connectivity is one of the strengths of Power BI, due to the vast list of standard data source connectors included in Power BI Desktop, in addition, to support for **Open Database Connectivity (ODBC)** and **Object Linking and Embedding, Database (OLE DB)** connections. The breadth of data connectivity options is further bolstered by the ability for developers to create custom Power BI data connectors for a specific application, service, or data source. Custom data connectors, the data retrieval processes created for all data sources for Power BI, and other Microsoft applications are developed with the M language.

Power BI's data connectors are consistently extended and improved with each monthly release of Power BI Desktop. New data sources are commonly added as a preview or beta release feature and previous beta connectors are moved from beta to general availability.

In the following example from the October 2017 release of Power BI Desktop, the connector for **Google BigQuery** is in beta while Amazon Redshift has been generally available since the June 2017 release:

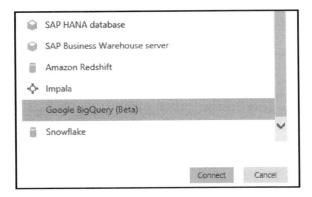

Beta and generally-available data connectors in Power BI Desktop

 Beta connectors should only be used for testing purposes, as differences between the beta release and the subsequent generally-available connector may cause queries dependent on the beta version to fail.

The data connector icons exposed in the **Get Data** graphical interface of Power BI Desktop are associated with the data access functions of M, such as `Sql.Database()`.

Authentication

Power BI Desktop saves a data source credential, or sign-in identity, for each data source connection used. These credentials and settings are not stored in the PBIX file but rather on the local computer specific to the given user.

An authentication dialog specific to the data source is rendered if the user hasn't accessed the data source before or if the user has removed existing permissions to the data source in Power BI Desktop's **Data source settings** menu. In the following example, an Sql.Database() M query function references the AdventureWorksDW SQL Server database on the ATLAS server.

In this scenario, the user has not previously accessed this data source (or has cleared existing source permissions), and thus executing this query prompts the user to configure the authentication to this source as shown in the following image:

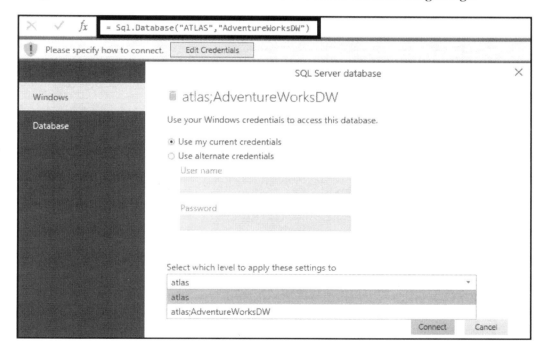

Edit Authentication Credentials in Power BI Desktop

Most relational database sources have similar authentication options. For SQL Server, the user can choose between the default Windows-integrated authentication (that is, **Use my current credentials**) or database authentication if the database is in Mixed Mode. Additionally, the credentials can be saved exclusively to the specific database or be reused for other databases on the same server.

Data source settings

The **Data source settings** menu provides access to the authentication and privacy levels configured for each data source within the current file and the saved permissions available to all of the user's Power BI Desktop files.

This menu can be accessed under the **Edit Queries** drop-down on the **Home** tab of Power BI Desktop's report view or from the **Home** tab of the **Query Editor**, as shown in the following screenshot:

Data source settings menu in Power BI Desktop

In this example, the user chose to save the Windows authentication to the ATLAS server rather than the specific database (AdventureWorksDW) on the server. The **Edit Permissions...** command button provides the ability to revise the authentication, such as from Windows to database or to enter a new username and password.

The **Edit...** command of the **Edit Permissions** menu, highlighted in the following image, prompts the same SQL Server credential menu that was used when originally configuring the method of authentication to the data source:

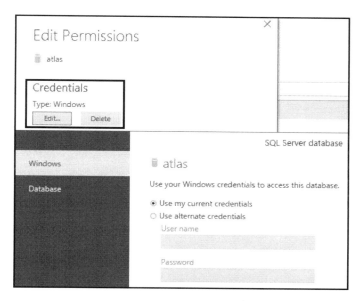

Edit credentials accessed via Edit Permissions

Many organizations set policies requiring users to regularly revise their usernames or passwords for certain data sources. Once these credentials have been updated, the user should utilize the **Edit Permissions** menu to ensure that the updated credentials will be used for M queries against this data source. Depending on the security policy of the data source, repeated failures to authenticate due to the outdated credentials saved in Power BI Desktop can cause the user's account to be temporarily locked out of the data source.

Privacy levels

In addition to the authentication method and user credentials for a data source, Power BI also stores a privacy level for each data source. Privacy levels define the isolation level of data sources and thus restrict the integration of data sources in M queries.

For example, in the absence of privacy levels, an M query that merges a CSV file with a publicly available online database could result in the data from the CSV file being passed to the online database to execute the operation. Although this default behavior is preferable from a query performance and resource utilization standpoint, the CSV file may contain sensitive information that should never leave the organization or even an individual user's machine. Applying privacy levels, such as **Private** for the CSV file and **Public** for the online database, isolates the two sources during query execution thus preventing unauthorized access to sensitive data.

The privacy level of a data source can be accessed from the same **Edit Permissions** dialog available in the **Data source settings** menu as shown in the following screenshot:

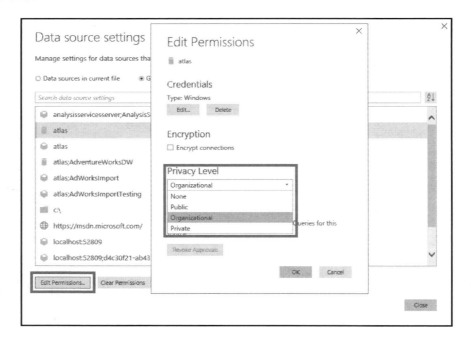

Privacy Level options per data source

The default **Privacy Level** for data sources is **None**. Therefore, dataset designers should revise privacy levels when first configuring data sources in Power BI Desktop based on the security policies for the given sources.

Four privacy levels are available:

- **Public**: A public data source is not isolated from other public sources, but data transfer from organizational and private data sources to public data sources is prevented. Public source data can be transferred to an organizational data source but not to a private data source.
- **Organizational**: An organizational data source is isolated from all public data sources but is visible to other organizational data sources. For example, if a CSV file is marked as organizational, then a query that integrates this source with an organizational SQL Server database can transfer this data to the database server to execute the query.
- **Private**: A private data source is completely isolated from all other data sources. Data from the private data source will not be transferred to any other data sources, and data from public sources will not be transferred to the private source.
- **None**: The privacy level applied is inherited from a separate data source, or not applied if the separate parent source has not been configured. For example, the privacy level for an Excel workbook stored on a network directory could be set to **None**, yet the isolation level of **Private** would be enforced if a data source for the root directory of the file is set to **Private**.

In this project, the Excel workbook containing the `Annual Sales Plan` is not merged with any queries accessing the SQL Server data warehouse and thus the privacy levels do not impact any queries. However, as with all other data security issues, such as **row-level security** (**RLS**) roles, the dataset designer should be mindful of privacy levels and apply the appropriate setting per data source.

 Restrictive privacy levels that do not directly reject queries that can only be executed by violating the privacy (isolation) level of a data source may still prevent query folding from occurring and thus significantly reduce performance and reliability. For example, if an Excel workbook is isolated from a SQL Server data source due to a **Private** privacy level, then the local resources available to the M engine will be used to execute this operation rather than the SQL Server database engine. If the source data retrieved from SQL Server is large enough, the resource requirements to load this data and then execute this operation locally could cause the query to fail.

Power BI as a data source

Over 59 distinct cloud services are available to Power BI, such as Google Analytics and Dynamics 365. Most importantly for this project, the Power BI online service is a fully supported data source enabling report development in Power BI Desktop against published datasets. As shown in the following screenshot, the datasets contained in Power BI App Workspaces in which the user is a member are exposed as data sources:

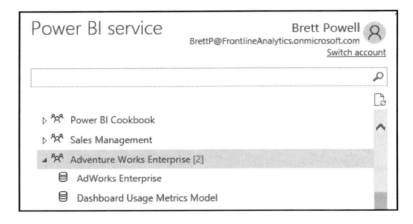

Power BI service data connector in Power BI Desktop

 Connecting to a dataset published to Power BI establishes a Live connection for the given report, just like connections to SQL Server Analysis Services. With Live connections, all data retrieval and modeling capabilities are disabled and the queries associated with report visualizations are executed against the source database.

Leveraging published datasets as the sources for reports provides a natural isolation between the dataset design and report development processes. For example, a dataset designer can implement changes to a local Power BI Desktop file (PBIX), such as the creation of new DAX measures, and re-publish the dataset to make these measures available to report authors. Additionally, these connections provide report authors with visibility to the latest successful refresh of the dataset if the dataset is configured in import mode.

Power BI Desktop options

Dataset designers should be aware of the global and current file settings available to manage the Power BI Desktop environment. Among other options, these settings include the implementation of the privacy levels described earlier, the DAX functions available to DirectQuery datasets, auto recovery, preview features, and whether M queries will be executed in parallel or not.

Power BI Desktop options can be accessed from the **File** menu as follows (**File | Options and settings | Options**):

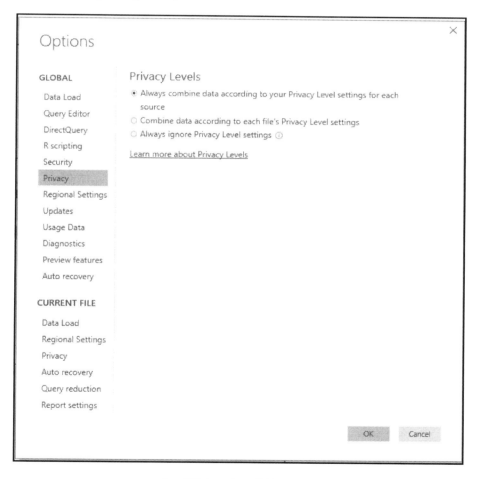

Power BI Desktop options – GLOBAL Privacy

By setting the global **Privacy Levels** option to **Always combine data according to your Privacy Level settings for each source**, the current file privacy setting options are disabled. For all development and project activities, it's recommended to apply the privacy levels established per data source rather than each PBIX file's privacy settings.

It's outside the scope of this chapter to provide details of each Power BI Desktop option, but the following two sections recommend settings that are relevant to dataset design.

Global options

Global options only need to be set once and concern fundamental settings, including data source privacy levels and security:

1. Set the **DirectQuery** option to **Allow unrestricted measures in DirectQuery mode**
2. Configure the security options to require user approval for new native database queries and to use the ArcGIS Maps for Power BI
3. Set the privacy option to always combine data according to privacy level settings for each source
4. Configure the Power Query Editor options to display the **Query Settings** pane and the **Formula Bar**
5. Click the **OK** button in the bottom-right corner of the **Options** dialog to apply these settings:
    * It may be necessary to restart Power BI Desktop for the revised settings to take effect

For DirectQuery datasets, not all DAX functions can be translated to a SQL statement for execution by the data source. When DAX measures use these non-optimized functions, especially against larger or unfiltered tables, the local execution can result in poor performance. However, when used appropriately, such as against pre-filtered or aggregated data, unrestricted measure expressions can add to the analytical value of the dataset without negatively impacting performance. See the official documentation for DAX-formula compatibility with DirectQuery models `http://bit.ly/2oK8QXB`.

CURRENT FILE options

The **CURRENT FILE** options must be set per the Power BI Desktop file and are particularly important when creating a new dataset:

1. Disable the automatic column type and header detection for unstructured sources
2. Disable all relationship options, including the import of relationships from data sources and the detection of new relationships after data is loaded
3. Assuming a date dimension table is available to the dataset, disable the **Auto Date/Time** option
4. For larger import datasets with many queries, disable the parallel loading of tables
5. Click the **OK** button in the bottom-right corner of the **Options** dialog to apply these settings:

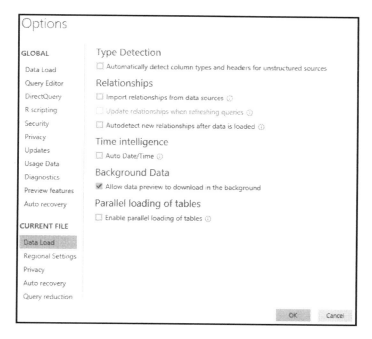

Power BI Desktop Options – CURRENT FILE Data Load

The dataset designer should explicitly apply the appropriate data types within the M queries, accessing any unstructured sources, such as Excel files. Likewise, the dataset designer should have access to data source documentation or subject matter experts regarding table relationships. Furthermore, the columns and hierarchies of the dataset's date dimension table can be used instead of the automatic internal date tables associated with the **Auto Date/Time** option.

Large Power BI datasets with multiple fact tables can contain many queries which, if executed in parallel, can overwhelm the resources of the source system resulting in a data refresh failure. Disabling the parallel loading of tables, therefore, improves the availability of the dataset and reduces the impact of the refresh process on the source server.

When Power BI Desktop is being used for report development rather than dataset development, the **Query reduction** in **CURRENT FILE** options can benefit the user experience. These options, including the disabling of cross-highlighting by default and the use of an **Apply** button for slicer and filter selections, result in fewer report queries being generated. Particularly for large and DirectQuery datasets, these options can contribute to more efficient and responsive self-service experiences with reports.

SQL views

As described in the *Dataset planning* section of Chapter 7, *Planning Power BI Projects*, a set of SQL views should be created within the data source and these objects, rather than the database tables, should be accessed by the Power BI dataset. Each fact and dimension table required by the Power BI dataset should have its own SQL view and its own M query within the dataset that references this view. The SQL views should preferably be assigned to a dedicated database schema and identify the dimension or fact table represented as shown in the following screenshot:

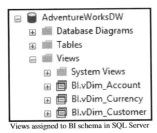

Views assigned to BI schema in SQL Server

A common practice is to create a database schema specific to the given dataset being created or to the specific set of reports and dashboards required for a project. However, as suggested in the *Data Warehouse Bus Matrix* section of

Chapter 7, *Planning Power BI Projects* there shouldn't be multiple versions of dimensions and facts across separate datasets—version control is a top long-term deliverable for the BI team. Therefore, a single database schema with a generic name (BI in this example) is recommended.

The existence of SQL view objects declares a dependency to source tables that are visible to the data source owner. In the event that a change to the source tables of a view is needed or planned, the SQL view can be adjusted, thus avoiding any impact to the Power BI dataset, such as a refresh failure or an unexpected change in the data retrieved. As shown in the following SQL Server dialog, a view (**BI.vDim_Promotion**) is identified as a dependent object of the **DimPromotion** dimension table:

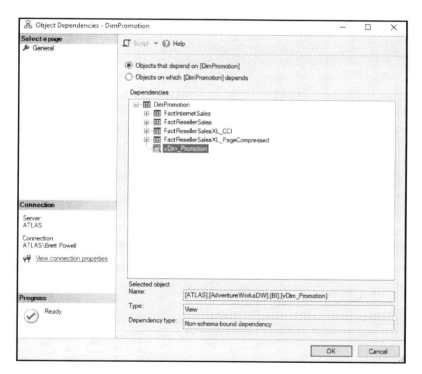

SQL Server Object Dependencies

For mature data warehouse sources, the simple query logic contained in each SQL view is sufficient to support the needs of the dataset. However, with Power BI (and SSAS Tabular 2017), BI teams can also leverage M functions to further enhance the value of this data.

SQL views versus M queries

A common question in Power BI projects specific to data retrieval is whether to implement any remaining transformation logic outside the data source in SQL views, within the M queries of the dataset, or both. For **SQL Server Analysis Services (SSAS)** projects prior to SQL Server 2017, the layer of SQL views was the only option to implement any transformations and some BI teams may prefer this more familiar language and approach. In other scenarios, however, the SQL views may not be accessible or the dataset designer may have a particular strength in M query development relative to SQL. Additionally, given the expanded role of M queries in the Microsoft ecosystem, such as the Common Data Service, as well as support for M query development in Visual Studio, other BI teams may see long-term value in M queries for lightweight data transformation needs.

Ideally, an organization's data warehouse already includes necessary data transformations and thus minimal transformation is required within SQL or M. In this scenario, the M query for the table can simply reference the SQL view of the table, which itself contains minimal to no transformations, and inherit all required columns and logic. As a secondary alternative, the SQL views can be modified to efficiently implement the required logic thus isolating this code to the data source. As a third design option, M queries can implement the required logic and, via query folding, generate a SQL statement for execution by the source. Yet another design option, though less than ideal, is to implement part of the required logic in the SQL view and the remaining logic in the M query.

The guiding principle of the data retrieval process for the import mode dataset is to leverage the resources and architecture of the data source. The M queries of the Power BI dataset, which access the layer of SQL views in the source system, ultimately represent the fact and dimension tables of the data model exposed for report development and ad hoc analysis. This model should address all data transformation needs, thus avoiding the need for DAX-calculated columns and DAX-calculated tables.

Additionally, the data model in Power BI (or Analysis Services) should remain aligned with the architecture and definitions of the data warehouse. If a gap is created by embedding data transformation logic (for example, new columns) into the Power BI dataset that is not present in the data warehouse, plans should be made to eventually migrate this logic to the data warehouse to restore alignment.

In other words, a user or tool should be able to return the same results of a Power BI report based on the Power BI dataset by issuing a SQL query against the source data warehouse. This is particularly essential in environments with other BI and reporting tools built on top of the data warehouse.

 If it's necessary to use both SQL views and M functions to implement the data transformation logic, then both queries should be documented and, when possible, this logic should be consolidated closer to the data source.

As shown in the *Dataset Planning Architecture* diagram from `Chapter 7`, *Planning Power BI Projects*, there are six layers in which data logic can be implemented:

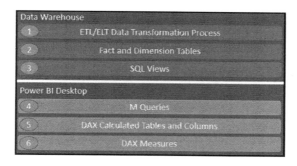

Dataset planning architecture

Data retrieval processes should strive to leverage the resources of data sources and avoid or minimize the use of local resources. For example, a derived column implemented within either a **SQL Views** (layer 3) or within an **M Queries** (layer 4) which folds its logic to the data source is preferable to a column created by a **DAX Calculated Tables and Columns** (layer 5). Likewise, if data transformation logic is included within M queries (for example, joins, group by), it's important to ensure these operations are being executed by the source system as described in the *Query folding* section later in this chapter. These considerations are especially critical for large tables given the relatively limited resources (for example, CPU, Memory) of a Power BI dataset or the On-premises data gateway if applicable.

Additionally, the dimension and fact tables of the Power BI dataset and the DAX measures created should represent a single version for the organization—not a customization for a specific team or project sponsor. Therefore, although the combination of SQL views and M queries provides significant flexibility for implementing data transformations and logic, over time this logic should be incorporated into corporate data warehouses and **extract-transform-load** (ETL) processes so that all business intelligence tools have access to a common data source.

> Incrementally migrate transformation logic closer to the corporate data warehouse over time. For example, a custom column that's originally created within an M query via the `Table.AddColumn()` function and a conditional expression (`if...then`), could first be built into the SQL view supporting the table, thus eliminating the need for the M query logic.

> In a second and final stage, the column could be added to the dimension or fact table of the corporate data warehouse and the conditional expression could be implemented within a standard data warehouse ETL package or stored procedure. This final migration stage would eliminate the need for the SQL view logic, improve the durability and performance of the data retrieval process, and in some scenarios also increase the feasibility of a DirectQuery dataset.

SQL view examples

Each SQL view should only retrieve the columns required for the dimension or fact table. If necessary, the views should apply business-friendly, unambiguous column aliases with spaces and proper casing. Dimension table views should include the surrogate key used for the relationship-to-fact tables, as well as the business or natural key column if historical tracking is maintained as will be shown by the customer dimension example later in this section.

Fact table views should include the foreign key columns for the relationships to the dimension tables, the fact columns needed for measures, and a WHERE clause to only retrieve the required rows, such as the prior three years. Given the size of many data warehouse fact tables and the differences in how this data can best be accessed per the Query design per dataset mode section earlier, dataset designers should ensure that the corresponding SQL views are efficient and appropriate for the dataset.

A robust date dimension table is critical for all datasets and thus its SQL view and/or M query has a few unique requirements. For example, it should include integer columns that can define the default sort order of weekdays as well as sequentially increasing integer columns to support date intelligence expressions. The date table should also include a natural hierarchy of columns (that is, `Year`, `Year-Qtr`, `Year-Mo`, `Year-Wk`) for both the Gregorian (standard) calendar as well as any custom fiscal calendar. These columns enable simple drill-up/down experiences in Power BI and report visualizations at different date granularities that span multiple time periods, such as the prior two years by week.

Given the static nature of the `Date` (and `Time`) dimension tables, their minimal size, and their universal application in reports and dashboards, it's usually a good use of IT/BI resources to enhance the source date table in the data warehouse. This could include any derived columns currently supported via SQL views or M queries as well as columns uniquely valuable to the organization, such as company holidays. Additionally, any dynamic columns, such as `Calendar Month Status` (`Current Month`, `Prior Month`) can be computed within a SQL-stored procedure or an ETL package and this processing can be scheduled to update the source date table daily.

Date dimension view

The following sample from a date dimension SQL view includes several columns that will be needed by the Power BI dataset:

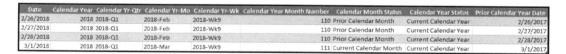

Date	Calendar Year	Calendar Yr-Qtr	Calendar Yr-Mo	Calendar Yr-Wk	Calendar Year Month Number	Calendar Month Status	Calendar Year Status	Prior Calendar Year Date
2/26/2018	2018	2018-Q1	2018-Feb	2018-Wk9	110	Prior Calendar Month	Current Calendar Year	2/26/2017
2/27/2018	2018	2018-Q1	2018-Feb	2018-Wk9	110	Prior Calendar Month	Current Calendar Year	2/27/2017
2/28/2018	2018	2018-Q1	2018-Feb	2018-Wk9	110	Prior Calendar Month	Current Calendar Year	2/28/2017
3/1/2018	2018	2018-Q1	2018-Mar	2018-Wk9	111	Current Calendar Month	Current Calendar Year	3/1/2017

Sample date dimension columns

The `Calendar Year Month Number` column can be used to define the default sort order of the `Calendar Yr-Mo` column and can also support date intelligence DAX measure expressions that select a specific time, frame such as the trailing four months. Likewise, a prior calendar year date (or prior fiscal year date) column can be referenced in date intelligence measure expressions.

The `Calendar Month Status` and `Calendar Year Status` columns make it easy for report authors to define common filter conditions, such as the current and prior month or the current year excluding the current month. Additionally, since the values for these columns are updated either by a daily job in the source database or computed within the SQL view for the date dimension, the filter conditions for these columns only need to be set once.

 Power BI Desktop supports relative date filtering conditions for date columns by default. Similar to the `Calendar Month` and `Year Status` columns identified earlier, this feature is also useful in defining many common report filter conditions, such as the last 20 days. However, the filter conditions available in relative date filtering are not comprehensive and typical conditions, such as all of last year and all dates from the current year, can only be defined via the status columns. Additional details regarding relative date filtering are available in `Chapter 11`, *Creating and Formatting Power BI Reports.*

The following T-SQL from the date dimension view (`BI.vDim_Date`) leverages the `CURRENT_TIMESTAMP()` function to compute two dynamic columns (`Calendar Year Status`, `Calendar Month Status`) and the `DATEPART()` function to retrieve the date rows from January 1st of three years ago through the current date:

```
SELECT
  D.Date
,
  CASE
     WHEN YEAR(D.[Date]) = YEAR(CURRENT_TIMESTAMP) THEN 'Current
Calendar Year'
     WHEN YEAR(D.[Date]) = YEAR(CURRENT_TIMESTAMP)-1 THEN 'Prior
Calendar Year'
     WHEN YEAR(D.[Date]) = YEAR(CURRENT_TIMESTAMP)-2 THEN '2 Yrs Prior
Calendar Year'
     WHEN YEAR(D.[Date]) = YEAR(CURRENT_TIMESTAMP)-3 THEN '3 Yrs Prior
Calendar Year'
     ELSE 'Other Calendar Year'
  END AS [Calendar Year Status]
,
  CASE
     WHEN YEAR(D.[Date]) = YEAR(CURRENT_TIMESTAMP) AND MONTH(D.Date) =
MONTH(CURRENT_TIMESTAMP) THEN 'Current Calendar Month'
     WHEN YEAR(D.[Date]) = YEAR(DATEADD(MONTH,-1,CAST(CURRENT_TIMESTAMP
AS date))) AND
        MONTH(D.[Date]) = MONTH(DATEADD(MONTH,-1,CAST(CURRENT_TIMESTAMP AS
date))) THEN 'Prior Calendar Month'
```

```
    WHEN YEAR(D.[Date]) = YEAR(DATEADD(MONTH,-2,CAST(CURRENT_TIMESTAMP
AS date))) AND
    MONTH(D.[Date]) = MONTH(DATEADD(MONTH,-2,CAST(CURRENT_TIMESTAMP AS
date))) THEN '2 Mo Prior Calendar Month'
    WHEN YEAR(D.[Date]) = YEAR(DATEADD(MONTH,-3,CAST(CURRENT_TIMESTAMP
AS date))) AND
    MONTH(D.[Date]) = MONTH(DATEADD(MONTH,-3,CAST(CURRENT_TIMESTAMP AS
date))) THEN '3 Mo Prior Calendar Month'
    ELSE 'Other Calendar Month'
  END AS [Calendar Month Status]
FROM
DBO.DimFinDate as D
WHERE
D.[Calendar Year] >= DATEPART(YEAR,CURRENT_TIMESTAMP)-3 AND D.Date <=
CAST(CURRENT_TIMESTAMP as date);
```

Provided that the scheduled refresh of the import mode dataset is successful, reports with filter conditions defined against the dynamic date columns, such as `Calendar Month Status`, will be updated automatically.

If the date columns in the SQL Server data source are only available as integers in `YYYYMMDD` format, the following T-SQL expression can be used to produce a date data type within the SQL view:

```
CONVERT(date,CAST(F.OrderDateKey AS nvarchar(8)),112)
```

However, the **Mark as Date Table** feature can be used to leverage existing `YYYYMMDD` integer columns for date relationships, as described in the following section.

Mark As Date Table

Most data warehouses store date columns as integers for query performance reasons. For example, an `Order Date Key` column on a fact table would store the `20180225` (`YYYYMMDD`) value as an integer data type to represent February 25th, 2018. Likewise, an existing date dimension table in the data warehouse usually also contains a `YYYYMMDD` date key column to support the join to these fact tables in SQL queries. If this date dimension table also contains a date column and meets essential data integrity criteria, the **Mark as Date Table** feature in Power BI Desktop can be used to leverage existing integer/whole number columns representing dates for relationships.

In the following screenshot, the **Date** table has been selected in the **Fields** list in Power BI Desktop and the **Mark as Date Table** icon has been selected from the modeling tab of the ribbon:

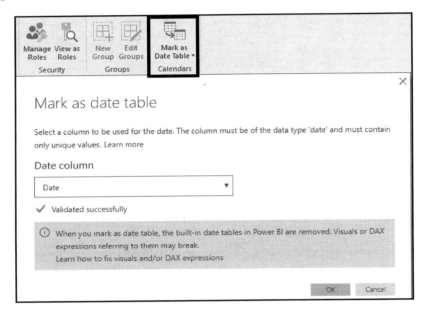

Mark as Date Table

As shown in the preceding screenshot, the column named **Date**, which is stored as a **Date** data type, has been specified as the **Date column** to use by the **Mark as Date Table** feature. Power BI validates that this column meets the required criteria to function properly.

In addition to relationships based on YYYYMMDD columns, this feature enables DAX Time Intelligence functions, such as SAMEPERIODLASTYEAR(), to work properly. Power BI will use the date column specified by the model author in the **Mark as Date Table** setting in executing these expressions.

To utilize the **Mark as Date Table** feature, the **Date column** (**Date** data type) specified for the **Mark as Date Table** feature must meet the following criteria:

- No null values.
- No duplicate values.
- Contiguous date values:
  - There must be a single date value for each date from the earliest date to the latest date. In other words, there can't be any gaps or missing dates.
- If a date/time column is used, the timestamp must be the same for each value of the column.

Product Dimension view

As shown in the database diagram schema referenced in `Chapter 7`, *Planning Power BI Projects*, it's recommended to provide a consolidated or de-normalized dimension for datasets. In the following view (`BI.vDim_Product`), three product dimension tables are joined and a logical column, `Product Category Group`, is created to support a common reporting and analysis need:

```
SELECT
  P.ProductKey as 'Product Key'
, P.ProductAlternateKey as 'Product Alternate Key'
, P.EnglishProductName AS 'Product Name'
, ISNULL(S.EnglishProductSubcategoryName, 'Undefined') 'Product
Subcategory'
, ISNULL(C.EnglishProductCategoryName, 'Undefined') AS 'Product
Category'
, CASE
  WHEN C.EnglishProductCategoryName = 'Bikes' THEN 'Bikes'
  WHEN C.EnglishProductCategoryName IS NULL THEN 'Undefined'
  ELSE 'Non-Bikes'
  END AS 'Product Category Group'
FROM
DBO.DimProduct AS P
LEFT JOIN DBO.DimProductSubcategory AS S
ON P.ProductSubcategoryKey = S.ProductSubcategoryKey
LEFT JOIN DBO.DimProductCategory AS C
ON S.ProductCategoryKey = C.ProductCategoryKey
```

In this example, it's necessary to use LEFT JOIN since the product dimension table in the data warehouse allows for null values in the foreign key column (ProductSubcategoryKey). Retrieving the product rows that haven't yet been assigned a subcategory or category is necessary for certain reports that highlight future products. For these products, an ISNULL() function is used to replace null values with an undefined value. Additionally, similar to the **Date** view, a CASE expression is used to generate a column that groups the product rows into two categories (Bikes and Non-Bikes).

Slowly-changing dimensions

The product and customer dimension views retrieve both the surrogate key column used for relationships in the dataset as well as the business key that uniquely identifies the given product or customer, respectively. For example, the same product (FR-M94B-38) is represented by three product dimension rows (304, 305, 306) due to changes in its list price over time:

Product Key	Product Alternate Key	Product Name	Product List Price	Product Start Date	Product End Date	Product Status
304	FR-M94B-38	HL Mountain Frame - Black, 38	$1,191	7/1/2011	12/28/2011	NULL
305	FR-M94B-38	HL Mountain Frame - Black, 38	$1,227	12/29/2011	12/27/2012	NULL
306	FR-M94B-38	HL Mountain Frame - Black, 38	$1,350	12/28/2012	NULL	Current

Slowly-changing dimension processing applied to Product Dimension

As discussed in Chapter 7, *Planning Power BI Projects*, the historical tracking of core business entities, such as customers and products, via slowly-changing dimension ETL processes is an essential requirement for data warehouses. The ability to insert and update rows based off of changes in specific columns is well outside the scope of SQL views and M query transformations.

DAX measures will reference the business key or alternate key column of these dimension tables to compute the discount count of these entities. For dimensions without slowly-changing dimension processing applied, the foreign key column of the related fact table can be used to compute the distinct count of dimension values associated with the given fact or event. Greater detail on these measures is included in Chapter 10, *Developing DAX Measures and Security Roles*.

M queries

With the SQL views created, the data sources configured, and the Power BI Desktop environment options applied, the dataset designer can finally develop the data retrieval queries and parameters of the dataset.

Within the Power Query Editor of Power BI Desktop, group folders can be used to organize M queries into common categories such as **Data Source Parameters**, **Staging Queries**, **Fact table Queries**, **Dimension Table Queries**, and **Bridge Table Queries** as shown in the following screenshot:

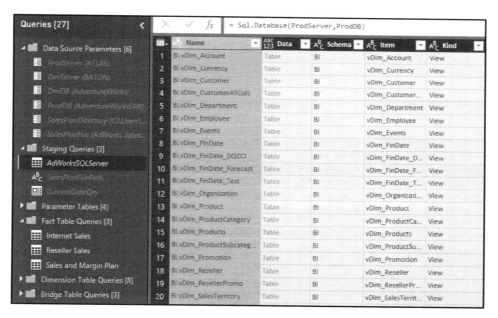

Power Query Editor in Power BI Desktop with group folders

The parameters and queries displayed with a gray font are included in the refresh process of the dataset but not loaded to the data modeling layer. For example, the `AdWorksSQLServer` query displayed in the preceding image merely exposes the objects of the SQL Server database via the `Sql.Database()` M function for other queries to reference. This query, along with the data source parameters, all have a gray font and are used to streamline the data retrieval process such that a single change can be implemented to update many dependent queries.

Right-click a query or parameter in the queries list to expose the **Enable load** and **Include in report refresh** properties as shown in the following screenshot:

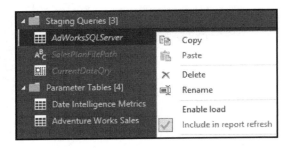

Enable load and Include in report refresh

For many datasets, the only queries that should be loaded to the data model are the dimension and fact table queries and certain parameter table queries. For this dataset, three bridge tables will also be loaded and included in the report refresh to support the analysis of `Internet Sales` and `Reseller Sales` data versus the annual `Sales and Margin Plan`.

 The parameter table queries, as described in the following **Parameters** table section, do not contain data and are merely used as placeholders for related DAX measures in the Power BI **Fields** list, similar to display folders.

Data Source Parameters

Parameters are special M queries that do not access an external data source and only return a scalar or individual value, such as a specific date, number, or string of text characters. The primary use case for parameters is to centrally define a common and important value, such as a server name or the name of a database, and then reference that parameter value in multiple other queries. Like global variables, parameters improve the manageability of large datasets as the dataset designer can simply revise a single parameter's value rather than manually modify many queries individually.

Query parameters can be created and modified via the **Manage Parameters** dialog available on the **Home** tab of the Power Query Editor. The following image of **Manage Parameters** identifies the six parameters defined for the SQL Server database and the Microsoft Excel workbook:

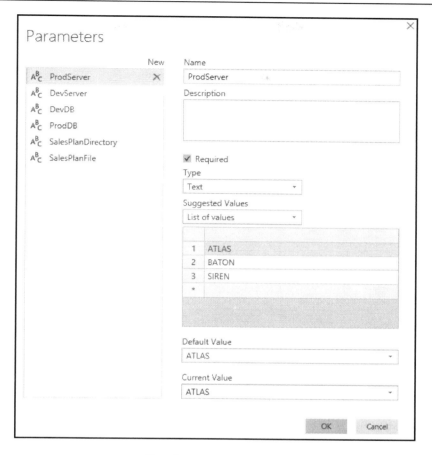

Manage Parameters in Power Query Editor

For this dataset, development and production environment database parameters (for example, **ProdServer** and **ProdDB**) are configured with a list of valid possible values to make it easy and error-free when switching data sources. For the same purpose, both the name of the Excel workbook containing the annual `Sales and Margin Plan` and its file directory are also stored as parameters.

The **Suggested Values** dropdown provides the option to allow any value to be entered manually, for a value to be selected from a hardcoded list of valid values, and for a query that returns a list (a value type in M, such as a table and a record), to dynamically populate a list of valid parameter values. Given the small number of valid server names in this example and the infrequency of changing production and development server names, the three suggested values have been entered manually.

Parameters are often used with **Power BI Template (.PBIT)** files to enable business users to customize their own reports with pre-defined and pre-filtered queries and measures. For example, the user would open a template and select a specific department, and this selection would be used to filter the M queries of the dataset.

Additionally, parameters can be useful in defining the values used in the filtering conditions of queries, such as the starting and ending dates and in the calculation logic used to create custom columns in M queries. Parameters are usually only used by other queries and thus not loaded (gray font) but they can be loaded to the data model as individual tables with a single column and a single row. If loaded, the parameters can be accessed by DAX expressions just like other tables in the model.

Staging Queries

With the data source parameters configured, staging queries can be used to expose the data sources to the dimension and fact table queries of the dataset. For example, the `AdWorksSQLServer` staging query merely passes the production server and production database parameter values into the `Sql.Database()` M function as shown in the earlier image of the Power Query Editor interface. This query results in a table containing the schemas and objects stored in the database, including the SQL views supporting the fact and dimension tables.

The **SalesPlanFilePath** staging query used for the `Annual Sales Plan` Excel workbook source is very similar in that it merely references the file name and file directory parameters to form a complete file path, as shown in the following screenshot:

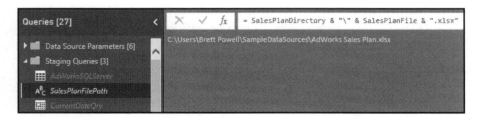

Annual Sales Plan Staging Query—Excel Workbook

The third and final staging query, `CurrentDateQry`, simply computes the current date as a date value:

Current Date Staging Query

Just like parameters, the results of staging queries, such as `CurrentDateQry`, can be referenced by other queries, such as the filtering condition of a fact table. In the following sample M query, the `Table.SelectRows()` function is used in the `Internet Sales` query to only retrieve rows where the `Order Date` column is less than or equal to the value of the `CurrentDateQry` (10/16/2017):

```
let
    Source = AdWorksSQLServer,
    ISales = Source{[Schema = "BI", Item =
"vFact_InternetSales"]}[Data],
    CurrentDateFilter = Table.SelectRows(ISales, each    [Order Date]
<=
    CurrentDateQry)
in
    CurrentDateFilter
```

In this simple example, the same filter condition can easily be built into the SQL view (`vFact_InternetSales`), supporting the fact table and this approach would generally be preferable. However, it's important to note that the M engine is able to convert the final query variable (`CurrentDateFilter`), including the reference to the staging query (`CurrentDateQry`), into a single SQL statement via Query Folding. In some data transformation scenarios, particularly with rapid iterations and agile project lifecycles, it can be preferable to at least temporarily utilize efficient M queries within the Power BI dataset (or Analysis Services model) rather than implement modifications to the data source (for example, data warehouse tables or views).

As you will see in the *Query folding* section later in this chapter, if it's necessary to use M to implement query transformations or logic, the dataset designer should be vigilant in ensuring this logic is folded into a SQL statement and thus executed by the source system. This is particularly important for large queries retrieving millions of rows, given the limited resources of the on-premises gateway server (if applicable) or any provisioned capacities (hardware) with Power BI Premium.

DirectQuery staging

The database staging query for a DirectQuery dataset is slightly different than an import mode dataset. For this query, an additional variable is added to the let expression, as shown in the following example:

```
let
    Source = Sql.Database(ProdServer, ProdDB),
    DummyVariable = null
in
    Source
```

The additional variable (DummyVariable) is ignored by the query and the same Sql.Database() function that references the server and database parameters for the import mode dataset can also be used for the DirectQuery dataset.

Fact and dimension queries

For larger datasets with multiple fact tables, most M queries will access a single SQL view, apply minimal to no transformations, and then expose the results of this query to the data model as a dimension or fact table. For import mode datasets, the M query is executed upon a scheduled refresh and the query results are loaded into a compressed, columnar format. For DirectQuery mode datasets, the M queries with the **Enable load** property set only define the SQL statement representing the given dimension or fact tables. The DirectQuery data source will utilize these SQL statements to create SQL queries necessary to resolve report queries, such as joining the Internet Sales query with the Product query.

Source Reference Only

The following M query references the SQL view (`BI.vDim_Customer`) via the staging query (`AdWorksSQLServer`) and does not apply any further transformations:

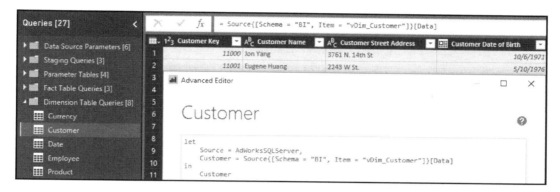

Customer Dimension Query

The customer query accesses the unique M record associated with the schema (BI) and SQL view (`vDim_Customer`) from the table produced by the staging query (`AdWorksSQLServer`). This record contains all field names of the staging table query including the `Data` field that stores the SQL view. Referencing the `Data` field of the M record retrieves the results of the SQL view.

Since no M transformations are applied, the M query reflects the source SQL view and changes to the SQL view such that the removal of a column will be automatically carried over to the Power BI dataset upon the next refresh. The one-to-one relationship between the SQL view and the M query is one of the primary reasons to favor implementing, or migrating, data transformation logic within the data warehouse source rather than in the Power BI dataset.

M query summary

In summary, the Power Query Editor interface in Power BI Desktop should contain the following types or groups of queries:

- **Parameters**:
    - These will be used to store individual values essential to the data retrieval that could change, such as the names of servers, databases, and file paths.

- **Staging Queries**:
    - These queries will not be loaded to the data model but will contain logic used by one or many other queries.
    - For example, a staging query will connect to a specific SQL Server database based on two parameters (server and database) and this staging query will be used by the fact and dimension table queries.

- **Fact and Dimension Queries**:
    - These queries will define the tables exposed to the data model layer and optionally the reporting interface.
    - It's essential that these queries contain columns supporting the relationships of the data model as well as all columns needed for calculations/aggregations, grouping, and filtering in reports.

- **Parameter Tables (optional)**:
    - Additional tables can be loaded to the data model that don't contain relationships but are used for other purposes, such as the user interface as a placeholder for hidden logic.

Excel workbook – Annual Sales Plan

For the import mode dataset, the annual `Sales and Margin Plan` data is retrieved from a table object within an Excel workbook. In the following fact table query (`Sales and Margin Plan`), the `SalesPlanFilePath staging query` is referenced within an `Excel.Workbook()` data access function:

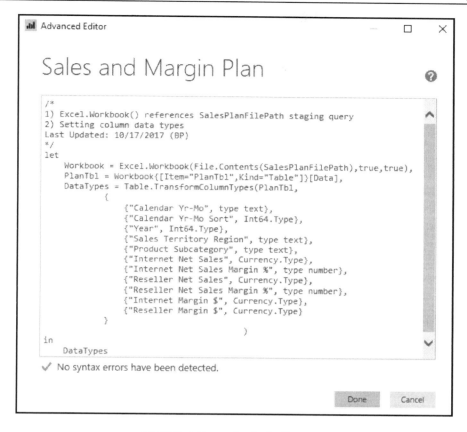

Sales and Margin Plan query from Excel workbook source

As you saw in the Power BI Desktop settings section earlier in this chapter, the automatic data type detection option for unstructured sources should be disabled. It's, therefore, necessary to explicitly define the appropriate data type for each column of the Excel table via the `Table.TransformColumnTypes()` function. The `Int64.Type`, `Currency.Type`, and `type number` arguments used in this function correspond to the `Whole Number`, `Fixed Decimal Number`, and `Decimal Number` data types, respectively.

For a DirectQuery dataset, the `Sales and Margin Plan` data would be retrieved from a SQL view within the same database as the other fact and dimension tables as shown in the following screenshot:

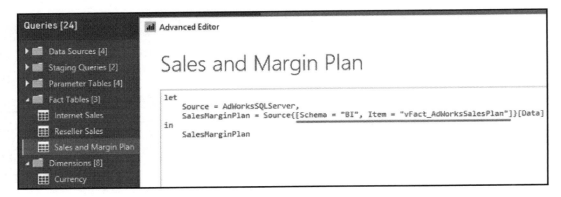

Sales and Margin Plan M query for DirectQuery dataset

The cost and time required to integrate the `Sales and Margin Plan` data into the data warehouse database are one of the reasons that the default import mode dataset was chosen for this project. The limitation of a single database within a single data source is currently one of the primary limiting factors for DirectQuery datasets. In the following screenshot, an error is thrown when trying to utilize two databases from the same database server for a DirectQuery dataset:

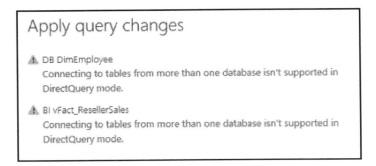

DirectQuery limitation – Single Database

DirectQuery is a strategic priority for Microsoft and thus current limitations may be eliminated in the near future.

Data types

For structured data sources, such as SQL Server, the source column data types will determine the data types applied in Power BI. For example, a money data type in SQL Server will result in a `Fixed Decimal Number` data type in Power BI. Likewise, the integer data types in SQL Server will result in a `Whole Number` data type and the numeric and decimal data types in SQL Server will result in `Decimal Number` data types in Power BI.

When an M query is loaded to the data model in a Power BI dataset, a `Fixed Decimal Number` data type is the equivalent of a (19,4) numeric or decimal data type in SQL Server. With four digits to the right of the decimal place, the use of the `Fixed Decimal Number` data type avoids rounding errors. The `Decimal Number` data type is equivalent to a floating point or approximate data type with a limit of 15 significant digits. Given the potential for rounding errors with `Decimal Number` data types and the performance advantage of `Fixed Decimal Number` data types, if four digits of precision is sufficient, the `Fixed Decimal Number` data type is recommended to store numbers with fractional components. All integer or whole number numeric columns should be stored as `Whole Number` types in Power BI.

Numeric columns in M queries can be set to `Whole Number`, `Fixed Decimal Number`, and `Decimal Number` data types via the following expressions, respectively—`Int64.Type`, `Currency.Type`, and `type number`. The `Table.TransformColumnTypes()` function is used in the following M query example to convert the data types of the `Discount Amount`, `Sales Amount`, and `Extended Amount` columns:

```
let
    Source = AdWorksSQLServer,
    Sales = Source{[Schema = "BI", Item =
"vFact_InternetSales"]}[Data],
    TypeChanges = Table.TransformColumnTypes(Sales,
            {
                {"Discount Amount", Int64.Type}, // Whole Number
                {"Sales Amount", Currency.Type}, // Fixed Decimal
Number
                {"Extended Amount", type number} // Decimal Number
            })
in
    TypeChanges
```

As M is a case-sensitive language, the data type expressions must be entered in the exact case, such as `type number` rather than Type Number. Note that single-line and multi-line comments can be included in M queries. See the *M query examples* section later in this chapter for additional details.

Given the impact on performance and the potential for rounding errors, it's important to check the numeric data types defined for each column of large fact tables. Additional details on data types are included in Chapter 9, *Designing Import and DirectQuery Data Models*.

Item access in M

Accessing records from tables, items from lists, and values from records are fundamental to M query development. In the following example, the results of the `BI.vDim_Account` SQL view are returned to Power BI using slightly different M syntax than the customer dimension query from the previous section:

```
let
    Source = AdWorksSQLServer,
    AccountRecord = Source{[Name = "BI.vDim_Account"]},
    Account = AccountRecord[Data]
in
    Account
```

For this query, a record is retrieved from the `AdWorksSQLServer` staging query based only on the Name column. The `Data` field of this record is then accessed in a separate variable (`Account`) to return the results of the `BI.vDim_Account` SQL view to Power BI. BI teams or the dataset designer can decide on a standard method for accessing the items exposed from a data source staging query.

The following sample code retrieves the `"Cherry"` string value from an M list:

```
let
    Source = {"Apple","Banana","Cherry","Dates"},
    ItemFromList = Source{2}
in
    ItemFromList
```

M is a zero-based system such that `Source{0}` would return the `"Apple"` value and `Source{4}` would return an error since there are only four items in the list. Zero-based access also applies to extracting characters from a text value. For example, the `Text.Range("Brett",2,2)` M expression returns the `et` characters.

> The list value type in M is an ordered sequence of values. There are many functions available for analyzing and transforming list values, such as `List.Count()` and `List.Distinct()`. List functions that aggregate the values they contain (for example, `List.Average()`) are often used within grouping queries that invoke the `Table.Group()` function.

DirectQuery report execution

In the following database trace from **SQL Server Profiler**, a DirectQuery dataset has translated a Power BI report query into a SQL statement, which joins the SQL statements associated with the `Reseller Sales`, **Reseller**, and **Date** M queries:

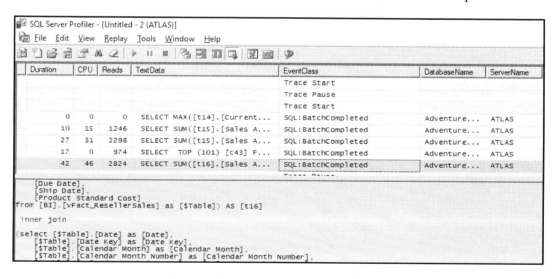

SQL Server Profiler trace – Power BI DirectQuery report visualization

For DirectQuery datasets, it's important to understand both the individual queries associated with each table of the model as well as how the data source is utilizing these queries in resolving report queries. In this example, the three table queries are used as derived tables to form the FROM clause of the outer SQL statement. Additionally, though not included in the trace image, the WHERE clause reflects a slicer (filter) selection for a specific calendar year in a Power BI report.

Bridge Tables Queries

The analysis of actual or historical Sales and Margin Plan versus the Annual Sales Plan is one of the top requirements for this dataset. Given the granularity of the annual Sales and Margin Plan (Calendar Month, Product Subcategory, Sales Territory Region), it's necessary to create bridge tables reflecting the unique values of these columns.

The three bridge tables, which can be hidden from the user interface, enable relationships between the Date, Product, and Sales Territory dimension tables with the Sales and Margin Plan fact table.

In the following example, the Sales Territory dimension table query is referenced as a source and the unique values of the Sales Territory Region column are retrieved via the Table.Distinct() function:

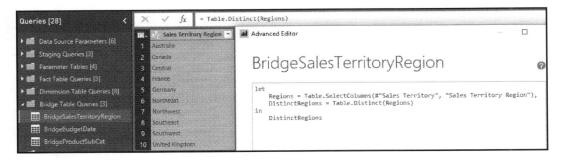

Sales Territory Bridge Table query for actual versus plan analysis

In the data model, the bridge tables will have one-to-many relationships with both the Annual Sales Plan fact table and their associated dimension tables. The relationship between the bridge tables and the dimensions will be set to allow bidirectional cross-filtering such that a filter selection for a Product Category (for example, Bikes) will impact both the historical sales fact tables as well as the Sales and Margin Plan. Greater details of this model will be discussed in Chapter 9, *Designing Import and DirectQuery Data Models*. The **Enable load** and **Include in Report Refresh** properties for each bridge table query (accessible via the right-click menu) should be set to true.

All three bridge table M queries result in simple SQL statements, such as the following, via Query Folding:

```
"Select distinct [Sales Territory Region] from
BI.vDim_SalesTerritory"
```

Therefore, all three bridge table queries can be used in a DirectQuery dataset. Additionally, these bridge queries could be stored as new SQL views in the source database to eliminate the dependency on M functions.

Parameter Tables

The final group of M queries, parameter table queries, are developed for usability and manageability purposes. From a usability standpoint, the Date Intelligence Metrics and Adventure Works Sales queries serve to consolidate similar DAX measures in the **Fields** list. Additionally, the CurrentDate query is used to provide reports with a text message advising of the latest data refresh date. From a manageability standpoint, the Measure Support query can be used to centralize intermediate or branching DAX expressions that can be referenced by many DAX measures.

As shown in the following example of the `Adventure Works Sales` query, a trivial expression can be used for three of the four queries since the purpose of the query is simply to provide a table name to the data model:

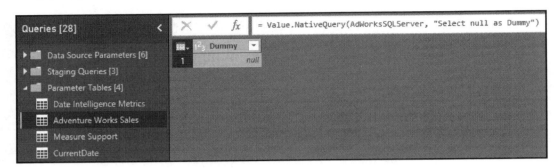

Adventure Works Sales Parameter Tables query

The `Date Intelligence Metrics`, `Adventure Works Sales`, and `Measure Support` queries can all retrieve a blank value and the **Include in report refresh** property can be disabled. The following two chapters will demonstrate how these blank tables can be utilized as data model metadata, and DAX measures are added to the dataset in `Chapter 9`, *Designing Import and DirectQuery Data Models*, and `Chapter 10`, *Developing DAX Measures and Security Roles,* respectively.

The `CurrentDate` query is the only parameter table query that needs to be executed with each report refresh. The following M script for the `CurrentDate` query produces a table with one column and one record, representing the current date as of the time of execution:

```
let
    RefreshDateTime = DateTime.LocalNow(),
    TimeZoneOffset = -5,
    RefreshDateTimeAdjusted = RefreshDateTime +
#duration(0,TimeZoneOffset,0,0),
    RefreshDateAdjusted = DateTime.Date(RefreshDateTimeAdjusted),
    TableCreate = Table.FromRecords({[CurrentDate =
RefreshDateAdjusted]}),
    DateType = Table.TransformColumnTypes(TableCreate,{"CurrentDate",
type date})
in
    DateType
```

All reported times in Microsoft Azure are expressed in **Coordinated Universal Time (UTC)**. Therefore, timezone adjustment logic can be built into the M query to ensure the last refreshed date message reflects the local timezone. In the preceding example, five hours are reduced from the `DateTime.LocalNow()` function reflecting the variance between US Eastern Standard Time and UTC. The adjusted datetime value is then converted into a date value and a table is built based on this modified date value.

As shown in the following image, the `Adventure Works Sales` and `Date Intelligence Metrics` queries are represented in the **FIELDS** list and the `CurrentDate` query is used by a DAX measure to advise of the last refreshed date:

Parameter Tables in Fields list and Data Refresh Message

The DAX expression supporting the last refreshed message is as follows:

```
Last Refresh Msg =
    VAR CurrentDateValue = MAX('CurrentDate'[CurrentDate])
    RETURN "Last Refreshed: " & CurrentDateValue
```

An additional example of using DAX to return a string value for title or label purposes is included in the *Drillthrough Report Pages* section of `Chapter 12`, *Applying Custom Visuals, Animation, and Analytics.*

As datasets grow larger and more complex, BI teams or dataset designers may add or revise group names to better organize M queries. For example, the four parameter group queries in this section serve three separate functions (`fields list`, `last refreshed date`, and `DAX logic centralization`).

To experienced Power BI and SSAS Tabular developers, a parameter table is understood as a custom table of parameter values loaded to a model and exposed to the reporting interface. DAX measures can be authored to detect which value (parameter) has been selected by the user (for example, 10% growth, 20% growth) and dynamically compute the corresponding result. For this dataset, the concept of **Parameter Tables** is extended to include any query that is loaded to the data model but not related to any other table in the data model.

Security Tables

Based on the data security needs for this project described in Chapter 7, *Planning Power BI Projects*, it's not necessary to retrieve any tables for the purpose of implementing a **row-level security (RLS)** role. As shown in the *Sample Power BI project template* section in Chapter 7, *Planning Power BI Projects*, the sales managers and associates should only have access to their `Sales Territory` groups, while the Vice Presidents should have global access. With these simple requirements, the security groups of users (for example, North America, Europe, the Pacific region) can be created and assigned to corresponding RLS roles defined in the data model. See Chapter 10, *Developing DAX Measures and Security Roles*, for details on implementing these security roles.

In projects with more complex or granular security requirements, it's often necessary to load additional tables to the data model such as a `Users` table and a `Permissions` table. For example, if users were to be restricted to specific postal codes rather than sales territory groups, a dynamic, table-driven approach that applies filters based on the user issuing the report request would be preferable to creating (and maintaining) a high volume of distinct RLS roles and security groups. Given the importance of dynamic (user-based) security, particularly for large-scale datasets, detailed examples of implementing dynamic security for both import and DirectQuery datasets are included in Chapter 10, *Developing DAX Measures and Security Roles*.

Query folding

Query folding is one of the most powerful and important capabilities of the M language as it translates M expressions into SQL statements that can be executed by the source system. With query folding, M serves as an abstraction layer to implement both common and complex data cleansing and transformation operations while still leveraging source system resources. When implementing any remaining logic or data transformations via M functions, a top priority of the dataset designer is to ensure that these operations are folded to the data source.

In the following M query, a `Table.RemoveColumns()` M function is applied against the SQL view for the `Internet Sales` fact table to exclude three columns that are not needed for the dataset:

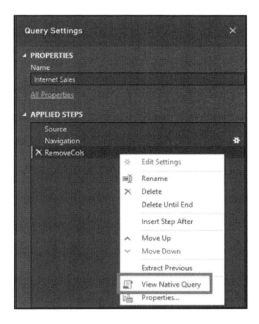

Power Query Editor: View Native Query

The additional step is translated to a SQL query that simply doesn't select the three columns. The specific SQL statement passed to the source system can be accessed by right-clicking the final step in the **Query Settings** pane and selecting **View Native Query**. If the **View Native Query** option is grayed out, this indicates that the specific step or transformation is executed with local resources.

Selecting one of the **APPLIED STEPS** in the **Query Settings** pane displays a preview of the results of the query of the given step. Particularly for queries with several steps, the ability to quickly walk through the transformations or view the query results at any given step is very helpful in analyzing and debugging M queries. Note that the names of the variables used in the M query will be reflected in the **APPLIED STEPS** pane, further underscoring the importance of applying intuitive variable names in M queries.

Query folding is limited by the data source of the M expression with relational databases, such as SQL Server and Oracle, supporting the most query folding. Alternatively, no query folding is possible when an Excel workbook or a text file is the data source of a query. The M queries against these file sources will use local M engine resources and thus the volume of data imported as well as the complexity of the query should be limited. Other sources, such as SharePoint lists, Active Directory, and Exchange, support some level of query folding, though significantly less than relational databases.

Partial query folding

Dataset designers should check the final step of each query in the dataset to ensure that query folding is occurring. If all required transformations or logic of an M query cannot be folded into a single SQL statement, the dataset designer should attempt to re-design the query to obtain as much query folding as possible. For example, all common or simple transformations can be implemented in the first four steps of the query so that **View Native Query** will be visible for the fourth step. The remaining logic can be added as the fifth step of the query and this locally executed step or transformation will be applied against the results of the SQL statement generated from the fourth step of the query.

The `Value.NativeQuery()` M function can be used to pass a SQL statement to the data source. However, any further transformations applied to the results of this function in the M query will exclusively use local resources. Therefore, if implemented, the SQL statement passed to the data source should either include all required logic for the query or return a small result set that can be further processed with local resources.

M Query examples

The M query language includes hundreds of functions and several books have been written about to its application. The greater purpose of this chapter is to understand M queries in the context of a corporate Power BI solution that primarily leverages an IT-managed data warehouse. As shown in the examples shared in the *M Queries* section earlier, the combination of a mature data warehouse and a layer of SQL view objects within this source may eliminate any need for further data transformations. However, Power BI Dataset designers should still be familiar with the fundamentals of M queries and their most common use cases, as it's often necessary to further extend and enhance source data.

The following sections demonstrate three common data transformation scenarios that can be implemented in M. Beyond retrieving the correct results, the M queries also generate SQL statements for execution by the source system via query folding, and comments are included for longer-term maintenance purposes.

 If you're new to M query development, you can create a blank query from the **Other category of data source connectors** available within the **Get Data** dialog. Alternatively, you can duplicate an existing query via the right-click context menu of a query in the Power Query Editor and then rename and revise the duplicate query.

Trailing three years filter

The objective of this example is to retrieve dates from three years prior to the current year through the current date. For example, on October 18th, 2017, the query should retrieve January 1st, 2014 through October 18th, 2017. This requirement ensures that three full years of historical data, plus the current year, is always available to support reporting.

The starting date and current date values for the filter condition are computed via `Date` and `DateTime` M functions and assigned variables names (`StartDate`, `CurrentDate`). Since the starting date will always be on January 1st, it's only necessary to compute the starting year and pass this value to the `#date` constructor. Finally, the two date variables are passed to the `Table.SelectRows()` function to implement the filter on the `Reseller Sales` fact table view:

```
let
//Trailing Three Year Date Values
    CurrentDate = DateTime.Date(DateTime.LocalNow()),
    StartYear = Date.Year(CurrentDate)-3,
```

```
        StartDate = #date(StartYear,1,1),
    //Reseller Sales View
        Source = AdWorksSQLServer,
        ResellerSales = Source{[Schema = "BI", Item =
    "vFact_ResellerSales"]}[Data],
    //Trailing Three Year Filter
        FilterResellerSales =
            Table.SelectRows(ResellerSales, each [Order Date] >= StartDate
    and [Order Date] <= CurrentDate)
    in
        FilterResellerSales
```

As shown in the **View Native Query** dialog available in the **Applied Steps** window of the Power Query Editor, the custom filter condition is translated into a T-SQL statement for the source SQL Server database to execute:

```
from [BI].[vFact ResellerSalesXL CCI] as [_]
where [_].[Order Date] >= convert(datetime2, '2014-01-01 00:00:00') and [_].[Order Date] <= convert(datetime2, '2017-10-18 00:00:00')
```

Query Folding of three-year filter condition

Note that the order of the variables in the expression doesn't impact the final query. For example, the two `Reseller Sales` view variables could be specified prior to the three date variables and the final `FilterResellerSales` variable would still generate the same SQL query. Additionally, be advised that M is a case-sensitive language. For example, referencing the variable defined as `StartDate` via the name `Startdate` will result in a failure.

 Single-line comments can be entered in M queries following the double forward slash (//) characters per the trailing three years example. Multiline or delimited comments start with the (/*) characters and end with the (*/) characters, just like T-SQL queries for SQL Server.

If the requirement was only to retrieve the trailing three years of data relative to the current date (for example, October 18th, 2014 through October 18th, 2017) the `StartDate` variable could be computed via the `Date.AddYears()` function, as follows:

```
    //Trailing three years (e.g. October 18th, 2014 through October 18,
    2017)
        CurrentDate = DateTime.Date(DateTime.LocalNow()),
        StartDate = Date.AddYears(CurrentDate,-3)
```

Customer history column

In this example, the goal is to add a column to the customer dimension table that groups the customers into four categories based on the date of their first purchase. Specifically, the new column needs to leverage the existing first purchase date column and assign the customer rows to one of the following four categories—First Year Customer, Second Year Customer, Third Year Customer, Legacy Customer. Since the column will be computed daily with each scheduled refresh, it will be used by the sales and marketing teams to focus their efforts on new and older customer segments.

A combination of date functions and conditional logic (if..then..else) is used with the Table.AddColumn() function to produce the new column:

```
let
// Customer History Date Bands
    CurrentDate = DateTime.Date(DateTime.LocalNow()),
    OneYearAgo = Date.AddYears(CurrentDate,-1),
    TwoYearsAgo = Date.AddYears(CurrentDate,-2),
    ThreeYearsAgo = Date.AddYears(CurrentDate,-3),
//Customer Dimension
    Source = AdWorksSQLServer,
    Customer = Source{[Schema = "BI", Item = "vDim_Customer"]}[Data],
    CustomerHistoryColumn = Table.AddColumn(Customer, "Customer
History Segment",
    each
    if [Customer First Purchase Date] >= OneYearAgo then "First Year
Customer"
    else if [Customer First Purchase Date] >= TwoYearsAgo and
[Customer First Purchase Date] < OneYearAgo then "Second Year
Customer"
    else if [Customer First Purchase Date] >= ThreeYearsAgo and
[Customer First Purchase Date] < TwoYearsAgo then "Third Year
Customer"
else "Legacy Customer", type text)
in
    CustomerHistoryColumn
```

As shown in the following image from the Power Query Editor, the `Customer History Segment` produces one of four text values based on the `Customer First Purchase Date` column:

Customer History Segment column in Power Query Editor

In this example, the customer `Alan Zheng` falls into the `Third Year Customer` segment since his first purchase date (10/20/2014) is after 10/18/2014 - three years prior to the current date (10/18/2017). When the dataset is refreshed on 10/21/2017, `Alan Zheng` will be re-classified as a `Legacy Customer` by the `Customer History Segment` column since his first purchase date will be more than three years old at that time.

Like the previous M query example of a trailing three year filter, the conditional logic for the derived customer column is also translated into T-SQL via query folding:

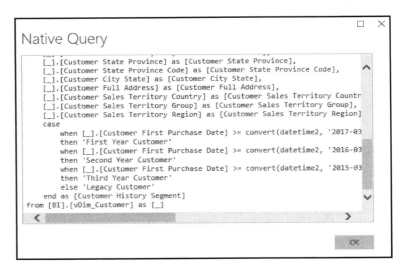

Native SQL Query generated by Customer M Query

> The two dynamic columns (`Calendar Year Status`, `Calendar Month Status`) included in the date dimension SQL view earlier in this chapter could also be computed via M functions.

Derived column data types

The final parameter to the `Table.AddColumn()` function is optional but should be specified to define the data type of the new column. In the customer history column example, the new column is defined as a text data type. If a whole number column was created, an `Int64.Type` would be specified, such as the following example:

```
MyNewColumn = Table.AddColumn(Product, "My Column", each 5,
Int64.Type)
```

If the data type of the column is not defined in the `Table.AddColumn()` function or later in the query via the `Table.TransformColumnTypes()` function, the new column will be set as an **Any** data type, as shown in the following screenshot:

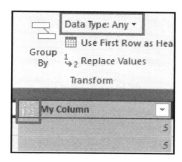

Data Type of Any

Columns of the **Any** data type will be loaded to the data model as a text data type. Dataset designers should ensure that each column in every query has a data type specified. In other words, the **Any** (that is, unknown) data type should not be allowed in M queries.

Product dimension integration

The SQL view for the product dimension referenced earlier in this chapter contained the following four operations:

1. Join the `Product`, `ProductSubcategory`, and `ProductCategory` dimension tables into a single query
2. Create a custom product category group column (for example, `Bikes` versus `Non-Bikes`)
3. Apply report-friendly column names with spaces and proper casing
4. Replace any null values in the `Product Subcategory` and `Product Category` columns with the `'Undefined'` value

Like almost all operations available to SQL `SELECT` queries, the same query can also be created via M functions. If the SQL view for the product dimension cannot be created within the data source, the following M query produces the same results:

```
let
    Source = AdWorksSQLServer,
//Product Dimension Table Views
    Product = Source{[Schema = "BI", Item = "vDim_Products"]}[Data],
    ProductSubCat = Source{[Schema = "BI", Item =
"vDim_ProductSubcategory"]}[Data],
    ProductCat = Source{[Schema = "BI", Item =
"vDim_ProductCategory"]}[Data],

//Product Outer Joins
    ProductJoinSubCat =
Table.NestedJoin(Product,"ProductSubcategoryKey",ProductSubCat,"Produc
tSubcategoryKey","ProductSubCatTableCol",JoinKind.LeftOuter),
    ProductJoinSubCatCol =
Table.ExpandTableColumn(ProductJoinSubCat,"ProductSubCatTableCol",{"En
glishProductSubcategoryName","ProductCategoryKey"},{"Product
Subcategory", "ProductCategoryKey"}),

    ProductJoinCat =
Table.NestedJoin(ProductJoinSubCatCol,"ProductCategoryKey",ProductCat,
"ProductCategoryKey","ProductCatTableCol",JoinKind.LeftOuter),
    ProductJoinCatCol =
Table.ExpandTableColumn(ProductJoinCat,"ProductCatTableCol",{"EnglishP
roductCategoryName"},{"Product Category"}),

//Select and Rename Columns
    ProductDimCols =
Table.SelectColumns(ProductJoinCatCol,{"ProductKey","ProductAlternateK
```

```
ey","EnglishProductName","Product Subcategory","Product Category"}),
    ProductDimRenameCols = Table.RenameColumns(ProductDimCols,{
        {"ProductKey", "Product Key"},{"ProductAlternateKey","Product
Alternate Key"},{"EnglishProductName","Product Name"}
    }),

//Product Category Group Column
    ProductCatGroupCol = Table.AddColumn(ProductDimRenameCols,"Product
Category Group", each
        if [Product Category] = "Bikes" then "Bikes"
        else if [Product Category] = null then "Undefined"
        else "Non-Bikes"
,type text),

//Remove Null Values
    UndefinedCatAndSubcat =
Table.ReplaceValue(ProductCatGroupCol,null,"Undefined",Replacer.Replac
eValue,{"Product Subcategory","Product Category"})
in
    UndefinedCatAndSubcat
```

The three product dimension tables in the dbo schema of the data warehouse are referenced from the `AdWorksSQLServer` staging query described earlier in this chapter.

The `Table.NestedJoin()` function is used to execute the equivalent of the LEFT JOIN operations from the SQL View, and the `Table.ExpandTableColumn()` function extracts and renames the required `Product Subcategory` and `Product Category` columns. Following the selection and renaming of columns, the `Product Category` group column is created via a conditional expression within the `Table.AddColumn()` function. Finally, the `Table.ReplaceValue()` function replaces any null values in the `Product Category` and `Product Subcategory` columns with the `'Undefined'` text string. The Power Query Editor provides a preview of the results:

Power Query Editor preview of Product M Query

Despite the additional steps and complexity of this query relative to the previous M query examples (trailing three years filter, Customer History Segment column), the entire query is translated into a single SQL statement and executed by the source SQL Server database. The **View Native Query** option in the **Applied Steps** pane of the Power Query Editor reveals the specific syntax of the SQL statement generated via query folding:

```
Native Query

select [_].[ProductKey] as [Product Key],
    [_].[ProductAlternateKey] as [Product Alternate Key],
    [_].[EnglishProductName] as [Product Name],
    case
        when [_].[EnglishProductSubcategoryName] is null
        then 'Undefined'
        else [_].[EnglishProductSubcategoryName]
    end as [Product Subcategory],
    case
        when [_].[EnglishProductCategoryName] is null
        then 'Undefined'
        else [_].[EnglishProductCategoryName]
    end as [Product Category],
    case
        when [_].[EnglishProductCategoryName] = 'Bikes' and [_].[EnglishProductCategoryName] is not null
        then 'Bikes'
        when [_].[EnglishProductCategoryName] is null
        then 'Undefined'
        else 'Non-Bikes'
    end as [Product Category Group]
from
```

Part of Native Query generated from Product M Query

Note that a dedicated SQL view object in the BI schema (for example, BI.vDim_ProductSubcategory) is accessed for each of the three product dimension tables. Per the SQL views section earlier in this chapter, it's recommended to always access SQL views from Power BI datasets, as this declares a dependency with the source tables.

Note that the `Table.Join()` function could not be used in this scenario given the requirement for a left outer join and the presence of common column names. With a left outer join, the presence of common column names, such as `ProductSubcategoryKey` or `ProductCategoryKey`, for the tables in the join operation would cause an error. Additionally, although a left outer join is the default behavior of the `Table.NestedJoin()` function, it's recommended to explicitly specify the join kind (for example, `JoinKind.Inner`, `JoinKind.LeftOuter`, `JoinKind.LeftAnti`) as per the `ProductJoinSubCat` and `ProductJoinCat` variables of the M query.

Whenever any unstructured or business-user-owned data sources are used as sources for a Power BI dataset, it's usually appropriate to implement additional data quality and error-handling logic within the M query. For example, a step that invokes the `Table.Distinct()` function could be added to the `Sales and Margin Plan` query that retrieves from the Excel workbook to remove any duplicate rows. Additionally, the third parameter of the `Table.SelectColumns()` function (for example, `MissingField.UseNull`) can be used to account for scenarios in which source columns have been renamed or removed.

M editing tools

Power BI Desktop stores the M code for queries created via the Power Query Editor graphical interface or the Advanced Editor within M documents for repeatable execution. Similar to other languages and project types, code editing tools are available to support the development, documentation, and version control of M queries. Dataset designers can use Visual Studio or Visual Studio Code to author and manage the M queries for Power BI and other Microsoft projects. These tools include common development features, such as IntelliSense, syntax highlighting, and integrated source control.

Advanced Editor

In Power BI Desktop, the M code for each query can be accessed from the Advanced Editor window within the Power Query Editor. With the Power Query Editor open, select a query of interest from the list of queries on the left and click on the Advanced Editor icon from the **Home** tab to access the following window:

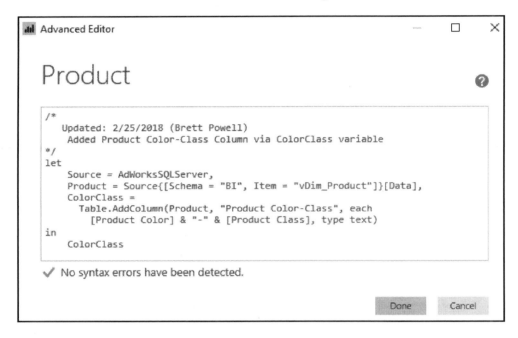

Advanced Editor in Power BI Desktop

As of the October 2017 release of Power BI Desktop, the Advanced Editor is limited to checking the syntax of the query. The colorization or highlighting of keywords, surrounding detection, and IntelliSense features available to DAX expressions is not yet available in Power BI Desktop. Given the importance of M queries to Power BI projects, as well as SQL Server Analysis Services 2017 and other Microsoft applications, external M editing tools, such as Visual Studio Code, are frequently used by dataset designers.

Experienced M query authors will often use the data transformation icons available in the Power Query Editor to quickly produce an initial version of one or a few of the requirements of the query. The author then uses the Advanced Editor or an external M editing tool to analyze the M code generated by the Power Query Editor and can revise or enhance this code, such as by changing variable names or utilizing optional parameters of certain M functions.

For the most common and simple data transformation tasks, such as filtering out rows based on one value of a column (for example, `State = "Kansas"`), the M code generated by the Power Query Editor usually requires minimal revision. For more complex queries with custom or less common requirements, the Power Query Editor graphical interface is less helpful and a greater level of direct M development is necessary.

Visual Studio Code

Visual Studio Code is a free, lightweight code-editing tool from Microsoft that's available on all platforms (Windows, Mac, Linux). Power Query M Language is an extension to Visual Studio Code that provides code-editing support for M queries, as shown in the following screenshot:

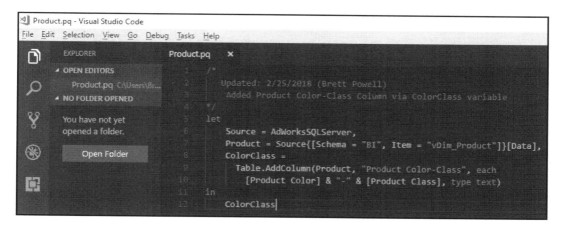

M Query in Visual Studio Code

In this example, the same `Internet Sales` query viewed in the Advanced Editor of Power BI Desktop has been copied into a Visual Studio code file and saved with a (`.pq`) file extension. Once saved in a supported file extension, code-editing features, such as colorization, auto-closing, and surrounding detection, are applied. M query files can be opened and saved with the following four file extensions—`.m`, `.M`, `.pq`, and `.PQ`.

 Since the `.pq` file extension is used by the Power Query SDK for Visual Studio, as described in the following section, this file extension is recommended for storing M queries.

In the initial release of the extension (v 1.0.0), IntelliSense is limited to the terms within the query. Future updates will likely include IntelliSense support for the standard library of M functions and common M syntax, similar to the Power Query SDK for Visual Studio. To install the Power Query M Language extension for Visual Studio Code, open the Extensions Marketplace in Visual Studio Code (**View** | **Extensions**) and search for the name of the extension.

 Prior to the M extension for Visual Studio Code and the Power Query SDK for Visual Studio, M developers commonly utilized the free Notepad++ code editor application. Since M is not a standard supported language for this tool, developers would create a user-defined language by pasting or typing in a list of M functions and keywords. The following blog post from Lars Schreiber, MS MVP, walks through the M for Notepad++ setup process: `http://ssbi-blog.de/technical-topics-english/power-query-editor-using-notepad/`.

Visual Studio

For Visual Studio 2015 and 2017, the Power Query SDK can be used to create Data Connector and M query projects, as shown in the following screenshot:

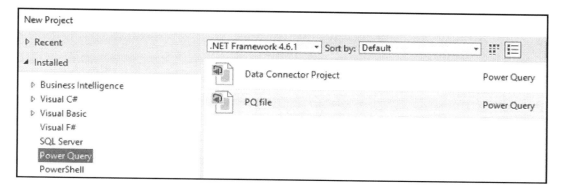

Power Query project types in Visual Studio

With a new PQ file solution and project in Visual Studio, the M queries of a Power BI dataset can be added as separate (.pq) files, as shown in the following screenshot:

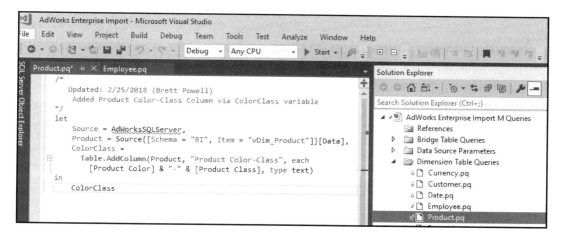

Power Query project in Visual Studio 2017

Unlike the extension for Visual Studio Code, the file extension types for Power Query projects are exclusive to (.pq). Most importantly, full M language Intellisense is supported, making it dramatically easier to find M functions relevant to specific data transformation operations. Moreover, unlike the extension for Visual Studio Code, M queries can be executed from within Visual Studio via the Power Query SDK for Visual Studio. To execute an M query in Visual Studio, such as in the preceding example, click the Start button on the toolbar (green play icon) or hit *F5*. You can also right-click the Power Query project (for example, AdWorks Enteprise Import) to configure properties of the M query project, such as the maximum output rows to return and whether native queries can be executed.

To install the Power Query SDK for Visual Studio, access the Visual Studio Marketplace (**Tools** | **Extensions and Updates**) and search for the name of the extension (Power Query SDK).

As per the lock icons next to the project files in the Solution Explorer window, the Power Query SDK for Visual Studio enables standard integration with source control and project management tools, such as **Team Foundation Server (TFS)** and **Visual Studio Team Services (VSTS)**.

Summary

In this chapter, we've covered all the components of the data retrieval process used to support the dataset for this project as described in Chapter 7, *Planning Power BI Projects*. This includes the layer of SQL views within a database source, source connectivity parameters in Power BI Desktop, and the M queries used to define and load the dimension and fact tables of the dataset. In constructing a data access layer and retrieval process for a dataset, we've also discussed the design considerations relative to import and DirectQuery datasets, Power BI Desktop configuration options, and data source privacy levels. Additionally, we've reviewed the core concepts of the M language, including query folding, item access, and data types. Moreover, we've reviewed three examples of efficiently implementing impactful data transformation logic via M queries as well as the tools for developing and editing M queries.

In the next chapter, we'll leverage the M queries and design techniques described in this chapter to create import and DirectQuery data models. Specifically, the dimension and fact table M queries will become the dimension and fact tables of the data model, and relationships will be defined to form multiple star schemas. Additionally, the bridge table M queries will be used to support the analysis of historical sales and margin results versus the annual sales and margin plan.

9
Designing Import and DirectQuery Data Models

This chapter utilizes the queries described in `Chapter 8`, *Connecting to Sources and Transforming Data with M,* to create both an import and a DirectQuery Data Model. Relationships are created between fact and dimension tables to enable business users to analyze the fact data for both `Internet Sales` and `Reseller Sales` simultaneously by using common dimension tables and across multiple business dates. A combination of relationships, bidirectional cross-filtering, and DAX measures will be used to support the analysis of actual sales data versus the Annual Sales and Margin Plan. Additionally, the product dimension table is enhanced with a hierarchy to enable simple drill up/down, and a custom sort order is applied to columns in the date dimension table.

This chapter also includes recommended practices for model metadata, such as data categories, and tips to improve the usability of Data Models, such as a simplified field list. Finally, we will review common performance analysis tools and optimization techniques for import and DirectQuery Data Models. As described in the *Dataset planning* section of `Chapter 7`, *Planning Power BI Projects*, a DirectQuery model relies on the data source of the dataset (for example, a SQL Server-relational database) to execute report queries while an import model loads (copies) the source data into a columnar compressed in-memory data store. The implications of this decision significantly influence many factors of Power BI solutions, such as modifications to data source systems to support DirectQuery datasets and the configuration of scheduled refresh processes to support import mode datasets.

In this chapter, we will review the following topics:

- Dataset objectives
- Views in Power BI Desktop
- Fact table design
- Relationships
- Hierarchies
- Custom sort orders
- Bidirectional cross-filtering
- Model metadata
- Performance optimization

Dataset layers

As we saw in Chapter 7, *Planning Power BI Projects*, and Chapter 8, *Connecting to Sources and Transforming Data with M*, Power BI datasets are composed of three tightly integrated layers, all included within a Power BI Desktop file. The M Queries described in Chapter 8, *Connecting to Sources and Transforming Data with M*, connect to data sources and optionally apply data cleansing and transformation processes to this source data to support the Data Model. The Data Model, the subject of this chapter, concerns the relationships defined between fact and dimension tables, hierarchies of related columns, and metadata properties that define default behaviors, such as the sorting of column values. The final layer of datasets discussed in Chapter 10, *Developing DAX Measures and Security Roles,* **Data Analysis Expressions** (**DAX**) Measures, leverages the Data Model (and thus the M Queries) to deliver analytical insights for presentation in Power BI and other tools.

The term *Data Model* is often used instead of dataset, particularly in the context of Analysis Services. Both Azure Analysis Services models and **SQL Server Analysis Services** (**SSAS**) models created in Tabular mode include the same three layers of Power BI datasets. In other contexts, however, *Data Model* refers exclusively to the relationships, measures, and metadata, but not the source queries. For this reason, and given the use of the term datasets in the Power BI service, the term dataset (and *dataset designer*) is recommended.

The following diagram summarizes the role of each of the three dataset layers:

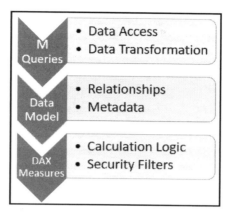

Three layers of datasets

At the **Data Model** layer, all data integration and transformations should be complete. For example, it should not be necessary to define data types or create additional columns at the **Data Model** level.

Ensure that each layer of the dataset is being used for its intended role. For example, DAX Measures should not contain complex logic, so as to avoid unclean or inaccurate data. Likewise, DAX Measure expressions should not be limited by incorrect data types (for example, a number stored as text) or missing columns on the date table. Dataset designers and data source owners can work together to keep the analytical layers of datasets focused exclusively on analytics.

Dataset objectives

For both Power BI projects and longer-term deployments, it's critical to distinguish Power BI datasets from Power BI reports and dashboards. Although Power BI Desktop is used to develop both datasets and reports, a Power BI dataset is an SSAS Data Model internally. Similar to an SSAS Data Model developed and maintained by IT, the intent of the Power BI dataset is to provide a simplified layer for reporting and analysis and to embed corporate-approved logic and security. Power BI reports, which are also saved as `.pbix` files, will only connect to the dataset and thus will exclusively leverage Power BI Desktop's visualization features, such as **Bookmarks** and **Slicer** visuals.

As per `Chapter 7`, *Planning Power BI Projects*, datasets and reports are also associated with unique technical and non-technical skills. A Power BI report developer, for example, should understand visualization standards, the essential logic and structure of the dataset, and how to distribute this content via Power BI Apps.

However, the report developer doesn't necessarily need to know any programming languages and can iterate very quickly on reports and dashboards. A Power BI dataset designer, conversely, must have a fundamental knowledge of DAX and is very well served by the M (Power Query) language and standard SQL. Additionally, the dataset designer is not able to iterate as quickly as the report developer given the technical dependencies within a dataset and the longer-term objectives for the dataset.

Given that the dataset serves as the bridge between data sources and analytical queries, it's important to proactively evaluate datasets relative to longer-term objectives. Large, consolidated datasets should be designed to support multiple teams and projects and to provide a standard version or definition of core metrics. Although organizations may enable business users to create datasets for specific use cases, corporate BI solutions should not utilize datasets like individual reports for projects or teams.

The following table summarizes the primary objectives of datasets and identifies the questions that can be used to evaluate a dataset in relation to each objective:

Objective	Success criteria
User interface	How difficult is it for business users to build a report from scratch? Are users able to easily find the measures and columns needed?
Version control	Do our measures align with an official, documented definition? Are we reusing the same dimensions across multiple business processes?
Data security	Have we implemented and thoroughly tested **Row-level security (RLS)** roles? Are we using **Azure Activity Directory (AAD)** security groups to implement security?
Performance	Are users able to interact with reports at the speed of thought? Are our core DAX Measures efficient and utilizing all CPU cores available?
Scalability	Can the dataset support additional business processes and/or history? Can the dataset support additional users and workloads?
Analytics	Does the dataset deliver advanced insights (out of the box)? Are any local (report-level) measures or complex filters being used?
Availability	How confident are we in the data sources and data retrieval process? Are there dependencies we can remove or potential errors we can trap?
Manageability	How difficult is it to implement changes or to troubleshoot issues? Can existing data transformation and analytical logic be consolidated?

Several of the objectives are self-explanatory, but others, such as availability and manageability, are sometimes overlooked. For example, the same business logic may be built into many individual DAX Measures, making the dataset more difficult to maintain as requirements change. Additionally, there may be certain hardcoded dependencies within the M Queries that could cause a dataset refresh to fail. Dataset designers and BI teams must balance the needs to deliver business value quickly while not compromising the sustainability of the solution.

To simplify individual measures and improve manageability, common logic can be built into a small subset of hidden DAX Measures. The DAX Measures visible in the fields list can reference these hidden measures and thus will automatically update if any changes are necessary. This is very similar to parameters and data source staging queries in M per Chapter 8, *Connecting to Sources and Transforming Data with M*. Examples of centralizing DAX logic are provided later in this chapter within the *Parameters table* section.

Competing objectives

As a dataset is expanded to support more dimension and fact tables, advanced analytics, and more business users, it can be necessary to compromise certain objectives to deliver others. A common example of this is the implementation of date intelligence measures. For instance, five DAX Measures with their own date intelligence calculation (for example, Year-to-Date, Prior Year-to-Date), may be created for each existing measure thus causing a dataset with 20 measures to contain 120 measures. Since Power BI does not currently support display folders for measures, this can negatively impact the usability or user interface objective. Another example is the performance of complex DAX Measures relative to the scale of the dataset. Advanced, statistical calculations can be embedded in datasets but performance is limited by the size of the dataset and the volume of users that utilize this logic.

A method or work-around for providing the essential effect of measure-display folders can be achieved with parameter tables. Essentially, an empty table can be loaded to the model with a table name that describes a type of DAX Measure. DAX Measures can then be assigned to this table via the **Home Table** property. See the *Parameter tables* section for additional details.

External factors

Just like any other database, a well-designed Power BI dataset can still fail to deliver its objectives due to external factors. For example, Power BI reports can be created that generate a wide and long table of many columns and many metrics. These data extracts and other dense visualizations that plot many different points are very resource-intensive relative to card- and summary-level chart visualizations. Additionally, even when the compression of an import mode dataset is maximized and the DAX Measures are efficient, there may be insufficient hardware resources available to support the given reporting workload. It's the responsibility of the Power BI admin, as described in Chapter 7, *Planning Power BI Projects*, and potentially any delegated capacity administrators to utilize the monitoring capabilities of Power BI and to provision the necessary resources to ensure sufficient performance.

The Data Model

The Data Model layer of the Power BI dataset consists of the Relationship View, the Data View, and the fields list exposed in the Report View. Each of the three views in Power BI Desktop is accessible via an icon in the top-left menu below the toolbar, although the Data View is exclusively available to import mode datasets.

The Relationships View

The Relationships View provides the equivalent of a database diagram specific to the tables loaded to the model for the dataset. The relationship lines distinguish the one, or parent, table of each relationship from the many, or child, table. A solid line indicates that the relationship is active, while a dotted line denotes an inactive relationship that can only be activated via the USERELATIONSHIP() DAX expression. Additionally, the arrow icons on the relationship lines advise whether cross-filtering is single-directional (one arrow → one way) or bidirectional (two arrows).

In the following screenshot from the Relationships View, only the `Reseller` to `Reseller Sales` relationship is bidirectional and the relationships between all tables displayed are active:

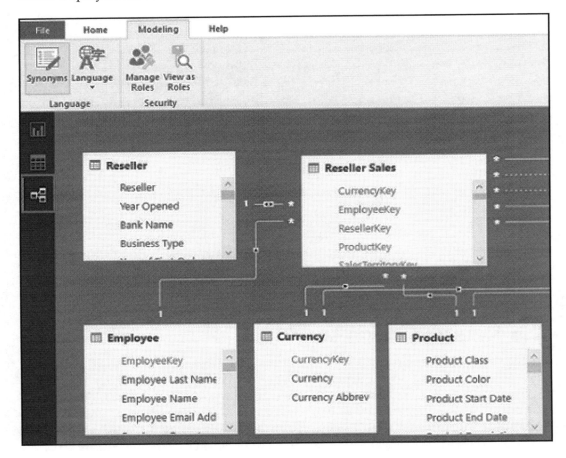

Relationships View

Given the bidirectional cross-filtering relationship, a filter applied to the `Employee` table would filter the `Reseller Sales` table and then also filter the `Reseller` dimension table. Double-clicking a relationship line prompts the Edit Relationship dialog to optionally modify the columns defining the relationship, the cross-filtering behavior (single or bidirectional), and whether the relationship is active or passive.

The bidirectional relationship between `Reseller` and `Reseller Sales` from this example is only intended to demonstrate the graphical representation of relationships in the Relationships View. Bidirectional relationships should only be applied in specific scenarios, as described in the *Bidirectional relationships* section later in this chapter.

A gray font indicates that the given column is not visible in the Report View. For certain tables that are only used for internal logic, such as bridge tables or measure support, the entire table will be grayed out and invisible to the Report View. Synonyms can only be accessed via the Relationships View and can serve to improve the accuracy of Power BI's Q & A natural language queries by associating terms with tables, columns, and measures of the Data Model.

The Data View

The Data View provides visibility to the imported rows for each table as well as important metadata, such as the count of rows and the distinct values for columns. In the following screenshot, the `Freight` column of the `Reseller Sales` table has been selected in the Data View, as indicated by the table icon on the far left:

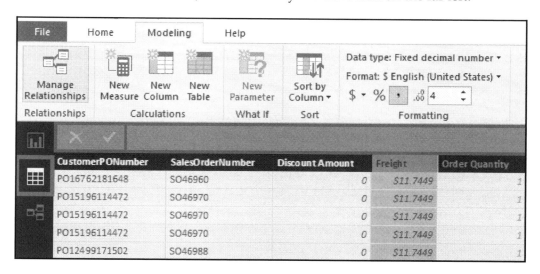

Data View

Metadata of the column and/or table selected is displayed at the bottom of the Data View window. For example, selecting the `Freight` column per the preceding image results in a status message noting 53,207 rows for the `Reseller Sales` table and 1,394 distinct values for the `Freight` column. If only the table name is selected from the fields list, only the count of rows imported to the table is displayed at the bottom.

> The count of rows, and particularly the count of distinct values in a column, is of critical importance to import mode datasets. Columns with many unique values, such as primary keys or highly precise numeric columns (that is, 3.123456), will consume much more memory. Additionally, as a columnar database, the columns with a larger memory footprint will also require more time to scan to resolve report queries.

DirectQuery datasets do not include Data View and thus common modeling features, such as setting the data format of columns and measures, can be accessed via the **Modeling** tab in the Report View. The dataset designer of a DirectQuery dataset would select the column or measure from the Fields list in the Report View and then access the relevant metadata property from the **Modeling** tab, such as **Data Category** and **Sort by Column**. The availability of Data View and its supporting metadata (for example, count of rows, discount count of values) is a modeling convenience of import mode datasets over DirectQuery datasets. In the absence of the Data View, DirectQuery modelers can use table report visuals on the Report View to sample or preview the values and formatting of columns and measures.

The Report View

The Report View is primarily used for developing visualizations, but it also supports modeling features, such as the creation of user-defined hierarchies. In the following screenshot of a DirectQuery dataset, the `Customer City` column of the `Customer` table is selected from the fields list:

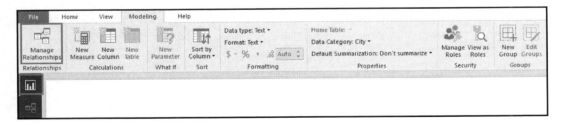

Modeling options in Report View

The **Data Category** and **Default Summarization** properties for the `Customer City` column have been set to **City** and **Don't summarize**, respectively. The **Modeling** tab of the Report View provides both import and DirectQuery datasets with access to all common modeling features, such as managing relationships, creating new DAX Measures, and accessing RLS roles.

Note that the **New Table** option is grayed out for DirectQuery datasets since DAX-calculated tables are exclusively able to import models. However, as explained in both the chapters `Chapter 7`, *Planning Power BI Projects* and `Chapter 8`, *Connecting to Sources and Transforming Data with M*, DAX-calculated columns and tables should be rarely used. M queries, SQL views, and data warehouse objects are almost always preferable alternatives to support the needed columns and tables.

In terms of data modeling, the Relationships View and the following **Manage relationships** dialog are the most fundamental interfaces as these definitions impact the behavior of DAX Measures and report queries:

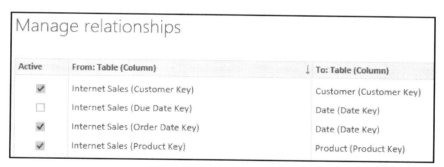

Manage relationships dialog

Relationships can be created, edited, and deleted from the **Manage relationships** dialog. For larger models with many tables and relationships, the dataset designer can utilize both the Manage relationships dialog and the Relationships View.

Dynamic Management Views (DMVs), such as TMSCHEMA_RELATIONSHIPS, can be used to analyze Power BI datasets, just as they're used with other SQL Server products. To get started, simply open the DAX Studio application while the Power BI Desktop (PBIX) file is open and connect to the running dataset. You can then query the DMVs (that is, select * from $SYSTEM.TMSCHEMA_RELATIONSHIPS). For longer-term projects, it can be worthwhile to create a Power BI dataset that exclusively retrieves from DMVs data and supports updated documentation reports, such as the tables, columns, and measure definitions included in a dataset. An example of this is included in the *Microsoft Power BI Cookbook* (https://www. packtpub.com/big-data-and-businessintelligence/microsoft-power-bi-cookbook).

Fact tables

There are three fact tables for this dataset—Internet Sales, Reseller Sales, and the Sales and Margin Plan. The ability to analyze and filter two or all three of these tables concurrently via common dimensions, such as Date, Product, and Sales Territory, is what gives this dataset its analytical value to the business. A Power BI report, which is always connected to a single dataset, could contain visualizations comparing total Adventure Works Sales (Internet Sales plus Reseller Sales) to the overall Sales and Margin Plan. This same report could also include detailed visualizations that explain higher-level outcomes, such as the growth in online customers or changes in the Reseller Sales margin rates:

	SHARED DIMENSIONS							
BUSINESS PROCESSES	Currency	Customer	Date	Employee	Product	Promotion	Reseller	Sales Territory
Internet Sales	✔	✔	✔		✔	✔		✔
Reseller Sales	✔		✔	✔	✔	✔	✔	✔
Sales and Margin Plan			✔		✔			✔

Data Warehouse Bus Matrix

Each checkmark symbol represents the existence of a relationship implemented either directly between the fact and dimension tables in the Data Model or, in the case of the Sales and Margin Plan, via bridge tables. See Chapter 7, *Planning Power BI Projects*, for more details on the Data Warehouse Bus Matrix.

The `Sales and Margin Plan` is at a lower grain than the `Internet Sales` and `Reseller Sales` fact tables and thus cannot be filtered directly by columns such as `Product Name`. For the `Sales and Margin Plan` fact table, an alternative model design, including bridge tables and conditional DAX Measures, is used to support cross-filtering from the Product, Sales Territory, and Date dimension tables. See the *Bridge tables* section later in this chapter for more details.

Fact table columns

Fact tables should only contain columns that are needed for relationships to dimension tables and numeric columns that are referenced by DAX Measures. In some models, an additional column that isn't modeled in a dimension table and is needed for analysis, such as `Sales Order Number`, may also be included in a fact table.

Given their size and central role in the dataset, fact tables receive much greater analysis to deliver optimal performance and scalability.

In the following T-SQL query of the `Reseller Sales` source fact table, columns are computed that produce the same values as the `ExtendedAmount`, `SalesAmount`, and `TotalProductCost` columns:

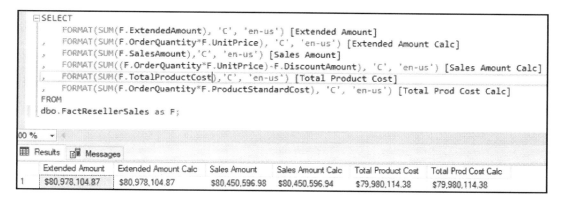

Reseller Sales fact column logic

Only the `UnitPrice`, `OrderQuantity`, `DiscountAmount`, and `ProductStandardCost` columns are needed for the import mode dataset since DAX Measures can be written to embed the necessary logic (for example, `UnitPrice *` `OrderQuantity`) for the `ExtendedAmount`, `SalesAmount`, and `TotalProductCost` columns. By not importing these columns to the Data Model, a significant amount of data storage is saved and query performance is not compromised. Columns with few unique values, such as `OrderQuantity`, can be highly compressed by import mode datasets and thus are lightweight to store and fast to scan to resolve report queries.

> The same three columns can also be removed from the `Internet Sales` fact table. The `SUMX()` function will be used in the DAX Measures and only reference the source columns (`OrderQuantity`, `UnitPrice`, and `ProductStandardCost`).

> The $0.04 difference between the sum of the `Sales Amount` column and the `Sales Amount Calc` expression is caused by the `DiscountAmount` column being stored as a float (approximate) data type. In almost every scenario, a variance this small ($.04 out of $80.4 M) is acceptable to obtain the scalability benefit of not importing a fact table column.

If the SQL View for the fact table is exclusively utilized by this dataset, then the three columns can be removed there. If the SQL View cannot be modified, then the three columns can be removed via the M Query for the fact table, as shown in the following screenshot:

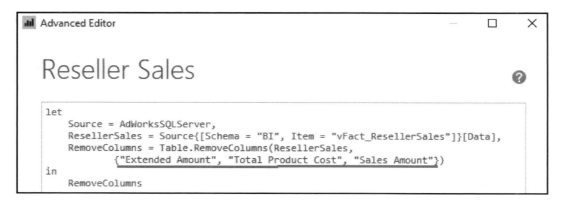

Fact table columns excluded from the dataset

As shown in the previous screenshot, the `Table.RemoveColumns()` function excludes three columns from the source SQL View, as these columns only represent derived values from other columns that are included in the query. Therefore, for an import mode dataset, DAX Measures can be written to efficiently implement these simple calculations via the source columns, such as `Unit Price` and `Order Quantity`. However, for a DirectQuery dataset, these derived columns (for example, `Total Product Cost`) would not be removed due to the performance advantage of the `SUM()` SQL expressions referencing individual columns. The following chapter contains details on implementing these DAX measures and other measure expressions.

Fact column data types

It's essential that the numeric columns of fact tables are assigned to the appropriate data types. All integer columns, such as `Order Quantity`, should be stored as a whole number data type, and decimal numbers will be stored as either fixed decimal numbers or as decimal numbers. If four decimal places is sufficient precision, a **Fixed decimal number** type should be used to avoid rounding errors and the additional storage and performance costs of the decimal number type.

In the following screenshot, the `Freight` column is stored as a **Fixed decimal number** type and, thus, despite a format of six decimal places, only four significant digits are displayed to the right of the decimal place:

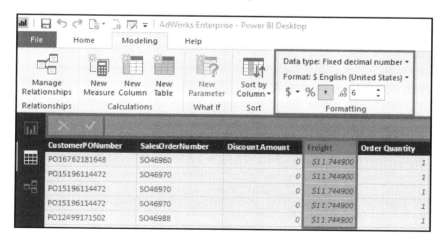

Fixed decimal number data type

Dataset designers should check the numeric columns of fact tables and ensure that the appropriate data type has been assigned for each column. For example, certain scientific columns may require the deep precision available for decimal number types (15 significant digits), while accounting or financial columns generally need to be exact and thus the internal (19, 4) data type of a **Fixed decimal number** type is appropriate. Note that the result of aggregated expressions against this fixed decimal column will be a number of the same type and, therefore, to avoid overflow calculation errors, will also need to fit the (19, 4) data type. The *Data types* section in Chapter 8, *Connecting to Sources and Transforming Data with M* provides details on the relationship between M data types and data types in the Data Model, as well as the function for converting column types in M Queries.

The Data View from the **Fixed decimal number** data type image is not available for DirectQuery datasets. For DirectQuery datasets, the data types of columns should be set and managed at the data source table level such that Power BI only reflects these types. Revising data types during report query execution, either via SQL views in the data source or the M Queries in Power BI, can significantly degrade the performance of DirectQuery datasets.

Fact-to-dimension relationships

To create the Data Model relationships identified in the Data Warehouse Bus Matrix image:

1. Click **Manage Relationships** from the **Modeling** tab in Report View.

2. From the **Manage Relationships** dialog, click the **New** command button at the bottom to open the **Create relationship** interface. Choose the fact table, such as Internet Sales, for the top table via the dropdown and then select the dimension table as shown in the following screenshot:

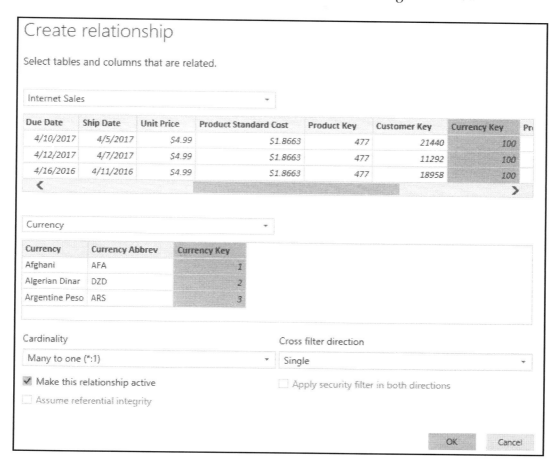

Creating a relationship for the import mode dataset

If the relationship columns have the same name, such as `Currency Key` in this example, Power BI will automatically select the columns to define the relationship. Almost all relationships will follow this **Many to one(*:1)** or fact-to-dimension pattern with the **Cross-filter direction** property set to **Single** and the relationship set to active.

The two columns used for defining each relationship should be of the same data type. In most relationships, both columns will be of the whole number data type as only a numeric value can be used with slowly changing dimensions. For example, a `Product Key` column could use the values 12, 17, and 27 to represent three time periods for a single product as certain attributes of the product changed over time.

Prior to the **Mark as Date Table** feature described in the previous chapter, a date column stored as a date data type was used for relationships in Power BI datasets as this enables the time intelligence functions of DAX to work correctly. Given this feature, however, whole number (integer) columns stored in YYYYMMDD format (for example, 20180225 for February 25th, 2018) can be used for fact-to-date table relationships in Power BI datasets. Details on utilizing this feature and other considerations for date dimension tables are included within the *SQL views* section of `Chapter 8`, *Connecting to Sources and Transforming Data with M*.

As more relationships are created, it can be helpful to switch to the Relationships view and move or organize the dimension tables around the fact table. Relationships view can make it clear when additional relationships need to be defined and can be useful in explaining the model to report authors and users.

Click **OK** to create the relationship and repeat this process to build the planned star schema relationships for both the `Internet Sales` and `Reseller Sales` fact tables, as shown in the following screenshot of `Internet Sales`:

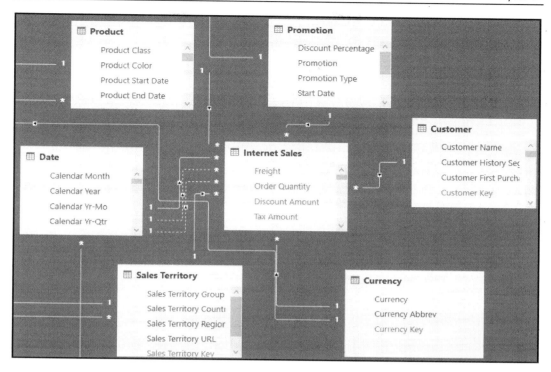

Internet Sales relationships

All relationships from `Internet Sales` to a dimension table are active (solid line) except for two additional relationships to the Date dimension table. In this dataset, the `Order Date` is used as the active relationship, but two additional inactive (dotted line) relationships are created based on the `Due Date` and `Ship Date` columns of the fact table. DAX Measures can be created to invoke these alternative relationships via the `USERELATIONSHIP()` DAX function, as shown in the following example:

```
Internet Net Sales (Due Date) =
CALCULATE([Internet Net Sales], USERELATIONSHIP('Internet Sales'[Due
Date Key],'Date'[Date Key]))

Internet Net Sales (Ship Date) =
CALCULATE([Internet Net Sales],USERELATIONSHIP('Internet Sales'[Ship
Date Key],'Date'[Date Key]))
```

The inactive relationships and their corresponding measures enable report visualizations based on a single-date dimension table, such as in the following table:

	2017-Jan	2017-Feb	2017-Mar	2017-Apr	2017-May	Total
Internet Net Sales	$1,130,732	$1,193,634	$1,405,413	$512,907	$549,225	**$4,791,911**
Internet Net Sales (Due Date)	$1,100,752	$1,155,753	$1,395,318	$814,995	$549,701	**$5,016,519**
Internet Net Sales (Ship Date)	$1,115,703	$1,183,442	$1,409,425	$682,072	$533,160	**$4,923,803**

Measures with active and inactive relationships

In this scenario, the `Internet Net Sales` measure uses the active relationship based on `Order Date` by default, but the other measures override this relationship via the `CALCULATE()` and `USERELATIONSHIP()` functions.

A common alternative approach to inactive relationships is to load additional date dimension tables and create active relationships for each additional date column on the fact table (for example, `Due Date`, `Ship Date`) to these tables. The columns for these additional date tables can be named to avoid confusion with other date columns (for example, `Ship Date Calendar Year`) and some teams or organizations are more comfortable with table relationships than DAX Measures. Additionally, this design allows for intuitive matrix-style visualizations with two separate date dimensions (`Ship Date`, `Order Date`) on the *x* and *y* axis filtering a single measure via active relationships.

For DirectQuery datasets, the **Assume referential integrity** relationship property is critical for performance as this determines whether inner- or outer-join SQL statements are generated to resolve report queries. When enabled, as shown in the following screenshot, inner-join SQL queries will be passed to the source system when report queries require columns or logic from both tables of the relationship:

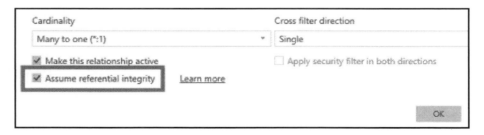

Assume referential integrity

If **Assume referential integrity** is not enabled, outer-join SQL queries will be generated to ensure that all necessary rows from the fact table or many sides of the relationship are retrieved to resolve the report query. The query optimizers within supported DirectQuery sources, such as SQL Server and Oracle, are able to produce much more efficient query execution plans when presented with inner-join SQL statements. Of course, improved performance is of no value if the outer join is necessary to return the correct results, thus it's essential for referential integrity violations in the source system to be addressed.

Bridge tables

For this dataset, bridge tables are used to link three dimension tables (`Sales Territory`, `Product`, and `Date`) to the `Sales and Margin Plan` fact table. As shown in the following screenshot from the Relationships View, the bridge tables are hidden from the fields list in the Report View (gray shading) and bidirectional cross-filtering is enabled between the dimension and bridge tables:

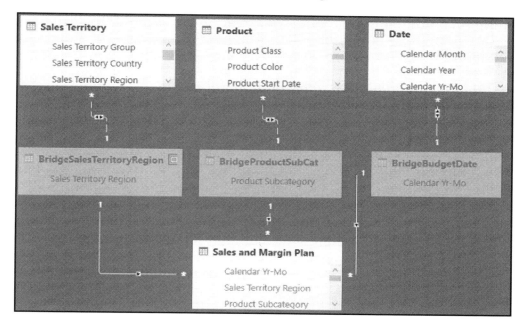

Bridge tables hidden from the Report View

The bidirectional relationships enable filter selections on the three dimension tables (Sales Territory, Product, and Date) to impact the Sales and Margin Plan fact table as well as the Internet Sales and Reseller Sales fact tables. Given the higher granularity of the dimension tables relative to the Sales and Margin Plan (for example, individual dates versus months), the bridge tables with distinct values (the one side) and bidirectional cross-filtering support the core requirement of analyzing historical sales data (Internet and Reseller Sales) versus the Sales and Margin Plan.

As described in the *Bridge Tables Queries* section of Chapter 8, *Connecting to Sources and Transforming Data with M*, a Table.Distinct() M function can be used against the column from the given dimension table query that aligns with the granularity of the Sales and Margin Plan table.

For example, the Sales and Margin Plan fact table contains rows per Product Subcategory, thus the Product Subcategory bridge table contains one row for each unique Product Subcategory value via the following M expression:

```
let
    SubCats = Table.SelectColumns(Product, {"Product Subcategory"}),
    DistinctSubCats = Table.Distinct(SubCats)
in
    DistinctSubCats
```

The existing M Query for the Product dimension table, which references the data source staging query (AdWorksSQLServer) and the SQL view of the dimension (BI.vDim_Product), is leveraged by the bridge table query. The M Queries for the bridge tables generate simple SQL statements ("Select Distinct..") for execution by the source system. Additionally, with the **Include in report refresh** query property set to true, any new dimension values are automatically retrieved into the dataset.

Parameter tables

Unlike the bridge tables, there are no relationships between the four parameter tables and any other tables in the model, as shown in the following screenshot from the Relationships View:

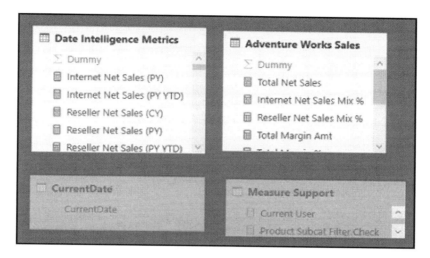

Parameter tables

Measure groups

The Date Intelligence and Adventure Works Sales tables only serve to provide an intuitive name for users to find related DAX Measures. For example, several of the most important DAX Measures of the dataset will include both Internet Sales and Reseller Sales. It wouldn't make sense for these consolidated measures, such as Total Net Sales, to be found under the Internet Sales or Reseller Sales fact tables in the field list.

For similar usability reasons, the Date Intelligence Metrics provides an intuitive name for users and report developers to find measures, such as year-to-date, prior year-to-date, and year-over-year growth. The two parameter tables, Date Intelligence Metrics and Adventure Works Sales, effectively serve as display folders, as shown in the following screenshot of the Fields list from the Report View:

Fields list with parameter tables

To obtain the calculator symbol icon in the fields list, all columns have to be hidden from the Report View and at least one DAX Measure must reference the table in its **Home Table** property. Once these two conditions are met, the show/hide pane arrow of the fields list highlighted in the image can be clicked to refresh the fields list.

In this example, the Adventure Works Sales and Date Intelligence Metrics tables both contain only a single column (named Dummy) that can be hidden via the right-click context menu accessible in the Relationships View, the fields list of Report View, and for import datasets the Data View as well.

The columns of the three fact tables (Internet Sales, Reseller Sales, and Sales and Margin Plan) are also hidden to provide users with an intuitive display of groups of measures at the top of the fields list followed by dimensions and their hierarchies.

The **Home Table** for a measure can be set by selecting it from the fields list and choosing a table from the **Home Table** dropdown on the **Modeling** tab in the Report View. As shown in the following screenshot, the `Internet Net Sales (PY YTD)` measure is selected and `Date Intelligence Metrics` is configured as its home table:

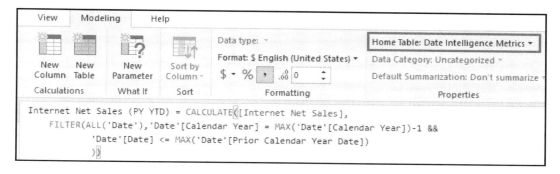

Home Table property for DAX Measures

Last refreshed date

The `CurrentDate` table, as described in the *Data Source Parameters* section of `Chapter 8`, *Connecting to Sources and Transforming Data with M*, contains only one column and one row, representing the date at the time the source M Query was executed. With this date value computed with each dataset refresh and loaded into the Data Model, a DAX Measure can be written to expose the date to the Power BI report visuals. In the following screenshot from the Report View, a measure named `Last Refresh Msg` uses a DAX variable to reference the parameter table and then passes this variable to a text string:

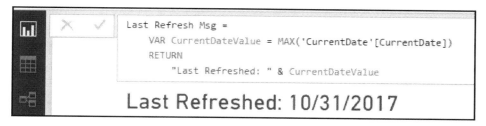

Last refreshed message via the parameter table

It's common to include a last refreshed text message on at least one report page of every published report. In the event the source dataset has failed to refresh for several days or longer, the text message will advise users of the issue. See Chapter 10, *Developing DAX Measures and Security Roles* for more information on DAX variables.

For DirectQuery datasets, the M Query for the CurrentDate parameter table uses standard SQL syntax within the Value.NativeQuery() function, such as the following:

```
let Source = AdWorksSQLServer,
    View =   Value.NativeQuery(Source, "Select CAST(Current_Timestamp
as date) as [CurrentDate]")
in  View
```

The Source variable references the AdWorksSQLServer staging query, as described in the previous chapter. The *Data Source Parameters* section of Chapter 8, *Connecting to Sources and Transforming Data with M*, contains the M Query for the CurrentDate parameter table in the import mode datasets.

Measure support logic

The purpose of the Measure Support table is to centralize DAX expressions that can be reused by other measures. Since DAX variables are limited to the scope of individual measures, a set of hidden, intermediate measures avoids the need to declare variables for each measure. The intermediate, or branching, DAX measure expressions also make it easy and less error-prone to implement a change as all dependent DAX measures will be updated automatically. In this way, the Measure Support table serves a similar function to the parameter and staging query expressions, described in the previous chapter, for M Queries.

For this dataset, DAX expressions containing the ISFILTERED() and ISCROSSFILTERED() functions can be used to determine the granularity of the filter context for the Product, Sales Territory, and Date dimension tables. If the user or report developer has applied a filter at a granularity not supported by the Sales and Margin Plan fact table, such as an individual product or date, a blank should be returned to avoid confusion and incorrect actual versus plan comparisons. The following DAX Measure tests the filter context of the Date dimension table and returns one of two possible text values—Plan Grain or Actual Grain:

```
Date Grain Plan Filter Test = SWITCH(TRUE(),
    NOT(ISCROSSFILTERED('Date')),"Plan Grain",
```

```
      ISFILTERED('Date'[Calendar Week in Year]) ||
   ISFILTERED('Date'[Date]) || ISFILTERED('Date'[Weekday])
   ||ISFILTERED('Date'[Calendar Yr-Wk]), "Actual Grain", "Plan Grain")
```

Similar filter test measures can be created for the `Sales Territory` and `Product` dimension tables. All three measures should be hidden from the Report View, and the **Home Table** property should be set to **Measure Support**. Once these dimension-specific measures have been defined, a final support measure can integrate their results, as shown in the following example:

```
Plan Grain Status = IF([Date Grain Plan Filter Test] = "Plan Grain" &&
[Product Grain Plan Filter Test] = "Plan Grain" && [Sales Territory
Grain Plan Filter Test] = "Plan Grain", "Plan Grain", "Actual Grain")
```

Given the logic built into the four hidden measure support expressions, DAX Measures can reference the results and deliver the intended conditional behavior in report visualizations, as shown in the following example of a variance-to-plan measure:

```
Internet Net Sales Var to Plan = IF([Plan Grain Status] = "Actual
Grain",BLANK(),
[Internet Net Sales] – [Internet Net Sales Plan Amt])
```

In the following report, the `Internet Net Sales Plan` and `Internet Net Sales Var to Plan` measures both return blank values when a product color or calendar year-week value has been selected from either slicer visual:

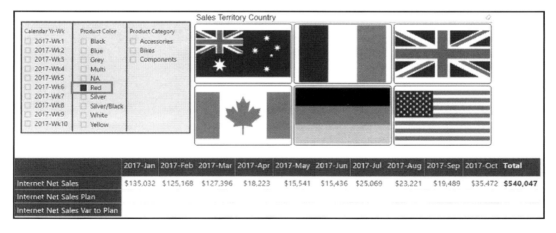

Sales and Margin Plan measures are blank due to the Product Color filter

The `Product Category` and `Sales Territory` country visuals do not cause the sales plan measures to return blank values since these columns are within the granularity of the `Sales and Margin Plan` fact table.

Relationships

Relationships play a central role in the analytical behavior and performance of the dataset. Based on the filters applied at the report layer and the DAX expressions contained in the measures, relationships determine the set of active rows for each table of the model to be evaluated. It's critical that the dataset designer understands how relationships drive report behavior via cross-filtering and the rules that relationships in Power BI must adhere to, such as uniqueness and non-ambiguity.

Uniqueness

Relationships in Power BI Data Models are always defined between a single column from each of the two tables. One of these two columns must uniquely identify the rows of its table, such as the `Currency Key` column from the `Currency` table in the *Fact-to-dimension relationships* section earlier in this chapter. Power BI will throw an error message if a row with a duplicate value for the relationship column is attempted to be loaded to the one side of the relationship, as shown in the following screenshot:

Apply query changes

 Currency
Column 'Currency Key' in Table 'Currency' contains a duplicate value '3' and this is not allowed for columns on the one side of a many-to-one relationship or for columns that are used as the primary key of a table.

Uniqueness enforced in relationships

Power BI and SSAS Tabular models do not enforce or require referential integrity as with relationship uniqueness, however. For example, a sales fact table can contain transactions for a customer that is not present in the customer dimension table. No error message will be thrown and DAX measures that sum the sales table will still result in the correct amount, including the new customer's transactions. A blank row is added to the customer dimension table by default for these scenarios (also known as early-arriving facts) and this row is visible when the measure is grouped by columns from the customer dimension table in report visualizations. If missing dimensions is an issue, the dataset designer can work with the data source owner and/or the data warehouse team to apply a standard foreign key value (for example, -1) to these new dimension members within an **extract-transform-load** (ETL) process and a corresponding row can be added to dimensions with an unknown value for each column.

In the rare event that a text column is used for a relationship, note that DAX is not case-sensitive like the M language. For example, M functions that remove duplicates, such as `Table.Distinct()`, may result in unique text values (from M's perspective), such as `Apple` and `APPLE`. When these values are loaded to the data model, they will be considered duplicates and thus relationships will not be allowed. To resolve this issue, a standard casing format can be applied to the column within a `Table.TransformColumns()` function via text functions, such as `Text.Proper()` and `Text.Upper()`. Removing duplicates after the standard casing transformation will result in a column of unique values for the data model.

Ambiguity

Data model relationships must result in a single, unambiguous filter path across the tables of the model. In other words, a filter applied to one table must follow a single path to filter another table—the filter context cannot branch off into multiple intermediate tables prior to filtering a final table. In the following screenshot from the Relationships View, only one of the two relationships to the `Auto Accidents` fact table is allowed to be active (solid line):

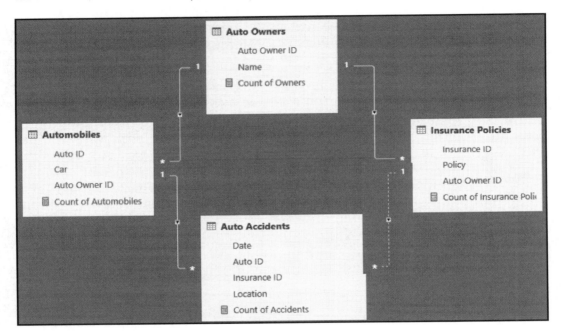

Ambiguous relationships avoided

When a filter is applied to the `Auto Owners` table, the inactive relationship between `Insurance Polices` and `Auto Accidents` provides a single, unambiguous filter path from `Auto Owners` to `Auto Accidents` via relationships with the `Automobiles` table. If the model author tries to set both relationships to the `Auto Accidents` table as active, Power BI will reject this relationship and advise of the ambiguity it would create, as shown in the following screenshot:

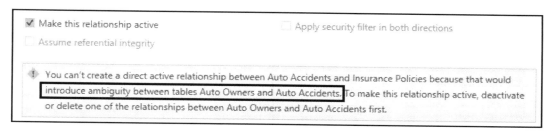

Ambiguity error in the Edit Relationship Dialog

Given the active relationship between the `Automobiles` and `Auto Accidents` tables, if the relationship between `Insurance Policies` and `Auto Accidents` was active, the `Auto Owners` table would have two separate paths to filter the `Auto Accidents` table (via `Insurance Policies` or via `Automobiles`).

Model metadata

The consistent and complete application of metadata properties, such as **Default Summarization** and **Data Category**, greatly affect the usability of a dataset. With a solid foundation of tables, column data types, and relationships in place, dataset designers and BI teams should consider all primary metadata properties and their implications for user experience as well as any additional functionality they can provide.

Visibility

Every table, column, and measure that isn't explicitly needed in the Report View should be hidden. This usually includes all relationship columns and any measure support tables and measure expressions.

If a column is rarely needed or only needed for a specific report, it can be temporarily unhidden to allow for this report to be developed and then hidden again to maximize usability. Numeric fact table columns that are referenced by DAX Measures (for example, quantity) should be hidden from the fields list, as the measures can be used for visualizing this data.

As discussed in the *Parameter tables* section, when all columns of a table are hidden from the Report View and at least one DAX Measure identifies the given table as its home table, a measure group icon (calculator symbol) will appear in the fields list. This clear differentiation between the measures and dimension columns (attributes) is recommended, especially if business users will be developing their own reports based on the dataset.

 Tables with both visible columns and measures will force business users and report developers to navigate between these different elements in the fields list. This can be onerous given the volume of DAX Measures for common fact tables. If it's necessary to expose one or a few fact table columns permanently, consider migrating some or all of the DAX Measures for the table to a parameter table to simplify navigation.

Column metadata

Dataset designers should review the columns of each table exposed to the Report View and ensure that appropriate metadata properties have been configured. These settings, including any custom sorting described earlier, only need to be applied once and can significantly improve the usability of the dataset.

Default Summarization

The **Default Summarization** property should be revised from Power BI's default setting to the **Do not summarize** value for all columns. Power BI will apply a **Default Summarization** setting of **Sum** for all columns with a numeric data type (whole number, fixed decimal number, decimal number) when a table is first loaded to the data model.

As shown in the following screenshot, a summation symbol (Σ) will appear next to the field name in the fields list if a **Default Summarization** other than **Do not Summarize** is enabled:

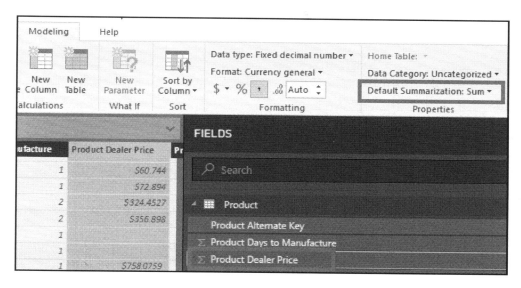

Default Summarization for numeric columns

As illustrated in the previous image, the **Default Summarization** property for a column can be accessed via the **Modeling** tab of the Data View. Additionally, as with other metadata properties, **Default Summarizaton** can also be accessed from the Report View. As mentioned in the *Data View* section earlier, implementing metadata changes, such as **Default Summarization** and **Data Category**, via the **Modeling** tab from the Report View is the only option for DirectQuery models.

If a user selects a column with **Default Summarization** enabled, the specific aggregation specified by the property (for example, **Sum**, **Average**) will be returned rather than the grouping behavior of **Do not summarize**. In many cases, the numeric column is only used to group measures, such as `Internet Net Sales` by `Product Dealer Price`, and DAX Measures can be written for any needed calculation logic. Additionally, **Default Summarization** can create confusion, such as when a user expects a sum aggregation based on the summation symbol but the model author has applied an alternative default summarization (for example, **Minimum**, **Average**). Alternatively, the names assigned to DAX measures, such as `Average Product Dealer Price`, make it clear which aggregation is being applied.

For these reasons, it's recommended to convert the default summarization setting to **Do not Summarize**. A broader concept of this recommendation is to build essential DAX Measure expressions into the dataset, as described in Chapter 10, *Developing DAX Measures and Security Roles,* to make Power BI datasets more flexible and powerful for users and report developers.

Data format

The default formatting Power BI applies to columns and measures should also be revised to a corporate standard or a format applicable to the column or measure. For example, the default full date format of 'Friday July 1, 2011' can be revised to the more compact (mm/dd/yyyy) format of 7/1/2011. Likewise, the currency format for measures calculating financial data can be revised to display two decimal places and the thousands separator can be added to numeric measures.

Business users and report developers do not have the ability to change column and measure formatting when connecting to the published dataset from Power BI or Excel. Therefore, it's important to choose widely accepted data formats and formats that lend themselves to intuitive data visualizations.

Data category

By default, Power BI does not assign columns to any of the 13 available data categories. Assigning geographic categories, such as City, to columns helps Power BI determine how to display these values on map visualizations. For example, certain city names, such as Washington, are also associated with state or province names and without an assigned data category, map visuals would have to guess whether to plot the city or the state.

 Currently 10 of the 13 column data categories are related to geography, including **County**, **Country/Region**, **Continent**, **City**, **Latitude**, **Longitude**, **Postal Code**, **Address**, **Place**, and **State or Province**.

The **Web URL Data Category** can be used to enable the initiation of emails from Power BI report visuals. In the following table visual, the `Employee Email Link` column contains `mailto` values (that is, `mailto://John@adworks.com`) and the URL icon property under **Values** has been set to **On**:

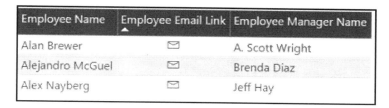

Web URL Data Category for Mailto Link column

Without specifying the **Web URL Data Category** of the `Employee Email Link` column, the values will appear as normal text. With the **Web URL Data Category** specified, the full `mailto` link will be displayed in the table visual by default; this can also be used to initiate an email. Both the **Web URL Data Category** specification and the URL icon property (set to **On**) are required to display the email icon.

The **Image URL Data Category** can be used to expose images in report visualizations, such as the following example with the custom Chiclet slicer:

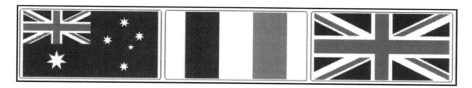

Image URL Data Category used for Chiclet slicer visual

See `Chapter 12`, *Applying Custom Visuals, Animation, and Analytics* for additional details on the Chiclet slicer.

The **Barcode Data Category**, the only other non-geographic category beyond **Web URL** and **Image URL**, can be used by the Power BI mobile applications to scan individual items from mobile devices.

Field descriptions

Descriptions can be added to the measures and columns of a data model to aid users during report development. Once descriptions have been applied and the dataset has been published to the Power BI service, users connected to the dataset via reports can view the descriptions as they hover over the fields in the fields list. This feature is particularly useful in communicating the business logic contained in measures, such as whether discounts are included or excluded in the `Internet Net Sales` measure.

Although field descriptions are recommended, particularly for measures that contain custom or complex logic, they are not a substitute for the formal documentation of a dataset. In most scenarios, the field description will only be used as a convenient reminder of the essential logic or meaning and thus can be more concise than the official corporate definition of the column or measure. A detailed example of developing documentation reports of a Power BI Dataset via **Dynamic Management Views (DMVs)** and Power BI Desktop can be found in Chapter 10 of *Microsoft Power BI Cookbook* (`https://www.packtpub.com/big-data-and-business-intelligence/microsoft-power-bi-cookbook`) by *Packt Publishing*.

In the following example, a report author is connected to a published Power BI dataset and has hovered over the `Internet Gross Product Margin` measure:

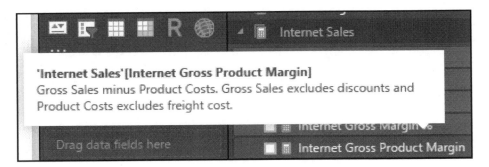

Field Descriptions as Tooltips in the fields list

The descriptions can only be viewed from Power BI Desktop or the Power BI service. Users connecting to the dataset from Excel via the Power BI Publisher for Excel can't see the descriptions. Additionally, field descriptions are exclusive to the fields list and are not displayed in visuals on the report canvas. Chapter 11, *Creating and Formatting Power BI Reports,* contains additional information on Power BI reports created via Live connections to published Power BI datasets.

Descriptions can be applied by enabling the **FIELD PROPERTIES** pane from the **View** tab in the Report View. In the following screenshot, the **FIELD PROPERTIES** pane exposes the **Name** and **Description** of the selected measure (Internet Gross Product Margin):

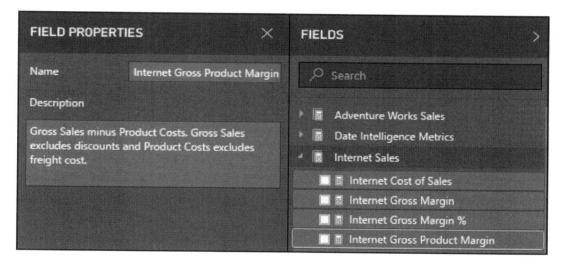

FIELD PROPERTIES pane

Users connected to the dataset via Live connections can view the descriptions via the **FIELD PROPERTIES** pane. In this context, the **Name** and **Description** properties are read-only.

DMVs can be used to retrieve the descriptions applied to measures and columns of a dataset. With the dataset open in Power BI Desktop, the user can connect from a client application, such as DAX Studio, to execute the relevant DMV. The **Description** field of both the MDSCHEMA_MEASURES and the TMSCHEMA_MEASURES DMVs contains the description that has been applied to DAX Measures. The **Description** field in the TMSCHEMA_COLUMNS DMV provides the description applied to columns.

Optimizing performance

One of the main reasons for creating a dataset, particularly an import mode dataset, is to provide a performant data source for reports and dashboards. Although Power BI supports traditional reporting workloads, such as email subscriptions and view-only usage, Power BI empowers users to explore and interact with reports and datasets. The responsiveness of visuals for this self-service workload is largely driven by fundamental data model design decisions, such as the granularity of fact and dimension tables.

Additional performance factors outside the scope of this chapter include the hardware resources allocated to the dataset, such as with Power BI Premium capacities (v-cores, RAM), the efficiency of the DAX Measures created for the dataset, the design of the Power BI reports that query the dataset, and the volume and timing of queries generated by users. Beyond the DAX measures described in Chapter 10, *Developing DAX Measures and Security Roles* these other factors are outside the control of the dataset designer and will be addressed in other chapters, such as Chapter 19, *Scaling up with Premium and Analysis Services.*

Import

The performance of an import mode dataset is largely driven by fundamental design decisions, such as the granularity of fact and dimension tables. For example, large dimension tables with more than a million unique values, such as customer IDs or product IDs will produce much less performant report queries than small dimensions with only 100 to 1,000 unique values. Likewise, DAX Measures that access columns containing thousands of unique values will perform much more slowly than measures that reference columns with a few unique values. A simplistic but effective understanding is that higher levels of cardinality (unique values) result in greater memory consumption via reduced compression and CPUs require additional time to scan greater amounts of memory.

An import mode designer should be cautious about the performance implications of relationships to large dimension tables. Although usability is somewhat compromised, a separate but less granular dimension containing only the most common columns can be created to drive more efficient report queries. For example, business users may rarely need to access individual product SKUs and would prefer the performance benefit provided by a smaller dimension table that contains only product categories and product subcategories.

Columnar compression

It's important to understand the columnar layout and internal storage of the import mode datasets. Power BI creates individual segments of approximately one million rows and stores separate memory structures for column data, the dictionary of unique values for columns, relationships, and hierarchies.

In the following diagram, three segments are used to store a fact table of 2.8 million rows:

	Date	Price	Qty	Sales	Order #
Segment 1 1 M Rows	2015	1.5	2	3	1234
Segment 2 1 M Rows	2016	1.8	3	5.4	1235
Segment 3 1 M Rows	2017	1.9	2	3.8	1236

Columnar storage of import mode datasets

Since only the columns required for a query are scanned during query execution, a relatively expensive column in terms of memory consumption (due to many unique values), such as Order #, can be stored in the dataset without negatively impacting queries that only access other columns. Removing fact table columns or reducing the cardinality of fact table columns that are not used in queries or relationships will nonetheless benefit the storage size and resources required to refresh the dataset. Fewer fact table columns may also enable Power BI to find a more optimal sort order for compression and thus benefit the query performance.

Eliminate any DAX-calculated column on fact tables as these columns are not compressed as efficiently as imported columns. If necessary, replace DAX-calculated columns with the equivalent expression in the source M Query or SQL View. Additionally, per the *Fact table columns* section earlier in this chapter, remove columns that can be computed within DAX Measures via simple expressions (+,-,/,*). For example, the Sales column from the Columnar Storage example image can be excluded from the Import dataset given the Price and Qty columns.

During query execution over tables with more than one segment, one CPU thread is associated per segment. This parallelization is limited by the number of CPU threads available to the dataset (for example, Power BI Premium P1 with four backend v-cores), and the number of segments required to resolve the query. Therefore, ideally, the rows of fact tables can be ordered such that only a portion of the segments are required to resolve queries. Using the example of the 2.8M-row fact table, a query that's filtered on the year 2017 would only require one CPU thread and would only scan the required column segments within Segment 3.

The internal order of fact table rows cannot be dictated by the dataset designer as Power BI determines the optimal order that will lead to the highest compression during dataset refreshes. However, dataset designers can add a sorting transformation to the M query of a fact table (Table.Sort()) such that Power BI will, at a minimum, consider this particular order during its processing. Whether Power BI used the particular sort order can be determined by analyzing the memory footprint of the sorted column before and after the data is loaded. If the size of the sort by column is significantly reduced following the refresh operation, Power BI took advantage of the order by.

Memory analysis via DMVs

The same DMVs that provide information about SSAS Tabular databases are also available for Power BI datasets. Querying these DMVs can provide schema information, such as the columns used to define relationships, the definitions of DAX Measures, and the memory usage of columns and other structures. From a memory analysis standpoint, the two most important DMVs are DISCOVER_STORAGE_TABLE_COLUMNS and DISCOVER_STORAGE_TABLE_COLUMN_SEGMENTS.

In the following query from DAX Studio, the dictionary size of each column of a Power BI dataset is retrieved via the DISCOVER_STORAGE_TABLE_COLUMNS DMV:

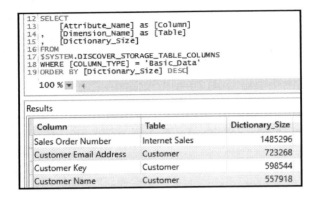

Dictionary size by Column

With the Power BI dataset (the PBIX file) open on the local machine, the DAX Studio application can connect to the dataset and SQL queries can be executed against the DMVs, just like normal DAX queries.

The DISCOVER_STORAGE_TABLE_COLUMN_SEGMENTS DMV contains information on four separate memory structures: user hierarchies, system hierarchies, relationships, and the compressed data segments per column. Dataset designers are generally most interested in the size and distribution of data segments by column and this can be retrieved with the following SQL query:

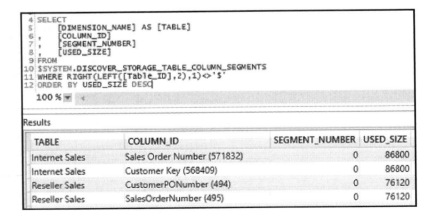

Data size per Column Segment

The first two characters of the `Table_ID` column identify the data structure represented by the row. For example, `H$` refers to system column hierarchies, `U$` refers to user-defined hierarchies, and `R$` refers to relationships. All other rows of the DMV, the rows in which the second character is not a dollar sign, refer to column data segments. In this query, the `WHERE` clause containing the `LEFT()` and `RIGHT()` text functions and the `<>'$'` condition is used to retrieve only the column data segments.

The `Dictionary_Size` column and the `Used_Size` column from the two respective DMVs are stored in bytes. For a more intuitive analysis of this data, particularly with large datasets, it can be helpful to convert from bytes to megabytes by dividing by 1,048,576.

Fact and dimension tables with over a million rows will contain more than one segment with each segment representing approximately one million rows. To analyze the DMV query results with multiple segments, it's necessary to group the result set by column and use aggregation functions (sum, average) against the `Used_Size` column. Analyzing the memory usage data from SSAS DMVs is generally performed outside of DAX Studio in tools such as Excel or Power BI.

A separate Power BI dataset (the PBIX file) exclusively dedicated to analyzing the memory usage of Power BI datasets can be an effective method of streamlining the data retrieval and visualization process. A detailed example of developing and maintaining one of these datasets is included in Chapter 10 of the *Microsoft Power BI Cookbook* (`https://www. packtpub. com/big-data-and-businessintelligence/microsoft-power-bi-cookbook`). At a high level, this solution involves executing M Queries against a running Power BI dataset to retrieve DMVs, such as the two DMVs identified, and then model and visualize this data.

DirectQuery

The dataset designer has less control over the performance of DirectQuery datasets given that data storage and query execution is the responsibility of the source system. However, dataset designers can ensure that the DAX functions used in measures take advantage of the source system resources and can partner with source system owners and experts to test alternative data source optimizations, such as the columnstore index for SQL Server. Additionally, as advised earlier regarding the Assume Referential Integrity relationship property, performance can be significantly improved by generating inner-join SQL statements.

Optimized DAX functions

If the allowed unrestricted measures for DirectQuery mode setting is enabled in Power BI Desktop, all DAX functions can be used in measures. However, only certain DAX functions are natively converted to SQL expressions for execution by the source system. The list of these optimized functions is available in the MS documentation: http://bit.ly/2oK8QXB. To the greatest extent possible, dataset designers should ensure that optimized functions are leveraged in measures and that non-optimized functions are only used on small, pre-filtered or aggregated query results.

Columnstore and HTAP

Business intelligence queries generated from tools such as Power BI are more suited for columnar data stores and most DirectQuery source systems offer a columnar feature to deliver improved query performance. For Microsoft SQL Server, the columnstore index is recommended for large fact tables and this index eliminates the need to maintain traditional B-tree indexes or to apply row or page compression. Additionally, a combination of non-clustered columnstore indexes and in-memory table technologies can be used to support **hybrid transactional and analytical processing (HTAP)** workloads. For example, the Power BI queries against the DirectQuery dataset would utilize the columnstore index without impacting the OLTP workload of the database.

The details of these features and configurations are outside the scope of this book but at a minimum the owners or experts on the DirectQuery data source should be engaged on the performance of the Power BI dataset. The following URL provides guidance on designing columnstore indexes for SQL Server database services (for example, Azure SQL Database, Azure SQL Data Warehouse) and on-premises SQL Server database environments: http://bit.ly/2EQon0q.

The **Related Tasks** section of the *Columnstore indexes – Design guidance* documentation referenced in the preceding URL contains links for the T-SQL DDL statements associated with implementing the columnstore index. In most scenarios, the dataset designer in a Power BI project or the author of an Analysis Services model is not responsible or authorized to optimize data sources such as with the columnstore index. However, the dataset designer can regularly collaborate with this subject matter expert or team as the demands and requirements of the dataset change. For example, the dataset designer can use tools, such as DAX Studio and SQL Server Profiler as described in the *Microsoft Power BI Cookbook* (`https://www.packtpub.com/big-data-and-business-intelligence/microsoft-power-bi-cookbook`), to capture the common or important SQL queries generated by Power BI reports and then share this information with the data warehouse team.

Alternatively, the database or data warehouse team can run a trace against a data source system per the *DirectQuery report execution* section of `Chapter 8`, *Connecting to Sources and Transforming Data with M*, during a test query workload from Power BI. This trace data could be used to identify the specific columns, tables, or expressions associated with slow queries and thus inform database modification decisions.

Summary

This chapter built on the queries from `Chapter 8`, *Connecting to Sources and Transforming Data with M*, to implement import and DirectQuery analytical data models. Relationships were created between fact and dimension tables as well as between bridge tables and the `Sales and Margin Plan` to enable actual versus plan reporting and analysis. Additionally, the fundamentals of designing Power BI models and all top features were reviewed, including bidirectional cross-filtering, inactive relationships, and hierarchies. Moreover, detailed guidance on metadata, such as data categories and DMVs available for analyzing memory usage, was provided.

The following chapter continues to build on the dataset for this project by developing analytical measures and security models. The DAX expressions implemented in this chapter will directly leverage the relationships defined in this chapter and ultimately drive the visualizations and user experience demonstrated in later chapters.

10
Developing DAX Measures and Security Roles

This chapter will detail the implementation of DAX measures and security roles for the dataset developed in the previous two chapters. First, a set of base measures for each business process are created, representing business definitions such as gross and net sales, cost of sales, and margin percentages. The base measures are then leveraged in the development of date intelligence calculations including **year-to-date** (**YTD**) and **year-over-year** (**YOY**) growth. Additionally, a set of customs measures are created, including exceptions, rankings, and KPI targets to further extract insights from the dataset and simplify report visualizations.

This chapter will also contain examples of dynamic security models in which the identity of the logged in user is used to filter the dataset. Finally, guidance will be provided on testing the performance of DAX expressions with DAX Studio.

In this chapter, we will review the following topics:

- DAX measures
- Filter and row contexts
- DAX variables
- Base measures
- Date intelligence metrics
- Dimension metrics
- Ranking metrics
- Security roles
- Dynamic row-level security
- Performance testing

DAX measures

All analytical expressions ranging from simple sums and averages to custom, complex statistical analyses are implemented within DAX measures. Most measure expressions will reference and aggregate the numeric columns of fact tables, which are hidden from the Report View, as we have seen in per the previous chapter. Additional DAX measures can include filtering conditions which supplement or override any filters applied in Power BI reports, such as the net sales amount for first-year customers only. Measures can also evaluate text columns from dimension tables, such as the count of states or provinces with sales and return text and date values.

Just like the M query language, DAX is a rich, functional language that supports variables and external expression references. Multiple variables can be defined within a DAX measure to improve readability, and the results of other measures can be referenced as well, such as the Plan Grain Status measure in Chapter 9, *Designing Import and DirectQuery Data Models*. These layers of abstraction and the built-in code editing features of Power BI Desktop including IntelliSense and colorization, enabling dataset designers to embed powerful yet sustainable logic into datasets.

In addition to the DAX measures authored for a Power BI Dataset, Power BI Desktop's **Analytics** pane can be used to create metrics specific to a given visual, such as the trend line, min, max, an average of a metric on a line chart. The **Analytics** pane is reviewed in Chapter 12, *Applying Custom Visuals, Animation and Analytics*.

Measure evaluation process

Each value in the report, such as the $600 from the matrix visual, is computed according to the following four-step process:

1. **Initial Filter Context**:
     - This includes all filters applied within and outside the report canvas by the report author
     - Selections on slicer visuals and the rows and columns of the table and matrix visuals represent on-canvas filters
     - Report, page, visual, and drillthrough filters represent off-canvas filters that also contribute to the initial filter context

2. **Filter Context Modified via DAX**:
   - For base measures and other simplistic expressions, the initial filter context from the report is left unchanged
   - For more complex measures, the CALCULATE() function is invoked to further modify the initial filter context:
     - Via CALCULATE(), the initial filter context can be removed, replaced, or supplemented with an additional filter condition
     - In the event of a conflict between the initial filter context from the report (for example, slicers, report level filters) and the filter condition embedded in the DAX measure, by default, the DAX measure will override the report filter condition

3. **Relationship Cross-Filtering**:
   - With each table filtered from steps *1* and *2*, the filter context is transferred across cross-filtering relationships
   - In most cases, the filtered dimension tables filter the related fact tables via single direction cross-filtering
   - However, as described in Chapter 9, *Designing Import and DirectQuery Data Models*, bidirectional cross-filtering allows the filter context to also transfer from the many side of a relationship to the one side

4. **Measure Logic Computation**:
   - The computation logic of the measure (for example, DISTINCTCOUNT(), COUNTROWS()) is finally evaluated against the remaining active rows for the given table or column referenced
   - For common and base measures, this is simply the set of remaining or active fact table rows
   - However, as shown in the following *Dimension metrics* section, other DAX measures will reference dimension tables, and thus it's important to understand how these tables are impacted by relationship filtering and DAX expressions

This four-step process is repeated for each value of the report independently. Consequently, reports and visuals which are dense in values require more computing resources to refresh and update based on user filter selections. Large tabular report visuals with many columns and rows are particularly notorious for slow performance, as this forces the DAX engine to compute hundreds or thousands of individual values.

Although report authors and business analysts will not create DAX measures, it's important that they have a basic understanding of the filter context and measure evaluation processes. For example, the report author should understand the cross-filtering relationships of the data model (single or bidirectional) and how certain DAX measures impact the filters applied in reports. Similarly, business analysts should be able to explain to business users why certain report behaviors and results occur.

Row context

In addition to filter context, several DAX functions such as FILTER() and SUMX() are iterators and execute their expressions per row of a given table. The set of rows to evaluate from this table is always defined by the filter context which was described earlier in this chapter. The expression parameter of iterating functions can aggregate the rows of a table or can invoke the filter context of the specific row being iterated via the CALCULATE() function or a measure reference.

Calculated DAX columns are used to illustrate row context. In the following screenshot, four calculated columns have been added to a Date table and reference the Weekday Sort column:

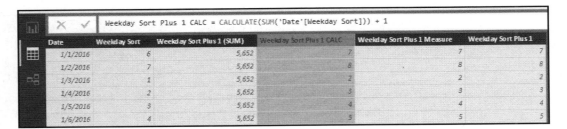

The row context in calculated columns

All four calculated columns simply add the value 1 to the Weekday Sort column, but achieve their results via distinct expressions:

```
Weekday Sort Plus 1 (SUM) = SUM('Date'[Weekday Sort]) + 1
Weekday Sort Plus 1 CALC = CALCULATE(SUM('Date'[Weekday Sort])) + 1
Weekday Sort Plus 1 Measure = [Weekday Sort Summed] + 1
Weekday Sort Plus 1 = 'Date'[Weekday Sort]+1
```

The Weekday Sort Plus 1 CALC column and the Weekday Sort Plus 1 Measure column represent the concept of context transition. These two columns invoke the filter context (context transition) of the given row via the CALCULATE() function or implicitly via the reference of an existing measure, respectively:

- Weekday Sort Plus 1 (SUM) computes the sum of the Weekday Sort column plus one and repeats this value for each row
- Weekday Sort Plus 1 CALC embeds a SUM() function within the CALCULATE() function prior to adding one
- Weekday Sort Plus 1 Measure references an existing measure which sums the Weekday Sort column and then adds one
- Weekday Sort Plus 1 references the Weekday Sort column of the Date table and adds one

The Weekday Sort Plus 1 (SUM) expression demonstrates that aggregation functions, in the absence of CALCULATE() or the implicit CALCULATE() when invoking measures, ignore row context. The three other columns all operate on a per-row basis (row context) but achieve their results via three different methods. The Weekday Sort Plus 1 column represents the default behavior of expressions executing in a row context such as calculated columns, FILTER(), and other iterating DAX functions.

To develop more complex DAX measures, it can be necessary to ignore the row context of the input table, such as the Weekday Sort Plus 1 SUM() example or explicitly invoke the row context of the table.

Scalar and table functions

The majority of DAX functions return a single value based on an aggregation or a logical evaluation of a table or column. For example, the COUNTROWS() and DISTINCTCOUNT() functions return individual numeric values based on a single table and a single column input parameter, respectively. The DAX functions which return individual values as their output, including information functions, such as ISBLANK() and LOOKUPVALUE(), are referred to as scalar functions. For relatively simple datasets and at early stages in projects, most DAX measures will reference a single scalar function with no other modifications, such as with CALCULATE().

In addition to scalar functions, many DAX functions return a table as the output value. The tables returned by these functions, such as FILTER() and ALL(), are used as input parameters to other DAX measure expressions to impact the filter context under which the measure is executed via the CALCULATE() function. The DAX language has been extended to support many powerful table functions, such as TOPN(), INTERSECT(), and UNION(), thus providing further support for authoring DAX measures.

 In addition to serving as table input parameters to DAX measures, the results of DAX table functions can be returned and exposed to client reporting tools. The most common example of this is in developing a paginated reporting services report either with **SQL Server Reporting Services** (**SSRS**) or the Power BI Report Server based on an Analysis Services Tabular model. Additionally, DAX table functions can return a summarized or filtered table within a Power BI dataset based on the other tables in the dataset.

As models grow in complexity and as model authors become more familiar with DAX, new measures increasingly leverage a combination of scalar functions (or existing measures based on scalar functions) and table functions. Per the *DAX Variables* section later in this chapter, both scalar and table values (based on scalar and table functions, respectively) can be stored as variables to further support abstraction and readability.

The CALCULATE() function

The CALCULATE() function is the most important function in DAX as it enables the author to modify the filter context under which a measure is evaluated. Regardless of the fields used and filters applied in reports, the filter parameter input(s) to CALCULATE() will be applied. Specifically, the CALCULATE() function will either add a filter to a measure expression (for example, Color = "Red"), ignore the filters from a table or column (for example, ALL(Product)), or update/overwrite the filters applied within a report to the filter parameter specified in CALCULATE().

The syntax of CALCULATE() is the following CALCULATE(<expression>, <filter1>, <filter2>). Any number of filter parameters can be specified including no filter parameters such as CALCULATE(SUM(Sales[Sales Amount])). When multiple filter parameters have been specified, the function will respect all of them together as a single condition via internal AND logic. The expression parameter is evaluated based on the new and final filter context applied via the filter parameters.

In the following measure, any filter applied to any column from the Product or Sales Territory tables will be ignored by the calculation:

```
ISales Row Count (Ignore Product and Territory) =
CALCULATE(COUNTROWS('Internet Sales'),ALL('Product'),ALL('Sales
Territory'))
```

The preceding measure represents one simple example of a table function (ALL()) being used in conjunction with a scalar function (COUNTROWS()) via CALCULATE(), as described in the previous session.

There are multiple forms of the ALL() function beyond ALL(table). The ALL() function can be used to ignore the values from a single column or multiple columns, such as, the following two examples: (All('Customer'[Customer City]) and ALL('Customer'[Customer City], 'Customer'[Customer Country]). Additionally, the ALLEXCEPT() function only allows certain columns specified to impact the filter context, and the ALLSELECTED() function ignores filters from inside a query but allows filters from outside the query.

Just as the CALCULATE() function is used to modify the filter context of scalar value expressions, the CALCULATETABLE() function is used to modify the filter context of expressions which return tables. For example, the following query expression returns all columns from the product dimension table and only the rows which match the two filter parameter conditions specified:

```
EVALUATE
CALCULATETABLE('Product',
'Product'[Product Category] = "Bikes",
'Product'[Product Dealer Price] > 2100)
```

The modified table result from CALCULATETABLE() can then be used as a parameter input to another table function such as FILTER() or as a filter parameter to CALCULATE().

Related tables

It's possible to reference other tables in the data model from within a row context via the RELATED() and RELATEDTABLE() functions. In the following screenshot from Data View of an import mode dataset, three calculated columns have been added to a Date dimension table with expressions referencing the Freight column of the Internet Sales fact table:

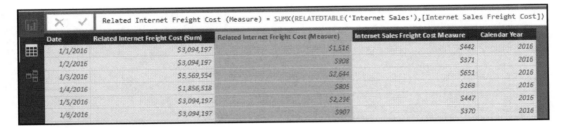

Row context with RELATEDTABLE()

The DAX expressions used for each column are as follows:

```
Related Internet Freight Cost (Sum) =
SUMX(RELATEDTABLE('Internet Sales'),(SUM('Internet Sales'[Freight]))))
Related Internet Freight Cost (Measure) =
SUMX(RELATEDTABLE('Internet Sales'),[Internet Sales Freight Cost])
Internet Sales Freight Cost Measure = [Internet Sales Freight Cost]
```

Only the `Internet Sales Freight Cost Measure` returns the correct freight cost amount for each date. The `Related Internet Freight Cost (Sum)` column computes the total freight cost on the entire `Internet Sales` table and uses this value for each related row before summing the result. For example, nine rows on the `Internet Sales` table have a date of `1/3/2016` and the sum of the `Freight` column on the `Internet Sales` table is `$618,839`. Given the `SUMX()` function, the `$5,569,554` value is the result of 9 (rows) multiplied by `$618,839`.

The `Related Internet Freight Cost (Measure)` also overcounts the freight cost for the day, specifically, whenever multiple rows of the same date have the same freight cost, the sum of these values is counted for each row. For example, five rows on the `Internet Sales` table have a date of `1/2/2016` and three of these rows have the same freight cost of `$89.46`. Given the `SUMX()` function, the value *$268.37 (3 * $89.46)* is added three separate times prior to adding the other two freight cost values (`$17.48` and `$85.00`) to produce `$908`.

The `RELATEDTABLE()` function is used to reference tables on the many sides of one-to-many relationships. Likewise, the `RELATED()` function is used to reference tables on the one side of many-to-one relationships. For example, a calculated column or the row context of an iterating function such as `SUMX()` on the Internet Sales fact table would use `RELATED()` to access a dimension table and apply logic referencing the dimension table per row of the Internet Sales table.

The FILTER() function

The `FILTER()` function is one of the most important and powerful functions in DAX in that it allows complex logic to fully define the set of rows of a table. `FILTER()` accepts a table as an input and returns a table with each row respecting its defined condition. The `FILTER()` function is almost always used as a parameter to a `CALCULATE()` function and can add to the existing filter context or redefine the filter context by invoking `ALL()` as its table input. The date intelligence measures described later in this chapter utilize `FILTER()` to fully define the set of `Date` rows for the filter context.

In the following DAX measure, the `FILTER()` function is utilized against the `Date` table and implements a condition based on the existing `Internet Gross Sales` measure:

```
Days with over 15K Gross Internet Sales =
    CALCULATE(COUNTROWS('Date'),
        FILTER('Date', [Internet Gross Sales] > 15000))
```

The ability to directly reference DAX measures is unique to the `FILTER()` function. For example, the following measure expression is not allowed by the DAX engine: `CALCULATE(COUNTROWS('Date'), [Internet Gross Sales] > 15000).`

The `Days with over 15K Gross Internet Sales` measure and the `Internet Gross Sales` base measure are used in the following Power BI report:

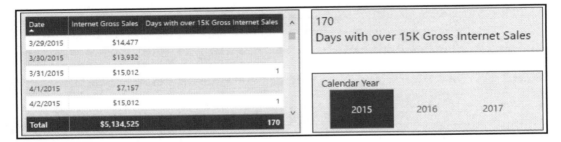

DAX measure with FILTER

Given that the `FILTER()` function simply references the `Date` table and does not remove any filters via `ALL()`, the measure executes on each date contained in the matrix visual to return a 1 or a blank. When no dates are on the visual such as the subtotal row or the card visual, the total number of days that meet the condition (170 for the year 2015) is returned. If the `Internet Gross Sales` measure was not included in the table visual, by default Power BI would only display the dates with a 1 value for the `Days with over a 15K Gross Internet Sales` measure.

Given both its iterative (row-by-row) execution and the potential to apply complex measures to each row, it's important to use the `FILTER()` function carefully. For example, DAX measures should not use `FILTER()` directly against large fact tables. Additionally, `FILTER()` should not be used when it's not needed for simple measures such as the following two examples
```
CALCULATE([Internet Gross Sales],'Product'[Product
Category] = "Bikes")
CALCULATE([Reseller Gross Sales],'Product'[Product
Color] IN {"Red", "White"},Promotion[Discount
Percentage] > .25).
```

DAX variables

Variables can be defined within DAX measures and primarily serve to improve the readability of DAX expressions. Rather than creating and referencing separate DAX measures, variables provide an inline option, thereby limiting the volume of distinct measures in a dataset. As a basic example of variable syntax, the `"Last Refreshed"` text message described in the *Parameter Tables* section of Chapter 8, *Connecting to Sources and Transforming Data with M*, uses a DAX variable in its expression, as follows:

```
Last Refresh Msg =
    VAR CurrentDateValue = MAX('CurrentDate'[CurrentDate])
    RETURN
    "Last Refreshed: " & CurrentDateValue
```

The `VAR` function is used to name a variable and the `RETURN` keyword allows for the variable's result to be referenced by this name. In this example, the `CurrentDateValue` variable retrieves the date stored in the `CurrentDate` parameter table, and a string of text is concatenated with the variable to generate the text message.

Variables can sometimes be implemented to improve the performance of slow measures. Variables are only evaluated once and their resulting values (a scalar value or a table) can be referenced multiple times. Measures which produce fewer storage engine queries will almost always execute faster and make better use of hardware resources. Therefore, any DAX measure or query which makes multiple references to the same expression logic can be a good candidate for DAX variables.

A common use case for DAX variables is to split up the components of an otherwise more complex DAX expression. In the following example, six DAX variables are used to produce a filtered distinct count of accessory products and a filtered distinct count of clothing products:

```
Reseller High Value Accessory and Clothing Products =
/*
Accessory category products with over 20K in net sales and over 32%
net margin since last year
Clothing category products with over 55K in net sales and over 28% net
margin since last year
Enable filtering from dimension tables related to Reseller Sales
*/
VAR AccessorySales = 20000 VAR AccessoryNetMargin = .32
VAR ClothingSales = 50000 VAR ClothingNetMargin = .28
//Distinct Accessory Products
VAR AccessoryProducts =
CALCULATE(DISTINCTCOUNT('Product'[Product Alternate Key]),
    FILTER(
    SUMMARIZE(
    CALCULATETABLE('Reseller Sales',
      'Date'[Calendar Year Status] IN {"Current Calendar Year", "Prior
Calendar Year"},
      'Product'[Product Category] = "Accessories"),
      'Product'[Product Alternate Key]),
      [Reseller Net Margin %] >= AccessoryNetMargin && [Reseller Net
Sales] >= AccessorySales))
//Distinct Clothing Products
VAR ClothingProducts =
CALCULATE(DISTINCTCOUNT('Product'[Product Alternate Key]),
    FILTER(
    SUMMARIZE(
    CALCULATETABLE('Reseller Sales',
      'Date'[Calendar Year Status] IN {"Current Calendar Year", "Prior
Calendar Year"},
      'Product'[Product Category] = "Clothing"),
      'Product'[Product Alternate Key]),
      [Reseller Net Margin %] >= ClothingNetMargin && [Reseller Net
Sales] > ClothingSales))
RETURN
AccessoryProducts + ClothingProducts
```

With the variables named and evaluated, the RETURN keyword simply adds the results of the two distinct count expressions contained within the AccessoryProducts and ClothingProducts variables. The multi-line comment at the top of the expression denoted by /* and */ makes the DAX measure easier to understand in the future. Single-line comments have been added using // to precede the distinct accessory and clothing products. With the variables declared in this structure, it becomes very easy to adjust the measure to different input thresholds such as a higher or lower net sales value or net margin rates.

The most efficient filtering conditions of measures should be implemented in measures first. Efficient filter conditions are those which don't require the FILTER() function, such as the calendar year status and product category filter conditions in the Reseller High Value Accessory and Clothing Products measure. Once the sufficient filters have been applied, more complex but less performant filtering conditions can operate on smaller sets of data, thus limiting their impact on query performance.

A Power BI report can leverage the measure in a Visual level filter to only display the specific products that meet the criteria of the measure. In the following table visual, only five products (2 Accessories, 3 Clothing) are displayed given the filter on the Reseller High Value Accessory and Clothing Products measure:

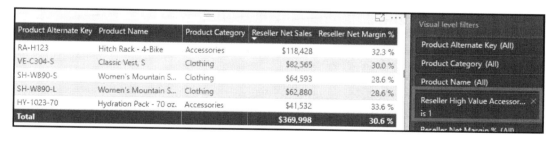

Variable-based DAX measure as a Visual level filter

The filter context of the Reseller Sales fact table is respected via the SUMMARIZE() function. Just like bidirectional cross-filtering via the CROSSFILTER() function and bidirectional relationships, other dimensions related to the Reseller Sales fact table can be used for filtering the measure. For example, a filter on the Sales Territory Country column for the United States would result in only one product.

It's necessary to reference the alternate key of the product dimension given the implementation of slowly changing dimension logic, as described in `Chapter 7`, *Planning Power BI Projects*. A single product can have multiple rows in its dimension table, reflecting various changes such as with list prices and product weight. These unique product keys would be reflected in the fact table, and so using the product key column would result in counting different versions of the same product multiple times.

In addition to scalar values like DAX measures, DAX variables can also store table values such as a specific set of customer key values or filter set of product rows. DAX measures can then reference and apply aggregation functions against this set of tables.

In the following example, two distinct sets of customer keys (tables) are computed via variables and then combined via the UNION() function to drive the filter context of the measure:

```
Internet Sales First Year and Accessory Customers =
VAR FirstYearCustomers =
SUMMARIZE(
  CALCULATETABLE('Internet Sales',
    'Customer'[Customer History Segment] = "First Year Customer"),
  'Customer'[Customer Alternate Key])
VAR AccessoryCustomersThisYear =
SUMMARIZE(
CALCULATETABLE('Internet Sales',
    'Date'[Calendar Year Status] = "Current Calendar
Year",'Product'[Product Category] = "Accessories"),
  'Customer'[Customer Alternate Key])
VAR TargetCustomerSet =
DISTINCT(UNION(FirstYearCustomers,AccessoryCustomersThisYear))
RETURN
CALCULATE(DISTINCTCOUNT(Customer[Customer Alternate
Key]),TargetCustomerSet)
```

The DISTINCT() function is applied against the result of the UNION() function since duplicate rows are retained by the UNION() function in DAX. Just like the previous example with variables, the SUMMARIZE() function is used to both embed filter conditions and to respect the filter context of the Internet Sales fact table. In this example, SUMMARIZE() allows selections on dimension tables related to the Internet Sales fact table, such as Sales Territory to also impact the measure.

In the following matrix visual of a Power BI report, the `Sales Territory Country` column from the `Sales Territory` dimension is used as the column header and the results from the measure reflect each individual country:

	United States	Australia	United Kingdom	Germany	France	Canada
Internet Sales First Year and Accessory Customers	4,452	1,966	1,159	1,035	989	964
Internet Sales Orders	7,197	5,224	2,382	1,937	1,877	2,402

Table-valued DAX variable-based measure

The filter context embedded into both variables (`FirstYearCustomers` and `AccessoryCustomersThisYear`) of the measure provides the equivalent behavior of bidirectional cross-filtering between `Internet Sales` and the `Customer` dimension. The `SUMMARIZE()` function is used rather than `CROSSFILTER()` when given a performance advantage. See the *Performance testing* section later in this chapter for additional details on performance testing.

> The combination of table-valued DAX variables and set-based DAX functions such as `UNION()`, `INTERSECT()`, and `EXCEPT()` support a wide variety of analytical operations. Authors of DAX measures should familiarize themselves with the essentials of DAX as a query language, particularly the `SUMMARIZE()` and `SUMMARIZECOLUMNS()` functions. Custom tables resulting from DAX queries are often needed by DAX measure expressions and can also be used in other applications such as SSRS.

Base measures

Before any custom or complex DAX measures can be developed, a set of relatively simple base measures must be implemented first. These measures represent the metrics from the *Define the facts* section of Chapter 7, *Planning Power BI Projects*, and thus contain validated and approved business definitions. For Adventure Works, a set of 12 base measures related to sales, cost, and margins are applicable to both the `Internet Sales` and `Reseller Sales` fact tables, such as the following:

```
Reseller Gross Sales = SUMX('Reseller Sales',
    'Reseller Sales'[Unit Price]*'Reseller Sales'[Order Quantity])
Reseller Net Sales = [Reseller Gross Sales] - [Reseller Sales
Discounts]
Reseller Sales Product Cost = SUMX('Reseller Sales',
```

```
'Reseller Sales'[Order Quantity]*'Reseller Sales'[Product Standard
Cost])
Reseller Cost of Sales = [Reseller Sales Product Cost] + [Reseller
Sales Freight Cost]
Reseller Gross Product Margin = [Reseller Gross Sales] - [Reseller
Sales Product Cost]
Reseller Gross Product Margin % = DIVIDE([Reseller Gross Product
Margin],[Reseller Gross Sales])
Reseller Net Product Margin = [Reseller Net Sales] - [Reseller Sales
Product Cost]
Reseller Net Product Margin % = DIVIDE([Reseller Net Product
Margin],[Reseller Net Sales])
Reseller Gross Margin = [Reseller Gross Sales] - [Reseller Cost of
Sales]
Reseller Gross Margin % = DIVIDE([Reseller Gross Margin],[Reseller
Gross Sales])
Reseller Net Margin = [Reseller Net Sales] - [Reseller Cost of Sales]
Reseller Net Margin % = DIVIDE([Reseller Net Margin],[Reseller Net
Sales])
```

As shown in the *Fact table columns* section from Chapter 9, *Designing Import and DirectQuery Data Models*, three fact table columns (Extended Amount, Sales Amount, and Total Product Cost) were excluded from the Power BI fact table to save resources. The SUMX() function is used to compute the equivalent values from these three columns to support the Gross Sales, Net Sales, and Product Cost measures, respectively.

 Sales discounts and freight costs, both simple sums of their respective fact table columns, are the two measures that create differences among the base measures. Discounts separate gross sales from net sales and freight costs separate the cost of sales from product costs only. The distinct definitions of the base measures support common analysis needs, such as the profitability (margin) of sales inclusive or exclusive of freight costs.

With base measures created for both `Reseller Sales` and `Internet Sales` fact tables, an additional set of base measures can be created for Adventure Works as an organization. Several of these measures can simply sum the `Reseller Sales` and `Internet Sales` measures as shown in the following examples:

```
AdWorks Net Sales = [Internet Net Sales] + [Reseller Net Sales]
AdWorks Cost of Sales = [Internet Cost of Sales] + [Reseller Cost of Sales]
AdWorks Net Margin = [AdWorks Net Sales] – [AdWorks Cost of Sales]
AdWorks Net Margin % = DIVIDE([AdWorks Net Margin],[AdWorks Net Sales])
```

Additional DAX measures with specific filtering or evaluation logic such as date intelligence metrics can reference the base measures in their expressions. Via this measure branching, any subsequent changes to the definition of the base measures will be automatically reflected in other dependent measures. Additionally, the readability of the custom measures is improved, as these expressions only contain their specific logic.

Measure support expressions

Large and complex Power BI datasets with many measures may have one or multiple measure support tables. As shown in the previous chapters, these hidden tables don't contain data and aren't refreshed with the dataset, but serve as the home table for commonly used DAX expressions. Unlike DAX variables, hidden DAX measure expressions are globally available to other DAX measures and queries. Measure support expressions, therefore, serve as a staging and consolidation layer to simplify DAX measures.

The measure support table may contain any of the following types of expressions:

- KPI targets
- Current and prior periods
- Filter context information

The two measures described in the *Measure support logic* section of Chapter 9, *Designing Import and DirectQuery Data Models*, represent the filter context information type of measure support. These measures typically use the ISFILTERED() or ISCROSSFILTERED() functions and are referenced within conditional expressions of other measures. Additionally, the USERPRINCIPALNAME() function is a good candidate for the Measure Support table if dynamic RLS is needed, or if other, user-based functionality is built into the dataset.

The ISFILTERED() function is limited to a specific column and only returns a true value when the given column is directly filtered. The ISCROSFFILTERED() function can reference a column or a table and returns true when one of the following three conditions are met:

- The column referenced is directly filtered
- A column on the same table as the column referenced is filtered
- A column on a table which has a cross-filtering relationship to the table or column referenced is filtered

KPI Targets

The standard **Key Performance Indicator** (**KPI**) visual in Power BI Desktop compares an indicator measure relative to a Target measure. The variance between the indicator and the target is displayed in the visual and is used to drive the color formatting (for example, red = bad; green = good). For many measures, a corresponding target measure may need to be created that applies some calculation logic to an existing measure. The following measure is simply 10% greater than the previous year's year-to-date net sales:

```
Target: 10% Above PY YTD Internet Sales = [Internet Net Sales (PY
YTD)] * 1.10
```

In a standard KPI visual, the target measure is displayed as the goal and used to calculate the variance percentage between the indicator and the target. In the following example, a $9.2M indicator value `Internet Net Sales` (YTD) is 5.8% below the 10% growth target measure of $9.8M:

Standard KPI Visual

Several other common visuals in Power BI benefit from target measures, including the bullet chart and the gauge visual. Several of these visuals can use multiple target measures to define alternative thresholds, such as the min and max values displayed.

In certain scenarios, a dedicated table of corporate target measures can be added to a dataset. For example, a table may contain columns for expected or target customer counts, products sold, and other metrics at a given date's granularity. Target measures can be created to access the values of this table via utility functions, such as LOOKUPVALUE().

The LOOKUPVALUE() function is particularly useful because it ignores the current filter context. As shown in the examples in the following section, the LOOKUPVALUE() function can be relied on to provide the same input value to other measures, such as a date or a number referring to specific date rows, regardless of any filters applied in the report.

Current and prior periods

A common requirement of date intelligence metrics is to compare the YTD total for a measure versus the equivalent time period of the prior year. For example, on November 14, 2017, the visual would compare January through October of 2017 versus January through October of 2016. Without any external filtering, however, a standard YTD measure would include the 14 days of November in 2017 and would capture the entire year of 2016 if the year 2016 was in the filter context. To deliver equivalent or *apples to apples* comparisons of equal time periods, the filter context of measures can be further customized.

The following measures retrieve the year-to-date net sales through the prior calendar month and prior calendar week. For example, throughout the month of November, the YTD Last Month measure would, at most, only retrieve the net sales through the month of October. Likewise, the YTD Last Week measure would, at most, only include the net sales through the end of the prior week of the year (45):

```
Prior Calendar Month Number =
VAR CurrentDay = TODAY()
RETURN
IF (
LOOKUPVALUE('Date'[Calendar Month Number],'Date'[Date],CurrentDay) =
1,12,
LOOKUPVALUE('Date'[Calendar Month Number],'Date'[Date],CurrentDay)-1
)
Prior Calendar Week Number =
VAR CurrentDay = TODAY()
RETURN
IF(
LOOKUPVALUE('Date'[Calendar Week Number in
Year],'Date'[Date],CurrentDay) = 1, CALCULATE(MAX('Date'[Calendar Week
Number in Year]),FILTER(ALL('Date'),'Date'[Calendar Year] =
MAX('Date'[Calendar Year]) - 1)),
LOOKUPVALUE('Date'[Calendar Week Number in
Year],'Date'[Date],CurrentDay)-1)

Internet Net Sales (YTD Last Month) =
IF([Prior Calendar Month Number] <> 12,
CALCULATE([Internet Net Sales], FILTER(ALL('Date'),'Date'[Calendar
Year] = MAX('Date'[Calendar Year]) &&
    'Date'[Date] <= MAX('Date'[Date]) && 'Date'[Calendar Month Number]
<= [Prior Calendar Month Number])),
CALCULATE([Internet Net Sales], FILTER(ALL('Date'), 'Date'[Calendar
Year] = MAX('Date'[Calendar Year])-1 && 'Date'[Date] <=
MAX('Date'[Date]) && 'Date'[Calendar Month Number] <= [Prior Calendar
Month Number])))
```

```
Internet Net Sales (YTD Last Week) =
VAR CurrentWeek = LOOKUPVALUE('Date'[Calendar Week Number in
Year],'Date'[Date],TODAY())
RETURN
IF(CurrentWeek <> 1,
CALCULATE([Internet Net Sales], FILTER(ALL('Date'),'Date'[Calendar
Year] = MAX('Date'[Calendar Year]) &&
    'Date'[Date] <= MAX('Date'[Date]) && 'Date'[Calendar Week Number
in Year] <= [Prior Calendar Week Number])),
CALCULATE([Internet Net Sales], FILTER(ALL('Date'),'Date'[Calendar
Year] = MAX('Date'[Calendar Year])-1 && 'Date'[Date] <=
MAX('Date'[Date]) && 'Date'[Calendar Week Number in Year] <= [Prior
Calendar Week Number])))
```

For any prior calendar year in the filter context, the (YTD Last Month) measure would only include January through October for this given year. Likewise, the (YTD Last Week) measure would only include weeks 1 through 45 of the given year. By embedding this dynamic filtering logic, it's possible to use these measures in report visuals without applying any additional filters.

 The TODAY() function combined with the LOOKUPVALUE() function makes it possible to retrieve values at query time relative to the current date. In the previous example, the month and week number columns of the current year (for example, October = 10) are queried via LOOKUPVALUE() based on the current date. With these values retrieved, subtracting one from the results provides the value associated with the prior month and prior week, respectively. These measures are then referenced in the FILTER() function of their respective year-to-date measures.

Similar to this simple example, dynamically computed dates and other values make it possible to create measures for the current date and yesterday:

```
Internet Net Sales (Today) = CALCULATE([Internet Net Sales],
FILTER(ALL('Date'),'Date'[Date] = TODAY()))
```

```
Internet Net Sales (Yesterday) = CALCULATE([Internet Net Sales],
FILTER(ALL('Date'),'Date'[Date] = TODAY()-1))
```

Along with the date intelligence metrics described in the following section, a rich set of date-based metrics give users of Power BI reports and dashboards visibility for both short and long-term results.

Date intelligence metrics

Date intelligence metrics are typically the first set of measures to be added to a dataset following base measures. These measures reference the base measures and add a custom filtering condition to the Date dimension table, thus providing visibility to multiple distinct time intervals, such as year-to-date and the previous year-to-date. Given their built-in date filtering logic, Power BI reports and dashboards can be developed faster and without manual maintenance costs of updating date filter conditions.

The following four measures apply custom filter contexts to either return the current year, month, and week by default, or the latest of these time intervals given the date filters applied in a report:

```
Internet Net Sales (CY) = CALCULATE([Internet Net
Sales],FILTER(ALL('Date'),
   'Date'[Calendar Year] = MAX('Date'[Calendar Year]) &&
   'Date'[Date] >= MIN('Date'[Date]) && 'Date'[Date] <=
MAX('Date'[Date])))

Internet Net Sales (YTD) = CALCULATE([Internet Net Sales],
   FILTER(ALL('Date'),'Date'[Calendar Year] = MAX('Date'[Calendar
Year]) &&
     'Date'[Date] <= MAX('Date'[Date])))

Internet Net Sales (MTD) = CALCULATE([Internet Net Sales],
   FILTER(ALL('Date'),'Date'[Calendar Year Month Number] =
MAX('Date'[Calendar Year Month Number]) &&
     'Date'[Date] <= MAX('Date'[Date])))

Internet Net Sales (WTD) = CALCULATE([Internet Net Sales],
   FILTER(ALL('Date'),'Date'[Calendar Year Week Number] =
MAX('Date'[Calendar Year Week Number]) &&
     'Date'[Date] <= MAX('Date'[Date])))
```

The use of the MIN() and MAX() functions within the FILTER() function invokes the filter context of the report query. For example, if a report page is filtered to the second quarter of 2016 (2016-Q2), the CY measure will only return the sales from these three months while the YTD measure will include both the first and second quarter of 2016. The **month-to-date (MTD)** and **week-to-date (WTD)** measures will return the sales for June of 2016 and Week 27 of 2016, the last month and week in the filter context.

The date dimension table only contains rows through the current date. Therefore, in the absence of any other date filters applied in a report, these measures default to the current YTD, MTD, and WTD totals for net sales per the following multi-row card visual:

$50,822	$368,073	$9,119,671
Internet Net Sales (WTD)	Internet Net Sales (MTD)	Internet Net Sales (YTD)

Date intelligence metrics for the current year

The (CY) measure returns the same value as the YTD measure when no other date filters are applied.

 The MTD and WTD measure both references a numeric column on the date table that corresponds to the given granularity. For example, December of 2016 and January of 2017 are represented by the values 96 and 97 in the Calendar Year Month Number column. As shown in the previous chapter, these sequential columns are critical for date intelligence and are also used by the Sort By column property.

The following set of DAX measures return the prior year, month, and week given the filter context of the report:

```
Internet Net Sales (PY) = CALCULATE([Internet Net
Sales],FILTER(ALL('Date'),
   CONTAINS(VALUES('Date'[Prior Calendar Year Date]),'Date'[Prior
Calendar Year Date],'Date'[Date])))

Internet Net Sales (PYTD) = CALCULATE([Internet Net Sales],
   FILTER(ALL('Date'),'Date'[Calendar Year] = MAX('Date'[Calendar
Year])-1 &&
     'Date'[Date] <= MAX('Date'[Prior Calendar Year Date])))

Internet Net Sales (PMTD) = CALCULATE([Internet Net Sales],
   FILTER(ALL('Date'),'Date'[Calendar Year Month Number] =
```

```
MAX('Date'[Calendar Year Month Number])-1 &&
        'Date'[Date] <= MAX('Date'[Prior Calendar Month Date])))

Internet Net Sales (PWTD) = CALCULATE([Internet Net Sales],
    FILTER(ALL('Date'),'Date'[Calendar Year Week Number] =
MAX('Date'[Calendar Year Week Number])-1 &&
        'Date'[Date] <= MAX('Date'[Prior Calendar Week Date])))
```

The `Calendar Year`, `Calendar Year Month Number`, and `Calendar Year Week Number` columns used by the current period measures are also referenced by the prior period measures. However, the prior period measures subtract a value of one from the result of the `MAX()` function to navigate to the given preceding period.

In the PY measure, the `CONTAINS()` function used within the filtering parameter of the `FILTER()` function returns a true or false value for each prior calendar year date based on the date column. The date column reflects the filter context of the report query and thus only the corresponding prior year dates are passed to `FILTER()` as the modified filter context.

DAX provides a number of functions dedicated to date intelligence, such as `DATEADD()` and `SAMEPERIODLASTYEAR()`. These functions are much less verbose than the techniques from these examples, but they're also generally limited to standard calendars. The approach described in this section leveraging core DAX functions, such as `FILTER()` and `ALL()`, can also be applied to financial calendars. Additionally, the filter navigation (for example, `MAX() - 1`) implemented in the prior period measures is applicable to more advanced date intelligence expressions.

Each prior period measure references a column containing date values that have been adjusted relative to the date column. The following screenshot of the date dimension table in SQL Server highlights these three columns relative to the date column:

Date	Prior Calendar Year Date	Prior Calendar Month Date	Prior Calendar Week Date
2017-11-15	2016-11-15	2017-10-15	2017-11-08
2017-11-14	2016-11-14	2017-10-14	2017-11-07
2017-11-13	2016-11-13	2017-10-13	2017-11-06

Prior date columns in the date dimension

Given the value of date intelligence measures and the relative static nature of the date dimension, it's recommended to develop a robust date dimension table. If the necessary columns cannot be implemented in the source database itself, the columns can be computed within the SQL view or the M query of the `Date` table.

Current versus prior and growth rates

With date intelligence measures developed for the current and prior periods, growth or variance measures can be added to the dataset, comparing the two values. In the following example, a **year-over-year** (YOY) and a **year-over-year year-to-date** (YOY YTD) measure have been created based on the current year and prior year measures from the preceding section:

```
Internet Net Sales (YOY) = [Internet Net Sales (CY)] - [Internet Net
Sales (PY)]
Internet Net Sales (YOY YTD) = [Internet Net Sales (YTD)] - [Internet
Net Sales (PY YTD)]
```

Finally, growth percentage measures can be added, which express the variance between the current and prior period measures as a percentage of the prior period. The following measures reference the above YOY measures as the numerator within a DIVIDE() function:

```
Internet Net Sales (YOY %) = DIVIDE([Internet Net Sales
(YOY)],[Internet Net Sales (PY)])
Internet Net Sales (YOY YTD %) = DIVIDE([Internet Net Sales (YOY
YTD)],[Internet Net Sales (PY YTD)])
```

The DIVIDE() function returns a blank value if the denominator is zero or a blank value by default. The divide operator (/), however, will return an infinity value when dividing by zero or a blank. Given the superior error-handling behavior and performance advantages of DIVIDE(), the DIVIDE() function is recommended for computing division in DAX.

Rolling periods

Rolling period and trailing average measures are also very common in datasets, as they help to smooth out individual outliers and analyze longer-term trends. For example, a significant business event or variance 10 months ago will have a relatively small impact on a trailing 12 month total. Additionally, this variance will not impact trailing 30 day or 3, 6, and 9-month rolling period measures.

The following two measures capture the trailing 60 days of sales history and the 60 days of history prior to the trailing 60 days:

```
Internet Net Sales (Trailing 60 Days) =
VAR MaxDate = MAX('Date'[Date])
VAR StartDate = MaxDate - 59
RETURN
CALCULATE([Internet Net Sales],FILTER(ALL('Date'),'Date'[Date] >=
StartDate && 'Date'[Date] <= MaxDate))

Internet Net Sales Trailing (60 to 120 Days) =
VAR MaxDate = MAX('Date'[Date])
VAR EndDate = MaxDate - 60
VAR StartDate = EndDate - 59
RETURN
CALCULATE([Internet Net Sales],FILTER(ALL('Date'), 'Date'[Date] >=
StartDate && 'Date'[Date] <= EndDate))
```

The two 60-day measures compute the dates for the filter condition within DAX variables and then pass these values into the FILTER() function. The two measures help to answer the question "Is Internet sales growth accelerating?". The following table visual in Power BI Desktop displays the measures by date and as a subtotal value:

Date	Internet Net Sales (Trailing 60 Days)	Internet Net Sales Trailing (60 to 120 Days)
11/15/2017	$1,750,742	$1,664,879
11/14/2017	$1,764,882	$1,644,292
11/13/2017	$1,771,927	$1,617,369
11/12/2017	$1,791,173	$1,603,709
Total	**$1,750,742**	**$1,664,879**

Trailing 60 and 60 to 120-day measures

With this logic, the value for the trailing 60 days measure on November 15th, 2017 includes Internet sales since September 17th, 2017. The 60 to 120 days measure, however, includes sales history from July 19th, 2017 through September 16th, 2017. The subtotal value reflects the latest date in the filter context—November 15th, 2017, in this example.

Rolling period or trailing average measures generally require the sequential numeric date dimension columns in the date suggested in both previous chapters. Very similar to the prior period measures from the previous section (for example, PY YTD), rolling period measures can reference sequential columns for the given granularity and modify the date filter by adding or subtracting values.

Dimension metrics

The majority of DAX measures will apply aggregating functions to numeric columns of fact tables. However, several of the most important metrics of a dataset are those which identify the presence of dimensions in fact tables such as the count of customers who've purchased and those who haven't. It can also be necessary to count the distinct values of a dimension column such as the number of postal codes sold to or the number of distinct marketing promotions over a period of time.

In the dataset for this project, the customer dimension table is exclusive to the Internet Sales fact table, and the measure should only count customers with internet sales history. Additionally, slowly changing dimension logic has been implemented so that a single customer defined by the Customer Alternate Key column could have multiple rows defined by the Customer Key column.

The following two DAX measures count the number of unique customers and products with internet sales history:

```
Internet Sales Customer Count =
CALCULATE(DISTINCTCOUNT(Customer[Customer Alternate Key]), 'Internet
Sales')
```

```
Internet Sales Products Sold Count =
CALCULATE(DISTINCTCOUNT('Product'[Product Alternate Key]),'Internet
Sales')
```

By invoking the Internet Sales fact table as a filtering parameter to CALCULATE(), any filter applied to a related dimension table such as Sales Territory will also impact the measure. This behavior is the same as bidirectional cross-filtering between the Internet Sales and Customer table. However, in the event that no filters have been applied in the reporting tool (for example, Power BI or Excel), the Internet Sales table filter ensures that only customers with Internet Sales histories are counted.

Missing dimensions

Missing dimension measures are commonly used in churn and exception reporting and analyses. For example, a report may be needed which displays the specific products that haven't sold or the past customers who haven't made a purchase in a given filter context. Additionally, missing dimension measures give greater meaning to other dimension measures. For instance, the count of products sold in a period may not be as useful without knowing how many products were not sold over this same period.

The following DAX measure counts the number of unique customers without Internet Sales history:

```
Internet Sales Customers Missing =
CALCULATE(DISTINCTCOUNT('Customer'[Customer Alternate Key]),
    FILTER(VALUES('Customer'[Customer Alternate Key]),
        ISEMPTY(RELATEDTABLE('Internet Sales'))))

Internet Sales Products Missing =
CALCULATE(DISTINCTCOUNT('Product'[Product Alternate Key]),
    FILTER(VALUES('Product'[Product Alternate Key]),
        ISEMPTY(RELATEDTABLE('Internet Sales'))))
```

The Internet Sales Customers Missing measure references the 'Internet Sales' fact table like the customer count measure does, but only within the ISEMPTY() function. The ISEMPTY() function operates as the filter parameter of the FILTER() function and returns a true or a false value for each distinct Customer Alternate Key provided by the VALUES() function. Only the customer rows without any related rows in the Internet Sales fact table are marked as true and this filtered set of customer rows is passed to the DISTINCTCOUNT() function. The same methodology is applied to the Internet Sales Products Missing measure.

The following matrix visual of a Power BI report has been filtered to four calendar quarters and broken out by the `Sales Territory Group`:

Sales Territory Group	2016-Q3	2016-Q4	2017-Q1	2017-Q2	Total
Europe					
Internet Sales Customer Count	869	941	1,021	610	2,993
Internet Sales Customers Missing	17,615	17,543	17,463	17,874	15,491
North America					
Internet Sales Customer Count	1,144	1,146	1,352	1,057	4,316
Internet Sales Customers Missing	17,340	17,338	17,132	17,427	14,168
Pacific					
Internet Sales Customer Count	597	689	750	492	2,151
Internet Sales Customers Missing	17,887	17,795	17,734	17,992	16,333
Internet Sales Customer Count	**2,610**	**2,776**	**3,123**	**2,159**	**9,460**
Internet Sales Customers Missing	**15,874**	**15,708**	**15,361**	**16,325**	**9,024**

Internet Sales Customers and Customers Missing

Any other dimension table with a relationship to the `Internet Sales` fact table, such as `Promotion` and `Product` could also be used to filter the metrics.

In this dataset, the customer dimension has 18,484 unique customers as defined by the `Customer Alternate Key`. Therefore, the sum of the customer count and customers missing measures is always equal to 18,484. As explained in the *Filter context* section, the subtotal values execute in their own filter context. For example, only 9,024 did not make an online purchase in any of the four quarters, while over 15,000 customers did not make a purchase in each of the four quarters.

Once core dimension metrics have been established such as in the previous examples, additional metrics can be developed which leverage their logic. The following measures identify the count of first-year internet sales customers and the count of accessories products which have not sold online, respectively:

```
Internet Sales First Year Customer Count =
CALCULATE([Internet Sales Customer Count],'Customer'[Customer History
Segment] = "First Year Customer")
```

```
Internet Sales Products Missing (Accessories) =
CALCULATE([Internet Sales Products Missing],'Product'[Product
Category] = "Accessories")
```

Dimension metrics, just like the base measures described earlier, may be used in reporting by themselves or may be referenced by other measures. This branching of measures underlines the importance of clearly defining, documenting, and testing the foundational measures of a dataset.

Ranking metrics

Many reports and analyses are built around the ranking of dimensions relative to measures, such as the top 10 salespeople based on YTD sales. Ranking measures can also help deliver more clean and intuitive report visualizations as they substitute small integer values for large numbers and decimal places. Ranking measures can be as simple as specifying a column and a measure, or more complex with unique ranking logic applied in distinct filter contexts.

Ranking measures in DAX are implemented via the RANKX() function, which is an iterator like SUMX() and FILTER(). As an iterating function, two required input parameters include a table and the expression to be evaluated for each row of the table. The following two measures rank products based on the Internet Net Sales measure:

```
Internet Net Sales Product Rank =
RANKX(ALL('Product'[Product Alternate Key]),[Internet Net
Sales],,DESC,Skip)
```

```
Internet Net Sales Product Rank (All Products) =
VAR ProdRankTable =
ALL('Product'[Product Alternate Key],'Product'[Product
Name],'Product'[Product Category
```

```
Group],'Product'[Product Category],'Product'[Product
Subcategory],'Product'[Product Name])
RETURN
RANKX(ProdRankTable, [Internet Net Sales],,DESC,Skip)
```

As with date intelligence and other measures, ALL() is used to remove the filters applied to a table. The ALL() function both removes a filter and returns a table which can then be evaluated by other functions. ALL() can remove filters from an entire table, multiple columns of the same table, or a single column from a table. Additionally, the ALLEXCEPT() function can be used remove filters from the current and any future columns of a table, except for one or a specific set of columns.

In the Internet Net Sales Product Rank measure, the ALL() function returns a table of the unique product's alternate key values. Since only a single column is referenced by ALL() in this measure, other columns from the Product dimension table are allowed into the filter context. For example, in the following table, the Product Category column impacts the Internet Net Sales Product Rank measure so that the HL-U509-R product is ranked first given that it's the highest selling product in the Accessories category:

Product Category	Product Alternate Key	Internet Net Sales	Internet Net Sales Product Rank	Internet Net Sales Product Rank (All Products)
Bikes	BK-R50B-60	$57,158	61	61
Bikes	BK-R50R-58	$56,347	62	62
Accessories	HL-U509-R	$55,774	1	63
Bikes	BK-R50R-44	$54,530	63	64
Accessories	HL-U509	$52,800	2	65

Ranking measures

The Internet Net Sales Product Rank (All Products) measure, however, ranks the product relative to all other products including products in the Bikes category. The group of columns specified in the ALL() function (the table parameter to RANKX()), defines the set of rows that the ranking expression will be evaluated against.

For ranking and certain other scenarios, it's necessary to apply alternative logic for subtotals. For example, the total row of the previous table visual would show a ranking value of 1 without any modification to the DAX. A common pattern to address subtotal values is to check whether an individual item of a column is in the filter context via HASONEVALUE(). The following revised measure uses an IF() conditional function to apply the ranking for individual products, but otherwise returns a blank value:

```
Internet Net Sales Product Rank =
IF(HASONEVALUE('Product'[Product Alternate Key]),
RANKX(ALL('Product'[Product Alternate Key]),[Internet
Net Sales],,DESC,Skip),BLANK())
```

As shown in this example, it's essential to understand the intended ranking logic and it may be necessary to store alternative ranking measures to suit the requirements of different reports and projects.

The RANKX() function has five parameters, but only the first two—the table and the expression to evaluate—are required. In this example, the third parameter is skipped via the comma and the measure is set to rank in descending order of the expression. Additionally, the final parameter (Skip or Dense) determines how tie values are treated. For example, if two products are tied for the highest sales, both products will be ranked 1, and the next-highest product will be ranked 3. Descending order and the skip tie behavior are both defaults, but it's a good practice to explicitly define these settings in the measures.

Dynamic ranking measures

The ranking measures in the previous section are specific to individual products. These measures cannot be used, for example, to rank product subcategories or product categories. Rather than develop many separate measures targeted at one specific column, logic can be embedded in DAX measures to dynamically adjust to the columns in the filter context.

In the following measure, a ranking is applied based on the filter context from three levels of a product hierarchy:

```
Internet Net Sales Product Rank (Conditional) =
VAR ProductFilter = ISFILTERED('Product'[Product Name])
VAR SubCatFilter = ISFILTERED('Product'[Product Subcategory])
VAR CatFilter = ISFILTERED('Product'[Product Category])
RETURN
Switch(TRUE(),
  ProductFilter = TRUE(), RANKX(ALL('Product'[Product Name]),[Internet
Net Sales],,DESC,Skip),
  SubCatFilter = TRUE(), RANKX(ALL('Product'[Product
Subcategory]),[Internet Net Sales],,DESC,Skip),
  CatFilter = TRUE(), RANKX(ALL('Product'[Product Category]),[Internet
Net Sales],,DESC,Skip),
  BLANK())
```

The measure checks for the existence of a filter on the `Product Name`, `Product Subcategory`, and `Product Category` columns within a `SWITCH()` function via the `ISFILTERED()` function. The first logical condition to evaluate as true will result in the corresponding `RANKX()` expression being executed. If no condition is found to be true, then the `BLANK()` value is returned.

The dynamic ranking measure can be used in report visuals which drill up/down through the product hierarchy or in separate visuals dedicated to specific columns. In the following screenshot, distinct table visuals representing the three levels of the product hierarchy utilize the `Internet Net Sales Product Rank (Conditional)` measure:

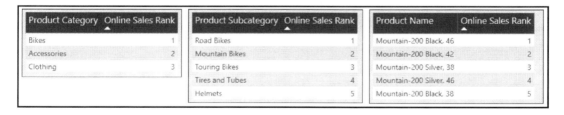

Product Category	Online Sales Rank
Bikes	1
Accessories	2
Clothing	3

Product Subcategory	Online Sales Rank
Road Bikes	1
Mountain Bikes	2
Touring Bikes	3
Tires and Tubes	4
Helmets	5

Product Name	Online Sales Rank
Mountain-200 Black, 46	1
Mountain-200 Black, 42	2
Mountain-200 Silver, 38	3
Mountain-200 Silver, 46	4
Mountain-200 Black, 38	5

Dynamic ranking measure

For the visuals in the preceding table, a shorter and more intuitive name was used instead of the full measure name (`Internet Net Sales Product Rank (Conditional)`). To change the name of a measure or column used in a report visual, double-click the name of the measure or column in the **Values** bucket of the **Visualizations** pane. The revised name only applies to the specific visual, and hovering over the revised name identifies the source measure or column.

Similar to the `Internet Net Sales Product Rank` measure from the previous section, the conditional measure allows for other columns to impact the filter context. For example, if both the `Product Category` and `Product Subcategory` columns are included in the same table visual, the conditional measure will rank the subcategories relative to other subcategories of the same `Product Category`. With this dataset, the Tires and Tubes subcategory, which is ranked fourth overall per the above table, would be ranked number one for the `Accessories` product category.

Security roles

Per `Chapter 7`, *Planning Power BI Projects*, the required data security for this project is to limit the visibility of the Adventure Works sales team users to their respective sales territory groups. There are three sales territory groups (`North America Sales Group`, `Europe Sales Group`, and `Pacific Sales Group`), and, as described in the previous chapter, cross-filtering relationships exist between the `Sales Territory` dimension table, and all three fact tables (`Internet Sales`, `Reseller Sales`, and `Sales and Margin Plan`). Therefore, security roles with a filter condition on the given sales territory group will also filter the fact tables, and business users mapped to these roles will only see data associated for their `Sales Territory` group.

Security roles are defined in Power BI Desktop via the **Manage roles** dialog of the
Modeling tab as shown in the following screenshot:

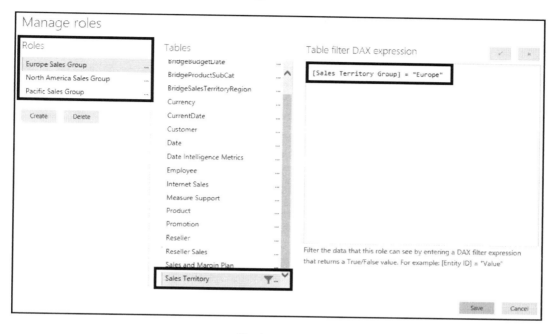

Managing security roles

 In this example model, the Sales Territory dimension table has a
single direction one-to-many relationship with the Internet
Sales and Reseller Sales fact tables. For the Sales and
Margin Plan fact table, the Sales Territory filter first flows to
the bridge table and then uses a bidirectional cross-filtering
relationship from the Sales Territory bridge to Sales and
Margin Plan. Therefore, a user mapped to the Europe Sales
Group role will only have access to the Internet Sales, Reseller Sales,
and Sales Plan data associated with Europe.

Just like a filter selection on a column of the Sales Territory table in a report, a
security filter also flows across the cross-filtering relationships of the data model.
However, unlike report filters, security filters cannot be overridden by DAX
measures. Security filters are applied to all report queries for the given dataset and
any additional filtering logic or DAX expression respects the security role definition.

Given the automatic filtering of security role conditions, it's important to implement efficient security filters and to test the performance of security roles. For example, a complex filter condition applied against a large dimension table could significantly degrade the performance of reports and dashboards for users or groups mapped to this security role.

In addition to defining security roles, security roles can also be tested in Power BI Desktop via the **View as roles** command on the **Modeling** tab. In the following screenshot, a chart that displays sales by the sales territory country is only displaying the countries associated with the European Sales Territory group due to the **View as roles** selection:

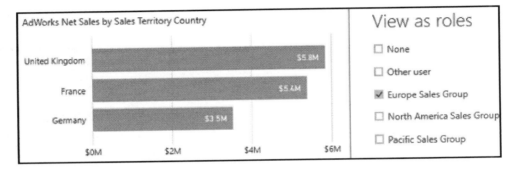

View as roles in Power BI Desktop

Similar to the **View as roles** feature in Power BI Desktop, a **Test as role** option is available in the Power BI service. This feature can be accessed from the ellipsis next to each RLS role in the **Security** dialog for the dataset. Additionally, other users can test the security roles by connecting to published Power BI apps. In this testing scenario, the user would not be a member of the app workspace, but a member of an Azure Active Directory Security group which is mapped to a security of the dataset.

Individual users and groups of users are mapped to security roles in the Power BI service. For this project, and as a strongly recommended general practice, **Azure Active Directory (AAD)** security groups should be created for the users accessing Power BI content. The following screenshot from AAD displays the properties of a `North America Sales` security group:

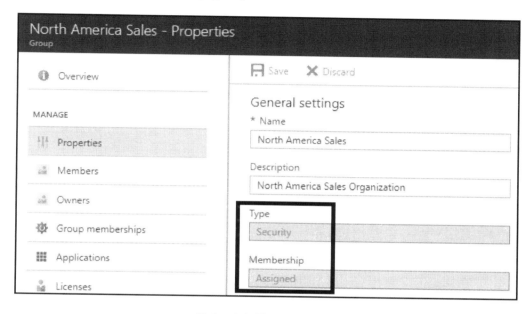

The Azure Active Directory security group

Users can be added or removed from AAD security groups in the Azure portal or via PowerShell scripts. In the previous screenshot, the **Assigned** membership type is used but alternatively, a **Dynamic User** membership type can be created based on a membership rule query. With Dynamic User AAD security groups, a user can be automatically added or removed from groups as their role in the organization changes.

The AAD security groups can then be mapped to their respective security roles for the published dataset in Power BI. In the following screenshot, the North America Sales AAD security group is recognized as a potential group to be added as a member of the North America Row-Level Security (RLS) role:

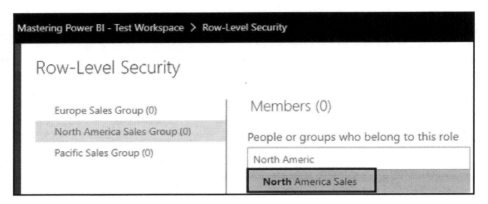

Member assignment to Row-Level Security roles

With the Azure AD security groups created and mapped to their corresponding RLS roles of the Power BI dataset, security filters will be applied based on the user's membership of the Azure AD group. When RLS roles have been applied to a dataset, the users accessing the reports and dashboards based on that dataset will need to be mapped to at least one of the roles. For example, if a Power BI app is distributed to a user who is not included in one of the Azure AD security groups mapped to one of the RLS roles, and this user account is not mapped individually to one of these RLS roles, the user will receive the following error message in the Power BI service:

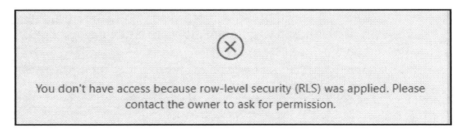

Error message: User Not mapped to an RLS role

In the event that a user is mapped to multiple RLS roles, such as both the North America Sales Group and the Europe Sales Group, that user will see data for both Sales Territory groups (and not Pacific Sales Group). For users that require access to the entire dataset, such as administrators or executives, an RLS role can be created on the dataset that doesn't include any filters on any of the tables. Chapter 17, *Creating Power BI Apps and Content Distribution*, and Chapter 18, *Administering Power BI for an Organization*, contain additional details on Azure AD's relationship to Power BI and the role of security groups in securely distributing Power BI content to users.

Dynamic row-level security

Dynamic row-level security (DRLS) models identify the user connected to the dataset via the USERPRINCIPALNAME() function and apply filters based on this identity. These models can use DAX functions or tables and relationships to implement a filter context specific to the given user. For example, a user and a permissions table could be added to the dataset (and hidden) so that the user table would first filter the permissions table, and the permission table would then filter the dimension to be secured, such as a Sales Territory Country.

In the following example of a permissions table, Jen Lawrence is associated with Germany, Australia, and the United States, and thus should only have visibility to these countries in any Power BI report or dashboard built on top of the dataset:

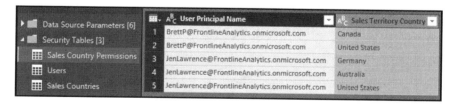

User permissions table

The other two tables in the Security Tables query group include a distinct list of **User Principal Names (UPNs)** and a distinct list of Sales Territory Country. The Sales Country table is necessary because the Sales Territory dimension table is more granular than the country one. The Sales Country table receives the filter context from the permissions table and uses a simple one-to-many cross-filtering relationship with the Sales Territory dimension table to filter the fact tables.

The dynamic RLS role will be defined with the User Principal Name column of the Users table equal to the USERPRINCIPALNAME() function. The relationships, and, more specifically, the cross-filtering from the Permissions table, will deliver the intended filter context for the given user. In the following screenshot from the Relationship view, a bidirectional cross-filtering relationship is defined between Sales Country Permissions and Sales Countries so that only the countries associated with the user will filter the Sales Territory dimension table:

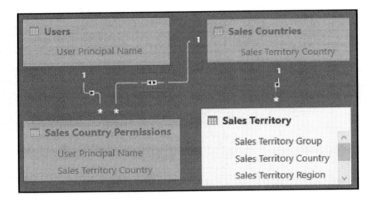

Dynamic RLS model relationships

The **Apply security filter in both directions** property of the bi-directional relationship between Sales Country Permissions and Sales Countries is enabled by default. This property and the relationships-based filtering design is applicable to both import and DirectQuery datasets. The gray shading indicates that all three security tables should be hidden from the Report View.

With users or groups assigned to the dynamic security role in the Power BI Service, the role can be tested via the **Test as role** feature in Power BI. In the following screenshot, the user Brett is able to test the dynamic role as himself (Canada, United States), but can also view the dynamic role as though Jennifer is logged in, viewing the reports:

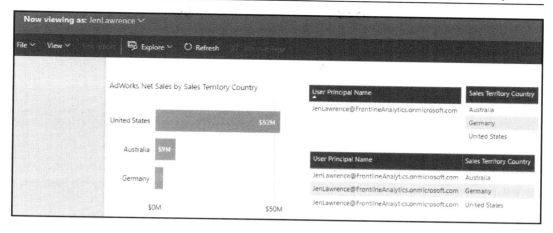

Testing dynamic row-level security in Power BI

In this security testing sample, the chart only displays the sales territory countries associated with `Jennifer`, and the three tables to the right reflect the three security tables added to the dataset. As expected, all three security tables are filtered based on Jennifer's UPN, and this filter flows through the rest of the data model via relationships among the `Sales Territory` dimension and all three fact tables.

It can be useful to create a dedicated security testing report that can be leveraged as security roles are created and modified. The report may contain multiple pages of visualizations representing all primary tables and any sensitive metrics or columns from across the dataset. On this project, a business analyst or a QA Tester, such as `Stacy Loeb`, can be mapped on to the security role and use the report to confirm that the filter context from the security role has been implemented successfully.

Performance testing

There are often many available methods of implementing business logic and custom filter contexts into DAX measures. Although these alternatives deliver the essential functional requirements, they can have very different performance characteristics, which can ultimately impact user experience and the scalability of a dataset. When migrating a self-service dataset to a corporate solution or preparing a large and highly utilized dataset, it's always a good practice to test common queries and the DAX measures used by those queries.

For example, the same common dimension grouping (for example, `Product Category` and `Year`) and the same filter context (`Year = 2018`) could produce dramatically different performance results based on the measures used in the query, such as `Net Sales` versus `Count of Customers`. The alternative performance statistics associated with different measures such as duration and the count of storage engine queries generated could then be used to focus performance tuning efforts.

In some cases, the DAX measures associated with slow queries cannot be significantly improved, but the data obtained from the performance testing results can drive other changes. For example, report authors could be advised to only use certain measures in less performance intensive visuals such as Cards, or in reports that have been substantially filtered. In a DirectQuery model, the data source owner of the dataset may be able to implement changes to the specific columns accessed via the slow-performing measures.

DAX Studio

DAX Studio is a lightweight (5 MB), open source client tool for executing DAX queries against Power BI datasets and other sources which share the Microsoft Analysis Services Tabular database engine, such as SSAS in Tabular mode and Azure Analysis Services. DAX Studio exposes the metadata of the source model (for example, tables, measures, hierarchies), includes reference panes for DAX functions and Tabular **Dynamic Management Views** (**DMVs**), and also provides query formatting, syntax highlighting, and IntelliSense for developing DAX queries. Additionally, DAX Studio supports performance tuning as it can execute traces against its data sources and displays useful performance statistics, as well as the query plans used to execute the query.

The **Server timings** and **Query plan** panes in DAX Studio expose the storage engine and formula engine query plans, respectively. In most performance-testing scenarios, the storage engine versus formula engine results of a trace (for example, 50 ms in the storage engine, 10 ms in the formula engine) will lead the user to focus on either the slowest storage engine queries or the most expensive operations in the formula engine.

For these reasons, despite improvements to DAX authoring in **SQL Server Management Studio** (**SSMS**), DAX Studio is very commonly used by Microsoft BI developers in Analysis Services and Power BI environments. Specifically, BI developers will store the DAX queries created within DAX Studio as `.dax` or `.msdax` files and later open these files from DAX studio for performance testing or troubleshooting scenarios. For example, a team may have a DAX query that returns the count of rows for three fact tables of a data model by calendar date, and use this query to troubleshoot issues related to a data-loading process. Additionally, just as M queries saved within `.pq` files can be added to version control systems, DAX query files can be added to version control systems, such as Visual Studio Team Services.

DAX Studio can be downloaded from `http://daxstudio.org`.

Tracing a Power BI dataset via DAX Studio

The following steps can be used to trace and analyze a Power BI dataset via DAX Studio:

1. Within the Power BI Desktop file containing the dataset (import or DirectQuery), create report pages and visuals which represent the most common reporting and analysis use cases:
   - To simplify this effort, access two or three existing Power BI reports which are highly utilized by business users and create the same visuals in the dataset file.
   - The formatting of these visuals is not important, but it's essential that the visuals include the most common DAX measures, filters, and granularity.

2. Open the Power BI Desktop file containing the dataset and the sample report visuals from step *1*:
   - Power BI Desktop files which do not include a dataset, such as a file with a Live connection to Analysis Services or a Live connection to a published Power BI dataset, will not be visible to DAX Studio.

3. Open DAX Studio and click the Connect icon on the right-hand side of the Home ribbon:

   - Specify the Power BI dataset from the **Connect** dialog as shown in the following screenshot:

Connecting to the Power BI dataset via DAX Studio

4. As shown in the preceding image, DAX Studio can connect to **Tabular Server,** and even **PowerPivot Model**, if DAX Studio is launched from an Excel Workbook containing a PowerPivot model.

5. Click **Connect** and observe the tables of the Power BI dataset displayed in the metadata pane on the left.

6. Click the **All Queries** icon within the group of Traces icons on the **Home** tab:

   - The **Output** window at the bottom will explain that the query trace has started.
   - Select the **All Queries** tab at the bottom (to the right of **Query History**).

7. In the Power BI Desktop file, apply a filter to a slicer or select one of the values within the visuals to cross-highlight the other visuals:

   - The intent of these actions is to mimic normal user behavior when accessing the Power BI report visuals.

- These actions will generate DAX queries which will be displayed in the **All Queries** pane of DAX Studio, as shown in the following screenshot:

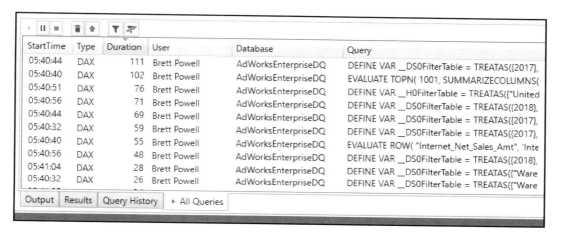

StartTime	Type	Duration	User	Database	Query
05:40:44	DAX	111	Brett Powell	AdWorksEnterpriseDQ	DEFINE VAR __DS0FilterTable = TREATAS({2017},
05:40:40	DAX	102	Brett Powell	AdWorksEnterpriseDQ	EVALUATE TOPN(1001, SUMMARIZECOLUMNS(
05:40:51	DAX	76	Brett Powell	AdWorksEnterpriseDQ	DEFINE VAR __H0FilterTable = TREATAS({"United
05:40:56	DAX	71	Brett Powell	AdWorksEnterpriseDQ	DEFINE VAR __DS0FilterTable = TREATAS({2018},
05:40:44	DAX	69	Brett Powell	AdWorksEnterpriseDQ	DEFINE VAR __DS0FilterTable = TREATAS({2017},
05:40:32	DAX	59	Brett Powell	AdWorksEnterpriseDQ	DEFINE VAR __DS0FilterTable = TREATAS({2017},
05:40:40	DAX	55	Brett Powell	AdWorksEnterpriseDQ	EVALUATE ROW("Internet_Net_Sales_Amt", 'Inte
05:40:56	DAX	48	Brett Powell	AdWorksEnterpriseDQ	DEFINE VAR __DS0FilterTable = TREATAS({2018},
05:41:04	DAX	28	Brett Powell	AdWorksEnterpriseDQ	DEFINE VAR __DS0FilterTable = TREATAS({"Ware
05:40:32	DAX	26	Brett Powell	AdWorksEnterpriseDQ	DEFINE VAR __DS0FilterTable = TREATAS({"Ware

Output | Results | Query History | ▶ All Queries

Tracing results in DAX Studio – All Queries pane

8. The **All Queries** pane can be sorted by the `Duration` column to quickly identify the slowest query, as illustrated in the preceding screenshot. Additionally, hovering over the `Query` field displays a formatted version of the DAX query, thus making it easy to identify the DAX measure(s) involved.

9. Stop the trace via the stop icon in the **All Queries** pane (above **StartTime**).

10. Double-click a value from the row of the **All Queries** pane representing the slowest query (for example, Duration = 111) to add this query to the editor window:
    - The values in the `User`, `Database`, and `Query` fields can all be used to add the query to the editor window.
    - Alternatively, the Copy All icon (up arrow) in the **All Queries** pane can be used to add all queries from the trace to the editor window.

11. Select the Server Timings icon in the middle of the **Home** tab to start a new trace:
    - Select the **Server Timings** pane that appears at the bottom (to the right of **All Queries**)

12. With the slowest query from step 7 in the editor window, click the **Run** icon, or hit *F5* to execute the DAX query.

In the following screenshot, the query from the original trace against the Power BI Desktop file (`AdWorksEnterpriseDQ`), which required 111 ms in duration, was executed in 106 ms from DAX Studio:

The Server Timings window in DAX Studio

As shown in the preceding image, the editor window displays the `Internet Net Sales Amt` measure, and the **Server Timings** pane at the bottom identifies the duration of the query (**106 ms**). Given that the dataset for this example is in DirectQuery mode against a SQL Server database, the T-SQL statement generated and passed to the database server is displayed in the `Query` field and window to the right (not shown). This T-SQL statement can be easily copied into another application, such as **SQL Server Server Management Studio** (**SSMS**), and executed directly against the source or saved as its own `.sql` file.

For DirectQuery datasets, use traces in DAX Studio to collect the SQL statements associated with the slowest-performing DAX queries. The team responsible for the DirectQuery source (for example, Teradata) may be able to identify the cause of the issue such as the columns referenced in the filter condition. Additionally, if referential integrity is enforced in the DirectQuery data source, ensure that the SQL statements generated use inner join conditions. Inner join SQL statements will be generated if the Assume referential integrity property of the Edit relationship window has been enabled.

As an alternative to the **All Queries** trace of a Power BI dataset, a new DAX measure could be tested against an existing DAX query. For example, a common grouping query built with the SUMMARIZECOLUMNS() DAX function and stored in a .dax or .msdax file could be opened in DAX Studio. The new DAX measure contained in the dataset could be referenced in the editor window and the query could be executed with a trace running (via **Server Timings**). The performance results of the new measure could be compared against the baseline results from common measures (for example, Net Sales and Count of Orders) to obtain a sense of relative performance.

Additionally, two DAX measures which return the same results but utilize distinct logic or functions could be tested against each other in DAX Studio to determine which measure is more performant. DAX measures already added to the Power BI dataset can be accessed via the Metadata pane, and DAX measures can also be defined within the Power Query Editor window via the DEFINE clause.

The following URL contains the full syntax of using DAX as a query language http://bit.ly/2FoRF2y.

Summary

This chapter developed and described several common classes of DAX measures, including date intelligence, dimension metrics, and ranking metrics. These measures utilized the fact and dimension tables accessed in Chapter 8, *Connecting to Sources and Transforming Data with M*, as well as the data model relationships defined in Chapter 9, *Designing Import and DirectQuery Data Models*. In addition to detailed measure examples, primary concepts of the DAX including filter context, row context, measure evaluation, and DAX variables were also reviewed. Moreover, examples of standard and DRLS models were shared, and DAX Studio was presented as a tool for testing and tuning DAX.

In the following chapter, Power BI reports will be created which leverage the dataset that has been incrementally developed since Chapter 8, *Connecting to Sources and Transforming Data with M*. Report-authoring features, such as the visualization types in Power BI Desktop, will access the DAX measures from this chapter and the dimensions from previous chapters to deliver business insights and intuitive, self-service functionality.

11
Creating and Formatting Power BI Reports

In this chapter, we will create Power BI reports based on the dataset developed over the past three chapters and published to the Power BI service. We will review a report-planning and design process as well as all primary report formatting features in the context of visualization best practices. Additionally, we will look at report behavior and functionality features, such as alternative filter scopes, slicers, and conditional formatting options.

This chapter also highlights several of the latest and most powerful Power BI report features, including visual interactions, top N, relative date filters, and What-if parameters. The reports developed in this chapter can be further supplemented with custom visuals and advanced analytics from the following chapter to serve as a supporting analysis layer to Power BI dashboards.

In this chapter, we will review the following topics:

- Report planning
- Live connections to Power BI datasets
- Visualization best practices
- Choosing the visual
- Visual interactions
- Slicers
- What-if parameters
- Report filter scopes
- Relative date filtering
- Conditional formatting
- Mobile-optimized reports

Report planning

Power BI reports can take on a variety of forms and use cases, ranging from executive-level dashboard layouts to highly detailed and focused reports. Prior to designing and developing Power BI reports, some level of planning and documentation is recommended to ensure that the reports are well aligned with the needs of the users and the organization.

Effective report planning can be encapsulated in the following five steps:

1. Identify the users or consumers of this report:
   - Senior managers generally prefer less self-service interactivity and value simple, intuitive visuals, such as KPIs.
   - Analysts often require significant flexibility to filter and interact with more detailed reports. For example, reports used by analysts generally include more slicer visuals and may include table or matrix visuals as well.

   Separating reports by user role or group serves to keep reports focused for users and more manageable for BI teams. In many scenarios, an organizational hierarchy provides a natural demarcation such that reports can be designed for specific roles or levels within an organization.

   In the project example for the Adventure Works sales team, reports could align with the `Sales Territory` hierarchy (`Sales Territory Group` | `Sales Territory Country` | `Sales Territory Region`). The vice president of group sales will value high-value corporate-wide metrics and intuitive dashboard reports. A sales analyst in the United States, however, will likely need to break out individual regions and even analyze specific zip codes or individual products.

2. Define the business question(s) that the report should answer or support:
   - Confirm with the business user(s) or project sponsors that this is the appropriate focus and scope of the report:
     - A report architecture diagram described in the next section can support this communication.
     - For example, the user could be advised that a particular business question or metric will be included in a different report but will be featured on the same dashboard and will be easily accessible within the same Power BI app.

- The most important business question (for example, *What were our sales?*) will be addressed in the top-left corner of the report canvas, likely with a KPI or card visual.

Similar to separating reports by user role or group, a report should not attempt to resolve widely disparate business questions. A sales report can, for example, provide high-level metrics on other business processes, such as customer service, inventory, or shipping. However, the supporting visuals of a report should almost always be derived from the same business processes and fact tables as the primary business question, such as `Internet Sales` and `Reseller Sales`.

3. Confirm that the dataset supports the business questions:
    - The report author should ensure that the dataset includes measures such as **year-over-year** (**YOY**) sales and the dimension columns (for example, `Product Category`) necessary to visualize the business questions.

It's very important that report authors have a solid understanding of the Power BI dataset. This knowledge includes the logic and business definitions of DAX measures, the relationships defined between fact and dimension tables, and any data transformation logic applied to the source data. In many projects, report authors will regularly collaborate with business stakeholders or project sponsors in gathering requirements and demonstrating report iterations. Therefore, the authors will need to explain the values and behaviors of Power BI reports as well as any current limitations in the dataset, such as the years of history supported and any DAX logic or measures not yet created:

- If a gap exists between the dataset and the measures required for the report, the team can determine whether the dataset should be extended or whether the measure should be created local to the report
- Only measures can be created within Power BI Live connection reports
- Any new columns, tables, or modifications to existing tables or columns must be implemented within the source dataset

The set of base measures described in Chapter 10, *Developing DAX Measures and Security Roles*, as well as the dynamic date dimension columns described in Chapter 8, *Connecting to Sources and Transforming Data with M* (for example, Calendar Month Status = 'Prior Calendar Month'), should support the most common needs of reports. If a measure required for a report is considered to be common to other future reports, and if the measure doesn't violate the single corporate definition of an existing measure, the measure should generally be added to the dataset. However, if the report requirement is considered rare or if a measure definition has been approved only for the specific report, then the measure(s) can be created local to the report. For version control and manageability reasons, report authors should not have to implement complex filtering logic or develop many local report measures. Report authors should communicate with dataset designers and the overall team if a significant gap exists or is developing between reports and the dataset.

4. Determine how the report will be accessed and the nature of any user interactivity:
   - Reports and dashboards can be optimized for mobile device consumption if this use case is expected
   - Power BI Desktop supports slicer visuals, a What-if parameter, and visual interaction options as standard features:
     - Reports can, therefore, be designed for static consumption or to support rich data exploration

5. Draw a sketch of the report layout:
   - At least for the primary page of the report, document how the area of the report canvas will be allocated

The following sample sketch is created within a PowerPoint
presentation file via the standard shape objects:

Sales (YTD)	Margin % (YTD)		Sales by Product Category Comparison
Sales (YOY)	Margin % (YOY)	Sales versus Plan by Month	
Calendar Year-Mo Slicers			
Distribution of Unit Prices		Sales and Margin % Comparison by Country	Margin % by Product Category Breakdown

Sample report layout sketch

- Per the sample layout, the critical sales and margin measures
  are located in the top-left corner of the report page:
  - Slicer (filter) visuals are planned for below
    these KPI or card visuals and other visuals will
    add further context
  - Greater space is allocated to the two visuals in
    the middle of the page given their importance
    to the report
- The report layout sketch can be used exclusively for planning
  purposes or can be set as the background for a report page
  - For example, a PowerPoint slide of the same
    shapes, background shading, and borders can
    be saved to a network directory as a PNG file

- In Power BI Desktop, the PNG file can be imported via the **Add Image formatting** option under **Page Background** or via the insert an image icon on the **Home** tab in Report view
- Page background images with proper alignment, spacing, and colors can expedite quality report development

Be willing to modify a report layout or even start afresh with a new layout based on user feedback. Unlike dataset development, which can require significant time and expertise (for example, DAX, M, SQL), reports can be developed in a rapid, agile delivery methodology. Report authors can engage directly with users on these iterations and, although recommended practices and corporate standards can be communicated, ultimately the functional value to the user is the top priority. It's important to distinguish flexibility in report layout and visualization from the report's target users and business questions. Second and third iterations of reports should not, for example, call for fundamentally different measures or new report pages to support different user groups. Report authors and BI teams can work with users and project sponsors to maintain the scope of IT-supported reports. The interactivity built into Power BI reports and the self-service capabilities provided by Power BI Pro licenses can broaden the reach of projects without requiring new or additional reports.

Power BI report architecture

Similar to the data warehouse bus matrix described in Chapter 7, *Planning Power BI Projects,* a report architecture diagram can be helpful for planning and communicating Power BI projects with both business and IT stakeholders. This diagram serves to maintain the scope and focus of individual reports. For example, certain business questions or entities (such as Customers, Products) can be assigned to dedicated reports and the individual pages of these reports can visualize these questions or entities at varying levels of detail.

Most commonly, a single report page will address the top priority of a report at a summary level. This page includes cards and/or KPI visuals at the top-left of the page and charts rather than tables or matrices that visualize these metrics at a high level. Additional report pages, usually 3-4 maximum, would be designed to provide a greater level of detail supporting the summary page. With this report structure, a user can naturally start their analysis from an intuitive and visually appealing summary page and then, if necessary, navigate to pages exposing greater levels of detail.

In addition to supporting report pages with greater detail, Drillthrough report pages can be designed to display the details for an individual item, such as a specific product or a combination of items, for example, the year 2018 and a specific product. The *Drillthrough report pages* section of Chapter 12, *Applying Custom Visuals, Animation, and Analytics* provides details and examples of this feature.

In the absence of a report architecture or diagram, reports can quickly become less user-friendly as many report pages are added that address unrelated business questions. Additionally, the lack of scope or focus for a report can lead to duplicated efforts with the same business question being visualized in multiple reports.

Guidance from stakeholders on the visuals to be included in or featured on a dashboard can strongly inform the report design process. If several dashboard tiles, particularly those intended in the top or left section of the dashboard, are closely related (for example, profitability %) then it's likely that multiple reports, each with multiple pages, should be designed to support further related analysis of these tiles. However, if only one dashboard tile relates to a particular business question or entity, such as resellers, then the supporting report may only need 1-2 pages and provide relatively less detail.

In the following basic example, four reports and one dashboard are planned for the German sales team:

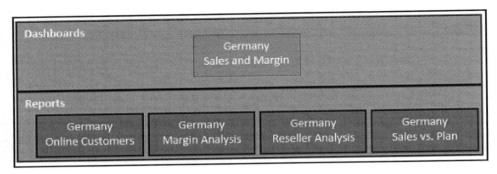

Sample report architecture diagram

In this sample, at least one visual from each of the four reports would be pinned as a tile on the `Germany Sales and Margin` dashboard. By default, this would link the reports to the dashboard such that a user could access the details of any of the four reports by clicking on a related dashboard tile. Visuals from a single report can be pinned as tiles to multiple dashboards. Additionally, a dashboard tile can be linked to a separate dashboard or to a separate report in the Power BI service. `Chapter 13`, *Designing Power BI Dashboards and Architectures* include additional details and examples of Power BI report and dashboard architectures.

The four reports and the dashboard from the preceding example could be included in a dedicated app workspace for the German sales team or within a broader workspace that supports multiple sales teams and related content (for example, marketing) in the organization. If a Power BI dataset is used as the source for Power BI reports, then consolidating reports and dashboards into a broader app workspace avoids the need to duplicate this dataset across other workspaces given the current dependency between Power BI Live connection reports and datasets within the same workspace. Information on app workspaces and content distribution via apps are provided in `Chapter 14`, *Managing Application Workspaces and Content* and `Chapter 17`, *Creating Power BI Apps and Content Distribution*. The following section describes Live connection reports to Power BI datasets published to the Power BI service.

Understand and communicate the differences between Power BI reports and dashboards. Although report pages can look like dashboards to users, Power BI dashboards are generally best suited to integrating the essential visuals from multiple reports. Dashboards deliver a holistic, at-a-glance view of strategic metrics while reports are more narrowly focused on specific business questions. Additionally, reports provide interactive, analytical features (for example, slicer visuals) for users to leverage in a self-service.

Live connections to Power BI datasets

One of the most important features released in 2017 was the ability to use published Power BI datasets as a source for Power BI reports. With Live connections to Power BI datasets, report authors can develop reports in Power BI Desktop files containing only the visualization layer (for example, report pages of visuals) while leveraging a single dataset.

The dataset, which is generally developed and managed by a different user or team, already includes the data retrieval supporting tables and columns, the data model relationships, and the DAX measures or calculations as described in previous chapters. Once the Live connection report is developed and published to Power BI, it will maintain its connection to the source dataset and will be refreshed with the refresh schedule configured for the dataset.

Prior to Live connection reports to Power BI datasets, users within teams would frequently create multiple versions of the same dataset in order to create different reports. As both a report and a dataset, each individual report would require its own scheduled refresh process (in import mode), its own data storage, and would create version control problems as the report author could modify the underlying dataset. Live connection reports therefore severely reduce resource requirements and promote a single version of the truth. Moreover, Live connection reports facilitate the isolation of report design and development from dataset design and development.

Most Power BI report authors will not be interested in or responsible for dataset design topics, such as data retrieval with M queries, data modeling, and DAX measures. Likewise, a dataset designer is often less interested in or responsible for visualization best practices and the engagement with the actual users of reports and dashboards. As advised in Chapter 7, *Planning Power BI Projects,* it's important for the alternative roles (dataset designer, report author) to regularly collaborate, such as by identifying measures or columns that need to be added to the dataset to support reports and dashboards.

To create a Live connection report with a published Power BI dataset as the source, the report author needs a Power BI Pro license and will need to be a member of the app workspace hosting the dataset with edit rights.

In the following example, the report author is a member of the Corporate Sales app workspace and creates a new report in Power BI Desktop by connecting to the AdWorks Enterprise dataset within this workspace:

Power BI service   Jennifer Lawrence
JenLawrence@FrontlineAnalytics.onmicrosoft.com
Switch account

⊿ 📊 Microsoft Power BI service [5]
  ▷ 👥 My workspace
  ▷ 👥 Mobile Testing
  ⊿ 👥 Corporate Sales [1]
    🗄 AdWorks Enterprise
  ▷ 👥 North America Sales
  ▷ 👥 Europe Sales

Creating a Live connection to the Power BI dataset

After selecting the **Power BI service** from the list of **Online Services** within the **Get Data** dialog, the list of the workspaces of which the report author is a member is prompted. In this example, either double-clicking the `AdWorks Enterprise` dataset or clicking the **Load** button will establish the Live connection per the status bar in Power BI Desktop:

Connected live to the Power BI dataset: AdWorks Enterprise in Corporate Sales

Live connection status bar

The same field list of measures and tables is exposed in Report View but the Relationship View and Data View do not appear. Likewise, once the Live connection has been established, the **Get Data** dialog is also grayed out. Live connection reports to Power BI datasets and **SQL Server Analysis Services** (**SSAS**) databases are always limited to a single data model as a source.

Live connection reports are published to the same app workspace as their source dataset. In the following example, a report file named `USA Sales and Margin`, which is connected to the `AdWorks Enterprise` dataset in the `Corporate Sales` workspace has been published from Power BI Desktop:

Published Live connection report

Per the preceding image, the report will appear in the workspace of the source dataset (Corporate Sales) in Power BI. Since the report was published from Power BI Desktop, the report (.pbix file) can be downloaded by opening the report and clicking **Download report** from the **File** menu.

It's possible to create reports based on Power BI datasets within the Power BI online service. However, the .pbix files for these reports cannot be downloaded and thus all edits must be implemented within the service without version history. Additionally, several important report authoring features in Power BI Desktop are not supported in the service, including the alignment of objects and local report measures. Given these considerations, Power BI Desktop is recommended for any report development beyond personal or ad hoc use. Guidance on version history for Power BI Desktop files (reports and datasets) is included in Chapter 14, *Managing Application Workspaces and Content.*

Customizing Live connection reports

Although data modeling and retrieval capabilities are removed in Live connection reports, report authors have the ability to create new measures specific to the given report via the New Measure icon under the **Modeling** tab. Additionally, report authors can change the names of measures and columns displayed in reports.

In the following example, the `Internet Net Sales` measure and the `Customer Country` column have been renamed to `Net Sales` and `Country`, respectively:

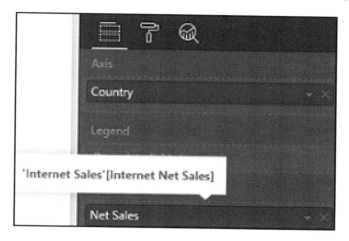

Renamed measure and column in Visual

Double-clicking the name of the column or measure in the field well(s) for the visual exposes an input box for the revised name. Per the preceding image, the revised names will appear in the report visual and the **Tooltips** in the field wells will indicate the source column or measure. In this example, the `Internet Net Sales` measure, with a home table of the `Internet Sales` fact table, is the source for the `Net Sales` alias name.

Although the flexibility to create measures and apply names within reports is helpful and appropriate in certain scenarios, these revisions can create complexity and version control issues. For example, users can become accustomed to specific measures and names that the dataset designer is not aware of and that may conflict with other measures or names in the dataset. Therefore, it's generally recommended to incorporate the necessary measure logic and standard names into the source dataset.

Switching source datasets

In many project scenarios, a Power BI report will initially be built against a development or testing dataset. After this report has been validated or received the proper approvals, the report's source dataset can be switched to a production dataset and the report can then be published to the production app workspace used for distributing Power BI content to users.

To switch the Power BI dataset of a Live connection report, click the **Data Source settings** icon under the **Edit Queries** drop-down menu under the **Home** tab. In the following two steps with supporting images, a report is switched from a dataset in the `Corporate Sales` workspace to a dataset in the `North America Sales` workspace:

1. Open the Power BI service data source window via **Data source settings**:

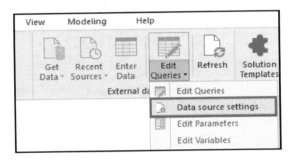

Data source settings for a Live connection report

2. Select the new dataset to use as the source for the report:
   - Either double-click the dataset or click the **Load** command button to establish the connection:

Power BI dataset sources

3. Confirm the source dataset has changed via the status bar:

Connected live to the Power BI dataset: AdWorks Enterprise in North America Sales

Source Power BI dataset switched

See `Chapter 14`, *Managing Application Workspaces and Content* for details on Power BI project life cycles, such as migrating from development to production environments and version control.

Visualization best practices

Effective reports are much more than simply answering documented business questions with the available measures and columns of the dataset. Reports also need to be visually appealing and provide a logical structure that aids in navigation and readability. Business users of all backgrounds appreciate a report that is clear, concise, and aesthetically pleasing.

Now that the report-planning phase described earlier is complete, the following list of 15 visualization practices can guide the report development process:

1. Avoid clutter and minimize nonessential details:
    - Each visual should align with the purpose of the report—to gain insight into a business question:
        - Visualizations should not represent wild guesses or functionality that the author finds interesting
    - Eliminate report elements that aren't essential for gaining understanding:
        - Gridlines, legends, axis labels, text boxes, and images can often be limited or removed
    - The report should be understandable at a glance, without supporting documentation or explanation.

A simple but helpful test is to view a Power BI report on a laptop screen from a distance of 12 to 15 feet, such as from the opposite end of a conference room. At this distance, it will be impossible to read any small text and only the shapes, curves, and colors will be useful for deriving meaning. If the report is still meaningful, this suggests the report is effectively designed visually.

2. Provide simple, clear titles on report pages and visuals:
    - Text boxes can be used to name or describe the report, report page, and provide the last-refreshed date

3. For chart visuals, use the length of lines and the two-dimensional position of points to aid visual comprehension:
    - In line charts, users can easily perceive trends and the divergence of lines relative to each other
    - In column or bar charts, users can easily distinguish relative differences in the length of bars
    - In scatter charts, users can quickly interpret the two-dimensional position of data points relative to each other

The purpose of these two attributes (line length, 2-D position) as the primary communication mechanism is to guide the user to an accurate assessment with minimal effort. Other visual attributes such as color, shape, and size can also be beneficial, particularly when these properties are driven by the data, such as with conditional formatting and KPIs. However, line length and 2-D position (X, Y coordinates) have a natural advantage in visual perception. For example, the differences between three items on a clustered column chart are much more obvious than the same three items presented on a pie chart.

4. Position and group visuals to provide a logical navigation across the canvas:
    - The most important visuals should be positioned in the top-left corner of each report page
    - If multiple visuals are closely related, consider grouping them within a shape object

5. Use soft, natural colors for most visuals:
    - Avoid overwhelming users with highly saturated bright or dark colors

- Only use more pronounced colors when it's necessary to make an item stand out, such as conditional formatting

6. Only apply distinct colors to items in chart visuals when the colors convey meaning:
    - For example, three colors might be useful for the data points of three separate product categories

7. Align visuals to common and *X* and *Y* pixel positions:
    - For example, if a visual in the top-left corner of a page has *X* and *Y* position values of 20 and 40, respectively, then other visuals on the left side of the canvas should also have an **X Position** of 20
    - Likewise, the top visual(s) on the right side of the canvas should align with the left visuals at a Y position of 40

8. Distribute visuals vertically and horizontally to create an equal amount of space between visuals:
    - The amount of spacing should be adequate to clearly distinguish the visuals as separate entities

With one or multiple visuals selected in Power BI Desktop, a **Format** tab will appear on the ribbon per the following image:

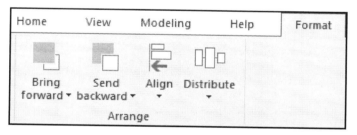

Alignment, distribution, and Z-order format options

The three format options (**Align**, **Distribute**, and **Bring forward** and **Send backward** (Z-order)) are consistent with common MS Office applications, such as Excel and PowerPoint. Between these formatting options and the four properties available under the general formatting card for all visuals (**X Position**, **Y Position**, **Width**, and **Height**). Report authors can ensure that visuals are properly aligned and spaced. The **Show gridlines** and **Snap objects to grid** options under the **View** tab also support alignment.

9. Choose a page background color that will naturally contrast with visuals, such as the default white or a very light gray.

10. For column and bar charts, sort visuals by their measure to provide an implicit ranking by the given measure:

   - This sorting is only applicable to nominal categories, such as product categories, when the individual items in the category don't need to follow a custom sort order

11. Fill the available report canvas space; avoid large blank spaces in report pages.

12. Provide supporting context via tooltips and additional lines in charts, such as target values and the min, max, and average:

   - Several measures related to a given visual can be displayed via tooltips without incurring performance penalties
   - The Power BI Analytics pane provides several support lines, including a trend line and a predictive forecast line

13. All report pages should follow a common design theme and color palette:

   - Preferably all reports in a project and even for an organization should follow the same basic design guidelines

A **Switch Theme** icon on the **Home** tab of Power BI Desktop in Report View exposes options for importing a report theme and thus overriding the default color and formatting properties:

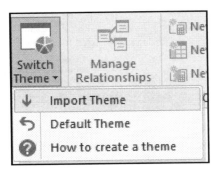

Import report theme

Custom Report Themes are a preview feature as of the November 2017 release of Power BI Desktop and allow organizations to apply a custom set of formatting properties to Power BI reports. For example, an organization can embed its corporate colors into a report theme (a JSON file) to apply this set of colors to all Power BI reports. Additionally, more elaborate formatting properties can be specified in report themes to standardize report development, such as the font family and font sizes. Existing report themes are available for download from the Power BI Report Theme Gallery (`http://bit.ly/2pyUKpl`). Additionally, tools and documentation are available for easily generating report themes, such as the Power BI Tips Color Theme Generator (`https://powerbi.tips/tools/color-theme-generator/`).

14. The quantitative scale for column and bar charts must start at zero:
    - Custom quantitative scales, such as from 12% to 15%, can be applied to line, scatter, and bubble charts to emphasize specific ranges of values

Consider two items, `Product A` and `Product B`, of a clustered column chart with margin percentage values of 32% and 34%, respectively. With a base of zero, the two items would correctly appear similar for the given measure. However, if the base value of the visual starts at 31% and the max value of the scale is set to 35%, `Product B` would visually appear as a dramatically higher value. This distortion is the reason that quantitative scales for column and bar charts must start at zero.

15. Lines should only be used to connect interval scale data points, such as time series and ordered bins of values:
    - A line should not, for example, represent the sales for different product categories
    - A line should, however, represent the sales of products by unit price bins (for example, $0 to $10, $10 to $20, and so forth)

Visualization anti-patterns

In addition to report planning and generally aligning reports with visualization best practices, it can be helpful to acknowledge and avoid several common visualization anti-patterns. For many reports, particularly when report development time and Power BI experience is limited, simply avoiding these anti-patterns coupled with adequate planning and appropriate visual type choices is sufficient to deliver quality, sustainable content.

Six of the most common visualization anti-patterns include the following:

- A cluttered interface of many visuals and report elements that's complex or difficult to interpret:
    - This is often the result of too many visuals per report page or too high a precision being displayed
    - Separate reports, report pages, and the removal of unnecessary details and precision can improve usability
- A lack of structure, order, and consistency:
    - Each report page should naturally guide the user from the essential top-left visuals to the supporting visuals
    - A failure to align visuals or to provide proper spacing and borders can make reports appear disorganized
    - Mixing widely disparate grains of detail on the same report page can be disorienting to users
- High density and/or high detail visualizations, such as large table visuals or thousands of points on a scatter chart or map:
    - The need for a scrollbar is a strong indication that a visual contains too many values
    - A table visual should not be used as a raw data extract of many columns and rows
    - High density visuals, such as line and scatter charts with thousands of data points, can cause poor performance

The following table visual with six dimension columns and three measures is an example of a data extract anti-pattern:

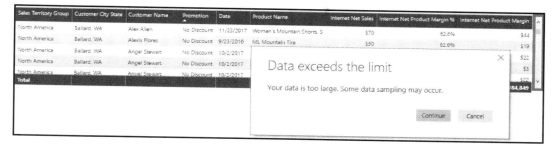

Data extract anti-pattern

The small scrollbar on the right indicates that many rows are not displayed. Additionally, the export data option prompts the warning message (data exceeds the limit) suggesting the visual contains too much data.

- The excessive use of fancy or complex visuals and images:
    - Reports can be aesthetic and engaging but the priority should be to inform users, not to impress them.
    - For example, a column chart or a stacked column chart will usually be more effective than a treemap.
- Suboptimal visual choices such as pie charts, donut charts, and gauges:
    - Column or bar charts are easier to interpret than the circular shapes of pie and donut charts.
    - KPI visuals provide more context than gauge visuals including the trend of the indicator value.
- The misuse of colors, such as utilizing more than five colors and overwhelming users with highly saturated colors:
    - Colors should be used selectively and only when the few alternative colors convey meaning.

Choosing the visual

With the report planning phase completed, an essential task of the report author is to choose the visual(s) best suited to gain insight into the particular questions within the scope of the report. The choice of the visualization type, such as a column chart or a matrix visual, should closely align with the most important use case, the message to deliver, and the data relationship to represent.

Visualization types have distinct advantages in terms of visual perception and types of data relationships such as part-to-whole and comparisons. Additionally, although several formatting options are common to all visuals, certain options such as the line style (solid, dashed, dotted) of a line chart are exclusive to specific visuals.

A standard visual selection process is as follows:

1. Plan and document the business question(s) and related measures and dimension columns.
2. Determine whether a table, a chart, or both will be needed to best visualize this data.
3. If a chart is needed, choose the chart visual that's best aligned with the relationship (for example, trend, comparison, correlation).

Following these three steps helps to ensure that effective reports are developed with efficient resources. Many other visualization and analysis features can be used to further enhance reports but these should only supplement report planning and design.

 Power BI currently supports 25 standard visualizations, and many more custom visualizations can be imported from the MS Office Store. The standard visuals are aligned with the most common analytical representations including trend, rankings, part-to-whole, exceptions, geospatial, and distribution. Several of these visuals can be further enhanced via the Analytics pane and a vast array of custom visuals can be easily imported to reports from the MS Office Store. See the following chapter for additional details on the **Analytics** pane in Power BI Desktop and custom visuals.

Tables versus charts

An initial step in the visualization selection process is to determine whether a table, a chart, or a combination of both is most appropriate. Power BI's table visual provides simple row groups of dimension values and measures, and the matrix visual supports both an *X* and a *Y*-axis field like a pivot table in Excel. Both the table and the matrix visuals are superior to charts in enabling users to look up specific data points. However, despite conditional formatting options available to table and matrix visuals, charts are superior to table and matrix visuals in displaying trends, comparisons, and large volumes of distinct data points.

The following matrix visual breaks down the `AdWorks Net Sales` measure by two product dimension columns and two promotion dimension columns:

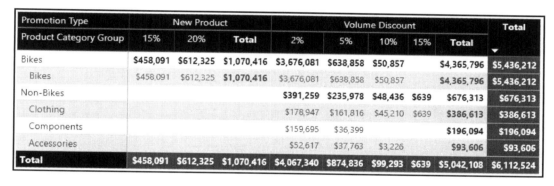

Promotion Type	New Product			Volume Discount					Total
Product Category Group	15%	20%	Total	2%	5%	10%	15%	Total	▼
Bikes	$458,091	$612,325	$1,070,416	$3,676,081	$638,858	$50,857		$4,365,796	$5,436,212
Bikes	$458,091	$612,325	$1,070,416	$3,676,081	$638,858	$50,857		$4,365,796	$5,436,212
Non-Bikes				$391,259	$235,978	$48,436	$639	$676,313	$676,313
Clothing				$178,947	$161,816	$45,210	$639	$386,613	$386,613
Components				$159,695	$36,399			$196,094	$196,094
Accessories				$52,617	$37,763	$3,226		$93,606	$93,606
Total	$458,091	$612,325	$1,070,416	$4,067,340	$874,836	$99,293	$639	$5,042,108	$6,112,524

Matrix visual

The product hierarchy created in `Chapter 9`, *Designing Import and DirectQuery Data Models* is used as the rows' input and a promotion table hierarchy is used as the columns' input. Via the expand all down feature for both the rows and the columns, the matrix provides easy access to specific data points, including subtotals by both product categories and promotion types. Although it's clearly possible to visualize the same data with a chart, a matrix visual (or a table visual) makes it easy to locate individual values and to display the exact values with no rounding.

Additionally, if a table or matrix is needed to reference individual values but less precision is required, the field formatting card in the formatting pane allows the report author to define the display units (for example, thousands (K), millions (M)) and the number of decimal places for the measure. The same two formatting properties (display units and value decimal places) are also accessible for chart visuals via the data labels formatting card in the formatting pane.

Although they're rarely used in Power BI dashboards, Power BI's table and matrix visuals were significantly enhanced throughout 2017 to provide more granular formatting controls. Matrix features, such as showing values (for example, multiple metrics) as individual rows, as a percentage of column or row totals, and full control over subtotals positions Power BI matrix visuals as an alternative to many Excel pivot tables and matrix reports in **SQL Server Report Services (SSRS)**. Additionally, table and matrix visuals are interactive such that user selections on a row, a specific value, or a row or column header will filter other visuals.

The following line chart visual breaks down the AdWorks Net Sales measure by the calendar year week:

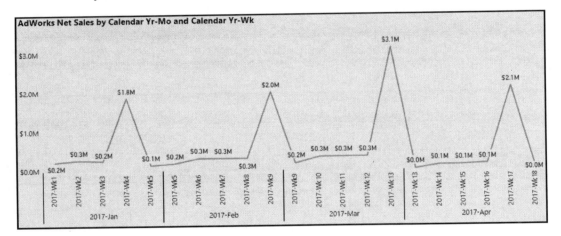

Line chart visual

With 18 different data points displayed, the periodic spikes of the line help to identify the specific weeks with relatively higher net sales. In this example, the AdWorks Net Sales measure is highest in the fourth or last week of the month and is especially higher at the end of March—the first quarter. The drawback or tradeoff of this visual relative to the prior matrix visual is the lack of subtotals and the loss of precision given the rounding to one decimal place.

Line charts are uniquely advantaged to call out patterns, trends, and exceptions in measures across time. More generally, chart visualizations (for example, bar, column, scatter) are recommended over table and matrix visuals when the shape or position of the data, such as trends, comparisons, correlations, and exceptions, is more valuable than the individual values.

 With a date hierarchy or the date columns in the chart axis input field, the concatenate labels property in the X-axis formatting card should be turned off to provide the grouped layout per the preceding line chart example. Additionally, also included in the line chart example visual, the X-axis gridlines can be turned on to separate the parent values (for example, **2017-Feb**).

Chart selection

Chart visuals can broadly be categorized into the following four types of data relationships:

- **Comparison**: How items compare against each other or over time
- **Relationship**: How items relate (or correlate) to one another across multiple variables
- **Distribution**: The most common values for a variable and the concentration of values within a range
- **Composition**: The portion of a total that an item represents relative to other items, possibly over time

The following table associates specific visuals to these categories and briefly describes their top use cases:

Chart	Category	Example Use Cases
Line chart	Comparison	• Display the fluctuation and trend of a value over time. • Compare the trends of multiple items over time.
Column chart	Comparison	• Rank items based on a value and display precise data points. • Use a bar chart if there are many items or if item data labels are long.
Combination chart	Comparison	• Compare items against two values with disparate scales. • For example, display sales by country as columns across time but also show the margin % as a line on the secondary axis.
Scatter charts and bubble charts	Relationship	• Display the relative position of items (data points) on two variables such as products by sales and sales growth %. • Optionally drive the size of the data points by a third variable.
Pie charts and doughnut charts	Composition	• Commonly used for part-to-whole relationships. • Column, bar and stacked column and bar charts are recommended alternatives to pie and doughnut charts.
Histograms	Distribution	• Display a frequency distribution such as the count of items sold by different list prices or list price bins on the X axis. • In Power BI, use a column chart, line chart or custom visual.
Waterfall charts and funnel charts	Composition	• Use waterfall charts to break out the changes in a value over time based on a category. • Use a funnel chart to display variances in the stages of a process.

Chart visuals by category

As a table of chart types, map visuals, and the three standard single number visuals provided in Power BI Desktop—Cards, Gauge, and KPI, are excluded. Single number visuals are commonly used in dashboards, mobile optimized reports, and in the top-left section of report pages to deliver easy access to important metrics.

The standard single number visuals (Card, Gauge, KPI) can also be used to create data alerts when these visuals are pinned to Power BI dashboards. Alerts can be created and managed in both the Power BI service and on the Power BI mobile applications. With an alert set on a dashboard tile representing one of these visuals, whenever the number of the visual crosses a defined condition (for example, above 100), a notification will be raised and optionally an email will be sent as well.

Details on standard map visuals are included in the *Map visuals* section of this chapter and the *ArcGIS Map visual for Power BI* is reviewed in `Chapter 12`, *Applying Custom Visuals, Animation and Analytics*.

There are several publicly available resources on visualization practices and visual selection. The *Chart Suggestions* diagram from Extreme Presentation (`http://bit.ly/1xlXh1x`) provides additional details on the visuals and visual categories described in this section. Additionally, the SQL BI team provides a *Power BI Visuals Reference* (`http://bit.ly/2ndtcZj`) that categorizes visuals at a more granular level than the table in this section.

Visual interactions

By default, the filter selections applied to a single visual, such as clicking a bar on a column chart or a row on a table, will impact all other data visualizations on the given report page with relationships to the selection. In the following example, the bar representing the United States sales territory country has been selected and this causes the product category chart to highlight the portion of each product category related to the United States sales territory country ($31.3M):

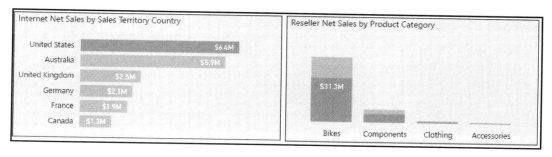

Visual Interactions – Highlighting

Multiple values from the same column can be selected (for example, `France` and `Canada`) and the values from separate columns of the same visual, such as the dimension columns of a table visual, can also cross-filter other visuals on the report page. The ability to drive visual interactions from the selections of two or more visuals (for example, `United States` and `Bikes`) is not currently supported excluding slicers.

The highlight interaction option from the preceding example is available and enabled by default for column, bar, treemap, pie, and donut charts. Only the filter and the none interaction options are available for cards, KPIs, and line and scatter chart visuals.

Per prior chapters, the Sales Territory, Product, and Date dimension tables are related to all three fact tables—Internet Sales, Reseller Sales, and Sales and Margin Plan. Therefore, the filters and selections applied to the columns of these tables will simultaneously impact measures from other fact tables. This integration within the dataset supports robust analyses but can also require some training or explanation to users as they may not initially expect or understand the cross-filtering behavior.

Edit interactions

Report authors can modify the visual interaction behavior such that selections (user clicks) on certain visuals don't impact other visuals or only impact certain visuals. Additionally, for the visuals set to the highlight interaction by default, report authors can revise the interaction behavior to filter.

In the following example, the United States selection in the middle bar chart has no impact on the multi-row car visual but causes a filter interaction (rather than highlight) on the product category chart:

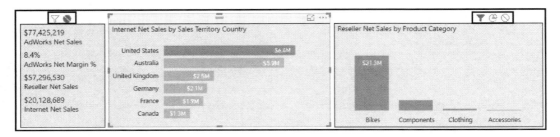

Edit interactions in Power BI Desktop

To edit visual interactions, select the visual that will receive the selections and then enable the `Edit interactions` command under the **Format** tab in Power BI Desktop. In this example, the None interaction icon has been selected for the multi-row card visual and the Filter interaction icon has been selected for the `Product Category` column chart.

Like the preceding example, it's often appropriate to disable visual interactions from impacting the card or KPI visuals in the top-left corner of the reports. These values can be impacted exclusively by the filters defined outside of the report canvas, such as report and page level filters, and will not change during user sessions like other visuals on the page.

Regardless of the design decision, if users will regularly interact with reports, such as clicking on slicers and other visuals, it's important to briefly review or explain the visual interaction behavior. This is especially necessary with new users and with more customized designs, such as 2-3 visuals with interactions enabled and 2-3 visuals with interactions disabled.

What-if parameters

Power BI Desktop provides a user interface for more easily creating What-if parameters than the custom slicer parameter demonstrated earlier in this chapter. This option is currently limited to numeric parameter values but automatically creates a single column table and a DAX measure that retrieves the input value.

In the following example, two What-if parameters are used to calculate alternative unit price and unit cost values thereby driving a hypothetical product margin % measure:

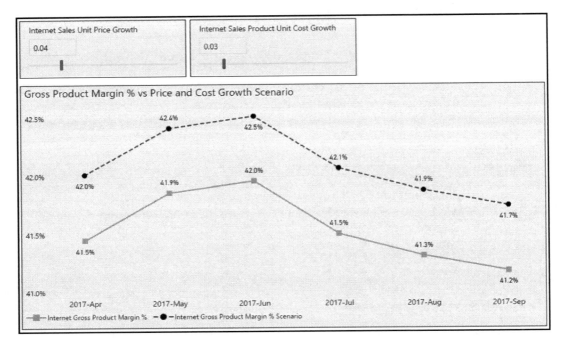

What-if parameters applied in report visuals

By adjusting the two slider bars, a user is able to quickly model an alternative gross product margin % scenario, as illustrated by the dotted line in the line chart visual. The slider bar for modifying a single value is unique to slicers for What-if parameter columns.

To create a `What-if` parameter, click the **New Parameter** icon on the **Modeling** tab in Report View to launch the following dialog:

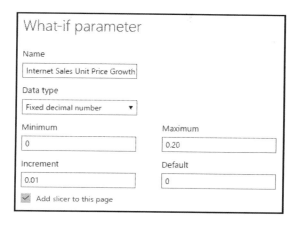

Creating a What-if parameter

Based on the minimum, maximum, and increment input values specified, a new table with a single column of values will be created within the Power BI dataset. For the `Unit Price Growth` parameter, this column has 20 rows from 0 to .19 with each value representing a full percentage point (for example, 0% to 19%). Additionally, a new DAX measure is created automatically to retrieve the user selection, per the following expressions:

```
Internet Sales Unit Price Growth Value =
SELECTEDVALUE('Internet Sales Unit Price Growth'[Internet Sales Unit
Price Growth], 0)
```

```
Internet Sales Product Unit Cost Growth Value =
SELECTEDVALUE('Internet Sales Product Unit Cost Growth'[Internet Sales
Product Unit Cost Growth], 0)
```

With the second argument to both functions set to 0, both growth values will return zero if a selection hasn't been made or if multiple values have been selected. The same `SELECTEDVALUE()` function, which was added to the DAX language in 2017, was also used in the custom slicer parameters example earlier in this chapter.

The only remaining step is to create one or more measures that reference the parameter values in their calculation logic. In this example, the Unit Price and Unit Cost growth parameters are applied to gross sales and product cost scenario measures, respectively. These two scenario measures are then used to compute a product margin scenario measure and a product margin % scenario measure, per the following expressions:

```
Internet Gross Sales Scenario = SUMX('Internet Sales','Internet
Sales'[Order Quantity]*
   ('Internet Sales'[Unit Price]*(1 + [Internet Sales Unit Price Growth
Value])))

Internet Sales Product Cost Scenario = SUMX('Internet Sales','Internet
Sales'[Order Quantity] *
   ('Internet Sales'[Product Standard Cost] * (1 + [Internet Sales
Product Unit Cost Growth Value])))

Internet Gross Product Margin Scenario =
[Internet Gross Sales Scenario] - [Internet Sales Product Cost
Scenario]

Internet Gross Product Margin % Scenario =
DIVIDE([Internet Gross Product Margin Scenario],[Internet Gross Sales
Scenario])
```

Although it's possible and sometimes necessary to create parameter columns and measures manually, the **What-if** parameter feature in Power BI Desktop can simplify this process for many modeling scenarios. Additionally, the slider bar slicer exclusive to the **What-if** parameter columns is the most user-friendly option for selecting parameter values.

To change the range of values available to the parameter, select the parameter column in the Fields list and modify the min, max, or increment arguments to the GENERATESERIES() function. Based on the user interface selections from the Unit Price Growth parameter, Power BI built the following function: GENERATESERIES(0,20,.01).

Slicers

Slicer visuals represent a central element of self-service functionality in Power BI in addition to the *Visual interactions* behavior described in the previous section. The standard slicer visual displays the unique values of a single column enabling report users to apply their own filter selections. Additionally, Power BI Desktop provides several formatting and filter condition options available based on the data type of the column. The following image contains three sample slicer visuals with each slicer representing a different data type (text, number, date):

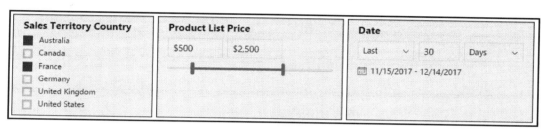

Slicer visuals

In this example, the three slicers filter for two sales territory countries (Australia and France), a range of product list prices ($500 to $2,500), and the last 30 days inclusive of the current date (**11/15/2017** to **12/14/2017**). Filter condition rules are available for numeric and date columns in slicers, such as greater than or equal to $500 and after 5/1/2017, respectively.

The numeric range slicer, such as the preceding $500 to $2,500 example, is a preview feature as of the November 2017 release for Power BI Desktop. In its current state, the numeric range slicer is exclusive to Power BI Desktop and will appear as a standard list slicer in the Power BI service. Additionally, only numeric columns can be used for the numeric range slicers - DAX measures are not supported.

See the *Report filter conditions* and *Relative date filtering* sections later in this chapter for additional details on relative date filters.

By default, the **Single Select** option under the **Selection Controls** formatting card is enabled and the **Show "Select All...** option is disabled. These settings require users to hold down the Ctrl key to select multiple items. For slicer visuals with many unique values, and when users regularly need to exclude only one or a few items, enabling the **Show "Select All...** option can improve usability. Additionally, for slicers based on text data-type columns, users can search for values via the ellipsis in the top-right corner of the visual.

To preserve space on the report canvas, the slicer visual supports a drop-down option for all column data types. In the following example, a single value is selected for the country and date slicers but multiple values are selected for the price slicer:

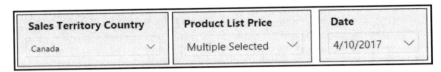

Slicer visuals as dropdown

The drop-down option is most applicable to columns with many unique values. Slicers are generally appropriate to empower users with self-service capabilities such that they're not limited to filter conditions defined outside the report canvas.

It's recommended to group slicer visuals together near the edge of a report page. Slicers are most commonly aligned on the left side of the page below the visuals in the top-left corner. If vertical canvas space is limited, slicers displayed in list format can be presented horizontally rather than vertically. The orientation formatting property (vertical or horizontal) is available under the General formatting card.

Unlike other visuals (for example, charts, maps, tables), visual-level filters cannot be applied to slicer visuals. Report and page-level filters are required to reduce the available values displayed on a slicer visual. Additional information on these filter scopes and associated filter conditions supported are included in the *Report filter scopes* section later in this chapter.

One of the most powerful features of slicers is the ability to filter both the current report page and optionally other report pages from a single slicer visual. The details of utilizing this feature referred to as Slicer synchronization, are included in the following section.

Slicer synchronization

By default, slicer visuals only filter the other visuals on the same report page. However, via the **Sync Slicers** pane, report designers can synchronize a slicer visual to also filter all other report pages or only specific report pages. This feature eliminates the need to include the same slicer on multiple report pages and thus simplifies the user experience. For example, a common report may utilize three slicers (for example, `Year`, `Product Category`, `Sales Country`) and include four report pages. With slicer synchronization configured, the report user would only need to select values from these slicers on a single report page and the visuals from all four report pages would be updated to reflect these selections.

The **Sync slicers** pane can be accessed from the **View** tab of the ribbon in Report View per the following image:

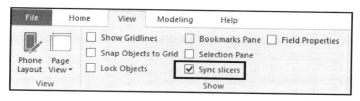

Sync slicers pane

Once selected per the preceding image, the **Sync slicers** pane will appear to the right of the report page. A slicer visual from the current report page can then be selected to configure its synchronization with other pages.

In the following image, the `Sales Territory Group` slicer on the `AdWorks Sales` report page has been selected but has not yet been synchronized with other report pages:

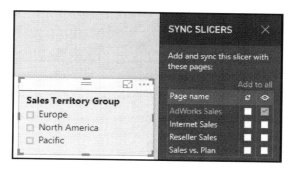

Sync slicers Pane with slicer selected

To quickly synchronize the slicer to all other report pages, simply click the **Add to all** link above the Sync and Visible icons. In this example, the **Add to all** command would apply checkmarks under the Sync icon for all four report pages. The Sales Territory Group slicer would now filter all four report pages but would only be visible on the AdWorks Sales page per the single checkmark under the Visible icon.

 Several other report design features are accessible from the **View** tab, such as the **Bookmarks** and **Selection** panes, **Show gridlines**, and **Snap objects to grid**. The **Bookmarks** and the **Selection** Pane are described in the *Bookmarks* section of the following chapter. The **Field Properties** pane is described in the *Metadata management* section of Chapter 14, *Managing Application Workspaces and Content.*

Alternatively, the **Sync slicers** pane can be used to customize the synchronization and visibility properties of the slicer per report page. For example, the Sales Territory Group slicer could be set to only filter (synchronize) three of the four report pages by selecting or unselecting the checkmarks for these pages. Additionally, checkmarks can be added to the Visible property to display the slicer on other pages. With this approach, the user would still only need to make a slicer selection once via synchronization but could view the slicer on other report pages to understand the current slicer selection(s) impacting the given report page.

For reports with several report pages and common slicers, a single report page could be dedicated to slicer selections and not contain any other visuals. Report designers could configure synchronization for each slicer on this page and instruct users to only use this page for applying their filter selections for all pages of the report. Moreover, a back button could be added to report pages allowing the user to easily navigate back to the dedicated slicer report page. An example of using a back button image is included in the *Drillthrough Report Pages* section of Chapter 12, *Applying Custom Visuals, Animation, and Analytics.*

Custom slicer parameters

A powerful use case for slicer visuals is to expose a custom list of parameter values and drive one or multiple DAX measures based on the user's selection. In the following example, a slicer visual contains six date intelligence periods and a custom DAX measure references the date intelligence measure corresponding to the user's selection:

Slicer as a measure parameter

The table used for the slicer values could be defined within a source system and retrieved during data refresh like other tables. Alternatively, since the parameter values are unlikely to change, the table could be created within Power BI Desktop and loaded to the model but not included in a data refresh. Like all parameter tables, no relationships would be defined with other tables.

The custom measure, User Selected Internet Net Sales, utilizes the SELECTEDVALUE() and SWITCH() functions to retrieve the user selection and then apply the appropriate date intelligence measure. In this implementation, a DAX variable is used to store the period selection value, per the following expression:

```
User Selected Internet Net Sales =
VAR PeriodSelection = SELECTEDVALUE('Date Parameter'[Date Period
Selection],"Year to Date")
RETURN
SWITCH(TRUE(),
  PeriodSelection = "Week to Date", [Internet Net Sales (WTD)],
  PeriodSelection = "Month to Date", [Internet Net Sales (MTD)],
  PeriodSelection = "Year to Date", [Internet Net Sales (YTD)],
  PeriodSelection = "Prior Week to Date", [Internet Net Sales (PWTD)],
  PeriodSelection = "Prior Month to Date", [Internet Net Sales
(PMTD)],
  PeriodSelection = "Prior Year to Date", [Internet Net Sales (PYTD)]
  )
```

The second parameter to the SELECTEDVALUE() function ensures that the Year to Date measure will be used if multiple values have been selected or if no values have been selected. If several additional DAX measures will be driven by the parameter selection, a dedicated measure could be created that only retrieves the selected value. This supporting measure would then eliminate the need for the variable since the support measure could be referenced directly within the SWITCH() function.

See `Chapter 10`, *Developing DAX Measures and Security Roles* for example expressions of date intelligence measures as well as measure support expressions. It's, of course, possible to fully define each date intelligence expression within the parameter-driven measure but, for manageability reasons, it's almost always preferable to leverage an existing measure. This is particularly the recommendation when the required measures represent common logic, such as month-to-date.

Report filter scopes

A fundamental skill and practice in Power BI report development is utilizing the report filter scopes and the filter conditions available to each scope. For example, a report intended for the European sales team can be filtered at the report level for the European sales territory group and specific report pages can be filtered for France, Germany, and the United Kingdom. Reports can be further customized by implementing filter conditions to specific visuals, applying more complex filter conditions, and providing drillthrough report pages to reflect the details of a unique item, such as a product or a customer.

Unlike the slicer visuals and visual interactions reviewed earlier in this chapter, report filter scopes are defined outside of the report canvas. Report filter scopes, therefore, provide report authors with the option to eliminate or reduce the need for on-canvas user selections as well as the canvas space associated with slicer visuals.

In addition to meeting functional requirements and delivering a simplified user experience, report filter scopes can also benefit performance. Using the European sales report as an example, the simple filter conditions of `Sales Territory Group = Europe` (Report-level filter) and `Sales Territory Country = France` (Page-level filter) are efficiently implemented by the Power BI in-memory engine (import mode) and almost all DirectQuery data sources. Even if the DAX measures used on the report page for France are complex, the report filters will contribute to acceptable or good performance.

With a visual selected on the canvas in the Report View, a filters pane below the visualizations icon presents the following four input field wells:

- **Report-level filters**:
    - The filter conditions defined impact all visuals on all report pages
- **Page-level filters**:
    - The filter conditions defined impact all visuals on the given report page
    - Report-level filter conditions are respected by the page-level filters as well
    - Any Drillthrough filter conditions defined for the report page are also respected
- **Visual-level filters**:
    - The filter conditions defined only impact the specific visual selected
    - Report and page-level filter conditions are respected by the visual-level filters as well
    - Any Drillthrough filter conditions defined for the report page of the given visual are also respected
- **Drillthrough filters**:
    - The filter condition, a single value from a column, impacts all visuals on the given report page.
    - Report-level filter conditions are respected by the Drillthrough filters as well.
    - Any page and visual-level filter conditions defined for the given report page are respected

Per the prior two chapters, filters are applied to Power BI visuals via the relationships defined in the dataset (via single or bidirectional cross-filtering) as well as any filtering logic embedded in DAX measures. All four of the preceding filters (**Report**, **Page**, **Visual**, **Drillthrough**) contribute to the initial filter context as described in the *Measure Evaluation Process* of Chapter 10, *Developing DAX Measures and Security Roles*. Therefore, just like filters applied on the report canvas (for example, Slicers), the filter logic of DAX measures can supplement, remove, or replace these filters conditions. In the event of a conflict between any report filter and a DAX measure expression that utilizes the CALCULATE() function, the DAX expression will supersede or override the report filter.

Report filter conditions

Different types of filter conditions can be defined for the distinct filter scopes. For example, report and page-level filters are limited to relatively simple filter conditions that reference individual columns of a dataset. However, more complex and powerful conditions such as filtering by the results of a DAX measure and top N filters can be applied via visual level filters.

The following outline and matrix (filter conditions by filter scope) summarize the filtering functionality supported:

- **Basic Filtering**:
    - A single equality condition for a column to a single value or set of values, such as "is North America or Europe"
    - A single inequality condition for a column to a single value or set of values, such as "is not $25 or $35"

- **Advanced Filtering**
    - Several condition rules per data type, such as "starts with" for text and "is greater than or equal to" for numbers:
        - Supports filtering for blank and non-blank values
    - Optionally apply multiple conditions per column via logical operators (and, or)

- **Relative Date Filtering**:
    - Supports three filter condition rules (is in this, is in the last, is in the next) for days, weeks, months, and years
    - Partial period and complete period filter conditions can be defined
    - The same filter condition rules are available to slicers with date data-type columns

- **Top N Filtering**:
    - Filter a visual to a defined number of top or bottom values of a column based on their values for a measure
    - For example, the top 10 products based on net sales can be set as a visual-level filter condition

- **Filter by Measure**:
    - Filter a visual by applying advanced filtering conditions to the results of a DAX measure
    - For example, greater than 45% on the Internet Net Margin % measure can be set as a visual-level filter condition

The following table summarizes the preceding filter conditions available to each of the three primary report filter scopes:

Filter Conditions	Report Level	Page Level	Visual Level
Basic Filtering	Yes	Yes	Yes
Advanced Filtering	Yes	Yes	Yes
Relative Date Filtering	Yes	Yes	Yes
Top N Filtering	No	No	Yes
Filter by Measure	No	No	Yes

Filter conditions by filter scope

Multiple filter conditions can be defined per report filter scope. For example, a report-level filter could include two basic filter conditions and an advanced filter condition. Additionally, the same column can be used in multiple filter scopes, such as a report-level filter and a page-level filter on the product subcategory column. All defined filter conditions are applied to the visuals within their scope provided that the DAX measures included in the visuals don't contain filtering logic in conflict with the report filter conditions. Additionally, the columns and measures referenced in the filter conditions do not need to be displayed in the report visuals. For the top N Filtering condition, the column to be filtered only has to be displayed in the visual when the filter condition is initially defined.

A good indicator of Power BI development and solution-specific knowledge is the ability to accurately interpret the filters being applied to a given visual on a report page. This includes all Power BI report filters (report-level, page-level, visual-level), any slicer selections or cross-highlighting, the filter logic of the DAX measures, the cross-filtering applied via relationships in the data model, and any filter logic built into the M queries of the dataset. Complex reports and datasets will utilize all or many of these different layers in various combinations to ultimately affect the values displayed in report visuals.

BI teams will want to limit the complexity built into reports, both for users and the report authors or developers responsible for the reports. For example, if visual-level filter conditions are applied to many visuals of a report, the filter condition for each visual will need to be modified if the requirement(s) of the report change or the columns or measures used by the filter condition change. Dataset designers and data warehouse teams can often implement changes or enhancements to simplify the filter conditions needed by report authors.

As one example, a filter condition implemented in multiple reports that specifies several product categories (hardcoded) could be replaced with a new column on the product dimension table. The new column would distinguish the group of product categories that meet this criteria relative to those that don't, and logic could be built into the data source or retrieval process to dynamically include additional product categories that later meet the given criteria.

Drillthrough filters, which are used to define drillthrough report pages as described in Chapter 12, *Applying Custom Visuals, Animation, and Analytics*, are unique in that they can be used to implement basic filtering conditions at the page level as well as their more common filter of a single column value. For example, three countries can be selected in a Drillthrough filter condition and the visuals on this report page will reflect these three countries. However, a user can only drill to the report page from the context of a single column value. The source drillthrough value (for example, Germany), will replace the three countries in the previous filter condition on the drillthrough page when the drillthrough action is executed.

Additionally, multiple columns can be used as Drillthrough filters and the values of both columns from a separate report page are applied to the drillthrough page when a drillthrough action is executed. If only one value is present from the source report page, the drillthrough action will only filter this column and remove any filter defined for the other Drillthrough filter column. See Chapter 12, *Applying Custom Visuals, Animation, and Analytics* for additional details on drillthrough report pages.

Report and page filters

Report and page level filters are most commonly used to apply the fundamental filter context for the report. Columns with few unique values such as `Sales Territory Country` are good candidates for report level filters while more granular columns such as `Sales Territory Region` are better suited for page level filters.

In the following example, the individual report pages are named according to the report and page filters applied:

Power BI report pages

In the absence of any custom DAX measures that retrieve the filter selections applied, users of the report will not see the report, page, and visual-level filters applied. Therefore, it's important to assign intuitive names to each report page per the preceding example and to include a brief title for each report page via text box.

The following image represents the report and page filters applied to the Northeast report page of a `United States` sales report:

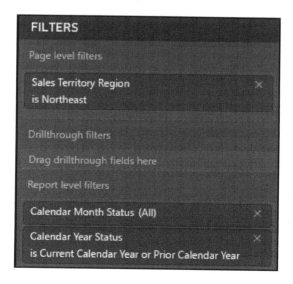

Report and page-level filters

Each report page would be filtered for a different sales territory region except the USA page, which would not contain a page level filter. The `Calendar Year Status` column, which was described in the *Date dimension view* section of `Chapter 8`, *Connecting to Sources and Transforming Data with M*, restricts all visuals to only the current and prior calendar year. One or two years of history is sufficient for many reports given the pace of change in business environments and strategies. Additionally, the report-level date filter promotes both query performance and low maintenance since the dates filtered reflect the latest dataset refresh.

Report filters are not a long-term substitute for poor data quality or a suboptimal dataset (data model, retrieval queries). If it's necessary to implement many filter conditions or complex filtering conditions within reports to return accurate results, it's very likely that the dataset or the source system itself should be revised. Similarly, if many filter conditions or complex filter conditions are needed to retrieve the desired results, it's likely that the dataset can be enhanced (for example, new column, new measure) to simplify or eliminate these report filter conditions.

Power BI report authors should communicate to the dataset designer(s) and BI team whenever complex or convoluted report filters are being applied. Given limited team resources, it may be sufficient to use report filters to support rare or uncommon reports. For common reporting needs, however, it's generally appropriate to build or revise the necessary logic in the data source or dataset.

Page filter or slicer?

Slicer visuals can serve as an alternative to distinct or dedicated report pages. With a slicer, a user has the flexibility to select one or multiple values on the same report page, such as Northeast and Southwest, without needing to navigate to a dedicated page. Additionally, by consolidating dedicated report pages, slicers can simplify report development and management.

Slicers are often the best choice when there's nothing unique to the different values of the slicer. For example, if all sales regions are always analyzed by the same measures, dimensions, and visuals it may be unnecessary to duplicate these pages of visuals. Slicers are also very helpful or necessary when users regularly need to analyze the data by the same dimensions or by custom dimensions, such as price and date ranges.

However, dedicated report pages are valuable for supporting email subscriptions, data alerts, and dashboard visuals specific to a particular value such as a sales region. In the following image from the Power BI service, an email subscription can be set to any of the report pages within the **USA SALES AND MARGIN** report:

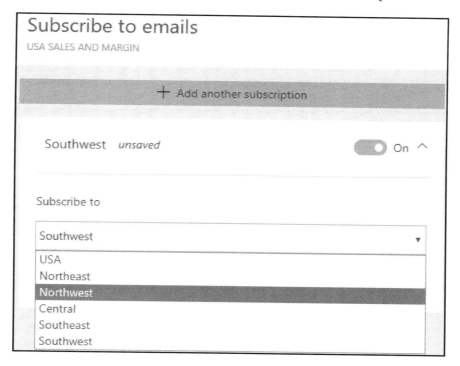

Email subscription in Power BI

As one example, the visuals from the **Northeast** report page could potentially be pinned to a Northeast dashboard (or other dashboard) and used in data alerts and notifications for the Northeast team as well. These region-specific capabilities are made possible by the distinct report pages of visuals filtered for the given sales territory region.

Relative date filtering

Relative date filtering is available for date columns at all filter scopes (report, page, and visual) and for slicer visuals. These dynamic filter conditions, such as the last 30 days (relative to the current date) promote both data freshness and query performance since the minimal amount of history required can be retrieved. Additionally, relative date filters can often avoid the need to create custom DAX measures to support specific date filter conditions.

In the following example, five report pages are dedicated to a specific relative date filter condition:

Relative date filter conditions per page

A page-level filter is used for each report page with the following conditions, per the following example:

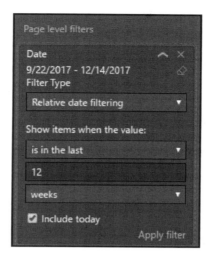

Relative date filter condition

As of 12/14/2017, the five report pages are filtered to the following date ranges with the Include today option enabled:

- Is in the last 12 months 12/15/2016 through 12/14/2017
- Is in the last 12 weeks 9/22/2017 through 12/14/2017
- Is in this month 12/1/2017 through 12/31/2017
- Is in the next 12 weeks 12/14/2017 through 3/7/2018
- Is In the next 12 months 12/14/2017 through 12/13/2018

A report design such as this would make it simple for users to analyze immediate, near-term, and longer-term trends and issues.

Three types of relative date filter conditions can be set—**is in the last, in this**, and **in the next**. Each of these filter conditions supports day, week, month, and year intervals. For the in the last and in the next filter conditions, calendar week, month, and year conditions can also be specified. These conditions represent full or completed calendar periods only. For example, as of November 28th, 2017, the last one-calendar month and last one-calendar year would include all dates of October 2017 and all dates of 2016, respectively. The week of 11/19/2017 through 11/25/2017 would represent the last one-calendar week.

Visualization formatting

A final step in report development is configuring the formatting options for each visual. Several of these options, such as data labels, background colors, borders, and title are common to all visuals and are often essential to aid comprehension. Several other formatting options, such as fill point for scatter charts, are exclusive to particular visuals and report authors are well served to be familiar with these features.

In addition to giving reports a professional appearance, features such as tooltips can be used to provide visuals with additional or supporting context. Furthermore, formatting features can be used to implement conditional logic to dynamically drive the color of data points by their values.

Visual-level formatting

Formatting visuals primarily refer to modifying the format properties of a visual via the format cards associated with that visual. Additionally, report authors can use the options exposed on the **Format** tab in the Report View of Power BI Desktop to control the alignment, distribution, and Z-position of visuals.

Whenever a visual is selected on the canvas, the **Format** pane presents a number of formatting cards specific to the visual. In the following image, the 10 formatting cards currently available to the Power BI column chart visual are displayed:

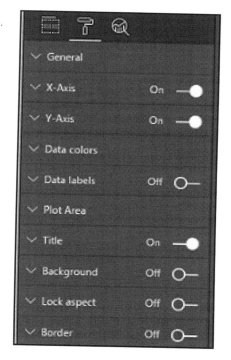

Visual formatting cards

Expanding and enriching the available formatting options across all visuals has been a priority for the Power BI team. As an example, for the column chart, the **X-Axis** card includes a concatenate labels property that can be useful for maintaining context while navigating through the levels of a hierarchy. Additionally, the **Data labels** card contains options for positioning labels inside the base of the column and changing the scale (for example, thousands, millions) and decimal places of the values displayed.

 For some visuals, such as column, line, and scatter charts, the **Analytics** pane (next to the **Format** pane) provides additional formatting options. These options are reviewed in the following chapter.

Line and column charts

Line, column, and bar charts are the most common chart visualization types given their advantages in visual perception, as explained in the *Visualization best practices* section. Power BI includes clustered and stacked versions of column and bar charts in addition to two combination charts that display both a line and either a clustered or stacked column.

The ribbon chart visualization was added to Power BI Desktop in September 2017 and represents a variation of the stacked column chart. Unlike the stacked column chart, the ribbon chart sorts the category items within each column based on their values and connects the items across columns with a ribbon.

In the following example of a ribbon chart, four product subcategories are displayed across months by their net sales:

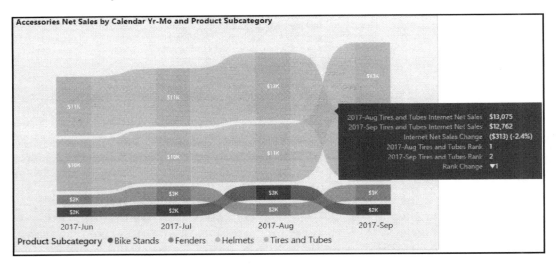

Ribbon chart

Helmets subcategory overtook the **Tires and Tubes** category in September 2017 to become the top-selling product subcategory in the visual. Per the tooltip included in the preceding image, hovering over the curved ribbon connecting the months on the X-axis displays the values for each month, the variance and percentage change between the months, and the change in rank for the given category (for example, from first to second for **Tires and Tubes**). Insights into the rankings of categories and their changes across periods wouldn't be as easily identified in a standard stacked column chart.

The ribbons formatting card allows for spacing, transparency, and a border to further aid comprehension. In the example visual, the ribbon border is enabled, the transparency of the ribbon is set to 50, and the ribbon spacing is set to 5. Currently, unlike the stacked column chart, the Ribbon chart doesn't include a *Y*-axis to identify the total value of each column. Additionally, the individual ribbons are currently distinguished by color. Formatting options available to other visuals, such as customizing each series or the legend using alternative styles and markers, are not yet supported.

Tooltips

Chart and map visuals include a **Tooltips** field well in the **Fields** pane to allow report authors to define additional measures that will display when the user hovers over the items in the visual. These tooltip values will reflect the same filter context of the data labels for the visual and thus provide the user with additional context. In the following example, four measures have been added to the **Tooltips** field well for a column chart:

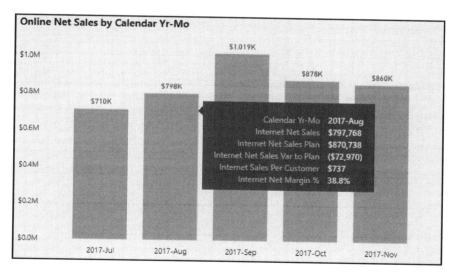

Additional measures displayed as tooltips

By hovering over the column for online net sales in August of 2017, the tooltip is displayed, which includes both the `Internet Net Sales` measure used for the chart as well as the four tooltip measures.

In this example, the tooltip measures indicate that `Internet Net Sales` was below the plan for this month by $72,970 in addition to other potentially useful metrics (`Intenet Sales Per Customer`, `Internet Net Margin %`). In the absence of the tooltips, the user may have to search for other reports or visuals to find this information or may miss important insights related to the visual.

Tooltips are a great way to enhance the analytical value of a visual without adding complexity or clutter. Additionally, given the features of the DAX query engine, such as measure fusion, the additional measures displayed as tooltips will generally not negatively impact performance. For example, the internet sales and margin measures are based on the same fact table. Therefore, the necessary source columns for both measures will be accessed by one storage engine query via measure fusion.

Report page tooltips

The standard tooltips described in the previous section may be sufficient for most reporting scenarios. However, Power BI Desktop also provides report page tooltips that allow report authors to display a custom page of report visuals as an alternative to the default tooltips. The following steps can be used to configure a report page tooltip:

1. Add a new blank report page to a report.
2. On the **Format** pane for the report page, enable the **Tooltip** property under the **Page Information** formatting card.

3. Also on the **Format** pane, specify a **Tooltip** page size per the following image:

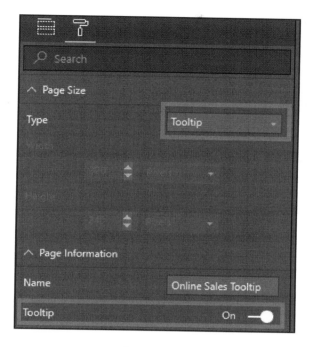

Report page tooltip

4. On the Tooltip page from step 3, set the **Page View** to **Actual Size** via the **Page View** icon on the **View** tab.

5. From the **Fields** pane of the Tooltip page, drag a measure or multiple measures to the tooltip **Fields** field well:
    - Columns can also be specified as tooltip fields (for example, `Product Name`)

6. Create report visuals on the tooltip report page that relate to the tooltip field well measure(s) or column(s):
    - For example, if the tooltip page will support a sales measure, consider building visuals that display sales versus plan, budget, or sales growth measures
    - Given the limited size of the Tooltip report page, KPI and card visuals are recommended

By default, other visuals in the report that utilize the measure(s) or column(s) specified as tooltip fields in step 5 will display the tooltip report page when the user hovers over the items of the visual.

The **Tooltip Page Size** from step 3 is not required for utilizing tooltip report pages. However, this property makes the purpose of the page clear to the other report authors and has been provided by the Power BI team as at a good starting point for most report page tooltips. Likewise, viewing the report page tooltip in actual size per step 4 is technically not required but is very helpful in designing these pages.

Alternatively, a tooltip formatting card is available at the bottom of the **Format** pane for charts and map visuals. This formatting card can be used to specify a particular tooltip report page for the given visual or to disable tooltip report pages. If report page tooltips have been disabled for a visual, the visual will display the default tooltips as described in the previous section.

Column and line chart conditional formatting

Column and line charts are two of the most common visuals in reports given their flexibility and advantages in visualizing comparisons and trends. However, these classic visuals don't have to be static or simple—report authors can embed custom rules to dynamically drive formatting properties based on source data. Similar to tooltips, conditional formatting techniques help users more quickly derive insights from visuals without the added complexity of more data points or additional visuals.

Column chart conditional formatting

Conditional formatting can be applied to column charts by specifying a measure, such as product margin in the color saturation field well. By default, the value of this measure will drive the saturation of color for each column in the visual. To take further control of the formatting or to apply a conditional formatting rule, the **Diverging** formatting options under the **Data colors** card can be modified.

In the following example of a column chart, a product margin percentage measure is used as the Color saturation field (above tooltips) and threshold values have been entered to define the formatting rule:

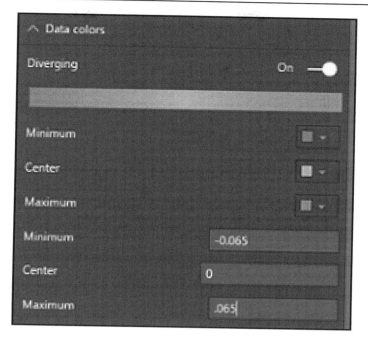

Diverging Data colors formatting

With the **Diverging** property enabled this rule associates three colors (red, yellow, and green) with **Minimum**, **Center**, and **Maximum** values of -6.5%,0%, and 6.5%, respectively. This rule will make it easy for users to distinguish the columns, such as fiscal periods or product categories, associated with low, average, and high product margins.

 By disabling the **Diverging** property, a rule can be specified for only a minimum and a maximum value. This can be useful to change the color of a column only when a threshold is reached. In other words, the chart will at most display two distinct colors with one of the colors (for example, red) flagging the exceptions. To implement this rule, simply specify the same value for both minimum and maximum inputs and then associate different colors for each.

Line chart conditional formatting

Conditional formatting can be applied to line charts by applying distinct colors to separate DAX measures. In the following example, a DAX measure is created that only returns the sales per order value when its value is below $600:

```
Internet Net Sales Per Order Below $600 =
IF([Internet Net Sales Per Order] < 600,[Internet Net Sales Per
Order],BLANK())
```

Using this measure and the `Internet Net Sales Per Order` measure on the same line chart allows for separate colors to be applied:

Contrasting colors for line chart measures

For this example, a default light green can be used for the `Internet Net Sales Per Order` measure and red can be applied for the below $600 measure. Additionally, the below $600 line can be formatted with a slightly larger stroke width and a dotted line style via the customize series formatting options to better contrast these values.

The line chart will appear as a single line that changes colors and styles when it goes below $600:

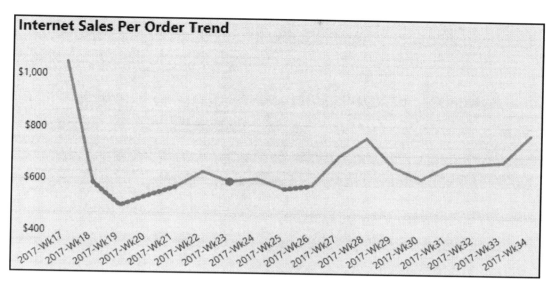

Conditionally-formatted line chart

The stroke width, join type, line style, and marker shape formatting properties provide a wide range of options for contrasting lines beyond their colors. These additional properties are recommended to aid general comprehension and to support users who cannot easily distinguish colors.

Table and matrix

Per the *Choosing the visual* section earlier in this chapter, table and matrix visuals are good for looking up individual values and for displaying precise values. For example, all seven digits of the value $7,847,292 would be displayed on a table or matrix visual but this same value would likely need to be rounded to $7.8M in a column or line chart to maintain readability.

Table and matrix visuals support the same **Display units** and **Value decimal places** formatting properties as other visuals. In the following example from a table visual, both measures have been formatted to display their values in terms of millions with one decimal place:

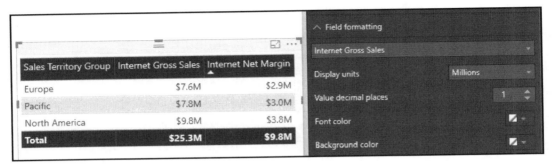

Display Units and Decimal Places for Table and Matrix Visuals

Per the preceding example, these properties are available within the **Field formatting** card of the **Format** pane. Display unit options range from the thousands (K) to the trillions (T). By default, the **Display units** property is set to **None** for table and matrix visuals and thus displays the full value.

Prior to the availability of the **Display units** and **Value decimal places** properties, it was necessary to use the FORMAT() function in separate DAX measures to display custom formats in table or matrix visuals. The following two measures apply a custom rounded currency format to the results of the Internet Net Sales measure:

```
Internet Net Sales (Format Thousands) = FORMAT([Internet Net
Sales],"$0,.0K")

Internet Net Sales (Format Millions) = FORMAT([Internet Net
Sales],"$0,,.0M")
```

Both measures use the FORMAT() function to convert the input value (the Internet Net Sales measure) to a string in a custom, rounded format. Specifically, the comma or commas immediately to the left of the decimal are used to divide the value by 1,000 and round as necessary. The zero to the right of the decimal displays a digit or a zero. For example, the $541,613 value would be displayed as $541.6K and $0.5M by the format thousands and format millions of measures, respectively.

Table and matrix conditional formatting

Default and custom conditional formatting rules can be applied to table and matrix visuals to make it easier to identify exceptions and outlier values. Power BI currently supports background color scales, font color scales, and data bar conditional formatting for table and matrix visuals. To apply conditional formatting to a table or matrix, click the drop-down arrow next to the field name of the measure (for example, `Internet Net Sales`) in the `Values` field well of the **Visualizations** pane. A conditional formatting menu item will appear with an arrow providing access to the three types of conditional formatting.

In the following table, data bar conditional formatting has been applied to four measures related to internet sales:

Top 10 French State Provinces by Internet Net Sales				
Customer State Province	Internet Net Sales	Internet Sales Customer Count	Internet Sales Per Customer	Internet Net Sales (YOY YTD %)
Seine (Paris)	$422,298	298	$1,417	4.5%
Seine Saint Denis	$290,668	227	$1,280	7.2%
Nord	$278,709	216	$1,290	23.9%
Essonne	$202,682	122	$1,661	-11.1%
Hauts de Seine	$195,506	158	$1,237	-10.9%
Yveline	$168,968	125	$1,352	-15.7%
Loiret	$74,133	54	$1,373	5.9%
Seine et Marne	$68,884	45	$1,531	29.1%
Moselle	$68,772	42	$1,637	-32.0%
Garonne (Haute)	$37,245	23	$1,619	-47.6%
Total	**$1,807,865**	**1,310**	**$1,380**	**-0.0%**

Data bars conditional formatting

Although the visual has been filtered to the top 10 customer state provinces for France, it would be difficult or time-consuming to gain insight from the 40 distinct data values. The length of the data bars helps to call out high or low values and alternative colors can be applied per measure.

The direction of data bars is particularly helpful in distinguishing negative from positive values per the `Internet Net Sales (YOY YTD %)` measure in the preceding example visual. For large table and matrix visuals with many values, or when the relative differences between values are more important than the individual values themselves, the option to show only the data bar can be very useful.

Custom conditional formatting rules can be applied to the background and font color scales of table and matrix visual cells similar to Microsoft Excel. In the following example, the **Color by rules** option is enabled and **Rules** are defined to format the cells of a measure as green if over 25%, yellow when between -25% and 25%, and red if the value is less than -25%:

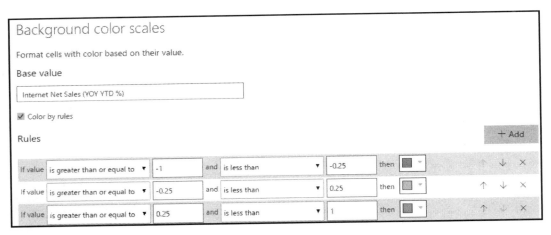

Custom conditional formatting rules

The conditional formatting rules are evaluated from the bottom to the top. Therefore, if a cell meets the condition of multiple rules, the lower rule will be applied. The order of rules can be adjusted via the up and down arrows to the right of the color icons.

Multiple conditional formatting types can be applied against the same measure. For example, the same three conditional rules used for the background color scales in the preceding image could also be implemented as font color scale rules. However, the font colors specified for each rule (for example, white) could be chosen to contrast with the conditional background colors (for example, red) to further help call attention to the value.

As of the November 2017 release of Power BI Desktop, only hardcoded values can be specified in the custom formatting rules. In a future release, DAX measures will likely be supported as inputs to conditional formatting rules. This functionality would make it easier to implement more complex rules, such as greater than the prior year-to-date sales value.

Values as rows

An additional and highly requested enhancement to matrix visuals is the ability to show measures as rows. The following matrix visual breaks out six DAX measures by a date hierarchy across the columns:

Calendar Yr-Qtr	2017-Q1				2017-Q2				Total
	2017-Jan	2017-Feb	2017-Mar	Total	2017-Apr	2017-May	2017-Jun	Total	
AdWorks Net Sales	$2,694,687	$3,058,913	$4,286,165	$10,039,766	$2,500,780	$3,214,876	$4,768,418	$10,484,073	$20,523,838
Reseller Net Sales	$1,563,955	$1,865,278	$2,880,753	$6,309,986	$1,987,873	$2,665,651	$4,212,972	$8,866,495	$15,176,481
Internet Net Sales	$1,130,732	$1,193,634	$1,405,413	$3,729,780	$512,907	$549,225	$555,446	$1,617,578	$5,347,357
AdWorks Net Margin %	17.5%	16.5%	14.0%	15.7%	10.0%	-1.0%	-2.9%	0.8%	8.1%
Reseller Net Margin %	1.7%	1.9%	1.5%	1.7%	2.6%	-9.3%	-8.5%	-6.2%	-2.9%
Internet Net Margin %	39.2%	39.3%	39.5%	39.3%	39.0%	39.4%	39.5%	39.3%	39.3%

Values on rows in matrix visual

Displaying multiple measures as rows, particularly with one or multiple date dimension fields across the columns, is a very common layout for Excel pivot table reports. To enable this feature in Power BI, simply enable the Show on rows feature within the values formatting card of the matrix visual.

Scatter charts

Scatter charts are very effective at explaining the relationship or correlation between items against two variables. Optionally, a third variable can be used to drive the size of the data points and thereby convert the visual to a bubble chart.

In the following example, three countries from the `Sales Territory Country` column are used as the details input to a scatter chart:

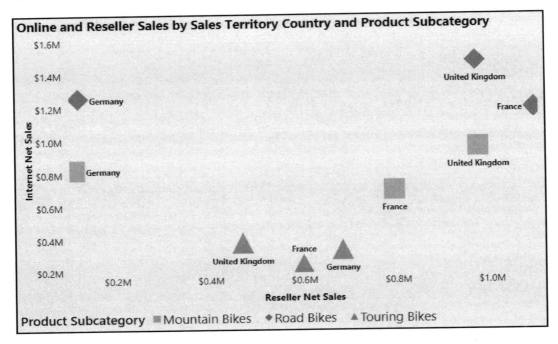

Scatter chart

To provide additional detail, three product subcategories are included in the legend input, such that nine total points (3 X 3) are plotted on the chart. The scatter chart naturally calls out the differences among the items based on their **X Position** (`Reseller Net Sales`) and **Y Position** (`Internet Net Sales`). Moreover, to make the visual even easier to interpret, the marker shapes have been customized for each product subcategory (for example, triangles, diamonds, squares) and the size of the shapes have been increased to 40%.

By default, Power BI applies different colors to the items in the legend. If the legend is not used, the report author can customize the colors of the individual items from the details input column. Although color can be effective for differentiating values, customized marker shapes, such as this example, are helpful for users with visual disabilities.

Map visuals

As of the November 2017 release, Power BI currently provides four map visuals including the bubble map, filled map, shape map (in preview), and the ArcGIS Map. The bubble map plots location points over a world map and varies the size of the bubbles based on a value. The points on bubble maps can also be broken out across a dimension to provide additional context. The filled map and shape map visuals are forms of heat maps that use color and color intensity to distinguish specific areas of a map by a value, such as postal codes by population.

The ArcGIS Map visual is the most powerful of the available geospatial visualizations and several custom map visuals are available in the Office Store including the Globe Map and the Flow Map. See Chapter 12, *Applying Custom Visuals, Animation, and Analytics* for details on the ArcGIS Map visual and using custom visuals. The **Shape Map** visual is currently still in preview and thus should only be used for testing purposes. The following URL provides documentation on the **Shape Map** http://bit.ly/2zS2afU.

Per the *Data category* section in Chapter 9, *Designing Import and DirectQuery Data Models*, it's important to assign geographic data categories to columns. This information aids the map visuals in plotting the correct location when a value is associated with multiple locations (ambiguous locations). The following image from the Data view highlights the city category for a column:

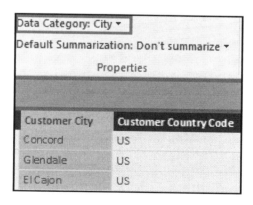

Data category per column

Data categories can be assigned to columns from the modeling tab in Data view or the Report View. For DirectQuery datasets, these metadata properties can only be assigned from the Report View. Report authors should engage the dataset designer or BI team responsible for a dataset if data categories have not been assigned to columns needed for report development.

Additionally, for bubble and filled map visuals, hierarchies can be added to the location field well to avoid ambiguous results. For example, by adding the following hierarchy to the `Location` field well, the map visuals will only use the locations associated with their parent values, such as only the states of Australia.

Geographic hierarchies in map visuals

 For greater precision and performance with map visuals (excluding the Shape Map), latitude and longitude input field wells are available as alternative inputs to **Location**.

Bubble map

Bubble maps are particularly useful when embedding an additional dimension column or category to the legend input. When a geographic boundary column, such as country or postal code, is used as the location input, the added dimension converts the bubbles to pie charts of varying sizes. Larger pie charts reflect the measure used for the `Size` input field and the components of each pie are color-coded to a value from the legend column providing even greater context.

The following bubble map example uses the postal code as the location input, the `Internet Net Sales` measure as the size input, and the `Customer History Segment` column as the legend input:

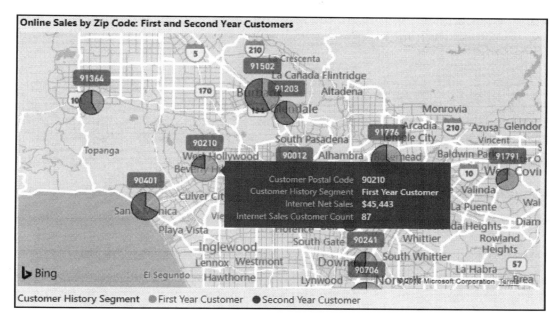

Map visual

For this map, the **Grayscale** theme is applied from the Map styles formatting card and the **auto-zoom** property under the **Map controls card** has been disabled. These two settings, along with a bubble size of 15% via the **Bubbles** card, makes it easy for users to analyze the data associated with postal codes north of Los Angeles.

The bubble map also includes a color saturation input to help distinguish bubbles beyond their relative sizes. This input, however, can only be used when the legend field well is not used.

See the **Customer history** column section of `Chapter 8`, *Connecting to Sources and Transforming Data with M* for details on creating a history segment column within an M query.

Filled map

A filled map visual includes several of the same formatting properties of a bubble map but utilizes color as its primary means to contrast the locations. In the following filled map, a diverging color scheme has been applied via the **Data colors** formatting card to highlight individual states based on their online net sales:

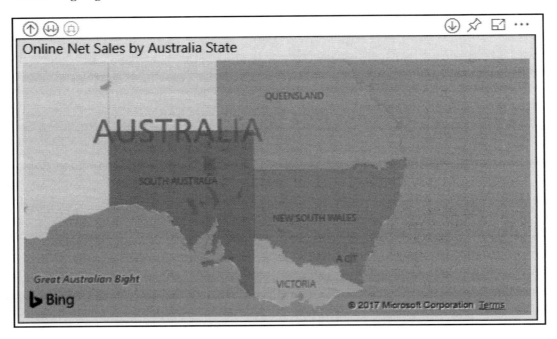

Filled map visual with diverging colors

Exactly like the color scheme described in the column and line chart conditional formatting section, three distinct numeric values and colors are assigned to the **Minimum**, **Center**, and **Maximum** properties. For this visual, the values of $1M, $2M, and $3M are associated with red, yellow, and green; this causes the South Australia state to appear as red while the New South Wales states are green.

Additionally, like the previous bubble map example, a grayscale map-style theme has been applied and the **auto-zoom** property has been disabled. Other map themes, such as dark, light, road, and aerial, are also available for filled and bubble maps. These alternative themes, particularly when contrasted with the bright or rich colors of a filled map, can significantly add to the aesthetic appeal of a report.

Per the drill-up/down icons above the visual, a hierarchy of geographical columns (`Country`, `State`, `City`) has been added to the location field well. These additional columns help the Bing Maps API to display the correct location, such as only Victoria in Australia. To ensure that Bing Maps respects the parent column (for example, `Country`) when plotting child locations (for example, States/Provinces), the user can enable the drill mode via the drill-down button in the top-right corner of the visual. With drill mode enabled, the user can click the specific parent value on the map, such as the United States, and Bing will plot states by only searching for states within the United States.

Alternatively, with drill mode not enabled, the user can click the expand all down one level icon in the top-left of the visual. From the initial state of the parent value (country), this will also plot the states within each parent value. The other drill option at the top-left of the visual, the go to the next level drill, only plots the child values without the context of the parent value.

Mobile-optimized reports

A critical use case for many reports is mobile access via the Power BI mobile applications for iOS, Android, and Windows platforms. A report that is perfectly designed for a laptop or PC monitor may be difficult to use on a tablet or mobile device. To account for multiple form factors, including both small and largescreen phones, report authors can create mobile-optimized reports via the **Phone Layout** view in Power BI Desktop.

In the following example, the **Phone Layout** of a report page in Power BI Desktop is accessed via the **View** tab:

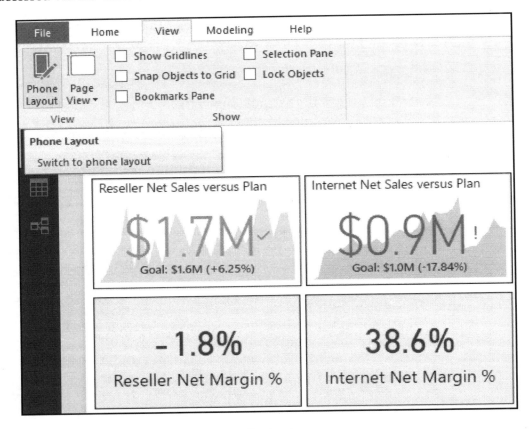

Phone Layout

From the **Phone Layout** view, the visuals created and formatted for the report page can be arranged and sized on a mobile layout grid. In the following example, the two KPI and card visuals included in the preceding image from the Report View, as well as a line chart, are arranged on the phone canvas:

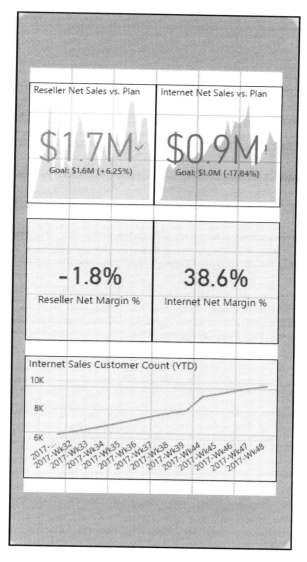

Phone Layout

Single-number visuals, such as cards and KPIs, are natural candidates for mobile-optimized layouts. More complex and data-intensive visuals, such as scatter charts and combination charts, are generally less effective choices for mobile layouts. Given the one-to-one relationship between report pages and the phone layout, one design option is to create a dedicated report page with the visuals needed for the phone layout.

The size and position of visuals can be adjusted by dragging visual icons along the phone layout grid. A mobile-optimized layout can be defined for each report page or any number of the pages contained in a report. The formatting and filter context of report visuals is always aligned between the **Phone Layout** and the default Report View. For example, to change the format or filter for a visual accessed via the **Phone Layout**, the visual can be modified from the standard Desktop Layout view.

When a report page is accessed from the Power BI mobile application, the **Phone Layout** created in Power BI Desktop will be rendered by default in the phone report mode. If a phone-optimized layout doesn't exist, the report opens in landscape view.

Power BI dashboards can also be optimized for mobile devices. The mobile layout for dashboards is implemented in the Power BI service and is reviewed in Chapter 13, *Designing Power BI Dashboards and Architectures*.

Responsive visuals

Certain Power BI visuals, such as line, column, and scatter charts, can be configured to dynamically display the maximum amount of data possible given the available screen size. For example, a responsive column chart visual will display fewer gridlines and columns as the height and width properties of the visual are reduced. This setting can benefit the mobile layouts for both reports and dashboards as visuals will retain their most valuable elements as they're resized.

To enable the responsive feature, select the visual on the report page in Desktop Layout and enable the **Responsive (Preview)** property under the **General** formatting card, per the following example:

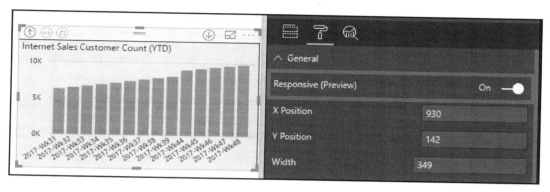

Responsive visuals property

The **Responsive (Preview)** formatting property, currently in preview, is disabled by default and can only be enabled per report visual.

Report design summary

As a data visualization and analytics platform, Power BI provides a vast array of features and functionality for report authors to develop compelling content to help users derive insights. Given the volume of features and possible formatting configurations, report authors and BI teams will want to follow a set of report planning and design practices to ensure consistently, quality report content is delivered to stakeholders. These practices include report planning in terms of scope, users and use cases, data visualization practices, and the selection of visuals.

The *Report planning, Visualization best practices*, and *Choosing the visual* sections earlier in this chapter provided details on many of the recommended practices to develop effective and sustainable report content. At a standard summary-level review of a report and the implementation of these practices, perhaps at the conclusion of a development phase and prior to deployment, the following list of questions can be asked:

1. Does the report have a clear scope and use case?
    - The report addresses specific business questions of value to specific users or teams that will consume the report
    - The relationship and distinction between this report and other reports or dashboards that the users will have access to is understood
    - The pages of the report naturally relate to one another to address the same or closely-related business questions, perhaps at alternative levels of detail

2. Have standard visualization practices been followed?
    - The visuals have proper spacing, alignment, and symmetry
    - The reports use colors selectively and there are clear titles on report pages and visuals
    - The report is intuitive and not cluttered with unnecessary details

3. Have the right visuals been chosen to represent the data?
    - Tables and matrices were used when cross-referencing or looking up individual values was necessary
    - The type of data relationship to represent (for example, comparison) and the relative advantages of the different visuals, such as line charts for the trends of a value, drove the visual choice

4. Does the report enable the user to easily apply filters and explore the data?
    - Slicer visuals for common or important columns have been utilized and are easily accessible to users
    - The filtering and cross-highlighting interactions between the visuals on the report pages have been considered and configured appropriately
    - Hierarchies of columns have been built into certain visuals to allow a simple drill-up and drill-down experience

5. Does the report aid the user in identifying insights or exceptions?
    - Dynamic formatting, such as with KPI visuals and conditional formatting rules and techniques, has been applied
    - Tooltips have been added to report visuals to provide the user with additional context hovering over the visual such as the columns in a column chart or the data points in a line chart.

6. Have simple and sustainable filter conditions been applied at the appropriate scope?
    - Report and page-level filter scopes have been applied to minimize the resources required by the queries generated by the report:
        - Visual-level filters are only used when the visual needs to reflect an alternative filter context of the report and page-level filter scopes
    - Report filter conditions are not being used to address issues with data quality or the source dataset:
        - Efforts have been made (or will be made) to enhance the source dataset to better support the report
    - Filter conditions on the date dimension are dynamic and sustainable (for example, `Current Year` and `Prior Year`) rather than hardcoded values (for example, 2018 and 2017)

Summary

In this chapter, we walked through the fundamental components of Power BI report design, including visualization best practices, Live connections to Power BI datasets, and the filter scopes available in Power BI Desktop. We reviewed top report development techniques and examples, such as conditional formatting, tooltips, and user parameters. Furthermore, we looked at powerful self-service and mobile report features, including slicers, visual interactions, and mobile-optimized reports.

The following chapter is also dedicated to the report development but goes well beyond the fundamental design concepts and features introduced in this chapter. That chapter will leverage the latest, most powerful report authoring features of Power BI, including drillthrough report pages, bookmarks, the analytics pane, and custom visuals.

12
Applying Custom Visuals, Animation, and Analytics

The previous chapter's emphasis on report planning, visualization best practices, and standard visuals in Power BI Desktop serve as a foundation for effective Power BI report development. However, more advanced visualization and report development features, such as the Analytics pane, Bookmarks, and drillthrough report pages are available to create even more compelling and insightful content. Additionally, a vast array of custom visuals created by Microsoft and a community of third parties can be leveraged to address specific use cases or provide extended functionality.

This chapter reviews many of the latest and most powerful analytical and visualization features in Power BI. This includes the design and utilization of drillthrough report pages, the ArcGIS Map for Power BI, and the use of Bookmarks and related features to easily store and share the insights contained in reports. Additionally, several of the more powerful and popular custom visuals are described including the Power KPI by Microsoft and the Impact Bubble Chart.

In this chapter, we will review the following topics:

- Drillthrough report pages
- Bookmarks
- Custom report navigation
- The Analytics Pane
- Quick Insights

- Trend and prediction lines
- Custom visuals
- ArcGIS Map visual for Power BI
- Waterfall chart
- Microsoft Power KPI visual
- Animation and storytelling visuals

Drillthrough report pages

Drillthrough report pages enable report authors to anticipate the needs of users to view the details associated with a particular item such as a product or customer. Since it's unknown which specific item the user will need to analyze during a self-service session in Power BI, generic drillthrough report pages can be designed that highlight the most relevant dimensions and metrics such as the product list price or the first purchase date of the customer. Drillthrough report pages update to reflect the filter context of the user's selection (for example, Product ABC) on a separate report page.

 Drillthrough was one of the most requested features in 2017 and its availability closes a gap with other Microsoft BI products. In paginated **SQL Server Reporting Services (SSRS)** reports, drillthrough actions can be defined in a source report to open a target report based on the parameters of the source report. The **Drillthrough filters** defined in Power BI report pages serve the same purpose as the parameters defined in the target reports of SSRS drillthrough actions.

In the following example, a report page has been designed with a drillthrough filter set to the Product Name column:

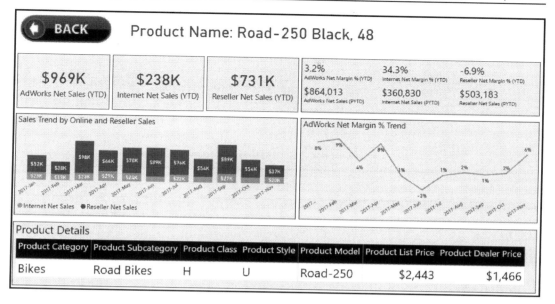

Drillthrough report page

The drillthrough report page provides a mix of high-level sales and margin metrics as well as seven product dimension columns in the `Product Details` table at the bottom. With the drillthrough report page configured, when the `Product Name` column is exposed on a separate page within the report, the user will have a right-click option to drill to this page as per the following image:

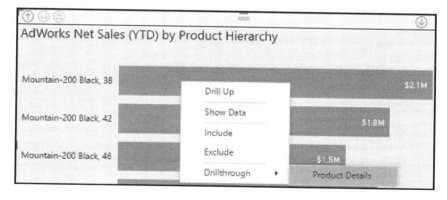

Drillthrough source page

Only the column or columns specified as **Drillthrough filters** can be used as drill columns. For example, even if the product's Alternate key column has a 1-to-1 relationship with the Product Name column, the drillthrough option will not be available to visuals based on the product alternate key column unless it's also been specified as a drillthrough filter like the Product Name column. Therefore, if some report visuals use Product Name and others use the product alternate key, both columns can be configured as **Drillthrough filters** on the drillthrough report page to support both scenarios.

In the preceding example, the user has drilled down through the four levels of the product hierarchy created in Chapter 9, *Designing Import and DirectQuery Data Models* (Product Category Group, Product Category, Product Subcategory, Product Name) to display a bar chart by the Product Name column. The same right-click drillthrough option is exposed via table, matrix, and other chart visuals including the scatter chart and the stacked column and bar charts.

The Bottom level column of a hierarchy such as the preceding Product Name example is often a good candidate to support with a drillthrough report page. For example, a common analysis pattern is to apply a few slicer selections and then to drill down through the hierarchy levels built into chart and matrix visuals. Each level of the hierarchy provides supporting context for its parent value, but ultimately the report user will want to investigate a specific value (for example, Customer 123) or a specific combination of values (Customer 123 and Calendar Year 2018).

Custom labels and the back button

Two of the most important components of the drillthrough report page include the Custom Product Name and back button image at the top of the report page. The Product Name message at the top of the page uses the following DAX Measure expression:

```
Selected Product Name =
VAR ProdName = SELECTEDVALUE('Product'[Product Name], "Multiple
Product Names")
RETURN "Product Name: " & ProdName
```

The SELECTEDVALUE() function returns either the single value currently selected for a given column or an alternative expression if multiple values have been selected. For drillthrough report pages, it's a given that the drill column will only have a single value as each drillthrough column is limited to a single value. To provide a dynamic label or title to the page, the DAX variable containing the Product Name expressions is concatenated with a text string. In this example, the Selected Product Name measure is displayed in a similar card visual.

The custom back button image was added to the report via the insert image command on the **Home** tab of the Report view. Once positioned in the top left of the page, selecting the image exposes the format image formatting cards. As per the following image, the **Link** formatting card is enabled and the **Type** is set to **Back**:

Back button image

The Power BI Desktop adds a back button arrow shape by default when a drillthrough page is created, but this shape is less intuitive for users than the custom image. With the back button configured, *Ctrl* + click is used to return to the source page in Power BI Desktop. Only a single click is needed to use the back button in the Power BI service.

The single row Product Details table at the bottom of the drillthrough report page has been filtered to only display the current, active values of the product. As described in the *Slowly changing dimensions* section of Chapter 8, *Connecting to Sources and Transforming Data with M*, the Products table contains multiple rows per product, representing different points in time. To ensure that only one row is displayed by the table visual, a visual level filter was applied, setting the Product Status column equal to Current. Alternatively, the visual level filter condition could specify that the Product End Date column is blank via the advanced filter condition type.

Multi-column drillthrough

In many scenarios, a more specific filter context is needed for drillthrough report pages to resolve analyses. For example, the user may be interested in one specific year for a given `Product Subcategory`. To support these needs, multiple columns can be added as drillthrough page filters. When one or both columns are exposed in a report visual on a separate page, the drillthrough right-click option can be used to apply multiple filter selections to the drillthrough page.

In the following stacked column chart of `Internet Sales` by year and `Product Subcategory`, right-clicking on the `Road Bikes` column for 2015 ($4.2M) exposes the **Drillthrough** option to the **Subcategory-Year Details** drillthrough report page:

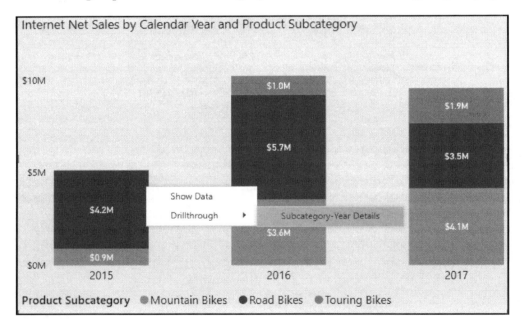

Drillthrough by multiple columns

The **Subcategory-Year Details** report page contains **Drillthrough filters** for both the `Calendar Year` and the `Product Subcategory` columns. Report visuals which only expose one of these two columns can still drill to this multi-column drillthrough report page. In this scenario, no filter would be applied to the column not contained in the source visual.

Executing the drillthrough action from the preceding chart results in the drillthrough report page filtered for both column values:

Multi-column drillthrough report page

The drillthrough report page (**Subcategory-Year Details**) in this scenario would be designed to display the values of the two drillthrough columns and provide supporting analysis for this given filter context. In the following example, the $4.2M of `Internet Net Sales` from the source page is identified in a card visual and also visualized by the calendar months of 2015 in a stacked column chart to break out the product models for the `Road Bikes` subcategory:

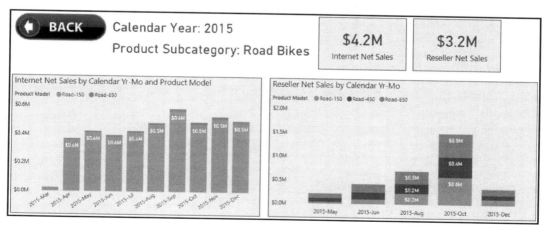

Multi-column drillthrough report page

In the preceding drillthrough report example, the user obtains details on both `Internet Net Sales` and `Reseller Net Sales` for the given year and `Product` category. Visuals which utilize measures from any fact table (for example, `Sales Plan`) with a cross-filtering relationship to the drillthrough column tables can be added to the drillthrough report page to provide additional context.

In addition to stacked column charts, matrix visuals are also a common choice for initiating a drillthrough action based on two columns. For example, the `Calendar Year` column could be the columns input and the `Product Subcategory` could be the rows input. Additionally, a pie chart with the two columns used in the legend and detailed input fields can also be used to drillthrough based on two columns.

Bookmarks

Bookmarks enable report authors to save specific states of reports for easy access and sharing with others. For example, an important or common view of a report page which involves filter conditions across several columns can be saved as a bookmark for easy access at a later time. By persisting the exact state of a report page, including any cross-highlighting, drilling, and sorting, each bookmark can serve as a distinct report page, thus amplifying the scope and usability of Power BI reports.

By default, bookmarks represent the entire state of a report page, including all filter selections and the properties of the visuals (for example, hidden or not). However, bookmarks can also optionally be associated with only a few visuals on a report page. Additionally, report authors can choose to avoid persisting any filter or slicer selections and rather only save visual properties on the page. These granular controls, along with the Selections pane and linking support from images and shapes, enable report authors to create rich and compelling user experiences.

In the following example, 12 Bookmarks have been created for a European sales report:

Bookmarks Pane

Bookmarks are created via the **Add** icon at the top of the **Bookmarks Pane**. With the **Bookmarks Pane** visible via the **View** tab in Report view, a report author can develop a report page with the filters and visual layout required and then click the **Add** icon to save these settings as a bookmark. As per the preceding image, the ellipsis at the right of the bookmark's name can be used to update Bookmarks to reflect the current state and to rename and delete visuals. Additionally, the second and third groups of bookmark options allow report authors to customize what is stored by the bookmark.

The **Data** category includes report, page, and visual level filters, slicer selections, the drill location if a visual has been drilled into, any cross-highlighting of other visuals, and any sort orders applied to visuals. The **Display** category includes whether a visual is hidden or not, the Spotlight property, focus mode, and the Show Data view. By disabling the **Data** category for a bookmark, a user's selections on slicers or other visuals will not be overridden when the bookmark is accessed.

In the preceding report, three Bookmarks have been applied for each of four report pages—Europe, United Kingdom, Germany, and France. For example, selecting the **France: Bikes Only** bookmark from the **Bookmarks Pane** displays the France report page filtered for both France and Bikes, as per the following image:

Bookmarks and Filters Pane

Switching to the **France: Excluding Bikes** book simply changes the filter condition on the Product Category Group column to Non-Bikes and selecting the **France: Summary** bookmark removes the Product Category Group filter. By using **Page level filters** within Bookmarks, a single report page (France) can more easily be re-used to address additional business questions. Additionally, Bookmarks and off-canvas filters avoid the need for users to interact with slicer visuals and also eliminates the canvas space that slicer visuals would otherwise consume.

Selection pane and the Spotlight property

The **Selection Pane** and the Spotlight property for visuals are both closely related features to Bookmarks. For example, with the **Selection Pane** exposed via the **View** tab of the Report view, certain textboxes on a report page can be hidden while a specific text box associated with a bookmark is left visible.

In the following example, three textboxes have been created for the Europe report page, but only one of the three textboxes is visible for each of the three Europe Bookmarks:

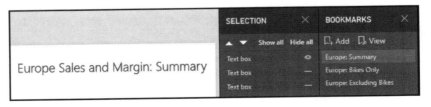

Selection Pane and Bookmarks Pane

The **Selection Pane** can be accessed via the **View** tab in Report view and displays all objects of the selected report page including visuals, images, and shapes. Although most commonly used with Bookmarks, the **Selection Pane** is also helpful when developing report pages that contain many visuals and objects. Selecting an object from the **Selection Pane** provides access to the properties associated with that object (for example, field inputs, formatting cards) as though the object was selected on the report canvas.

The icons next to the objects can be toggled between visible (eye symbol) and hidden (dash symbol). In the preceding example, only the text box containing the title `Europe Sales and Margin: Summary` is visible for the **Europe: Summary** bookmark. The other two textboxes on the Europe report page contain a title corresponding to the other two Europe Bookmarks (**Europe: Bikes Only**, **Europe: Excluding Bikes**). Like the **Europe: Summary** bookmark, only the text box containing the title associated with the given bookmark is visible for these two other Bookmarks.

The Spotlight property, accessed via the ellipsis in the top-right corner of each visual, draws attention to the specific visual by making all other visuals on the report page fade into the background.

Spotlight is particularly useful in supporting presentations via Bookmarks. For example, in the View mode described later in this section, one bookmark could display a report page of visuals normally and the following bookmark could highlight a single visual to call out a specific finding or an important trend or result. Spotlight may also be helpful for presenters to explain more complex visuals with multiple metrics and/or dimension columns.

As an alternative to Spotlight, Focus mode can also be saved as a bookmark. Focus mode can be applied via the diagonal arrow icon in the top right corner of chart visuals and fills the entire report canvas with the single visual.

In the following example, the Spotlight property has been enabled for a scatter chart on the Europe report page:

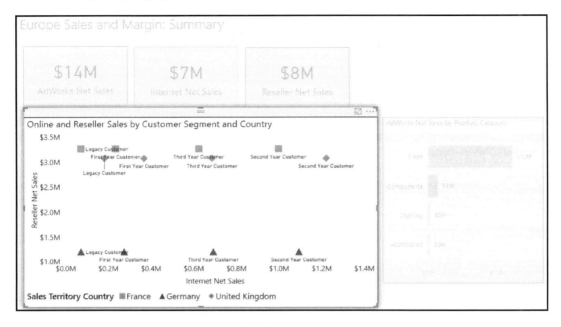

Report page with Spotlight enabled on the scatter chart

In the preceding report page, four other visuals (three cards and a bar chart) are still visible, but the scatter chart is emphasized via the Spotlight property. With Spotlight enabled, the report author could add a bookmark with an intuitive name (for example, `Europe Summary: Customer Segment and Country Scatter`) to save this specific view. Referencing this bookmark in a meeting or presentation makes it easier to explain the meaning and insights of the scatter chart.

Custom report navigation

Bookmarks can also be assigned as links to shapes and images. With multiple Bookmarks created across multiple report pages, a visual table of contents can be created to aid the user's navigation of a report. Rather than opening and browsing the **Bookmarks Pane**, users can simply click images or shapes associated with specific Bookmarks, and a back button can be used to return to the table of contents page.

In the following example, nine images have been positioned within a rectangle shape and linked to Bookmarks in the report:

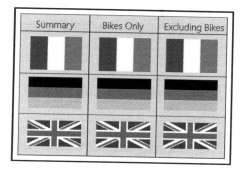

Custom navigation to Bookmarks

 The rectangle shape and three line shapes are used to form the matrix of icons. Shapes and images can be added from the insert group of icons on the **Home** tab of Report view. With a shape or image selected, the **Format** tab appears, allowing the author to align and distribute the objects as well as move certain objects forward or backward on the canvas. Grouping similar objects within shapes is a common practice to improve usability.

With an image or a shape selected, a **Link** formatting card can be enabled to choose between a **Bookmark** link and a **Back** link. In the following example, the France flag image positioned in the top right of the table of contents is linked to the **France: Excluding Bikes** bookmark:

Link formatting card for images and shapes

In this report, the back button image introduced in the *Drillthrough report pages* section earlier in this chapter is also inserted in each page of the report. Rather than return to the source page of a drillthrough action, a **Back** type link is set to allow users to return to the table of contents.

In the following image, a custom back button image has been inserted and set as a **Back** type link to aid navigation:

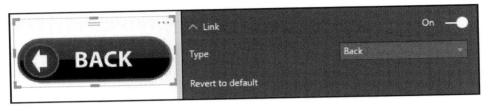

Back link for an image

The combination of custom navigation and Bookmarks representing many specific views or reports contributes to an easier, more productive experience for users. When designed properly, the user often doesn't need to know which page or bookmark to navigate to or which filters to apply as this logic is already built into the report.

View mode

The **View** icon in the **Bookmarks Pane** can be used in both Power BI Desktop and in the Power BI service to navigate between visuals similar to a slideshow. When **View** mode is enabled, the following navigation bar appears at the bottom of the screen and the user can close other panes and/or launch full screen mode in the Power BI service to further support the presentation:

View mode navigation

As per the preceding image, the number and order of Bookmarks, bookmark names, and navigation arrows are included in the **View** mode navigation. Bookmarks are ordered based on their position in the **Bookmarks Pane** from the top to the bottom. To revise the order, Bookmarks can be dragged and dropped to higher or lower positions in the **Bookmarks Pane**.

ArcGIS Map visual for Power BI

The ArcGIS Map visual for Power BI enables report authors to develop map visualizations far beyond the capabilities of the bubble and filled map visuals described in Chapter 11, *Creating and Formatting Power BI Reports*. Created by Esri, a market leader in **Geographic Information Systems (GIS)**, the ArcGIS Map supports all standard map types (for example, bubble and heatmap), but also provides many additional features including a clustering map theme for grouping individual geographic points and the ability to filter a map by the points within a geographical area. The ArcGIS Map also enables deep control over the logic of the size and color formatting, such as the number of distinct sizes (classes) to display and the algorithm used to associate locations to these classes. Additionally, reference layers and cards of demographic and economic information can be embedded into visuals to provide greater context.

The ArcGIS Map visual is included in the standard visualizations pane and enabled by default in Power BI Desktop. However, as noted in Chapter 16, *Deploying the Power BI Report Server*, the ArcGIS Map visual is not currently supported for the Power BI Report Server and thus is not available in the Power Desktop application optimized for the Power BI Report Server. Additionally, an option is available in the **Tenant settings** page of the Power BI admin portal to enable or disable the use of the ArcGIS Maps visual. Details on utilizing the Power BI admin portal to configure tenant settings and other options are included in Chapter 18, *Administering Power BI for an Organization*.

In the following example, customer addresses in the state of Washington have been plotted as diamonds of different sizes and colors based on the `Internet Sales` measure and the `Customer History Segment` column, respectively:

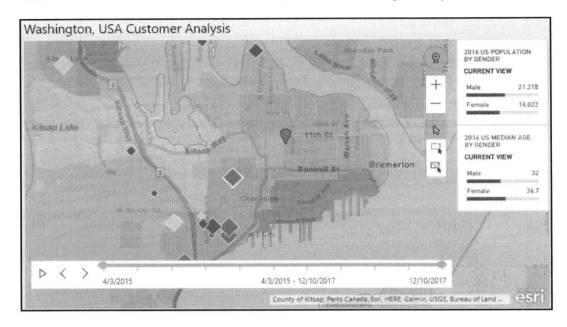

ArcGIS Map visual for Power BI

For the most visually engaging ArcGIS Map, use the **Dark Gray Canvas** basemap and bright, saturated colors for the data points plotted. The **Light Gray Canvas** basemap, however, avoids the risk of overwhelming the user with colors, as described in the previous chapter. The **Streets** and **OpenStreetMap** basemap types are practical choices whenever transportation between the data points or pinned locations is expected. In the preceding example, the **Streets** basemap supports the sales team that may drive from the pinned office location on 11th street in Bremerton, Washington to the plotted customer addresses.

The visual has been zoomed into the Bremerton, Washington area near several large customers and a fictional sales office location denoted by a red pin icon on 11th street near downtown Bremerton. Pin locations are often used in conjunction with the **Drive Time** feature to plot an area relative to specific locations such as the group of customers who are within a 20-minute drive of an office.

To configure these options and all other layout and formatting settings, click the ellipsis in the top right corner and select **Edit**. The following image displays the edit mode of an ArcGIS visual with the **Pins** menu selected:

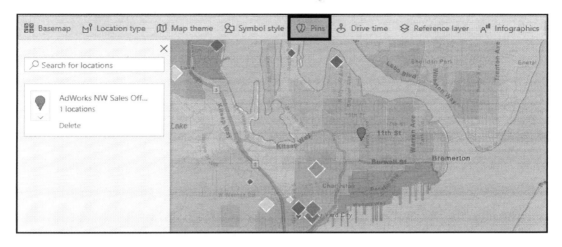

ArcGIS Map for Power BI toolbar options

For this visual, the **Streets** basemap type has been selected and the **Map theme** is set to **Size & Color**. The reference layer **USA Median Age** is used to distinguish areas based on age (via color intensity). Finally, two infographic cards have been selected—population and age by gender—to display these specific metrics as the user selects and hovers over the map.

A column named `Customer Full Address` has been applied to the **Location** input field. This column includes the street address, city, state, and postal code such as the following example: 1097 Kulani Lane, Kirkland, WA, 98033.

The **Data Category** for this column has been set to **Address** in Power BI Desktop to further improve the accuracy of the geocoding process in which the location input value (the address) is converted to a latitude and longitude. Latitude and longitude fields are available as well, and these inputs are recommended over street addresses for greater performance and scale. A max of 1,500 street addresses can be geocoded without a plus subscription and up to 5,000 addresses can be geocoded with a monthly plus subscription.

The Customer History Segment column, described in Chapter 8, *Connecting to Sources and Transforming Data with M*, evaluates to one of four values based on the relationship between the Current Date and the Customer First Purchase date column. In this example, first year, second year, and third year customers are assigned the colors purple, green, and blue, respectively. Legacy customers have been formatted as orange. The size and color formatting can be customized via the **Symbol Style** menu, and these options alone make it relatively easy for users to gain insights from the visual such as identifying the location of first year customers.

To provide greater analytical flexibility and to support presentations, the Date column from the Date dimension table has been applied to the Time input field, thus creating the timeline scrollbar. Similar to the play axis of the scatter chart described later in this chapter, the timeline for the ArcGIS Map supports both animation via the play and pause buttons and slider controls to define a specific time frame.

The left and right end points of the timeline can be used in combination with the animated playback. For example, a time frame of three months can be defined at the beginning of the timeline, and each frame of the animation will represent a distinct three month time frame. At each frame, the user can optionally pause the animation to call attention to specific points on the visual. These intervals can be set for 3, 6, 9, and 12 months.

The timeline and two measures are further supplemented with two date intelligence measures in the **Tooltips** field input. In the following example, the user has hovered over the address location of a First Year Customer (a purple diamond) and the two date intelligence measures (year-to-date and prior year-to-date), as well as the Date column from the timeline, which leads to them being exposed:

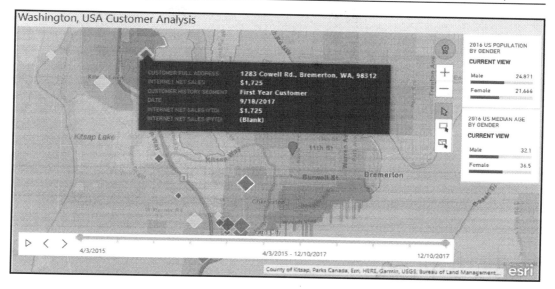

ArcGIS visual with Tooltips

To avoid the limit of addresses geocoded (1,500, or 5,000 with a Plus subscription), and to focus the visual on more meaningful data points, a visual level filter can be applied to a measure. In this example, a visual level filter has been applied to the `Internet Net Sales` measure to only include data points (customer addresses) with over $100. By removing the small customers, this filter reduced the count of addresses from 1,799 to 921 and retained over 97 percent of the `Internet Sales`.

Selections of ArcGIS Map locations also impact other visuals on the report page. For example, the selection of one address location on the map could cause a bar chart visual to filter or highlight the specific product subcategories associated with that location. Additionally, rather than selecting one location at a time, areas of locations can be selected via the **Select Multiple Locations** option and the areas of a reference layer can also be used to select locations. The multi-select options under the cursor icon and the cross-filtering of other related Power BI visuals provide powerful self-service geospatial analysis capabilities.

The **Use ArcGIS Maps for Power BI** option should be checked in the Global **Security** options of Power BI Desktop. An equivalent option is exposed in the Power BI service via the **Settings** menu (Gear icon | **Settings** | **ArcGIS Maps for Power BI**), and this should be checked as well to render ArcGIS Maps in the online service.

 Additionally, a **Use ArcGIS Maps for Power BI** setting is available in the **Tenant settings** page of the Power BI admin portal. Power BI service administrators can optionally disable this feature to prevent all users from using **ArcGIS Maps for Power BI**. The configuration of **Tenant settings** in the Power BI admin portal is described in Chapter 18, *Administering Power BI for an Organization*. The ArcGIS Map visual is the only standard Power BI visual not currently supported by the Power BI Report Server.

ArcGIS Maps Plus subscriptions

The ArcGIS Map visual is free, and Power BI reports using the ArcGIS Map visual can be published for users to view in the Power BI service and on mobile devices at no extra cost. However, in many scenarios, the limit of 1,500 geocoding addresses may prove insufficient. Additionally, the four basemaps available (**Light Gray Canvas**, **Dark Gray Canvas**, **Streets**, and **OpenStreetMap**) may not provide the desired details, such as satellite imagery.

With an ArcGIS Plus subscription, currently priced at $5 per user, per month, up to 5,000 addresses can be geocoded and plotted on a map. In the following image, the Plus icon appears above the zoom buttons of an ArcGIS Map visual:

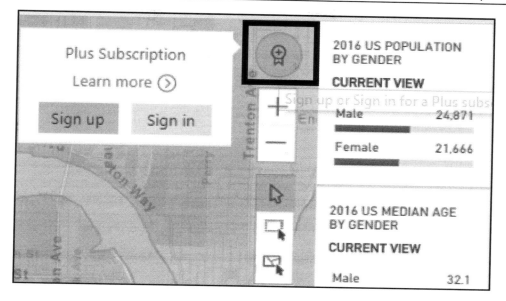

ArcGIS Plus subscription icon

Plus subscriptions also enable eight additional basemaps, several of which including satellite imagery and access to many additional reference layers and infographics. The following site maintained by Esri provides further details on Plus subscriptions: `http://arcg.is/2jG5DnG`.

 It's necessary for both report authors and users or consumers of the Power BI reports containing the ArcGIS Map visual to have Plus subscriptions. When an ArcGIS Maps visual contains premium content (via a Plus subscription), that content is only visible to other subscribed Plus users.

Waterfall chart breakdown

The waterfall chart is one of the most powerful standard visuals in Power BI given its ability to compute and format the variances of individual items between two periods by default. The items representing the largest variances are displayed as columns of varying length, sorted and formatted with either an increase (green) or decrease (red) color. This built-in logic and conditional formatting makes waterfall charts both easy to create and intuitive for users.

In the following example, the `Internet Sales` of the last two completed months is broken down by `Sales Territory Country`:

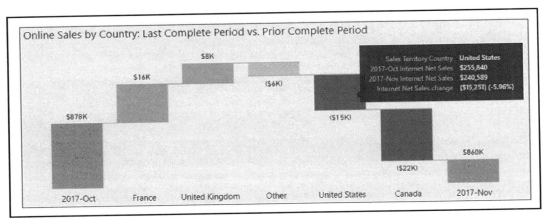

Waterfall chart with breakdown

The waterfall chart naturally walks the user from the starting point category on the left (**2017-Oct**) to the ending point category on the right (**2017-Nov**). As per the preceding image, hovering the cursor over a bar results in the details for this item being displayed as a tooltip. In this example, hovering over the (**$15K**) red bar for the **United States** displays the `Internet Sales` for both months, the variance, and the variance as a percentage. These four tooltip values are provided by default and report authors can optionally add measures to the **Tooltips** field to deliver even greater context.

The `Internet Net Sales` measure is applied to the y-axis input field, and the `Calendar Yr-Mo` and `Sales Territory Country` columns are applied to the `Category` and `Breakdown` input fields, respectively. For this visual, the Max breakdowns property available under the Breakdown formatting card is set to **4** and thus only four countries are displayed. The other breakdown item, formatted in yellow by default, is used to summarize the variances for all items not displayed as a breakdown column. In the preceding example, the relatively smaller variances from Australia and Germany are automatically rolled into the other item.

As with other visuals, a **Show Data** and an **Export data** option is available in both Power BI Desktop and when viewing the visual in the Power BI service. These options are exposed under the ellipsis (three dots) in the top right corner of each visual. As one example, the user could select **Show Data** for the waterfall chart to view the sales data for all the countries (including Germany and Australia) in a table format. Report authors can adjust the Max breakdowns property to display greater detail and reduce the size of the other breakdown. However, waterfall charts with fewer breakdown columns are easier for users to interpret.

As per the following image, a filter is applied to the `Calendar Month Status` column to only include the `Prior Calendar Month` and the `2 Mo Prior Calendar Month` values:

Filter impacting the waterfall chart

This filter results in only two month values being available to the visual and ensures that the visual will update over time. For example, in March of 2018, the visual will automatically update to compare January of 2018 versus February of 2018. This filter can be applied at the report level, page level, or visual level scope, depending on the scenario.

Details on building date dimension columns such as `Calendar Month Status` into a Power BI dataset are included in the *Date dimension view* section of `Chapter 8`, *Connecting to Sources and Transforming Data with M*. Additionally, filter scopes and the filter conditions available to each scope was reviewed in the *Report filter scopes* section in `Chapter 11`, *Creating and Formatting Power BI Reports*.

Analytics pane

In addition to the Field and Formatting panes used to create report visuals, an Analytics pane is also available for cartesian visuals such as Line and clustered column charts. This pane allows report authors to add constant and dynamic reference lines such as average, max, and min to visuals to provide greater context and analytical value. Additionally, trend and forecast lines can be added to display the results of advanced analytical techniques such as exponential smoothing to support predictive analytics.

A simple but important use case of the Analytics pane, exemplified in the *Trend lines* section below, is to add a constant line that represents a goal or threshold to compare a measure against. Dynamic reference lines representing an aggregation (for example, a median) behave just like DAX measures and thus, in some scenarios, avoid the need to create new DAX measures into the source dataset.

The reference lines available in the Analytics pane depend on the type of visual. For example, reference lines are currently not supported for any custom visuals and only a constant line can be applied to the stacked column and bar charts. Additionally, the trend line is exclusive to the Line and clustered column chart, while the forecast line is exclusive to the line chart. Moreover, a date or a numeric column is required in the axis to utilize the trend and forecast lines.

New features and capabilities are planned for the Analytics pane, including an expanded list of visuals supported. Similar to the Tooltips feature described in the previous `Chapter 11`, *Creating and Formatting Power BI Reports*, Power BI report authors should be conscious of the Analytics pane and its ability to enhance report visuals with additional context and insights.

Trend Line

A **Trend Line** is available in the Analytics pane for the clustered column chart and the line chart. The **Trend Line** is particularly valuable when a chart contains many data points and significant variation exists among the points, making it difficult to observe the trend of the metric visually.

In the following example, a trend line and two additional reference lines (average and constant) have been added to a clustered column chart to provide greater insight and context:

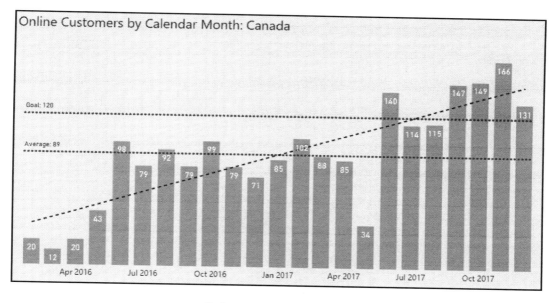

Trend, constant, and average reference lines

The **Label Density** property of the **Data labels** formatting card has been set to 100 percent. Additionally, the position property of the data labels has been set to an inside end with a white color and text size of 11. Clear visibility of the data labels for each column, in addition to the two reference lines (Average and Goal), avoids the need to display the **Y-AXIS** and gridlines.

Excluding the three reference lines from the Analytics pane, the clustered column chart simply plots the `Internet Sales Customer Count` measure against the `Calendar Month Ending Date` column. The `Calendar Month Ending Date` column (for example, `11/30/2017`) is required for the axis input in this scenario as both the trend line and the forecast line require either a date or a number data type for the axis. For example, if the `Calendar Yr-Mo` column was used for the axis (for example, `2017-Oct`), both the trend line and the forecast line cards would not appear in the Analytics pane.

The DAX expression used for this measure is included in the *Dimension metrics* section of `Chapter 10`, *Developing DAX Measures and Security Roles*. To ensure that the current month's data does not impact on the trend line, the `Calendar Month Status` column was used as a page level filter. The filter condition applied (**Is Not Current Calendar Month**) excludes the latest month from the visual and any other visuals on the report page. Additional information on the `Calendar Year` and `Month Status` columns is included in `Chapter 8`, *Connecting to Sources and Transforming Data with M*.

With the essential column chart built, the three reference lines can be added from the Analytics pane per the following image:

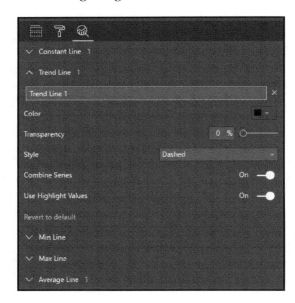

Analytics pane

As per the preceding image, the **Style** of the **Trend Line** is set to **Dashed** with a transparency of **0** percent. This formatting ensures that the trend reference line can be easily distinguished from other data on the chart such as the other two reference lines. The **Combine Series** property is not relevant to this visual as there is only one series (`Internet Sales Customer Count`), and **Use Highlight Values** is the default setting for calculating the **Trend Line**.

The numeric symbols (**1**) next to the **Constant Line** and **Average Line** cards denote that a reference line of each type has also been applied to the visual. For these reference lines, a **Dotted line** style has been used, and custom names have been configured (for example, **Goal**, **Average**) to be displayed via **Data labels**. These two additional lines make it easy for users to identify the columns which are above or below the average value for the visual (89) and the constant goal value of 120.

Forecast line

The **Forecast** line, exclusive to standard line chart visuals, utilizes predictive forecasting algorithms to generate both specific forecast data points as well as upper and lower boundaries. The report author has control over the number of data points to forecast, the confidence interval of the forecast (for example, 80 percent, 95 percent), and can apply formatting to distinguish the forecast from the actual data points. Additionally, the forecasting feature allows authors to optionally exclude a number from the last data points. This **Ignore last** property is useful for excluding incomplete periods as well as evaluating the accuracy of the forecast relative to recently completed periods.

In the following example, the clustered column chart from the *Trend Lines* section has been switched to a Line chart and a **Forecast** line for the next two months has been added:

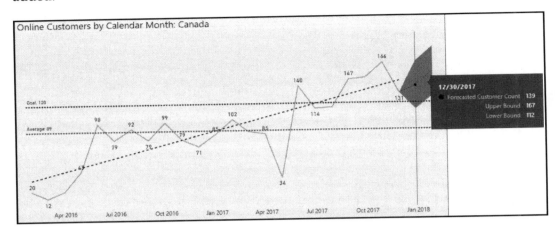

Forecast line

By hovering over the first forecast point, December of 2017, the **Forecasted Customer Count** value of **139** is displayed along with the upper (**167**) and lower (**112**) boundaries. The user can easily distinguish the last actual data point, 131 for November of 2017, from the forecast via the **Dotted** style of the **Forecast** line and the dark fill of the **Confidence band style**. The **Trend**, **Average**, and **Goal** reference lines applied in the previous section provide further context to the **Forecast**.

Like the *Trend Lines* section example, the `Calendar Month Ending Date` column is used as the axis, and the `Current Month` (2017-Dec) has been excluded with a page level filter condition on the `Calendar Month Status` column. This filter condition avoids the need to utilize the **Ignore last** property of the forecast analytics card. The **Label Density** property has been reduced to 72 percent to reduce clutter given in the additional reference line.

As per the following image, the **Forecast length, Confidence interval,** and a custom name (`Forecasted Customer Count`) have been applied to the **Forecast** line:

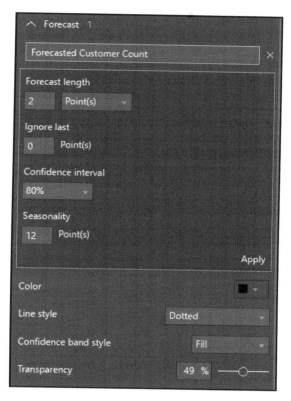

Forecast properties in the Analytics pane

The **Seasonality** property is optional, but since the data reflects calendar months, a value of **12** overrides the automatically detected season value. Likewise, for quarterly data, a value of 4 could be applied.

The **Confidence interval** property defines the distance between the upper and lower boundaries from the forecasted data points. For example, the minimum confidence interval of 75 percent would produce a more narrow range, and the maximum confidence interval of 99 percent would widen the boundaries of the first forecast point to an upper limit of 194 and a lower limit of 84.

The **Ignore last** property can be used to evaluate how accurately the forecast would've predicted recent data points. In this example, an **Ignore last** value of **2** would result in forecast values for October and November of 2017—the last two completed months. The forecast algorithm would use all available data points through September of 2017 to generate the two forecast points.

If the actual data points for these two months fall outside the confidence interval (upper and lower bounds) of the forecast, the forecast may not be valid for the given data, or the **Confidence Interval** may be too narrow. This testing technique is referred to as **hindcasting**.

Quick Insights

Quick Insights is one of the most analytically advanced features in Power BI as it enables sophisticated machine learning algorithms to be executed against datasets or specific subsets of those datasets. The results of these computations automatically generate highly formatted Power BI visuals which can be integrated into reports as though they were created from scratch. **Quick Insights** is only generally available in the Power BI service for import mode datasets and dashboard tiles reflecting those datasets. However, the essential capabilities of **Quick Insights** are also now available in preview for Power BI Desktop.

In the following image, **Quick Insights** has been executed against the AdWorks Enterprise dataset in the Power BI service:

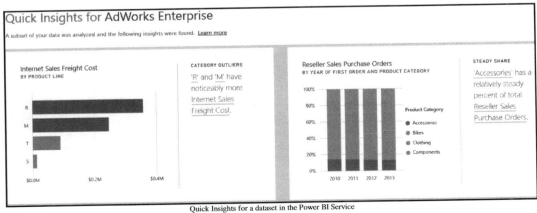

Quick Insights for a dataset in the Power BI Service

To execute **Quick Insights** against an entire dataset, see the **Get quick insights** option under the Actions ellipsis menu in the Power BI service. Once the insights have been generated, a **View insights** menu option replaces the **Get quick insights** option. The visuals generated from the insights, such as the clustered bar chart on the left, advise of the algorithm used (for example, outlier, cluster, and correlation). Most importantly, the visuals can be pinned to dashboards and are displayed without the supporting text like normal dashboard tiles. In Power BI Desktop, **Quick Insights** are currently limited to specific data points represented by report visuals.

Quick Insights cannot be executed against datasets which contain row-level security roles as described in `Chapter 10`, *Designing DAX Measures and Security Roles*. Additionally, **Quick Insights** cannot be executed against DirectQuery datasets, Live connection datasets to Analysis Services models, and realtime streaming datasets.

Explain the increase/decrease

Quick Insight features are enabled in Power BI Desktop by default, allowing users to right-click data points in visuals and execute the relevant analysis. In the following example, the user has right-clicked the data point for **2017-Apr**, and as a result, an option to explain the decrease is exposed in the **Analyze** menu:

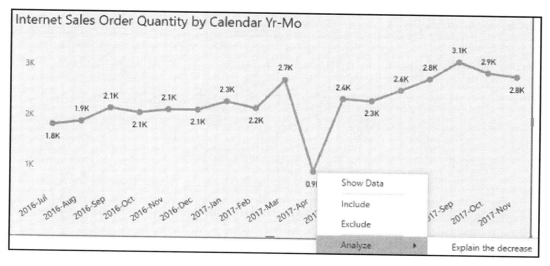

Explaining the decrease in Power BI Desktop

Clicking **Explain the decrease** executes machine learning algorithms against the dataset and populates a window with visuals representing the insights retrieved. The user can scroll vertically to view the different insights obtained such as the `Customer Gender` column accounting for a majority of the decrease, or `Product Name XYZ`, which had the largest decrease among all products.

By default, a waterfall visual is used to display each insight, but other visuals such as the scatter chart and the 100 percent stacked column chart are available too. In the following example, the user has scrolled to an insight based on the `Customer History Segment` column and views the data as a waterfall chart:

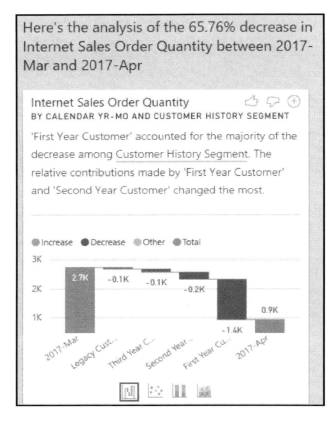

Explain the decrease in Power BI Desktop

Clicking the plus sign at the top right corner of the text box explaining the insight adds the visual to the report page. Adding the visual to the report page automatically populates the associated field wells and visual level filters as though the visual was created manually. If necessary, the report author can apply further formatting to align the visual with the design and layout of the page.

Currently, **Quick Insights** in Power BI Desktop is limited to the local dataset and is exclusive to import mode datasets. For example, the **Explain the decrease** option will not appear when connecting to a published Power BI dataset or a SSAS database via Live connection. Given the importance of isolating reports from a central dataset as described in the previous Chapter 11, *Creating and Formatting Power BI Reports* this limitation represents a significant obstacle to utilize this feature in corporate deployments.

Additionally, there are several limitations on the kinds of measures and filters supported. For example, measures which use the DISTINCTCOUNT() and SUMX() functions are not supported, and measures containing conditional logic (for example, IF()) cannot be either.

Custom visuals

In addition to the standard visuals included in the **Visualizations** pane of Power BI Desktop, a vast array of custom visuals can be added to reports to deliver extended functionality or to address specific use cases. These visuals, many of which have been created by Microsoft, are developed with the common framework used by the standard visuals and are approved by Microsoft prior to inclusion in Microsoft AppSource. Given the common framework, custom visuals can be integrated into Power BI reports with standard visuals and will exhibit the same standard behaviors such as filtering via slicers and report and page filters.

This section highlights four powerful custom visuals and the distinct scenarios and features they support. Power BI report authors and BI teams are well-served to remain conscience of both the advantages and limitations of custom visuals. For example, when several measures or dimension columns need to be displayed within the same visual, custom visuals such as the Impact Bubble Chart and the Dot Plot by Maq Software may exclusively address this need. In many other scenarios, a trade-off or compromise must be made between the incremental features provided by a custom visual and the rich controls built into a standard Power BI visual.

Custom visuals available in AppSource and within the integrated custom visuals store for Power BI Desktop are all approved for running in browsers and on mobile devices via the Power BI mobile apps. A subset of these visuals have been certified by Microsoft and support additional Power BI features such as email subscriptions and export to PowerPoint. Additionally, certified custom visuals have met a set of code requirements and have passed strict security tests. The list of certified custom visuals and additional details on the certification process is available at the following link: `http://bit.ly/2AFAC9W`.

Adding a custom visual

Custom visuals can be added to Power BI reports by either downloading `.pbiviz` files from Microsoft **AppSource** or via the integrated Office Store of custom visuals in Power BI Desktop. Utilizing **AppSource** requires the additional step of downloading the file; however, it can be more difficult to find the appropriate visual as the visuals are not categorized. However, **AppSource** provides a link to download a sample Power BI report (`.pbix` file) to learn how the visual is used, such as how it uses field inputs and formatting options. Additionally, **AppSource** includes a short video tutorial on building report visualizations with the custom visual.

The following image reflects Microsoft **AppSource** filtered by the **Power BI visuals Add-ins** category:

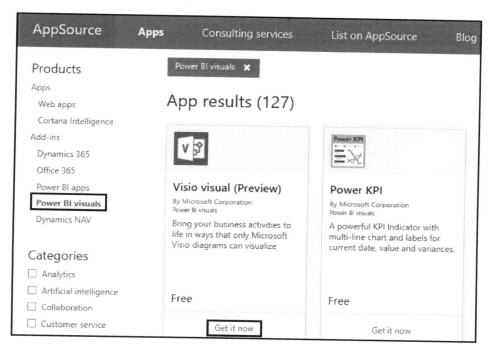

Power BI custom visuals in AppSource

The following link filters **AppSource** to the Power BI custom visuals per the preceding image: `http://bit.ly/2BIZZbZ`.

The search bar at the top and the vertical scrollbar on the right can be used to browse and identify custom visuals to download. Each custom visual tile in **AppSource** includes a **Get it now** link which, if clicked, presents the option to download either the custom visual itself (`.pbiviz` file) or the sample report for the custom visual (`.pbix` file). Clicking anywhere else in the tile other than **Get it now** prompts a window with a detailed overview of the visual, a video tutorial, and customer reviews.

To add custom visuals directly to Power BI reports, click the **Import from store** option via the ellipsis of the Visualizations pane, as per the following image:

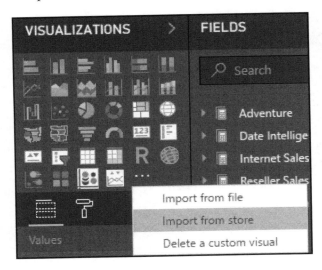

Importing custom visuals from the store

 If a custom visual (`.pbiviz` file) has been downloaded from **AppSource**, the **Import from file** option can be used to import this custom visual to the report. Additionally, both the **Import from store** and **Import from file** options are available as icons on the **Home** tab of the Report view in Power BI Desktop.

Selecting **Import from store** launches an MS Office Store window of **Power BI Custom Visuals**. Unlike **AppSource**, the visuals are assigned to categories such as **KPIs**, **Maps**, and **Advanced Analytics**, making it easy to browse and compare related visuals. More importantly, utilizing the integrated **Custom Visuals** store avoids the need to manage `.pbiviz` files and allows report authors to remain focused on report development.

As an alternative to the **VISUALIZATIONS** pane, the **From Marketplace** and **From File** icons on the **Home** tab of the Report view can also be used to add a custom visual. Clicking the **From Marketplace** icon in the follow image launches the same MS Office Store window of **Power BI Custom visuals** as selecting **Import from store** via the **VISUALIZATIONS** pane:

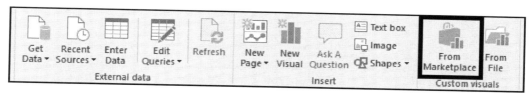

From Marketplace ribbon icon

In the following image, the **KPIs** category of **Custom visuals** is selected from within the MS Office store:

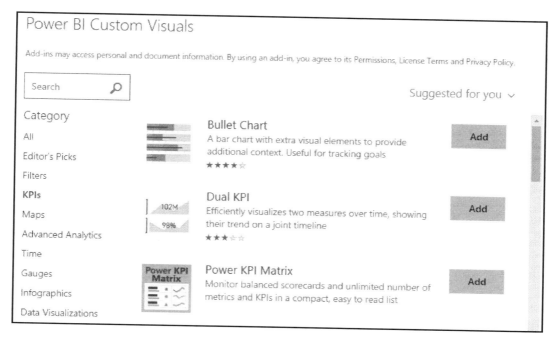

Custom visuals via the Office Store in the Power BI Desktop

The **Add** button will directly add the custom visual as a new icon in the Visualizations pane. Selecting the custom visual icon will provide a description of the custom visual and any customer reviews. The Power BI team regularly features new custom visuals in the blog post and video associated with the monthly update to Power BI Desktop. The visual categories, customer reviews, and supporting documentation and sample reports all assist report authors in choosing the appropriate visual and using it correctly.

Organizations can also upload custom visuals to the Power BI service via the organization visuals page of the Power BI Admin portal. Once uploaded, these visuals are exposed to report authors in the **MY ORGANIZATION** tab of the custom visuals **MARKETPLACE** as per the following example:

My Organization custom visuals

This feature can help both organizations and report authors simplify their use of custom visuals by defining and exposing a particular set of approved custom visuals. For example, a policy could define that new Power BI reports must only utilize standard and organizational custom visuals. The list of organizational custom visuals could potentially only include a subset of the visuals which have been certified by Microsoft. Alternatively, an approval process could be implemented so that the use case for a custom visual would have to be proven or validated prior to adding this visual to the list of organizational custom visuals. Additional details on managing organizational custom visuals are included in Chapter 18, *Administering Power BI for an Organization.*

Power KPI visual

Key Performance Indicators (KPIs) are often prominently featured in Power BI dashboards and in the top left area of Power BI report pages, given their ability to quickly convey important insights. Unlike card and gauge visuals which only display a single metric or a single metric relative to a target respectively, KPI visuals support trend, variance, and conditional formatting logic. For example, without analyzing any other visuals, a user could be drawn to a red KPI indicator symbol and immediately understand the significance of a variance to a target value as well as the recent performance of the KPI metric. For some users, particularly executives and senior managers, a few KPI visuals may represent their only exposure to an overall Power BI solution, and this experience will largely define their impression of Power BI's capabilities and the Power BI project.

Given their power and important use cases, report authors should become familiar with both the standard KPI visual and the most robust custom KPI visuals such as the Power KPI Matrix, the Dual KPI, and the Power KPI. Each of these three visuals have been developed by Microsoft and provide additional options for displaying more data and customizing the formatting and layout.

The **Power KPI Matrix** supports scorecard layouts in which many metrics can be displayed as rows or columns against a set of dimension categories such as Operational and Financial. The **Dual KPI**, which was featured in the *Microsoft Power BI Cookbook* (`https://www.packtpub.com/big-data-and-business-intelligence/microsoft-power-bi-cookbook`), is a good choice for displaying two closely related metrics such as the volume of customer service calls and the average waiting time for customer service calls.

One significant limitation of custom KPI visuals is that data alerts cannot be configured on the dashboard tiles reflecting these visuals in the Power BI service. Data alerts are currently exclusive to the standard card, gauge, and KPI visuals.

In the following Power KPI visual, `Internet Net Sales` is compared to `Plan`, and the prior year `Internet Net Sales` and **Year-over-Year Growth percent** metrics are included to support the context:

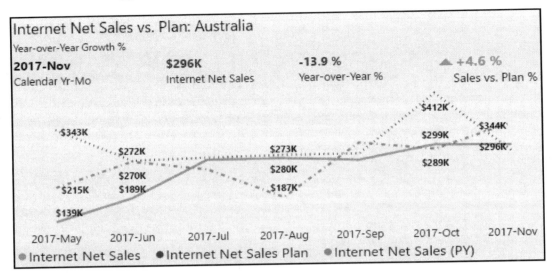

Power KPI custom visual

The `Internet Net Sales` measure is formatted as a solid, green line whereas the `Internet Sales Plan` and `Internet Net Sales (PY)` measures are formatted with **Dotted** and **Dot-dashed** line styles respectively. To avoid clutter, the **Y-Axis** has been removed and the **Label Density** property of the **Data labels** formatting card has been set to 50 percent. This level of detail (three measures with variances) and formatting makes the Power KPI one of the richest visuals in Power BI.

The Power KPI provides many options for report authors to include additional data and to customize the formatting logic and layout. Perhaps its best feature, however, is the Auto Scale property, which is enabled by default under the Layout formatting card. Similar to the responsive visuals feature described in the *Mobile optimized reports* section of the previous `Chapter 11`, *Creating and Formatting Power BI Reports*, Auto Scale causes the visual to make intelligent decisions about which elements to display given the available space.

For example, in the following image, the Power KPI visual has been pinned to a Power BI dashboard and resized to the smallest tile size possible:

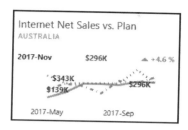

Minimal Power BI dashboard tile

As per the preceding dashboard tile, the less critical data elements such as July through August and the year-over- year % metric were removed. This auto scaling preserved space for the KPI symbol, the axis value (**2017-Nov**), and the actual value (**$296K**). With Auto Scale, a large Power KPI custom visual can be used to provide granular details in a report and then re-used in a more compact format as a tile in a Power BI dashboard.

Another advantage of the Power KPI is that minimal customization of the data model is required. The following image displays the dimension column and measures of the data model mapped to the field inputs of the aforementioned Power KPI visual:

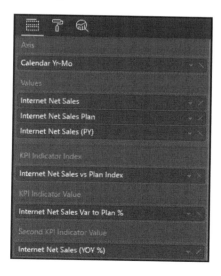

Power KPI field inputs

As described in previous chapters, the `Sales and Margin Plan` data is available at the monthly grain and thus the `Calendar Yr-Mo` column is used as the **Axis** input. In other scenarios, a `Date` column would be used for the **Axis** input provided that the actual and target measures both support this grain.

The order of the measures used in the **Values** field input is interpreted by the visual as the actual value, the target value, and the secondary value.

In this example, `Internet Net Sales` is the first or top measure in the **Values** field and thus is used as the actual value (for example, **$296K** for November). A secondary value as the third measure in the **Values** input (`Internet Net Sales (PY)`) is not required if the intent is to only display the actual value versus its target.

The **KPI Indicator Value** and **Second KPI Indicator Value** fields are also optional. If left blank, the Power KPI visual will automatically calculate these two values as the percentage difference between the actual value and the target value, and the actual value and the secondary value respectively. In this example, these two calculations are already included as measures in the data model and thus applying the `Internet Net Sales Var to Plan %` and `Internet Net Sales (YOY %)` measures to these fields further clarifies how the visual is being used.

If the metric being used as the actual value is truly a critical measure (for example, revenue or count of customers) to the organization or the primary user, it's almost certainly appropriate that related target and variance measures are built into the Power BI dataset. In many cases, these additional measures will be used independently in their own visuals and reports. Additionally, if a target value is not readily available, such as the preceding example with the `Internet Net Sales Plan`, BI teams can work with stakeholders on the proper logic to apply to a target measure, for example, 10 percent greater than the previous year.

The only customization required is the **KPI Indicator Index** field. The result of the expression used for this field must correspond to one of five whole numbers (1-5) and thus one of the five available KPI Indicators. In the following example, the KPI Indicators **KPI 1** and **KPI 2** have been customized to display a green caret up icon and a red caret down icon respectively:

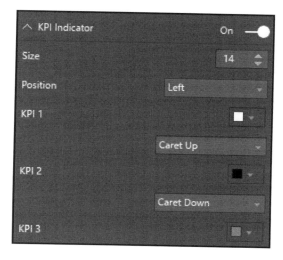

KPI Indicator formatting card

Many different **KPI Indicator** symbols are available including up and down arrows, flags, stars, and exclamation marks. These different symbols can be formatted and then displayed dynamically based on the **KPI Indicator Index** field expression. In this example, a KPI index measure was created to return the value 1 or 2 based on the positive or negative value of the Internet Net Sales Var to Plan % measure respectively:

```
Internet Net Sales vs Plan Index = IF([Internet Net Sales Var to Plan
%] > 0,1,2)
```

Given the positive **4.6 percent** variance for November of 2017, the value **1** is returned by the index expression and the green caret up symbol for **KPI 1** is displayed. With five available KPI Indicators and their associated symbols, it's possible to embed much more elaborate logic such as five index conditions (for example, poor, below average, average, above average, good) and five corresponding KPI indicators.

Four different layouts (**Top**, **Left**, **Bottom**, and **Right**) are available to display the values relative to the line chart. In the preceding example, the **Top** layout is chosen as this results in the last value of the **Axis** input (**2017-Nov**) to be displayed in the top left corner of the visual. Like the standard line chart visual in Power BI Desktop, the line style (for example, **Dotted**, **Solid**, **Dashed**), color, and thickness can all be customized to help distinguish the different series.

Chiclet Slicer

As per the previous chapter, the standard slicer visual can display the items of a source column as a list or as a dropdown. Additionally, if presented as a list, the slicer can optionally be displayed horizontally rather than vertically. The custom Chiclet Slicer, developed by Microsoft, allows report authors to take even greater control over the format of slicers to further improve the self-service experience in Power BI reports.

In the following example, a Chiclet Slicer has been formatted to display calendar months horizontally as three columns:

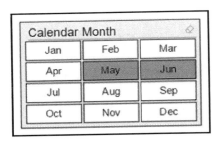

Chiclet Slicer

Additionally, a dark green color is defined as the **Selected Color** property under the Chiclets formatting card to clearly identify the current selections (**May** and **June**). The **Padding** and **Outline Style** properties, also available under the Chiclets card, are set to **1** and **Square** respectively, to obtain a simple and compact layout.

Like the slicer controls in Microsoft Excel, Chiclet Slicers also support cross highlighting. To enable cross highlighting, specify a measure which references a fact table as the **Values** input field to the Chiclet Slicer. For example, with the `Internet Net Sales` measure set as the **Values** input of the Chiclet Slicer, a user selection on a bar representing a product in a separate visual would update the Chiclet Slicer to indicate the calendar months without `Internet Sales` for the given product. The **Disabled Color** property can be set to control the formatting of these unrelated items.

Chiclet Slicers also support images. In the following example, one row is used to display four countries via their national flags:

Chiclet Slicer with images

For this visual, the **Padding** and **Outline Style** properties under the Chiclets formatting card are set to **2** and **Cut** respectively. Like the **Calendar Month** slicer, a dark green color is configured as the **Selected Color** property helping to identify the country or countries selected—**Canada**, in this example.

The Chiclet Slicer contains three input field wells—**Category**, **Values**, and **Image**. All three input field wells must have a value to display the images. The **Category** input contains the names of the items to be displayed within the Chiclets. The **Image** input takes a column with URL links corresponding to images for the given category values. In this example, the `Sales Territory Country` column is used as the **Category** input and the `Internet Net Sales` measure is used as the **Values** input to support cross highlighting. The `Sales Territory URL` column, which is set as an **Image URL** data category, is used as the **Image** input. For example, the following `Sales Territory URL` value is associated with the United States: `http://www.crwflags.com/fotw/images/u/us.gif`.

A standard slicer visual can also display images when the data category of the field used is set as **Image URL**. However, the standard slicer is limited to only one input field and thus cannot also display a text column associated with the image. Additionally, the standard slicer lacks the richer cross-highlighting and formatting controls of the Chiclet Slicer.

Impact Bubble Chart

One of the limitations with standard Power BI visuals is the number of distinct measures that can be represented graphically. For example, the standard scatter chart visual is limited to three primary measures (**X-AXIS**, **Y-AXIS**, and **SIZE**), and a fourth measure can be used for color saturation. The Impact Bubble Chart custom visual, released in August of 2017, supports five measures by including a left and right bar input for each bubble.

In the following visual, the left and right bars of the Impact Bubble Chart are used to visually indicate the distribution of `AdWorks Net Sales` between `Online` and `Reseller Sales` channels:

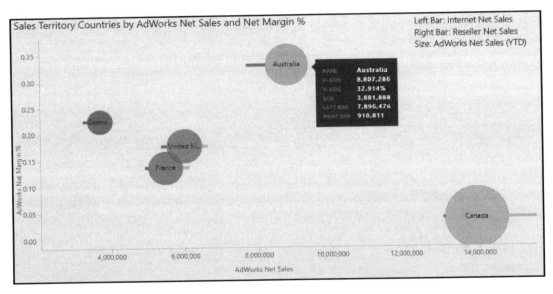

High Impact Bubble Chart

The Impact Bubble Chart supports five input field wells: **X-AXIS**, **Y-AXIS**, **SIZE**, **LEFT BAR**, and **RIGHT BAR**. In this example, the following five measures are used for each of these fields respectively: `AdWorks Net Sales`, `AdWorks Net Margin %`, `AdWorks Net Sales (YTD)`, `Internet Net Sales`, and `Reseller Net Sales`.

The length of the left bar indicates that Australia's sales are almost exclusively derived from online sales. Likewise, the length of the right bar illustrates that Canada's sales are almost wholly obtained via `Reseller Sales`. These graphical insights per item would not be possible for the standard Power BI scatter chart. Specifically, the `Internet Net Sales` and `Reseller Net Sales` measures could only be added as Tooltips, thus requiring the user to hover over each individual bubble.

In its current release, the Impact Bubble Chart does not support the formatting of data labels, a legend, or the axis titles. Therefore, a supporting text box can be created to advise the user of the additional measures represented. In the top right corner of this visual, a text box is set against the background to associate measures to the two bars and the size of the bubbles.

Dot Plot by Maq Software

Just as the Impact Bubble Chart supports additional measures, the Dot Plot by Maq Software allows for the visualization of up to four distinct dimension columns. With three **Axis** fields and a **Legend** field, a measure can be plotted to a more granular level than any other standard or custom visual currently available to Power BI. Additionally, a rich set of formatting controls are available to customize the Dot Plot's appearance, such as orientation (horizontal or vertical), and whether the **Axis** categories should be split or stacked.

In the following visual, each bubble represents the internet sales for a specific grouping of the following dimension columns: Sales Territory Country, Product Subcategory, Promotion Type, and Customer History Segment:

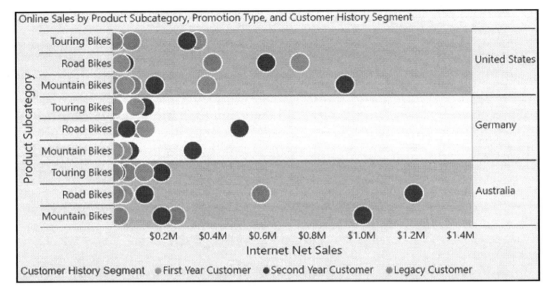

Dot Plot by Maq Software

For example, one bubble represents the Internet Sales for the Road Bikes Product Subcategory within the United States Sales Territory Country, which is associated with the volume discount promotion type and the first year Customer History Segment. In this visual, the Customer History Segment column is used as the legend and thus the color of each bubble is automatically formatted to one of the three customer history segments.

In the preceding example, the **Orientation** property is set to **Horizontal** and the **Split labels** property under the **Axis** category formatting card is enabled. The **Split labels** formatting causes the Sales Territory Country column to be displayed on the opposite axis of the Product Subcategory column. Disabling this property results in the two columns being displayed as a hierarchy on the same axis with the child column (Product Subcategory) positioned inside the parent column (Sales Territory Country).

Despite its power in visualizing many dimension columns and its extensive formatting features, data labels are currently not supported. Therefore, when the maximum of four dimension columns are used, such as in the previous example, it's necessary to hover over the individual bubbles to determine which specific grouping the bubble represents, such as in the following example:

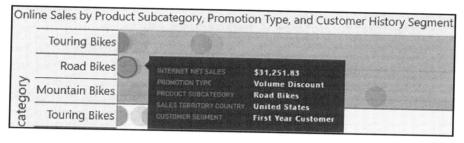

Four dimension columns per bubble of the Dot Plot visual

If only three dimension columns are used, which is still a detailed grain, then the lack of data labels is much less of a limitation. For example, the `Sales Territory Country` and `Product Subcategory` columns could be applied to the Axis category I and Axis category II field wells respectively, and the promotion type column could be added to the **Legend**. The two axis labels and the color of each bubble (per promotion type) would visually indicate the three-column grouping each bubble represents.

Animation and data storytelling

A top responsibility for many data professionals is the ability to convey their findings to others in a clear and compelling fashion. Common scenarios for data storytelling include recurring performance review meetings (for example, fiscal period close) and special project or ad hoc meetings with senior managers and executives. For these meetings, the data professional or team has already identified the insights to highlight, but must plan to properly communicate this message to the specific stakeholders or audience.

Power BI animation features, including bookmarks described earlier in this chapter, provide powerful support for data storytelling. In addition to the play axis available to the standard Scatter chart visual, many custom visuals support animation features such as the LineDot Chart and the Pulse Chart.

Play axis for scatter charts

The scatter chart is the only standard visual in Power BI Desktop which supports animation. By applying a time series column to the scatter chart's **Play Axis** field, animated playback and trace features are enabled. For example, a visual can be paused at a specific point along the time series, allowing the user to provide additional context. The user can also select one or multiple items which have been plotted (for example, product categories) to display data points representing the previous time periods.

In the following visual, the user has paused the animation on the month of September via the **Play Axis** and selected the icon associated with the `Touring Bikes` product subcategory:

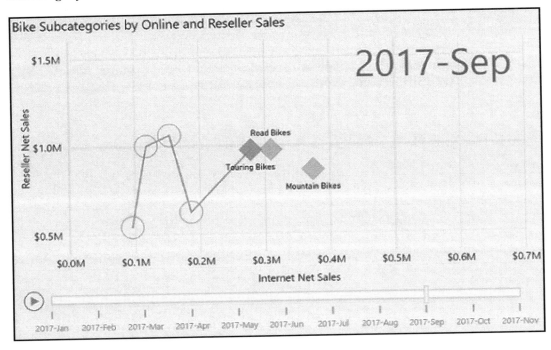

Scatter chart with Play axis

With the `Touring Bikes` subcategory selected, a trace line appears connecting the latest data point for this subcategory to its preceding data points. In this example, the user can explain that `Touring Bikes` weren't introduced until May of 2017 (the first data point), but by September was almost equal to the `Road Bikes` subcategory for both `Online` and `Reseller Sales`. Additionally, the user can hover the cursor over the four preceding data points representing May through August to provide the details for these months.

 Date, number, and text columns can be used in the **Play Axis** for the scatter chart. As per `Chapter 9`, *Designing Import and DirectQuery Data Models,* the **Sort By** column property can be used to define a logical sort order for text columns such as sorting a `Month name` column by a `Month number` column.

Pulse Chart

The Pulse Chart custom visual, developed by Microsoft, provides both animation and annotation features to support data storytelling. The Pulse Chart animates the value of a single measure over time and pauses at dates associated with events to display pop-up boxes of annotations describing these events. During this pause, which can also be applied manually via playback buttons, other Power BI visuals on the same report page are filtered by the event date. Additionally, a second measure can be visualized as a counter at the top of the chart via the **Runner Counter** field.

In the following example, a **year-to-date (YTD)** online sales measure and four events with annotations are plotted on a Pulse Chart:

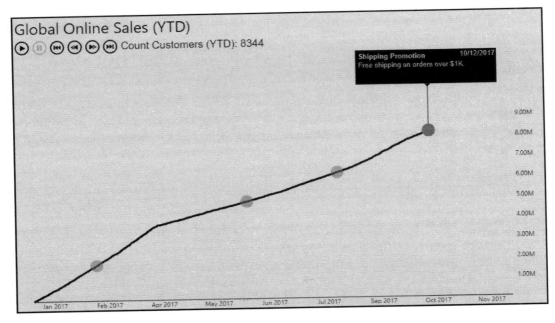

Pulse Chart

The YTD sales measure is visualized via the animated line (and dots) in relation to the Y axis. For this example, a YTD customer count measure has also been applied to the **Runner Counter** field input. With the visual paused on the shipping promotion event of October 12, 2017, the Y axis indicates a sales value of approximately **$8.00 M**, and the **Runner Counter** displays a count of 8,344 customers. Alternatively, the same measure can be applied to both the **Values** and **Runner Counter** fields, thus providing the precise value at each pause in addition to the trend via the line. Examples of defining YTD and customer count measures are included in Chapter 10, *Developing DAX Measures and Security Roles*.

If event annotations are not needed, only the **Timestamp** and **Values** input fields are required to render the Pulse Chart. Event Title, Event Description, and Event Size input fields are available to display events and annotations as pop-up boxes. Additionally, the formatting pane provides several cards for defining the look and behavior of the Pulse Chart, including the size and color of the pop-up textboxes and the speed of the animation. For example, white text at size 14 can be formatted against a black fill background and the pause at each event can be set to four seconds.

To support the Pulse Chart in the preceding example, a separate table of events has been added to the dataset as per the following image:

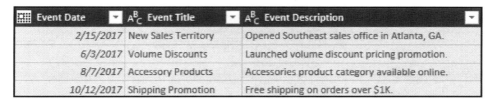

Event Date	Event Title	Event Description
2/15/2017	New Sales Territory	Opened Southeast sales office in Atlanta, GA.
6/3/2017	Volume Discounts	Launched volume discount pricing promotion.
8/7/2017	Accessory Products	Accessories product category available online.
10/12/2017	Shipping Promotion	Free shipping on orders over $1K.

Events table

The Event Date column is used to define a one-to-many relationship from the Events table to the Date dimension table with single direction cross-filtering. The Date column from the Date dimension table is applied to the Pulse Chart's **Timestamp** input field, and the Event Title and Event Description columns from the events table are applied to their respective input fields.

The formatting options for the X and Y axes of the Pulse Chart are much less robust than the standard line chart. As one example, the **Y Axis** gridlines cannot be disabled. Gridlines are not visible in the preceding example purely because the axis color was set to match the background color. Additionally, the second and later lines of event descriptions in pop-up boxes are displayed without spaces. Report authors can adjust the width of pop-ups or reduce the length of event descriptions to account for this.

Summary

This chapter reviewed many advanced analytical and visualization features that are available to deliver powerful and compelling report content. This included the design of drillthrough report pages, the configuration of custom navigation controls via Bookmarks, and advanced analytics such as predictive forecasting with the Analytics pane. Additionally, the ArcGIS Map visual for Power BI and custom visuals was introduced as a means to support specific use cases and to extend solutions beyond the capabilities of Power BI's standard visuals.

The next chapter utilizes the report visualizations and design patterns described in this chapter and the previous chapter to create Power BI dashboards. This includes simple, single dashboard projects and more elaborate multi-dashboard architectures representing different levels of detail. Although some users may only view or interact with Power BI via dashboards, the quality and sustainability of this content, and particularly the ability to analyze the supporting details, is largely driven by the report design concepts and features from Chapter 11, *Creating and Formatting Power BI Reports*.

13
Designing Power BI Dashboards and Architectures

This chapter leverages the dataset and report development features and concepts from prior chapters to plan and develop Power BI dashboards. Alternative dashboard architectures are described, including an organizational methodology that seeks to align business teams at various levels within an organization to a common set of corporate KPIs. The design and implementation of these dashboards, including layout, custom links, and mobile-optimized dashboards are described in this chapter. Additionally, other top features and capabilities of dashboards are reviewed, including live report pages and the integration of content from other report types, including **SQL Server Reporting Services (SSRS)** paginated reports and Microsoft Excel workbooks.

In this chapter, we will review the following topics:

- Dashboards versus reports
- Multi-dashboard architectures
- Dashboard tiles
- Custom links
- Live report pages
- Mobile-optimized dashboards
- SQL Server Reporting Services integration
- Excel Workbook integration

Dashboards versus reports

Executives and high-level stakeholders require a holistic yet streamlined view of the top metrics, or **Key Performance Indicators (KPIs)**, established by their organization. While Power BI reports deliver a rich, self-service analytical experience, optionally at a very detailed level, Power BI dashboards provide an integrated and simplified consumption layer. From a technical architecture standpoint, Power BI dashboards are exclusive to the Power BI online service and are primarily composed of tiles representing visuals from one or many reports. Although each Power BI report is limited to a single source dataset, a dashboard's tiles can represent multiple datasets from highly disparate sources to help provide a 360 degree view on a single canvas.

To less experienced users and BI team members, the terms and capabilities associated with dashboards and reports can be misunderstood.

For example, the data-driven alert is exclusive to Power BI dashboards, while embedding in SharePoint online is specific to reports. More fundamentally, the user experience with slicer selections, bookmarks, and cross-highlighting available in reports and Power BI Desktop is not available in dashboards, exclusive of pinned live report pages.

Although several capabilities, such as email subscriptions and printing, are common to reports and dashboards, BI teams are well served to design dashboards and reports according to their distinct roles in Power BI. For example, a dashboard should not contain granular details or complex visuals, but rather the essential metrics describing the stakeholder's area of responsibility or influence.

Data-driven alerts are exclusive to Power BI dashboards in the Power BI service. Data alerts and their corresponding notifications are not available to Power BI reports, including reports published to the Power BI Report Server. The ability to embed custom alert rules and the deep integration of data alerts with the Power BI mobile apps is a top reason to leverage dashboards in the Power BI service. Data alerts and email subscriptions to reports and dashboards in the Power BI service is reviewed in Chapter 17, *Creating Power BI Apps and Content Distribution*.

The subsequent sections of this chapter describe many core dashboard features and capabilities including dashboard tiles, mobile optimizations, and alternative sources, including Excel and SSRS.

Multi-dashboard architectures

For small projects and the early iterations of an agile BI project, a single dashboard and a few supporting reports may be sufficient. For many dashboard users, however, multiple dashboards with their own distinct reports are needed to adequately reflect the broader set of metrics they're responsible for. Both of these approaches, single dashboard, and multiple dashboards are geared towards a specific stakeholder or group of consumers, such as the vice presidents of sales group. Although these methodologies may meet the needs of their intended users, a potential risk is a lack of coordination across teams.

For example, business units would reference distinct metrics included in their dashboard and these metrics may not be included in the dashboards of senior managers or other business units.

To promote greater consistency and coordination across groups of users, BI teams can pursue an integrated, organizational dashboard architecture. In this approach, the same metrics and KPIs considered strategic for the organization are available in multiple dashboards specific to levels in an organizational hierarchy or distinct business units. The **Global** sales dashboard, described in the *Dashboard design* section earlier, represents this methodology as separate dashboards specific to individual sales territory groups that would include the same KPIs as the global dashboard. This approach ensures that dashboard tiles are relevant to the specific users and make it possible to analyze up and down a natural organizational hierarchy. Additionally, a common dashboard layout with integrated KPIs makes Power BI solutions much easier to manage with limited BI resources.

Single-dashboard architecture

In the following diagram, a single dashboard focused on `Reseller Sales` contains tiles representing report visuals from four separate Power BI reports:

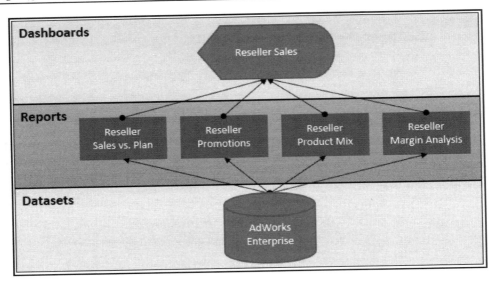

Single-dashboard architecture

By default, a user selection on any of the dashboard tiles opens the report page of the underlying report. For example, a dashboard tile reflecting the percentage of bike sales versus other product categories would be linked to the Reseller Product Mix report and the specific page of this report containing the source visual.

Each Power BI report is based on a Live connection to the AdWorks Enterprise dataset. As described in the *Live connections to Power BI datasets* section in Chapter 11, *Creating and Formatting Power BI Reports*, leveraging this feature avoids the duplication of datasets since each Power BI Desktop report file (PBIX) only contains the visualization layer (for example, visuals, formatting). Although relatively simple to build and support, the single Reseller Sales dashboard architecture provides both a summary overview of a diverse set of essential metrics and visuals (represented as dashboard tiles) as well as an entry point to reports containing the details supporting this dashboard. As described in the previous two chapters, the Power BI reports could include multiple report pages of visuals related to the dashboard and leverage interactive features, such as slicers and bookmarks, to enable users to more easily explore these reports.

 All of the content in this architecture - the dashboard, reports, and dataset would be hosted in a single app workspace in the Power BI service. Chapter 14, *Managing Application Workspaces and Content* explains the role and configuration of app workspaces.

Multiple-dashboard architecture

In the following diagram, a `Reseller Margin` dashboard and a `Reseller Margin Trends` report have been added to the solution described in the previous section:

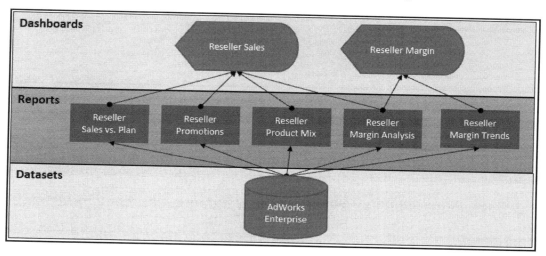

Multiple-dashboard architecture

In this design, a visual from the `Reseller Margin Analysis` report has been pinned to both the `Reseller Sales` and the `Reseller Margin` dashboards, per the preceding diagram. This is not required but is recommended for usability such that users can maintain context as they navigate between both dashboards. The new `Reseller Margin Trends` report, built via a Live connection to the published `AdWorks Enterprise` dataset, exclusively supports the `Reseller Margin` dashboard.

This architecture extends the scope of the solution to provide greater visibility to margin metrics and trends not available via the single dashboard. For example, rather than navigating through the multiple pages of the two reseller margin reports (`Reseller Margin Analysis`, `Reseller Margin Trends`), users could access the `Reseller Margin` dashboard for a more simplified dashboard experience. In addition to user convenience and the limited scope of a single dashboard, utilizing dashboards and their cached data helps to reduce the workload on the underlying dataset and resources.

Like the single dashboard architecture, all content (**Dashboards**, **Reports**, **Datasets**) from this multi-dashboard architecture is included in the same app workspace in the Power BI service. Given this common workspace, each dashboard tile can be linked to a report or dashboard in the same workspace. For example, the one margin-related tile on the sales dashboard could be linked to the margin dashboard rather than the default source report. The *Dashboard tiles* section later in this chapter contains an example of configuring custom links.

Organizational dashboard architecture

In the following diagram, four dashboards contain corporate KPIs at the global level and for the three sales territory groups:

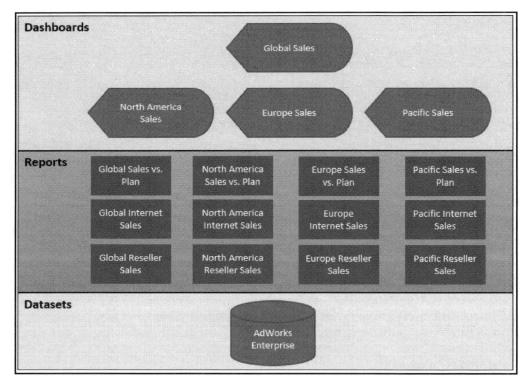

Organizational dashboard architecture

Since the same KPIs or metrics are included in each of the four dashboards, users of these dashboards are able to remain aligned with the same goals and can more clearly share their findings and results across teams and levels in the organization. From the perspective of an executive at the global level, the **Global Sales** dashboard provides an intuitive entry point into the individual sales territory groups and potentially further layers, if necessary.

For example, the `Europe Sales` territory group missed the total net sales plan by 11.6% for the month of November 2017, per the **Global Sales** dashboard described in the *Dashboard design* section. The executive could simply click this tile to access the **Europe Sales** dashboard to determine whether the sales miss was driven by a particular country (for example, France, Germany, United Kingdom) and how European sales performed across the online and reseller sales channels.

The following **European** sales dashboard follows the design (layout, visual selection) of the **Global** sales dashboard:

Europe sales dashboard

The three tiles aligned at the top of the **Europe** sales dashboard are exactly the same tiles as presented on the **Global** sales dashboard. The only difference is that the values are formatted in thousands rather than millions, given the smaller numbers for several of the **European** sales dashboard tiles. In this example, the executive interested in the -11.6% miss to sales plan for November of 2017 could access the Europe sales dashboard with a single click from the **Global** sales dashboard and determine that **Germany** and **France** were responsible for the underperformance with misses of -15% and -19.8%, respectively.

The three tiles representing the second row of the **Global** and **Europe** sales dashboard (Net Sales YTD versus Plan, Net Margin % YTD versus Plan, Sales Channel Mix) do not have to be the same across the dashboards since these are not the approved KPIs for the organization. Maintaining a 1:1 match in terms of tiles across the dashboards can be beneficial as this allows users to navigate between dashboards for further analysis of any given tile. However, in many scenarios, there are metrics or visuals that are more pertinent to the given business unit and users may rarely need to analyze non-KPIs across multiple dashboards.

Per the organizational dashboard architecture diagram, a set of three dedicated European sales reports support the **Europe** sales dashboard. The pages of these reports may provide sufficient detail or, depending on the organizational structure and requirements, an additional layer of dashboards dedicated to each sales territory country could be added. Other forms of the organizational dashboard architecture include dedicated dashboards by product group, such as Bikes, Clothing, and Accessories in the case of Adventure Works. Ultimately, these implementations serve to align the different business units on common corporate goals while also providing a rich set of insights relevant to each business unit or organizational level.

Multiple datasets

A single dataset, AdWorksEnterprise, was utilized to support all reports and dashboards in each of the three dashboard architectures reviewed in the previous sections. This level of integration is not technically necessary and there are valid scenarios where multiple datasets could be used in the same Power BI solution and even by the same dashboard. However, additional or multiple datasets can quickly create problems due to separate data refresh processes, separate data source dependencies, and separate data security rules to implement.

Additionally, version control issues can arise as each dataset may include differences in the structure and definitions of tables common to both datasets. Moreover, the integration of visuals from the separate dataset on a dashboard may be insufficient to support analytical requirements.

In many cases, business users eventually need to analyze the data stored in separate datasets in the same report. For example, viewing dashboard tiles based on shipment and sales reports may be a helpful starting point but ultimately a user will need to filter both tables by product category, date, department, and other dimensions common to both business processes. A Power BI report is always limited to a single dataset as its source and thus an integrated dataset is always required whenever cross-analysis is required.

As one use case for multiple datasets, an organization may not have a particular data source, such as an Oracle database, integrated into its data warehouse system (for example, Teradata) but still wish to provide essential visualizations of this data in Power BI to supplement other reports and dashboards. In this scenario, a Power BI dataset could be built against the Oracle database, and reports utilizing this dedicated dataset could then support one or multiple dashboards. Once the necessary data warehouse integration was completed, the dedicated dataset could be retired and its reporting replaced with new reports based on an Analysis Services model (which uses Teradata as its source) that supports other Power BI reporting content for the organization.

The import versus DirectQuery dataset decision described earlier in this book significantly impacts the need for multiple datasets. For example, if the default import mode is used, a BI team could choose to load the separate data source (for example, Oracle) into the same dataset containing data from Teradata or another source. If a DirectQuery model was created, however, this model would be limited to its own source and database thus implying a separate dataset to support the Oracle database source.

In other scenarios, a dataset is chosen (or was already implemented) for one or a few business processes that aren't closely related to other business processes. For example, one dataset was built to include sales- and marketing-related data, while a separate dataset includes inventory and shipment data. The reasoning for this isolation may have been that the users of each dataset don't need access to the other dataset or that a large, integrated dataset would be complex to develop and use.

For example, it's not uncommon for datasets with multiple fact tables to require hundreds of DAX measures and Power BI Desktop currently doesn't support display folders or perspectives, such as Analysis Services, to help simplify the user interface. Additionally, if the Power BI Premium capacity is not available and Power BI datasets are used, the 1 GB file limit could force a team to utilize separate Power BI files to store the required data.

In general, corporate BI projects should limit the use of multiple datasets for the reasons described and the long-term value of a centralized data store. However, in environments lacking a data warehouse and other scalable resources, such as an Analysis Services instance or Power BI Premium capacity, multiple datasets can be considered as an option and potentially the only option to support one or multiple dashboards in the same Power BI solution.

Dashboard tiles

Most dashboard tiles are created in the Power BI service by pinning a visual, image, or shape from a report to a new or existing dashboard in the same app workspace. However, dashboard tiles can also be created by adding a tile directly from the dashboard itself and by pinning from an Excel Workbook or an SSRS report.

With a report open in the Power BI service, hovering over the top-right corner of a visual exposes the Pin visual icon, per the following image from the `Global Reseller Sales` report:

Pin visual icon for report visual

Report visuals can be pinned to dashboards from both the **Reading view** and the **Editing view**. The preceding image is from the **Reading view**, but clicking the **Edit report** button next to the **File** and **View** drop-downs menus opens the **Editing view**. Reports generally open by default in the **Reading view**, and the **Editing view** is only available to the user who created the report or members and admins of the app workspace for the report, such as AdWorks Enterprise Sales in this example.

The following URL from MS Docs provides a complete comparison of the functionality differences between the **Reading view** and **Editing view** for Power BI reports `http://bit.ly/2HztVsY`.

Power BI Desktop is always in the **Editing view** and offers more report-editing functionality than the **Editing view** in the Power BI service, such as the ability to write DAX-measure expressions scoped to the specific report. Additionally, since reports created in the Power BI service cannot be downloaded as PBIX files, almost all report creation and edit activities occur in Power BI Desktop. Dashboards, workspaces and all content distribution options, such as Power BI apps are configured in the Power BI service, described in later chapters.

Once pinned to the dashboard, several options are available for configuring tiles depending on the type of tile and the content it contains. In the **Global** and **Europe** sales dashboards described in previous sections, for example, a subtitle was added to each tile (for example, France) and custom links were applied to allow direct navigation from the **Global** dashboard to the **Europe** dashboard.

SSRS 2016, and later versions, support integration with the Power BI service. Once integration has been configured in the Report Server Configuration Manager, certain SSRS report items, such as charts and maps, can be pinned to Power BI dashboards. A reporting services subscription is automatically created for pinned report items to manage the data refresh of the dashboard tile.

The Power BI publisher for Excel add-in, available for Excel 2007 and later, allows users to pin Excel ranges and objects, such as pivot tables and charts, directly from Excel workbooks to dashboards. This add-in includes the ability to update pinned items and to connect to published datasets in the Power BI service to create pivot-table Excel reports. Additionally, ranges within Excel workbooks uploaded to the Power BI service can also be pinned to dashboards.

The details of creating SSRS and Excel-based dashboard tiles is beyond the scope of this chapter. However, several examples of these integrations were included in the *Microsoft Power BI Cookbook* (`https://www.packtpub.com/big-data-and-business-intelligence/microsoft-power-bi-cookbook`). Additionally, the Power BI Report Server, which includes the full SQL Server Reporting Services functionality, is described in `Chapter 16`, *Deploying the Power BI Report Server*.

Dashboard tiles can be thought of as snapshots of a specific visual and filter context. When a visual is pinned from a report to a dashboard, the specific filter context (for example, slicers, page-level filters), visualization, and formatting at that time are captured by the dashboard. Subsequent changes to the report, such as a modified filter or a different visualization type, are not reflected by the dashboard tile. The dashboard tile will, however, continue to reflect the latest data refreshes of the underlying dataset. Additionally, by default, the dashboard tile will continue to be linked to the report from which the visual was pinned.

To maintain the synchronization between report visuals and dashboard tiles, changes to reports that impact the pinned visuals require the updated report visual to be pinned again. The existing dashboard tile, reflecting the original filter context and visualization, can be deleted. One exception to the snapshot behavior of dashboard tiles is live report pages, as described later in this chapter.

One exception to the snapshot behavior of dashboard tiles is live report pages. When an entire report page has been pinned as a single tile to a dashboard, any changes to the report page are automatically reflected on the dashboard as well. The *Live report pages* section later in this chapter includes additional details and an example.

Tile details and custom links

Custom links are an important component of multi-dashboard architectures, and particularly the organizational dashboard architecture described in the previous section. In the absence of custom links, clicking a dashboard tile opens the report page from which the visual was pinned to the dashboard. Custom links allow BI teams to take control of the navigation experience and enable users to navigate directly to another dashboard with related information or even to an external site, such as a team site on SharePoint Online.

Tile details can be accessed by hovering over the top-right corner of a dashboard tile, clicking the ellipsis, and then selecting **Edit details**. In the following image from the **Tile details** window, a **Subtitle** (Europe) is added to one of the `Total Net Sales vs. Plan` KPI tiles:

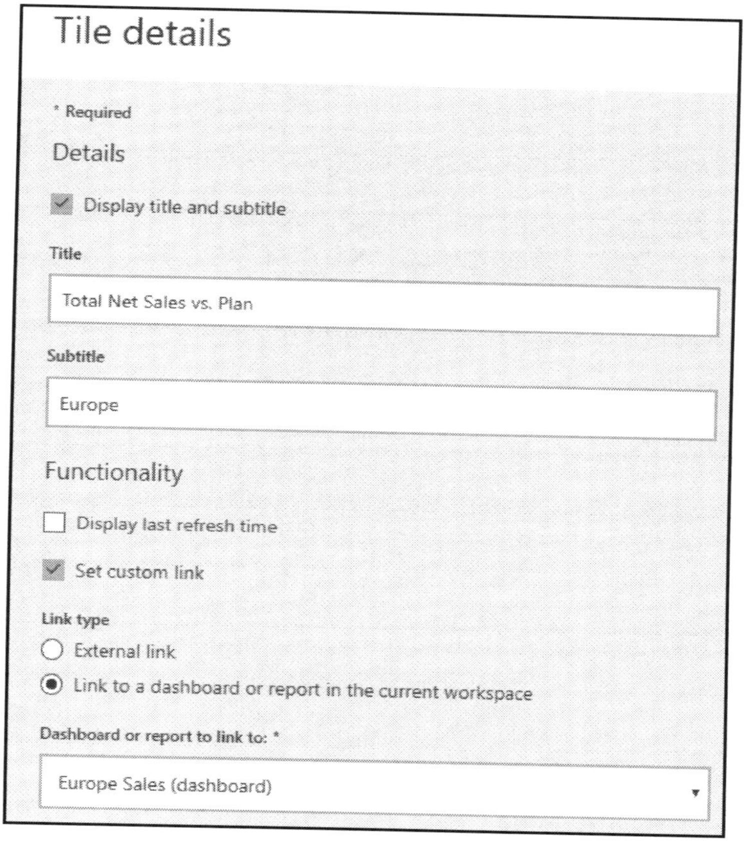

Tile details

Additionally, per the preceding **Tile details** image, the **Set custom link** property has been enabled and the **Europe Sales (dashboard)** has been selected for the target of the link. Clicking **Apply** at the bottom of the dialog (not included in the preceding screenshot) confirms the selection. Different options are available in the tile details window for widgets added directly on the dashboard (not pinned), such as text boxes and images, per the following section.

Images and text boxes

In addition to pinning custom images with text, as described in the *Supporting tiles* section, it may be necessary to add supporting widget tiles directly on the dashboard. These widgets, created via the Add tile icon above each dashboard, can include web content, images (via URL), text boxes, video, and real-time data.

The following three tiles represent the video, image, and text box widgets created via the **Add tile** functionality:

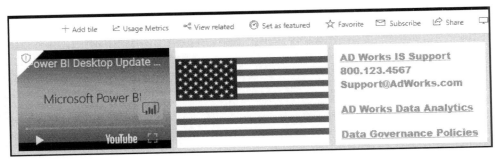

Image and text box tiles

The tile details for the video and image flag include a required URL input box to reference. For the video, the URL must reference either YouTube or Vimeo. Other common tile details can be configured as well, including title, subtitle, and a custom link. Likewise, the video widget tile includes a required video URL to either Youtube or Vimeo (`https://vimeo.com/210508392`).

The text box tile supports common text formatting options as well as hyperlinks, per the following image:

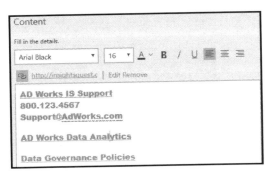

In the preceding text box, hyperlinks are provided to IS Support, a company data and analytics site, and a data governance site. A common text box with essential links to documentation and support can be applied to all corporate BI-supported dashboards.

SQL Server Reporting Services

SSRS 2016, and later versions as well as the Power BI Report Server, supports integration with the Power BI service. Once integration has been configured between the on-premises report server and the Power BI tenant, certain SSRS report items, such as charts and maps, can be pinned to Power BI dashboards. Additionally, a reporting services subscription is automatically created for pinned report items, allowing for report server administrators to manage the data refresh schedule of the dashboard tile.

In the following image of the **Report Server Configuration Manager**, a Power BI Report Server has been configured:

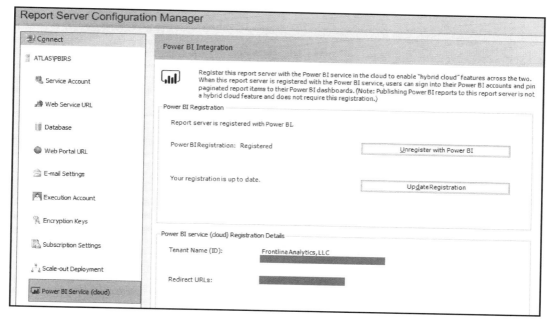

Power BI integration with Power BI Report Server

In the preceding image, the **Power BI Report Server (PBIRS)** instance installed on the ATLAS server has been configured for integration with the Power BI service. The same Power BI integration is available for SQL Server Reporting Services 2016 and 2017 via the same interface in the Report Server Configuration Manager. The following documentation includes all the requirements for integration with the Power BI service as well as technical details on the integration and pinning process `http://bit.ly/2CnCkOU`.

 As described in `Chapter 16`, *Deploying the Power BI Report Server*, the Power BI Report Server includes all the functionality of the SSRS, including paginated (RDL) reports, report subscriptions, folder security, and the reporting services web portal. Power BI Report Server, however, provides several additional features and benefits, with the ability to view and interact with Power BI reports (PBIX files) topping this list.

In the following image from the Power BI Report Server web portal, a paginated (RDL) report containing a map has been opened:

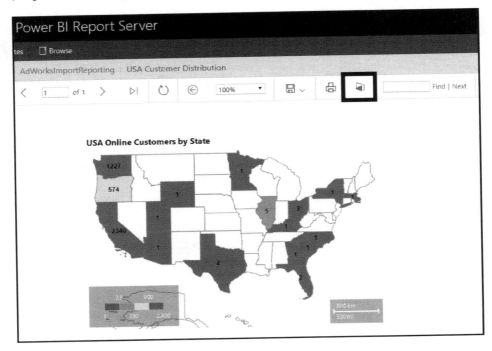

Pin to Power BI icon in Power BI Report Server

Selecting the Pin to Power BI Dashboard icon in the top-right window prompts the user to select the specific report item to pin. In this report, the map is selected and this launches the following dialog for identifying the dashboard in the Power BI service as well as defining the refresh schedule of the tile:

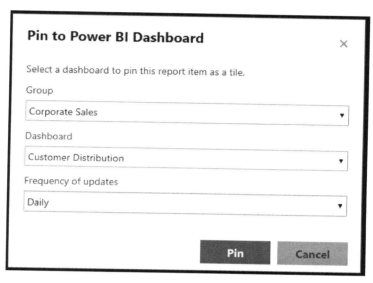

Pin to Power BI Dashboard   ✕

Select a dashboard to pin this report item as a tile.

Group

| Corporate Sales | ▾ |

Dashboard

| Customer Distribution | ▾ |

Frequency of updates

| Daily | ▾ |

[Pin] [Cancel]

Pin SSRS item to Power BI Dashboard

In this example, the map is pinned to the **Customer Distribution** dashboard in the `Corporate Sales` app workspace. The **Daily**, **Hourly**, and **Weekly** tile refreshes can be configured via the **Frequency of updates** drop-down menu and this setting defines the report subscription supporting the tile. Report subscriptions can be managed via the **My Subscriptions (Settings | My Subscriptions)** interface on the Reporting Services web portal.

 App workspaces replaced group workspaces in 2017 and are utilized by Power BI Pro users to create and manage content. App workspaces and related topics (for example, version control) are explained in `Chapter 14`, *Managing Application Workspaces and Content*.

Unlike visuals from Power BI reports, which can only be pinned to dashboards in the workspace of the given report, SSRS report items can be pinned to any dashboard in any workspace. In the following image from the Power BI service, the dashboard tile reflecting the pinned SSRS report item has been moved and sized to the top-left corner of the canvas:

SSRS report item as Power BI Dashboard tile

By default, the SSRS-based dashboard tile is linked back to the on-premises SSRS report. This link, as well as the title and subtitle for the tile, can be modified via the **Tile details** window like other dashboard tiles.

Paginated SSRS reports (RDL files) created with **SQL Server Data Tools** (**SSDT**) for Visual Studio or SQL Server Report Builder cannot currently be published to the Power BI service. However, just as Power BI reports (PBIX files) can now be published to the Power BI Report Server, the Power BI and Reporting Services teams have advised that support for RDL files in the Power BI service is planned. Once this is accomplished, the three primary Microsoft report types (Power BI, Excel, and SSRS) will all be available in both the Power BI cloud service as well as on-premises via the Power BI Report Server.

Additional information on the Power BI Report Server including the deployment and scheduled refresh of Power BI reports is included in `Chapter 16`, *Deploying the Power BI Report Server.*

Excel workbooks

The Power BI Publisher for Excel add-in, available for Excel 2007 and later, allows Power BI Pro users to pin Excel ranges and objects, such as pivot tables and charts, directly from local Excel workbooks to Power BI dashboards in app workspaces. This add-in includes the ability to update pinned items and to connect to published datasets in the Power BI service to create pivot-table Excel reports. Additionally, report content from Excel workbooks published to the Power BI service can also be pinned to dashboards.

Scheduled data refreshes can be configured in the Power BI service for Excel workbooks containing data models. However, given the size limitations of Excel data models as well as the additional capabilities of Power BI reports, such as custom visuals, role security, and advanced analytics, it's generally recommended to migrate Excel data models to Power BI datasets (PBIX files). Per the following image, the Power BI content contained in an Excel workbook can be imported to a Power BI Desktop file:

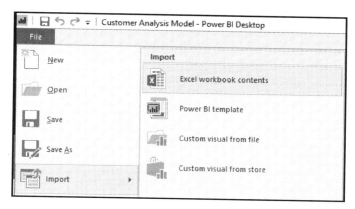

Import Excel to Power BI

The migration process includes the data retrieval M queries, data model tables and relationships, DAX measures, and even any Power View report pages contained in the source workbook.

Only when Excel reports are deeply dependent on Excel-specific functionality, such as worksheet formulas and customized conditional formatting rules, should the model not be migrated to Power BI. Power BI Desktop's enhanced table and matrix visuals and conditional formatting options now support many of the most common Excel report use cases. Therefore, the usually limited effort is required to develop the equivalent or a preferable report in Power BI Desktop relative to Excel.

In the following image, the filtered Excel pivot table is pinned to the **Customer Distribution** dashboard in the `Corporate Sales` workspace via the Power BI Publisher for Excel:

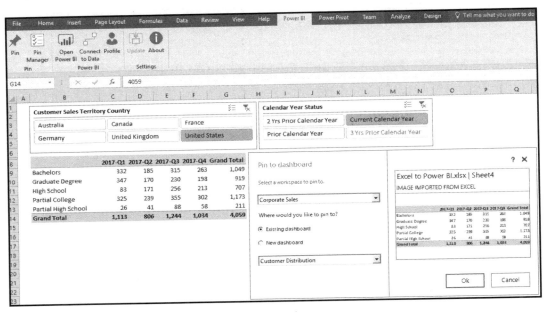

Pin Excel content to Power BI Dashboard

Just like SSRS report items, Excel content can also be pinned to any dashboard in any workspace in the Power BI service. However, when pinning from a local workbook, such as this example, the owner of the Excel workbook is responsible for updating the dashboard tile with any data refreshes or changes in filter conditions. The push updates from the user's workbook to the dashboard in the Power BI service can be executed via the **Pin Manager** dialog. This interface, which also provides visibility to pinned Excel items in any workspace, is accessed via the Power BI ribbon of the Power BI Publisher for Excel add-in, per the preceding image.

In the following image of the **Customer Distribution** dashboard, a custom title and subtitle have been applied to the tile containing the pinned Excel pivot table:

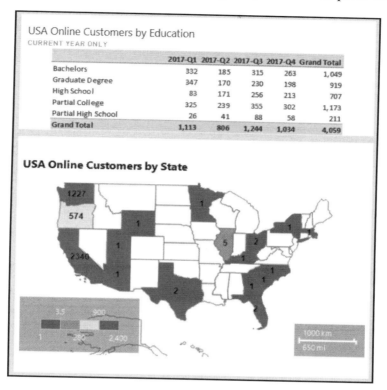

Power BI Dashboard with Excel and SSRS content

Also like SSRS-based dashboard tiles, the details of dashboard tiles containing Excel content can be configured, including title, subtitle, and a custom link. Moreover, Excel and SSRS dashboard tiles can also be included in dashboard layouts dedicated to consumption via smartphones. The *Mobile-optimized dashboards* section later in this chapter describes this feature.

Although Excel and SSRS report content are not designed to be as visually engaging as Power BI visuals, the ability to leverage these common reporting tools and to consolidate their distinct content on the same dashboard is a unique capability of Power BI. Additionally, the data refresh of Excel workbooks containing external connections to sources, such as Power BI datasets and Analysis Services data models, is a highly requested feature that may be delivered by the fall of 2018.

Per the following image, only workbooks containing data models can currently be refreshed:

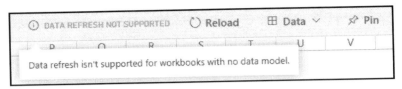

External workbook connections not supported

Given this current limitation, the two slicers above the pivot table (`Country`, `Calendar Year Status`) from the earlier example cannot be used in the Power BI service. This is because the Excel report was based on a connection to a published Power BI dataset via Power BI Publisher for Excel.

The details of developing SSRS and Excel-based content as complements to a Power BI solution is beyond the scope of this chapter. However, several examples of these integrations, as well as considerations in choosing among the three tools, were included in the *Microsoft Power BI Cookbook* (`https://www.packtpub.com/big-data-and-business-intelligence/microsoft-power-bi-cookbook`).

Live report pages

For some users, the self-service data exploration experience provided within Power BI report pages is the most valuable use case of Power BI content. Although a dashboard of tiles may initiate or contribute to an analysis, these users often have more complex and unpredictable analytical needs such that greater flexibility is needed. Additionally, these users are generally much more comfortable and experienced in interacting with Power BI content, such as modifying slicer selections and drilling up and down through hierarchies.

To provide both the self-service experience of a report page as well as the consolidation benefits of a dashboard, an entire report page can be pinned as a single tile to a dashboard. In the following dashboard for the **United States**, a live report page of eight visuals has been pinned to supplement the corporate standard KPI tiles:

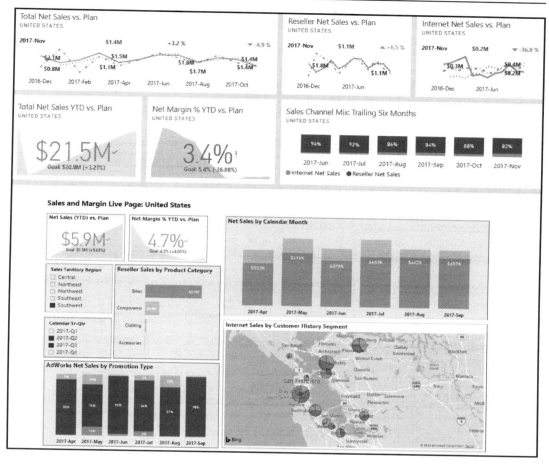

Dashboard with live report page

In this dashboard, the user can leverage the robust filtering options on the sales and margin live page to explore the dataset while maintaining visibility to standard metrics via the top six tiles. In the preceding example, the user has filtered on the Southwest sales territory region, the second and third quarters of the year (2017-Q2 and 2017-Q3), and also selected the Bikes product category via the bar chart. These selections impact the other five visuals on the page via either highlighting, in the case of the Net Sales by Calendar Month column chart, or filtering, in the case of the other four visuals. Filter selections on the live page do not, however, impact dashboard tiles outside of the live page.

Defining the interaction behavior between visuals, such as switching between highlight and filter, is described in the *Visual interactions* section of `Chapter 11`, *Creating and Formatting Power BI Reports*.

Like standard dashboard tiles, a live page tile can be moved around the canvas and the title and subtitle can be configured via the **Tile details** window. However, custom links cannot be configured for live report pages. In the **United States** dashboard example, the report page itself included a textbox with a title and thus the display title and subtitle property of the dashboard tile has been disabled.

Unlike the snapshot behavior of normal dashboard tiles, any saved changes to the report containing the live report page, such as a different filter condition, are automatically reflected by the live page tile on the dashboard. This automatic synchronization avoids the need to delete dashboard tiles reflecting the original state of the report and re-pinning visuals to reflect changes in the source report.

Just like individual visuals within reports, a report page can be pinned from both the **Reading view** and the edit mode in the Power BI service. The Pin Live Page menu icon, next to the refresh icon in **Reading view**, generates the following window:

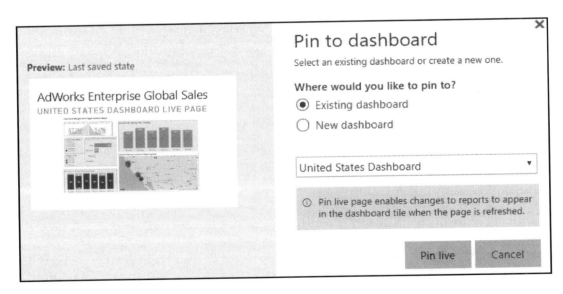

Pin Live Page

Live report page tiles can also be included in mobile-optimized views of dashboards. However, given their size, live pages are generally more valuable in larger form factors and with full screen mode.

Mobile-optimized dashboards

Just like the phone layout view in Power BI Desktop described in `Chapter 11`, *Creating and Formatting Power BI Reports*, the Power BI service provides a phone view to customize a mobile-optimized layout for dashboards. With a phone view configured for a dashboard, the specific tiles, sizes, and order of tiles defined for the phone view will be presented to the user when the dashboard is accessed via the Power BI mobile app on their phone.

The **Phone view** can be accessed via the drop-down menu of **Web view** in the top-right corner of the dashboard, per the following image:

Dashboard Phone view

Once in **Phone view**, the same drag and resize options available in phone layout for Power BI Desktop are also available for the dashboard. In the following example, the three most important total net sales KPI visuals from the **Global Sales** dashboard have been positioned at the top of the phone view (**Global, North America, Europe**) and several less important tiles have been unpinned:

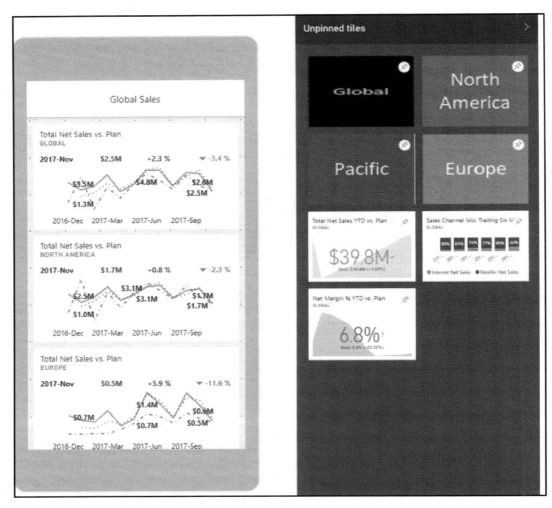

Phone view of dashboard in Power BI service

Power BI saves the phone layout automatically and the defined **Phone view** will be the new default view for phones accessing the dashboard. However, the user can still turn their phone sideways to view the dashboard in the standard web view.

The subtitles applied to the dashboard tiles are particularly valuable in **Phone view**. In the standard web view, the four supporting tiles with custom images (**Global**, **North America**, **Europe**, **Pacific**) make it easy to determine the scope of each tile. These image tiles are likely not, however, desired in **Phone view** and thus the subtitles can be relied on to convey the scope of each tile.

Summary

This chapter demonstrated how dashboards can be planned and developed as part of a large, integrated corporate BI solution. All essential features and processes of Power BI dashboards were highlighted, including the configuration of dashboard tiles, their links to other dashboards and reports, and mobile-optimized dashboards. Additionally, the unique capability of dashboards to integrate BI content from the SSRS reports and Excel workbooks was reviewed.

The next chapter transitions from the development of Power BI content to the management of Power BI content. This includes the application of version control to Power BI Desktop files and the migration of content across test and production environments with app workspaces.

14
Managing Application Workspaces and Content

The preceding six chapters have focused on the design and development of Power BI datasets, reports, and dashboards. While the creation of impactful and sustainable content is essential, this chapter reviews the processes and features that IT organizations can leverage to manage and govern this content through project life cycles and ongoing operational support. This includes application workspaces in the Power BI service, staged deployments between test and production environments, and maintaining version control of Power BI Desktop files. Additional features and practices highlighted in this chapter include data classifications for dashboards, documenting Power BI datasets, and utilizing the Power BI REST API to automate and manage common processes.

In this chapter, we will review the following topics:

- Application workspaces
- Workspace roles and rights
- Staged deployments
- Power BI REST API
- OneDrive for Business version history
- Source control for M and DAX code
- Dashboard data classifications
- Dataset field descriptions
- Metadata reporting

Application workspaces

Application workspaces are containers in the Power BI service of related content (reports and dashboards). As a Power BI Pro feature as discussed in the *Power BI licenses* section of Chapter 7, *Planning Power BI Projects*, members of application workspaces, are able to create and test content, such as new dashboards and changes to reports, without impacting the content being accessed by users outside of the workspace. Once the new or revised content in the workspace is determined to be ready for consumption, the workspace can be published or updated as a Power BI app, as described in Chapter 17, *Creating Power BI Apps and Content Distribution*.

> *"We intend workspaces just for creation...it's the place where content gets created in Power BI."*
>
> *– Ajay Anandan, Senior Program Manager.*

In addition to the default isolation or staging between content creation (workspaces) and content consumption (apps), BI teams can utilize multiple app workspaces to stage their deployments as per the *Staged deployments* section later in this chapter. For example, reports and dashboards can be initially created in a development workspace, evaluated against requirements in a test workspace, and finally deployed to a production workspace. The production app workspace would support the app which large numbers of business users would access and therefore could be assigned to Power BI Premium capacity to provide dependable performance and the flexibility to scale resources according to the needs of the workload.

Chapter 19, *Scaling with Premium and Analysis Services*, provides details on the features and benefits of Power BI Premium. These include the cost advantage of capacity-based pricing versus per-user licensing in large-scale deployments, managing Premium capacities (hardware), such as scaling up or out, and assigning workspaces to Premium capacities. Additional capabilities exclusive to content stored in Premium capacity, such as incremental data refresh, larger Power BI datasets, and more frequent scheduled data refreshes (for example, every 30 minutes), are also described in Chapter 19, *Scaling with Premium and Analysis Services*.

The following diagram and four-step process depicts the essential role of app workspaces in the life cycle of Power BI content:

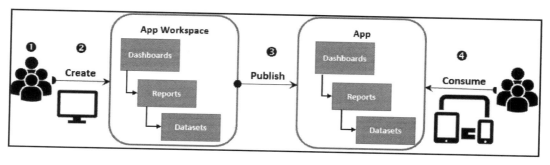

App workspaces and apps

1. A Power BI Pro user creates an **App Workspace** and adds other Power BI Pro users as members with edit rights
2. The members of the **App Workspace** publish reports to the workspace and create dashboards in the workspace
3. All content or a subset of the content in the **App Workspace** is published as a Power BI app
4. Users or groups of users access content in the published app from any device

All users within the **app workspace** will need a Power BI Pro license. All users consuming the published Power BI app will also need a Power BI Pro license, unless the **app workspace** has been assigned to Power BI Premium capacity. If the **app workspace** has been assigned to Power BI Premium capacity, users with Power BI (free) licenses and, optionally, external guest users from outside the organization with free licenses, can read or consume the Power BI app. As described in Chapter 19, *Scaling with Premium and Analysis Services*, it is, of course, necessary to provision the appropriate resources (for example, CPU cores and RAM) to support the workload generated by the Power BI app.

In small team scenarios (5–15 users) in which maximum self-service flexibility is needed, all users can be assigned Pro licenses and collaborate on content within the app workspace. This approach negates the isolation benefit of workspaces from apps but provides immediate visibility to the latest versions of the content. Additionally, Power BI Pro users within the workspace can create their own Power BI and Excel reports based on connections to the published dataset in the workspace.

Workspace roles and rights

Every app workspace has one or multiple administrators who manage the access of other Power BI Pro users to the workspace. The user who initially creates the app workspace is the workspace admin by default and can add other users as members of the workspace, thus providing access to the datasets contained in the workspace. With the privacy level of the workspace set to allow members to edit content, workspace members can create and store content in the workspace as well as publishing content from the workspace to a Power BI app.

Workspace admins

Workspace admins can modify the name of the workspace, the privacy level for workspace members (edit or view only), and the role of each member (admin or member). For example, once users have been added to the workspace as members, the workspace admin can revise the role of one or multiple users from members to admins so that this user(s) can add other members and contribute to the management of the workspace.

If Power BI Premium capacity has been provisioned for the organization and if the workspace administrator has been granted assignment permissions to Premium capacity, the workspace admin can assign the workspace to a Premium capacity. This action moves the content in the workspace to dedicated hardware (capacity) exclusive to the organization and enables many additional features, such as the distribution of apps to Power BI free users. Further information on the assignment of app workspaces to Power BI Premium capacity is included in Chapter 18, *Administering Power BI for an Organization*. The additional capabilities provided by Power BI Premium and considerations in allocating Premium capacity are included in Chapter 19, *Scaling with Premium and Analysis Services*.

Workspace admins also have the exclusive right to delete an app workspace and thus remove all of its content (dashboards, reports, and datasets) from the Power BI service. Additionally, workspace admins can only leave an app workspace if another user has been assigned as an admin of the workspace.

Prior to deleting an app workspace, check to see if an app has been published from the workspace. If an app has been published, unpublish this app via the ellipis (three dots) next to the **Update app** button. If the app workspace has been deleted but the published app has not been unpublished, users of the published app will see errors when attempting to access or refresh its content.

The following screenshot displays the app workspace options available to a workspace administrator:

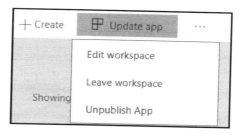

App Workspace options for workspace admin

The **Edit workspace** dialog, as illustrated in the following section, is exclusively available to workspace administrators. Workspace members (non-admins) with edit rights, however, can also update and unpublish apps as well as leave the app workspace.

Workspace members

The members added to the workspace are most commonly report authors who will connect to dataset(s) to develop reports in Power BI Desktop. These reports can then be published back to the app workspace and their visuals can be pinned to dashboards in the Power BI service as per the previous Chapter 13, *Designing Power BI Dashboards and Architectures.*

Since app workspaces have a one-to-one relationship with Power BI apps, workspace administrators are often familiar with the users or groups of users who will consume the content as well as other subject matter experts, such as the dataset designer described in the *Project roles* section of Chapter 7, *Planning Power BI Projects.*

In the following screenshot, **Jennifer** has created an app workspace and added Mark as a member with edit rights:

Edit app workspace

The **Edit workspace** dialog is exclusive to workspace admins. In this example, Mark's edit rights as a member may be sufficient or Jennifer can revise Mark's role from **Member** to **Admin** so that he can also add other members. A security group in Azure Active Directory cannot be used to add members to a workspace. However, security groups can be referenced when publishing an app workspace as a Power BI app to enable groups of users to view the content of the workspace.

In almost all scenarios, only users who create and manage Power BI content are added as members of app workspaces. However, if a report page from the app workspace is going to be embedded in a SharePoint Online site, the members of the SharePoint Online site will need to be added as members of the app workspace. Both Power BI Pro and Power BI free users can view embedded Power BI content from SharePoint Online. In the case of Power BI free users, however, the app workspace containing the embedded content needs to be assigned to Power BI Premium capacity. Additional information on embedding Power BI content in SharePoint Online is included in `Chapter 17`, *Creating Power BI Apps and Content Distribution.*

Users with Power BI free licenses can technically be added to app workspaces via the **Edit workspace** dialog. The free user will see the name of the app workspace in the Power BI service but the following dialog will be prompted when trying to access the workspace:

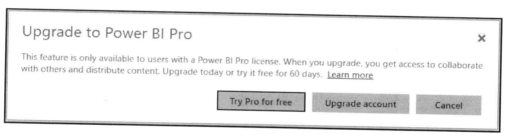

Power BI free user attempting to access an app workspace

The preceding dialog is also prompted to free users when trying to utilize other Power BI Pro features, such as sharing a dashboard, accessing a shared dashboard from shared (non-Premium) capacity, or creating an email subscription to a report or dashboard.

 Administrators of Power BI deployments have the ability to view the creation of Pro trial versions via the Office 365 audit logs. For example, a user assigned to the Power BI admin role (a role in Office 365), could analyze the level of activity for Pro trial users and assign available Pro licenses. Additionally, the process of assigning Pro licenses to users can be automated via PowerShell scripts so that administrators can focus on other governance and security issues. The Office 365 audit logs and options for accessing this data is described in `Chapter 18`, *Administering Power BI for an Organization.*

My Workspace

All Power BI users, including those with free licenses, are assigned a **My Workspace** in the Power BI service. This workspace should only be used and thought of as a private scratchpad for content specific to the individual user. **My Workspace** can be accessed via the same **Workspaces** menu as **APP WORKSPACES**, as shown in the following screenshot:

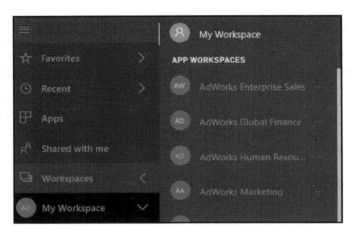

My Workspace

Any Power BI content which requires access by other users should be stored in an app workspace and distributed from the app workspace. Although **My Workspace** can host the same content types as **APP WORKSPACES**, any content distributed from **My Workspace**, such as via the dashboard sharing feature described in Chapter 17, *Creating Power BI Apps and Content Distribution*, is dependent on the individual user's account. Additionally, Power BI apps are exclusive to **APP WORKSPACES** and the Power BI team has advised that future administration and governance features will also be exclusive to **APP WORKSPACES**.

 The Power BI team has advised of a future setting in the Power BI admin portal allowing administrators to disable the **My Workspace** for Power BI free users. If enabled, Power BI free users would only see the four consumption-related menu items (**Favorites**, **Recent**, **Apps**, **Shared with me**) and the user experience for these items will remain simple and intuitive. Application workspaces, denoted by the darker shading, will increasingly contain more options for report authors and content creators to customize their solutions.

Staged deployments

Multiple application workspaces and their corresponding apps can be used to stage and manage the lifecycle of Power BI content. Similar to the development, test, and production release cycles familiar to IT professionals, staged deployments in the Power BI service are used to isolate data, users, and content appropriate to each stage of the process. Effectively implementing a staged Power BI deployment serves to raise the quality of the content delivered as well as the productivity of project team members.

The following diagram and nine-step process describe the primary elements of a staged deployment lifecycle:

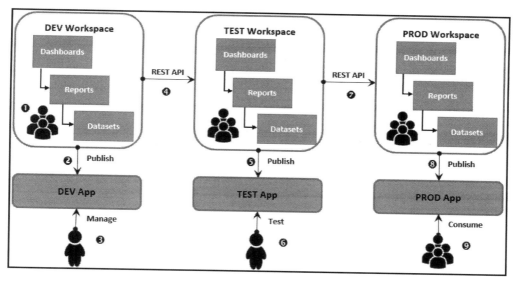

Staged deployment lifecycle

1. A development app workspace is created and Power BI content is built into the workspace:

   - A Power BI Desktop file containing the dataset is published to the development workspace
   - Reports are developed in Power BI Desktop based on Live connections to the development workspace dataset
   - Dashboards are created within the development workspace in the Power BI service

2. An app is published or updated and made available to a small number of users for their review

3. The BI manager or project lead reviews the status of content being developed and provides feedback to the developers:

   - In other scenarios, certain business stakeholders are allowed early access to content under development

4. The Power BI REST API is used to migrate completed content from the development workspace to the test workspace:

   - Supported REST API operations, such as a clone report and a rebind report, are called via PowerShell scripts

5. A **TEST App** is published or updated and made available to a small number of users for their review

6. A **user acceptance testing** (**UAT**) user or team reviews the content relative to requirements and provides feedback:

   - If necessary, revisions are implemented in the **TEST Workspace** and the **TEST App** is updated for further review

7. The Power BI REST API is used to migrate approved content from the **TEST Workspace** to the production workspace:

   - Supported REST API operations, such as a clone report and rebind report, are called via PowerShell scripts

8. A production app is published or updated and made available to groups of users for their consumption:

   - Publishing and accessing apps is described in Chapter 17, *Creating Power BI Apps and Content Distribution*

9. Groups of business users access and consume the dashboards and reports via the production app from any device:

   - Measuring and monitoring the usage of the published app is also described in Chapter 17, *Creating Power BI Apps and Content Distribution*

Creating and managing app workspaces as well as publishing apps for testing or consumption are all simple processes that can be handled via the user interface in the Power BI service. Properly utilizing the Power BI REST API to copy or migrate content across workspaces, however, requires some level of custom scripting. IT organizations familiar with managing Azure and on-premises resources via Windows PowerShell can leverage these skills as well as sample scripts provided by the Power BI team as per the *Power BI REST API* section later in this chapter.

Workspace datasets

As per the staged deployment lifecycle diagram, this architecture requires distinct Power BI datasets per app workspace. To minimize resource usage and for data security reasons, the development workspace dataset could include the minimal amount of data necessary and exclude all sensitive data. This would allow the organization to comfortably provide development access to teams of content developers, potentially from outside of the organization. Access to the test workspace could be limited to a small number of trusted or approved users within the organization and thus could include sensitive data. Finally, the production workspace dataset would have the same schema as the other datasets but include the full volume of data as well as sensitive data.

If a common schema exists between the different datasets in each workspace, the source dataset of a Power BI Desktop report file can be revised to a dataset in a separate workspace as per the *Switching source datasets* section in `Chapter 11`, *Creating and Formatting Power BI Reports*.

For example, the report file (`.pbix`) approved for migration from the development workspace to the test workspace could be opened, modified to reference the test workspace dataset, and then published to the test workspace. This approach represents a manual alternative to the Power BI REST API described in the following section.

A new feature is expected in 2018 that will allow a Power BI report to reference a dataset in an external app workspace. The availability of this feature will help eliminate the resource cost and manageability issues of duplicated datasets across multiple app workspaces.

For example, distinct Power BI apps developed for the finance, sales, and marketing teams could all leverage a single production dataset in a dedicated workspace rather than individual datasets within each workspace. The availability and implementation of this feature will revise the architecture of staged deployments of Power BI content via large Power BI datasets.

Another alternative to avoid the duplication of a dataset across multiple apps is Analysis Services. With Analysis Services, either on-premises via SSAS or in the cloud via AAS, Power BI reports can be created with Live connections to development, test, and production data models. Information on utilizing Analysis Services and its advantages as the data modeling tool and engine for Power BI is included in Chapter 19, *Scaling with Premium and Analysis Services.*

Power BI REST API

The Power BI REST API provides programmatic access to resources in the Power BI service including content (datasets, reports, and dashboards), application workspaces, and the users of these resources. This access enables organizations to automate common workflows, such as cloning a report to a different workspace or triggering a dataset refresh operation via familiar tools, such as Windows PowerShell. The goal of the REST API is to fully support all functionality available in the Power BI service, including capabilities exclusive to the Power BI admin portal, thus providing complete administrative and automation capabilities. The following URL provides updated documentation on the REST API including the request syntax and a sample result set for each operation: http://bit.ly/2AIkJyF.

As more REST API operations are developed, they will initially be exposed exclusively via REST API calls. This allows organizations comfortable with the programmatic interface to get started with automation scripts and for a user interface to be developed on top of the API operations. The following sections describe the components needed to get started with the REST API, including the ID for a registered application, the IDs for core Power BI objects, and sample PowerShell scripts provided by the Power BI team.

Windows PowerShell is a task-based command-line shell and scripting language. It's primarily used by system administrators to automate administrative tasks. For example, PowerShell script files (.ps1) are commonly used in scheduled data refresh processes for SSAS models.

Client application ID

To use the Power BI REST API, a client application ID must be obtained by registering an application with Azure Active Directory. This registration can be completed via the four-step process at the following portal: `https://dev.powerbi.com/apps`:

1. Sign in with the Azure Active Directory account:

   - This is the account used for logging into the Power BI service

2. Describe the application being registered:

   - Provide an application name and **Home Page URL**
   - Select **Native app** from the **App Type** dropdown
   - Use the following **Redirect URL**:
     `urn:ietf:wg:oauth:2.0:oob`

3. Choose the Power BI APIs to access:

   - Select all available boxes (**Dataset APIs**, **Report and Dashboard APIs**, and **Other APIs**)

4. Click **Register App**

Once the app is registered, the **Client ID** required for authentication will be exposed at the bottom, as shown in the following screenshot:

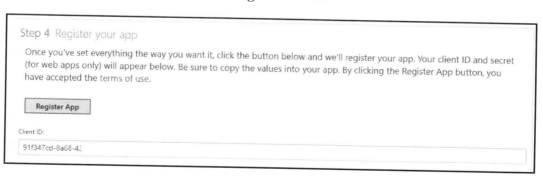

Power BI app Registration portal

Alternatively, an application can be registered via the **App registrations** menu of Azure Active Directory. Registered applications can be managed in the Azure portal, as shown in the following screenshot of the **Frontline Power BI Automation** app:

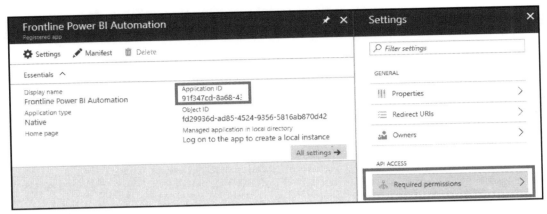

Registered app in Azure Active Directory

In addition to the **Application ID** property, which is the **Client ID** to use for authentication, the **Required permissions** menu in Azure Active Directory provides access to all Power BI APIs including those currently in preview. For example, the permissions of the **Frontline Power BI Automation** app from the preceding image could be expanded to include the view all reports API currently in preview.

Workspace and content IDs

In addition to the client ID of the registered application, the REST API operations require an ID associated with the given object or collection of objects referenced by the API operation. For example, to clone a report to a separate app workspace and then bind the report to a dataset in the new workpace, the IDs (GUID values) associated with the report, the source and target workspace, and the dataset must be obtained. These ID values can then can be passed into the variables of PowerShell script files and executed on demand or as part of a scheduled process, such as with dataset refresh operations.

The IDs for Power BI objects can be obtained by executing scripts which reference the appropriate REST API, such as Get Reports. Alternatively, the necessary IDs can be found by navigating to the specific object or collection of objects in the Power BI service and noting the URL.

For example, to retrieve both the group ID and the dataset ID, navigate to an app workspace and open the **Settings** menu for a dataset, as shown in the following screenshot:

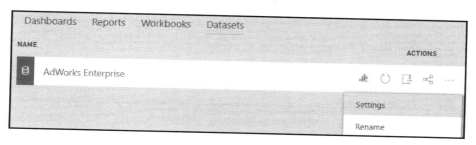

Access to dataset Settings

In this example, opening the **Settings** menu for the `AdWorks Enterprise` dataset of the `AdWorks Global Sales` workspace results in the following URL in the address bar of the browser `https://app.powerbi.com/groups/c738f14c-648d-47f5-91d2-ad8e f234f49c/settings/datasets/61e21466-a3eb-45e9-b8f3-c015d7165e57`

Based on this URL, the following two IDs can be used in PowerShell scripts calling the REST APIs:

- `AdWorks Global Sales` (app workspace): `c738f14c-648d-47f5-91d2-ad8ef234f49c`

- `AdWorks Enterprise` (dataset): `61e21466-a3eb-45e9-b8f3-c015d7165e57`

Just as the terms *groups* and *datasets* precede the IDs for these objects, respectively, the term *reports* precedes the ID for a specific report the URL when a report is selected in the Power BI service.

PowerShell sample scripts

Several self-documenting sample PowerShell scripts that leverage the Power BI REST API are available at the following GitHub repository `https://github.com/Azure-Samples/powerbi-powershell`.

As shown in the following screenshot, this repository includes PowerShell scripts (`.ps1` files) for the refresh of a dataset, the rebinding of a report (to a dataset), and other common use cases:

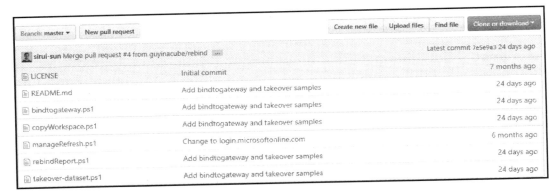

Power BI REST API samples

In addition to Windows PowerShell or the PowerShell **Integrated Scripting Environment** (**ISE**), Azure PowerShell cmdlets must also be installed to execute the REST API scripts. The following links can be used to install the necessary components:

- Windows PowerShell: `http://bit.ly/2FkaSmc`
- Azure PowerShell cmdlets: `https://aka.ms/webpi-azps`

The necessary cmdlets can also be installed from PowerShell via the following commands:

```
Install-Module AzureRM
Install-Module AzureAD
```

The variables in each sample advise of the parameters needed to successfully execute the script, such as the client ID of the registered application. The following sample script includes a variable for the client ID of the registered application described earlier and a function for authenticating against Azure Active Directory with this client ID:

```
$clientId = " FILL ME IN "
function GetAuthToken
{
    $adal =
"${env:ProgramFiles}\WindowsPowerShell\Modules\AzureRM.profile\4.1.1\M
icrosoft.IdentityModel.Clients.ActiveDirectory.dll"
    $adalforms =
"${env:ProgramFiles}\WindowsPowerShell\Modules\AzureRM.profile\4.1.1\M
icrosoft.IdentityModel.Clients.ActiveDirectory.WindowsForms.dll"
    [System.Reflection.Assembly]::LoadFrom($adal) | Out-Null
    [System.Reflection.Assembly]::LoadFrom($adalforms) | Out-Null
    $redirectUri = "urn:ietf:wg:oauth:2.0:oob"
    $resourceAppIdURI = "https://analysis.windows.net/powerbi/api"
    $authority =
"https://login.microsoftonline.com/common/oauth2/authorize";
    $authContext = New-Object
"Microsoft.IdentityModel.Clients.ActiveDirectory.AuthenticationContext
" -ArgumentList $authority
    $authResult = $authContext.AcquireToken($resourceAppIdURI,
$clientId, $redirectUri, "Auto")
    return $authResult
}
$token = GetAuthToken
```

The sample PowerShell script files can be edited to contain the appropriate variable (for example, client IDs and group IDs) and then saved to a secure network location. The user with rights to the Power BI resources, such as a BI manager or an IT administrator assigned the Power BI admin role, can run the PowerShell scripts as an administrator.

A top use case for the Power BI REST API is to synchronize the data refresh of Power BI datasets with the refresh process of data sources utilized by those datasets. For example, the refresh for certain production datasets in the Power BI service can be dynamically triggered to begin once the update process for a data source is completed, such as a nightly data warehouse **extract-transform-load** (ETL) or **extract-load-transform** (ELT) process or job. This synchronization ensures that Power BI reports and dashboards reflect the latest possible updates.

Additionally, the dynamic refreshes help to eliminate variances between Power BI reports and dashboards and any reporting tools which generate queries directly against the data source. Data refresh synchronization, along with incremental data refresh (expected in 2018), reduces one of the advantages of DirectQuery datasets relative to import mode datasets.

 The refresh dataset API requires the group ID for the given app workspace and the dataset ID. These values can be obtained manually as per the *Workspace and content IDs* section earlier or via the Get Groups and Get datasets API operations, respectively. The following URL contains documentation on the *Refresh dataset* operation: `http://bit.ly/2EpWLKL`

Dashboard data classifications

Dashboard data classifications allow administrators of Power BI to define data security classifications for dashboards in the Power BI service. Once configured in the Power BI admin portal, Power BI Pro users responsible for creating and editing dashboards in app workspaces can associate one of the available classifications to each dashboard. Additionally, the classification tags can be linked to external URLs to provide users with additional information, such as the organization's definitions and policies for each data classification.

The data security tags, such as **Confidential** or **Public**, serve to raise awareness regarding the sensitivity of the content and thus reduce the risk that protected data is inappropriately exposed or distributed.

For example, an organization could allow certain security groups of users to share Power BI content with users outside of the organization but, as an organizational policy, require that this content matches certain data classifications, such as public or low business impact.

In the following screenshot from the Power BI admin portal, four dashboard data classifications have been configured:

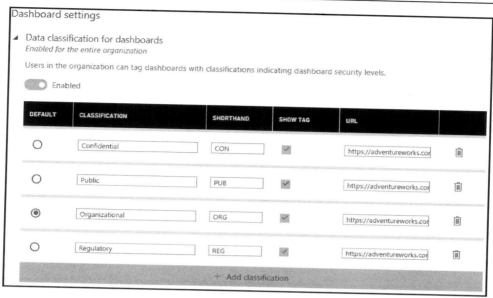

Dashboard data classifications

In the preceding example, the **Organizational** classification has been defined as the default data classification. This setting causes all new dashboards and any existing dashboard which have not been assigned to a different classification to be tagged as **Organizational**. For usability and reference purposes, a three-letter shorthand acronym and a URL link to a corporate site have been assigned to each classification, respectively.

> The Power BI admin portal can be accessed via the Settings (gear) icon in the top-right corner of the Power BI service. Only Office 365 global admins or users mapped to the Power BI admin role will have visibility to tenant settings within the Power BI admin portal, which includes data classification for dashboards.

 Chapter 18, *Administering Power BI for an Organization*, reviews the Power BI admin role as well as the settings available in the Power BI admin portal extensively. Additionally, the *Power BI project roles* section in Chapter 7, *Planning Power BI Projects*, introduces the Power BI admin role and contains an example of assigning the Power BI service administrator role to a user in the Office 365 admin center.

With the data classifications for the organization configured, a user with edit rights to a dashboard can assign a classification via the **Dashboard settings** menu, as shown in the following screenshot:

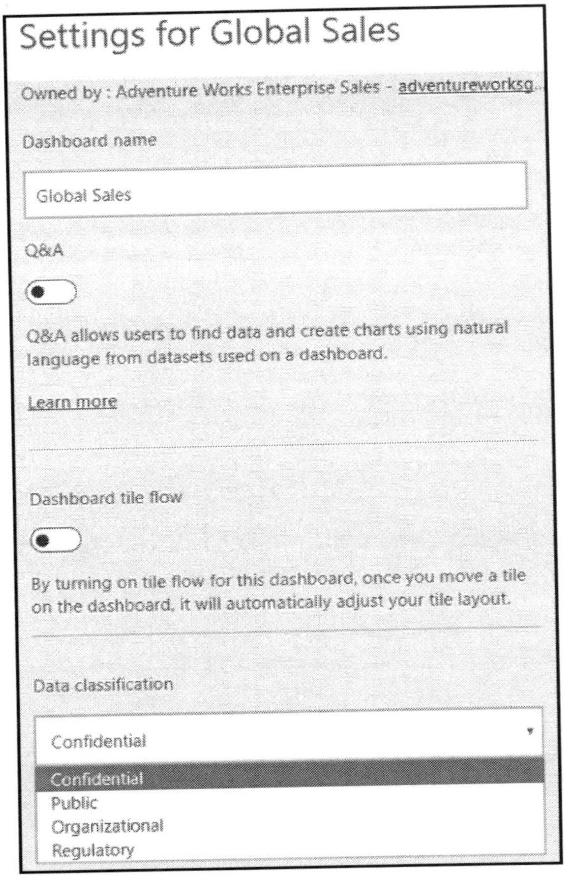

Settings for Global Sales

Owned by : Adventure Works Enterprise Sales - adventureworksg.

Dashboard name

Global Sales

Q&A

Q&A allows users to find data and create charts using natural language from datasets used on a dashboard.

Learn more

Dashboard tile flow

By turning on tile flow for this dashboard, once you move a tile on the dashboard, it will automatically adjust your tile layout.

Data classification

Confidential

| Confidential |
| Public |
| Organizational |
| Regulatory |

Dashboard settings

In the preceding example for the Global Sales dashboard, the default **Organizational** classification is switched to **Confidential**. The **Dashboard settings** menu can be accessed from within a dashboard by clicking the ellipsis (three dots) to the right of the **Web view/Phone view** dropdown. Alternatively, the settings for a dashboard can be accessed from outside the dashboard via the gear icon in the **ACTIONS** group within the app workspace.

In the following screenshot, the shorthand tag of the **Data classification** assigned to each dashboard is populated in the workspace:

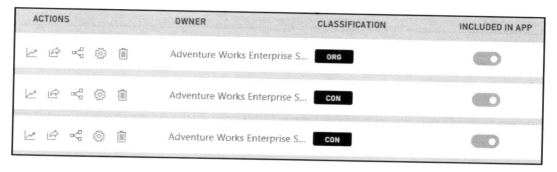

Dashboards in app workspace

Just like the icons under the **ACTIONS** group, hovering the cursor over the **CLASSIFICATION** tag (for example, **CON**,) creates a pointing icon and displays the full name of the classification (**Confidential**) as a tool tip. Clicking the tag will open the URL associated with the given classification in a separate browser tab.

Data classifications are deleted if the feature is turned off in the Power **Admin Portal**. Additionally, if a classification is removed, any dashboards assigned to the removed classification will be assigned back to the default until the dashboard owner changes the classification. Finally, if the default classification is changed, all dashboards that weren't already assigned a classification type will change to the new default.

Given the importance of data security and the risk involved in re-creating work for both the Power BI Admin(s) and report and dashboard authors, the teams responsible for deploying Power BI should ensure these classifications align with corporate data governance standards.

Version control

Version history and source control are very common, highly valued elements of an IT organization's **application lifecycle management** (ALM).

For example, changes to an Analysis Services data model, such as new DAX measures, are typically committed to a source control repository and tools such as **Visual Studio Team Services (VSTS)** provide features for teams to manage and collaborate on these changes. Perhaps most importantly, these tools enable teams to view and revert back to prior versions.

Power BI Desktop files (.pbix) do not integrate with these robust systems and are not expected to in the foreseeable future. As an alternative, Microsoft recommends OneDrive for Business, given its support for version history and its current 15 GB file size limit. Additionally, for longer term and larger scale projects, BI teams can optionally persist the core DAX and M code contained in a dataset into a structure suitable for implementing source control.

OneDrive for Business version history

In the following screenshot, a Power BI Desktop file containing an import mode dataset has been uploaded to a OneDrive for Business folder:

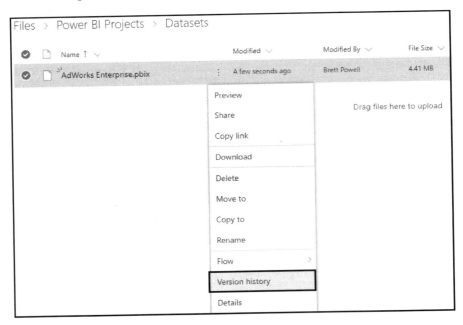

OneDrive for Business file options

Selecting the ellipsis (three dots) exposes several file options including **Version history**. As changes are implemented and saved in the PBIX file, such as a revised DAX measure or a new M query, the updated PBIX file could be uploaded to `OneDrive for Business`. Given the same name as the existing file, `OneDrive for Business` will require the user to confirm that the file should be replaced, as illustrated in the following screenshot:

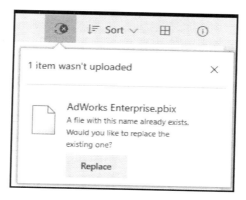

Uploading updated PBIX file

Once the replacement is confirmed, only the new file is accessible from the folder but the prior file and other versions of the file are still accessible via **Version history**. As shown in the following screenshot, the **Version History** window makes it easy to view the history of changes to a file and to restore an earlier version:

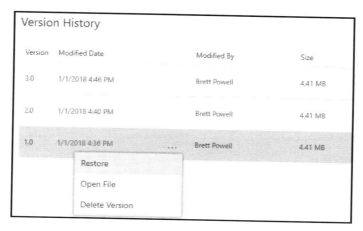

File options in Version History

In this example, selecting the ellipsis (three dots) for the Version **1.0** row exposes three file options, including **Restore**. Selecting **Restore** creates a new version (Version 4.0), which is an exact copy of the file restored. This restored file replaces the current file accessible in the OneDrive for Business folder. Finally, from the standard folder view in OneDrive for Business, the **Download** option displayed in the first image of this section can be used to retrieve the restored PBIX file.

As described in the *Live connections to Power BI datasets* section in Chapter 11, *Creating and Formatting Power BI Reports*, reports should be created with Power BI Desktop files rather than within the Power BI service to enable **Version history**. However, as per the previous chapter, dashboards are exclusively created within the Power BI service. Therefore, while **Version history** can be maintained with datasets and reports, **Version history** is currently not possible with dashboards.

Source control for M and DAX code

Although the version history of M and DAX code within Power BI Desktop files is technically available via OneDrive for Business, some BI organizations may also choose to utilize more robust version control tools on essential queries and measures. For example, the M query used to retrieve the Customer dimension table could be saved as a .pq file and synchronized with a team project code repository in VSTS. This approach would improve the visibility of the code to project team members and, for M queries, provide the code editing benefits of colorization and IntelliSense.

In the following screenshot, a Power Query project containing multiple folders of PQ files (M queries) has been added to a solution in Visual Studio and synchronized with a Git repository in a VSTS project:

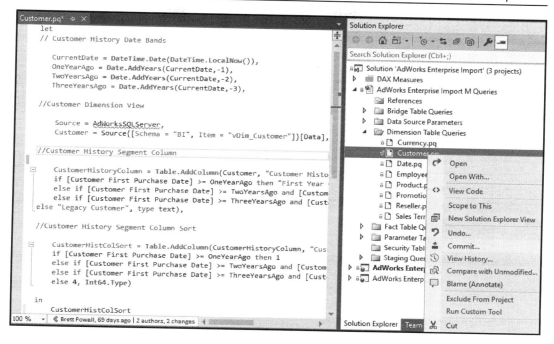

Power Query project in Visual Studio

In this example, all M queries (.pq files) are checked into source control via the lock icon in the **Solution Explorer** window except for the Customer query which is pending an edit (checkmark icon). The revised Customer dimension table query would be implemented within the Power BI Desktop file first but also saved within the Power Query project in Visual Studio.

As an enterprise tool, many version control options are available in Visual Studio, including **Compare with Unmodified...** and **Blame (Annotate)**. By clicking **Commit**, a message describing the change can be entered and the updated file can be synced to the source control repository in VSTS.

In the following screenshot from VSTS, the updated Customer dimension query file (`Customer.pq`), including the latest commit date (**5 minutes ago**), is visible:

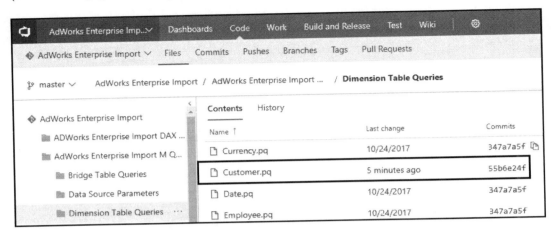

Files view in VSTS

Given the additional maintenance overhead, enterprise source control tools may not be suitable for smaller, simpler Power BI projects or the very early stages of projects. In addition to sound requirement gathering efforts, teams can minimize the maintenance effort required of the version control project by only including the essential M queries and DAX measures. For example, only the DAX measures containing fundamental business logic, such as the base measures described in `Chapter 9`, *Designing Import and DirectQuery Data Models*, could be saved as (`.msdax`) files.

Metadata management

As Power BI projects grow to support more teams and business processes, the dataset(s) supporting the reports and dashboards for these projects will also grow. For example, integrating the general ledger into the existing AdWorks Enterprise dataset would require new fact and dimension tables, new relationships, and additional measures with their own unique business rules or definitions. Additionally, it's common for hundreds of DAX measures to be built into datasets over time to support more advanced analytics and address new requirements.

Given this added complexity, BI teams and specifically the dataset designer described in Chapter 7, *Planning Power BI Projects* can embed descriptions to aid report authors incorrectly utilizing the data model. Additionally, the **dynamic management views (DMVs)** for Analysis Services models can be leveraged to generate metadata reports providing detailed visibility to all essential objects of the dataset. The combination of field descriptions and metadata reporting can help drive consistent report development as well as facilitate effective collaboration within the project team and between the project team and other stakeholders.

Field descriptions

A **FIELD PROPERTIES** pane in the Report view of Power BI Desktop allows dataset designers to enter descriptions for the measures, columns, and tables of a dataset. This metadata is then exposed to report authors who connect to this dataset as they hover over these objects in the **FIELDS** list and within the input field wells of visualizations. Although field descriptions are not a full substitute for formal documentation, descriptions of the logic, definition, or calculation of various objects enable report authors to develop content more efficiently. For example, rather than searching an external resource such as a data dictionary or contacting the dataset designer, the report author could simply hover over measures and column names from within Power BI Desktop.

Creating descriptions

To create a description, open the Power BI Desktop file containing the dataset and enable the **FIELD PROPERTIES** pane under the **View** tab of the Report view. In the following screenshot, the Internet Gross Sales measure is selected on the **FIELDS** List and a sentence is entered into the description box of the **FIELD PROPERTIES** pane:

FIELD PROPERTIES pane

Just like the preceding example with measures, selecting a table or a column in the **FIELDS** list will expose the name of this object and a description box in the **FIELD PROPERTIES** pane. Table and column descriptions can be valuable but measures are likely the best use case for this feature given the volume of measures in a dataset and the variety of calculations or logic they can contain.

Identify the most important measures in a dataset and apply concise, consistent descriptions using business-friendly terms. The set of measures described in the *Base measures* section of Chapter 10, *Developing DAX Measures and Security Roles,*would represent good candidates for descriptions as these measures are often reused in many other custom measures, such as date intelligence measures. For example, it's essential that the report author knows that the net sales measure includes discounts while the gross sales measure does not.

Although the **Name** field in the **FIELD PROPERTIES** pane can also be used to revise the names for measures, columns, and tables, this is rarely necessary as these changes can be implemented in other ways. Particularly for tables and columns, the Power Query Editor described in Chapter 8, *Connecting to Sources and Transforming Data with M*, should be used to define table and column names.

It's likely that a future release of Power BI Desktop will expose the **FIELD PROPERTIES** window to the Data view and/or the Relationships view as well. Additionally, other metadata properties may be added to the **FIELD PROPERTIES** pane, such as formatting and data categories, giving dataset designers a more centralized and robust means to configure dataset objects.

View field descriptions

The descriptions embedded in Power BI datasets can be viewed in the **FIELDS** lists, the input field wells of visualizations, and the **FIELD PROPERTIES** pane as well. With a Power BI report based on a Live connection to a published Power BI dataset, as described in the *Live connections to Power BI datasets* section in Chapter 11, *Creating and Formatting Power BI Reports*, the report author can view but not edit the descriptions.

In the following screenshot, the report author has built a matrix visual and hovers over the `Customer History Segment` column used in the **Rows** input field well:

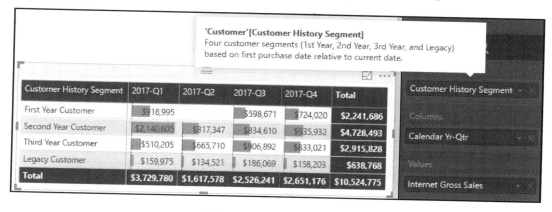

Field description via visualization field wells

As shown in the preceding image, the report author can view the description of the field (column or measure) via the tool tip to understand the essential definition, such as first purchase date relative to current date in this example. Likewise, the author can also hover over the `Internet Gross Sales` measure in the **Values** field well to view this description or hover over the measures, columns, and table names in the in the **FIELDS** list, as shown in the following screenshot:

Description of measure via FIELDS list

For the `Internet Gross Product Margin` measure and other measures in the dataset, the description applied uses proper casing when referring to DAX measures. This approach helps to keep each description concise and advises the user of the other measures they may need to review. In this example, the user may need to hover over the `Internet Gross Sales` measure and/or the `Internet Sales Product Cost` measure to fully understand the `Internet Gross Product Margin` measure.

Although it's likely unnecessary, the report author can also view the descriptions via the **FIELD PROPERTIES** pane. When the **FIELD PROPERTIES** pane is enabled from a Live connection report, Power BI Desktop advises that these properties are read-only given that they are from a model stored outside of the Power BI Desktop file.

Field descriptions cannot be viewed by hovering over names or values in the visuals themselves on the report canvas. However, as per the *Visualization formatting* section of Chapter 11, *Creating and Formatting Power BI Reports*, chart visuals contain a **Tooltips** input field well that provide a very similar experience to viewing field descriptions. **Tooltips** are typically used to display DAX measures related to the measures in the visual, such as the net margin percentage for a chart that visualizes net sales. However, measures can also return text strings and, thus, if necessary to aid the users viewing reports, measures can be created containing field descriptions and utilized as **Tooltips**.

In the following screenshot, a DAX measure containing the description of the Internet Gross Product Margin measure is used as an input to the **Tooltips** field well:

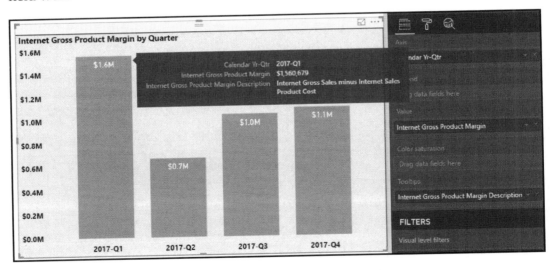

Field description measure as tooltip

In the preceding screenshot, hovering over the individual columns (or points if a line chart) displays the description built into the dedicated measure (Internet Gross Product Margin description). Although potentially useful for report consumers, BI teams should be cautious that the DAX measures used for descriptions are isolated from the actual field descriptions. Therefore, in the event of a change in description, both the description measure and the field description would need to be updated. Additionally, if measures containing descriptions are used extensively, a dedicated measure support table, as described in Chapter 8, *Connecting to Sources and Transforming Data with M*, and Chapter 9, *Designing Import and DirectQuery Data Models*, may be necessary to organize these measures.

 Field descriptions applied to Analysis Services data models will also flow through to Power BI reports just like the examples in this section with a Power BI dataset. However, field descriptions applied to Power BI datasets are not visible when connecting via Microsoft Excel.

Metadata reporting

Analysis Services DMVs are available to retrieve the descriptions applied to datasets and related information. These DMVs can be leveraged for both simple, ad hoc extracts via common dataset tools, such as DAX Studio, as well as more robust and standardized reports in Power BI or Excel. Official documentation of Analysis Services DMVs, including a reference and description of each DMV, query syntax, and client-tool access is available via the following link: http://bit.ly/2A81lek

Query field descriptions

The following query can be used to retrieve the measures in a dataset with descriptions as well as their DAX expression:

```
SELECT
        [Name] as [Measure Name]
    ,   [Description] as [Measure Description]
    ,   [Expression] as [DAX Expression]
FROM
$SYSTEM.TMSCHEMA_MEASURES
WHERE  LEN([Description]) > 1
ORDER BY [NAME];
```

As shown in the following screenshot, the query can be executed from DAX Studio against the open Power BI Desktop file:

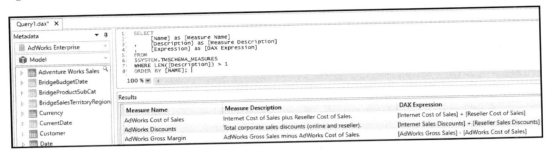

Measure descriptions via DMV query in DAX Studio

The WHERE clause in this query ensures that only measures with a description applied are returned. Removing or commenting out this clause (for example, --WHERE LEN([Description]) > 1) will return all measures whether they have a description or not. Additionally, column aliases of Measure Name, Measure Description, and DAX Expression improve the usability of the DMV columns.

Just as measure descriptions can be retrieved via the TMSCHEMA_MEASURES DMV, the following query retrieves the column descriptions from the TMSCHEMA_COLUMNS DMV:

```
SELECT
        [ExplicitName] as [Column Name]
    ,   [Description] as [Column Description]
FROM $SYSTEM.TMSCHEMA_COLUMNS
WHERE LEN([Description]) > 1
ORDER BY [ExplicitName];
```

As per the official documentation referenced earlier in this section, the query engine for DMVs is the Data Mining parser and the DMV query syntax is based on the SELECT (DMX) statement. Therefore, although the queries appear to be standard SQL statements, the full SQL SELECT syntax is not supported, including the JOIN and GROUP BY clauses. For example, it's not possible to join the TMSCHEMA_COLUMNS DMV with the TMSCHEMA_TABLES DMV within the same SELECT statement to retrieve columns from both DMVs. Given these limitations, it can be helpful to build lightweight data transformation processes on top of DMVs, as described in the following section.

Standard metadata reports

For larger datasets with many measures, relationships, and tables, a dedicated metadata report can be constructed using Power BI. In this approach, the Analysis Services data connector is used to access the DMVs of the Power BI dataset and this data is transformed via M queries. Finally, a set of report pages are created to visualize the primary objects of the model and support common ad hoc questions, such as which relationships use bidirectional cross-filtering?

Implementing the DMV-based Power BI report consists of the following four steps:

1. Obtain the server and database parameter values of the Power BI dataset
2. Query the DMVs of the Power BI dataset from a separate Power BI Desktop file
3. Integrate and enhance the DMV data to support the visualization layer
4. Develop the report pages

Server and database parameters

The server value of the Power BI dataset is visible in the status bar (bottom-right corner) when connected to the dataset from DAX Studio, as shown in the following screenshot:

Server value of Power BI dataset via DAX Studio

In the following code, the server parameter is **localhost:52809**. To obtain the database parameter, run the following query in DAX Studio:

```
SELECT
    [CATALOG_NAME]
,   [DATABASE_ID]
FROM $SYSTEM.DBSCHEMA_CATALOGS
```

Both columns will retrieve the same GUID value that can be used as the database parameter.

There are other methods of obtaining the server parameter, such as finding the process ID (PID) in **Task Manager** and then running `netstat -anop tcp` from Command Prompt to find the port associated with the PID. Connecting to the dataset from DAX Studio is more straightforward and it's assumed that experienced Power BI dataset designers will have at least a basic familiarity with DAX Studio.

The server parameter (for example, **localhost:52809**) can also be used to connect to the running Power BI dataset via SQL Server Profiler. This can be useful for identifying the DAX queries generated by report visuals and user interactions. Alternatively, Power BI Desktop can generate a trace file via the **Enable tracing** setting within the **Diagnostics option** (**File** | **Options and Settings** | **Diagnostics**).

Querying the DMVs from Power BI

With the server and database known, parameters and queries can be created in Power BI Desktop to stage the DMV data for further transformations. In the following screenshot from the Power Query Editor, three query groups are used to organize the parameters, the DMV queries, and the enhanced queries (`Metadata Report Tables`) used by the report:

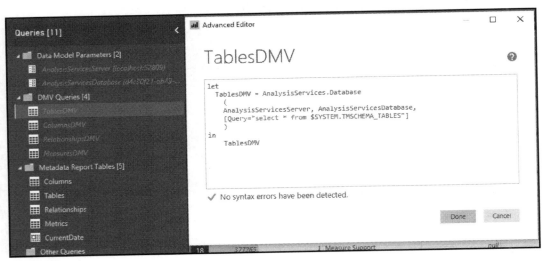

Power Query Editor in Power BI Desktop

As per the `TablesDMV` query, the two parameters (`AnalysisServicesServer` and `AnalysisServicesDatabase`) are passed to the `AnalysisServices.Database()` function for each DMV query. As indicated by the gray font of the DMV queries and the parameters, these queries are not loaded to the data model layer.

To update the metadata report in a future session to reflect changes to the dataset, the server and database parameter values would need to be retrieved again. These values could then be passed to the data model parameters, thus allowing all queries to update. This manual update process is necessary with Power BI Desktop files, given changes to the port and database ID, but is not necessary for metadata reports based on Analysis Services models.

Given the small size of the DMV data and the limitations of SQL `SELECT` queries against DMV data, a simple `SELECT *` is used to expose all columns and rows. The `Metadata Report Table` queries contain all the joins and transformations to prepare the data for reporting.

Integrating and enhancing DMV data

The following M query produces the `Relationships` table by implementing joins to retrieve the table and column names on each side of each relationship:

```
let
    FromTableJoin = Table.NestedJoin(
RelationshipsDMV,{"FromTableID"},TablesDMV,{"ID"},"TableDMVColumns",
JoinKind.Inner),
    FromTable = Table.ExpandTableColumn(FromTableJoin,
"TableDMVColumns", {"Name"}, {"From Table"}),
    ToTableJoin = Table.NestedJoin(
        FromTable,{"ToTableID"},TablesDMV,{"ID"},"TableDMVColumns",
JoinKind.Inner),
    ToTable = Table.ExpandTableColumn(ToTableJoin, "TableDMVColumns",
{"Name"}, {"To Table"}),
    FromColumnJoin = Table.NestedJoin(
        ToTable,{"FromColumnID"},ColumnsDMV,{"ID"},"ColumnsDMVColumns",
JoinKind.Inner),
    FromColumn = Table.ExpandTableColumn(FromColumnJoin,
"ColumnsDMVColumns",
        {"ExplicitName"}, {"From Column"}),
    ToColumnJoin = Table.NestedJoin(
        FromColumn,{"ToColumnID"},ColumnsDMV,{"ID"},"ColumnsDMVColumns",
JoinKind.Inner),
```

```
    ToColumn = Table.ExpandTableColumn(ToColumnJoin,
"ColumnsDMVColumns",
        {"ExplicitName"}, {"To Column"}),
    CrossFilteringColumn = Table.AddColumn(ToColumn, "Cross-Filtering
Behavior", each
        if [CrossFilteringBehavior] = 1 then "Single Direction"
        else if [CrossFilteringBehavior] = 2 then "Bidirectional" else
"Other", type text),
    RenameActiveFlag =
Table.RenameColumns(CrossFilteringColumn,{{"IsActive", "Active
Flag"}})
in
    RenameActiveFlag
```

The Relationships DMV (TMSCHEMA_RELATIONSHIPS) includes table and column ID columns, which are used for the joins to the tables (TMSCHEMA_TABLES) and columns (TMSCHEMA_COLUMNS) DMVs, respectively. Additionally, a more intuitive cross-filtering behavior column is added based on a conditional (if..then) expression.

Metadata report pages

With the enhanced DMV data loaded, report pages can be created, visualizing the most important columns. In the following screenshot, the table and column names retrieved via the M query joins in the previous section, *Integrating and enhancing the DMV data*, are included in a simple table visual:

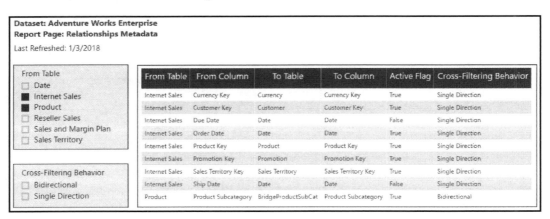

Metadata report page

In the slicer visual on the left, the table is filtered to only display relationships in which the `Internet Sales` and `Product` tables are on the **From Table** side of the relationship. In other words, only the relationships in which the `Internet Sales` and `Product` tables are on the many side of a one-to-many relationship are displayed. The `Active Flag` column identifies the two inactive date relationships based on `Due Date` and `Ship Date`. Additionally, the cross-filtering behavior column and slicer makes it easy to identify any relationships with bidirectional cross-filtering enabled.

A Power BI Desktop file containing the M queries and report pages from this example is included with the code bundle for this book. Additionally, `Chapter 8`, *Connecting to Sources and Transforming Data with M*, and `Chapter 9`, *Designing Import and DirectQuery Data Models*, describe the essential concepts of M queries and relationships contained in this section, respectively.

Summary

This chapter introduced application workspaces and their fundamental role in managing and delivering Power BI content to groups of users in the Power BI service. A staged deployment architecture across development, test, and production workspaces was described, including calls to the Power BI REST API to manage this process. Additionally, several features and processes related to content management and governance were reviewed, including version history via OneDrive for Business, field descriptions, and accessing the DMVs of datasets to document datasets.

The next chapter examines the On-premises data gateway and the configuration of data refresh processes in the Power BI service. This includes the administration of the gateway, such as authorizing users and data sources, as well as monitoring gateway resource utilization.

Managing the On-Premises Data Gateway

15

For many organizations, the data sources for Power BI datasets or reports are located in on-premises environments. The On-premises data gateway provides a means to securely connect to these sources to support scheduled data refreshes or, in the case of DirectQuery and Analysis Services Live connections, only return the results of queries requested by users in the Power BI service. As a critical component of many Power BI solutions and potentially other solutions utilizing Microsoft cloud services, such as Azure Analysis Services, MS Flow, and PowerApps, a sound understanding of the On-premises data gateway is essential.

This chapter reviews the architecture and behavior of the On-premises data gateway in the context of Power BI. End-to-end guidance and best practices are provided across the primary stages of deployment, from planning to installation, and setup to management and monitoring.

In this chapter, we will review the following topics:

- On-premises data gateway planning
- Gateway clusters and architectures
- Configuration of the On-premises data gateway
- Dashboard tile cache refresh
- Managing gateway clusters
- Monitoring gateway usage
- Live connections to Analysis Services models
- Single sign-on DirectQuery

On-premises data gateway planning

Planning for the On-premises data gateway involves identifying which data sources require a gateway and understanding the role of the gateway in each deployment scenario. For example, if an import mode Power BI dataset or an import mode Azure Analysis Services model simply needs to be refreshed with on-premises data every night, then gateway resources (hardware) should be provisioned to support this specific nightly workload. This deployment scenario, with the refreshed and in-memory data model hosted in the cloud, is preferable from a user experience or query performance standpoint, as the queries generated in the Power BI service do not have to access the on-premises source via the On-premises data gateway.

Alternatively, when the data model or data source accessed directly by Power BI reports is located in an on-premises environment, the On-premises data gateway is used to facilitate data transfer between the data source and the queries from the Power BI service. For example, a DirectQuery Power BI dataset built against on-premises Teradata database results in report queries being sent from the Power BI service to the Teradata database via the On-premises data gateway and the results of those queries being returned to the Power BI service via the On-premises data gateway. This deployment scenario can naturally require alternative gateway resources, such as additional CPU cores, given the potentially high volume of queries being generated dynamically based on user activity.

In addition to on-premises data sources, data sources residing in **Infrastructure-as-a-Service (IaaS) virtual machines (VMs)** also require a data gateway. This is an important exception as cloud data sources generally do not require a gateway. For example, **Platform-as-a-Service (PaaS)** sources, such as Azure SQL Database, and **Software-as-a-Service (SaaS)** solutions, such as Google Analytics, do not require a gateway.

The following two sets of questions address essential, high-level planning topics including the administration of the installed gateway. The following section, *Top gateway planning tasks*, as well as the *Gateway architectures* section later in this chapter, contain higher detail to support gateway deployment:

1. Where is the data being used by the Power BI dataset?
   - Confirm that a gateway is needed to access the data source from Power BI
   - This access includes both scheduled data refresh and any DirectQuery or Live connections to the data source

- Additional details on sources requiring a gateway are provided in the next section

2. If a gateway is needed, is the data source supported with a **generally available (GA)** data connector?
    - If a source-specific connector is not available, the gateway supports **Open Database Connectivity (ODBC)** and OLE DB connections as well
    - The current list of supported data sources is available at `http://bit.ly/2EN1BCg`
    - Data connectors labeled as (`Beta`) in the **Get Data** window of Power BI Desktop should only be used for testing

3. Is the on-premises data or the IaaS data being imported to the Power BI dataset(s) or an Azure Analysis Services model?
    - If yes, the gateway will support the scheduled refresh/processing activities for these datasets
    - If no, the gateway will support user queries of the data source via DirectQuery or Live connections

4. Will a standard On-premises data gateway be used or will a personal gateway (personal mode) be used?
    - In all corporate BI deployments, the default and recommended on-premises gateway will be installed by the IT organization on IT-owned and maintained servers.
    - However, in certain business-led self-service projects or in scenarios in which an IT-owned gateway server is not available, the personal gateway could be installed on a business user's machine, allowing that user to configure scheduled refreshes of import mode datasets.

A single gateway can be used to support multiple datasets, both import and DirectQuery. However, it can be advantageous to isolate the alternative Power BI workloads across distinct gateway clusters, such as with an import gateway cluster and a DirectQuery or Live connection gateway cluster. Without this isolation, the scheduled refresh activities of import mode datasets (Power BI or Azure Analysis Services) could potentially impact the performance of user queries submitted via DirectQuery and Live connection datasets. Additionally, as mentioned earlier, scheduled refresh activities can require far different gateway resources (for example, memory) than the queries generated via DirectQuery datasets or Live connections to on-premises **SQL Server Analysis Services (SSAS)** databases.

In addition to provisioning hardware and installing the gateway(s) for each scenario, BI teams must also plan for the administration and management of the gateway. Answering the following five questions contributes to planning the implementation:

1. Which users will administer the gateway in Power BI?
   - This should be more than one user; preferably, a security group of multiple gateway admins can be configured
   - These users do not need Power BI Pro licenses if they're only administering gateway clusters

   In larger Power BI deployments, distinct users or security groups could be assigned as administrators of different gateways. For example, two users could administer a gateway cluster utilized by enterprise or corporate-owned BI content while two other users could administer a gateway cluster used to support self-service BI content and projects.

    This isolation of hardware resources between corporate and self-service BI (that is, business user/team owned) can also be implemented with Power BI Premium capacities, as described in Chapter 19, *Scaling with Premium and Analysis Services*. The essential goal of this isolation is to provide the self-service projects with resources aligned to these needs while ensuring that high priority and widely utilized corporate BI assets are not impacted by self-service content or activities.

2. Which authentication credentials or method will be used to configure the gateway data sources?
   - For SSAS and Azure Analysis Services, this should be a server administrator of the Analysis Services instance
   - For certain DirectQuery data sources, a **single sign-on** (**SSO**) option is supported in which the Power BI user's identity is passed to the source system, thus leveraging the source system's security.
   - The *DirectQuery datasets* section later in this chapter contains details of this configuration

3. Which users will be authorized to use the gateway?
   - Users or security groups of users must be mapped to the data source of a gateway

- These are usually report authors with Power BI Pro licenses

4. Where will the gateway recovery key be stored?
    - This will be necessary for migrating, restoring, or taking over an existing gateway

5. Who will be responsible for updating the On-premises data gateway as new versions are released?
    - Just like Power BI Desktop, a new version of the On-premises data gateway is made available each month and includes new features and improvements, such as the support for datasets with both cloud and on-premises data sources
    - The Power BI team recommends staying up to date with new releases and will not support old gateway versions
    - For example, as of March 15, 2018, gateway versions older than the August 2017 release will not be supported

 Each monthly gateway version includes the same M Query engine utilized by that month's release of Power BI Desktop. Examples and considerations for M Queries were described in `Chapter 8`, *Connecting to Sources and Transforming Data with M.*

In the following image, two users are added to a security group in **Azure Active Directory (AD)**, dedicated to the administration of the On-premises data gateway:

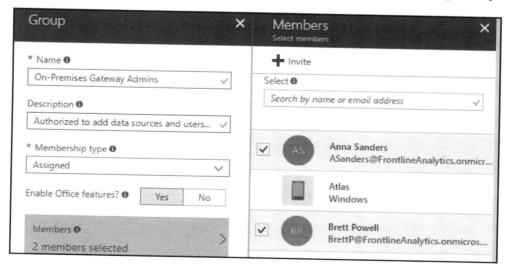

Security group in Azure Active Directory

In this example, mapping the `On-Premises Gateway Admins` security group to a gateway in Power BI would allow Anna and Brett to configure data sources for the gateway and to authorize users or security groups of users to utilize the gateway. The *Managing gateway clusters* section later in this chapter includes details on using the gateway portal in the Power BI service.

Top gateway planning tasks

Since the gateway relates to different areas of IT, including infrastructure, networking, and data security, subject matter experts in these areas often inquire about the technical requirements of the gateway and its functionality. Additionally, business intelligence teams want to ensure that the gateway doesn't become a bottleneck to query performance and that dependencies on an individual gateway are avoided. Therefore, the BI/IT teams responsible for deploying Power BI solutions with on-premises data (or IaaS data) must partner with these other IT stakeholders to resolve questions and to provision the appropriate resources for the On-premises data gateway.

This section addresses three of the most common gateway planning questions. Information related to high availability and security is included in the gateway clusters and architectures, and gateway security sections, respectively.

Determining whether a gateway is needed

As one would expect, an On-premises data gateway is usually not required for connectivity to cloud data sources. PaaS offerings, such as Azure SQL Database, and SaaS solutions, such as Salesforce, do not require a gateway.

However, data sources that reside in an IaaS VM do require a gateway. Additionally, the `Web.Page()` function used in M Queries also requires a gateway. This function is used by the **Web Data Connector (WDC)** (**Get Data | Web**) to return the contents of an HTML web page as a table, as shown in the following M Query:

```
// Retrieve table of data access M functions and their descriptions
let
  Source =
Web.Page(Web.Contents("https://msdn.microsoft.com/en-US/library/mt2966
15.aspx")),
  PageToTable = Source{0}[Data],
  ChangedType = Table.TransformColumnTypes(PageToTable,
```

```
                  {{"Function", type text}, {"Description", type text}}})
    in
      ChangedType
```

In the preceding example, a two-column table (`Function`, `Description`) of M functions is retrieved from an MSDN web page and imported into a table in Power BI.

Additionally, all data sources for a dataset that accesses an on-premises data source must be added to the list of data sources in the gateway management portal. For example, if a dataset uses both SharePoint (on-premises) and an Azure SQL database, the URL for the Azure SQL database must also be added as a data source (via the SQL Server data source type) in the gateway management portal. If one of the data sources for the dataset is not configured for the gateway, the gateway will not appear in the dataset settings to support a refresh.

Identifying where the gateway should be installed

Gateways should be installed in locations that minimize the distance between the Power BI service tenant, the gateway server, and the on-premises data source. Reduced physical distance between these three points results in less network latency and thus improved query performance. Minimizing this latency is especially important when the gateway is used to support interactive report queries from Power BI to on-premises DirectQuery sources and Live connections to on-premises SSAS models.

Network latency from an IP location to Azure data regions can be tested at `http://azurespeed.com`.

For example, via this free tool, it can quickly be determined that the average latency to the West US region is 100 ms while the East US region is only 37 ms. The lower latency of the East US region is due to the physical proximity of this region to the source IP location (near Boston, MA).

For example, if the Power BI tenant for your organization is located in the **North Central US** region in Microsoft Azure and your on-premises data source (for example, Oracle) is also located in the upper Midwest region of the United States, then the gateway should be installed on a server near or between these two locations.

The location of a Power BI tenant can be found by clicking the **About Power BI** menu item via the question mark icon in the top-right corner of the Power BI service:

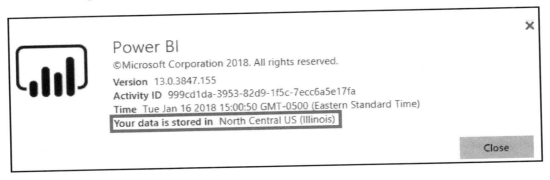

About Power BI: tenant location

In this example, the Power BI content for the organization is being stored in the **North Central US (Illinois)** Azure region. Therefore, the gateway should be installed on a location that minimizes the distance between Illinois and the location of the data source. One example of this would be to install the gateway on the same subnet of the production data source server. It's not necessary, or recommended, to install the gateway on the same server as the production data source.

 Currently, there are 36 Azure regions globally with six new regions planned. This link identifies the Azure regions and the criteria for choosing a specific region: http://bit.ly/2B598tD.

Defining the gateway infrastructure and hardware requirements

The recommended starting point for the server on which the gateway will be installed is eight CPU cores, 8 GB of memory, and the 64-bit version of Windows 2012 R2 (or later). However, hardware requirements for the gateway server will vary significantly based on the type of dataset supported (import versus DirectQuery/Live connection), the volume of concurrent users, and the queries requested.

For example, if an M Query or part of an M Query is not folded back to the source system, as described in `Chapter 8`, *Connecting to Sources and Transforming Data with M*, the gateway server will be required to execute the non-folded M expressions during the scheduled refresh (import) process. Depending on the volume of data and the logic of these expressions, a greater amount of RAM would better support these local operations. Similarly, if many users will be interacting with reports based on a DirectQuery dataset or a Live connection to a SSAS model (on-premises), additional CPU cores will result in better throughput.

It's strongly recommended to avoid a single point of failure by installing instances of the On-premises data gateway on separate servers. These multiple instances can serve as a single gateway cluster of resources available to support data refreshes and queries against on-premises data sources. Gateway clusters and architectures consisting of separate gateway clusters are described in later sections of this chapter.

Performance counters associated with the gateway and the gateway server can be used to determine whether adjustments in available resources (RAM and CPU) are necessary. Guidance on interpreting these counters and a technique to integrate and visualize this data via Power BI is included in the *Monitoring gateway usage* section later in this chapter.

In terms of network configuration, the gateway creates an outbound connection to the Azure Service Bus and does not require inbound ports. The gateway communicates on the following outbound ports: TCP 443 (default), 5671, 5672, and 9350 through 9354. It's recommended that organizations whitelist the IP addresses for the data region of their Power BI tenant (for example, North Central US) within their firewall. The list of IP addresses for the Azure data centers can be downloaded via the following URL `http://bit.ly/2oeAQyd`.

The downloaded list of Azure IP addresses is contained within an XML file which can be easily accessed via Power BI Desktop, as shown in the following image:

A^B_C Name	A^B_C Region	A^B_C IP Address
Region	usnorth	20.190.135.0/24
Region	usnorth	23.96.128.0/17
Region	usnorth	23.98.48.0/21

Azure datacenter IP addresses

The gateway installs on any domain-joined machine and cannot be installed on a domain controller. Additionally, only one gateway can be installed per computer per gateway mode (enterprise versus personal). Therefore, it's possible to have both an enterprise mode and a personal mode gateway running on the same machine.

On-premises data gateway versus personal mode

The first configuration setting when installing a gateway is the mode of the gateway, as depicted in the following image:

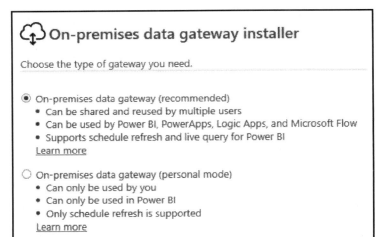

On-premises data gateway installer

The default and recommended gateway mode (commonly referred to as the enterprise mode) provides all the functionality of the **personal mode** plus many more features and management capabilities. These additional benefits include support for DirectQuery and Live connection datasets, several other Azure services, such as MS Flow, and the management capabilities described in the *Managing gateway clusters* section later in this chapter.

A single **personal mode** gateway can be installed per Power BI user account and can only be used for the on-demand or scheduled refresh of the import mode Power BI datasets. Most importantly, the **personal mode** gateway is completely tied to the individual user and cannot be shared. For example, if the gateway is installed in the **personal mode** on a user's laptop, that laptop will need to be on and connected to the internet to support any scheduled data refreshes. Additionally, unlike the administrators of the **On-premises data gateway**, a **personal mode** user cannot authorize other users to leverage the **personal mode** gateway and its configured data sources.

In the following image, both a **personal mode** gateway and a standard **On-premises data gateway** are available to refresh a dataset:

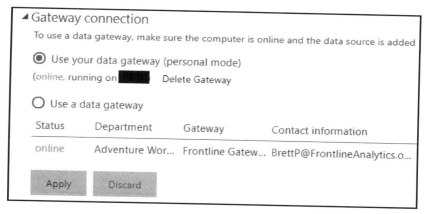

Dataset gateway connection

In the preceding example, if the user was not authorized to use the **On-premises data gateway (Frontline Gateway)**, the **personal mode** gateway could be used to complete the refresh. This assumes the user has the necessary privileges to the on-premises data sources of the import mode dataset.

 Although the terms in the **Dataset settings** menu refer to single gateways (for example, **Gateway connection**, data gateway), the **Frontline Gateway** is actually a cluster of gateway resources. Specifically, the **Frontline Gateway** operates as a single logical unit but may have multiple gateways installed across separate servers. The *gateway clusters and architectures section* contains additional details on the configuration of multiple clusters and multiple gateways within a cluster.

The **personal mode** gateway is not intended for large datasets or datasets supporting reports and dashboards that many users depend on. The **personal mode** gateways should only be considered for enabling individual business users to work on personal or proof-of-concept projects. For example, the business user may have several Excel workbooks and other frequently changing local files that are not configured as data sources on an **On-premises data gateway**. If the user has been assigned a Power BI Pro license, the **personal mode** gateway allows the user to keep Power BI reports and dashboards based on these sources updated for review by colleagues. In the event that the user's content requires reliable, longer-term support, the BI/IT organization can add the data sources to an **On-premises gateway** (enterprise mode) and revise removing the dependency on the user's machine.

All the remaining sections of this chapter are exclusively focused on the **On-premises data gateway** (that is, the enterprise mode). Although there are overlapping characteristics with the **personal mode**, any reference to the **On-premises data gateway** in this chapter and elsewhere in this book refers to the default mode (enterprise).

Gateway clusters

Each Power BI dataset is associated with a single gateway cluster, which is composed of one or many gateway instances. For example, if a Power BI dataset (.pbix) imports data from both a SQL Server database and an Excel file, the same gateway cluster will be responsible for the import from both sources. Likewise, if hundreds of business users interact with reports based on the same DirectQuery dataset or a Live connection to an on-premises SSAS instance, these user interactions will generate query requests to the same gateway cluster.

Gateway clusters representing multiple gateways (for example, primary and secondary), each of which must be installed on separate machines as per the *Hardware and network requirements* section, provide both high availability and load balancing. From an availability standpoint, if an individual gateway instance within a cluster is not running, due to a server failure, for example, the data refresh and user query requests from the Power BI service will be routed to the other gateway instance(s) within the cluster. In terms of query performance and scalability, the Power BI service will distribute (load balance) the query requests across the multiple gateway instances within the cluster.

Data source configurations for the primary gateway of the cluster, which is the first gateway installed for the cluster, are leveraged by any additional gateways added to the cluster. For example, when a gateway cluster is first created on server abc and a data source (for example, SQL Server) is added to this cluster, the same data source settings (for example, the authentication method) will be used when another gateway on server xyz is added to the gateway cluster.

In the following image from the gateway installer application, a new gateway is added to an existing gateway cluster:

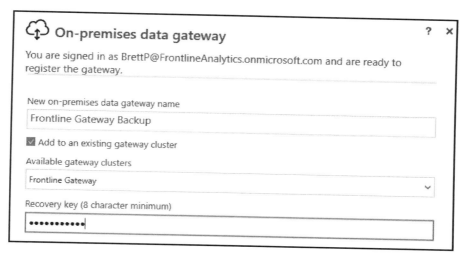

Adding a gateway to a gateway cluster

In this example, the new gateway (Frontline Gateway Backup) is added to the **Frontline Gateway** cluster as per the checkbox and **Available gateway clusters** selection. Note that the **Recovery key** for the primary gateway instance, which was created when the first gateway instance of the cluster was installed, is required to add a gateway to a cluster. Additionally, be aware that the gateway management portal in the Power BI service only displays the gateway clusters, not the individual gateways within each cluster. Both the gateway clusters and the individual gateways within each cluster can be accessed and managed via PowerShell scripts as per the *Managing gateway clusters* section.

Prior to the release of gateway clusters in late 2017, each Power BI dataset was dependent on a single gateway (and thus a single server). This was a significant limitation from both an availability and a performance standpoint as BI teams and projects would naturally prefer to reuse the same dataset for many reports and dashboards. Adding a gateway or multiple gateways from separate servers to a single gateway cluster eliminates this single point of failure and provides load balancing of the requested queries by default.

Before adding a gateway to a cluster, ensure that the new gateway instance will be able to connect to the same data sources configured for the cluster. As described in the *Top gateway planning tasks* section, the additional gateways added to gateway clusters should also be installed in locations that minimize the distance between the gateway server, the Power BI service tenant, and the data source(s).

Gateway architectures

For large-scale deployments of Power BI in which multiple types of datasets and workloads will be supported (import refreshes, as well as DirectQuery and Live connection queries), BI teams can consider multiple gateway clusters. In this approach, each gateway cluster is tailored to meet the specific resource needs (RAM and CPU) of the different workloads, such as large nightly refreshes or high volumes of concurrent queries in the early mornings.

For example, one gateway cluster could be composed of two gateway instances with a relatively high amount of available RAM on each gateway server. This cluster would have resources available during the most intensive scheduled refresh operations (for example, 4 A.M. to 6 A.M.) and would be exclusively used by import mode Power BI datasets and any Azure Analysis Services models that also regularly import data from on-premises sources. A separate gateway cluster would be created based on two gateway instances with a relatively high number of CPU cores on each gateway server. This gateway cluster would be used exclusively by DirectQuery Power BI datasets and any reports based on Live connection to an on-premises SQL Server Analysis Services instance.

A third gateway cluster, in addition to an import and a DirectQuery/Live connection cluster, could be dedicated to business-led BI projects. For example, as described in the *On-premises data gateway versus personal mode* section earlier in this chapter, certain data sources maintained by business teams (for example, Excel workbooks) may require the high availability and management benefits of the On-premises data gateway. Generally, this self-service cluster would be oriented toward scheduled refresh operations, but organizations may also want to empower business users to create DirectQuery datasets or reports based on Live connections to SSAS instances (on-premises).

In the following example from the **Manage gateways** portal in the Power BI service, two gateway clusters have been configured:

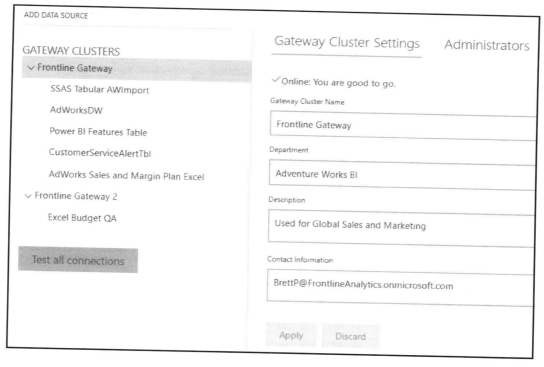

Manage gateways in Power BI service

As shown in the preceding image, the two Gateway Clusters (**Frontline Gateway** and **Frontline Gateway 2**) have been configured to support different data sources. As noted in the previous section, the individual gateway instances installed for each cluster are not currently accessible from the gateway portal but can be accessed via PowerShell scripts. Each cluster represents a single logical unit of gateway resources for its given data source(s).

If gateway clusters are created for specific workloads (for example, import versus DirectQuery), it can be helpful to note this both in the **Gateway Cluster Name** and in its **Description**. It's not recommended to allow a single point of failure but if only one gateway server is used in a cluster then the name of this server can be included in the cluster name and description.

The following diagram depicts a gateway cluster being used to support a scheduled data refresh of a Power BI dataset:

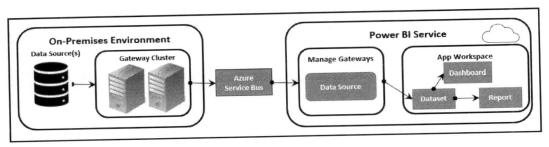

Scheduled data refresh via gateway cluster

With the data source(s) configured in the **Manage Gateways** portal in the **Power BI Service**, a scheduled data refresh for an import mode dataset can be configured to use the **Gateway Cluster**. The **Gateway Cluster** receives the query request at the scheduled time and is responsible for connecting to the data source(s) and executing the queries that load/refresh the tables of the Power BI dataset. Once the dataset in the **Power BI Service** is refreshed, dashboard tiles based on the dataset will also be refreshed and reports built against the dataset will issue queries against the dataset.

Given that the report queries are local to the refreshed dataset within the same **Power BI Service** tenant, and given the performance optimizations of the engine running within import mode Power BI datasets (that is, columnar compression, in-memory), query performance is usually very good with this deployment.

Currently, the entire Power BI dataset must be fully refreshed in each scheduled refresh operation. This is very inefficient, and in some scenarios infeasible, for large datasets as resources are needed to load both historical (unchanged) data and new data. However, incremental data refresh is a top feature identified on the Power BI Premium roadmap and, along with other roadmap features, will help support larger Power BI datasets. Additional details on Power BI Premium are included in Chapter 19, *Scaling with Premium and Analysis Services*.

The following diagram depicts two gateway clusters being used to support both the scheduled refresh of an import mode dataset and a Live connection to a SSAS tabular instance:

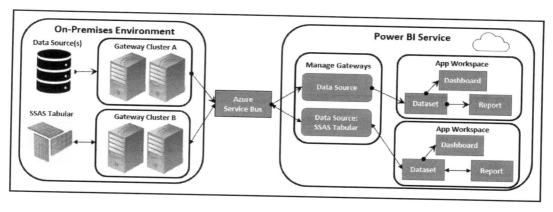

Multiple gateway clusters

Gateway Cluster A in the preceding diagram functions just like the previous diagram in supporting scheduled refreshes of import mode datasets. **Gateway Cluster B** has been created to exclusively support queries requested via Live connections to an on-premises SSAS database—an **SSAS Tabular** model in this scenario. Given the high volume of query requests generated by users interacting with Power BI reports based on the SSAS model, the servers used in **Gateway Cluster B** can be provisioned with additional CPU cores and actively monitored via performance counters for changes in utilization.

In addition to the interactive query requests from Live connection reports, owners of datasets can configure a scheduled refresh for the cache supporting dashboard tiles based on Live connection reports. Guidance on configuring this feature is included in the *Dashboard cache refresh* section at the end of this chapter.

The description of **Gateway Cluster B** is also generally applicable to DirectQuery datasets based on supported sources, such as SQL Server, Oracle, and Teradata. Just like Live connections to SSAS, reports built against these datasets will also generate high volumes of queries that must go through the gateway cluster and be returned to the Power BI service tenant.

Given the additional latency created by the requests for queries and the transfer of query results back to the Power BI service, it's especially important to develop and provision efficient data sources for DirectQuery and Live connection reports. Two examples of this include using the clustered columnstore index for SQL Server and optimizing the DAX expressions used for measures of an SSAS model.

Additionally, organizations can consider Azure ExpressRoute to create a fast, private connection between on-premises infastructure and Azure. The following URL provides documentation on this service: `http://bit.ly/2tCCwEv`.

Gateway security

Administrators of the **On-premises data gateway**, such as the security group mentioned in the *On-premises data gateway planning* section, are responsible for configuring the data sources that can be used with each gateway cluster. Additionally, gateway administrators have control over the users or security group(s) of users that can utilize a gateway data source.

As shown in the following image from the **Manage gateways** portal in the Power BI service, credentials entered for data sources are encrypted:

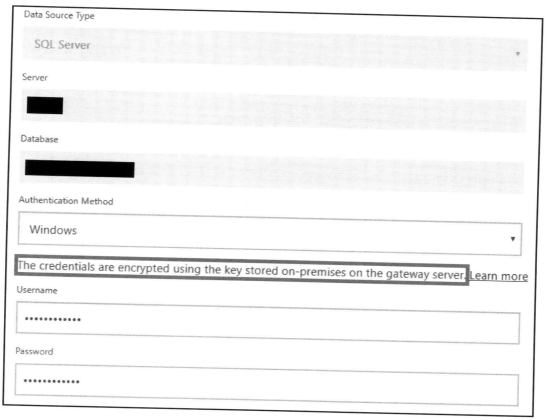

Encrypted data source credentials

The data source credentials are only decrypted once the query request reaches the on-premises gateway cluster within the corporate network. The gateway decrypts the credentials needed for query requests and, once the query has executed, it encrypts the results of these query requests prior to pushing this data to the Power BI service. The Power BI service never knows the on-premises credential values.

Technically, the following five-step process occurs to facilitate communication and data transfer between the Power BI service and the on-premises sources:

1. The Power BI service initiates a scheduled refresh or a user interacts with a DirectQuery or a Live connection report.

   In either event, a query request is created and analyzed by the data movement service in Power BI.

2. The data movement service determines the appropriate Azure Service Bus communication channel for the given query.

   A distinct service bus instance is configured per gateway.

3. The **On-premises data gateway** polls its service bus channel and obtains the pending request.

4. The gateway decrypts the credentials and then sends the query to the data source for execution.

5. The results of the query (data) are returned to the gateway, encrypted, and then pushed to the Power BI service.

The critical component of the gateway's security is the recovery key that's created during the installation and configuration process. In the following image, a user account has signed into the Power BI service and both a name for the gateway and a recovery key are required to configure the gateway:

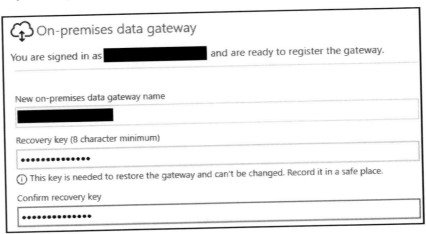

Configuration of an On-premises data gateway

The recovery key is used to generate strong RSA and AES encryption keys. As described earlier in this section, these encyrption keys never leave the gateway machine.

It's strongly recommended to store the gateway recovery key in a safe and secure location. This should be on a machine other than the gateway server itself as the recovery key can be used to migrate, restore, or take over an existing gateway, as described in the *Troubleshooting and monitoring gateways* section later in this chapter. Additionally, the recovery key is required when adding a gateway to a cluster to provide high availability and load balancing.

Gateway configuration

Once the gateway scenario and architecture has been planned per the previous sections, BI or IT administrators can download and install the gateway (or multiple gateways) on the chosen server(s). The gateway installation file to be downloaded is small (for example, 508 KB) and the installation process is quick and straightforward. However, gateway administrators should be aware of primary settings, such as the default Windows service account used by the gateway, and the option to change this account as well as the option to switch network communication from TCP to HTTPS.

The gateway installer application can be obtained via the **Download** dropdown in the Power BI service, as shown in the following image:

Download in Power BI service

The **Data Gateway** item from the download menu in the preceding image currently links to a **Power BI Gateway** page with a large **Download Gateway** button at the top. Selecting **Download Gateway** from this page allows the user to save the installer (`PowerBIGatewayInstaller.exe`) locally. If the gateway installation file is downloaded from a web page other than the **Power BI Gateway** page, such as Azure Logic Apps documentation, the option to install the gateway in **personal mode** will not be included.

The installation and configuration process via the installer application is very straightforward. Step-by-step instructions have been documented here (see *Install the gateway* section) `http://bit.ly/2rq22Ao`.

Once the installation and configuration is complete, an **On-premises data gateway** application will be available on the server machine to help manage the gateway, as shown in the following image:

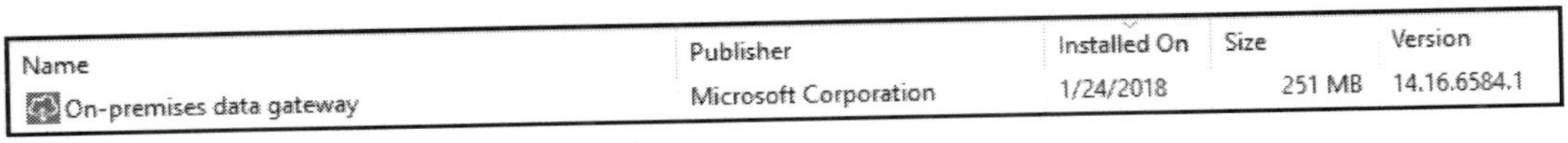

Name	Publisher	Installed On	Size	Version
On-premises data gateway	Microsoft Corporation	1/24/2018	251 MB	14.16.6584.1

On-premises data gateway application

Details on the settings available via this application are included in the *Troubleshooting and monitoring gateways* section later in this chapter. When first getting started with the gateway, you can launch the application after configuration and sign in with a Power BI service account to check the status of the gateway and to get familiar with the tool.

The same installation software can be downloaded and run to update an existing **On-premises data gateway** to the latest version. For example, the January 2018 version of the gateway corresponds to version **14.16.6584.1** and this includes the very latest data mashup engine, bug fixes, and new administrative features. The update process is very quick to complete and the **On-premises data gateway** application will reflect the new version number on the **Status** page, as shown in the following image:

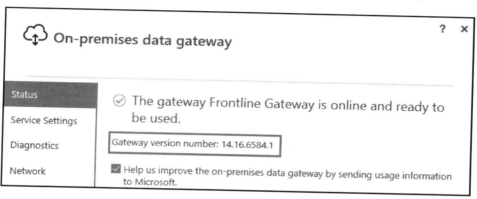

On-premises data gateway status

It's strongly recommended to regularly update the **On-premises data gateway** to the latest version. An out-of-date gateway will be flagged for updating on the **Status** page of the **On-premises data gateway** and may result in data refresh or connectivity issues.

Additionally, administrators should be aware of the following two XML configuration files for the gateway:

```
C:\Program Files\On-premises data
gateway\enterprisegatewayconfigurator.exe.config
C:\Program Files\On-premises data
gateway\Microsoft.PowerBI.EnterpriseGateway.exe.config
```

The `configurater.exe` file relates to the installation screens that configure the gateway. The `PowerBI.EnterpriseGateway.exe` file is for the actual Windows service that handles the query requests from the Power BI service.

The gateway service account

By default, the gateway runs under the **NT SERVICE\PBIEgwService** Windows service account. However, as shown in the following image from the **On-premises data gateway** desktop application, this account can be changed via the **Service Settings** tab:

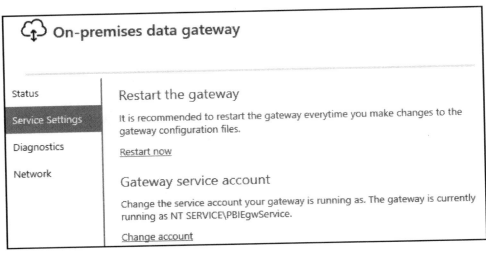

On-premises data gateway application

In the preceding example, a user has opened the gateway application from the server on which a gateway instance has been installed. Additionally, in order to change the service account, the user has signed into Power BI from the gateway application with the email address used to log in to the Power BI service.

If the default account (**NT SERVICE\PBIEgwService**) is able to access the internet and thus its Azure Service Bus, ensure that the account can also authenticate to the required on-premises data sources, such as the production SQL Server instance. In some environments, the default account cannot access the internet as it is not an authenticated domain user. In this scenario, the service account can be revised to a domain user account within the **Active Directory** domain. To avoid the need to routinely reset the password for the **Active Directory** account, it's recommended that a managed service account is created in **Active Directory** and used by the gateway service.

TCP versus HTTPS mode

By default, the gateway uses direct TCP network communication. However, as shown in the following image from the **On-premises data gateway** application, the gateway can be forced to exclusively use HTTPS via the **Network** tab:

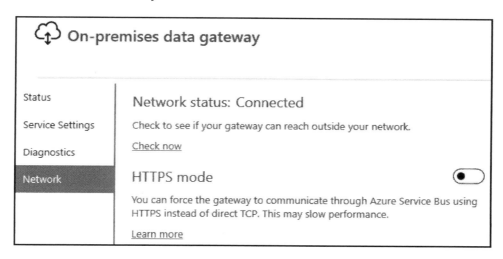

On-premises data gateway application

In the preceding example, a user has opened the gateway application from the server on which a gateway instance has been installed. Unlike modifying the service account per the previous section, however, the user does not need to sign in to Power BI from the gateway application to enable the HTTPS mode. A restart of the gateway is required to apply the change to the HTTPS mode and thus this modification should only be implemented when minimal or no query requests are being processed.

Once the HTTPS mode has been applied, the gateway will strictly use FQDN only and no communication will happen using IP addresses. As advised in the gateway application, enabling the HTTPS mode may slow the performance of gateway requests.

Managing gateway clusters

Once a gateway has been installed, the Power BI account used to register the gateway during installation can access the manage gateways portal in the Power BI service to assign administrators for the gateway. For example, if Anna Sanders' account was used to register the gateway during installation, as shown in the following image, Anna would initially be the only administrator of the gateway:

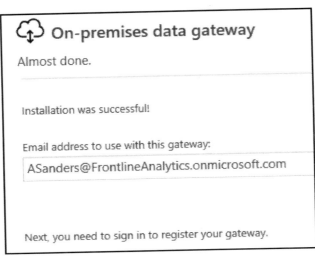

Account registering the gateway

Once registered, Anna can use the manage gateways portal to add a security group of users as administrators for the gateway. Anna can then optionally remove her individual account from the list of gateway administrators since she's either already included in the admin security group or it's not her role to administer this gateway.

The **Manage gateways** portal is available via the gear icon in the top-right corner of the Power BI service, as shown in the following image:

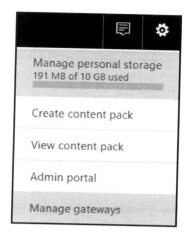

Manage gateways

The **Manage gateways** portal exposes all gateway clusters that the user is an administrator for. The primary functionality and tasks of gateway administrators are described in the following sections.

Gateway administrators

Administrators of gateway clusters have the ability to add or remove data sources, modify the authentication to those sources, and to enable or disable users or groups of users from utilizing the cluster. Given the importance of these responsibilities, more than one gateway administrator, such as a security group of admins, is strongly recommended. For example, in the event that the credentials for a data source need to be revised or when a data source needs to reference a different database, only an admin for the gateway will be able to implement these changes in the **Manage gateways** portal.

In the following image from the **Manage gateways** portal in Power BI, a single security group (**On-Premises Gateway Admins**) has been added as the administrator of the **Frontline Gateway** cluster:

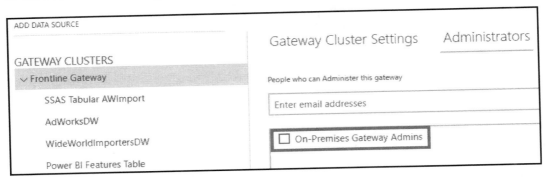

Power BI gateway administrators

As described in the *On-premises data gateway planning* section earlier in this chapter, this security group currently includes two users (Anna Sanders and Brett Powell).

Gateway data sources and users

The primary role of gateway administrators is to add data sources per the gateway cluster and to authorize (or remove) users or groups of users. With the gateway cluster selected within the **Manage gateways** portal, clicking **ADD DATA SOURCE** from the list of gateway clusters creates a blank new data source, as shown in the following image:

Adding a data source to a gateway cluster

New data sources can also be added via the ellipsis to the right of each cluster name in the **Manage gateways** portal. Once data sources have been added, the users who will publish reports and/or schedule data refreshes via the gateway can be added to the data source.

In the following example, a security group of users is added to the **AdWorksDW** data source of the **Frontline Gateway**:

Adding a security group of users to the gateway data source

The users included in the security group (for example, **AdWorks DW Sales Team**) will see the option to use the **Frontline Gateway** to configure scheduled refreshes in the **Data Source Settings** menu. For DirectQuery datasets and Live connections to on-premises SSAS databases, Power BI Desktop will advise that a gateway has been applied when the PBIX file is published.

PowerShell support for gateway clusters

A PowerShell script module is included in the installation of the **On-premises data gateway** to support the management of gateway clusters. Once the module is imported to a session of PowerShell in which the user has administrator privileges, a login command (`Login-OnPremisesDataGateway`) must be executed to enable other gateway management commands.

By default, the PowerShell module file (`.psm1`) can be imported from the following path:

On-premises gateway PowerShell module

Unlike the **Manage gateways** portal in the Power BI service, the PowerShell commands provide access to the specific gateway instances configured for each cluster. For example, properties of a specific gateway within an instance can be modified or a gateway instance can be removed from a cluster altogether.

In the following example from PowerShell, the gateway admin account (ASanders@FrontlineAnalytics.onmicrosoft.com) has been used for the Login-OnPremisesDataGateway command:

```
PS C:\Windows\System32> Login-OnPremisesDataGateway
cmdlet Set-OnPremisesDataGatewayUserAccount at command pipeline position 1
Supply values for the following parameters:
EmailAddress: ASanders@FrontlineAnalytics.onmicrosoft.com
Current backend is: https://wabi-us-north-central-redirect.analysis.windows.net/

PS C:\Windows\System32> Get-OnPremisesDataGatewayClusters


objectId    : 3b6f921a-1352-490c-83f9-2bc5bd372bc0
name        : Frontline Gateway
description : Used for Global Sales and Marketing
permission  : {
                  "objectId":  "f3ae71c5-6ee7-42be-b471-5ce1766800a7",
                  "principalType":  "Group",
                  "tenantId":
                  "role":  "Admin",
                  "allowedDataSourceTypes":  [

                                             ]

              }
gateways    : {
                  "gatewayId":  1593305,
```

Gateway cluster PowerShell commands

Once authenticated as Anna Sanders, the Get-OnPremisesDataGatewayClusters command has been used to retrieve the list of gateway clusters in which Anna is an administrator. The list of available gateway cluster PowerShell commands and their parameters can be found here: http://bit.ly/2BfXL2e.

Troubleshooting and monitoring gateways

For organizations with significant dependencies on the **On-premises data gateway**, it's important to plan for administration scenarios, such as migrating or restoring a gateway to a different machine. Gateway administrators should also be familiar with accessing and analyzing the gateway log files and related settings to troubleshoot data refresh issues. Finally, gateway throughput and resource availability can be consistently monitored via Windows' performance monitor counters associated with the gateway and the gateway server.

In the following image, the status and version number of an installed gateway is obtained via the **On-premises data gateway** desktop application:

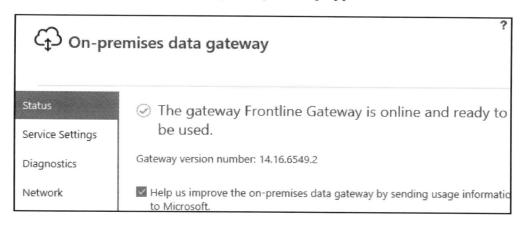

On-premises data gateway application

In the preceding example, a user has accessed the server on which the **Frontline Gateway** instance has been installed and then opened the **On-premises data gateway** application. To obtain the gateway's status (for example, green check mark), the user is required to sign in with the email address used to log in to the Power BI service. If the **Gateway version number** is out of date, a message will appear advising that a new version of the gateway is available. It's recommended to regularly update gateways to the latest versions.

Restoring, migrating, and taking over a gateway

In many scenarios, it's necessary to migrate or restore a gateway to a separate server. For example, a gateway may have initially been installed on a server with insufficient resources to support the current workload. In other cases, a hardware failure may have occurred on a gateway's server and thus it's necessary to quickly restore connectivity. Via the recovery key that's created when a gateway is first installed and configured, the data sources and their associated settings (authentication and credentials) can be restored on a new gateway machine.

In the following image, the gateway installation application (`PowerBIGatewayInstaller.exe`) provides the option to **Migrate, restore, or takeover an existing gateway** rather than register a new gateway:

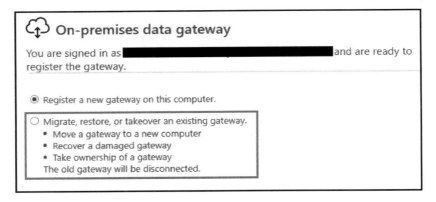

Gateway setup options

Choosing to **Migrate, restore, or takeover an existing gateway** will require the recovery key that is created when a gateway is originally configured. If this key is not available, the only option will be to install a new gateway and manually add the data sources and authorized users for that gateway. Additionally, only an administrator of a gateway can use the recovery key to restore a gateway to a different server.

Gateway log files

The **On-premises data gateway** desktop application makes it easy for gateway administrators to analyze gateway request activity. As shown in the following image, the **Diagnostics** tab allows admins to record additional details in the gateway log files and to export these files for analysis:

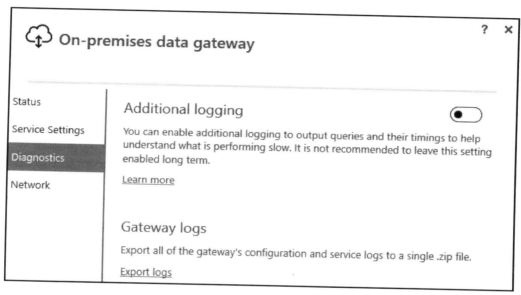

Diagnostics settings

Applying the additional logging setting requires the gateway to be restarted but provides visibility to the specific queries requested and the duration of their execution. In a typical troubleshooting or analysis scenario, a gateway admin would temporarily enable additional logging, execute a data refresh or query from the Power BI service, and then export the gateway log files to analyze this activity. Once the log files have been exported, additional logging should be disabled to avoid reduced query throughput.

Technically, the additional logging setting modifies the `EmitQueryTraces` and `TracingVerbosity` properties of the following two XML configuration files, respectively:
`Microsoft.PowerBI.DataMovement.Pipeline.GatewayCore.dll`
`Microsoft.PowerBI.DataMovement.Pipeline.Diagnostics.dll`

As an alternative to the gateway application setting, both configuration files can be accessed and modified at the installation location of the gateway, such as `C:\Program Files\On-premises data gateway`.

In the following example, a gateway log file with verbose logging has been copied into Excel and filtered for a specific request ID:

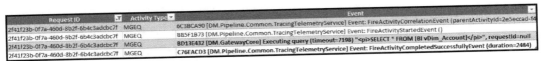

Request ID	Activity Type	Event
2f41f23b-0f7a-460d-8b2f-6b4c3adcbc7f	MGEQ	6C3BCA90 [DM.Pipeline.Common.TracingTelemetryService] Event: FireActivityCorrelationEvent (parentActivityId=2e5eccad-f4
2f41f23b-0f7a-460d-8b2f-6b4c3adcbc7f	MGEQ	BB5F1B73 [DM.Pipeline.Common.TracingTelemetryService] Event: FireActivityStartedEvent ()
2f41f23b-0f7a-460d-8b2f-6b4c3adcbc7f	MGEQ	BD13E432 [DM.GatewayCore] Executing query (timeout=7198) "<pi>SELECT * FROM [BI.vDim_Account]</pi>", requestId=null
2f41f23b-0f7a-460d-8b2f-6b4c3adcbc7f	MGEQ	C76EACD3 [DM.Pipeline.Common.TracingTelemetryService] Event: FireActivityCompletedSuccessfullyEvent (duration=2484)

Log file output

In the preceding example, a refresh process caused the `SELECT * FROM BI.vDim_Account` query to be executed against an on-premises source via the gateway. The duration of this query was 2.48 seconds (2,484 ms) per the final row containing the `FireActivityCompletedSuccessfullyEvent` log event. Note that column headers are not included in the log files and that the second column of the logs (a GUID) is the **Request ID**. This is the column that can be used to match a query with its completion event and duration.

Performance Monitor counters

Windows performance-monitor counters, specific to both the gateway service and the servers on which the gateway is running, are helpful in assessing workloads relative to available resources. For example, a BI team can determine whether a gateway server has adequate memory available to support the scheduled refreshes of large datasets. Likewise, the performance counters specific to the **On-premises data gateway** can be used to identify spikes or dips in query executions and failures throughout the day. The results of this analysis could suggest adding a gateway instance to a cluster or migrating a gateway instance to a server with additional CPU cores.

The Windows Performance Monitor tool can be used to create a collector set of the necessary counters, as shown in the following image:

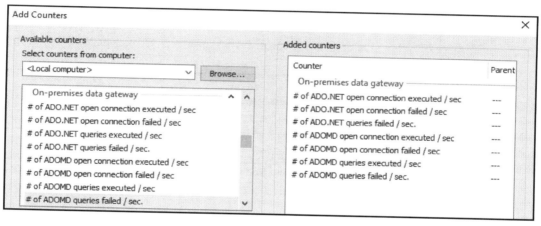

On-premises data gateway counters

As you can see in the preceding image, several of the same counters are available per query type, such as ADO.NET, ADOMD, OLEDB, and mashup. The ADO.NET counters are used by DirectQuery connections and the mashup counters relate to the refresh of imported datasets. Detailed descriptions of all counters and types can be obtained via the Power BI docs website under **Gateways**.

Power BI tools and services are well suited to integrating and analyzing performance-counter data. A detailed paper describing this solution, as well as a sample Power BI Desktop file, is available on the *Insight Quest* blog at `http://bit.ly/2Dssgbh`.

DirectQuery datasets

For datasets built with DirectQuery connections to on-premises sources, authorized users of the gateway source will receive the following message when publishing from Power BI Desktop:

Gateway assigned to the DirectQuery dataset

It's essential that the data source settings (for example, server name, database name) configured for the gateway data source exactly match the entries used by the Power BI dataset (`.PBIX`). Once the DirectQuery dataset has been published to the Power BI service, new reports can be built on top of this dataset via the Power BI service data source described in the *Live connections to Power BI datasets* section of `Chapter 11`, *Creating and Formatting Power BI Reports*.

Single sign-on to DirectQuery sources via Kerberos

Many organizations have made significant investments in scalable on-premises data sources and have implemented user security rules/conditions in these sources. For these organizations, it's often preferable to use DirectQuery data connections that leverage both the resources of the source and the custom security rules. To address this scenario, the **On-premises data gateway** now supports a single sign-on feature that passes the identity of the Power BI user to the data source via Kerberos constrained delegation.

In the following image from the **Manage gateways** portal, the single sign-on setting for a SQL Server data source is exposed:

Username

•••••••••••

Password

•••••••••••

⌄Advanced settings

☐ Use SSO via Kerberos for DirectQuery queries

This will only be applied for DirectQuery queries. Import will use the Username and Password specified in the data source details Learn more

Single sign-on for DirectQuery

By default, the **single sign-on** (**SSO**) feature is not enabled and thus all DirectQuery queries (from any user) will execute via the credentials specified in the source. If enabled, the **user principal name** (**UPN**) of the user viewing content in the Power BI service is mapped to a local Active Directory identity by the gateway. The gateway service then impersonates this local user when querying the data source.

Kerberos constrained delegation must be configured for the gateway and data source to properly use the SSO for DirectQuery feature. This involves changing the service account of the gateway to a domain account, as discussed in the *Configuration of on-premises gateway* section earlier in this chapter. Additionally, an SPN may be needed for the domain account used by the gateway service and delegation settings must be configured for this account as well. Detailed instructions on configuring Kerberos constrained delegation can be found here: http://bit.ly/2DsTI82.

Currently this feature is only available for SQL Server, SAP HANA, and Teradata sources, but Oracle and other common DirectQuery sources are planned.

Live connections to Analysis Services models

For on-premises SSAS models that Power BI users will access via Live connections, an SSAS data source must be added in the **Manage gateways** portal. Critically, the credentials entered for this data source in the **Manage gateways** portal must match an account that has server administrator permissions for the SSAS instance. The following image, from **SQL Server Management Studio (SSMS)**, exposes the server administrator accounts for the ATLAS instance of SSAS Tabular:

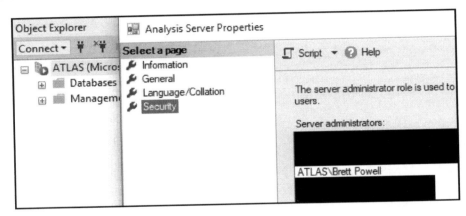

Analysis Services Server administrators

Both SSAS and Azure Analysis Services instances can be accessed via SSMS. Additionally, the **Analysis Server Properties** dialog from the preceding image can be accessed by right-clicking the instance name. Identification of the Power BI user by SSAS will only work if a server admin account is specified and thus used when opening connections.

User authentication to SSAS is based on the `EffectiveUserName` property of SSAS. Specifically, the user principal name (for example, `JenL@FrontlineAnalytics.onmicrosoft.com`) of the Power BI user is passed into this property and this email address must match a UPN within the local Active Directory. This allows the SSAS model to apply any row-level security roles built into the model for the given Power BI user.

Azure Analysis Services refresh

To support the data refresh operations of Azure Analysis Services models based on on-premises sources, an **On-premises data gateway** resource is created in Azure and associated with the Azure Analysis Services resource. As shown in the following image, the gateway resource is located in the same region (**North Central US**) as the Power BI service tenant:

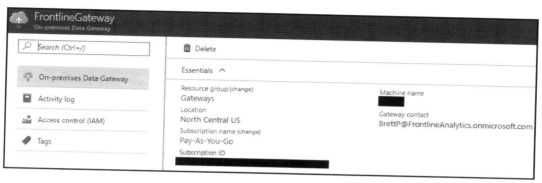

On-premises data gateway resource in Azure portal

To create a gateway resource in Azure (for example, **FrontlineGateway**), either search the Azure marketplace for **On-premises data gateway** in the Azure portal or use the link (**Create a gateway in Azure**) provided on the **Status** page of the **On-premises data gateway** application. Like other resources in Azure, an Azure subscription and resource group are required to create and configure the gateway resource. However, the gateway resource only stores metadata to reference an existing gateway installation and thus there are no billing charges associated with the gateway itself. The name of the existing (and running) gateway should appear on the **Installation name** property of the **Create connection gateway** blade in the Azure portal.

Once created, the gateway resource in Azure must be associated with the Azure
Analysis Services resource, as shown in the following image:

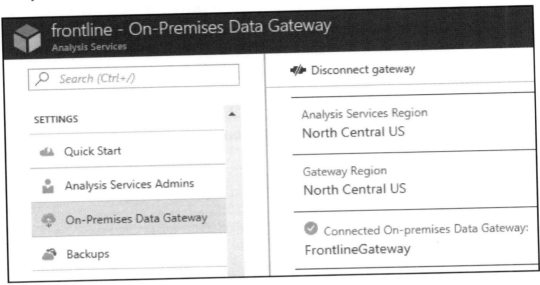

Azure Analysis Services connected to gateway

In the preceding example, the AAS resource (**frontline**) has been configured to use
the **FrontlineGateway** resource via the **On-premises data gateway** setting for AAS
resources. The **FrontlineGateway**, in turn, references an existing installation of the
On-premises data gateway. Because the AAS resource is associated with the gateway
in the Azure portal, it does not need to be added as a data source in the manage
gateways portal of Power BI.

From a user authentication and row-level security standpoint, Live connection
queries against AAS provide the Azure Active Directory account of the user.
Therefore, the row-level security models built into AAS models must reflect these
AAD identities to be enforced.

Dashboard cache refresh

Dashboard tiles based on import mode datasets are refreshed when the dataset itself is refreshed in the Power BI service. For dashboard tiles based on DirectQuery or Live connection datasets, however, the Power BI service maintains a scheduled cache refresh process for updating dashboard tiles. The purpose of this cache is to ensure dashboards are loaded extremely quickly since, as described in `Chapter 13`, *Designing Power BI Dashboards and Architectures,* many users, such as executives, exclusively rely on dashboards.

By default, the dashboard tile cache is refreshed once every hour. As shown in the following image, owners of these datasets can configure this refresh process to occur as frequently as every **15 minutes** or as infrequently as once per week:

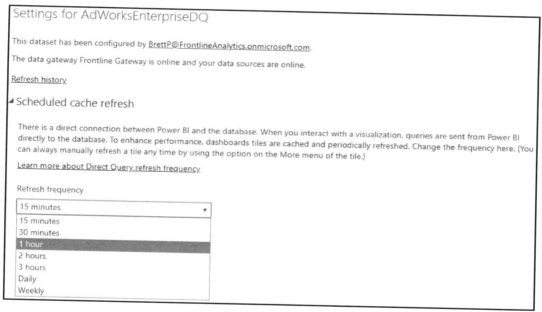

Scheduled cache refresh

In the preceding example, a Power BI dataset (`AdWorksEnterpriseDQ`) containing a DirectQuery connection to an on-premises SQL Server database has been published to an app workspace in Power BI. The **Scheduled cache refresh** option will not appear for datasets that import their data—these datasets can use the scheduled refresh dialog described earlier in this chapter. Per the settings dialog, the dataset is associated with an **On-premises data gateway (Frontline Gateway)**, thus allowing queries from the Power BI service to reach the on-premises database.

 It can be helpful to run a trace on the source system to capture the volume and performance characteristics of the queries associated with dashboard cache refreshes. If the dataset is used by several dashboards with many tiles and/or complex tiles with many data points, the cache refresh process can be expensive on the source system. The trace can be started immediately prior to a scheduled cache refresh or, if only one dashboard is being refreshed, prior to a manual dashboard tile refresh.

Switching the **Refresh frequency** to **15 minutes** causes the queries associated with each dashboard tile dependent on the DirectQuery dataset to be submitted in 15-minute intervals, as shown in the following image:

ACTIONS	LAST REFRESH	NEXT REFRESH
⬤ ○ ▢ ⤙ ⋯	1/15/2018, 8:34:10 PM	1/15/2018, 8:49:10 PM

Dataset menu in Power BI service

In addition to the **Last Refresh** and **Next Refresh** columns, dataset owners can also access the **Refresh history** from the same dataset settings menu used to configure the **Scheduled cache refresh**.

 Users can also manually refresh dashboard tiles via the **Refresh dashboard tiles** menu option. This option, exposed via the ellipsis in the top-right corner of dashboards, also sends queries to the DirectQuery or Live connection data source like the scheduled cache refresh.

Power BI reports (.PBIX files) containing either a Live connection to an Analysis Services server (AAS or SSAS) or a DirectQuery connection to the data source will be represented as distinct datasets in the Power BI service. Power BI reports created based on these published datasets will utilize the scheduled cache refresh configured for the given source dataset. The *Live connections to Power BI datasets* section in Chapter 11, *Creating and Formatting Power BI Reports* contains details and examples of these reports.

The optimal cache refresh frequency will depend on the business requirements for data freshness, the frequency with which the source database is updated, and the available resources of the source system. For example, if the top priority of the source system is OLTP transactions and the dashboard queries are resource intensive, it may be preferable to limit the refresh frequency to once a day. However, if the very latest data updates are of top value to the business users and ample resources are available to the source system, a 15-minute cache refresh schedule may be appropriate.

Unlike dashboards, a cache is not maintained for Power BI reports based on DirectQuery or Live connection datasets. These reports issue queries as the user interacts with report visuals and therefore can result in some latency. The degree of this latency depends on many factors, including the hardware resources of the data source, whether Power BI Premium capacity has been provisioned, and the complexity or density of the report visuals being analyzed. Chapter 19, *Scaling with Premium and Analysis Services* is dedicated to scalability and performance-related topics.

Summary

This chapter reviewed the primary planning and management scenarios for the On-premises data gateway. This included alternative-solution architectures requiring a gateway, methods for distributing workloads across multiple gateways, and ensuring high availability via gateway clusters. Additionally, this chapter described the process of administering a gateway, including the configuration of data sources and the authorization of users or groups to utilize the gateway per source. Finally, the primary tools and processes for troubleshooting and monitoring the gateway were reviewed.

While this chapter focused on using the Power BI Cloud service with on-premises data, the following chapter highlights the option to deploy Power BI exclusively on-premises via the Power BI Report Server. This includes the publication, refresh, and management of Power BI reports on-premises as well as the primary differences between the Power BI Report Server and the Power BI service.

16
Deploying the Power BI Report Server

The Power BI Report Server is a modern enterprise-reporting platform that allows organizations to deploy, manage, and view Power BI reports, in addition to other report types, internally. The Power BI Report Server allows large numbers of users to view and interact with the same reports created in Power BI Desktop in a modern web portal and via the same Power BI mobile applications used with the Power BI cloud service. The Power BI Report Server addresses a current and sometimes long-term need to maintain a fully on-premises BI solution that includes both data sources and reports. Additionally, the Power BI Report Server can be used in combination with the Power BI service to support scenarios in which only certain reports need to remain on premises.

The Power BI Report Server has been built on top of **SQL Server Reporting Services (SSRS)**, and therefore organizations can continue to utilize existing paginated SSRS reports and familiar management skills to easily migrate to the Power BI Report Server. In addition to Power BI and paginated reports, the **Office Online Server (OOS)** can be configured to allow for viewing and be interacting with Excel reports in the same report server portal, thus providing a consolidated hub of BI reporting and analysis. Moreover, when provisioned with Power BI Premium capacity, organizations can later choose to migrate on-premises Power BI reports to dedicated capacity in the Power BI service, without incurring an additional cost.

"Power BI Report Server is extending our journey of giving customers more flexibility in terms of being able to deploy some of their workloads on-premises behind their firewall."

– Riccardo Muti,
Group Program Manager

This chapter reviews the primary considerations in planning and deploying the Power BI Report Server. This includes feature compatibility with the Power BI service, licensing and configuration details, and an example deployment topology. Additionally, management and administration topics are reviewed, including the scheduled data refresh of Power BI reports and monitoring server usage via execution log data.

In this chapter, we will review the following topics:

- Planning for the Power BI Report Server
- Installation and configuration of Power BI Report Server
- Power BI Desktop for Power BI Report Server
- Power BI Report Server Portal
- Scheduled data refresh and Live connections
- Power BI mobile applications
- Power BI Report Server administration
- Scaling Power BI Report Server

Planning for the Power BI Report Server

Prior to any licensing or deployment planning, an organization should be very clear on the capabilities of the Power BI Report Server in relation to the Power BI cloud service. The Power BI Report Server does not include many of the features provided by the Power BI cloud service, such as the dashboards described in Chapter 13, *Designing Power BI Dashboards and Architectures*, or the apps, email subscriptions, Analyze in Excel, and data alert features reviewed in Chapter 17, *Creating Power BI Apps and Content Distribution*. Although new features are included with new releases of the Power BI Report Server, the Power BI Report Server is not intended or planned to support the features provided in the Power BI cloud service.

Additionally, for organizations using SSRS, it's important to understand the differences between the Power BI Report Server and SSRS, such as the upgrade and support lifecycle. Mapping the capabilities and the longer-term role of the Power BI Report Server in relation to a current and a longer-term BI architecture and cloud strategy is helpful in planning for the Power BI Report Server.

The following list of five questions can help guide the decision to deploy the Power BI Report Server:

- Do some or all reports currently need to stay on-premises and behind a corporate firewall?
    - Power BI Report Server is a fully on-premises solution designed to meet this specific scenario
    - Alternatively, organizations can deploy the Power BI Report Server to virtual machines provisioned in Azure
- Is SSRS currently being used?
    - Power BI Report Server includes SSRS and thus allows a seamless migration from an existing SSRS server
    - Paginated (.RDL) reports are not currently supported in the Power BI service
- Are the primary data sources for reports located on-premises and expected to remain on-premises?
    - As an on-premises solution, the On-premises data gateway is not required to connect to on-premises sources
    - As discussed in the previous chapter, some degree of query latency, hardware, and administrative costs are incurred by using on-premises data sources with the Power BI service
- Are there features exclusive to the Power BI Service that is needed?
    - The Power BI Report Server is limited to rendering Power BI reports (.PBIX) files, as will be discussed in the following section
- Will large import mode Power BI datasets be needed or will the Power BI reports use DirectQuery and Live connections?
    - The size of files that can be uploaded to the Power BI Report Server for **Scheduled refresh** is limited to 2 GB
    - Additionally, unlike the Power BI service, a single Power BI dataset cannot be used as a source for other reports
    - With Power BI Premium capacity in the Power BI Service, 10 GB and larger files (datasets) are supported

Given these considerations, organizations with significant on-premises investments or requirements should consider the Power BI Report Server as at least part of their BI architecture. One example of this is a large on-premises data warehouse with many existing paginated (.RDL) SSRS reports built against it.

As described in the *Hardware and user licensing* section later in this chapter, new Power BI reports deployed to the Power BI Report Server can later be migrated to the Power BI cloud service via the same licenses. For example, a group of related Power BI reports initially published to a folder on the Power BI Report Server could later be uploaded to an app workspace in the Power BI service. The app workspace could be assigned Power BI Premium capacity and thus the reports could be distributed to all users, including Power BI Free users, via an app, as per Chapter 17, *Creating Power BI Apps and Content Distribution*. In addition to a straightforward migration path, many features exclusive to the Power BI service, such as dashboards, can leverage reports originally deployed to the Power BI Report Server.

Feature differences with the Power BI service

The Power BI Report Server renders Power BI reports (PBIX files) for data visualization and exploration, just like the Power BI web service. In terms of Power BI features and functionality, this is the essential scope of the Power BI Report Server. For users or organizations inexperienced with Power BI concepts (datasets, reports, and dashboards) and the Power BI service, these reports may be considered to be dashboards, and many of the additional features provided by the Power BI service, such as dashboards, app workspaces, and apps may not be known or utilized.

Although viewing and interacting with Power BI reports is clearly central to Power BI, Power BI as a **Platform-as-a-Service (PaaS)** and **Software-as-a-Service (SaaS)** cloud offering provides many additional benefits beyond the standard infrastructure cost and maintenance benefits of a cloud solution. These additional features support content management, collaboration, and the managed distribution of content throughout the organization. Prior to committing to the Power BI Report Server, it's recommended to understand the role and benefit of features exclusive to the Power BI service.

The following list of features is exclusive to the Power BI service:

- Dashboards
- Data Alerts and Notifications
- Email Subscriptions to Dashboards and Reports
- App Workspaces and Apps
- Quick Insights
- Natural Language Query (Q & A)
- Content Packs
- Analyze in Excel
- Power BI Publisher for Excel
- Streaming Datasets
- ArcGIS Map Visual
- R Custom Visuals

The most straightforward guide to the Power BI features supported by the Power BI Report Server is the Power BI Desktop application. With the exception of new Power BI Desktop features (released in the last 1–3 months), which are not yet available in the latest release of the Power BI Desktop version optimized for the Power BI Report Server, almost all features in Power BI Desktop, including the great majority of custom visuals, are supported by the Power BI Report Server. One additional and important exception to this, however, is row-level security. As of the October 2017 release of the Power BI Report Server, row-level security roles implemented in Power BI Desktop, as described in Chapter 10, *Developing DAX Measures and Security Roles*, are not supported in the Power BI Report server.

Several of the Power BI service features not available to the Power BI Report Server have been reviewed in earlier chapters, such as dashboards (Chapter 13, *Designing Power BI Dashboards and Architectures*, and Chapter 14, *Managing Application Workspaces and Content*). Other features exclusive to the Power BI service, including email subscriptions to dashboards and reports, Power BI apps, and data alerts, are reviewed in the following Chapter 17, *Creating Power BI Apps and Content Distribution*. Finally, the ArcGIS Map Visual, which may be added to the Power BI Report Server in 2018, was included in Chapter 12, *Applying Custom Visuals, Animation, and Analytics*.

Content packs of pre-built Power BI datasets, reports, and dashboards for popular online services such as Google Analytics and Salesforce are available from the Microsoft AppSource portal (`http://bit.ly/2n5NB01`) and via the **Get Data** page of the Power BI service. These content packs, or apps, developed and maintained by third parties, allow organizations to get started quickly in analyzing this data with Power BI. Organizational content packs developed within an organization for the purpose of distributing content to users are being replaced by Power BI apps, as described in the following chapter.

As per the *Quick insights* section of `Chapter 12`, *Applying Custom Visuals, Animation, and Analytics*, certain Quick Insights features are now available in Power BI Desktop. Additionally, Q & A (natural language queries) is currently a preview feature in Power BI Desktop. Given the availability of these features in Power BI Desktop, a future release of Power BI Desktop optimized for the Power BI Report Server will very likely include support for these features as well.

Since the Power BI Report Server has been built on top of SSRS, a very mature and robust enterprise reporting platform, it includes several capabilities not currently available in the Power BI service. For example, paginated reports (`.RDLs`) developed by tools such as Report Builder and **SQL Server Data Tools (SSDT)** can be deployed to the Power BI Report Server but not the Power BI service. Additionally, the mobile reports introduced in SQL Server Reporting Services 2016 and built with the Mobile Report Publisher application are also fully supported.

Furthermore, if an **Office Online Server (OOS)** has been deployed on-premises, Excel workbooks with external data connections to sources such as **SQL Server Analysis Services (SSAS)** can also be published to the Power BI Report server portal and interacted with like other reports. The ability to view and interact with Excel reports containing external data connections is not currently available in the Power BI service, but is expected in 2018. Additionally, there are plans to bring SSRS reports (`.RDL` files) to the Power BI Service at some point in the future.

Per the Dynamics 365 Spring 2018 Release Notes (`https://aka.ms/ businessappsreleasenotes`), the ability to publish paginated SSRS reports (`.RDLs`) to Power BI Premium capacity in the Power BI service is expected later in 2018. This new capability will remove the requirement of deploying and managing a Power BI Report Server (or SSRS server) to support these report types. `Chapter 19`, *Scaling with Premium and Analysis Services,* contains additional details on Power BI Premium capabilities exclusive to the Power BI service.

Parity with SQL Server Reporting Services

A Power BI Report Server is 100% compatible with SSRS. A Power BI Report Server can be thought of as a superset of an SSRS server in the sense that both modern Power BI reports and all SSRS features through the latest release of SSRS are included. Therefore, it's not necessary to deploy both an SSRS report server and a Power BI Report Server to support existing SSRS workloads.

> *"There is no reason, except in some edge cases, for you to be running both SSRS and Power BI Report Server."*
>
> *– Christopher Finlan, Senior Program Manager for Power BI Report Server*

It's certainly possible to deploy the Power BI Report Server along with an instance of SSRS. For example, the Power BI Report Server could be dedicated to self-service BI reports built with Power BI Desktop, while the SSRS server could be dedicated to IT developed paginated (`.RDL`) reports.

For the majority of organizations, however, the Power BI Report Server and its modern web portal will be used to consolidate all report types.

There are three main differences between the Power BI Report Server and SQL Server Reporting Services (SSRS):

- Power BI Report (`.PBIX`) files can only be viewed from the Power BI Report Server's web portal
- Excel workbooks (`.XLSX`) can only be viewed from the Power BI Report Server's web portal:
    - This requires the OOS, as described in the *Configuration* section later in this chapter
- The upgrade and support cycles are significantly shorter for the Power BI Report Server:
    - A new version of the Power BI Report Server is released approximately every 4 months
    - Each new version of the Power BI Report Server is supported by Microsoft for 1 year

New versions of SSRS will continue to be tied to the release of SQL Server. For example, SSRS 2017 was made **generally available (GA)** on October 2nd, 2017, along with SQL Server 2017. Although the upgrade cycle has shortened for SQL Server, it doesn't match the pace of innovation from Power BI's monthly release cycles. Therefore, to make new Power BI features available to customers with on-premises deployments, a new Power BI Report Server is released approximately every 4 months.

Unlike versions of SSRS, which continue to receive support such as cumulative updates for years following their release, support for each Power BI Report Server release ends after one year. Therefore, while upgrading to each new version of the Power BI Report Server every 4 months is not required, organizations should plan to upgrade within one year of each version's release to maintain support. Additional information and considerations on upgrade cycles are included in the *Upgrade cycles* section later in this chapter.

 Support for multiple instances per server represents one additional difference between the Power BI Report Server and SSRS. Currently, only one instance of the Power BI Report Server can be installed per server. Therefore, unlike SSRS, virtual machines need to be configured if multiple instances are required for the same server.

There are no plans to deprecate SQL Server Reporting Services or replace it with the Power BI Report Server. However, given the additional features exclusive to the Power BI Report Server and the more frequent release cycle, there are strong reasons to choose Power BI Report Server over SSRS going forward. Additionally, an existing SSRS server can be easily migrated to Power BI Report Server as discussed in the *Migrating from SQL Server Reporting Services* section later in this chapter.

BI teams familiar with SSRS can quickly take advantage of mature features, such as report subscription schedules and role-based user permissions. For organizations running older versions of SSRS, the significant features introduced in SSRS 2016, including the modern web portal and KPIs, can further supplement their BI solution. In summary, the Power BI Report Server allows organizations to continue to fully support existing and new SSRS reports, while also enabling the self-service and data visualization features of Power BI reports.

Data sources and connectivity options

All three connectivity options for Power BI Reports (import, DirectQuery, and Live connection) are supported by the Power BI Report Server. As one example, corporate BI teams could develop DirectQuery and Live connection reports based on a Teradata database and a SQL Server Analysis Services model, respectively. Business users with Power BI Pro licenses, however, could import data from Excel and other sources to the Power BI Desktop version optimized for the Power BI Report Server and publish those reports to the Power BI Report Server.

Power BI reports deployed to the Power BI Report Server cannot currently utilize a single Power BI dataset (PBIX file) as their data source, as described in the Live connections to the *Power BI Datasets* section of `Chapter 11`, *Creating and Formatting Power BI Reports*. Given the resource limitations of the report server and the important goals of reusability and version control, this implies that DirectQuery and Live connection reports are strongly preferred for the current version of Power BI Report Server. However, the ability to reuse a published Power BI dataset (PBIX file) as a source for new Power BI reports is planned for a future release of the Power BI Report Server. Once released, BI teams will be able to isolate dataset design topics and users (such as relationships or DAX measures) from report authors just like with the Power BI service.

Imported Power BI datasets are currently limited to 2 GB file sizes. This compares to the 10 GB file size limit for Power BI datasets published to Premium capacity in the Power BI server. Therefore, if it's necessary to import data to a Power BI report for deployment to the Power BI Report Server; only include the minimal amount of data needed for the specific report.

 Avoid duplicating imported data across many reports by leveraging report pages, slicer visuals, and bookmarks. If import mode reports are required, such as when data integration is needed or when an Analysis Services model is not available, look for opportunities to consolidate report requests into a few PBIX reports that can be shared.

One advantage of the Power BI Report Server is that, as an on-premises solution, the *On-premises data gateway* section described in Chapter 15, *Managing the On-Premises Data Gateway* is not needed. The report server service account, running either as the Virtual Service Account or as a domain user account within the local Active Directory, will be used to connect to data sources. Additional information on this connectivity, including Kerberos constrained delegation, is included in the *Installation and Configuration* section.

Hardware and user licensing

The rights to deploy the Power BI Report Server to a production environment can be obtained by purchasing Power BI Premium capacity or via a SQL Server Enterprise Edition with the Software Assurance agreement. Power BI Premium is the primary and recommended method as this includes both Power BI service (cloud) dedicated capacity and the Power BI Report Server at the same cost. For example, a Power BI Premium P2 SKU includes 16 v-cores of dedicated capacity in the Power BI service, as well as the right to deploy the Power BI Report Server to 16 processor cores on-premises. Furthermore, the cores provisioned via Power BI Premium can be allocated to on-premises hardware; however, the organization chooses them, such as one Power BI Report server with all 16 cores, or two Power BI Report servers with eight cores, each in a scale-out deployment.

A **Power BI Premium P2** SKU is highlighted in the following screenshot from the **Purchase Services** page of the Office 365 admin center:

Power BI Premium P2

$9,995.00 instance/month

Power BI capacity dedicated to your organization, unlocking unlimited content distribution and dependable performance. P2 offers 16 virtual cor ...

Office 2016 desktop & mobile apps
Not included

Office 365 services

...

Power BI Premium SKU

As shown here, premium capacities represent a subscription-based model, such as $10,000 per month with an annual commitment. Currently, a month-to-month P1 SKU with eight v-cores (P1 for Students) is available, which doesn't require an annual commitment.

By licensing Power BI Report Server via Power BI Premium capacity, an organization can choose to migrate Power BI reports to the Power BI service (cloud) at a future date. For example, some or all of the Power BI reports deployed to the Power BI Report Server in 2018 could be migrated to app workspaces hosted in dedicated Power BI Premium capacity within the Power BI service in 2019. Additionally, as described in the *Hybrid Deployment Models* section later in this chapter, an organization could allow certain solutions to be developed with the dedicated Premium capacity in the Power BI cloud service, while other reports could remain on-premises on the Power BI Report server.

Once Power BI Premium capacity has been purchased, a product key required to install the report server will be available in the Power BI admin portal. The process for retrieving this key from within the Power BI service is included in the *Installation* section later in this chapter. Additionally, the details of Power BI Premium including the management of premium (dedicated) capacities and the additional capabilities enabled by Premium capacities for deployments to the Power BI service are included in Chapter 19, *Scaling with Premium and Analysis Services*.

As an alternative to licensing via Power BI Premium, organizations with SQL Server Enterprise Edition with Software Assurance can use their existing SQL Server licenses to deploy Power BI Report Server.

One of the benefits of the Software Assurance program has been to provide access to new versions of SQL Server as they're released, and this benefit has been extended to include the Power BI Report Server. For example, if an organization has already licensed 24 cores to run SQL Server Enterprise Edition, with a Software Assurance agreement they could allocate 8 of those 24 cores to a server for running Power BI Report Server. Just like current SQL Server licensing, additional SQL Server products (such as SQL Server Integration Services) could also be deployed on the same eight-core server. It's essential to realize that, unlike Power BI Premium, this licensing method does not provide access to the many additional features exclusive to the Power BI (cloud) service described earlier in this chapter.

Pro licenses for report authors

In addition to licensing for the Power BI Report Server, each user who will be publishing Power BI reports (PBIX files) to the report server's web portal will also require a Power BI Pro license. In most large deployments, these are typically a small number of BI report developers and self-service BI power users, as described in the Power BI Licenses section of Chapter 7, *Planning Power BI Projects*.

Users who only view and optionally interact with reports published to the Power BI Report Server do not require Power BI Pro licenses or even Power BI Free licenses. This licensing structure (Premium Capacity + Pro licenses for report authors) further aligns the Power BI Report Server with the Power BI service. For example, similar to the *Hybrid deployment models* described in the following section, a report author with a Power BI Pro license would have the ability to publish one report to the Power BI Report Server and a different report to an app workspace in the Power BI service.

Alternative and hybrid deployment models

The Power BI Report Server, along with the ability to embed Power BI content into custom applications, gives organizations the option to choose a single deployment model (such as Power BI Report Server only) or a combination of deployment models in which both the Power BI Report Server and the Power BI service are utilized for distinct scenarios or content.

With both the Power BI service and the Power BI Report Server available via Power BI Premium capacity, an organization could choose to match the deployment model to the unique needs of a given project, such as using the Power BI Report Server if traditional paginated reports are needed, or if the reports need to remain on-premises for regulatory reasons.

For example, one Power BI solution for the marketing organization could be completely cloud-based, such as using Azure SQL Database as the source for Power BI reports and dashboards hosted in the Power BI service. A different solution for the sales organization could use the On-premises data gateway to query a SQL Server Analysis Services model (on-premises) from the Power BI service, as described in Chapter 15, *Managing the On-Premises Data Gateway*. Finally, for scenarios in which both the data source(s) and the report/visualization layer must remain on-premises, such as for sensitive reports used by the human resources organization. Power BI reports developed against on-premises sources could be deployed to the Power BI Report server.

The following diagram describes the essential architecture of three distinct Power BI solutions: cloud only, cloud and on-premises, and on-premises only:

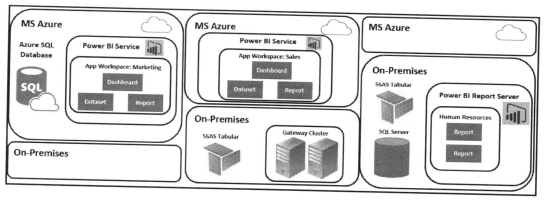

Power BI solutions by deployment model

In this example, Power BI reports and dashboards developed for the marketing department are hosted in the Power BI service and based on an Azure SQL Database. The sales team also has access to dashboards and reports in the Power BI service, but the queries for this content utilize a Live connection to an on-premises SSAS model via the On-premises data gateway. Finally, Power BI reports developed for the human resources department based on on-premises data sources are deployed to the Power BI Report Server.

BI solutions that utilize PaaS and SaaS cloud offerings generally deliver reduced the overall cost of ownership, greater flexibility (such as scale up/down), and more rapid access to new features. For these reasons, plans and strategies to migrate on-premises data sources to equivalent or superior cloud solutions, such as Azure SQL Data Warehouse and Azure Analysis Services, is recommended.

If multiple Power BI deployment models are chosen, BI teams should understand and plan to manage the different components utilized in different models. For example, identify the administrators, hardware, and users of the On-premises data gateway. Likewise, identify the Power BI service administrators and the tenant settings to apply, as described in Chapter 18, *Administering Power BI for an Organization*. Additionally, as discussed in the *Upgrade cycles* section later in this chapter, organizations can choose either a single Power BI Desktop version to utilize for both the Power BI Report Server and the Power BI service, or run separate versions of Power BI Desktop side by side.

BI teams responsible for managing these more complex deployments should have monitoring in place to understand the utilization and available resources of the alternative deployment models. For example, rather than adding resources to a Power BI Report Server or adding another report server in a scale-out deployment, certain Power BI reports could be migrated to available to premium capacity in the Power BI service. The Power BI Premium capacities section in Chapter 18, *Administering Power BI for an Organization*, includes details on the premium capacity monitoring provided in the Power BI service.

Report Server reference topology

The four main components of a Power BI Report Server deployment include the report server instance, the **Report Server Database**, **Active Directory**, and the data sources used by the reports. The **Active Directory** domain controller is needed to securely authenticate requests by both the data sources and the report server.

In the following diagram, a **SQL Server** database and an **SSAS Tabular** model are used as the data sources by the report server:

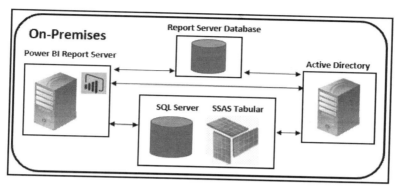

Power BI Report Server reference topology

In the diagram, the **Report Server Database** is hosted on a separate server than the **Power BI Report Server**. This is recommended to avoid competition for resources (CPU, memory, and network) between the **Power BI Report Server** and the **SQL Server** database engine instance required for the **Report Server Database**. Additional information on the **Report Server Database** and configuring this remote connection is included in the following sections.

Installation

Once capacity (cores) to deploy the Power BI Report Server has been obtained, teams can prepare to install and configure the environment by downloading the report server software and the version of Power BI Desktop optimized for the Power BI Report Server.

Both the report server installation software and the report server version of Power BI Desktop can be downloaded from the Microsoft download center (`http://bit.ly/2As4E4w`), as shown in the following screenshot:

Note: There are multiple files available for this download. Once you click on the "Download" button, you will be prompted to select the files you need.

Version:	Date Published:
14.0.600.442	1/10/2018
File Name:	**File Size:**
PBIDesktopRS.msi	132.4 MB
PBIDesktopRS_x64.msi	153.9 MB
PowerBIReportServer.exe	231.9 MB

Power BI Report Server installation files

Here, the **Details** menu exposes the version of the software associated with the given release. In this example, the version **14.0.600.442** corresponds to the October 2017 version of the Power BI Report Server. The **Advanced** download options link at the top of the Power BI Report Server site (`https://powerbi.microsoft.com/en-us/report-server`) also links to the MS download center.

To install Power BI Report Server to a production environment, a product key will need to be obtained from either the Power BI service or the Microsoft Volume Licensing Service Center. Additionally, teams should be aware of hardware and software requirements and other configuration settings, as described in the following sections.

Hardware and software requirements

An instance of the SQL Server Database Engine from 2008 or later must be available to configure the Power BI Report Server. Each Power BI Report Server instance, such as **ATLAS\PBIRS** requires both a Report Server Database and a related report server temporary database on the same instance of the database engine. The Report Server Database stores content, such as reports, schedule definitions, folders, data sources, and the credentials for report data sources. The report server temporary database stores cached reports, session and execution data, and work tables generated by the report server.

Both the Report Server Database and the report server temporary databases should be regularly backed up but not modified or tuned. In a restore operation, if the temporary database is not backed-up, it will have to be recreated. If a backed up temporary database is used in a restore operation, the contents of the database should be deleted and the report server windows service should be restarted.

The Power BI Report Server (and SSRS) also requires access to a Read-Write Domain controller to properly administer the service. The Netdom command-line tool for Windows Server can be used to determine whether the domain controller is read-only or read-write. Specifically, the `netdom query dc` command will return only writable domain controllers.

For the report server instance machine, an operating system of Windows Server 2012 or later is required, as is 1 GB of RAM, 1 GB of available hard-disk space, and an X64 processor with a clock speed of 1.4 GHz or higher. 4 GB of RAM and an X64 processor with a 2.0 GHz or a faster clock speed is recommended. Additional hard disk space will be required on the database server hosting the Report Server Database and the temporary database.

Analysis Services Integrated

The same columnar, in-memory OLAP database engine used by Analysis Services Tabular models and Power BI datasets is now built into the Power BI Report Server. This engine is used to render Power BI reports containing imported data (import mode) and DirectQuery connections. Therefore, if import mode Power BI datasets (PBIX files) will be deployed to the report server, especially large import mode files (100 MB+), a significantly greater amount of RAM will be needed on the server hosting the Power BI Report Server instance than typical reporting services deployments. Additionally, the **Scheduled refresh** operations for these large import mode reports will require both RAM and CPU resources, and this should be planned for.

The requirement for additional RAM could be significantly mitigated if the Live connections to Power BI datasets feature described in `Chapter 11`, *Creating and Formatting Power BI Reports*, is made available in a future release of the Power BI Report Server. In this scenario, similar to Power BI service deployments, a single import mode dataset (PBIX file) and its data refresh process could support many Power BI reports.

Alternatively, if the Power BI reports deployed to the Power BI Report Server will use Live connections or DirectQuery connections to data sources, the Power BI Report server will have significantly lower resource requirements. As with deployments to the Power BI service, the main driver of performance for Live connection and DirectQuery reports will be the data source receiving the query requests from the Power BI Report Server.

Retrieve the Report Server product key

If Power Premium capacity has been purchased, the Power BI Report Server product key can be retrieved from the Power BI admin portal. The Power BI admin portal can be accessed by either an Office 365 global administrator or a user assigned to the Power BI service administrator role. For these users, a link to the **Admin portal** will be exposed from the gear icon in the top-right corner of the Power BI service:

Power BI Admin portal link

The Power BI service administrator role and the assignment of this role in Office 365 were introduced in the *Power BI Project roles* section of Chapter 7, *Planning Power BI Projects*. Additionally, Chapter 18, *Administering Power BI for an Organization*, provides granular details on the **Tenant settings** available in the Power BI Admin portal and other topics related to governing Power BI deployments.

In the following screenshot, a Power BI service administrator has accessed the **Capacity settings** menu of the **Admin portal**:

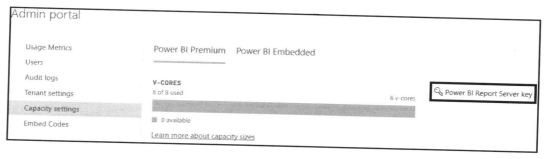

Power BI admin portal: Capacity settings

Clicking the **Power BI Report Server key** icon on the far right of the **Capacity settings** menu launches a dialog containing the key. This 25-character key value can be copied and used to complete the installation of the server:

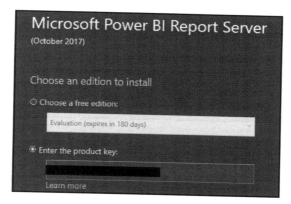

Installation of Power BI Report Server

If Power BI Report Server is being licensed via SQL Server Enterprise Edition with Software Assurance, the product key can be downloaded from the Microsoft **Volume Licensing Service Center** (**VLSC**) via the following link: http://bit.ly/2rqefW1.

An instance of the SQL Server Database Engine is not required to complete the standalone installation of the Power BI Report Server. However, as discussed in the *Hardware and software requirements* section, a SQL Server database engine instance is required to configure the report server. The report server is not available until it's been configured, as described in the *Configuration* section.

Migrating from SQL Server Reporting Services

There is not an in-place upgrade from SSRS to the Power BI Report Server. However, migrating an existing instance of SSRS running in **Native** mode to Power BI Report Server can be accomplished via the following steps:

1. Back up the database, application, and configuration files of the existing SSRS instance:
   - The encryption key of the SSRS instance should also be backed up
   - The configuration files can be found within the SQL Server installation directory (`<install directory>\Reporting Services\Report Server`), as shown in the following screenshot:

Name	Date modified	Type	Size
web	6/5/2016 10:36 AM	XML Configuration File	6 KB
rssrvpolicy	6/5/2016 10:36 AM	XML Configuration File	10 KB
rsreportserver	6/5/2016 10:44 AM	XML Configuration File	19 KB
ReportService2010	2/9/2016 7:19 PM	ASP.NET Web Service	1 KB
ReportService2006	2/9/2016 7:19 PM	ASP.NET Web Service	1 KB
ReportService2005	2/9/2016 7:19 PM	ASP.NET Web Service	1 KB
ReportExecution2005	2/9/2016 7:19 PM	ASP.NET Web Service	1 KB

Reporting Services config

   - The default installation directory for SSRS is `C:\Program Files\Microsoft SQL Server\MRS13.MSSQLSERVER`

2. Clone the Report Server Database hosting the reports for the instance of SSRS.

3. Install the Power BI Report Server instance via the `PowerBIReportServer.exe` file described earlier in this section; this installation can be on the same server as the existing SSRS instance.

4. Configure the Power BI Report Server instance to connect to the cloned database via the Report Server Configuration Manager application:
   - Additionally, also from the Report Server Configuration Manager, restore the backed-up encryption key
   - The reports from the existing SSRS instance will then appear in the Power BI Report Server web portal
   - The Report Server Configuration Manager is included with the installation of Power BI Report Server

The following screenshot from Report Server Configuration Manager gives the option to modify the database of the **ATLAS\PBIRS** Power BI Report Server instance:

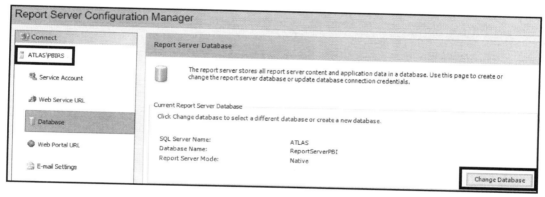

Report Server Configuration Manager

In scenarios where the hardware or topology of a Power BI Report Server deployment needs to change, the same four-step migration process outlined here applies when migrating an instance of Power BI Report Server to a different server. The only exception is that unlike the SSRS (**Native** mode) to Power BI Report Server migration, new and existing instances of Power BI Report Server must be installed on separate servers.

Migrating from SSRS instances in SharePoint-integrated mode is more complex, as it involves copying content from the SharePoint environment to the Power BI Report Server via report server command-line utilities, such as rs.exe. Of course, if the volume of reports (.RDL files) to be migrated is limited, the files could be downloaded manually. A sample script for copying SharePoint content to a report server and further documentation on this process is available at the following URL: http://bit.ly/2DoBIs9.

Configuration

Once the standalone installation of the new report server is complete (via the `PowerBIReportServer.exe` file), it's necessary to configure the report server with the Report Server Configuration Manager. This tool can be found within the `Microsoft Power BI Report Server` folder and includes an interface to 10 distinct groups of settings.

Several of these settings are outside the scope of this chapter, but configuring the following four are essential to make a report server operational:

- **Service Account**
- **Web Service URL**
- **Web Portal URL**
- **Database**

Default values are provided for the Web Service URL and Web Portal URL, such as a TCP Port of 80 and the URL of the web portal, respectively. When these four settings have been configured correctly, the Power BI Report Server portal should be accessible from a web browser, as shown in the following screenshot:

Power BI Report Server portal

The web portal for the Power BI Report Server instance here (**ATLAS\PBIRS**) uses the default URL (`<server>/reports`) and the default `brand` package of colors and a logo. Users assigned to the system administrator role of the report server can apply a custom brand package, such as a corporate logo and color scheme, by accessing the Site settings item from the web portal, as shown in the following screenshot:

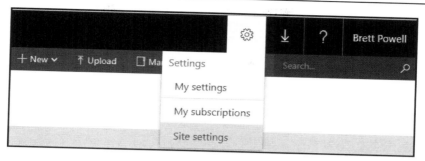

Power BI Report Server portal: Settings

Details on developing a `brand` package to upload and apply to a Power BI Report Server portal are included at the following URL: `http://bit.ly/2F35QcO`.

Service Account

As discussed in the Power BI *Report Server reference topology* section earlier in this chapter, the database server used to host the Report Server Database is usually a separate machine than the report server instance. Therefore, a domain account or a service account with network access must be used to support the remote connection from the report server to the database server containing the Report Server Database. The **Service Account** can be modified via the top tab of the Report Server Configuration Manager, as shown in the following screenshot:

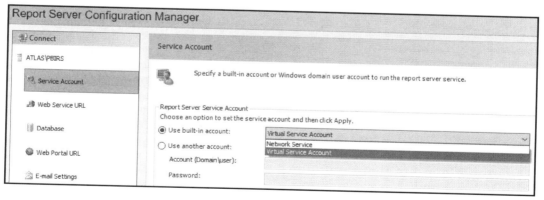

Report Server Service Account

The **Virtual Service Account** is selected as the default service account. If the Report Server Database is created on the same machine (such as **ATLAS**) as the report server instance, this account should have no issues. However, as shown in the preceding screenshot, a **Network Service** account or a domain account can be specified as well, which can access the Report Server Database on a remote server. Additional details and considerations on configuring a Report Server Database connection are included at the following URL: `http://bit.ly/2F5vXA1`.

Remote Report Server Database

If a remote database engine instance is being used, TCP/IP network connectivity will need to be enabled.

This can be accomplished by logging on to the database server and opening the SQL Server Configuration Manager tool, as shown in the following screenshot:

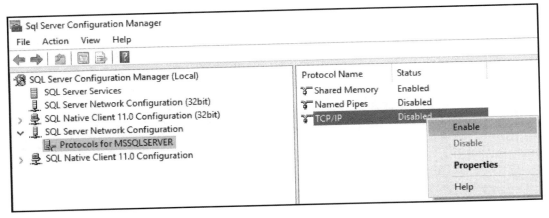

SQL Server Configuration Manager: TCP/IP

Per the screenshot, the SQL Server Network Configuration dropdown menu provides access to the protocols of the database instance (**MSSQLSERVER**). Once the **TCP/IP** protocol has been enabled (right-click | **Enable**), the database instance will need to be restarted. This option is available from the SQL Server Services menu, as shown in the following screenshot:

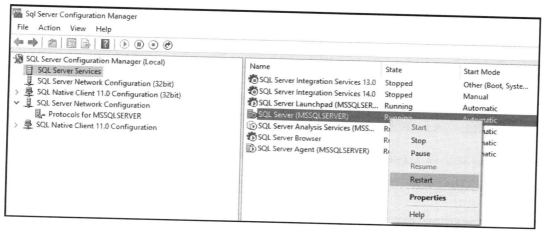

SQL Server Configuration Manager: Restart service

Finally, the port that the SQL Server instance listens on will need to be opened. This is typically port 1433 for **TCP/IP** connections for the default SQL Server database instance.

Office Online Server for Excel Workbooks

One of the most exciting Power BI Report Server features introduced in 2017 was the ability to publish and view Excel workbooks on the report server portal. Although Power BI Desktop is increasingly the preferred choice for data analysis, Excel workbooks and particularly Excel connections to **SQL Server Analysis Services** (**SSAS**) models are still very important to many business users as well. Having both Excel and Power BI in the same portal, in addition to paginated reports (.RDLs) gives BI teams the flexibility to meet many different needs from the same solution.

The **Office Online Server (OOS)** must be installed to enable Excel online functionality in the report server. The full process and technical details for deploying the Office Online Server are available at MS DOCs via the following URL: `https://docs.microsoft.com/en-us/power-bi/report-server/excel-oos`.

 If SQL Server Analysis Services is used as a data source, the account for the Office Online Server should be added as a server administrator for the instance of SSAS. SSAS admin accounts and how connections to SSAS models via these accounts enable row-level security roles to be applied to business users was described in the *Live connections to Analysis Services models* section of `Chapter 15,` *Managing the On-Premises Data Gateway*.

From a Power BI Report Server configuration perspective, the **Office Online Server Discovery Endpoint URL** must be added within the **Advanced** properties of **Site settings** as shown in the following screenshot:

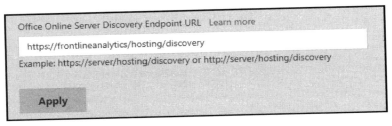

Office Online Server Discovery Endpoint URL   Learn more

https://frontlineanalytics/hosting/discovery

Example: https://server/hosting/discovery or http://server/hosting/discovery

Apply

Report Server portal: Site settings

This URL is the `InternalUrl` used when deploying the OOS server, followed by `/hosting/discovery`. As described at the beginning of this section, **Site settings** (Gear icon | **Site settings**) can only be accessed by users assigned to the **System Administrator** role.

Upgrade cycles

A new version of the Power BI Report Server is released approximately every 4 months. For example, the June 2017 release was followed by an October 2017 version, which included additional features, such as support for imported data in Power BI reports. As of this writing, the next version of Power BI Report Server (following October 2017) will likely be released in the first quarter of 2018. This new version is expected to incorporate the features introduced in the monthly updates to Power BI Desktop in Q4 of 2017, such as the Bookmarks feature described in `Chapter 12`, *Applying Custom Visuals, Animation, and Analytics*.

The following diagram describes the support provided for three hypothetical releases of the Power BI Report Server (October of 2017, February of 2018, and June of 2018):

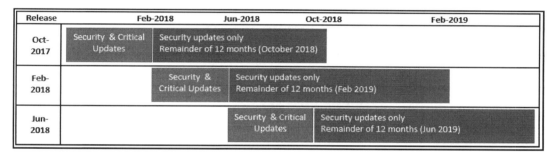

Support for Power BI Report Server releases

Per the diagram, a new release and version (for example, February 2018) are made available approximately four months following the prior version (from October 2017 to February 2018, from February 2018 to June 2018). The latest version of the Power BI Report Server receives both security and critical updates until a new version is available.

At that point, only security updates will be made available for the remainder of the 12 months. Therefore, assuming a new version is released in June of 2018, organizations with the February 2018 release would receive security updates from June of 2018 through February of 2019. At a minimum, these organizations would want to upgrade their environment prior to February of 2019 to maintain security support.

The upgrade cycle is one of the reasons for choosing the Power BI service as this process is managed by Microsoft. For example, new features are automatically added to the Power BI service each month and users can update to the latest release of Power BI Desktop automatically via the Windows Store in Windows 10 operating systems. The main reason Power BI Report Server is not released more frequently, such as every 2 months, is that most IT organizations will not want to upgrade their BI environments more than three to four times per year. Some organizations are expected to skip one or two of the releases per year to coincide with their internal upgrade policies and schedules.

With each release of the Power BI Report Server, a new version of the Power BI Desktop optimized for this version of the Power BI Report server is also released. This is a distinct application from the Power BI Desktop application, which can be downloaded directly from `PowerBI.com` and is described more fully in the following section.

To avoid report rendering errors, it's strongly recommended to synchronize the deployment of the Power BI Report Server with its associated version of the Power BI Desktop. For example, once an upgrade to the February 2018 version of the Power BI Report Server is complete, the February 2018 version of Power BI Desktop optimized for the Power BI Report server will be installed on users machines.

Report Server Desktop Application

As shown in the *Installation* section earlier, a `PowerBIDesktopRS_x64.msi` file is also available for download from the MS Download center. This is the application used to create Power BI reports to be published to this version (October 2017) of the Power BI Report Server.

As shown in the following screenshot, this application can be distinguished from the standard Power BI Desktop via the title bar (here, October 2017) and the **Save As** menu:

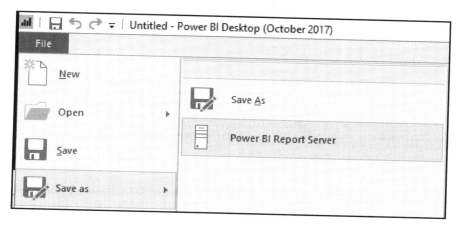

Power BI Desktop optimized for Power BI Report Server

As suggested by the **Save as** menu in the preceding screenshot, a report created via the Power BI Report Server optimized application can be saved directly to the report server. In other words, a PBIX file doesn't necessarily have to be saved to a user's machine—the Power BI Report Server can serve as a network file share. If a report needs to be modified, the user (with a Power BI Pro license), could open the file directly from the web portal described in the following section and save their changes back to the report server.

At some point in the future, a single version of Power BI Desktop that can be used for both the Power BI service and the Power BI Report Server may be released. This has been identified as an important goal that Power BI teams are currently working through, though no timelines have been suggested as of this writing.

Running desktop versions side by side

It's possible to install and run both versions of Power BI Desktop (standard and Report Server optimized) on the same machine. This can be useful in organizations deploying reports to both the Power BI service and the Power BI Report server, as described in the *Hybrid deployment models* section.

For example, the standard Power BI Desktop application could be used to create a new report for an app workspace in the Power BI service, which utilizes the very latest features. The report server optimized version, however, would be used to create or edit reports that are deployed to the Power BI Report Server.

In the following screenshot from a Windows 10 machine, both versions of Power BI Desktop are pinned to the **Start** menu:

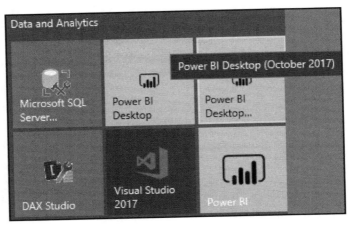

Side-by-side Power BI Desktop

In the preceding screenshot, hovering over the icon or just observing the three dots within the application tile makes it easy to distinguish the applications. As an alternative to running both applications side by side, an organization could choose to exclusively use the Power BI Report Server-optimized version of Power BI Desktop for reports published to both the Power BI service and the Power BI Report Server. This single application approach could simplify the management of the overall deployment but would prevent the utilization of the latest features available in the standard version of Power BI Desktop.

Report Server Web Portal

With the report server installed and configured, Power BI and other types of reports can be published or uploaded to the report server. This content can then be managed, organized into folders, and viewed by users from web browsers and the Power BI mobile application.

In the following screenshot, nine report items have been published to the **Home** page of the web portal:

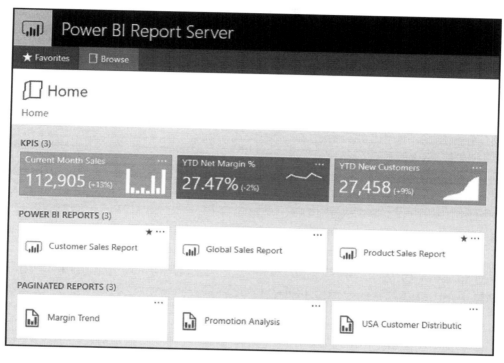

Power BI Report Server Web Portal

As illustrated here, Power BI reports can be easily distinguished from other report types and users can mark reports as favorites (star icon) for quick access from the **Favorites** page.

 KPIs are created exclusively in the web portal via the **New** dropdown at the top. Paginated reports (.RDL files) can be created with the Report Builder application and with Report Server projects in **SQL Server Data Tools** (**SSDT**) for Visual Studio. Additionally, Excel workbooks can be uploaded and the Mobile Report Publisher application can be used to create and publish mobile reports (.rsmobile files).

Clicking a Power BI report, such as the **Customer Sales Report**, opens this report in the browser and provides the same interactive experience of filtering and cross-highlighting available in Power BI Desktop and the Power BI service.

Scheduled data refresh

Power BI reports built with a DirectQuery or Live connection to their data sources execute their queries when the report is accessed by users. For import mode Power BI reports, a **Scheduled refresh** can be configured from the **Manage** page, as shown in the following screenshot:

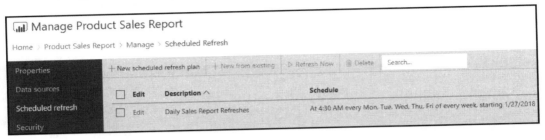

Scheduled refresh of Power BI report

The **Manage** page for a report can be accessed via the ellipsis (three dots) of the report icon or via right-clicking. A custom refresh schedule can be configured specific to a given report, or alternatively, a shared scheduled can be created in the **Site settings** menu (Gear icon | **Site settings**). In the preceding example, the **Product Sales Report** has been assigned to a shared schedule used by other import mode sales reports.

Given the RAM and CPU resources required to complete the refresh process for large import mode Power BI datasets, separate schedules may be configured to split this workload. Additionally, once the feature is available, a single Power BI dataset should be used as the source for other Power BI reports thus eliminating the need to refresh multiple files.

The refresh schedules created in the Power BI Report Server's web portal are implemented as SQL Server Agent jobs. The properties of these jobs (schedule and owner) can be accessed from **SQL Server Management Studio (SSMS)**.

Data source authentication

In addition to configuring a **Scheduled refresh**, report server administrators can use the **Manage** page to modify the data source properties of a report. For example, Power BI reports based on Live connections to **SQL Server Analysis Services (SSAS)** models will attempt to access the SSAS source as the user viewing the report by default. However, assuming that the SSAS instance is installed on a separate machine than the Power BI Report Server, **Kerberos Constrained Delegation (KCD)** is required for this impersonation to function. To enable this data source connection without KCD, while still respecting any row-level security defined in the SSAS model, an administrator can modify the data source properties of the report.

In the following screenshot from the **Manage** report page, a specific user credential is specified for accessing an SSAS source:

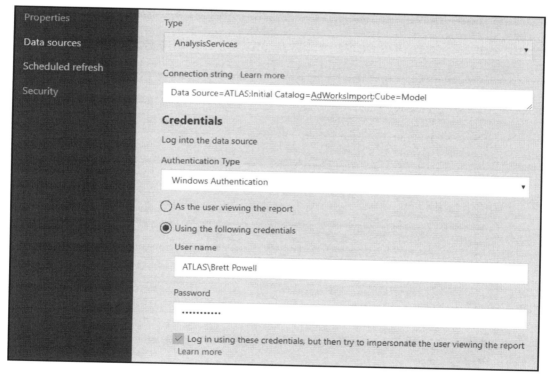

Manage report data source properties

With the check mark option enabled as in the preceding screenshot, once a connection has been opened to the SSAS model via the credential specified (`ATLAS\Brett Powell`), the identity of the user viewing the report can be passed to the source. In this scenario, the credential specified should be a server administrator for the source SSAS instance, thus enabling row-level security to be applied to the user viewing the report. Information on the SSAS server administrator role and user impersonation via the `EffectiveUserName` property is included in the Live connections to *Analysis Services Models* section of `Chapter 15`, *Managing the On-Premises Data Gateway*. Additionally, the following URL contains information on KCD in Windows Server 2012 (`http://bit.ly/2DMCKCj`).

Power BI mobile applications

The same Power BI mobile applications for iOS, Android, and Windows platforms used to access content published to the Power BI service can also be used with the Power BI Report Server. As shown in the following screenshot, the user has opened the **Settings** menu via the global navigation button (≡) to connect to a report server:

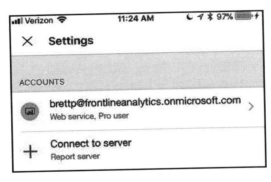

Power BI mobile app: Settings

From the global navigation page, the **Settings** menu can be accessed via the Gear icon at the top of the page. Clicking **Connect to server** opens a page to enter the report server address and to optionally provide a friendly name for the server, such as **AdWorks Report Server** . The server address entered should follow one of two formats:

```
http://<servername>/reports
https://<servername>/reports
```

The connection between the mobile application and the report server can be created by opening a port in the firewall, being on the same network (or VPN), or through a Web Application Proxy from outside the organization. Information on configuring OAuth authentication via Web Application Proxy is available at the following URL `http://bit.ly/2EepW4J`.

Regardless of the platform (iOS or Android), up to five concurrent connections can be created to different report servers. Each report server connection will appear in the Settings menu. Additionally, the **Favorites** menu will display reports and content marked as favorites, whether that content is hosted on a Power BI Report Server or in the Power BI service.

From a business user or consumption standpoint, the **Phone Layout** and the mobile optimizations described in the Mobile Optimized Reports section of `Chapter 11`, *Creating and Formatting Power BI Reports*, are reflected in Power BI reports accessed from the Power BI mobile app. Additionally, the KPIs that can be created in the Power BI Report Server's web portal and the mobile reports created via the Mobile Report Publisher application can also be viewed from the Power BI mobile app.

Report server administration

BI teams deploying the Power BI Report Server will want to limit user access to specific reports and groups of reports contained in folders. For example, users or groups of users in **Active Directory (AD)** will be granted the right to view certain Power BI reports, while other users or groups will have the right to edit content. Additionally, BI teams will be interested in understanding the usage and performance characteristics of the content deployed to the Power BI Report Server.

The Power BI Report Server inherits mature role-based permission features and the execution history log data of SSRS. For more granular analysis of report server activity, administrators can access the **Report Server Service Trace Log**, the **Windows Application Log**, and **Windows Performance Counters**. Additional details on these sources are available at the following URL: (`http://bit.ly/2DFed29`).

Securing Power BI report content

Several built-in security roles are available to assign to users or groups of users. This security assignment can be scoped at the folder level and is by default inherited by all reports within that folder or assigned to a specific report.

In the following screenshot, a security group (**AdWorksSales**) is assigned to the **Browser** role for the **Product Sales Report**:

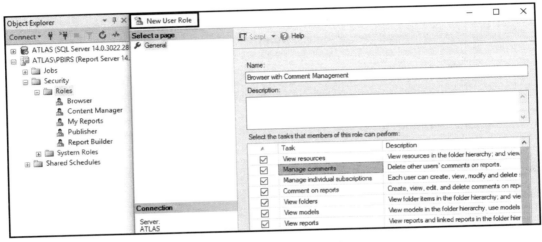

Role security in Power BI Report Server

The security configuration page for both reports and folders can be accessed via the **Manage** page, as described in the *Scheduled data refresh* section earlier in this chapter. By default, the **BUILTIN\Administrators** group is assigned to a **System Administrator system-level** role and the **Content Manager item-level** role of the **Home** folder.

Security roles can also be created and customized in **SQL Server Management Studio (SSMS)**. In the following example, a new user role is created that provides the same permissions as the default **Browser** role (such as **View Reports**), but also enables users to manage the comments posted to reports:

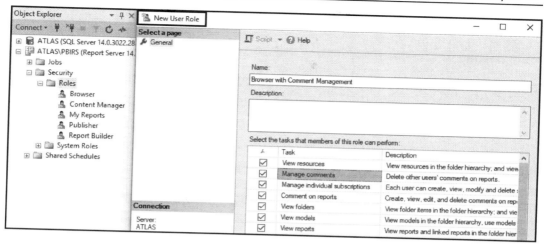

Power BI Report Server Security Roles

As shown in the preceding screenshot, the new role (`Browser with Comment Management`), is allowed to perform seven tasks including managing comments. There are 18 tasks, available to define a user role, which allow users to create, view, and manage report server content. This customization, along with default item level inheritance of a parent item's security, provides report server administrators with robust controls to implement role-based security.

Execution logs

Administrators of Power BI Report Servers can query and potentially build report server monitoring reports on top of execution log data maintained within the Report Server Database. This data, which is stored in the `ExecutionLogStorage` table, is exposed via **Views**, such as `dbo.ExecutionLog3`, and includes all essential attributes of report server execution history. This includes the report requested, the user requesting the report, the time, and the data size of the activity.

The names of the Report Server Database and its host server can be found via the **Database** page of the Report Server Configuration Manager application, as shown in the following screenshot:

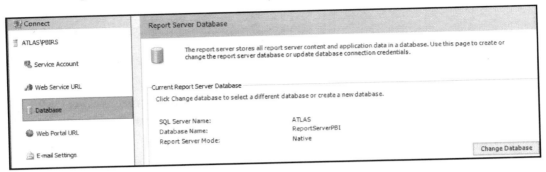

Report Server Configuration Manager: Database

In this example, any ad hoc analyses or standard monitoring reports based on execution log data will need to access the **ReportServerPBI** SQL Server database hosted on the ATLAS server. As described in the *Report Server reference topology* section, the Report Server Database is usually hosted on a separate server than the instance of the Power BI Report Server (**ATLAS\PBIRS**).

In the following screenshot from SQL Server Management Studio (SSMS), the ExecutionLog3 view of the **ReportServerPBI** database is queried to retrieve execution history:

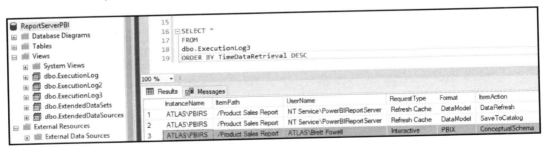

Report server execution log views

As shown in the preceding screenshot, the Format field can be used to query for specific report types, such as Power BI (such as PBIX). The list of columns available in the execution log view and their descriptions are documented at the following URL: (http://bit.ly/2nforva).

The `ExecutionLog` and `ExecutionLog2` views were created in older versions of SSRS. Therefore, if no dependencies exist on these views, `ExecutionLog3` is recommended.

By default, log entries are stored for 60 days. However, report server admins can modify this setting via the **Logging** page of **Server Properties**, as shown in the following screenshot:

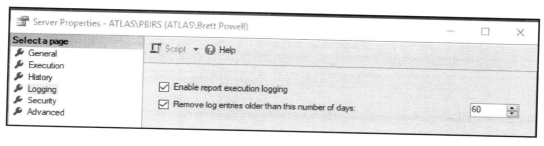

Power BI Report Server Logging properties

Server properties are accessible by right-clicking on the context menu of the Power BI Report Server instance in SSMS. As described in the *Report Server reference topology* section, the report server instance and the Report Server Database (which stores the log data) are usually on separate physical servers.

Scale Power BI Report Server

Both scale-up and scale-out options are available to Power BI Report Server deployments. In a scale-up scenario, additional CPU cores can be provisioned via Power BI Premium capacity or an existing SQL Server Enterprise Edition with Software Assurance agreement. For example, if 16 cores were obtained via Power BI Premium P2 SKU, an additional 8 cores could be purchased via a P1 SKU. Additionally, particularly if import mode Power BI datasets are used, additional RAM can be installed on report servers.

In a scale-out deployment, multiple instances of Power BI Report Server are installed on separate machines. These instances share the same **Report Server Database** and serve as a single logical unit exposed to business users via the web portal.

In the following diagram of a scale-out deployment, business user report requests are distributed between two different instances of the Power BI Report server via a network **Load Balancer**:

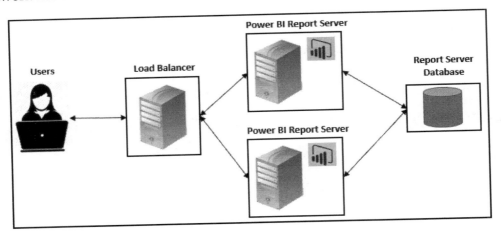

Scale-out Power BI Report Servers

Servers can be added or removed from a scale-out deployment via the **Scale-out Deployment** settings page of the Report Server Configuration Manager application. This is what points each server to the same Report Server Database. In addition, to support for more users and greater usage, scale-out deployment of the report server instances also increases the resiliency of the deployment. To avoid a single point of failure, the scale-out deployment of the report servers can be coupled with high availability features for the Report Server Database, such as SQL Server Always On availability groups or a failover cluster. Additional information on configuring **Always On availability** groups with a Report Server Database is available via the following URL: http://bit.ly/2rLtSqY.

Summary

This chapter reviewed the Power BI Report Server as Microsoft's modern, on-premises solution for enterprise and self-service BI. The main features of the report server and licensing requirements were described and contrasted with the Power BI cloud service. Furthermore, the core processes of installing, configuring, and administering the Power BI Report Server were detailed.

The next chapter returns to the Power BI (cloud) service and focuses on the distribution of published content to end users. This includes the delivery and management of packages of related Power BI content to large groups of users via Power BI apps. Additionally, other content delivery capabilities of the Power BI service are reviewed, including data-driven alerts and scheduled email subscriptions.

Creating Power BI Apps and Content Distribution

17

This chapter walks through all facets of Power BI apps as the primary method for distributing content to groups of users. Given the one-to-one relationship between apps and app workspaces, readers should review Chapter 14, *Managing Application Workspaces and Content*, prior to this chapter.

In addition to apps, other distribution and data access methods are described, including email subscriptions, data alerts, SharePoint Online embedding, and Analyze in Excel. Moreover, guidance is provided on leveraging Microsoft Flow to create custom email alert notifications. Distribution methods available to the Power BI Report Server and the technical details of integrating Power BI content into custom applications are outside the scope of this chapter.

In this chapter, we will review the following topics:

- Content distribution methods
- Power BI apps
- Sharing dashboards and reports
- Data Alerts and notifications
- SharePoint Online embedding
- Report and dashboard subscriptions
- Analyze in Excel
- Custom application embedding

Content distribution methods

One the of the main value propositions of Power BI is the ability for users to access relevant analytical content in a context that's best suited to their needs. For example, many read-only users may log into the Power BI service to view dashboards or reports contained within Power BI apps specific to their role or department. Other users, however, may only receive snapshot images of reports and dashboards via Email Subscriptions or respond to data alert notifications on their mobile device. In other scenarios, certain users may analyze a dataset hosted in Power BI from an Excel workbook while other users could observe a Power BI report embedded within a team SharePoint site.

Organizations can choose to distribute or expose their Power BI content hosted in the Power BI service in one or a combination of methods. The following table summarizes 11 methods of content distribution and data access:

#	Method	Summary Description
1	Power BI apps	• A group of related dashboards and reports within an app workspace is published. • The app can be published to security groups of users enabling wide distribution.
2	Embed in custom applications	• Power BI content is embedded in a custom application or a separate service from Power BI. • Power BI Premium capacity is required to host the embedded content.
3	Share dashboards and reports	• A dashboard and its underlying reports are shared with a user or a group of users. • Alternatively, an individual report can be shared with a user or a group of users.
4	Embed in SharePoint Online	• A Power BI report is embedded in a SharePoint Online site page via the Power BI web part. • Power BI Pro licenses or Power BI Premium capacity can be used to license site users.
5	Email subscriptions	• Subscriptions are configured for dashboards or individual pages of Power BI reports. • Users receive recurring emails with snapshot images of updated dashboard or report page(s).
6	Data alerts	• Alerts are configured for dashboard tiles in the Power BI web service or the mobile applications. • Users receive notification when the conditions the alert conditional rules are triggered.
7	Publish to web	• A Power BI report is made publicly available online via URL or embedding in a website. • The embed codes and the availability of this feature is administered in the Power BI service.
8	Analyze in Excel	• Users with Power BI Pro licenses connect to Power BI datasets via Excel. • The Power BI Publisher for Excel add-in can also be used to connect to Power BI.
9	Live connections in Power BI Desktop	• Users with Power BI Pro licenses connect to Power BI datasets from Power BI Desktop. • Users have the option of publishing PBIX files as reports back to the Power BI web service.
10	Windows Cortana	• The Windows 10 digital assistant is used to render Power BI content as search criteria results. • The Power BI dataset(s) in the Power BI service must be configured to allow Cortana access.
11	Microsoft Teams integration	• Power BI reports can be added as tabs in MS Teams, the Office 365 group chat application. • Power BI Pro licenses or Power BI Premium capacity can be used to license site users.

Content distribution methods in Power BI

The most common corporate BI distribution methods for supporting large numbers of users are Power BI apps and embedding Power BI content into custom applications, that is, embed in custom applications. Several other methods, however, are useful for small-scale and self-service scenarios, such as Analyze in Excel as well as supplements to larger Power BI solutions. Additionally, email subscriptions, data alerts, and embedding options can serve to streamline the analysis process and increase user productivity.

Organizational content packs are currently being replaced by **Power BI Apps** and thus are excluded from the preceding table. The ability to enable users to customize the content that has been distributed to them, which is currently supported via organizational content packs, will soon be supported by Power BI apps. Once Power BI apps deliver the same (and additional) capabilities as organizational content packs, the ability to create new organizational content packs will likely be removed from the Power BI service.

The Power BI mobile application aligns with and supports several of the primary distribution methods including Power BI apps, the sharing of dashboards and reports, and data alerts. Examples of the relationship between the Power BI service, Power BI mobile and other Microsoft applications and services are included in the following sections.

Power BI apps

A Power BI app is a published collection of content from an app workspace. The app can include all or a subset of the dashboards, reports, and any Excel workbooks within an app workspace. Just as app workspaces are intended for the creation and management of Power BI content, apps are intended for the distribution of that content to groups of users. With security and permission to view the app granted, users can view with the dashboards and reports of the app within the Power BI web service or via the Power BI mobile applications.

Microsoft has been clear that Power BI apps are the future of content consumption within organizations and that they will remain simple for users to access. The app workspaces used by report authors and BI professionals to define and manage the apps, however, will become more robust. Two examples of these enhancements include display folders for grouping content within an app as well as the automatic installation of published apps for users.

Licensing apps

Apps are particularly well-suited to large, corporate BI deployments that support the reporting and analysis needs of many users. In most of these scenarios, the great majority of users only need to view certain reports or dashboards and don't require the ability to edit or create any content like Power BI Pro users.

For example, a salesperson within the northwest region of the United States may only briefly access a few dashboards or reports 2 – 3 times per week and occasionally interact with this content, such as via slicer visuals. With the Power BI Premium capacity, these read-only users can be assigned Power BI Free licenses yet still be allowed to access and view published apps.

In the absence of the Power BI Premium capacity, a Power BI Pro license would be required for each user that needs to access the app. In small-scale scenarios, such as when organizations are just getting started with Power BI, purchasing Power BI Pro licenses for all users can be more cost-efficient than Power BI Premium capacities. However, at a certain volume of users, the Power BI Premium capacity becomes a much more cost-efficient licensing model. Additionally, Power BI Premium enables many other features intended to support enterprise deployments. The details of provisioning and managing Power BI Premium capacity is described in `Chapter 19`, *Scaling with Premium and Analysis Services*.

App deployment process

A Power BI app is published from an app workspace and inherits the name of its source workspace. Likewise, an app can only contain content from its source workspace. However, an app does not have to expose all the content of its source workspace. The members of the workspace responsible for publishing and updating the app can utilize the **Included in App** toggle switch to selectively exclude certain dashboards or reports. For example, two new reports that have yet to be validated or tested could be excluded from the app in its initial deployment. Following the validation and testing, the **Included in App** property (on the far right of each report and dashboard) can be enabled and the app can be updated, thus allowing users to access the new reports.

The one-to-one relationship between workspaces and apps underscores the importance of planning for the scope of an app workspace and providing a user-friendly name aligned with this scope. Too narrow a scope could lead to users needing to access many different apps for relevant reports and dashboards. Alternatively, too broad a scope could make it more difficult for users to find the reports and dashboards they need within the app. Additionally, the workspace and app-update process could become less manageable.

A simple publish (or update) process is available within the app workspace for defining the users or security groups who can access the app as well as adding a description and choosing a default landing page for users of the app. The details of the publish process are included in the *Publishing apps* section.

The following diagram and supporting five-step process describe the essential architecture of apps and app workspaces:

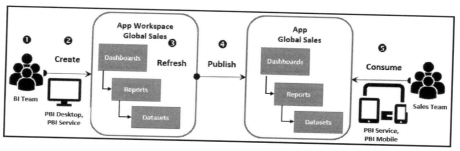

Global Sales app deployment process

In this example, the Global Sales app is accessed by the sales team consisting of 200 users, as per the *Sample Power BI Project template* section in Chapter 7, *Planning Power BI Projects*. Additionally, the row-level security roles described in Chapter 10, *Developing DAX Measures and Security Roles*, and the organizational dashboard architecture reviewed in Chapter 13, *Designing Power BI Dashboards and Architectures*, are utilized by the app.

1. An app workspace is created in the Power BI service and members are added with edit rights to the workspace.
   - Individual members (not security groups) can be added to app workspaces.
2. Members of the app workspace publish reports to the given workspace and create dashboards based on those reports.
   - Power BI Desktop is used to author and publish reports based on a Live connection to a Power BI dataset.
   - Visuals from the published reports are pinned to dashboards, such as European Sales.
      - Dashboards are not required to publish an app.
3. Scheduled data refresh or dashboard cache refresh schedules are configured and the workspace content is validated.
   - As an import mode dataset, the dashboards and reports are updated when the scheduled refresh is completed.

4. A workspace administrator or a member with edit rights publishes an app from the workspace.

- The app is distributed to one or multiple **Azure Active Directory (AAD)** security groups of users.

5. Members of the sales team view and optionally interact with the content in Power BI and Power BI mobile.
- The dashboards and reports would reflect the row-level security roles configured in the dataset.

Certain sales team users requiring Power BI Pro features, such as Analyze in Excel, could utilize the Power BI app as well. Additional content access methods exclusive to Power BI Pro users, such as Email Subscriptions to dashboards and reports, are described later in this chapter.

User permissions

BI teams distributing Power BI content via apps have two layers of control for granting users permission to view the app's dashboards and reports. The first layer is configured by choosing the users or security groups of users when publishing the app in the Power BI service.

In the following image, a security group from AAD (`Global Sales Team`) is specified when publishing the **Global Sales** workspace as an app:

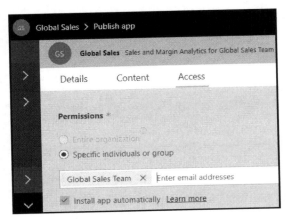

Publish app to a security group

In this example, a Power BI user will need to be included in the `Global Sales Team` security group to see and access the app. The user who published the app will also automatically be granted permission to the app. Additionally, as per the **Install app automatically** checkmark, the published app will be automatically installed for members of the `Global Sales Team`. These users will be able to access the installed app in the Apps menu between the **Recent** and **Shared with me** menu. An example of the Apps menu is included in the *Installing apps* section later in this chapter.

The **Install app automatically** option will only appear if this setting has been enabled in the Power BI admin portal. Specifically, a Power BI admin can enable the **Push apps to end users** setting in the **Tenant settings** page for an entire organization or for specific security groups of users. Microsoft recommends that apps should only be pushed to users during off hours and that teams should verify the availability of the app prior to communicating to a team that the published app is available. The configuration of **Tenant settings** in the Power BI admin portal is described in the following chapter.

The second layer of control is the **row-level security (RLS)** roles configured for the dataset supporting the reports and dashboards. If RLS has been defined within the dataset, all users accessing the app will need to be mapped to one of the RLS roles in the Power BI service.

In the following example, other Azure Active Directory security groups (for example, `BI Admin`) are mapped to four RLS roles:

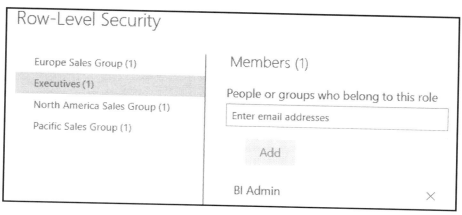

Dataset security role assignment

As per the preceding image, a `BI Admin` security group is mapped to the **Executives** security role. Unlike the other three security roles, which filter the `Sales Territory Group` column of the `Sales Territory` table, the **Executives** role does not have any filters applied.

The user accessing and consuming the app will, therefore, need to be a member of both the `Global Sales Team` security group and one or more of the security groups assigned to an RLS role. If the user is only a member of the `Global Sales Team` security group (from the **App Access** page), the visuals of the dashboard and report will not render.

Publishing apps

Apps are published from app workspaces in the following way:

1. A workspace member with edit rights clicks **Publish** in the top-right corner of the app workspace.
   - Three pages are launched for configuring the app: **Details**, **Content**, and **Access**.
2. On the **Details** page, a short description of the app is entered, such as the following example:

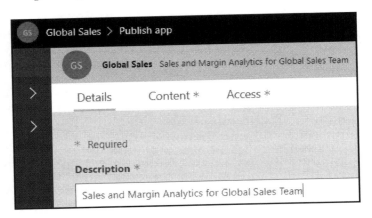

Publish app

3. In addition to the description, a background color for the app can be selected at the bottom of the **Details** page.

4. On the **Content** page, a specific **App landing page** is selected, such as the `Global Sales (dashboard)` in the following example:

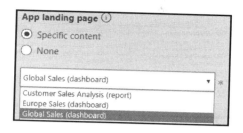

App landing page

In this example, users accessing the Global Sales app will land on the **Global Sales (dashboard)** by default. Alternatively, if **None** is selected, a list view of the dashboards and reports of the app will be exposed for the user to choose from. This setting is appropriate when an app contains many different dashboards and reports and diverse use cases. For example, if only a few users view the **Global Sales (dashboard)**, all other users will have to open the list view themselves to navigate to their report or dashboard.

The **Content** page also provides a consolidated view of the dashboards, reports, and datasets that will be included in the app given the current settings. In the event that any dashboard, report, or workbook is included that shouldn't be, the user can navigate to this item in the workspace and disable the **Included in App** property.

By default, the **Included in App** property for new reports and dashboards is enabled. Therefore, prior to publishing the app, ensure that this property has been disabled for any internal testing or development content.

5. On the **Access** page, the users or security groups who should have permission to the app are defined:
   - If the user publishing the app has the right to push apps to end users via the **Push apps to end users** in **Tenant settings** in the Power BI admin portal, the **Install app automatically** option will be appearing as well.
   - Click the Finish icon in the top-right corner of the **Access** page to publish the app.
   - An example of the **Access** page was included in the preceding *User permissions* section.

A URL to the app will be provided in a window along with a **SUCCESSFULLY PUBLISHED** message, as per the following example:

Published app

The published app can now be accessed by the users or groups of users defined on the **Access** page. If the **Install app automatically** option was used, the user or team publishing the app can verify with a few users that the app is indeed now installed and available. Depending on the number of items (reports, dashboards) included in the app, the automatic installation could take some time. Once the automatic installation has been confirmed, an email or other communication could then be sent to advise users of the availability of the published app.

The following section describes the installation of an app if the **Install app automatically** (**Push apps to end users**) feature was not used.

Installing apps

When an app has been published and not pushed to end users via the **Install app automatically** feature described in the previous section, a one-time install per user is necessary. This install can be completed by either sharing the URL for the app with users or by instructing users to add the app in the Power BI service.

In the following example, a user has logged into the Power BI service and clicked **Get apps** from the **Apps** menu to observe the Global Sales app:

Installing the Power BI app

The **Apps** menu can be found below the **Recent** menu and above the **Shared with me** menu. By clicking **Get it now**, the app will be added to the **Apps** menu of the user, as shown in the following screenshot:

App installed

Users can hover over the app icon, such as GS in this example, to either mark the app as a favorite or to remove the app. A new feature expected in 2018 is the ability to automatically install apps for users. For example, once the Global Sales app is published, all users assigned to the `Global Sales Team` security group would have the app.

A second option to install the app is to share the URL to the app provided in the Power BI service. As per the *Publishing apps* section, this URL is provided in a dialog when the app is first published. Additionally, this URL can be obtained from the **Access** page of the **Apps** menu, as per the following screenshot:

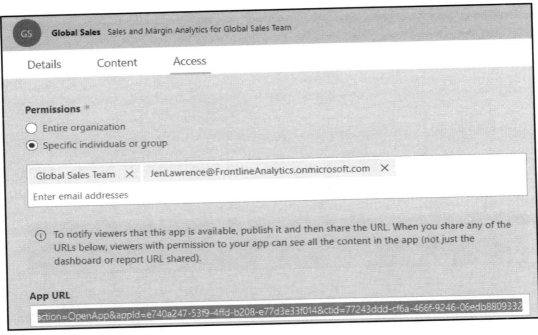

App URL

In the preceding example, a member of the Global Sales app workspace has clicked **Update app** from the top-right corner of the app workspace and navigated to the **Access** page. The **App URL**, as well as other URLs specific to dashboards and reports within the app, is located below the **Permissions** input box.

Apps on Power BI mobile

Just like the **Apps** menu item in the Power BI service, users can access published Power BI apps from the main menu within the Power BI mobile application. In the following image, a user has accessed the Global Sales app on the Power BI mobile application for iOS devices:

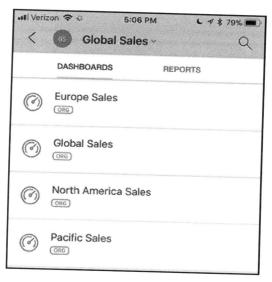

App on Power BI mobile

The user can easily swipe between dashboards and reports and take advantage of all standard mobile features, such as the ability to annotate and share both the annotations and the content with colleagues. Additionally, any mobile optimizations configured by the report authors for the reports and dashboards are also reflected through apps.

App updates

One of the main advantages of Power BI apps is their isolation from app workspaces. The members of the app workspace can continue to develop, test, and modify content in the app workspace while users only view the latest published app. This single level of built-in staging could be a sufficient alternative for some teams and projects relative to the multiple workspaces (Dev, Test, Prod) involved in a staged deployment life cycle, as described in Chapter 14, *Managing Application Workspaces and Content*.

After an app has been published, the Publish app icon in the top-right corner of the app workspace will be changed to an **Update app** icon, as shown in the following screenshot:

Update app

In the preceding screenshot, the ellipsis (three dots) to the right of the **Update app** icon has been selected from the context of the administrator for the workspace administrator. In addition to the options to edit and leave the workspace, an **Unpublish App** option exists to immediately remove user access to the published app. Workspace members (non-admins) can also unpublish the app and execute app updates.

Clicking **Update app** launches the same three pages (**Details**, **Content**, **Access**) described in the *Publishing apps* section. In the most common update scenarios, such as adding a new report or modifying a dashboard, it's unnecessary to change any of these settings and the **Update app** icon can be clicked a second time. However, these pages enable fundamental modifications to be implemented, including the users or groups with permission to access the app and the default landing page for the app.

Dataset-to-workspace relationship

As described in the *Workspace datasets* section of Chapter 14, *Managing Application Workspaces and Content*, the Power BI reports, based on Live connections to published Power BI datasets, are currently tied to the app workspace of the dataset. Therefore, in the absence of an Analysis Services database for Live connection reports or a supported DirectQuery data source, each app workspace and its corresponding app will require its own import mode dataset. The ability to utilize a single source Power BI dataset to support reports and dashboards across multiple app workspaces (and thus apps) is expected in 2018.

Prior to the availability of this centralized dataset workspace, BI teams can avoid duplicating datasets by deploying large, consolidated apps. These apps would contain the reports and dashboards relevant to multiple teams (for example, Sales, Finance), and the business users could use the Favorites feature to quickly access the most relevant content. Although not ideal, this would eliminate the need to manage multiple data-refresh schedules and to keep multiple datasets synchronized to the same business definitions.

Despite new features and capabilities that will increase the scalability of Power BI datasets, particularly Power BI Premium capacity, many organizations will choose either **SQL Server Analysis Services (SSAS)** or **Azure Analysis Services (AAS)** to support large-scale deployments.

For example, a BI project targeted at a particular business process and team, such as shipping for the supply chain team, may start out as a large Power BI dataset (.pbix). Once the Power BI dataset has proven to be valuable and stable in terms of business definitions and requirements, the dataset could be migrated to an Analysis Services model. The differences between Power BI datasets and Analysis Services models as well as migration considerations are contained in Chapter 19, *Scaling with Premium and Analysis Services*.

Self-Service BI workspace

As per the *Power BI deployment modes* section of Chapter 7, *Planning Power BI Projects*, some organizations may choose to empower certain business users to create and manage the visualization layer (Self-Service Visualization). This hybrid approach gives business users more flexibility to address rapidly changing analytical needs, yet leverages IT-supported and validated data sources and resources. When even greater business user flexibility is required, or when IT resources are not available, the Self-Service BI mode can be implemented via Power BI Pro licenses and an app workspace.

In the Self-Service BI deployment model, several business users (for example, five to ten) who regularly collaborate within a team or department are assigned Power BI Pro licenses. One of these users then creates an app workspace in the Power BI service and adds the other users who've been assigned Pro licenses as members with edit rights. The BI/IT team would typically require that at least one member of the BI organization be added as a workspace administrator. Additionally, if applicable, the BI/IT team would authorize a few business users in the workspace to utilize an On-premises data gateway for their required data sources.

Self-Service content distribution

Given that each user has a Pro license, members of the Self-Service BI Workspace (for example, Finance Team), a user has the full flexibility to view content in the Power BI service or mobile app as well utilize pro features, such as Analyze in Excel and Email Subscriptions. The users could choose to publish an app from the app workspace and advise workspace members to only use the published app for any production scenarios, such as printing reports or dashboards or referencing this content in meetings. As a small team, the users could delegate responsibilities for creating and testing the dataset(s), reports, dashboards, and any Excel workbooks hosted in the workspace.

A typical example of Self-Service BI is with advanced power users within finance and accounting functions. These users often have sophisticated and rapidly changing analytical needs that can't easily be translated into corporate BI-owned solutions. Additionally, the managers or stakeholders of this team's work may not require accessing this content themselves. For example, the analyst team could produce a monthly financial close package (that is, PowerPoint deck) or a project analysis and either present this content in person or distribute printed materials.

If it's determined that the business team requires additional resources, such as support for greater scale or sharing their content with users outside the workspace, the BI/IT team can consider assigning the workspace to the Power BI Premium capacity. Additionally, if the needs or the value of the workspace grows, the project could be migrated from Self-Service BI to one of the other deployment modes.

For example, the Power BI dataset created by the business team could be migrated to an Analysis Services model maintained by the BI team.

Risks to Self-Service BI

Perhaps no greater risk exists in business intelligence than the potential to motivate or drive an incorrect decision. Several of the chapters earlier in this book, particularly `Chapter 7`, *Planning Power BI Projects*, through `Chapter 10`, *Developing DAX Measures and Security Roles*, are dedicated to topics and practices that aim to reduce that risk. Although business users and analysts are often comfortable with the visualization layer, the quality and sustainability of this content rest on the planning, testing, and skills (for example, M queries, DAX measures) applied to the source dataset. A severe risk, therefore, to Self-Service BI projects is whether the business user(s) can build and maintain a source dataset that provides consistent, accurate information.

Another significant risk is a loss of version control and change management. The workspace users may not internally manage changes to content and thus inadvertently misinterpret or share content without the knowledge of changes implemented by other users. For example, rather than only using the published app for external communication and collaborating on any updates to the app, the users could view and edit the content of the app workspace itself thus eliminating all the staging of changes.

A final risk is that the self-service solution created may ultimately need to be discarded rather than migrated. For example, to quickly respond to new and changing analytical needs, the source dataset and reports may include many inefficient customizations and design patterns. These customizations can render the solution difficult to support and potentially consume unnecessary system resources. As more users and reports become dependent on these designs or anti-patterns, it can be more difficult and costly to migrate to a more sustainable solution.

Sharing dashboards and reports

In addition to Power BI apps, Power BI Pro users can share individual dashboards and reports directly to users, security groups of users, and even guest users from outside the organization. For example, unlike a Power BI app built for the sales organization containing several dashboards and many reports, a single dashboard or report could be shared with two or three users in the customer service department. In this scenario, the few customer service department users may have limited or undefined reporting needs or the corporate BI team may not have a full Power BI app for their department prepared yet.

Recipients of shared dashboards and reports receive the same essential benefits of Power BI apps in terms of easy access as well as the latest updates and modifications to the content. In terms of user access, the **Shared with Me** menu is positioned immediately following the **Apps** menu in both the Power BI service and the Power BI mobile applications.

In the following screenshot, the user has accessed the main menu of the Power BI mobile via the navigation icon (≡) at the top left:

Power BI mobile main menu

Recipients of shared dashboards and reports can also add this content to their list of **Favorites** just like Power BI apps.

The Power BI service gives content owners a properties pane to define the recipients of the shared content and whether the recipients will also be allowed to share the content. This pane can be accessed via the Share icon at the top right of the given report or dashboard when these items have been opened or from the **ACTIONS** group of the app workspace.

The following image identifies the share icon for two dashboards of the `Corporate Sales` app workspace:

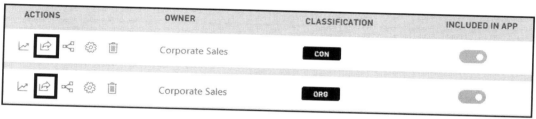

Share Action in Power BI service

The same sharing icon from the preceding image is also exposed in the **ACTIONS** workspace column for Power BI reports.

 Excel workbooks published to the Power BI service cannot be shared directly. To share a published Excel workbook (indirectly), a dashboard can be shared containing a tile that was pinned from the Excel workbook. The user receiving the shared dashboard can access the workbook via the dashboard tile, just like accessing a Power BI report based on a pinned report visual.

Once the sharing action has been selected, a sharing properties page is launched to define the recipients who will receive access. In the following example, the **CUSTOMER SERVICE TRENDS** dashboard is being shared with `Stacy Loeb` and `Brett Powell`:

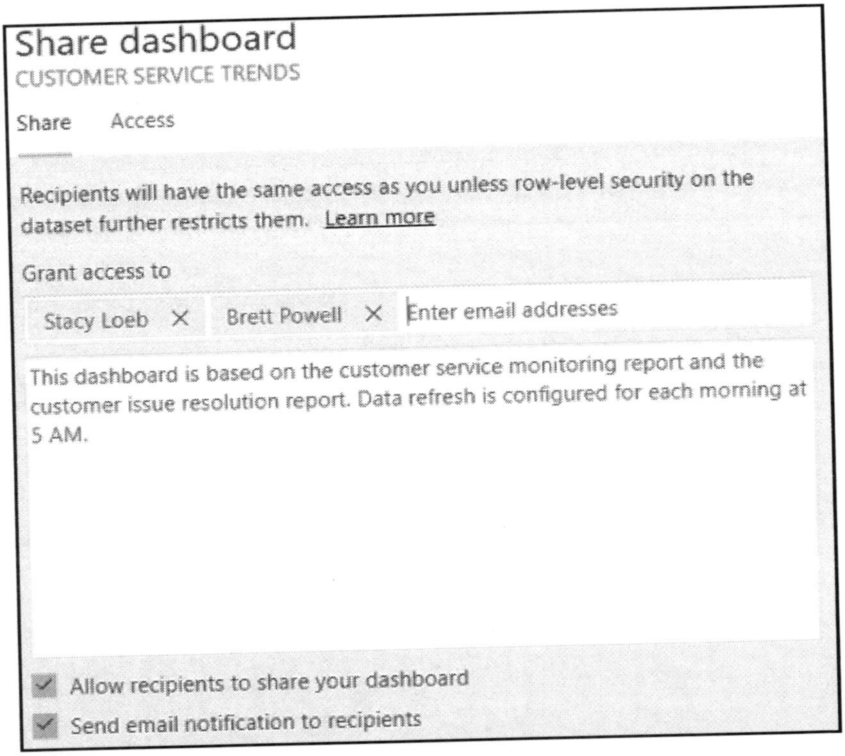

Share dashboard
CUSTOMER SERVICE TRENDS

Share   Access

Recipients will have the same access as you unless row-level security on the dataset further restricts them. Learn more

Grant access to

| Stacy Loeb ✕ | Brett Powell ✕ | Enter email addresses |

This dashboard is based on the customer service monitoring report and the customer issue resolution report. Data refresh is configured for each morning at 5 AM.

☑ Allow recipients to share your dashboard
☑ Send email notification to recipients

Share dashboard

As per the checkmark in the preceding image, the content owner has the option to allow recipients of the share to also share the dashboard themselves. This feature, referred to as resharing, expires one month after the share, if enabled originally.

Sharing dashboards and reports should only be generated from app workspaces and not from a user's private **My Workspace**. The app workspace allows the workspace members to manage both the content and its distribution, and thus eliminates a dependency on a single user.

Members with edit rights to the app workspace containing the shared dashboard or report can manage user access following the sharing of the content. For example, several days after the **CUSTOMER SERVICE TRENDS** dashboard was shared, it may be necessary to add or remove users from the share. Additionally, the ability of recipients to reshare the content can be revoked if this was enabled originally.

In the following image, a member of the **Customer Service** app workspace has again selected the Share action for the **CUSTOMER SERVICE TRENDS** dashboard but has now navigated to the **Access** pane:

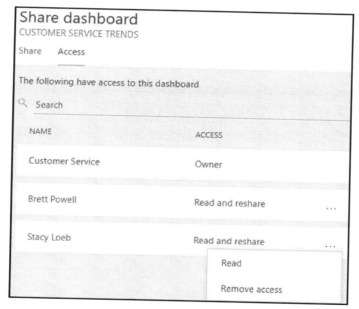

Manage shared access

By clicking the ellipsis next to each individual user, the app workspace member (with edit rights) has the option to remove the user's access altogether or to toggle the user's access between **Read** only and **Read and reshare**.

Sharing scopes

When a dashboard is shared, the reports containing the visuals pinned to that dashboard are shared as well. The recipient of the shared dashboard can, therefore, access and interact with the underlying reports by clicking the linked dashboard tile(s). The ability to share a report directly eliminates the need for the owners of a report to create a dashboard and for the recipients to leverage this dashboard when they only need to access the report. However, recipients of a shared dashboard can still add one or more of the underlying reports as favorites, thus providing the same ease of access as a shared report.

Although a single report may be all that's needed currently, sharing a dashboard provides greater scalability. For example, a shared dashboard may begin with only one report but visuals from two or three new reports could be pinned to the dashboard, thus granting access to these additional reports. This would negate the need to share each new report individually, and the dashboard could help summarize the reports for the user. When a report is shared, the only option for adding content is to add report pages to the existing report, and this can reduce the usability of the report.

Sharing versus Power BI apps

Just like Power BI apps, either Power BI Pro licenses or Power BI Premium capacity can be used to enable user access. In the example from this section, both `Stacy Loeb` and `Brett Powell` could be assigned Power BI Pro licenses to allow both users to view the shared content. Alternatively, the app workspace (**Customer Service**) of the shared content could be assigned to a Power BI Premium capacity, thus allowing Power BI Free users to access the content. The same licensing considerations for external guest users described in the *Power BI apps* section applies to sharing dashboards and reports.

Also, like Power BI apps, the recipients of the shared dashboard or report will need to be mapped to an RLS role if RLS has been configured on the source dataset. The users attempting to access the shared content will receive an error message if this mapping is not implemented within the security settings of the dataset, as described in the *User permissions* section earlier in this chapter.

Ultimately, Power BI apps provide the best long-term solution for content distribution, particularly for groups of users. Unlike sharing dashboards and reports, any number of new dashboards and reports can be added to Power BI apps as needs grow and change. Additionally, as described earlier in this chapter, owners of the app workspace can stage and test content prior to republishing the app via the app update process. In the case of shared dashboards and reports, any revision to the shared content is immediately visible to the user(s).

SharePoint Online embedding

Many organizations use team sites in SharePoint Online to facilitate collaboration between colleagues. These sites often contain important team or departmental documents (that is, Word, PowerPoint), calendars, and relevant links. Via the Power BI report web part for SharePoint Online, a Power BI report can be embedded into a SharePoint Online page to further enrich these sites.

 Yana Berkovich, Microsoft Data Platform MVP and collaboration consultant, has co-authored this section.

Technically, the SharePoint Online embedding process consists of two steps within the Power BI service and two steps within SharePoint Online. However, the following 12 step process can be used to effectively plan and implement the embedding:

1. Identify the business users of the team site who will need to view the embedded Power BI report.
2. Identify the app workspace and the report within that workspace that will be embedded in the team site.
3. Determine which of the following two options will be used to authorize the SharePoint Online site users:
    - Assign Power BI Pro licenses to each user and add these users as members of the app workspace.
    - Assign the app workspace to the Power BI Premium capacity such that Power BI Free users can view the content.

4. Open the report in the Power BI service and select **Embed in SharePoint Online** from the **File** menu dropdown:
   - The embed URL is provided via a dialog, per the following screenshot:

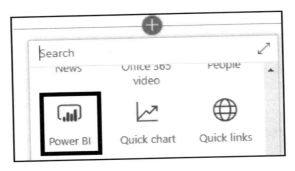

Embed link for SharePoint

Use the link below to securely embed this report in a SharePoint page. Learn more

https://app.powerbi.com/reportEmbed?reportId=be1932a5-49cb-4c4c-9f6a-681ff80afd39&groupId=4e8!

Embed link to Power BI report

5. In a modern SharePoint Online page, click the add (+) icon and select the **Power BI** web part, as shown in the following screenshot:

Add Power BI report web part

6. The add (+) icon to add a web part is provided by default for new site pages. For existing site pages, clicking the Edit icon in the top right will provide the same add (+) icon.

> **TIP**
>
> If the page's version hasn't already been set to modern, contact the SharePoint or Office 365 administrator as this is required to use the Power BI web part.

7. Select the **Add report** command button to access the web part property pane for configuring the embedded report.
   - This will launch the web part property pane on the right, including an input box for the Power BI Report URL.

8. Paste the Power BI report URL into the **Power BI report link** input box.
   - Use the **Page name** dropdown to select the default page that is shown on the report page.

9. Configure the web part via the **Display** (for example, **16:9**), **Show Navigation Pane**, and **Show Filter Pane** properties.
   - The **Show Navigation Pane** should be enabled if users require access to multiple pages of the report.

10. In the following screenshot, a Power BI report with two report pages (**General, Agents**) has been embedded into a SharePoint Online site page:

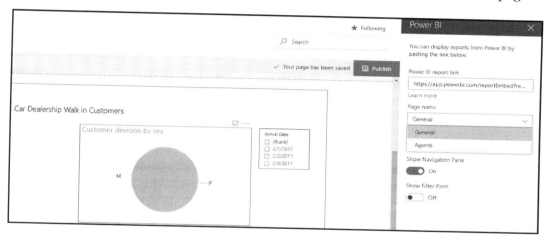

Power BI report embedded in SharePoint Online site page

11. Once embedded in the site page, the web part will reflect data refreshes and any report modifications implemented in Power BI.

12. Click the **Publish** button on the top-right of the site page to make the embedded report visible to site users.
   - When finished on the site page, click **Save and Close** on the left side of the page.

"Share Power BI reports where team collaboration is done to provide users with greater context and to drive overall productivity."

– Yana Berkovich, Microsoft Data Platform MVP

As described in Chapter 14, *Managing Application Workspaces and Content*, security groups are not supported for adding members to app workspaces. Therefore, if large numbers of users require access to Power BI reports via SharePoint Online, assigning the workspace(s) to the Power BI Premium capacity can both simplify management and reduce the cost of individual Power BI Pro licenses.

Custom application embedding

In addition to SharePoint Online embedding, the Power BI API can be leveraged to embed reports, dashboards, and individual dashboard tiles into any custom application. With the Power BI Premium capacity provisioned, content developed in the Power BI service can be embedded in new or existing applications for an organization so that Power BI Free users are able to view this content. Depending on the Power BI Premium SKU purchased, an organization can exclusively embed Power BI content in their application(s) or use embedding along with the Power BI service portal for content consumption.

Two kinds of Power BI Premium SKUs are available in the Office 365 portal that support embedding: P SKUs and EM SKUs. The EM SKUs are exclusive to custom applications and other **software as a service (SaaS)** offerings, such as SharePoint Online and teams. Power BI Free users are able to view embedded Power BI content in these applications but cannot view content in the Power BI service (PowerBI.com). Power BI Premium P SKUs, however, support both embedding content in custom applications as well as user access in the Power BI service, such as via Power BI apps. For example, an organization could use the same P3 SKU to support four Power BI apps and the embedding of content in a custom application.

 The third type of SKU that supports embedding Power BI content in custom applications is the A SKU. These SKUs are also referred to as Power BI Embedded and are exclusively available in the Microsoft Azure portal. A SKUs, or Power BI Embedded, are targeted at **independent software vendors (ISVs)** who will provide users from external organizations with access to the embedded content. As an Azure resource, the software vendor can utilize familiar development and operations processes, including the ability to scale up, down, and pause or resume the provisioned resources as workloads change.

Monthly billing and both monthly and yearly commitment options are available for Power BI Premium EM and P SKUs. Given their more limited scope, EM SKUs are significantly less expensive than P SKUs. In the following screenshot from the Office 365 admin center, the Power BI Premium EM SKU is available for purchase:

Power BI Premium – EM3

As shown in the preceding screenshot, the EM3 SKU provides four virtual cores and is available via month-to-month commitments. Currently, the EM3 SKU is the largest of the EM Premium SKUs in terms of virtual cores and memory but is the only EM SKU available in the Office 365 admin center. The EM1 and EM2 SKUs, which have fewer resources and thus lower prices, must be purchased through Microsoft volume licensing. For example, the EM1 SKU currently includes one virtual core, 3 GB of RAM, and is priced at $625 per month.

Publish to web

If enabled by the Power BI administrator, reports in the Power BI service can also be embedded on any website and shared via URL on the public internet. The **Publish to web** feature provides an embed code for the Power BI report, including iFrame HTML and a report URL. Organizations can utilize **Publish to web** to expose non-confidential or publicly available information on their public-facing corporate website.

In the following screenshot, a **Publish to web** embed code has been obtained in the Power BI service:

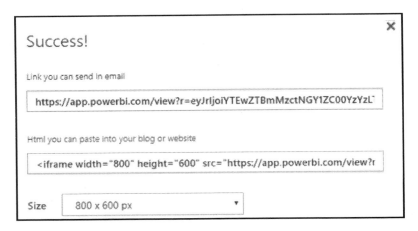

Publish to web embed code

The **Publish to web** feature is accessed via the **File** menu dropdown for a report, just like the SharePoint Online embedding URL from the previous section. However, unlike the SharePoint Online embedding feature, the Power BI service stores the **Publish to web** embed codes so that both administrators and users with edit rights to the reports can access and manage these codes.

For example, a member of an app workspace with edit rights can use the settings menu (Gear icon) to access a **Manage embed codes** page. This page allows the user to retrieve or delete any embed codes for the given app workspace.

 With the exception of custom visuals built with the R language, custom visuals are supported in Publish-to-web reports. This is the same limitation currently in place with the Power BI Report Server as described in Chapter 16, *Deploying the Power BI Report Server*. Reports based on datasets with row-level security roles configured and reports that use on-premises Analysis Services Tabular models are not supported.

Given the obvious potential risk of users accidentally sharing confidential or protected information over the public internet, Power BI administrators have granular controls over this feature including the ability to disable it for the entire organization. Details of these administrative settings are included in Chapter 18, *Administering Power BI for an Organization*.

Power BI reports accessed via embed codes will reflect the latest data refresh of the source dataset within approximately one hour of its completion. Additional documentation on Publish to web, including tips for fitting the iFrame into websites, is available at `http://bit.ly/2s2aJkL`.

Data alerts

Data-driven alerts are one of the top capabilities exclusive to dashboards in the Power BI service. For many users and business scenarios, data-driven alerts are a high-value complement, or even a substitute, to dashboards and reports as they help to avoid frequently accessing Power BI to search for actionable information. For example, rather than opening Power BI in the browser or on a phone every morning and looking for red colors or certain KPI symbols, the user could view certain dashboards or reports only once a week and otherwise only respond to data-driven alert notifications sent via email.

With a standard card, KPI, or gauge visual pinned to a dashboard, a data-driven alert can be configured either in the Power BI service or via the Power BI mobile app. In the following screenshot, a separate data alert has been configured for the gauge, the KPI, and the card visual reflecting the current day's average call length, staff versus target, and service calls, respectively:

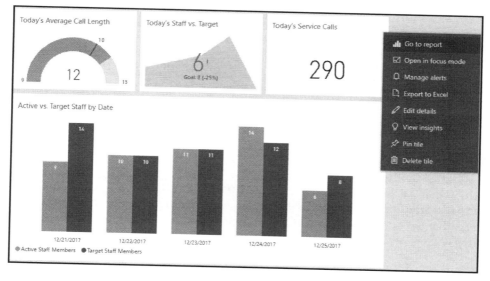

Manage alerts in Power BI service

The manage alerts option (bell icon), accessed by clicking the ellipsis in the top right corner of the tile, is only available for the standard gauge, KPI, and card visuals. In the following screenshot, an alert rule is set for the **Today's Call Length** measure, represented by the gauge visual:

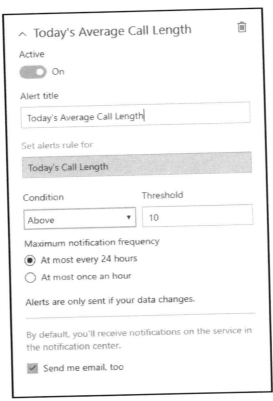

Setting an alert rule

In this screenshot, the target value from the gauge (**10**) is set as the threshold value of the alert rule by default. However, per the alert rule dialog in the preceding image, **Alert title**, the **Threshold** value, the **Condition** (**Above** or **Below**), the **Maximum notification frequency**, and the email notification can all be configured per alert rule. Only the **Set alerts rule for** input box is not configurable as this is based on the measure within the tile, in this case the **Today's Call Length** measure.

Each alert rule is limited to a single condition and thus additional alert rules can be configured for the same dashboard tile to provide notifications for multiple conditions. For example, a separate alert rule could be configured for the gauge tile with a condition of **Below 3**. When the underlying dataset of the dashboard tile is refreshed, a value for the **Today's Length Measure** of **Above 10** or **Below 3** would trigger an alert notification.

Data alerts and notifications are deeply integrated with the Power BI mobile applications. In the following screenshot from an iPhone, data alert notifications associated with each tile (3) are promoted to the Power BI mobile app icon:

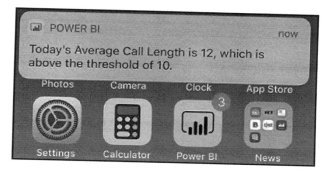

Data alert notification on iPhone

Additionally, as shown in the preceding screenshot, the notification associated with each alert rule is presented on the home screen including **ALERT TITLE**, **VALUE**, **CONDITION**, and **THRESHOLD**. Clicking on the Power BI mobile app icon provides access to the notifications pane that, like the Power BI Service, includes a link to the specific tile for further analysis. Between the mobile alert notifications, the notifications within the Power BI service, and the optional email delivery of the notification, users are able to respond quickly as significant data changes occur.

Microsoft Flow integration

Currently, the alert notification emails from Power BI are limited to the user who configured the data alert. In many scenarios, however, several users or a group email account should receive the notification email and it's not practical for each user to individually configure the data alerts.

Microsoft Flow provides a powerful but easy-to-use alternative to the standard Power BI alert email. For example, without any custom data connections or code, it enables a single user to fully define one or multiple email recipients of an alert notification and to customize the content of this message.

Microsoft Flow is an online service that enables the automation of workflows between applications and services. Since each MS flow is fundamentally composed of a trigger (starting action) and one or more corresponding actions, a top use case for MS Flow is to send custom email messages based on various trigger events. For example, when a sales lead is added in Salesforce, an email could be automatically sent to a sales team member via MS Flow.

Several pre-built MS Flow templates are available that leverage the Power BI data alert as a trigger. These templates make it easy to get started and to customize details, such as email addresses and the data from the alert to include. In the following MS Flow, the **Today's Average Call Length** alert described in the *Data alerts* section is used as the trigger of a customized email via an Office 365 for Outlook account:

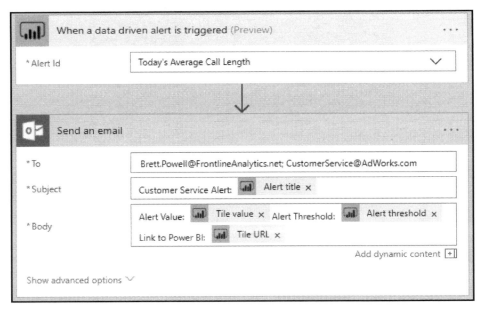

Power BI alert email via MS Flow

Power BI icons associated with the data alert trigger are available when populating the send email action via the Outlook for Office 365 connector. In the preceding screenshot, text labels with a closing colon are positioned in front of the icons to make the alert email messages easy to understand. The following sample email message reflects the preceding MS Flow configuration:

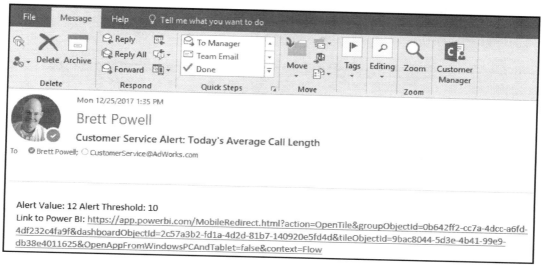

Power BI alert email message via MS Flow

MS Flow provides a rich platform for building both simple and complex workflows to obtain greater value from Power BI assets. Other common MS Flow and Power BI integrations, beyond custom email notifications, include posting messages to a Slack channel and triggering an alert in Microsoft Teams based on an alert in Power BI.

Email Subscriptions

Power BI also provides Email Subscriptions for Power BI Pro users of both reports and dashboards. With Email Subscriptions configured in the Power BI service, a user is sent a snapshot of either the report page or the dashboard canvas as well as a link to the content in the Power BI service. In the following service. In the following screenshot, a user with a Power BI Pro license has accessed the **Global Sales (dashboard)** described earlier in this chapter from within a Power BI app:

Subscribe to dashboard

Clicking the subscribe icon shown in the preceding image opens the following dialog to confirm the email subscription:

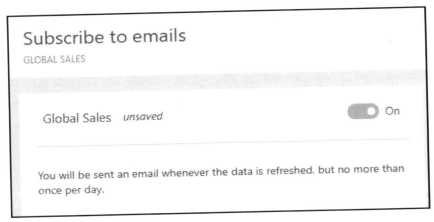

Dashboard Email Subscription

With the yellow slider set to **On**, selecting **Save and close** at the bottom of the dialog enables the email subscription to the dashboard. An email containing an image of the current state of the dashboard and a link to the dashboard in Power BI will then be sent when any of the underlying datasets change. If the source datasets refresh more than once per day, only the first email snapshot of the refresh will be sent.

A very similar subscription icon and dialog is also available for Power BI reports. The only significant difference with report subscriptions is that each subscription is associated with a single page. Therefore, the Power BI Pro user must choose the page for each subscription and configure multiple subscriptions to the same report if multiple pages of the report need to be emailed.

At this time, similar to data alerts, Email Subscriptions are only associated with the user who creates the subscriptions. However, the Power BI team has advised that they intend to enhance Email Subscriptions to include subscribing others to emails, such as security groups of users. Additionally, Email Subscriptions are currently sent with the report's default filter and slicer states. Per the Power BI team, this limitation is also expected to be addressed by allowing subscriptions to reports with specific slicer and filter states set.

Finally, emails are only sent to the **User Principal Name (UPN)** used to log into the Power BI service. For example, if the `Mark Langford` user doesn't receive email at his Power BI account (`Mlangford@AdWorks.onmicrosoft.com`), he will not receive Email Subscriptions. The Power BI documentation advises that the Power BI team is working to relax this limitation as well.

Email Subscriptions do not support most custom visuals. However, certified custom visuals, such as the Power KPI visual used in the **Global Sales (dashboard)**, are supported. Additional details on certified custom visuals can be found in the *Custom visuals* section of `Chapter 16`, *Deploying the Power BI Report Server*.

Analyze in Excel

Users with Power BI Pro licenses can connect to datasets hosted in the Power BI service from both Power BI Desktop and Microsoft Excel. Either of these tools will display the fields list of tables and measures for the dataset and, based on the report visuals created (for example, pivot tables), send queries to Power BI for execution by the source dataset. In the case of Power BI Desktop, these reports can be published back to the Power BI service and will retain their connection to the dataset, as recommended in the *Live connections to Power BI datasets* section of `Chapter 11`, *Creating and Formatting Power BI Reports*.

Excel reports based on these connections, however, currently do not retain their connection and thus cannot be refreshed or interacted with in the Power BI service. Despite this limitation, and the many additional analytical and visualization features of Power BI Desktop, Excel remains a very popular tool given its inherent flexibility and its mature, familiar features. Power BI's deep support for Excel, including both Analyze in Excel and the Power BI publisher for Excel, is an advantage over other BI platforms.

Additionally, the limitation of external data connections from Excel in the Power BI service is expected to be removed in 2018. The Power BI Report Server, for example, already supports Excel workbooks with Live connections as described in the *Office Online Server for Excel workbooks* section in `Chapter 16`, *Deploying the Power BI Report Server*.

Prior to broadly recommending Excel as a client-reporting tool, consider whether Power BI Desktop isn't better suited to common use cases, such as pivot tables. Many new features were added to Power BI Desktop in 2017 that targeted Excel pivot table scenarios, such as showing multiple metrics on rows, granular formatting, layout controls, and displaying values as a percentage of the total. Additionally, as the adoption of Power BI increases, Power BI reports built in Power BI Desktop provide a richer and more familiar user experience.

The Analyze in Excel feature is exposed as an action for Power BI reports via an Excel workbook icon in the Power BI service. The action is accessible in both app workspaces and in published apps for Power BI Pro users. In the following example from an app workspace, the option to analyze the `Monthly Sales Summary` report in Excel is available on the right:

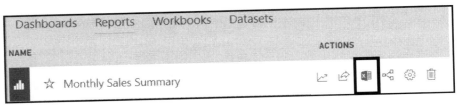

Analyze in Excel icon

Clicking the Analyze in Excel icon provides a **Microsoft Office Data Connection** (**ODC**) file that can be saved to the local machine. By default, opening this file launches Excel with a connection to the source dataset of the Power BI report. For example, even though the `Monthly Sales Summary` may only utilize a few measures and columns of the dataset, the entire fields list of the dataset will be exposed with a pivot table connection in Excel, as shown in the following screenshot:

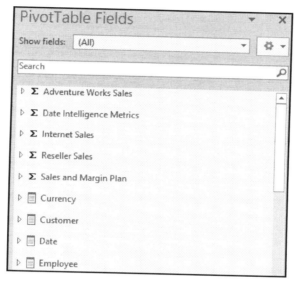

Excel connection to the Power BI dataset

Similar to the fields list in Power BI Desktop, Excel positions tables with only measures visible at the top of the list preceding the dimension tables. Just like standard Excel pivot tables, users can drag measures and columns to the field wells to structure each pivot table report. Right-clicking a column name, such as `Employee` department, presents the option to add the column as a slicer.

Just like interacting with a Power BI report, any RLS roles applied on the source dataset will be enforced on the user's report queries generated from Excel. The Excel workbook and any reports created based on the connection can be saved and shared like other Excel workbooks. However, for other users to refresh and query the source dataset from Excel, they will need access to the app or app workspace, a Power BI Pro license, and will need to be mapped to a security role if RLS has been configured.

Power BI Publisher for Excel

In addition to the Analyze in Excel feature from the Power BI service, even deeper integration with Excel is possible via the Power BI publisher for Excel add-in. This add-in can be downloaded from the Power BI service via the same drop-down menu used for the On-premises data gateway, as illustrated in the *Configuration of on-premises gateway* section of Chapter 15, *Managing the On-Premises Data Gateway*. Once downloaded and installed, a **Power BI** tab will be visible on the Excel ribbon:

Power BI Publisher for Excel

Via the **Connect to Data** button, users can access the reports and datasets of the app workspaces they have permissions to. For example, rather than navigating to the specific Power BI report of interest in the Power BI service to access the Analyze in Excel feature, the user could simply select the workspace and a report or dataset from a dropdown in Excel.

In the following screenshot, the user has clicked the **Connect to Data** button and navigated to the World Tour - New York app workspace:

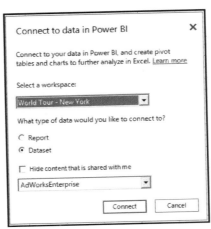

Connect to Data

The same Power BI workspaces and datasets accessible from Power BI Desktop can be accessed via the **Connect to Data** feature. Additionally, the Power BI publisher for Excel enables users to pin items, such as ranges of cells or charts, to dashboards in the Power BI service and to manage updates to these local items. Additional information on the Power BI publisher for Excel is available here: `http://bit.ly/2nuzQIt`.

Summary

This chapter provided a broad overview of Power BI's different content distribution and data access methods. Power BI apps were particularly emphasized as they represent the primary distribution mechanism supporting large groups of users going forward. The essential details of utilizing other distribution methods, such as email Subscriptions, data alerts, and sharing reports and dashboards were also reviewed. Furthermore, guidance was provided on analyzing the impact or usage of a published app as well as utilizing Microsoft Flow to drive custom email alerts.

The following chapter looks at Power BI deployments from an administration perspective. This includes the Power BI service administrator role and the controls available for administrators to define and manage authentication, monitor user activities, and limit or disable various features.

Administering Power BI for an Organization

18

The management and administrative processes described in previous chapters have primarily reflected the role of corporate business intelligence teams and BI professionals. In this chapter, the features and processes relevant to IT administrators are reviewed, to help organizations deploy and manage Power BI according to their policies and preferences. This includes data governance in the context of both self-service BI and corporate BI, the Power BI admin portal, monitoring user activity and adoption, and the administration of Power BI Premium capacity.

As in the previous chapter, this chapter exclusively covers the Power BI service. Administrative topics relevant to the on-premises deployments that were included in Chapter 16, *Deploying the Power BI Report Server*. Additionally, although data governance concepts and implementation guidance are included, readers are encouraged to review Microsoft documentation for further details on implementing data governance as part of Power BI deployments.

In this chapter, we will review the following topics:

- Data governance for Power BI
- Azure Active Directory conditional access policies
- Azure Active Directory B2B collaboration
- Power BI admin portal
- Power BI service Tenant settings
- Power BI activities in Audit Logs
- Using metrics reports
- Administering Power BI Premium capacities

Data governance for Power BI

Data governance is defined as a set of policies to secure an organization's data, ensure consistent and accurate decision making, and to manage access to data. Data governance is applicable to business intelligence generally, but organizations investing in Power BI for the long term should consider their data governance strategy and policies in the context of Power BI. A central component of data governance relates to the three deployment modes described at the beginning of `Chapter 7`, *Planning Power BI Projects*, and seeks to address the following question: "How can we ensure our data is secure and accurate while still providing the business with the access and flexibility it needs?"

It's generally understood that some level of **self-service BI (SSBI)** is appropriate and beneficial to empower business users to explore and discover insights into data. Tools, such as Power BI Desktop, and features in the Power BI web service, such as apps, make it easier than ever for business users to independently analyze data and potentially create and distribute content. However, experience with SSBI projects has also strongly suggested that IT-owned and managed administrative controls, enterprise-grade BI tools, and data assets, such as data warehouses, are still very much necessary. In response to the strengths and weaknesses of traditional IT-led BI and business-led SSBI, Microsoft has suggested and internally implemented a managed self-service approach to data governance.

From a BI architecture standpoint, managed self-service BI aligns represents a hybrid approach of both the Corporate BI and the Self-Service Visualization modes introduced in `Chapter 7`, *Planning Power BI Projects*. As shown in the following diagram, certain projects are carried out by the BI/IT department, while business users have the flexibility to analyze data and create their own reporting:

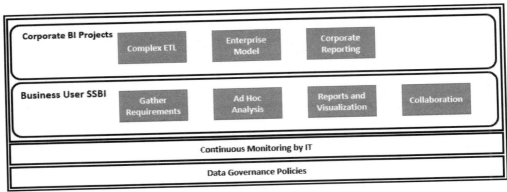

Multi-mode Power BI deployments

The three capabilities of **Corporate BI Projects** identified in the preceding screenshot address the limitations or weaknesses of self-service BI projects and tools. These limitations include data accuracy, scalability, complex data integration processes, and custom distributions of reports to groups of users. Certain projects requiring these skills and tools such as the integration of multiple source systems and the scheduled distribution of user-specific reports could be exclusively developed and managed by IT. Additionally, the business stakeholders for certain projects may prefer or insist that certain projects are wholly owned by IT. From an on-premises perspective, one example of this would include an **extract-transform-load** (ETL) package developed in **SQL Server Integration Service** (**SSIS**), an **SQL Server Analysis Services** (**SSAS**) data model, and a combination of paginated and Power BI reports developed for the Power BI Report Server.

 Some of the limitations, such as scalability and custom distributions of reports, may be mitigated in the near future by further enhancements to Power BI Premium and new features in the Power BI service. However, despite these new capabilities, certain projects and processes critical to a BI deployment are likely best suited for IT/BI professionals.

However, as shown in the **Business User SSBI** mode of the *Multi-mode Power BI deployments* diagram, business users are still empowered to leverage SSBI tools, such as Power BI Desktop, to conduct their own analysis and to internally determine requirements within their business unit. Most commonly, business users can leverage an IT-owned asset, such as an Analysis Services model, thus avoiding the data preparation and modeling components while retaining flexibility on the visualization layer. This Self-Service Visualization model is very popular and particularly effective when combined with Excel report connections.

Note that continuous monitoring and data governance policies are in effect across the organization regardless of Corporate BI or Business User SSBI. This is very important to detect any anomalies in user activity and as a first step in migrating a business developed solution to a corporate BI solution. For example, monitoring of the Office 365 Audit Log data for Power BI may indicate high and growing adoption of particular reports and dashboards based on a particular Power BI dataset. Given this query workload, or possibly other future needs for the dataset, such as advanced DAX measures, it may be appropriate to migrate this dataset to an Analysis Services model maintained by IT. An example of this migration process to an Azure Analysis Services model is included in Chapter 19, *Scaling with Premium and Analysis Services*.

Implementing data governance

With an overarching strategy in place for deploying Power BI, as shown in the previous section, concrete tasks can be defined for implementing data governance. Several of these tasks include the following:

1. Identify all data sources and tag sources containing sensitive data:
    - Additional access and oversight policies should be applied to data sources containing sensitive or protected data.
    - The classifications assigned to dashboards (Confidential, Organizational) in the *Dashboard data classifications* section of `Chapter 14`, *Managing Application Workspaces and Content*, is an example of data tagging.

2. Determine where critical data sources will be stored:
    - For example, determine whether the data warehouse will be hosted on-premises or in the cloud.
    - Power BI reporting can be deployed fully on-premises via the Power BI Report Server, fully in the cloud, or organizations can pursue hybrid deployment models. Examples of these deployment options are described in the *Hybrid deployment models* section of `Chapter 16`, *Deploying the Power BI Report Server*
    - Additionally, determine whether analytical (OLAP) BI tools such as Analysis Services and SAP BW will be used with these data sources and whether those tools will be stored on-premises or in the cloud.

3. Define who can access which data and how this access can be implemented:
    - Defining and managing security groups in **Azure Active Directory (AAD)** or **Active Directory (AD)** is strongly recommended.
    - Determine whether data security roles will be implemented in a data warehouse source such as Teradata or if row-level security roles will be implemented in analytical models such as Analysis Services.

4. Develop or obtain monitoring solutions to continuously monitor activities:
    - Visibility to the Office 365 Audit log data, as described later in this chapter, is an essential piece of this task.
    - Any high-risk or undesired activities should be automatically detected, enabling swift action.

5. Train business users on data governance and security:
   - This is particularly relevant for any dataset designers within business units who will leverage Power BI Desktop and to access shape, and model data.

The extent of data governance policies is driven by the size of the organization, its industry and associated regulations, and the desired data culture. For example, a large healthcare provider that wishes to pursue a more conservative data culture will implement many data governance policies to eliminate security risks and promote data quality and accuracy. However, a small to mid-sized company in a less regulated industry, and perhaps with less IT resources available, will likely implement less dense governance policies to promote flexibility.

For example, with Power BI Desktop and Power BI Premium capacity, a large analysis model containing complex M queries and DAX expressions could potentially be created and supported by a business user or team. However, the dataset designer of this model will need to be familiar with both the governance policy determining the level of visibility users of the dataset will have, as well as how to implement the corresponding row-level security roles. Additionally, business users with Power BI Pro licenses responsible for distributing content such as via Power BI apps will need to know the security groups that should have access to the app.

Azure Active Directory

As with other Microsoft Azure services, Power BI relies on Azure AD to authenticate and authorize users. Therefore, even if Power BI is the only service being utilized, organization's can leverage Azure AD's rich set of identity management and governance features, such as conditional access policies, **multi-factor authentication (MFA)** and business-to-business collaboration. For example, a conditional access policy can be defined within the Azure Portal which blocks access to Power BI based on the user's network location, or which requires MFA given the location and the security group of the user. Additionally, organizations can invite external users as guest users within their Azure AD tenant to allow for seamless distribution of Power BI content to external parties, such as suppliers or customers.

Guidance on configuring Azure AD security groups to support **row-level security (RLS)** is included in `Chapter 10`, *Developing DAX Measures and Security Roles*. This section reviews other top features of Azure AD in the content of Power BI deployments.

Azure AD B2B collaboration

Azure AD **business-to-business (B2B)** collaboration enables organizations using the Azure AD to work securely with users from any organization. Invitations can be sent to external users, whether the user's organization uses Azure AD or not, and once accepted the guest user can leverage their own credentials to access resources, such as dashboards and reports contained in a Power BI app. Just like users within the organization, guest users can be added to security groups and these groups can be referenced in the Power BI service.

 Prior to the existence of Azure AD B2B, it was necessary to create identities within Azure AD for external guest users, or even develop an application with custom authentication.

A guest user can be added to Azure AD by sending an invitation from Azure AD and by sharing content with the external user from the Power BI service. The first method, referred to as the planned invite method, involves adding a guest user from within Azure AD and sending an invitation to the user's email address. In the following screenshot from the Azure portal, **Azure Active Directory** has been selected and the **All users** page has been accessed from the **Manage users and groups** tab:

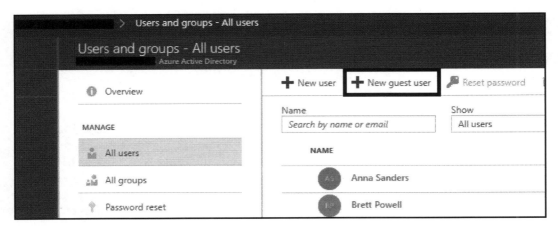

Add guest user in Azure AD

As shown in the preceding screenshot, the administrator can click **New guest user** to add the user, and enter an invitation message, such as in the following screenshot:

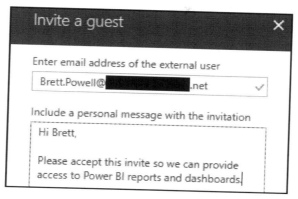

Invite a guest user to Azure AD

The guest or external user will be sent an invitation via email containing the personal message, as well as a **Get Started** button. The user will need to click **Get Started** and accept the invitation. Once accepted, the guest user can be managed and added to security groups for use in Power BI. In the following screenshot from the **All users** tab in Azure AD, the guest user (Brett.Powell@....) has accepted the guest user invite:

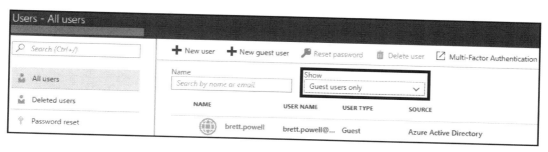

Guest User in Azure AD

Guest users are identified in Azure AD with a globe icon and with a **Guest** value in the **USER TYPE** property, as shown in the preceding screenshot.

As an alternative to the planned invite method via Azure AD described before, an invite to an external user can also be generated from the Power BI service directly. In this method, commonly referred to as ad hoc invites, a guest user's email address is specified when publishing or updating a Power BI app (via the **Access** page) or when sharing a Power BI dashboard or report. The external user would then receive an email invite to the specific content. Upon accepting this invite, the external user would be added as a guest user in Azure AD. Details on distributing content to users via apps and other methods are included in Chapter 17, *Creating Power BI Apps and Content Distribution.*

Organizations have the option to completely block sharing with external users via the Share content with external users setting in the Power BI admin portal. As shown in the following screenshot, this setting can be enabled or disabled for an entire organization, or limited to certain security groups:

Share content with external users setting in Power BI admin portal

In addition to the Power BI admin portal, additional management options over external guest users are available in Azure AD. These settings, including whether members in the organization (non-admins) can invite guest users, are available on the manage user settings page of Azure AD.

External B2B users are limited to consuming content that has been shared or distributed to them. For example, they can view apps, export data (if allowed by the organization) and create email subscriptions, but they cannot access app workspaces or create and publish their own content. Additionally, external users cannot currently access shared content via the Power BI mobile apps.

Licensing external users

In addition to authentication to the Power BI content, either a Power BI Pro license or Power Premium capacity is needed to allow the guest user to view the content. The following three licensing scenarios are supported:

1. The app workspace of the Power BI app can be assigned to Power BI Premium capacity:
    - Only Power BI Premium P SKUs support sharing with external users
    - Differences between P and EM SKUs were included in the *Custom application embedding* section in `Chapter 17`, *Creating Power BI Apps and Content Distribution*

2. The guest user can be assigned a Power BI Pro license by the guest user's organization

3. A Power BI Pro license can be assigned to the guest user by the sharing organization:
    - The Power BI Pro license only allows the user to access content within the sharing organization

In the following screenshot from Azure AD, a guest user (`Brett.Powell`) is assigned a Power BI Pro license:

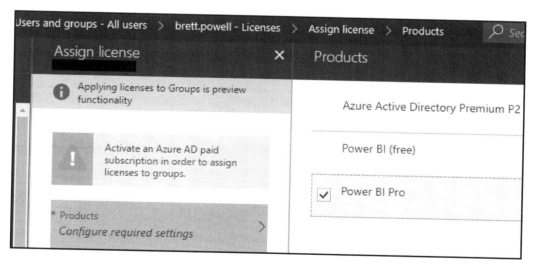

Power BI Pro license assignment in Azure AD

The License assignment for the guest user, as shown in the preceding screenshot, can be accessed via the **Manage Licenses** page for the given user in Azure AD. From this page, select the Assign icon (+) and then the **Products** tab to complete the assignment.

Conditional access policies

Administrators of Azure AD can configure conditional access policies to restrict user access to Power BI based on the user or security group, the IP address of the user sign-in attempt, the device platform of the user, and other factors. A very common scenario supported by conditional access policies is to either block access to Power BI from outside the corporate network or to require **multi-factor authentication (MFA)** for these external sign-in attempts. As a robust, enterprise-grade feature, organizations can use conditional access policies in conjunction with security groups to implement specific data governance policies.

Each Azure AD conditional access policy is composed of one or more conditions and one or more controls. The conditions define the context of the sign-in attempt such as the security group of the user and the user's IP address, while the controls determine the action to take given the context. For example, a policy could be configured for the entire organization and all non-trusted IP addresses (the conditions) that requires MFA to access Power BI (the control). The Azure portal provides a simple user interface for configuring the conditions and controls of each conditional access policy.

The following steps and supporting screenshots describe the creation of an Azure AD conditional access policy which requires MFA for users from the sales team accessing Power BI from outside the corporate network:

1. Log in to the Azure portal and select **Azure Active Directory** from the main menu

2. From the **SECURITY** group of menu items, select **Conditional access**, as shown in the screenshot:

Conditional access in Azure AD

3. Select the new policy icon at the top and enter a name for the policy, such as `Sales Team External Access MFA`

4. Set the users and group assignment property to an Azure AD security group (such as `AdWorks DW Sales Team`)

5. Set the **Cloud apps** assignment property to Microsoft Power BI service

6. On the **Conditions** assignment property, configure the locations to include any location and exclude all trusted locations:
    - With this definition, the policy will apply to all IP addresses not defined as trusted locations in Azure AD

7. On the **Grant** access control property, select the checkbox to require multifactor authentication

8. Finally, set the **Enable** policy property at the bottom to **On** and click the **Create** command button:

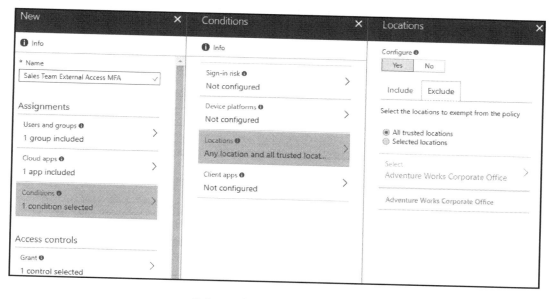

Configure new Azure AD conditional access policy

The minimum requirements to create new conditional access policies are the **Users and groups** property, the **Cloud apps** property (Power BI service), and at least one access control. As with all security implementations, conditional access policies should be tested and validated. In this screenshot, a user within the AdWorks DW Sales Team could attempt to log in to Power BI from outside the corporate network. The user should be prompted (challenged) to authenticate by providing a mobile device number and entering an access code sent via text message.

It's important to remember that conditional access policies are in addition to the user permissions defined in the Power BI service and the row-level security roles created in Power BI datasets or Analysis Services data models. The *User Permissions* section in Chapter 17, *Creating Power BI Apps and Content Distribution*, contains additional information on these security layers.

 Azure AD conditional access policies require either an Enterprise Mobility and Security E5 license or Azure AD Premium P2 license. **Enterprise Mobility and Security (EMS)** E5 licenses include Azure AD Premium P2 as well as Microsoft Intune, Microsoft's mobile device management service. Additional information on features, licensing, and pricing for EMS is available at the following URL http://bit.ly/2lmHDZt.

The following URL from MS Docs contains best practices for conditional access policies in Azure AD http://bit.ly/2nXAjlA.

Power BI Admin Portal

The Power BI Admin Portal provides controls for administrators to manage the Power BI tenant for their organization. This includes settings governing who in the organization can utilize which features, how Power BI Premium capacity is allocated and by whom, and other settings such as embed codes and custom visuals.

The admin portal is accessible to Office 365 Global Administrators and users mapped to the Power BI service administrator role. The Power BI service administrator role and the assignment of a user to this role in Office 365 was described in the *Power BI project roles* section of Chapter 7, *Planning Power BI Projects*. To open the admin portal, log in to the Power BI service and select the **Admin portal** item from the Settings (Gear icon) menu in the top right, as shown in the following screenshot:

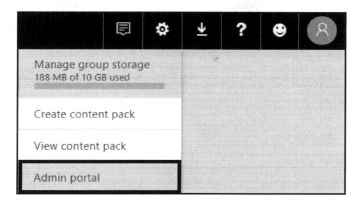

Admin portal in Settings menu

All Power BI users, including Power BI free users, are able to access the **Admin portal**. However, users who are not admins can only view the **Capacity settings** page. The Power BI service administrators and Office 365 global administrators have view and edit access to the following seven pages:

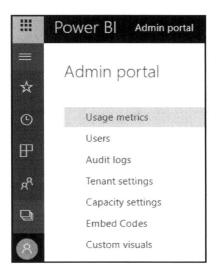

Admin portal pages

Administrators of Power BI most commonly utilize the **Tenant settings** and **Capacity settings** as described in the Tenant Settings and Power BI Premium Capacities sections later in this chapter. However, the admin portal can also be used to manage any approved custom visuals for the organization, as well as any embed codes associated with the **Publish to web** feature described in Chapter 17, *Creating Power BI Apps and Content Distribution.*

Usage metrics

The **Usage metrics** page of the **Admin portal** provides admins with a Power BI dashboard of several top metrics, such as the most consumed dashboards and the most consumed dashboards by workspace. However, the dashboard cannot be modified and the tiles of the dashboard are not linked to any underlying reports or separate dashboards to support further analysis. Given these limitations, alternative monitoring solutions are recommended, such as the Office 365 audit logs and usage metric datasets specific to Power BI apps. Details of both monitoring options are included in the app usage metrics and Power BI audit log activities sections later in this chapter.

Users and Audit logs

The **Users** and **Audit logs** pages only provide links to the Office 365 admin center. In the admin center, Power BI users can be added, removed and managed. If audit logging is enabled for the organization via the Create audit logs for internal activity and auditing and compliance tenant setting, this audit log data can be retrieved from the Office 365 Security & Compliance Center or via PowerShell. This setting is noted in the following section regarding the **Tenant settings** tab of the Power BI admin portal.

An Office 365 license is not required to utilize the Office 365 admin center for Power BI license assignments or to retrieve Power BI audit log activity. Examples of assigning Power BI Pro licenses and the Power BI service administrator role to users from within the Office 365 admin center are included in Chapter 7, *Planning Power BI Projects.* Retrieving and analyzing the Power BI audit log data is described in the Power BI Audit Log Activities section later in this chapter.

Tenant settings

The **Tenant settings** page of the Admin portal allows administrators to enable or disable various features of the Power BI web service. For example, an administrator could disable the **Publish to web** feature described in `Chapter 17`, *Creating Power BI Apps and Content Distribution*, for the entire organization. Likewise, the administrator could allow only a certain security group to embed Power BI content in SaaS applications such as SharePoint Online.

The following diagram identifies the 18 tenant settings currently available in the admin portal and the scope available to administrators for configuring each setting:

#	Setting Group	Setting	Scope
1	Export and Sharing	Share content with external users	Organization and Security Groups
2	Export and Sharing	Publish to web	Organization and Security Groups
3	Export and Sharing	Export data	Organization and Security Groups
4	Export and Sharing	Print dashboards and reports	Organization and Security Groups
5	Export and Sharing	Export reports as PowerPoint presentations	Organization and Security Groups
6	Content packs and apps	Publish content packs and apps to the entire organization	Organization and Security Groups
7	Content packs and apps	Create template organizational content packs and apps	Organization and Security Groups
8	Integration settings	Ask questions about data using Cortana	Organization only
9	Integration settings	Use Analyze in Excel with on-premises datasets	Organization and Security Groups
10	Integration settings	Use ArcGIS Maps for Power BI	Organization only
11	Integration settings	Use global search for Power BI	Organization only
12	Custom visuals settings	Custom visuals	Organization only
13	R visuals settings	Interact with and share R visuals	Organization only
14	Audit and usage	Create audit logs for internal activity auditing and compliance	Organization only
15	Audit and usage	Usage metrics for content creators	Organization and Security Groups
16	Audit and usage	Per-user data in usage metrics for content creators	Organization and Security Groups
17	Dashboard	Data classification for dashboards	Organization only
18	Developer	Embed content in apps	Organization and Security Groups

Power BI Tenant settings

From a data security perspective, the first seven settings within the **Export and Sharing** and **Content packs and apps** groups are most important. For example, many organizations choose to disable the **Publish to web** feature for the entire organization. Additionally, only certain security groups may be allowed to export data or to print hard copies of reports and dashboards. As shown in the **Scope** column of the previous table and the following example, granular security group configurations are available to minimize risk and manage the overall deployment.

Currently, only one tenant setting is available for custom visuals and this setting (**Custom visuals settings**) can be enabled or disabled for the entire organization only. For organizations that wish to restrict or prohibit custom visuals for security reasons, this setting can be used to eliminate the ability to add, view, share, or interact with custom visuals. More granular controls to this setting are expected later in 2018, such as the ability to define users or security groups of users who are allowed to use custom visuals.

In the following screenshot from the **Tenant settings** page of the **Admin portal**, only the users within the BI Admin security group who are not also members of the BI Team security group are allowed to publish apps to the entire organization:

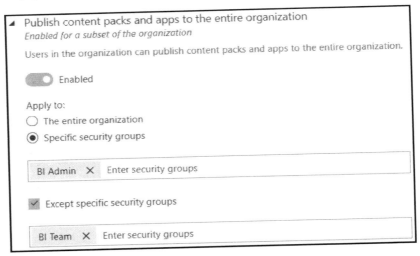

Security group permissions in Tenant settings

For example, a report author who also helps administer the On-premises data gateway via the **BI Admin** security group would be denied the ability to publish apps to the organization given membership in the **BI Team** security group. Many of the tenant setting configurations will be more simple than this example, particularly for smaller organizations or at the beginning of Power BI deployments. However, as adoption grows and the team responsible for Power BI changes, it's important that the security groups created to help administer these settings are kept up to date.

Embed Codes

Embed Codes are created and stored in the Power BI service when the **Publish to web** feature is utilized. As described in the *Publish to web* section of the previous chapter, this feature allows a Power BI report to be embedded in any website or shared via URL on the public internet. Users with edit rights to the workspace of the published to web content are able to manage the embed codes themselves from within the workspace. However, the admin portal provides visibility and access to embed codes across all workspaces, as shown in the following screenshot:

Embed Codes				
View embed codes that have been created by your organization. To change users ability to use publish to web, see <u>Tenant settings</u>.				
Report name	Workspace name	Published by	Status	Actions
M Function Reference Report	Insight Quest Public Content	Brett Powell	Active	↗ 🗑

Embed Codes in Power BI admin portal

Via the **Actions** commands on the far right of the **Embed Codes** page, a Power BI Admin can view the report in a browser (diagonal arrow) or remove the embed code. The **Embed Codes** page can be helpful to periodically monitor the usage of the **Publish to web** feature and for scenarios in which data was included in a publish to web report that shouldn't have been, and thus needs to be removed. As shown in the *Power BI Tenant settings* table referenced in the previous section, this feature can be enabled or disabled for the entire organization or for specific users within security groups.

Organizational Custom visuals

The **Custom Visuals** page allows admins to upload and manage custom visuals (`.pbiviz` files) that have been approved for use within the organization. For example, an organization may have proprietary custom visuals developed internally, which it wishes to expose to business users. Alternatively, the organization may wish to define a set of approved custom visuals, such as only the custom visuals that have been certified by Microsoft. The process of obtaining custom visuals via Microsoft AppSource and the details of certified custom visuals are included in the *Custom visuals* section of `Chapter 12`, *Applying Custom Visuals, Animation, and Analytics*.

In the following screenshot, the Chiclet Slicer custom visual is added as an organizational custom visual from the **Organizational visuals** page of the Power BI admin portal:

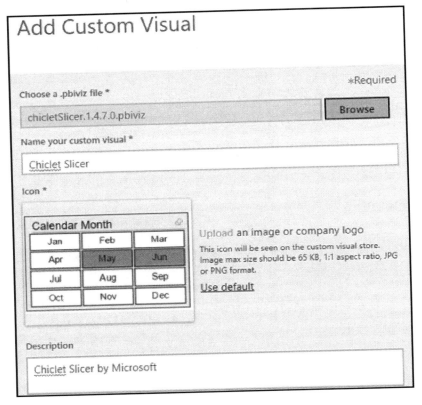

Add organizational custom visual

The **Organizational visuals** page provides a link (**Add a custom visual**) to launch the form and identifies all uploaded visuals, as well as their last update. Once a visual has been uploaded, it can be deleted but not updated or modified. Therefore, when a new version of an organizational visual becomes available, this visual can be added to the list of organizational visuals with a descriptive title (Chiclet Slicer v2.0). Deleting an organizational custom visual will cause any reports that use this visual to stop rendering.

The following screenshot reflects the uploaded Chiclet Slicer custom visual on the **Organization visuals** page:

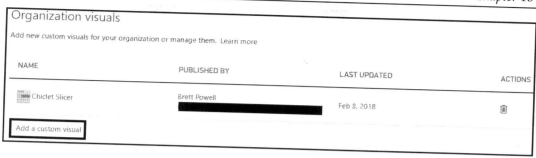

Organization Visuals page in Power BI admin portal

Once the custom visual has been uploaded as an organizational custom visual, it will be accessible to users in Power BI Desktop. In the following screenshot from Power BI Desktop, the user has opened the **MARKETPLACE** of custom visuals and selected **MY ORGANIZATION**:

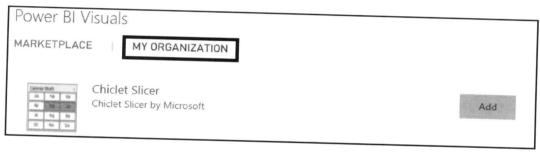

Power BI Custom visuals

In this screenshot, rather than searching through the **MARKETPLACE**, the user can go directly to visuals defined by the organization. The marketplace of custom visuals can be launched via either the **Visualizations** pane or the **From Marketplace** icon on the **Home** tab of the ribbon. Additional details on adding custom visuals are included in Chapter 12, *Applying Custom Visuals, Animation, and Analytics*.

Organizational custom visuals are not supported for reports or dashboards shared with external users. Additionally, organizational custom visuals used in reports that utilize the publish to web feature will not render outside the Power BI tenant. Moreover, Organizational custom visuals are currently a preview feature. Therefore, users must enable the My organization custom visuals feature via the Preview features tab of the Options window in Power BI Desktop.

Usage metrics reports

The Power BI service provides standard usage metrics reports for both dashboards and reports. These reports, which themselves are Power BI reports, provide quick insights to fundamental user adoption questions, such as how often the published content is being viewed and which users are viewing the content the most. These read-only reports can be generated for specific dashboards and reports and can also be personalized (edited) by saving a copy. Once a copy of a usage metrics report has been saved, a Power BI dataset of usage metrics will be created for either all the dashboards or all the reports in the app workspace. The usage metrics datasets, which are updated by the Power BI service for the last 90 days of activity, and the saved usage reports can then serve as a foundation for a lightweight but robust monitoring solution for the app workspace.

For example, the **Global Sales** app described in the previous chapter contains several dashboards and reports with some of the reports containing multiple report pages. The following 11-step process and supporting diagram walk through the creation of two usage metrics datasets (dashboards and reports), two usage metrics reports, and a dashboard summarizing usage metrics for the app workspace across dashboards and reports:

1. Access the app workspace in the Power BI service containing the content to monitor:
   - A Power BI Pro license and edit rights to the app workspace are required to access usage metrics data.
2. From the **Dashboards** page, select the View usage metrics report icon (line chart symbol) under **ACTIONS** for one of the dashboards, as shown in the following screenshot:

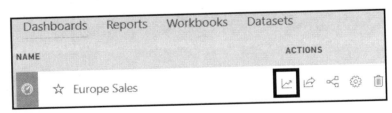

View usage metrics action

3. Once prompted, click the **View usage metrics** button on the **Usage metrics ready** popup textbox:
   - Alternatively, click the View usage metrics report icon again for any of the dashboards in the workspace.

   A Power BI report containing usage metrics for the selected dashboard will be displayed, such as the following:

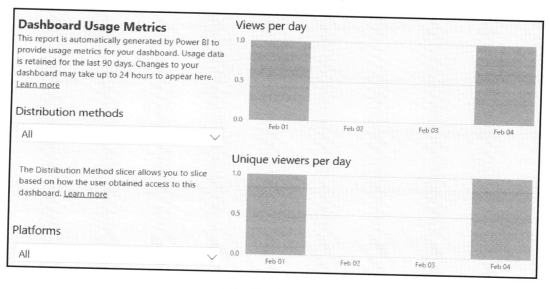

Dashboard Usage Metrics report

In addition to the slicers and visuals in the preceding screenshot, the usage metrics report page includes visuals for total views, total viewers (users), and views by user table that identifies the User Principal Name (login) and display name of the user.

At this point, usage metrics reports specific to each dashboard in the workspace will be accessible on demand via the View usage metrics report icon.

4. With the usage metrics report opened, click **Save as** from the **File** menu dropdown to save a copy of the report:
   - A report named **Dashboard Usage Metrics Report - Copy** will be saved in the reports group.

- Additionally, a dataset will be created named **Dashboard Usage Metrics Model - Copy**.
5. Open the report saved from step *4* and click **Edit report**.
6. In edit mode, remove the **Report level filters** that are specific to a single dashboard, as identified in the following screenshot:

Usage metrics report filtered for dashboard

7. Create a separate report page that uses the `DisplayName` column of the `Dashboards` table to analyze usage of the dashboards within the workspace.
8. Save the modifications from the file menu dropdown (**File | Save**).
9. Repeat steps *1* through *8* for a Power BI report in the same app workspace:
    - Use the `DisplayName` column from the `Reports` table and the `ReportPage` column from the `Views` table to design a usage metrics report for the reports in the workspace.
10. Create a new dashboard named `Usage Metrics`.
11. Pin report visuals from both the dashboard usage metrics report and the report usage metrics report to the **Usage Metrics** dashboard:
    - By default, the included in app property will be disabled for usage metrics reports, and the dashboard containing visuals from the usage metrics reports.

At this point, the workspace will include one usage metrics report for dashboards, one for reports, and two Power BI datasets supporting these usage reports, as shown in the following screenshot:

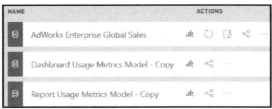

Report and dashboard usage metrics datasets

Via the Create report action icons (chart symbol) included in the preceding screenshot, additional usage reports can be created in the Power BI service. Additionally, new reports can be created in Power BI Desktop by connecting to either of these two datasets, as described in the *Live connections to Power BI datasets* section of `Chapter 11`, *Creating and Formatting Power BI Reports*.

Excluding any new reports or dashboards, the monitoring solution for the **Global Sales** workspace is structured as follows:

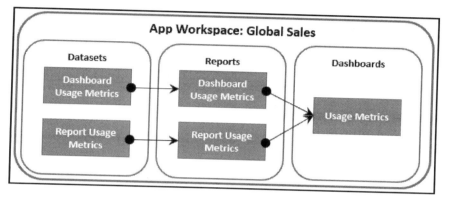

Usage metrics reporting: Global Sales workspace

Depending on the importance and size of the workspace, more reports and dashboards can be created to provide further insight into the adoption of the content. For example, the usage metric reporting may indicate that only one or two reports of an app workspace are being utilized, or that one particular report page of a report is most important to users. The BI team can use this information to engage with business stakeholders to better understand the reasoning behind the usage patterns reported.

The usage metrics data includes both Power BI Pro and Power BI Free users. For example, this includes Power BI Pro users who are members of the app workspace with edit rights to the content, as well as Power BI Free users who only access the content via a Power BI app. A `DistributionMethod` table in both the dashboard and report usage metrics datasets contains a `Name` field, which identifies how the user obtained access to view the specific item. This access will be one of the following three methods—as a member of the app workspace, as a recipient of a shared dashboard or report, or by installing an app.

User views of content through a Power BI app are currently counted as content packs but, as mentioned in the previous chapter, content packs are being replaced by apps. Additional information on the metrics and columns included in the usage metrics datasets is available in MS Docs via the following URL: `http://bit.ly/ 2nTyua4`.

Although very useful for app workspaces that support many users or important scenarios (such as executive dashboards), usage metrics reports are ultimately limited to individual workspaces. Additionally, the usage metrics don't include other activities of interest to administrators, such as when the newly scheduled refresh is configured or when a data source from a gateway is removed. A more comprehensive monitoring dataset inclusive of all app workspaces and all Power BI activities is available via the Office 365 audit logs for Power BI, as described in the following section.

Audit logs

Power BI activities stored in the Office 365 audit logs provide administrators with a complete view of user activities in the Power BI service. Each log event record identifies the user, the date and time of the activity, the type of activity, such as printed a report page, and the item in Power BI, such as the report that was printed. This level of detail at the tenant level across all primary activities helps administrators answer both high-level usage and adoption questions, as well as targeted compliance questions.

For example, the audit logs could prove that the volume of users and their level of engagement with Power BI reports and dashboards is increasing. Alternatively, an administrator could investigate the activities of just a few users to ensure they're only engaging in activities aligned with their role. Perhaps most importantly, an IT organization can understand what Power BI content is being utilized by the business. In the event that a few reports or dashboards become very popular, some level of engagement may be appropriate to ensure the underlying dataset is accurate and secure or migrate the content to an IT-supported solution.

Once enabled in the Power BI admin portal, the audit log data can be retrieved on an ad hoc basis or, more commonly, retrieved on a recurring basis as part of a continuous monitoring and governance solution. To minimize the setup and maintenance of these monitoring solutions, Microsoft has made available PowerShell scripts that export Power BI audit log data to a CSV file format. Additionally, a Power BI solution template is available with built-in audit log retrieval and prebuilt monitoring reports.

The first step in utilizing the audit logs is to enable the create audit logs setting in the Power BI admin portal. This setting in the **Audit** and **Usage settings** group of the **Tenant settings** page is set at the organizational level, as shown in the following screenshot:

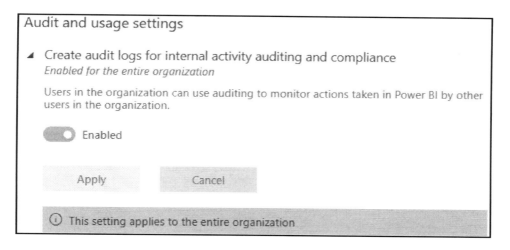

Enable Power BI audit logs

Once the audit log setting is enabled, user activities start to be recorded in the audit logs with a delay of 12 hours or less from their occurrence and will be stored for 90 days. This log data can be accessed directly from the Office 365 admin center or remotely via PowerShell scripts and solution templates. In terms of direct or ad hoc access, an Office 365 global administrator or a user with permission to the Security & Compliance Center can log in to Office 365 (www.office.com) and select the **Security & Compliance** app icon, as shown in the following screenshot:

Office 365 app menu

Alternatively, a link to the Office 365 admin center is provided on the Audit logs page of the Power BI admin portal. This links directly to the Audit log search interface of the Security & Compliance Center described later.

From the Security & Compliance Center, the **Search and Investigation** menu at the bottom (magnifying-glass icon) can be expanded to expose an **Audit log** search item. Select **Audit log search** and then specify the Power BI activities to search for, the start and end dates for the search, and, optionally the users, as shown in the following screenshot:

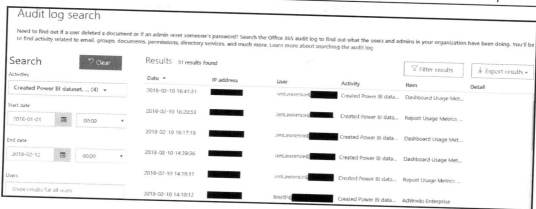

Audit log search in Security & Compliance Center

In this example, the following four activities are searched for—Created Power BI gateway, created Power BI dataset, deleted Power BI gateway, and deleted Power BI dataset. The **Filter results** button can be used to filter the results of the search by any of the search columns (User, Activity, Item). The **Export results** dropdown supports two formats to be exported to a **comma-separated value (CSV)** file. Specifically, the **Save loaded results** option exports only the columns displayed in the search. The **Download all results** option contains many more columns, such as the name of the app workspace and the user's web browser. However, these details are embedded in a single JSON column (AuditData), such as the following activity record:

```
{"Id":"9933734c-0dbd-
ba5b-41ce-42d89b7ac8cd","RecordType":20,"CreationTime":"2018-02-10T21:
17:18","Operation":"CreateDataset","OrganizationId":"77243ddd-
cf6a-466f-9246-06edb8809332","UserType":0,"UserKey":"10033FFFA28BA395"
,"Workload":"PowerBI","UserId":"JenLawrence@abcdef.onmicrosoft.com","C
lientIP":"12.123.645.99","UserAgent":"Mozilla\/5.0 (Windows NT 10.0;
Win64; x64) AppleWebKit\/537.36 (KHTML  like Gecko)
Chrome\/99.0.3539.132
Safari\/537.36","Activity":"CreateDataset","ItemName":"Dashboard Usage
Metrics Model","WorkSpaceName":"Global Sales","DatasetName":"Dashboard
Usage Metrics Model","WorkspaceId":"fb70ab4f-0daf-4aa8-
b704-7fae5ff9506f","ObjectId":"Dashboard Usage Metrics
Model","DatasetId":"4465997a-b043-4f7c-
b31f-82e9740ad4f1","DataConnectivityMode":"DirectQuery"}
```

As shown in the preceding activity record associated with the creation of a Power BI dataset, many more attributes of the activity are available in the audit logs which aren't displayed from the main **Audit log search** results interface. To view these additional details from the **Audit log search** page, one of the result records must be selected, thus prompting a **Details** window specific to this user activity.

> Object IDs such as `WorkspaceID` and `DatasetID` can be used to programmatically manage Power BI content via the Power BI REST API, as described in the Staged Deployments section of `Chapter 14`, *Managing Application Workspaces and Content*.

A BI team would expect the creation and deletion of datasets and gateways to be infrequent activities relative to the creation and deletion of reports and dashboards. If many datasets are being created, this could be a sign of inefficient resource utilization and version control issues. For example, rather than four reports using Live connections to a single published dataset, each report may have its own dataset, which requires its own resources and data refresh schedule (if import mode).

Excluding global admins, an Exchange Online license is required to access the auditing section of the Office 365 Security & Compliance Center. Additionally, administrators who are not global admins need to be mapped to an Exchange admin role that provides access to the audit log. As shown in the following screenshot, the **Permissions** menu of the Security & Compliance Center provides a link to the Exchange Admin center to add users to the necessary roles to access the audit logs:

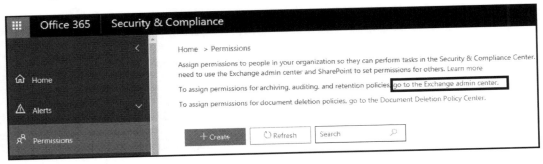

Security & Compliance Center: Permissions

Clicking the Exchange admin center link highlighted in the preceding screenshot allows a global admin to assign a user to an Exchange Online role group, such as Compliance Management, that includes access to audit logs.

 There are currently 45 distinct Power BI activities tracked in the audit logs, including the sharing of dashboards and reports, any updates to an organization's Power BI settings (**Tenant settings**), and activities related to the management of Power BI Premium capacities as described in the next section. The list of Power BI activities audited and their descriptions is available and updated at MS Docs via the following URL `http://bit.ly/2skXjAB`.

The maximum date range for an audit log search is 90 days and the date/time of each activity is presented in **Coordinated Universal Time (UTC)** format. Additionally, a maximum of 1,000 events (one user and one activity) can be displayed per audit log search. Given these limitations and the manual nature of audit log searches, a scheduled log retrieval process is necessary to support a more robust monitoring solution.

Audit log monitoring solutions

To internally develop a monitoring solution based on the audit log data, a PowerShell script which searches and exports the audit log data to a CSV file can be scheduled. This CSV file is then used as the source of an **extract-transform-load** (ETL) or **extract-load-transform** (ELT) process to persist the log data in a source system, such as a SQL Server database. Finally, Power BI Desktop can be used to implement remaining lightweight transformations, create DAX measures, and develop the monitoring reports.

The following list of steps and supporting screenshots describe the monitoring workflow in detail:

1. A PowerShell script (`.ps1`) is executed on a schedule and generates a CSV file of Power BI activities:

   The following sample script searches the audit log for Power BI activities since yesterday and exports the data to a CSV file:

   ```
   $UserCredential = Get-Credential
   $CurrentDate = get-date
   $Yesterday = $CurrentDate.AddDays(-1)
   $csvFile = "C:\Users\Brett
   ```

```
Powell\Desktop\PowerBIAuditLogs.csv"
$Session = New-PSSession -ConfigurationName
Microsoft.Exchange -ConnectionUri
https://outlook.office365.com/powershell-liveid/ -
Credential $UserCredential -Authentication Basic -
AllowRedirection

Import-PSSession $Session

$result = Search-UnifiedAuditLog -StartDate $Yesterday -
EndDate $CurrentDate -RecordType PowerBI -ResultSize 5000
| Export-Csv $csvFile
```

The `ResultSize` parameter (count of rows) of the `Search-UnifiedAuditLog` cmdlet is limited to 5,000. If not specified, the default value is 100. Depending on the level of usage in the organization, the frequency of executing the script and overall process will need to be adjusted accordingly to capture all Power BI activities.

2. An ETL (or ELT) process is executed to access the CSV file and load the new data to a data source:
   - The results of each audit log search can contain duplicate rows. However, the Identity column included in the search results can be used to eliminate these duplicate rows.

   In an on-premises MSBI environment, a combination of SQL Server Agent, **SQL Server Integration Services** (**SSIS**), and the SQL Server relational database engine could be used to implement the data retrieval process. For example, an Agent Services job could be scheduled to sequentially execute the PowerShell script, an SSIS package, and optionally a SQL Server stored procedure.

3. A Power BI dataset (`.PBIX`) with a connection to the data source in step 2 is refreshed:
   - The M query used to load the data model can include transformations to parse the JSON column and expose all columns to the data model, as shown in the following screenshot.
   - As an import mode dataset, additional data sources, such as Active Directory, could be included in the refresh process.

- Additionally, the refresh of this dataset could be triggered to execute immediately following the completion of step 2 via the Power BI Rest API, as described in the Power BI REST API section of `Chapter 14`, *Managing Application Workspaces and Content.*

In the following screenshot, audit log search result data has been connected to from Power BI Desktop:

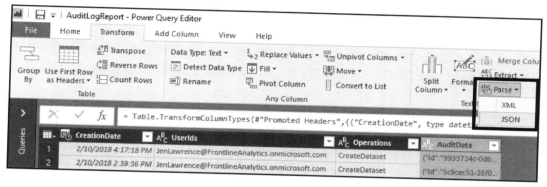

Power BI Desktop: Parse JSON transformation

As shown in the preceding screenshot, a Parse JSON command is available on the **Transform** tab of the **Power Query Editor**. Selecting the `AuditData` column containing the JSON and then the Parse JSON transform converts each cell value into a record value. Once parsed, select the outward facing arrows next to the `AuditData` column header to convert these records into individual columns.

 Technically, the two steps described here in the Power Query Editor are converted into M expressions, which utilize the `Table.TransformColumns()` and `Table.ExpandRecordColumn()` functions, respectively. As an essential M query to a monitoring solution, a review of the M syntax via the Advanced Editor and other enhancements, such as parameterizing the source file location, is recommended.

With the parsed JSON column expanded, 19 columns with an `AuditData` prefix will be available to load to the data model, as shown in the following screenshot:

Transformed audit log data

As shown in the preceding screenshot, the columns expanded will be of the Any data type in M (ABC123 icon). As `Any type` columns, these columns will be loaded to the data model as Text data type columns. Therefore, the `CreationDate` column, which is available outside the `AuditData` (JSON) column, should be used on the reporting layer as this column will be stored as a `Date/Time` type.

With a sound data retrieval process in place, DAX measures could be authored, such as the count of active users, the average number of users per day and per month, and the count of created reports or dashboards. To support security and compliance, measures and visualizations could be created targeting high-risk or undesirable activities, such as exporting report visual data or publishing reports to the web. For example, a card visual representing the count of data export activities could be pinned to a Power BI dashboard and a data alert could be configured against this dashboard tile.

Audit logs solution template

As an alternative to an internally developed monitoring solution, a Power BI solution template is now available containing an end-to-end MS Azure architecture for analyzing Power BI usage. The Power BI Usage metrics solution template created by Neal Analytics (with collaboration from Microsoft) allows the organization to leverage prebuilt data flows and Power BI usage reports as well as further customize the monitoring solution to meet their needs. Specifically, the solution template utilizes Azure Logic Apps for a recurring ETL process and Azure SQL Database to store the audit log data. Additionally, a robust Power BI dataset (relationships, measures, formatting) and several well-designed report pages will be included as a Power BI Desktop file.

The following screenshot is from the Apps Summary report page of the Power BI Usage metrics solution template:

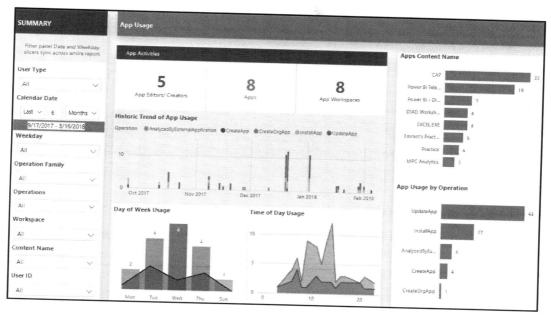

Power BI Usage metrics solution template

Several summary-level report pages similar to this example are included with the solution template, such as **Views Summary** and **Dataset Summary**. Additionally, the template contains multiple detail report pages (such as **User Details** and **Scheduling Details**) that expose all relevant attributes of specific user actions, or events in the Power BI service, such as editing a report or exporting a report. Between the dataset, the visualization layer, and the tested architecture in MS Azure, organizations can quickly derive value from the solution template and target their efforts to further improve monitoring visibility if necessary.

Links to Power BI solution templates in AppSource are available from PowerBI.com as well as Power BI Desktop. The following screenshot identifies the **Solution Templates** link under the **Solutions** menu in `PowerBI.com`:

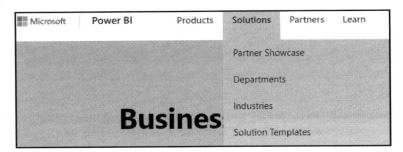

Power BI Solution Templates

In Power BI Desktop, a **Solution Templates** icon on the **Help** tab links to the solution templates in AppSource as well. The solution templates in AppSource include introductory videos, a **Test Drive** feature to interact with the Power BI report containing sample data, and a cost estimator document under the *Learn More* section.

Additionally, a **Get it Now** option provides further details on the architecture and the requirements of the template. In the following screenshot, the **Free Trial** option of the new Power BI Usage metrics solution template has been selected:

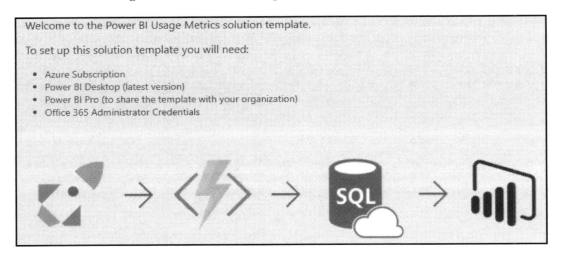

Power BI solution template: Get It Now

The preceding screenshot from the **Getting Started** tab is representative of the **Get it Now** option for other solution templates. Specifically, the templates connect to a specific source or service, process or transform that data, and load Azure SQL Database for analysis by a Power BI dataset and report. It's assumed that the current **Free Trial** option will be replaced with a **Get it Now** option later in 2018.

The natural trade-off for the solution template, of course, is the monthly cost of utilizing the underlying Azure resources. This cost will vary significantly based on the volume of users, and thus the volume of data to process and store. An estimate of this cost is not available as of this writing, but a cost estimator document is expected, similar to the documents available for other solution templates in Microsoft AppSource. For many organizations, this monthly cost (for example, $400) could be of great value relative to the development and operational costs associated with an internally developed monitoring solution.

Power BI Premium capacities

One of the most important responsibilities of a Power BI administrator is the management of Power BI Premium capacities. Power BI Premium is fully described in the following chapter but, from a Power BI service administration perspective, Power BI Premium can be thought of as an organization's dedicated hardware resources to support the use of the Power BI service. Not all of an organization's content needs to be hosted in premium capacity. However, these resources enable the distribution of content to read-only Power BI Free users and they provide more consistent performance, among other scalability and management benefits.

Power BI Premium SKUs (such as P1 and P2) are available on the Purchase services page of the Office 365 admin center. Given that Power BI Premium can also be used to deploy the Power BI Report Server, an example of a premium SKU was included in the *Power BI Report Server Licensing* section of `Chapter 16`, *Deploying the Power BI Report Server*. The specific actions involved in executing purchases of premium capacities, as well as cancellations of existing Premium subscriptions, is included via the following URL `http://bit.ly/ 2HeiXtG`.

Office 365 global administrators and users assigned to the Power BI service administrator role automatically have the right to administer premium capacities in the Power BI admin portal. An administrator's role in relation to premium capacity is to ensure that the provisioned resources are utilized according to the organization's policies, and that sufficient resources are available to support the existing workload.

Power BI Premium administrators should be familiar with the following list of responsibilities:

- Create a new capacity with the available (purchased) v-cores:
  - An organization may choose to dedicate a premium capacity to a specific project or application
  - In other scenarios, one capacity could be dedicated self-service projects while another capacity could be used by corporate BI projects.
    - See `Chapter 19`, *Scaling with Premium and Analysis Services* for additional details on allocating premium capacity.

- Grant capacity assignment permissions to users or security groups of users:
  - This enables Power BI Pro users who are also administrators of app workspaces to assign their workspaces to premium capacity
  - This setting can also be disabled or enabled for the entire organization

- Assign workspaces to premium capacity, or remove a workspace from premium capacity, in the Power BI admin portal:
  - This is an alternative and complementary approach to capacity assignment permissions
  - Power BI service administrators can manage existing capacities and assign workspaces in bulk:
    - These bulk assignments can be by user, by security group of users, or for the entire organization

- Monitor the usage metrics of premium capacities to ensure sufficient resources are available:
  - The Power BI Admin portal includes utilization monitoring for each premium capacity
  - Additionally, activities involving premium capacities such as the migration of an app workspace to a premium capacity are included in the audit logs described earlier in this chapter

- Change the size on an existing capacity to a larger (scale up) or smaller (scale down) capacity node:
  - As more users and content utilize a specific capacity, it may be necessary to scale up or to allocate certain app workspaces to a different premium capacity or to shared (free) capacity

- Assign a user or group of users as capacity administrators for a capacity:
  - This can be appropriate to support large, enterprise deployments with multiple capacities and many app workspaces

Given the importance of performance to any BI project, as well as the cost of Power BI Premium capacities, it's important for BI/IT teams to plan for an efficient, manageable allocation of premium capacity as described in the next chapter. This allocation plan and any project-specific decisions need to be communicated to the premium administrator(s) for implementation. The following sections describe the responsibilities identified here and related considerations in greater detail.

Capacity allocation

Power BI Premium provides organizations with significant flexibility for both allocating their resources to premium capacities, as well as assigning Power BI content to those capacities. A single premium capacity can be provisioned and created for an organization or, for larger and more diverse deployments, multiple premium capacities can be created with different sizes (CPU, memory, bandwidth) appropriate for their specific workloads.

In terms of allocating resources to premium capacities, an organization is only limited by the number of **virtual cores (v-cores)** that have been purchased. For example, an organization could initially purchase a P2 capacity, which includes 16 v-cores. Once purchased, a P2 capacity could be created in the **Capacity settings** page of the **Admin portal** that utilizes all of these cores. However, at some later date, this capacity could be changed to a P1 capacity which only uses 8 v-cores. This would allow the organization to create a second P1 capacity given the eight remaining v-cores available. Alternatively, a second P2 capacity could be purchased, providing another 16 v-cores. With 32 total v-cores purchased by the organization, an existing P2 capacity could be increased to a P3 capacity (32 v-cores).

The following diagram illustrates this example of capacity allocation:

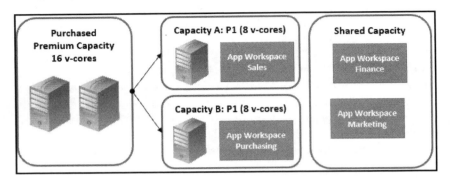

Power BI Premium capacity allocation

Regardless of the premium SKU (P1, P2, or P3), the combination of SKUs purchased in the Office 365 admin center, or the number of specific SKUs (instances), an organization can use the total number of v-cores purchased as it wishes. For example, purchasing a P3 SKU provides 32 v-cores, the same as purchasing four instances of a P1 SKU (8 X 4 = 32).

 For organizations getting started with Power BI and that are comfortable with actively managing their premium capacities, individual instances of the P1 SKU with no annual commitment (month-to-month) could make sense. For example, a single P1 instance could be purchased to start and then, if it's determined that more resources are needed, a second P1 instance could be purchased, making 16 cores available for either a P2 capacity or two P1 capacities.

In this diagram, an organization has chosen to isolate the sales and purchasing app workspaces to their own P1 capacities with eight v-cores each. This isolation ensures that the resources required for one workspace, such as the user's connection to the **Sales** app, will not impact the other workspace (**Purchasing**). Additionally, the **Finance** and **Marketing** workspaces have been left in shared (free) capacity for now, but could later be assigned to **Capacity A** or **Capacity B** if sufficient resources are available.

Whether Power BI workspaces (dashboards, reports, datasets) are allocated to premium capacity or shared capacity is transparent to end users. For example, the same login and content navigation experience in the Power BI web service and Power BI mobile apps applies to both premium and shared capacity. Therefore, organizations can selectively allocate certain workspaces, such as production workspaces accessed by many Power BI Free users, to premium capacity while allowing other small or team workspaces to remain in the shared capacity.

Different patterns for deploying premium capacity are discussed in the following chapters but, at a minimum, administrators should be familiar with the relationships between purchased premium capacity and premium capacities configured for an organization, as well as the assignment of app workspaces to those capacities.

Create, size, and monitor capacities

Office 365 global admins and Power BI service administrators can view, create, and manage all Power BI Premium capacities via the Admin portal. In the following screenshot from the **Capacity settings** page of the **Admin portal**, eight v-cores have been provisioned for the organization and a single P1 capacity has been created, which consumes all of these cores:

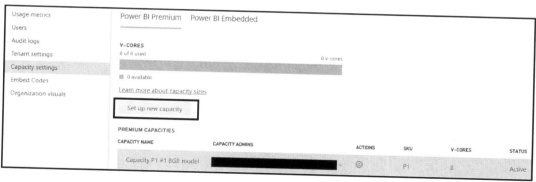

Admin portal: Capacity settings

As shown in the preceding screenshot, a **Set up new capacity** button is located above the list of premium capacities that have been configured. In this example, since all purchased v-cores have been used by a single capacity, the **Set up new capacity** button is grayed out. In the event that v-cores are available for a new capacity, clicking **Set up new capacity** button would launch a setup window, such as the following:

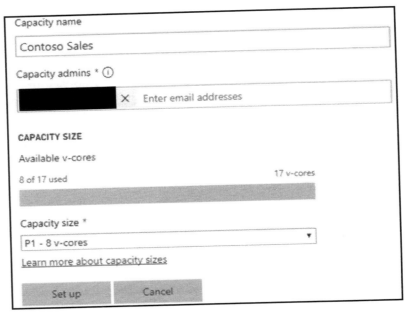

Set up new Premium Capacity

In this example, nine v-cores are available for the new capacity and thus a P1 capacity requiring eight v-cores can be created. The capacity is named and the capacity administrator(s) for the new capacity are defined. The **Capacity size** dropdown will expose all different capacity sizes (P2, P3) but sizes requiring more v-cores than the volume of v-cores currently available will be grayed out. Once these properties have been configured, click **Set up** to complete the process.

Note that the **Capacity size** and **Capacity admins** properties are required to set up the new capacity. Each capacity must have at least one capacity admin, who will have full administrative rights to the given capacity. Additional information on capacity admins is included in the *Power BI Capacity Admins* section later in this chapter.

Change capacity size

At some point after a capacity has been created, it may be necessary to change the size of the capacity. For example, given increased adoption of Power BI, the P1 SKU may be insufficient to support the current workload and thus an additional eight v-cores could be purchased with the intent to scale up the existing capacity to a P2 capacity size (16 v-cores). Alternatively, an admin may wish to view the recent utilization of a premium capacity to help determine whether additional app workspaces can be assigned to the capacity.

To change a capacity size and to view the utilization for a capacity, click the name of the capacity from the **Capacity settings** page described earlier. In the following screenshot, the **Capacity P1 #1 8GB model** from the **Capacity settings** screenshot earlier has been selected:

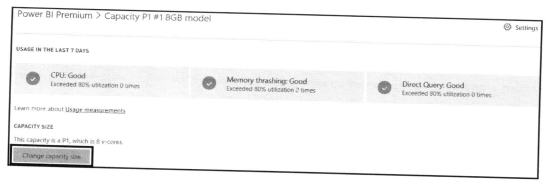

Manage premium capacity

A yellow **Change capacity size** button is exposed below the three usage metrics (**CPU**, **Memory thrashing**, and **Direct Query**). Selecting this button launches a simple window with a **Capacity size** dropdown, such as the **Capacity size** dropdown used for setting up a capacity. In this scenario, all capacity size options are grayed out in the **Change capacity size** window since the P1 capacity consumes all available v-cores. Nonetheless, with just a few clicks in the Admin portal, an admin can scale up or down a capacity.

Monitor premium capacities

The three usage metrics displayed in the manage capacity screen have built-in KPI formatting and conditional logic for good (green), marginal (yellow), and critical (red) statuses. Depending on the type of datasets (import, DirectQuery) and many other factors (such as usage patterns and query complexity), any of the three resources (CPU, memory, bandwidth) could represent a bottleneck.

For example, a P1 capacity has only 25 GB of RAM and thus will not be suitable for very large import (in-memory) datasets. It's recommended to monitor these metrics and to make adjustments if necessary to ensure users have an acceptable experience in terms of performance and responsiveness.

The usage metrics are driven by hourly time windows of activity for the given capacity over the past seven days. For example, the CPU usage metric (far left) will count the number of hours out of the last 168 hours (7 days * 24 hours) that experienced CPU utilization over 80%. These instances of high CPU utilization could be driven by the refresh process of an import mode dataset or users viewing and clicking through reports. During these high-CPU hours, users may experience poor performance when accessing or interacting with reports.

The refresh process for large, in-memory Power BI datasets and Analysis Services models is CPU intensive. For this reason, most scale out deployments of Analysis Services isolate the processing operations from the query workload. Specifically, a dedicated Analysis Services server would connect to the source(s) and refresh the model, and then the updated model would be synchronized to multiple separate servers which resolve user queries. This architecture is already available in Azure Analysis Services and a dedicated processing server is identified on the roadmap for Power BI Premium.

The memory thrashing usage metric (middle) measures how often in-memory datasets are evicted from memory. Premium capacities opportunistically keep frequently utilized datasets loaded to memory to reduce load performance. However, with multiple in-memory datasets assigned to a capacity, and given the fixed amount of RAM provided per capacity (such as 50 GB for P2), the service may unload a dataset from memory to use this memory for other datasets. Users requesting to access an unloaded dataset, such as viewing a report based on the dataset, could experience long wait times for the report to display data.

The Direct Query usage metric (far right) refers to throughput or concurrent queries over both Direct Query connections and Live connections to Analysis Services models. In addition to V-Cores and RAM, each premium capacity includes a connection limit for the maximum volume of DirectQuery/Live connection queries per second, such as 30 per second for a P1 capacity. In the event that this limit is exceeded, the incremental queries beyond the throughput limit will be forced to wait.

For example, in the event that 80 DirectQuery or Live connection queries are received by the P1 premium capacity, 30 queries will be executed in the first second with no delay. However, another 30 queries will have to wait one second before being executed, and finally, the remaining 20 queries will have to wait two seconds before executing. This wait time is in addition to the time required to execute the requested query by the data source system and thus represents a potential bottleneck for large-scale Power BI deployments with DirectQuery and Live connection data sources, if appropriate premium capacities are not provisioned.

As shown in the screenshots and diagram in this section, administrators have tools to monitor the performance of premium capacities and to scale up and down as an organization's needs and available resources allow. Once premium capacities have been created and sized, the next step is to assign app workspaces to these capacities so that an organization's content is moved from free (shared) capacity to the appropriate dedicated premium capacity.

Premium capacities can be allocated at a granular level, such as individual app workspaces, or broadly applied to all workspaces of an organization. Additionally, as described in the following sections, Power BI administrators can also delegate administrative rights over premium capacities, as well as authorize certain Power BI users to assign workspaces to premium capacity.

App workspace assignment

Just as organizations have the flexibility to allocate their purchased v-cores across one or multiple premium capacities, there are also multiple options for assigning app workspaces to premium capacity. To bulk assign multiple workspaces to a capacity within the Admin portal, click the **Assign workspaces** button for a capacity. This button and the list of workspaces already assigned to the capacity is below the **Change capacity size** button described in the previous section.

In the following screenshot, two workspaces have been selected for assignment to a premium capacity:

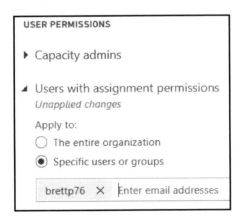

Assign workspaces

As shown in the preceding screenshot, the workspaces associated with individual users or groups of users can also be assigned to a premium capacity. If applied to specific users, any existing workspaces assigned to those users, including workspaces already in a separate capacity, will be moved to the capacity assigned.

As an alternative or complementary approach to assigning workspaces in the admin portal, administrators of a capacity can also grant users or groups of users the permission to assign workspaces to premium capacity. In the following screenshot, a user (**brettp76**) is granted assignment permission to a premium capacity:

Assignment Permissions

The **USER PERMISSIONS** options, which also includes **Capacity admins** described in the following section, is also just below the **Change capacity size** button, such as the **Assign workspaces** button. Users granted this permission will also require administrative rights to any app workspace they wish to assign to premium capacity.

In the following screenshot, a Power BI Pro user (**brettp76**) and administrator of an app workspace have opened the **Edit workspace** dialog to assign a workspace to premium capacity:

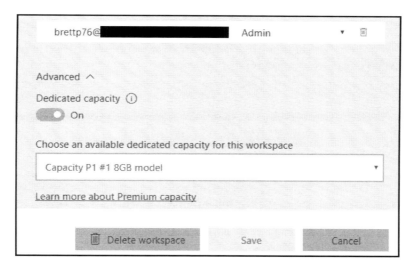

App workspace administrator: Assign to premium capacity

The differences between app workspace administrators and members were described in the Application Workspaces section of Chapter 14, *Managing Application Workspaces and Content*.

Capacity admins

One or more capacity admins are required for each premium capacity, and these users do not have to be an Office 365 global admin or a Power BI service admin. Users assigned as capacity administrators have the same administrative rights to the given capacity as Power BI Service admins, such as changing capacity size and assigning workspaces or user assignment permissions.

For example, a Power BI Pro user could be assigned as a capacity admin and could access this capacity via the Admin portal just like a Power BI admin. However, only the capacities for which the user is a capacity admin would appear on the **Capacity settings** page. Additionally, other pages of the **Admin portal**, such as **Tenant settings**, would not be visible or accessible to the capacity admin.

Summary

This chapter reviewed the features and processes applicable to administering Power BI for an organization. These included the configuration of tenant settings in the Power BI admin portal, analyzing the usage of Power BI assets, and monitoring overall user activity via the Office 365 audit logs. Additionally, important administrative capabilities of Azure Active Directory, such as conditional access policies and external guest users, were also described. Moreover, the tasks and options available to administer Power BI Premium capacity were also detailed.

The following chapter looks at the options for scaling Power BI to support increased user adoption, larger data sets, and enterprise BI solutions. This includes methodologies for allocating Power BI Premium capacity to workloads, leveraging the additional benefits of Power BI Premium, and migrating Power BI datasets to Analysis Services.

19
Scaling with Premium and Analysis Services

For many organizations, the deployment of Power BI entails the reporting and self-service needs of hundreds or even thousands of users, as well as massive datasets. Power BI Premium and Analysis Services are positioned to address these needs via workload-based pricing, flexible scale-up and scale-out options, and enterprise-grade semantic modeling features. Although organizations and certain projects may start out with Power BI Desktop and shared capacity in the Power BI service, the utilization of Power BI Premium capacity and optionally the migration to Analysis Services is often essential to deliver the scale, **return on investment (ROI)**, and administrative controls of an enterprise BI platform.

This chapter begins with a review of the capabilities enabled by Power BI Premium capacities and the top considerations in provisioning this capacity. In addition to premium capacities, **Azure Analysis Services (AAS)** and **SQL Server Analysis Services (SSAS)** are introduced as enterprise BI modeling tools with features that address limitations with Power BI Desktop. Finally, the steps and considerations in the migration of a Power BI Desktop file to an Analysis Services model are described.

In this chapter, we will review the following topics:

- Power BI Premium
- Power BI Premium provisioning factors
- Power BI Premium capacity allocation
- Analysis Services versus Power BI datasets
- Azure Analysis Services and SQL Server Analysis Services
- Migration from Power BI dataset to Analysis Services model

Power BI Premium

Power BI Premium consists of dedicated capacity (hardware) that an organization can provision to host some or all of its Power BI content (datasets, reports, and dashboards). As an alternative to the free clusters of capacity provided by Microsoft and shared by many organizations, premium capacities are isolated to a specific organization and thus are not impacted by the use of Power BI by other organizations. Another very important benefit of this isolation is that the provisioning organization can utilize their capacity as needed and is not constrained by the limits imposed on shared (free) capacity, such as dataset sizes and refresh frequencies. Additionally, as a cloud service managed by Microsoft, organizations have great flexibility to scale, allocate, and manage premium resources according to their preferred allocation methodology and changing requirements.

The top benefit of Power BI Premium is the ability to provide read-only access to Power BI Free users and thus cost-effectively scale Power BI deployments based on workloads rather than individual user accounts. This is particularly essential for large organizations with thousands of users, the majority of which only need the ability to view and optionally interact with content. If Power BI content is hosted in a premium capacity, the users consuming content such as via Power BI apps can view and interact with the content, such as making filter selections on a report or viewing a mobile-optimized dashboard on Power BI mobile applications. Power BI Premium enables organizations to limit the assignment of Power BI Pro users to those who will create and distribute content and to focus on provisioning and allocating premium resources according to the use cases and needs of workloads within the organization.

 Prior to Power BI Premium, the cost and management overhead of assigning pro licenses to all users in an organization was the main barrier to large-scale deployments. From a customer's perspective, it simply doesn't make sense to pay the same price for a user that only views a few reports and dashboards each week as for a BI developer who's working in Power BI constantly. Additionally, as usage patterns and the scope of BI solutions can change rapidly, the ability to quickly scale up or down premium resources and thus only pay for what's needed, similar to other cloud services, was a top request from customers.

Additionally, Power BI Premium capacity can be used to deliver Power BI content to users in applications and environments outside of the Power BI service. For example, premium capacity can be used to embed Power BI visuals in custom applications, in other SaaS applications such as SharePoint Online, and can be used to license the Power BI Report Server. Details regarding the Power BI Report Server and alternative content distribution methods are included in Chapter 16, *Deploying the Power BI Report Server*, and Chapter 17, *Creating Power BI Apps and Content Distribution*, respectively.

The premium capacity-based licensing model, which currently starts at $5,000 per month for a P1 SKU, implies the following three fundamental questions:

1. How much premium capacity should be provisioned?
2. How should provisioned capacity be allocated?
3. What can be done to minimize capacity utilization and thus resource costs?

Guidance and consideration of these questions are included in the following sections.

 Premium Embedded SKUs (EM3), which are exclusive to embedding Power BI content in applications or services such as SharePoint Online, have a lower starting price point and fewer resources. As most organizations will leverage the Power BI service and mobile apps for large-scale deployments, Power BI Premium P SKUs are the focus of this chapter.

Power BI Premium capabilities

Power BI Premium already provides several additional capabilities beyond the ability to distribute content to read-only Power BI Free users. As described in Chapter 18, *Administering Power BI for an Organization*, organizations have full control over their provisioned resources and therefore, unlike provisioning on-premises hardware, can quickly and easily adjust the amount and allocation of premium resources. For example, with v-core pooling, an organization can choose to distribute the 32 v-cores of a P3 capacity SKU across two P1 capacities and a single P2 capacity (8 + 8 +16 = 32). Likewise, with single-click scale up, an organization could provision an additional 8 v-cores by purchasing a P1 SKU and then change an existing P1 capacity to a P2 capacity, which requires 16 v-cores. The details of the hardware of each premium capacity node (CPU, RAM, and bandwidth) and the limits imposed on using those nodes are included in the *Premium capacity nodes* section.

The following table describes 12 capabilities of Power BI Premium that are either currently available or have been identified by the Power BI team as a potential capability in the future:

#	Capability	Detail	Available	Future
1	Content Distribution	Power BI Free users can view and interact with content hosted in premium capacities.	Yes	N/A
2	V-Core Pooling	The total number of provisioned v-cores can be allocated in any capacity configuration.	Yes	N/A
3	Single-Click Scale Up	If sufficient v-cores are available, an existing capacity can be modified to a larger capacity.	Yes	N/A
4	Large Datasets	Host Power BI datasets much larger than the 1GB limit in shared (free) capacity.	Yes – 10GB	Yes – 100GB+
5	Scheduled Data Refresh Frequency	Refresh Power BI datasets more frequently than the 8X per day limit in shared capacity.	Yes – 48X/day	Yes – More Frequently
6	Large Dataset Storage	Store large amounts of data beyond the 10GB per Pro user license limit in shared capacity.	Yes – 100TB per capacity	N/A
7	Single Dataset Across Workspaces	Publish reports to app workspaces based on a dataset in a separate app workspace.	No	TBD
8	Incremental Refresh	Define a rule for only refreshing new or changed data.	No	2018
9	Pin Dataset to Memory	Prevent a dataset from being evicted from memory to avoid inconsistent performance.	No	TBD – Roadmap
10	SQL Server Reporting Services Reports	Publish paginated SQL Server Reporting Services reports (.RDL format) to Power BI Premium workspaces.	No	2018
11	Connectivity Parity with Analysis Services	Connect to Power BI Premium workspaces from all tools supported by Analysis Services (SSMS, Visual Studio, Tableau, etc)	No	2018
12	Dedicated Data Refresh Nodes	Isolate report query activities from data refresh activities in scale out deployment.	No	TBD- Roadmap
13	Read-Only Replicas (Scale Out)	Copies of datasets automatically created within other capacity nodes of dedicated capacity. Query load balancing across the capacity nodes.	No	TBD- Roadmap
14	Geo-Replicas (Scale Out)	Replica is copied to a node in a separate data center region to reduce the distance between users and datasets.	No	TBD- Roadmap

Power BI Premium capabilities

Some of the capabilities identified in this table enable completely new scenarios for projects involving Power BI datasets created with Power BI Desktop. For example, up to a 10 GB dataset can be hosted in Premium capacity currently and much larger datasets will be supported in the future. Likewise, a dataset can be configured to refresh every 30 minutes in premium capacity and this frequency will also increase in the future. Incremental data refresh is expected to be delivered by mid-2018, and this will address a critical gap in the ability to leverage a large Power BI dataset. The following section, Corporate Power BI datasets, reviews the **Single Dataset Across Workspaces** (#7) limitation that may also support this deployment option.

The ability to publish **SQL Server Reporting Services (SSRS)** reports, also referred to as paginated reports or (`.RDL` reports), to the Power BI service will be especially valuable for organizations with significant SSRS investments. Without this capability, these organizations have needed to deploy the Power BI Report Server (or an SSRS server) as described in Chapter 16, *Deploying the Power BI Report Server*. Additionally, connectivity parity with Analysis Services will allow organizations to utilize familiar development and management tools such as Visual Studio and **SQL Server Management Studio (SSMS)** to apply lifecycle management processes to Power BI datasets as they would with Analysis Services models. Moreover, connectivity parity with Analysis Services will allow organizations to leverage other common data visualization and BI tools such as Tableau. For example, both Power BI and Tableau reports could be built against a Power BI dataset provided the dataset is assigned to a workspace in premium capacity.

To support the largest Power BI deployments, a scale-out option involving read-only replicas with load balancing and dedicated data refresh nodes is mentioned in the roadmap section of the Power BI Premium October 2017 whitepaper. This document and other Power BI whitepapers can be accessed at the following URL http://bit.ly/2Hu57DK.

Corporate Power BI datasets

Given the features described in the previous section, Premium capacity can be used to support entirely new scenarios with Power BI datasets. For example, rather than migrate a Power BI Desktop file (`.PBIX`) to an Analysis Services model, as described later in this chapter, an organization could choose to provision the necessary Premium capacity and leverage the scalability (that is, 10 GB+) and data refresh features available to content hosted in Premium capacity.

Limitation of Corporate BI datasets – Reusability

A significant barrier to leveraging a large Power BI dataset is the link between Power BI Live connection reports and the dataset(s) in their app workspace. For example, if an organization wishes to create three Power BI apps targeting three separate business units, a separate Power BI dataset currently needs to be hosted within the app workspace for each app. Naturally, any BI/IT organization would want to avoid creating (and managing) copies of a Power BI dataset, including its data model, queries, and measures.

This barrier or limitation is being worked on by the Power BI team so that, at some point in the future, a single Power BI dataset is expected to be able to support reports hosted in multiple workspaces. This isolation between visualizations (reports and dashboards) and datasets would lend itself to the following solution architecture:

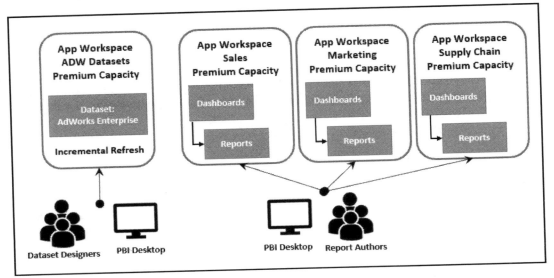

Power BI dataset supporting multiple app workspaces

As shown in the preceding diagram, a team's dataset designer(s) could be responsible for a single but potentially very large and complex Power BI dataset, including many fact and dimension tables. The dataset would be hosted in a premium capacity with v-cores and RAM aligned to its size and incremental data refresh could be configured to only load recent or new data. From a data visualization and distribution standpoint, report authors would create Live connection Power BI reports based on the large dataset (AdWorks Enterprise) and publish these reports to specific app workspaces. These reports would be refreshed based on the refresh schedule for the source dataset and, in the case of DirectQuery datasets, a scheduled cache refresh could be configured for the dashboards.

 Although the capability suggested previously is not yet available, it's assumed that both the dataset workspace and the visualization workspaces (reports, dashboards) would need to be assigned to the same Premium capacity.

As of February 2018, no timeline has been provided on the availability of this feature. Therefore, even with support for incremental data refresh and very large datasets, the need to maintain a single, consolidated data model will lead many organizations to choose Analysis Services models for corporate BI solutions. Additional reasons for choosing Analysis Services models over Power BI Desktop are included in the Analysis Services section later in this chapter.

Premium capacity nodes

A premium capacity node can be thought of as a fully managed server in the Azure cloud which runs the Power BI service. The capacity node is dedicated and isolated to the organization that provisioned the capacity and the same user experience and functionality is delivered as the shared (free) capacity provided by the Power BI service. Each capacity node has a set of processing and memory resources (v-cores and RAM), bandwidth limits, and a cost that aligns with these resources. For example, a P1 capacity node includes 8 v-cores and 25 GB of RAM at a cost of $5,000 per month, while a P2 capacity includes 16 v-cores and 50 GB of RAM at a cost of $10,000 per month. When app workspaces containing Power BI content (datasets, reports, and dashboards) are assigned to premium capacity nodes, the resources of the given capacity node are used to execute Power BI activities associated with this content, such as query processing and data refresh operations.

Chapter 18, *Administering Power BI for an Organization,* referred to the v-cores (virtual processing cores) of Premium capacity nodes but didn't provide details on other resources (RAM and bandwidth) and their relationship to Power BI workloads. For example, if all Power BI reports will utilize a DirectQuery dataset or a Live connection to an Analysis Services model, then the amount of RAM provided per capacity will be much less important than the limits on the number of connections and the max page renders at peak times. In these deployments, the resources provisioned for the data source system (CPU cores, clock speed, and RAM), as well as the latency and bandwidth of the connection between the source system and the data center region of the Power BI tenant, would largely drive query performance.

The following table identifies the resources associated the six EM and P Premium capacity nodes currently available:

Capacity Node	Total V-Cores	Frontend Cores	Backend Cores	RAM (GB)	DirectQuery / Live Connections Per Second	Max Page Renders at Peak Hour
EM1	1	.5	.5	2.5	3.75	150-300
EM2	2	1	1	5	7.5	301-600
EM3	4	2	2	10	N/A	601-1,200
P1	8	4	4	25	30	1,201-2,400
P2	16	8	8	50	60	2,401-4,800
P3	32	16	16	100	120	4,801-9,600

Premium capacity nodes

As shown in this table, as of February 2018 the largest premium capacity node includes 32 v-cores, 100 GB of RAM, and supports a max of 120 DirectQuery or Live connection queries per second. Larger capacity nodes, such as a P4 with 64 v-cores and 200 GB of RAM, will likely be released later in 2018 and will complement a scale out (multi-node) capacity as identified in the Power BI Premium whitepaper for October of 2017.

As shown in the *Custom application embedding* section of `Chapter 17`, *Creating Power BI Apps and Content Distribution*, EM SKUs are exclusive to embedding Power BI content in applications and do not support viewing content in the Power BI service or Power BI mobile apps. Given these more limited workloads, EM SKUs have significantly less resources and cost less to provision. Premium P SKUs (P1, P2, and P3), however, support both embedding content in applications and the usage of the Power BI service.

Microsoft Azure resources such as Azure Analysis Services or Azure SQL Database, which can be created within the same region as the Power BI service tenant, provide their own user interface and tools for scaling up and down as the needs of workloads dictate. Guidance on identifying the location of your Power BI tenant, and thus the preferred location for Power BI data sources, is included in the *Top gateway planning tasks* section of `Chapter 15`, *Managing the On-Premises Data Gateway*. The minimal distance between a Power BI tenant and an Azure data source in the same data center region provides a natural performance advantage over connections to on-premises sources via the On-premises data gateway.

Frontend versus backend resources

It's important to understand the composition of frontend and backend resources in relation to Power BI workloads. For example, although a P2 capacity provides 16 total v-cores, only 8 backend cores are dedicated to processing queries, refreshing datasets, and server-side rendering of reports. Additionally, only the backend of a premium capacity node, such as the 50 GB of RAM for a P2 capacity, is exclusive to the provisioning organization. If Power BI is only being used to create reports and dashboards against DirectQuery or Live connection sources, then these backend resources are less important and the connection limit (60 per second for a P2 capacity) would be the most relevant resource to understand and monitor.

The frontend cores (8 for a P2) are shared with other organizations in a pool of servers responsible for the web service, the management of reports and dashboards, uploads/downloads, and the user experience in navigating the Power BI service generally. Organizations that utilize Power BI datasets in the default import (in-memory) mode will want to ensure sufficient RAM and backend cores are available to support both the data refresh process and the query workloads.

The following diagram illustrates the distribution of frontend and backend resources for a P2 capacity node:

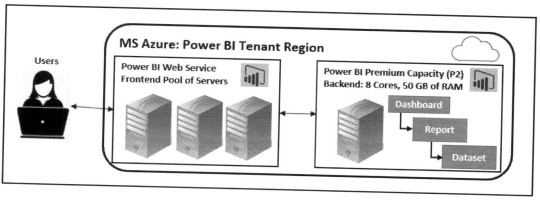

Power BI Premium Capacity node (P2)

As shown in this diagram, the backend of a capacity node can be thought of as a dedicated server or virtual machine with a fixed amount of CPU and RAM. It's the backend server which is responsible for the most resource-intensive or *heavy lifting* operations and thus should always be considered in relation to the resource needs of import mode datasets assigned to the given capacity.

In the near future, organizations will be able to fully utilize the memory included in their capacity to host even larger Power BI datasets (100 GB+), containing hundreds of millions or even billions of rows. To support these scenarios, BI teams will want to provision a capacity node with enough cores and RAM to support the data refresh operation and user queries against this dataset.

A factor of 2.5X is generally used to size the RAM requirements of in-memory Power BI datasets and Analysis Services Tabular models. For example, a 10 GB Power BI dataset (.PBIX), would require 25 GB of RAM (10 * 2.5 = 25). This estimate is based on 10 GB to store the dataset in-memory, another 10 GB for a copy of the dataset which is created during full refresh/processing operations, and an extra 5 GB to support temporary memory structures that can be required to resolve user queries.

Note that this example is exclusive to import mode datasets hosted in the Power BI premium capacity (the backend server). A separate architecture and considerations for capacity nodes apply when query requests are routed to Analysis Services models via Live connection or a DirectQuery data source such as Teradata or SAP HANA. From a premium capacity perspective, in these scenarios, the BI team would need to determine via load testing and the usage metrics described in the *Monitor premium capacities* section of Chapter 18, *Administering Power BI for an Organization*, whether the query throughput limit (60 per second for P2) to these sources will be sufficient. If this throughput level is sufficient yet performance is still unacceptable, several other components of the overall solution could represent the performance bottleneck and could be evaluated separately.

These other components or factors impacting performance include the design of the data model and the efficiency or complexity of DAX measures, the design of the data source and its available resources, the design of Power BI reports (for example, quantity and type of visuals), the resources and performance of the gateway server(s) if applicable, the network connection between the Power BI service and the data source, and the level of user interactivity with reports. Techniques and practices to optimize data models and the visualization layer in Power BI are provided in the *Data model optimizations* and *Report and visualization optimizations* sections later in this chapter, respectively.

Power BI Premium capacity allocation

Although it's possible to broadly assign all app workspaces (and thus all content) of an organization to a single premium capacity, most organizations will want to efficiently allocate and manage these resources. For example, certain Power BI reports and dashboards that are utilized by executives or which contribute to important business processes will be identified and prioritized for premium capacity. In an initial deployment of a premium capacity, a BI/IT team may exclusively assign the workspaces associated with content considered mission critical to this capacity. This capacity may remain isolated to the specific workload(s) or, based on testing and monitoring, the BI team may determine that sufficient resources are available to support additional workspaces and their associated resource requirements.

Similar to provisioning a premium capacity exclusive to high-value content, a premium capacity may be provisioned due to the unique requirements of a particular solution. As one example, a new Power BI dataset may be developed that represents a data source or business process not currently supported in the data warehouse. In this scenario, a large import mode Power BI dataset, perhaps initially developed by the business team, would serve as the source for reports and dashboards which require distribution to many Power BI Free users or even the entire organization. Given these characteristics, a premium capacity node could be provisioned and dedicated to the app workspace hosting this dataset and its visualizations so that no other solution could impact its performance.

The following section describes a capacity planning method.

Corporate and Self-Service BI capacity

As described in the *Data governance for Power BI* section of `Chapter 18`, *Administering Power BI for an Organization*, certain projects will likely be wholly owned by the BI/IT team including the report and visualization layer. Other projects, however, may be owned by business units or teams but still require or benefit from IT-provided resources such as the On-premises data gateway and premium capacity. The BI department can manage a continuous life cycle over both project types (Corporate BI, Self-Service BI) by validating use cases or requirements for premium capacity. Additionally, the migration of Power BI content across distinct premium capacities could become part of a standard migration process from a self-service solution to a corporate BI owned solution.

The provisioning and allocation of Power BI Premium capacity can further reflect an organization's support for both Corporate and Self-Service BI solutions. Typically the Power BI content created and managed by IT is considered mission critical to the organization or is accessed by a high volume of users. Self-service BI solutions, however, tend to utilize smaller datasets and usually need to be accessible to a smaller group of users.

The following example allocation includes two premium capacities, a **P3**, and a **P2**, dedicated to **Corporate BI Capacity** and **Self-Service BI Capacity** content, respectively:

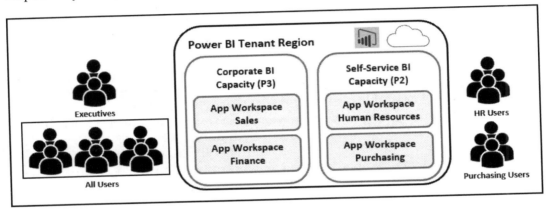

Power BI Premium Capacity allocation: Corporate and Self-Service BI

As shown in the diagram the sales, and a finance app workspace has been assigned to a P3 capacity dedicated to corporate BI solutions. As described in the *Premium capacity nodes* section earlier, a P3 capacity is currently the largest premium capacity available with 32 v-cores. These additional resources and limits, such as a max of 120 DirectQuery or Live connection queries per second, may be required to support organization-wide usage and an optimal user experience.

The Human Resources and Purchasing workspaces, however, have been assigned to a P2 Premium capacity dedicated to self-service BI projects. For example, certain Power BI Pro users in these departments have developed datasets and reports that have proven to be valuable to several stakeholders. The assignment of these workspaces to premium capacity enables these users to make this content accessible to a wider audience, such as the 20 Power BI Free users in the Purchasing department.

Remember that not all app workspaces will need to consume premium capacity resources. A team of Power BI Pro users may collaborate within an app workspace and still be effective with the content hosted in the shared capacity. Premium capacity is only needed in scenarios requiring broad distribution to read-only Power BI Free users or when the additional capabilities (for example, large datasets) identified in the *Power BI Premium capabilities* section earlier in this chapter are required.

In the event that one of the self-service solutions needs to be migrated to the corporate BI team, the BI team could re-assign the workspace to the existing P3 capacity. Alternatively, to avoid consuming any additional resources of the existing P3 capacity and potentially impacting these workloads, a new corporate BI capacity could be created for the workspace.

BI teams will consistently need to evaluate the trade-offs involved with isolating projects/solutions to specific premium capacities. Assigning a single workspace or multiple related workspaces to a dedicated capacity ensures that no other project or activity will impact performance. However, many dedicated premium capacities may become onerous to manage and could be an inefficient use of resources if the Power BI workload doesn't fully utilize the resources. Ultimately, teams will need to monitor capacity resource utilization and either re-allocate and re-assign capacities and workspaces, respectively, or provision additional premium resources (v-cores) and scale up existing capacities.

Power BI Premium resource utilization

Given the cost of premium capacity, BI teams will want to follow practices to ensure that these resources are actually required and not being used inefficiently. For example, with large import mode datasets, a simple design change such as the removal of unused columns from a fact table can significantly reduce the size of the dataset and thus the amount of memory needed. By following a series of recommended practices in terms of both modeling and report design, less premium capacity resources will be required to deliver the same query performance and scale.

With small-scale self-service BI datasets and reports, performance tuning and optimization is usually not necessary. Nonetheless, as these models and reports can later take on greater scale and importance, a basic review of the solution can be applied before the content is assigned to premium capacity. For example, the BI/IT team can identify a few small changes to be implemented prior to assigning the pro user's workspace to premium capacity.

The following two sections identify several of the top data modeling and report design practices to efficiently utilize hardware resources.

Data model optimizations

For many data models, particularly those that were developed as part of pilot projects or by business users, a number of modifications can be implemented to reduce resource requirements or improve query performance. Therefore, prior to concluding that a certain amount of Premium capacity (or Analysis Services resources) is required, data models can be evaluated against a number of standard design practices and optimization techniques such as the following:

- Avoid duplicate or near-duplicate data models:
    - Design and maintain a consolidated, standardized data model of fact and dimension tables.

- Remove tables and columns that aren't needed by the model:
    - For import mode models, columns with the unique values (cardinality) will be the most expensive to store and scan at query time.
    - The *Fact table columns* section of Chapter 9, *Designing Import and DirectQuery Data Models* provides examples of avoiding derived columns that, for import mode models, can be efficiently implemented via DAX measures.

- Reduce the precision and cardinality of columns when possible:
    - If four digits to the right of the decimal place are sufficient precision, revise a column's data type from a **Decimal number** to a **Fixed decimal number** (19, 4):
        - Apply rounding if even less precision is required.
    - Split columns containing multiple values such as a datetime column into separate columns (date and time).

- Limit or avoid high cardinality relationships, such as dimension tables with over 1.5 million rows:
    - Consider splitting very large dimension tables into two tables and defining relationships between these tables and the fact table. The less granular table (such as `Product Subcategory` grain) could support most reports while the more granular table (such as `Product`) could be used only when this granularity is required.
- Only use iterating DAX functions such as `SUMX()`, `RANKX()`, and `FILTER()` when either the table iterated over is small or when the row expression for these functions can be executed by the storage engine:
    - Simple expressions such as the multiplication of two columns from the table being iterated over can be executed by the storage engine.
- Use whole number (integer) data types instead of text data types whenever possible.
- If the data model uses a DirectQuery data source, optimize this source such as with indexes or columnar technologies available such as the `Clustered Columnstore Index` for SQL Server:
    - Additionally, ensure that the source database supports referential integrity and that the DirectQuery model assumes referential integrity in its defined relationships. This will result in inner join queries to the source.
        - The Fact-to-dimension relationships section of `Chapter 9`, *Designing Import and DirectQuery Data Models*, contains additional details.
- Avoid or limit `DISTINCTCOUNT()` measures against high cardinality columns:
    - For example, create the `DISTINCTCOUNT()` measure expression against the natural key or business key column identifying the dimension member (such as `Customer ABC`), rather than the columns used in the fact-to-dimension relationship. With slowly changing dimension processes, the relationship columns could store many more unique values per dimension member and thus reduce performance.

- Avoid the use of calculated DAX columns on fact tables:
    - Create these columns in the source system or in the queries used to load the model to allow for better data compression.
    - For DirectQuery models, avoid the use of DAX calculated columns for all tables.

Report and visualization optimizations

A well-designed analytical model with ample resources can still struggle to produce adequate performance due to an inefficient visualization layer. The following list of techniques can be applied to Power BI reports and dashboards to reduce the query workload and avoid slower resource-intensive queries:

- Create dashboards on top of reports to leverage cached query results representing the latest data refresh:
    - Unlike dashboards, report queries are sent and executed on the fly when Power BI reports are loaded.
    - Multiple dashboards can be linked together as described in Chapter 13, *Designing Power BI Dashboards and Architectures.*
    - If the dataset uses a DirectQuery or Live connection, take advantage of scheduled cache refresh as described in the *Dashboard cache refresh* section of Chapter 15, *Managing the On-Premises Data Gateway.*

- Avoid report visuals that return large amounts of data such as tables with thousands of rows and many columns:
    - Report visuals that require scrolling or which represent a data extract format should be filtered and summarized.
    - Report visuals that return more data points than necessary to address their business question can be modified to a lower granularity. For example, a dense scatter chart of individual products could be modified to use the less granular product subcategories column.

- Ensure that filters are being applied to reports so that only the required data is returned:
    - Apply report level filters to only return the time periods needed (such as current year and last year).
    - Use visual level filters such as a top N filter as described in the *Visual-level filtering* section of `Chapter 11`, *Creating and Formatting Power BI Reports*.
- Limit the volume of visuals used on a given report page:
    - Optionally remove the interactions between visuals (cross-highlighting) to further reduce report queries.
- Understand which DAX measures are less performant and only use these measures when required:
    - For example, only use expensive measures in card visuals or within highly filtered visuals exposing only a few distinct numbers.

Premium capacity estimations

The volume of factors involved in premium capacity utilization makes it difficult to forecast the amount of premium capacity (and thus cost) required. This complexity is particularly acute for large deployments with diverse use cases to support. Additionally, for organizations relatively new to Power BI, the level and growth of user adoption, as well as the requirements for future projects, can be unclear. Nonetheless, to provide an initial estimate of the cost of deploying Power BI with premium capacities, Microsoft has developed the Power BI Premium calculator. This online forecasting tool provides free estimates of the combined monthly cost of Power BI Pro licenses and Power BI Premium capacity.

In the following screenshot of the Power BI Premium calculator, the user has specified 2,500 total Power BI users and used the two slider bars to distribute those users among the following profiles—**Pro Users**, **Frequent Users**, and **Occasional Users**:

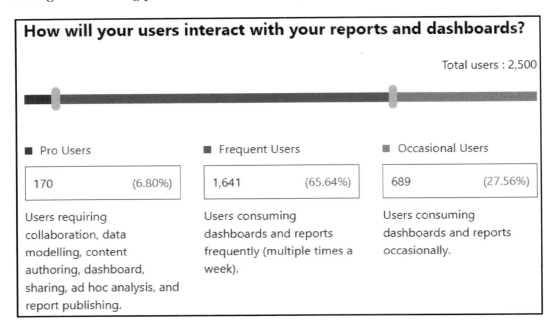

Power BI Premium calculator

In the example, 170 Pro Users results in 170 Pro licenses costing a total of $1,700 per month (170 * $10/mo). More importantly, the calculator estimates that two P1 nodes (8 v-cores) of Premium capacity will be required for the organization at a cost of $9,990 per month (2 * $4,995/mo). Therefore, an organization could use $11,690 per month as an initial and high-level estimate of their Power BI deployment. The Power BI Premium calculator is accessible at the following URL `http://bit.ly/2eKil1I`.

Thankfully the P1 month-to-month SKU eliminates the need for organizations to make large financial commitments in advance of actual usage. The 8 v-cores provided by a Premium P1 capacity (month-to-month) can be acquired in the Office 365 admin center as shown in the following screenshot:

Premium Capacity: Month to month

In a fiscally conservative approach, an organization could create a single P1 capacity and test this capacity against different workloads until both the usage metrics described in the previous chapter and actual load test experiences suggest additional capacity is needed. Load testing of premium capacity typically consists of multiple users simulating normal user behaviors in the Power BI service such as clicking a slicer, pausing to view the results of a selection, and then making another filter selection. Additional options and guidance for load testing premium capacity are included in the *Power BI Premium Capacity Planning and Deployment Whitepaper* available at the following URL http://bit.ly/2Hu57DK.

Once it's determined that additional capacity is needed, an organization can simply provision another instance of a P1 (month-to-month) thus obtaining 16 total v-cores. In the following image from the **Purchase services** page of the Office 365 admin center, the quantity of an existing P1 (month-to-month) SKU can be revised:

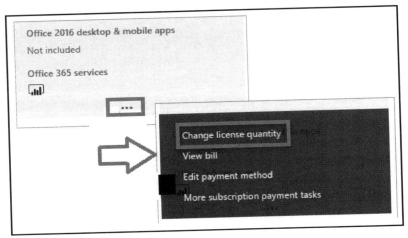

Purchasing additional premium capacity

Selecting the ellipsis (...) at the bottom of the Premium SKU exposes the Change license quantity option. Once the number of premium instances has been increased and submitted, the additional v-cores will be available in the Capacity settings page of the Power BI admin portal. Creating and managing premium capacities, including the assignment of app workspaces to premium capacities, was described in Chapter 18, *Administering Power BI for an Organization*.

With both v-core pooling and single-click scale up capabilities available in the Power BI admin portal it's very easy to reallocate premium capacity. In this example with 16 total v-cores purchased, an existing P1 capacity could be scaled up to a P2 capacity. Alternatively, a new and isolated P1 capacity could be created thus leaving two P1 capacities to handle the distinct workloads generated by different app workspaces.

The three-step process of purchasing additional v-cores, scaling up existing capacities or configuring new capacities, and testing workloads against premium capacities by assigning workspaces to those capacities will be repeated throughout the deployment lifecycle. In the event that usage or resource needs decline, the monthly price for a P1 month-to-month instance can be avoided thus reducing the amount of v-cores available.

The flexibility of premium capacity and other cloud services such as Azure Analysis Services naturally aligns with the frequently changing needs of BI projects. The following sections describe both AAS and SSAS as a primary tool to complement Power BI Premium and to support large-scale enterprise deployments of Power BI.

Analysis Services

Analysis Services has been Microsoft's enterprise **Online Analytical Processing (OLAP)** BI engine for many years. The Analysis Services Tabular model including the DAX programming language, in-memory and columnar storage, and columnar compression was first introduced with Microsoft's entry to self-service business intelligence with Power Pivot for Excel 2010. Analysis Services Tabular, which now includes the Power Query M programming language and the optional DirectQuery storage mode described earlier in this book, is the default installation mode of SSAS 2017. Additionally, the Analysis Services Tabular engine is built into Excel, Power BI, and the Azure Analysis Services PaaS offering.

The data model built into Excel workbooks is limited to in-memory storage mode and does not support bi-directional relationships. Additionally, Excel workbooks containing data models are limited to 250 MB and cannot be used as sources for Live connection Power BI reports or via Analyze in Excel like published Power BI datasets. For these reasons and many other features exclusive to Power BI Desktop and Power BI datasets, Power BI Desktop is recommended over Excel for creating data models in almost all scenarios.

SSAS also continues to support multidimensional mode instances, which consist of row and disk-based storage, and **Multidimensional Expressions (MDX)** for business logic. Despite structural advantages of tabular mode, multidimensional mode remains popular as it was available long before tabular mode and since it included many additional features relative to the initial releases of tabular mode. Power BI reports can leverage SSAS multidimensional models as Live connection data sources just like SSAS Tabular models and Microsoft has been clear that multidimensional mode will not be deprecated. However, multidimensional mode instances are currently not available in Azure Analysis Services and many new features and capabilities introduced in the past two years have been exclusive to tabular models.

Analysis Services Tabular, either via SSAS or **Azure Analysis Services (Azure AS)** instances, is recommended over multidimensional mode for new enterprise BI models. Similar to Power BI Desktop over Excel for self-service modeling and reporting, this recommendation is better aligned with Microsoft's BI roadmap and thus entails access to new features and capabilities. Additionally, given the common underlying engine between Power BI and Analysis Services Tabular, experience with Analysis Services Tabular positions organizations to better manage the relationship between Self-Service BI and Corporate BI.

Analysis Services Models versus Power BI Desktop

A local instance of Analysis Services Tabular is used by Power BI Desktop when creating both import and DirectQuery data models. When these models are published to the Power BI Service as Power BI Desktop (.PBIX) files, the Power BI service extracts the Analysis Services database from the Power BI Desktop file and provides an Analysis Services server instance for running the database in Power BI. However, despite this very deep integration with Analysis Services, Power BI Desktop is primarily targeted at business analysts and self-service BI, while Analysis Services is intended for business intelligence professionals and enterprise BI solutions.

Given these different target personas and use cases, many features and capabilities of Analysis Services Tabular models are not available to Power BI Desktop. For example, BI/IT organizations generally utilize robust version control systems such as **Visual Studio Team Services (VSTS)** and multiple tools and programmatic interfaces to manage and administer their solutions. Additionally, there are modeling features of Analysis Services including **Perspectives**, **Display Folders**, and **KPIs** that are currently not accessible to dataset designers of Power BI datasets.

The following table compares Power BI Desktop models to Analysis Services (Tabular) models across 19 features:

#	Feature	Power BI Desktop	Analysis Services
1	Table Partitions	No, but incremental data refresh coming to Power BI Premium in 2018.	Yes, with Standard tier instances (Azure AS) or with Enterprise Edition (SSAS).
2	In-Memory Mode	Yes	Yes
3	DirectQuery Mode	Yes	Yes
4	Version Control	No, limited to OneDrive for Business version history per PBIX file.	Yes, integration with version control systems such as Visual Studio Team Services (VSTS) and Team Foundation Server (TFS).
5	Scale Up	Yes, single-click scale up with Power BI Premium capacities	Yes, change to a larger instance (Azure AS) or add CPU or RAM (SSAS)
6	Scale Out	No, but scale out identified on roadmap.	Yes, up to 8 servers for Azure AS with automatic load balancing. Can configure scale out and sync with SSAS.
7	Row-level security	Yes	Yes
8	Object-level security	No	Yes
9	Detail Row Expressions	No	Yes
10	Perspectives	No	Yes
11	Display Folders	No	Yes
12	Hierarchies	Yes	Yes
13	Translations	No	Yes
14	KPIs	No, but can use standard and custom KPI visuals as alternatives.	Yes
15	Development Tools	Power BI Desktop	Visual Studio and SQL Server Data Tools (SSDT)
16	Management Tools	Dataset Settings in Power BI Service	SQL Server Management Studio (SSMS), Azure Portal
17	Automation Tools	No	Azure Functions, Azure Automation, SQL Server Agent, SQL Server Integration Services (SSIS), and Azure ARM.
18	Programmatic Interface	Power BI REST API	PowerShell, Tabular Object Model (TOM), Tabular Model Scripting Language (TMSL), and Azure Analysis Services REST API.
19	Monitoring	Power BI Premium Usage Measurements	Metrics in Azure Portal, Azure Log Analytics, Extended Events, and SQL Server Profiler.

Power BI Desktop versus Analysis Services feature matrix

As shown in the table, Analysis Services Tabular models, whether deployed to SSAS or Azure AS instances, are able to provide both maximum modeling functionality to aid the user experience as well as rich administrative tools and interfaces. It's outside the scope of this chapter to describe each feature, but the following three sections summarize the primary incremental benefits provided by Analysis Services over Power BI datasets built with Power BI Desktop.

Per the Power BI Premium capabilities section earlier in this chapter (see Capability #11), the same tools used to interface with Analysis Services servers will soon (2018) be available for app workspaces assigned to a Power BI premium capacity. For example, a BI team could use Visual Studio and **SQL Server Management Studio (SSMS)** for development and management of the Power BI dataset, respectively. Likewise, popular BI and data visualization tools such as Tableau could be used to connect to Power BI datasets stored in premium capacity.

In addition to the features identified in the table and described in the following sections, Analysis Services models avoid the dataset per app workspace limitation described in the Corporate Power BI datasets section earlier. A single Analysis Services model and its refresh process can be leveraged across multiple app workspaces and their corresponding Power BI apps.

Scale

Partitions are the key to scaling in-memory SSAS Tabular models as only certain partitions, such as the partitions representing the last two months of data, need to be included in a recurring refresh process.

These partitions can be defined in **SQL Server Data Tools (SSDT)** as shown in the following screenshot, and many patterns and practices have been documented for automating the management and refresh of partitions:

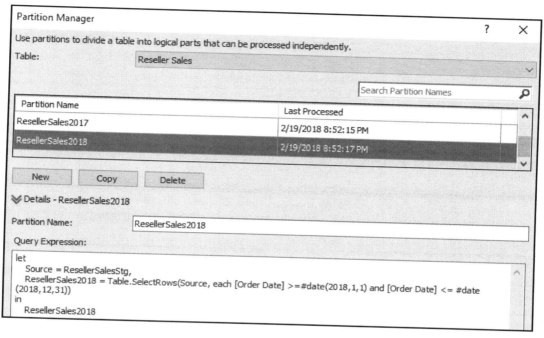

Partition Manager in SQL Server Data Tools (SSDT)

In the preceding screenshot, the `Reseller Sales` table is comprised of multiple yearly partitions (that is, **ResellerSales2018**). In most large models, the partitions would be much smaller (months, weeks) and logic would be built into a refresh process for dynamically determining which partitions to process and which (if any) to add or delete. Incremental data refresh for Power BI datasets hosted in Power BI Premium capacities is expected to offer the same essential as partitions in terms of minimizing refresh times and resources. However, it's unlikely that incremental data refresh will offer the same level of complete control.

Scaling out query workloads across multiple Analysis Services servers and implementing load balancing is also a very important feature of enterprise deployments. Azure Analysis Services greatly simplifies this setup and the planning involved by providing the following interface in the Azure portal:

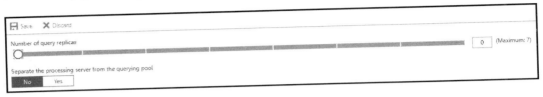

Scale out via Replicas in Azure Analysis Services

As shown in the preceding screenshot, up to seven query replicas of an Azure Analysis Services server can be created. If the processing server responsible for the data refresh process is not separated from the querying pool, a total of eight analysis services servers would be available in the Azure cloud to resolve queries from Power BI and other tools such as Excel and Tableau with load balancing provided automatically by Azure Analysis Services.

 In addition to the Azure portal interface, the Analysis Services REST API can be used to configure scale-out.

Scale out architectures are certainly also supported with SSAS Tabular in on-premises environments, but require significantly more planning and coordination to provision and configure the infrastructure.

Usability

Large enterprise models support many users from across the organization and typically each user only requires access to a section of the model. For example, a sales team member may only need to access a sales fact table and several dimension tables and thus shouldn't have to navigate through many other irrelevant tables that support other business teams. Perspectives in Analysis Services allow the modeler to map objects of the model (tables, columns, and measures) to a specific perspective such that users connecting to the model via the perspective only see those objects.

Display folders including hierarchies of folders (that is, subfolders) can be defined for Analysis Services models to simplify user access to measures and columns. In the following example from a Power BI Live connection report to an Analysis Services model, the measures associated with the `Internet Sales` and `Reseller Sales` fact tables have been grouped into display folders for each fact table:

Analysis Services Display Folders

Given the high volume of date intelligence measures, it's often best to isolate these measures so that the user can easily access the most common and basic measures such as total sales or the count of the products sold.

Another usability feature of Analysis Services not supported by Power BI currently includes support for multiple languages:

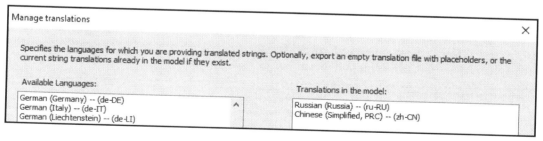

Multi-language support in Analysis Services

In Analysis Services projects within Visual Studio, the model author can export an empty JSON that contains placeholders for the translations, add string translations to the file, and then import the JSON file back to the model for access by users.

Development and management tools

Power BI Desktop is much closer to a Microsoft Office application than an **integrated development environment** (**IDE**) tool such as Visual Studio, which offers granular control over the data model. With Analysis Services, business intelligence developers and the teams responsible for Analysis Services models can take advantage of the rich development experience built into SSDT for Visual Studio, as well as familiar management capabilities available in **SQL Server Management Studio** (**SSMS**). Additionally, these same tools can be used for both AAS and SSAS models.

For example, the following screenshot from an Analysis Services project in Visual Studio 2017 exposes the **DAX Editor** window (left) and the Tabular Model Explorer interface (right):

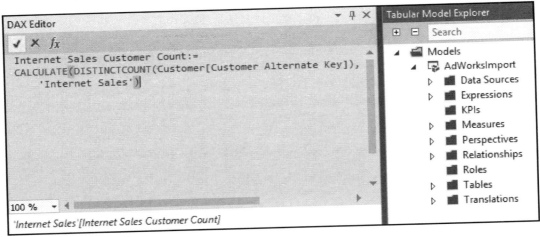

DAX Editor and Tabular Model Explorer in Visual Studio

With the Tabular Model Explorer, the model developer has a central location to find, view, and optionally edit the objects of the model. This interface, along with the DAX Editor window, is very helpful when working with large models containing many tables and complex DAX expressions.

In terms of managing deployed models, SSMS provides a familiar object explorer interface and enhanced support for DAX queries, as shown in the following screenshot:

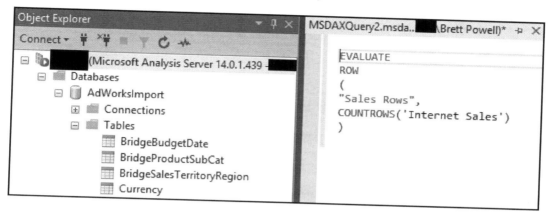

SQL Server Management Studio (SSMS)

In the preceding screenshot, the same data model (**AdWorksImport**) from Visual Studio is accessed from SSMS and an ad hoc DAX query is authored in the query window. In addition to the new .MSDAX files for DAX queries, **Tabular Model Scripting Language** (TMSL) commands can be scripted and executed in SSMS.

Azure Analysis Services versus SSAS

For many organizations, the Power BI service is only a part of an existing and broader cloud-based data and analytics environment. For example, the organization may already be using the **Azure Data Lake Store** (**ADLS**), Azure SQL Database, or Azure SQL Data Warehouse cloud services to store and process data for reporting analysis. In other organizations, the adoption of the Power BI service as a primary BI and collaboration platform may be part of a larger migration from an on-premises BI environment to the cloud. As one example of this migration, existing **extract-transform-load** (**ETL**) packages executed via on-premises **SQL Server Integration Services** (**SSIS**) servers could be moved (lift and shift) to **virtual machines** (**VMs**) in Azure and managed through the Azure Data Factory cloud service.

Even if neither of these two scenarios applies in the short term, an organization may still choose Azure Analysis Services over SSAS to reap the cost, performance, and agility benefits (scale-up/down) of this PaaS offering. With an Azure Analysis Services instance storing the data model(s) queried from Power BI within the same data region as the Power BI service tenant, the report and dashboard queries generated by Power BI avoid the latency incurred by accessing an on-premises SSAS instance via the On-premises data gateway. If data source(s) of the Analysis Services model remain on-premises, the same On-premises data gateway described in `Chapter 15`, *Managing the On-Premises Data Gateway*, can be used to support a recurring data refresh process of Azure Analysis Services models from on-premises sources.

Perhaps even more important than query performance, Azure Analysis Services dramatically reduces the following challenges with deploying SSAS at scale in enterprises:

1. Planning server resource requirements:
    - It's difficult to accurately predict how much CPU and RAM will be needed by an Analysis Services server, even for the next 1-2 years. Additionally, the optimal hardware for Analysis Services, such as CPU clock speed and NUMA Awareness, is sometimes not fully communicated or delivered when provisioning these servers.
    - With Azure AS, optimally tuned Analysis Services resources can be quickly and easily aligned to changing needs of the workload by switching pricing tiers.
    - BI teams can even schedule Azure AS resources to be scaled up at certain times to support high query volumes (such as every Monday morning) and then scaled down or even paused at times of low query volume such as nights and weekends.

2. Installation and server maintenance:
    - In an on-premises environment, SSAS has to be installed on the provisioned server and the server itself has to be managed and patched.
    - As a PaaS offering, Azure AS servers are fully installed once deployed and the underlying servers are maintained by Microsoft to support 99.9 percent availability.

3. Implementing scale-out:
   - Provisioning the read-only query servers, the processing servers, and configuring load balancing can take weeks or longer in on-premises environments.
   - As depicted in the Scale section earlier, Azure Analysis Services provides a graphical interface to easily configure a pool of read-only query replicas for distributing or balancing query requests.

These considerations specific to Analysis Services, as well as the broader advantages of a cloud architecture, serve as powerful motivation to choose Azure Analysis Services over SQL Server Analysis Services. For example, new features and enhancements to Azure Analysis Services are released more frequently than versions of SSAS, and some of these new features such as the Azure Analysis Services web designer are exclusive to the cloud service. Additionally, Azure AS instances are able to benefit from new capabilities and ongoing investments in other Azure services such as Azure Automation and Azure Functions. This is similar to the advantage of the Power BI service over the Power BI Report Server as described in `Chapter 16`, *Deploying the Power BI Report Server*.

SSAS to Azure AS Migration

Organizations with existing SSAS Tabular models may choose to migrate to Azure Analysis Services to support their Power BI deployment and for other reasons identified in previous sections. This can be accomplished by deploying an existing on-premises model (`.bim` file) to an Azure Analysis Services instance from SSDT in Visual Studio.

In the following screenshot, the deployment server of an existing SSAS model is changed to an Azure Analysis Services server:

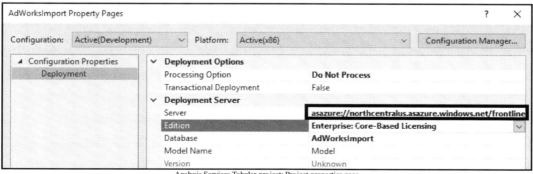

Analysis Services Tabular project: Project properties page

This page can be accessed by right-clicking the Analysis Services project name in SSDT and selecting **Configuration Properties**. Via the **Do Not Process** from the **Processing Option** property, only the metadata of the model will be deployed to the Azure Analysis Services server. Additionally, note that the server name to ensure should be the management server name provided by Azure Analysis Services in the Azure portal as described in the following section.

With a successful deployment of the model's metadata from SSDT, the user can manage and process the Azure Analysis Services model in SSMS. In the following screenshot, the same **AdWorksImport** model is now deployed to both an on-premises server (ATLAS) and the Azure Analysis Services server:

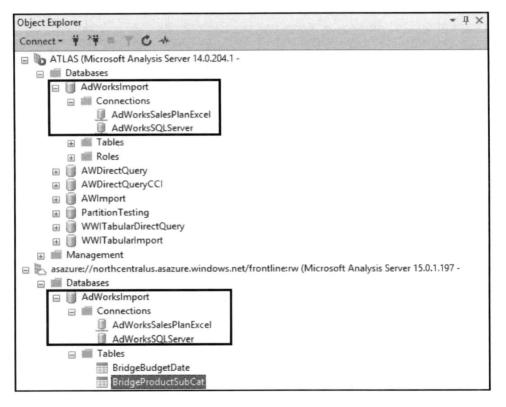

SSAS and Azure Analysis Services instances in SSMS

As shown in the preceding screenshot, the **AdWorksImport** database is now deployed to both an on-premises instance of SQL Server Analysis Services (Tabular) and an Azure Analysis Services instance. The same functionality SSAS developers and managers are familiar with in SSMS, such as viewing and processing partitions and tables of models, is still fully supported with Azure Analysis Services.

Provision Azure Analysis Services

Azure Analysis Services can be found within the **Data and Analytics** tab in the **Azure Marketplace**. Clicking the Analysis Services icon presents a configuration blade to define the new resource including its location (data center region) and pricing tier.

In the following screenshot, a new Azure AS instance (`Frontline`) is created in the **North Central US** region and for the **S0** pricing tier:

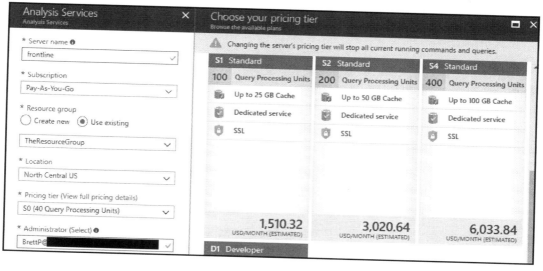

Provision Azure Analysis Services Instance

The view full pricing details link has been accessed in the preceding screenshot to expose additional SKUs currently supported. As of this writing, the largest Azure AS instance is an S9 with 640 **Query Processing Units (QPUs)** and 400 GB of memory. A single virtual core is currently approximately equal to 25 QPUs and thus an S9 server instance can be estimated at 25 to 26 virtual cores (640 / 25 = 25.6). The full list of SKUs, including the Basic tier (B1, B2) and additional details on pricing, is available at the Analysis Services Pricing page `http://bit.ly/2ooOKQI`.

> The location of the Azure Analysis Services instance should match the location of the Power BI service tenant. The location of the Power BI Service tenant can be found via the About Power BI menu item under the question mark icon in the Power BI Service as illustrated in the *Identify where the gateway should be installed* section of `Chapter 15`, *Managing the On-Premises Data Gateway*.

Once all required input boxes have been completed, clicking create starts the deployment process, which typically requires less than a minute. By default, the deployed Azure AS resource will be running but can be paused to avoid incurring any further charges, as shown in the following screenshot from the **Overview** page:

Deployed and running Azure Analysis Services instance

As shown in the preceding screenshot, both a **Server name** and a **Management Server Name** are provided on the **Overview** tab. The **Server name** is what should be used by client applications such as Power BI Desktop and Excel. The **Management Server Name**, which includes an **:rw** qualifier, should be used in SSMS, SSDT, and other operational or administrative tools such as PowerShell.

A server name alias can be created to provide a more friendly server name when creating reports. The alias created is specified as an endpoint using the `link://` format and the alias endpoint returns the real server name in order to connect to the server. Details on created Azure Analysis Services server aliases are available at the following URL `http://bit.ly/2EN2LC3`.

In addition to the Azure AS resource itself, if a data model on the Azure AS server needs to retrieve data from an on-premises source, it will be necessary to create an On-premises data gateway resource in the Azure portal as well. The Azure Analysis Services section of `Chapter 15`, *Managing the On-Premises Data Gateway*, includes details on creating and configuring this resource.

Migration of Power BI Desktop to Analysis Services

The Azure Analysis Services web designer, currently in preview, supports the ability to import a data model contained within a Power BI Desktop file. The imported or migrated model can then take advantage of the resources available to the Azure Analysis Services server and can be accessed from client tools such as Power BI Desktop. Additionally, Azure Analysis Services provides a Visual Studio project file and a `Model.bim` file for the migrated model that a corporate BI team can use in SSDT for Visual Studio.

The following process migrates the model within a Power BI Desktop file to an Azure Analysis Server and downloads the Visual Studio project file for the migrated model:

1. Open the Web designer from the **Overview** page of the Azure Analysis Services resource in the Azure portal
2. On the **Models** form, click **Add** and then provide a name for the new model in the **New model** form
3. Select the **Power BI Desktop File** source icon at the bottom and choose the file on the **Import** menu

4. Click **Import** to begin the migration process

The following screenshot represents these four steps from the Azure Analysis Services web designer:

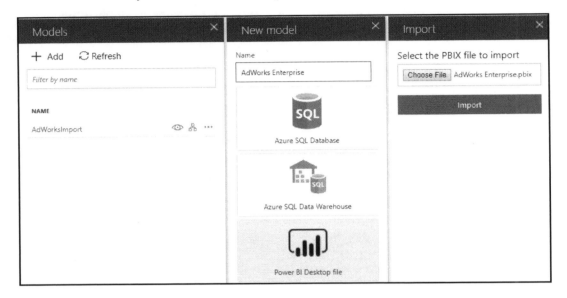

Create an Analysis Services model from a Power BI Desktop File

In this example, a Power BI Desktop file (`AdWorks Enterprise.pbix`) that contains an import mode model based on two on-premises sources (SQL Server and Excel) is imported via the Azure Analysis Services web designer.

Once the import is complete, the **Field** list from the model will be exposed on the right and the imported model will be accessible from client tools like any other Azure Analysis Services model. For example, refreshing the Azure AS server in SQL Server Management Studio will expose the new database (**AdWorks Enterprise**). Likewise, the Azure Analysis Services database connection in Power BI Desktop (**Get Data | Azure**) can be used to connect to the migrated model, as shown in the following screenshot:

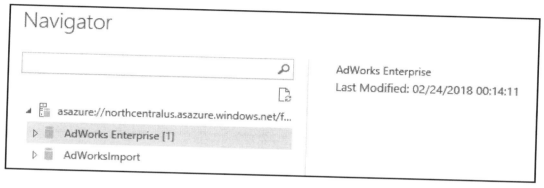

Migrated Model accessed from Azure as server in Power BI Desktop

Just like the SQL Server Analysis Services database connection (**Get Data | Database**), the only required field is the name of the server which is provided in the Azure portal as described in the *Provision Azure Analysis Services* section earlier.

5. From the **Overview** page of the Azure Analysis Services resource, select the **Open in Visual Studio** project option from the context menu on the far right, as shown in the following screenshot:

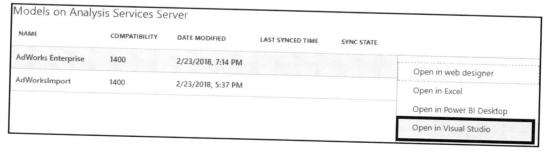

Context menu in Azure Portal for a model

6. Save the zip file provided by Azure Analysis Services to a secure local network location.

7. Extract the files from the zip file to expose the Analysis Services project and .bim file, as shown in the following screenshot:

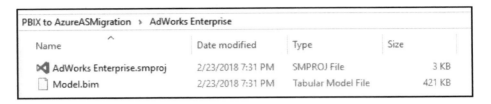

Folder contents downloaded from Azure Analysis Services

8. In Visual Studio, open a project/solution (**File | Open | Project/Solution**) and navigate to the downloaded project file (.smproj). Select the project file and click **Open**.

9. Double-click the Model.bim file in the Solution Explorer window to expose the metadata of the migrated model.

All of the objects of the data model built into the Power BI Desktop file including **Data Sources**, **Queries**, and **Measures** are accessible in SSDT just like standard Analysis Services projects, as shown in the following screenshot:

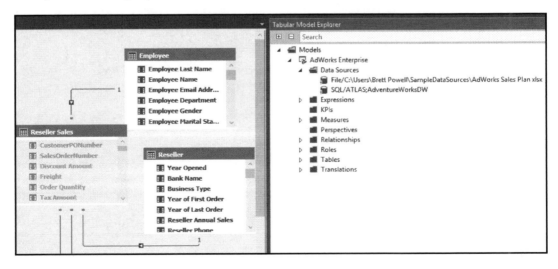

Migrated model opened as Analysis Services Project

The preceding screenshot from **Diagram** view in SQL Server Data Tools exposes the two on-premises sources of the imported PBIX file via the Tabular Model Explorer window. By default, the deployment server of the Analysis Services project in SSDT is set to the Azure Analysis Services server, but this can be revised as was described in the *SSAS to Azure AS Migration* section earlier.

 Since the ability to import a Power BI Desktop file directly in SSDT is not yet available, BI teams with on-premises SSAS environments could temporarily provision an Azure Analysis Services server to support migrations. Once the project file is downloaded from Azure, the Azure AS server could be paused or deleted and the deployment server property in the project could be revised to an SSAS server.

As an alternative to a new solution with a single project, an existing solution with an existing Analysis Services project could be opened and the new project from the migration could be added to this solution. This can be accomplished by right-clicking the existing solution's name in the Solution Explorer window and selecting the **Existing project** from the **Add** menu (**Add | Existing project**).

This approach allows the corporate BI developer to view and compare both models and optionally implement incremental changes, such as new columns or measures that were exclusive to the Power BI Desktop file.

The following screenshot from a solution in Visual Studio includes both the migrated model (via the project file) and an existing Analysis Services model (**AdWorks Import**):

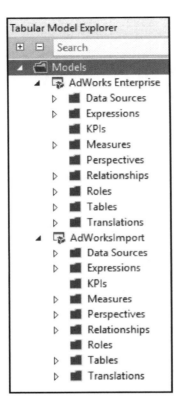

Tabular Model Explorer

The ability to quickly migrate Power BI datasets to Analysis Services models complements the flexibility and scale of Power BI Premium capacity in allowing organizations to manage and deploy Power BI on their terms.

Summary

This chapter reviewed Power BI Premium and Analysis Services as the primary means to deploy Power BI at scale and with enterprise BI tools and controls. The current and future features of Power BI Premium were described, as well as the factors to account for inefficiently provisioning and allocating premium capacity. Additionally, Analysis Services was contrasted with Power BI Desktop-based datasets to expose the features and benefits exclusive to Microsoft's enterprise BI modeling tool. Moreover, details were provided in comparing Azure Analysis Services with SSAS and in migrating a Power BI Desktop model to Analysis Services.

Power BI Premium and Analysis Services further Microsoft's goal of providing organizations with the flexibility to deploy Power BI on their terms. Organizations can quickly scale up a self-service solution to support many users and they can also migrate self-service content to IT-owned corporate BI solutions. The common modeling engine between Power BI and Analysis Services, as well as the elastic nature of cloud resources, serves to both reduce the friction between self-service and corporate BI, and reduce the time and costs associated with delivering BI solutions.

Other Books You May Enjoy

If you enjoyed this book, you may be interested in these other books by Packt:

Microsoft Power BI Cookbook
Brett Powell

ISBN: 978-1-78829-014-2

- Cleanse, stage, and integrate your data sources with Power BI
- Abstract data complexities and provide users with intuitive, self-service BI capabilities
- Build business logic and analysis into your solutions via the DAX programming language and dynamic, dashboard-ready calculations
- Take advantage of the analytics and predictive capabilities of Power BI
- Make your solutions more dynamic and user specific and/or defined including use cases of parameters, functions, and row level security
- Understand the differences and implications of DirectQuery, Live Connections, and Import-Mode Power BI datasets and how to deploy content to the Power BI Service and schedule refreshes
- Integrate other Microsoft data tools such as Excel and SQL Server Reporting Services into your Power BI solution

Mastering Qlik Sense
Martin Mahler, Juan Ignacio Vitantonio

ISBN: 978-1-78355-402-7

- Understand the importance of self-service analytics and the IKEA-effect
- Explore all the available data modeling techniques and create efficient and optimized data models
- Master security rules and translate permission requirements into security rule logic
- Familiarize yourself with different types of Master Key Item(MKI) and know how and when to use MKI.
- Script and write sophisticated ETL code within Qlik Sense to facilitate all data modeling and data loading techniques
- Get an extensive overview of which APIs are available in Qlik Sense and how to take advantage of a technology with an API
- Develop basic mashup HTML pages and deploy successful mashup projects

Leave a review - let other readers know what you think

Please share your thoughts on this book with others by leaving a review on the site that you bought it from. If you purchased the book from Amazon, please leave us an honest review on this book's Amazon page. This is vital so that other potential readers can see and use your unbiased opinion to make purchasing decisions, we can understand what our customers think about our products, and our authors can see your feedback on the title that they have worked with Packt to create. It will only take a few minutes of your time, but is valuable to other potential customers, our authors, and Packt. Thank you!

Index

L

Line charts 125
Live Connection
    about 21
    limitations 22
Live connection
    reports, customizing 362
    to Power BI datasets 359
live report pages 500, 503
Load Balancer 628

M

M editing tools
    about 251
    advanced editor 252
    Visual Studio 255
    Visual Studio Code 253
M formula language
    #shared 50
    about 48
M queries
    about 223
    Bridge Table Queries 236
    customer history column 245
    Data Source Parameters 224
    data types 233
    derived column data types 247
    dimension queries 228
    DirectQuery report execution 235
    DirectQuery staging 228
    examples 243
    excel workbook 230
    fact queries 228
    item, accessing 234
    parameter tables 237
    product dimension integration 248
    security tables 240
    Source Reference Only 229
    staging queries 226
    summary 230
    three years filter, trailing 243
    versus SQL views 214
many-to-many relationships
    about 61, 63

cross-filtering direction 63, 65
    filtering, enabling 66
Map visual 135
map visuals
    about 413
    bubble map 414
    filled map 416
Master Data Management (MDM) 185
Matrix visual 116, 117
measure evaluation process
    about 304
    Filter Context Modified via DAX 305
    Initial Filter Context 304
    Measure Logic Computation 305
    Relationship Cross-Filtering 305
measure support expressions
    about 319
    current period 322
    KPI targets 320
    prior period 322
Merging Queries 41
metadata management
    about 532, 533
    descriptions, creating 533, 534
    DMV data, enhancing 541
    DMV data, integrating 541
    DMVs, querying from Power BI 540
    field descriptions 533
    metadata, reporting 537
    query field descriptions 537, 538
    report pages 542, 543
    server parameters 539
    standard metadata reports 539
    view field descriptions 534, 535, 536, 537
Microsoft Flow integration 662
Microsoft Office Data Connection (ODC) 667
mobile-optimized dashboards 503, 505
mobile-optimized reports
    about 417
    responsive visuals 420
model metadata
    about 287
    column metadata 288
    field descriptions 292
    visibility 287

32469568R10435

Made in the USA
Lexington, KY
03 March 2019